ORLEY FARM

ORLEY FARM

by
Anthony Trollope

With 40 Illustrations by
John Everett Millais

Two Volumes Bound as One

DOVER PUBLICATIONS, INC.
NEW YORK

Published in Canada by General Publishing Company,
Ltd., 30 Lesmill Road, Don Mills, Toronto, Ontario.
Published in the United Kingdom by Constable and
Company, Ltd., 10 Orange Street, London WC2H 7EG.

This Dover edition, first published in 1981, is an unabridged republication of the work as published in two
volumes by Chapman and Hall, London, in 1862.

International Standard Book Number: 0-486-24181-5
Library of Congress Catalog Card Number: 81-66779

Manufactured in the United States of America
Dover Publications, Inc.
180 Varick Street
New York, N.Y. 10014

ORLEY FARM

VOLUME I

ORLEY FARM.

VOLUME I
CONTENTS.

CONTENTS.

ILLUSTRATIONS TO VOLUME I.

ILLUSTRATIONS.

ORLEY FARM.

CHAPTER I.

THE COMMENCEMENT OF THE GREAT ORLEY FARM CASE.

It is not true that a rose by any other name will smell as sweet. Were it true, I should call this story 'The Great Orley Farm Case.' But who would ask for the ninth number of a serial work burthened with so very uncouth an appellation? Thence, and therefore,—Orley Farm.

I say so much at commencing in order that I may have an opportunity of explaining that this book of mine will not be devoted in any special way to rural delights. The name might lead to the idea that new precepts were to be given, in the pleasant guise of a novel, as to cream-cheeses, pigs with small bones, wheat sown in drills, or artificial manure. No such aspirations are mine. I make no attempts in that line, and declare at once that agriculturists will gain nothing from my present performance. Orley Farm, my readers, will be our scene during a portion of our present sojourn together, but the name has been chosen as having been intimately connected with certain legal questions which made a considerable stir in our courts of law.

It was twenty years before the date at which this story will be supposed to commence that the name of Orley Farm first became known to the wearers of the long robe. At that time had died an old gentleman, Sir Joseph Mason, who left behind him a landed estate in Yorkshire of considerable extent and value. This he bequeathed, in a proper way, to his eldest son, the Joseph Mason, Esq., of our date. Sir Joseph had been a London merchant; had made his own money, having commenced the world, no doubt, with half a crown; had become, in turn, alderman, mayor, and knight; and in the fulness of time was gathered to his fathers. He had purchased this estate in Yorkshire late in life—we may as well become acquainted with the name, Groby Park—and his eldest son had lived there with such enjoyment of the privileges of an

English country gentleman as he had been able to master for himself. Sir Joseph had also had three daughters, full sisters of Joseph of Groby, whom he endowed sufficiently and gave over to three respective loving husbands. And then shortly before his death, three years or so, Sir Joseph had married a second wife, a lady forty-five years his junior, and by her he also left one son, an infant only two years old when he died.

For many years this prosperous gentleman had lived at a small country house, some five-and-twenty miles from London, called Orley Farm. This had been his first purchase of land, and he had never given up his residence there, although his wealth would have entitled him to the enjoyment of a larger establishment. On the birth of his youngest son, at which time his eldest was nearly forty years old, he made certain moderate provision for the infant, as he had already made moderate provision for his young wife; but it was then clearly understood by the eldest son that Orley Farm was to go with the Groby Park estate to him as the heir. When, however, Sir Joseph died, a codicil to his will, executed with due legal formalities, bequeathed Orley Farm to his youngest son, little Lucius Mason.

Then commenced those legal proceedings which at last developed themselves into the great Orley Farm Case. The eldest son contested the validity of the codicil; and indeed there were some grounds on which it appeared feasible that he should do so. This codicil not only left Orley Farm away from him to baby Lucius, but also interfered in another respect with the previous will. It devised a sum of two thousand pounds to a certain Miriam Usbech, the daughter of one Jonathan Usbech who was himself the attorney who had attended upon Sir Joseph for the making out of this very will, and also of this very codicil. This sum of two thousand pounds was not, it is true, left away from the surviving Joseph, but was to be produced out of certain personal property which had been left by the first will to the widow. And then old Jonathan Usbech had died, while Sir Joseph Mason was still living.

All the circumstances of the trial need not be detailed here. It was clearly proved that Sir Joseph had during his whole life expressed his intention of leaving Orley Farm to his eldest son; that he was a man void of mystery, and not given to secrets in his money matters, and one very little likely to change his opinion on such subjects. It was proved that old Jonathan Usbech at the time in which the will was made was in very bad circumstances, both as regards money and health. His business had once not been bad, but he had eaten and drunk it, and at this period was feeble and penniless, overwhelmed both by gout and debt. He had for many years been much employed by Sir Joseph in money matters, and it was known that he was so employed almost up to the day of his death. The question was whether he had been employed to make this codicil.

The body of the will was in the handwriting of the widow, as was also the codicil. It was stated by her at the trial that the words were dictated to her by Usbech in her husband's hearing, and that the document was then signed by her husband in the presence of them both, and also in the presence of two other persons—a young man employed by her husband as a clerk, and by a servant-maid. These two last, together with Mr. Usbech, were the three witnesses whose names appeared in the codicil. There had been no secrets between Lady Mason and her husband as to his will. She had always, she said, endeavoured to induce him to leave Orley Farm to her child from the day of the child's birth, and had at last succeeded. In agreeing to this Sir Joseph had explained to her, somewhat angrily, that he wished to provide for Usbech's daughter, and that now he would do so out of moneys previously intended for her, the widow, and not out of the estate which would go to his eldest son. To this she had assented without a word, and had written the codicil in accordance with the lawyer's dictation, he, the lawyer, suffering at the time from gout in his hand. Among other things Lady Mason proved that on the date of the signatures Mr. Usbech had been with Sir Joseph for sundry hours.

Then the young clerk was examined. He had, he said, witnessed in his time four, ten, twenty, and, under pressure, he confessed to as many as a hundred and twenty business signatures on the part of his employer, Sir Joseph. He thought he had witnessed a hundred and twenty, but would take his oath he had not witnessed a hundred and twenty-one. He did remember witnessing a signature of his master about the time specified by the date of the codicil, and he remembered the maid-servant also signing at the same time. Mr. Usbech was then present; but he did not remember Mr. Usbech having the pen in his hand. Mr. Usbech, he knew, could not write at that time, because of the gout; but he might, no doubt, have written as much as his own name. He swore to both the signatures—his own and his master's; and in cross-examination swore that he thought it probable that they might be forgeries. On re-examination he was confident that his own name, as there appearing, had been written by himself; but on re-cross-examination, he felt sure that there was something wrong. It ended in the judge informing him that his word was worth nothing, which was hard enough on the poor young man, seeing that he had done his best to tell all that he remembered. Then the servant-girl came into the witness-box. She was sure it was her own handwriting. She remembered being called in to write her name, and seeing the master write his. It had all been explained to her at the time, but she admitted that she had not understood the explanation. She had also seen the clerk write his name, but she was not sure that she had seen Mr. Usbech write, Mr. Usbech had had a pen in his hand; she was sure of that.

The last witness was Miriam Usbech, then a very pretty, simple girl of seventeen. Her father had told her once that he hoped Sir Joseph would make provision for her. This had been shortly before her father's death. At her father's death she had been sent for to Orley Farm, and had remained there till Sir Joseph died. She had always regarded Sir Joseph and Lady Mason as her best friends. She had known Sir Joseph all her life, and did not think it unnatural that he should provide for her. She had heard her father say more than once that Lady Mason would never rest till the old gentleman had settled Orley Farm upon her son.

Not half the evidence taken has been given here, but enough probably for our purposes. The will and codicil were confirmed, and Lady Mason continued to live at the farm. Her evidence was supposed to have been excellently given, and to have been conclusive. She had seen the signature, and written the codicil, and could explain the motive. She was a woman of high character, of great talent, and of repute in the neighbourhood; and, as the judge remarked, there could be no possible reason for doubting her word. Nothing also could be simpler or prettier than the evidence of Miriam Usbech, as to whose fate and destiny people at the time expressed much sympathy. That stupid young clerk was responsible for the only weak part of the matter; but if he proved nothing on one side, neither did he prove anything on the other.

This was the commencement of the great Orley Farm Case, and having been then decided in favour of the infant it was allowed to slumber for nearly twenty years. The codicil was confirmed, and Lady Mason remained undisturbed in possession of the house, acting as guardian for her child till he came of age, and indeed for some time beyond that epoch. In the course of a page or two I shall beg my readers to allow me to introduce this lady to their acquaintance.

Miriam Usbech, of whom also we shall see something, remained at the farm under Lady Mason's care till she married a young attorney, who in process of time succeeded to such business as her father left behind him. She suffered some troubles in life before she settled down in the neighbouring country town as Mrs. Dockwrath, for she had had another lover, the stupid young clerk who had so villainously broken down in his evidence; and to this other lover, whom she had been unable to bring herself to accept, Lady Mason had given her favour and assistance. Poor Miriam was at that time a soft, mild-eyed girl, easy to be led, one would have said; but in this matter Lady Mason could not lead her. It was in vain to tell her that the character of young Dockwrath did not stand high, and that young Kenneby, the clerk, should be promoted to all manner of good things. Soft and mild-eyed as Miriam was, Love was still the lord of all. In this matter she would not be persuaded; and eventually she gave her two thousand pounds to Samuel Dockwrath, the young attorney with the questionable character.

This led to no breach between her and her patroness. Lady Mason, wishing to do the best for her young friend, had favoured John Kenneby, but she was not a woman at all likely to quarrel on such a ground as this. 'Well, Miriam,' she had said, 'you must judge for yourself, of course, in such a matter as this. You know my regard for you.'

'Oh yes, ma'am,' said Miriam, eagerly.

'And I shall always be glad to promote your welfare as Mrs. Dockwrath, if possible. I can only say that I should have had more satisfaction in attempting to do so for you as Mrs. Kenneby.' But, in spite of the seeming coldness of these words, Lady Mason had been constant to her friend for many years, and had attended to her with more or less active kindness in all the sorrows arising from an annual baby and two sets of twins—a progeny which before the commencement of my tale reached the serious number of sixteen, all living.

Among other solid benefits conferred by Lady Mason had been the letting to Mr. Dockwrath of certain two fields, lying at the extremity of the farm property, and quite adjacent to the town of Hamworth in which old Mr. Usbech had resided. These had been let by the year, at a rent not considered to be too high at that period, and which had certainly become much lower in proportion to the value of the land, as the town of Hamworth had increased. On these fields Mr. Dockwrath expended some money, though probably not so much as he averred; and when noticed to give them up at the period of young Mason's coming of age, expressed himself terribly aggrieved.

'Surely, Mr. Dockwrath, you are very ungrateful,' Lady Mason had said to him. But he had answered her with disrespectful words; and hence had arisen an actual breach between her and poor Miriam's husband. 'I must say, Miriam, that Mr. Dockwrath is unreasonable,' Lady Mason had said. And what could a poor wife answer? 'Oh! Lady Mason, pray let it bide a time till it all comes right.' But it never did come right; and the affair of those two fields created the great Orley Farm Case, which it will be our business to unravel.

And now a word or two as to this Orley Farm. In the first place let it be understood that the estate consisted of two farms. One, called the Old Farm, was let to an old farmer named Greenwood, and had been let to him and to his father for many years antecedent to the

days of the Masons. Mr. Greenwood held about three hundred
acres of land, paying with admirable punctuality over four hundred
a year in rent, and was regarded by all the Orley people as an
institution on the property. Then there was the farm-house and the
land attached to it. This was the residence in which Sir Joseph
had lived, keeping in his own hands this portion of the property.
When first inhabited by him the house was not fitted for more
than the requirements of an ordinary farmer, but he had gradually
added to it and ornamented it till it was commodious, irregular,
picturesque, and straggling. When he died, and during the occupation of his widow, it consisted of three buildings of various
heights, attached to each other, and standing in a row. The lower
contained a large kitchen, which had been the living-room of the
farm-house, and was surrounded by bakehouse, laundry, dairy, and
servants' room, all of fair dimensions. It was two stories high,
but the rooms were low, and the roof steep and covered with tiles.
The next portion had been added by Sir Joseph, then Mr. Mason,
when he first thought of living at the place. This also was tiled,
and the rooms were nearly as low; but there were three stories,
and the building therefore was considerably higher. For five-and-
twenty years the farm-house, so arranged, had sufficed for the
common wants of Sir Joseph and his family; but when he determined to give up his establishment in the City, he added on another
step to the house at Orley Farm. On this occasion he built a good
dining-room, with a drawing-room over it, and bed-room over that;
and this portion of the edifice was slated.

The whole stood in one line fronting on to a large lawn which
fell steeply away from the house into an orchard at the bottom.
This lawn was cut in terraces, and here and there upon it there
stood apple-trees of ancient growth; for here had been the garden
of the old farm-house. They were large, straggling trees, such as
do not delight the eyes of modern gardeners; but they produced
fruit by the bushel, very sweet to the palate, though probably
not so perfectly round, and large, and handsome as those which the
horticultural skill of the present day requires. The face of the
house from one end to the other was covered with vines and passion-
flowers, for the aspect was due south; and as the whole of the
later addition was faced by a verandah, which also, as regarded the
ground-floor, ran along the middle building, the place in summer
was pretty enough. As I have said before, it was irregular and
straggling, but at the same time roomy and picturesque. Such was
Orley Farm-house.

There were about two hundred acres of land attached to it,
together with a large old-fashioned farm-yard, standing not so far
from the house as most gentlemen farmers might perhaps desire.
The farm buildings, however, were well hidden, for Sir Joseph,

though he would at no time go to the expense of constructing all anew, had spent more money than such a proceeding would have cost him in doctoring existing evils and ornamenting the standing edifices. In doing this he had extended the walls of a brewhouse, and covered them with creepers, so as to shut out from the hall door the approach to the farm-yard, and had put up a quarter of a mile of high ornamental paling for the same purpose. He had planted an extensive shrubbery along the brow of the hill at one side of the house, had built summer-houses, and sunk a ha-ha fence below the orchard, and had contrived to give to the place the unmistakable appearance of an English gentleman's country-house. Nevertheless, Sir Joseph had never bestowed upon his estate, nor had it ever deserved, a more grandiloquent name than that which it had possessed of old.

Orley Farm-house itself is somewhat more than a mile distant from the town of Hamworth, but the land runs in the direction of the town, not skirting the high road, but stretching behind the cottages which stand along the pathway; and it terminates in those two fields respecting which Mr. Dockwrath the attorney became so irrationally angry at the period of which we are now immediately about to treat. These fields lie on the steep slope of Hamworth Hill, and through them runs the public path from the hamlet of Roxeth up to Hamworth church; for, as all the world knows, Hamworth church stands high, and is a landmark to the world for miles and miles around.

Within a circuit of thirty miles from London no land lies more beautifully circumstanced with regard to scenery than the country about Hamworth; and its most perfect loveliness commences just beyond the slopes of Orley Farm. There is a little village called Coldharbour, consisting of some half-dozen cottages, situated immediately outside Lady Mason's gate,—and it may as well be stated here that this gate is but three hundred yards from the house, and is guarded by no lodge. This village stands at the foot of Cleeve Hill. The land hereabouts ceases to be fertile, and breaks away into heath and common ground. Round the foot of the hill there are extensive woods, all of which belong to Sir Peregrine Orme, the lord of the manor. Sir Peregrine is not a rich man, not rich, that is, it being borne in mind that he is a baronet, that he represented his county in parliament for three or four sessions, and that his ancestors have owned The Cleeve estate for the last four hundred years; but he is by general repute the greatest man in these parts. We may expect to hear more of him also as the story makes its way.

I know many spots in England and in other lands, world-famous in regard to scenery, which to my eyes are hardly equal to Cleeve Hill. From the top of it you are told that you may see into seven counties; but to me that privilege never possessed any value. I should not care to see into seventeen counties, unless the country which spread itself before my view was fair and lovely. The country which is so seen from Cleeve Hill is exquisitely fair and lovely ;—very fair, with glorious fields of unsurpassed fertility, and lovely with oak woods and brown open heaths which stretch away, hill after hill, down towards the southern coast. I could greedily fill a long chapter with the well-loved glories of Cleeve Hill; but it may be that we must press its heather with our feet more than once in the course of our present task, and if so, it will be well to leave something for those coming visits.

'Ungrateful! I'll let her know whether I owe her any gratitude. Haven't I paid her her rent every half-year as it came due? what more would she have? Ungrateful, indeed! She is one of those women who think that you ought to go down on your knees to them if they only speak civilly to you. I'll let her know whether I'm ungrateful.'

These words were spoken by angry Mr. Samuel Dockwrath to his wife, as he stood up before his parlour-fire after breakfast, and the woman to whom he referred was Lady Mason. Mr. Samuel Dockwrath was very angry as he so spoke, or at any rate he seemed to be so. There are men who take a delight in abusing those special friends whom their wives best love, and Mr. Dockwrath was one of these. He had never given his cordial consent to the intercourse which had hitherto existed between the lady of Orley Farm and his household, although he had not declined the substantial benefits which had accompanied it. His pride had rebelled against the feeling of patronage, though his interest had submitted to the advantages thence derived. A family of sixteen children is a heavy burden for a country attorney with a small practice, even though his wife may have had a fortune of two thousand pounds : and thus Mr. Dockwrath, though he had never himself loved Lady Mason, had permitted his wife to accept all those numberless kindnesses which a lady with comfortable means and no children is always able to bestow on a favoured neighbour who has few means and many children. Indeed, he himself had accepted a great favour with reference to the holding of those two fields, and had acknowledged as much when first he took them into his hands some sixteen or seventeen years back. But all that was forgotten now; and having held them for so long a period, he bitterly felt the loss, and resolved that it would ill become him as a man and an attorney to allow so deep an injury to pass unnoticed. It may be, moreover, that Mr. Dockwrath was now doing somewhat better in the world than formerly, and that he could afford to give up Lady Mason, and to demand also that his wife should give her up. Those trumpery presents from Orley Farm were very well while he was struggling for bare bread but now, now that he had

turned the corner,—now that by his divine art and mystery of law
he had managed to become master of that beautiful result of British
perseverance, a balance at his banker's, he could afford to indulge
his natural antipathy to a lady who had endeavoured in early life to
divert from him the little fortune which had started him in the world.

Miriam Dockwrath, as she sat on this morning, listening to her
husband's anger, with a sick little girl on her knee, and four or
five others clustering round her, half covered with their matutinal
bread and milk, was mild-eyed and soft as ever. Hers was a
nature in which softness would ever prevail;—softness, and that
tenderness of heart, always leaning, and sometimes almost
crouching, of which a mild eye is the outward sign. But her
comeliness and prettiness were gone. Female beauty of the
sterner, grander sort may support the burden of sixteen children,
all living,—and still survive. I have known it to do so, and to
survive with much of its youthful glory. But that mild-eyed, soft,
round, plumpy prettiness gives way beneath such a weight as that :
years alone tell on it quickly; but children and limited means
combined with years leave to it hardly a chance.

' I'm sure I'm very sorry,' said the poor woman, worn with her
many cares.

' Sorry; yes, and I'll make her sorry, the proud minx. There's
an old saying, that those who live in glass houses shouldn't throw
stones.'

' But, Samuel, I don't think she means to be doing you any
harm. You know she always did say ——. Don't, Bessy; how
can you put your fingers into the basin in that way ?'

' Sam has taken my spoon away, mamma.'

' I'll let her know whether she's doing any harm or no. And
what signifies what was said sixteen years ago ? Has she anything to
show in writing ? As far as I know, nothing of the kind was said.'

' Oh, I remember it, Samuel; I do indeed !'

' Let me tell you then that you had better not try to remember
anything about it. If you ain't quiet, Bob, I'll make you, pretty
quick; d'ye hear that ? The fact is, your memory is not worth a
curse. Where are you to get milk for all those children, do you
think, when the fields are gone ?'

' I'm sure I'm very sorry, Samuel.'

' Sorry; yes, and somebody else shall be sorry too. And look
here, Miriam, I won't have you going up to Orley Farm on any
pretence whatever; do you hear that ?' and then, having given that
imperative command to his wife and slave, the lord and master of
that establishment walked forth into his office.

On the whole Miriam Usbech might have done better had she
followed the advice of her patroness in early life, and married the
stupid clerk.

CHAPTER II.

LADY MASON AND HER SON.

I TRUST that it is already perceived by all persistent novel readers that very much of the interest of this tale will be centred in the person of Lady Mason. Such educated persons, however, will probably be aware that she is not intended to be the heroine. The heroine, so called, must by a certain fixed law be young and marriageable. Some such heroine in some future number shall be forthcoming, with as much of the heroic about her as may be found convenient; but for the present let it be understood that the person and character of Lady Mason is as important to us as can be those of any young lady, let her be ever so gracious or ever so beautiful.

In giving the details of her history, I do not know that I need go back beyond her grandfather and grandmother, who were thoroughly respectable people in the hardware line; I speak of those relatives by the father's side. Her own parents had risen in the world,—had risen from retail to wholesale, and considered themselves for a long period of years to be good representatives of the commercial energy and prosperity of Great Britain. But a fall had come upon them,—as a fall does come very often to our excellent commercial representatives—and Mr. Johnson was in the ' Gazette.' It would be long to tell how old Sir Joseph Mason was concerned in these affairs, how he acted as the principal assignee, and how ultimately he took to his bosom as his portion of the assets of the estate, young Mary Johnson, and made her his wife and mistress of Orley Farm. Of the family of the Johnsons there were but three others, the father, the mother, and a brother. The father did not survive the disgrace of his bankruptcy, and the mother in process of time settled herself with her son in one of the Lancashire manufacturing towns, where John Johnson raised his head in business to some moderate altitude, Sir Joseph having afforded much valuable assistance. There for the present we will leave them.

I do not think that Sir Joseph ever repented of the perilous deed he did in marrying that young wife. His home for many years had been desolate and solitary; his children had gone from him, and did not come to visit him very frequently in his poor home at the farm. They had become grander people than him, had been gifted with aspiring minds, and in every turn and twist which they took, looked to do something towards washing themselves clean from the dirt of the counting-house. This was specially the case with Sir Joseph's son, to whom the father had made over lands and money sufficient to enable him to come before the world as a country gentleman with a coat of arms on his coach-panel. It would be inconvenient for us to run off to Groby Park at the present moment, and I will therefore say no more just now as to Joseph junior, but will explain that Joseph senior was not made angry by this neglect. He was a grave, quiet, rational man, not however devoid of some folly; as indeed what rational man is so devoid? He was burdened with an ambition to establish a family as the result of his success in life; and having put forth his son into the world with these views, was content that that son should act upon them persistently. Joseph Mason, Esq., of Groby Park, in Yorkshire, was now a county magistrate, and had made some way towards a footing in the county society around him. With these hopes, and ambition such as this, it was probably not expedient that he should spend much of his time at Orley Farm. The three daughters were circumstanced much in the same way : they had all married gentlemen, and were bent on rising in the world : moreover, the steadfast resolution of purpose which characterized their father was known by them all,—and by their husbands : they had received their fortunes, with some settled contingencies to be forthcoming on their father's demise; why, then, trouble the old gentleman at Orley Farm?

Under such circumstances the old gentleman married his young wife,—to the great disgust of his four children. They of course declared to each other, corresponding among themselves by letter, that the old gentleman had positively disgraced himself. It was impossible that they should make any visits whatever to Orley Farm while such a mistress of the house was there ;—and the daughters did make no such visits. Joseph, the son, whose monetary connection with his father was as yet by no means fixed and settled in its nature, did make one such visit, and then received his father's assurance—so at least he afterwards said and swore—that this marriage should by no means interfere with the expected inheritance of the Orley Farm acres. But at that time no young son had been born,—nor, probably, was any such young son expected.

The farm-house became a much brighter abode for the old man, for the few years which were left to him, after he had brought his young wife home. She was quiet, sensible, clever, and unremitting in her attention. She burthened him with no requests for gay society, and took his home as she found it, making the best of it for herself, and making it for him much better than he had ever hitherto known it. His own children had always looked down upon him, regarding him merely as a coffer from whence money might be had; and he, though he had never resented this contempt, had in a certain measure been aware of it. But there was no such feeling shown by his wife. She took the benefits which he gave her graciously and thankfully, and gave back to him in return, certainly her care and time, and apparently her love. For herself, in the way of wealth and money, she never asked for anything.

And then the baby had come, young Lucius Mason, and there was of course great joy at Orley Farm. The old father felt that the world had begun again for him, very delightfully, and was more than ever satisfied with his wisdom in regard to that marriage. But the very genteel progeny of his early youth were more than ever dissatisfied, and in their letters among themselves dealt forth harder and still harder words upon poor Sir Joseph. What terrible things might he not be expected to do now that his dotage was coming on? Those three married ladies had no selfish fears—so at least they declared, but they united in imploring their brother to look after his interests at Orley Farm. How dreadfully would the young heir of Groby be curtailed in his dignities and seignories if it should be found at the last day that Orley Farm was not to be written in his rent-roll!

And then, while they were yet bethinking themselves how they might best bestir themselves, news arrived that Sir Joseph had suddenly died. Sir Joseph was dead, and the will when read contained a codicil by which that young brat was made the heir to the Orley Farm estate. I have said that Lady Mason during her married life had never asked of her husband anything for herself; but in the law proceedings which were consequent upon Sir Joseph's death, it became abundantly evident that she had asked him for much for her son,—and that she had been specific in her requests, urging him to make a second heir, and to settle Orley Farm upon her own boy, Lucius. She herself stated that she had never done this except in the presence of a third person. She had often done so in the presence of Mr. Usbech the attorney,—as to which Mr. Usbech was not alive to testify; and she had also done so more than once in the presence of Mr. Furnival, a barrister,—as to which Mr. Furnival, being alive, did testify—very strongly.

As to that contest nothing further need now be said. It resulted in the favour of young Lucius Mason, and therefore, also, in the favour of the widow ;—in the favour moreover of Miriam Usbech, and thus ultimately in the favour of Mr. Samuel Dockwrath, who is now showing himself to be so signally ungrateful. Joseph Mason, however, retired from the battle nothing convinced. His father, he said, had been an old fool, an ass, an idiot, a vulgar, ignorant fool; but he was not a man to break his word. That signature to the codicil might be his or might not. If his, it had been obtained by fraud. What could be easier than to cheat an old doting fool? Many men agreed with Joseph Mason, thinking that Usbech the attorney had perpetrated this villainy on behalf of his daughter; but Joseph Mason would believe, or say that he believed —a belief in which none but his sisters joined him,—that Lady Mason herself had been the villain. He was minded to press the case on to a Court of Appeal, up even to the House of Lords ; but he was advised that in doing so he would spend more money than Orley Farm was worth, and that he would, almost to a certainty, spend it in vain. Under this advice he cursed the laws of his country, and withdrew to Groby Park.

Lady Mason had earned the respect of all those around her by the way in which she bore herself in the painful days of the trial, and also in those of her success,—especially also by the manner in which she gave her evidence. And thus, though she had not been much noticed by her neighbours during the short period of her married life, she was visited as a widow by many of the more respectable people round Hamworth. In all this she showed no feeling of triumph; she never abused her husband's relatives, or spoke much of the harsh manner in which she had been used. Indeed, she was not given to talk about her own personal affairs ; and although, as I have said, many of her neighbours visited her, she did not lay herself out for society. She accepted and returned their attention, but for the most part seemed to be willing that the matter should so rest. The people around by degrees came to know her ways ; they spoke to her when they met her, and occasionally went through the ceremony of a morning call ; but did not ask her to their tea-parties, and did not expect to see her at picnic and archery meetings.

Among those who took her by the hand in the time of her great trouble was Sir Peregrine Orme of The Cleeve,—for such was the name which had belonged time out of mind to his old mansion and park. Sir Peregrine was a gentleman now over seventy years of age, whose family consisted of the widow of his only son, and the only son of that widow, who was of course the heir to his estate and title. Sir Peregrine was an excellent old man, as I trust may hereafter be acknowledged ; but his regard for Lady Mason was perhaps in the first instance fostered by his extreme dislike to her stepson, Joseph Mason of Groby. Mr. Joseph Mason of Groby was quite as rich a man as Sir Peregrine, and owned an estate which was nearly as large as The Cleeve property ; but Sir Peregrine would not allow that he was a gentleman, or that he could by any possible transformation become one. He had not probably ever said so in direct words to any of the Mason family, but his opinion on the matter had in some way worked its way down to Yorkshire, and therefore there was no love to spare between these two county magistrates. There had been a slight acquaintance between Sir Peregrine and Sir Joseph; but the ladies of the two families had never met till after the death of the latter. Then, while that trial was still pending, Mrs. Orme had come forward at the instigation of her father-in-law, and by degrees there had grown up an intimacy between the two widows. When the first offers of assistance were made and accepted, Sir Peregrine no doubt did not at all dream of any such result as this. His family pride, and especially the pride which he took in his widowed daughter-in-law, would probably have been shocked by such a surmise; but, nevertheless, he had seen the friendship grow and increase without alarm. He himself had become attached to Lady Mason, and had gradually learned to excuse in her that want of gentle blood and early breeding which as a rule he regarded as necessary to a gentleman, and from whicn alone, as he thought, could spring many of those excellences which go to form the character of a lady.

It may therefore be asserted that Lady Mason's widowed life was successful. That it was prudent and well conducted no one could doubt. Her neighbours of course did say of her that she would not drink tea with Mrs. Arkwright of Mount Pleasant villa because she was allowed the privilege of entering Sir Peregrine's drawing-room; but such little scandal as this was a matter of course. Let one live according to any possible or impossible rule, yet some offence will be given in some quarter. Those who knew anything of Lady Mason's private life were aware that she did not encroach on Sir Peregrine's hospitality. She was not at The Cleeve as much as circumstances would have justified, and at one time by no means so much as Mrs. Orme would have desired.

In person she was tall and comely. When Sir Joseph had brought her to his house she had been very fair,—tall, slight, fair, and very quiet,—not possessing that loveliness which is generally most attractive to men, because the beauty of which she might boast depended on form rather than on the brightness of her eye, or the softness of her cheek and lips. Her face too, even at that age, seldom betrayed emotion, and never showed signs either of anger or of joy. Her forehead was high, and though somewhat narrow, nevertheless gave evidence of considerable mental faculties; nor was the evidence false, for those who came to know Lady Mason well, were always ready to acknowledge that she was a woman of no ordinary power. Her eyes were large and well formed, but somewhat cold. Her nose was long and regular. Her mouth also was very regular, and her teeth perfectly beautiful; but her lips were straight and thin. It would sometimes seem that she was all teeth, and yet it is certain that she never made an effort to show them. The great fault of her face was in her chin, which was too small and sharp, thus giving on occasions something of meanness to her countenance. She was now forty-seven years of age, and had a son who had reached man's estate; and yet perhaps she had more of woman's beauty at this present time than when she stood at the altar with Sir Joseph Mason. The quietness and repose of her manner suited her years and her position; age had given fulness to her tall form; and the habitual sadness of her counte nance was in fair accordance with her condition and character. And yet she was not really sad,—at least so said those who knew her. The melancholy was in her face rather than in her character, which was full of energy,—if energy may be quiet as well as assured and constant.

Of course she had been accused a dozen times of matrimonia. prospects. What handsome widow is not so accused? The world of Hamworth had been very certain at one time that she was intent on marrying Sir Peregrine Orme. But she had not married, and I think I may say on her behalf that she had never thought of marrying. Indeed, one cannot see how such a woman could make any effort in that line. It was impossible to conceive that a lady so staid in her manner should be guilty of flirting; nor was there any man within ten miles of Hamworth who would have dared to make the attempt. Women for the most part are prone to love-making—as nature has intended that they should be; but there are women from whom all such follies seem to be as distant as skittles and beer are distant from the dignity of the Lord Chancellor. Such a woman was Lady Mason.

At this time—the time which is about to exist for us as the period at which our narrative will begin—Lucius Mason was over twenty-two years old, and was living at the farm. He had spent the last three or four years of his life in Germany, where his mother had visited him every year, and had now come home intending to be the master of his own destiny. His mother's care for him during his boyhood, and up to the time at which he became of age, had been almost elaborate in its thoughtfulness. She had consulted Sir Peregrine as to his school, and Sir Peregrine, looking to the fact of the lad's own property, and also to the fact, known by him, of Lady Mason's means for such a purpose, had recommended Harrow. But the mother had hesitated, had gently discussed the matter, and had at last persuaded the baronet that such a step would be in-injudicious. The boy was sent to a private school of a high character, and Sir Peregrine was sure that he had been so sent at his own advice. 'Looking at the peculiar position of his mother,' said Sir Peregrine to his young daughter-in-law, 'at her very peculiar position, and that of his relatives, I think it will be better that he should not appear to assume anything early in life; nothing can be better conducted than Mr. Crabfield's establishment, and after much consideration I have had no hesitation in recommending her to send her son to him.' And thus Lucius Mason had been sent to Mr. Crabfield, but I do not think that the idea originated with Sir Peregrine.

'And perhaps it will be as well,' added the baronet, 'that he and Perry should not be together at school, though I have no objection to their meeting in the holidays. Mr. Crabfield's vacations are always timed to suit the Harrow holidays.' The Perry here mentioned was the grandson of Sir Peregrine—the young Peregrine who in coming days was to be the future lord of The Cleeve. When Lucius Mason was modestly sent to Mr. Crabfield's establishment at Great Marlow, young Peregrine Orme, with his prouder hopes, commenced his career at the public school.

Mr. Crabfield did his duty by Lucius Mason, and sent him home at seventeen a handsome, well-mannered lad, tall and comely to the eye, with soft brown whiskers sprouting on his cheek, well grounded in Greek, Latin, and Euclid, grounded also in French, and Italian, and possessing many more acquirements than he would have learned at Harrow. But added to these, or rather consequent on them, was a conceit which public-school education would not have created. When their mothers compared them in the holidays, not openly with outspoken words, but silently in their hearts, Lucius Mason was found by each to be the superior both in manners and knowledge; but each acknowledged also that there was more of ingenuous boyhood about Peregrine Orme.

Peregrine Orme was a year the younger, and therefore his comparative deficiencies were not the cause of any intense sorrow at The Cleeve; but his grandfather would probably have been better satisfied —and perhaps also so would his mother—had he been less addicted to the catching of rats, and better inclined towards Miss Edgeworth's novels and Shakspeare's plays, which were earnestly recommended to him by the lady and the gentleman. But boys generally are fond of rats, and very frequently are not fond of reading; and therefore, all this having been duly considered, there was not much deep sorrow in those days at The Cleeve as to the boyhood of the heir.

But there was great pride at Orley Farm, although that pride was shown openly to no one. Lady Mason in her visits at The Cleeve said but little as to her son's present excellences. As to his future career in life she did say much both to Sir Peregrine and to Mrs. Orme, asking the council of the one and expressing her fears to the other; and then, Sir Peregrine having given his consent, she sent the lad to Germany.

He was allowed to come of age without any special signs of manhood, or aught of the glory of property; although, in his case,

SIR PEREGRINE AND HIS HEIR.

that coming of age did put him into absolute possession of his inheritance. On that day, had he been so minded, he could have turned
his mother out of the farm-house, and taken exclusive possession of
the estate; but he did in fact remain in Germany for a year
beyond this period, and returned to Orley Farm only in time to be
present at the celebration of the twenty-first birthday of his friend
Peregrine Orme. This ceremony, as may be surmised, was by no
means slurred over without due rejoicing. The heir at the time
was at Christchurch; but at such a period a slight interruption
to his studies was not to be lamented. There had been Sir
Peregrine Ormes in those parts ever since the days of James I.;
and indeed in days long antecedent to those there had been knights
bearing that name, some of whom had been honourably beheaded for
treason, others imprisoned for heresy; and one made away with on
account of a supposed royal amour,—to the great glorification of
all his descendants. Looking to the antecedents of the family, it
was only proper that the coming of age of the heir should be
duly celebrated; but Lucius Mason had had no antecedents; no
great-great-grandfather of his had knelt at the feet of an improper
princess; and therefore Lady Mason, though she had been at The
Cleeve, had not mentioned the fact that on that very day her son
had become a man. But when Peregrine Orme became a man—
though still in his manhood too much devoted to rats—she gloried
greatly in her quiet way, and whispered a hope into the baronet's
ear that the young heir would not imitate the ambition of his
ancestor. 'No, by Jove! it would not do now at all,' said Sir
Peregrine, by no means displeased at the allusion.

And then that question as to the future life of Lucius Mason
became one of great importance, and it was necessary to consult,
not only Sir Peregrine Orme, but the young man himself. His
mother had suggested to him first the law: the great Mr. Furnival,
formerly of the home circuit, but now practising only in London,
was her very special friend, and would give her and her son all
possible aid in this direction. And what living man could give better
aid than the great Mr. Furnival? But Lucius Mason would have none
of the law. This resolve he pronounced very clearly while yet in
Germany, whither his mother visited him, bearing with her a long
letter written by the great Mr. Furnival himself. But nevertheless
young Mason would have none of the law. 'I have an idea,' he said,
'that lawyers are all liars.' Whereupon his mother rebuked him
for his conceited ignorance and want of charity; but she did not gain
her point.

She had, however, another string to her bow. As he objected to
be a lawyer, he might become a civil engineer. Circumstances had
made Sir Peregrine Orme very intimate with the great Mr. Brown.
Indeed, Mr. Brown was under great obligations to Sir Peregrine,

and Sir Peregrine had promised to use his influence. But Lucius
Mason said that civil engineers were only tradesmen of an upper
class, tradesmen with intellects; and he, he said, wished to use his
intellect, but he did not choose to be a tradesman. His mother
rebuked him again, as he well deserved that she should,—and then
asked him of what profession he himself had thought. 'Philo
logy,' said he; 'or as a profession, perhaps literature. I shall
devote myself to philology and the races of man. Nothing considerable has been done with them as a combined pursuit.' And
with these views he returned home,—while Peregrine Orme at
Oxford was still addicted to the hunting of rats.

But with philology and the races of man he consented to combine
the pursuit of agriculture. When his mother found that he wished
to take up his abode in his own house, she by no means opposed
him, and suggested that, as such was his intention, he himself
should farm his own land. He was very ready to do this, and had
she not represented that such a step was in every way impolitic, he
would willingly have requested Mr. Greenwood of the Old Farm to
look elsewhere, and have spread himself and his energies over the
whole domain. As it was he contented himself with desiring that
Mr. Dockwrath would vacate his small holding, and as he was imperative as to that his mother gave way without making it the
cause of a battle. She would willingly have left Mr. Dockwrath in
possession, and did say a word or two as to the milk necessary for
those sixteen children. But Lucius Mason was ducal in his ideas,
and intimated an opinion that he had a right to do what he liked
with his own. Had not Mr. Dockwrath been told, when the fields
were surrendered to him as a favour, that he would only have them
in possession till the heir should come of age? Mr. Dockwrath had
been so told; but tellings such as these are easily forgotten by men
with sixteen children. And thus Mr. Mason became an agriculturist with special scientific views as to chemistry, and a philologist
with the object of making that pursuit bear upon his studies with
reference to the races of man. He was convinced that by certain
admixtures of ammonia and earths he could produce cereal results
hitherto unknown to the farming world, and that by tracing out the
roots of words he could trace also the wanderings of man since the
expulsion of Adam from the garden. As to the latter question his
mother was not inclined to contradict him. Seeing that he would
sit at the feet neither of Mr. Furnival nor of Mr. Brown, she had no
objection to the races of man. She could endure to be talked to
about the Oceanic Mongolidæ and the Iapetidæ of the Indo-Ger-
manic class, and had perhaps her own ideas that such matters,
though somewhat foggy, were better than rats. But when he
came to the other subject, and informed her that the properly
plentiful feeding of the world was only kept waiting for the

chemists, she certainly did have her fears. Chemical agriculture
is expensive ; and though the results may possibly be remunerative, still, while we are thus kept waiting by the backwardness of
the chemists, there must be much risk in making any serious expenditure with such views.

' Mother,' he said, when he had now been at home about three
months, and when the fiat for the expulsion of Samuel Dockwrath
had already gone forth, ' I shall go to Liverpool to-morrow.'

' To Liverpool, Lucius ?'

' Yes. That guano which I got from Walker is adulterated. I
have analyzed it, and find that it does not contain above thirty-two
and a half hundredths of—— of that which it ought to hold in a
proportion of seventy-five per cent. of the whole.'

' Does it not ?'

' No ; and it is impossible to obtain results while one is working
with such fictitious materials. Look at that bit of grass at the
bottom of Greenwood's Hill.'

' The fifteen-acre field ? Why, Lucius, we always had the
heaviest crops of hay in the parish off that meadow.'

' That's all very well, mother ; but you have never tried,—
nobody about here ever has tried, what the land can really produce.
I will throw that and the three fields beyond it into one ; I will get
Greenwood to let me have that bit of the hill-side, giving him compensation of course——'

' And then Dockwrath would want compensation.'

' Dockwrath is an impertinent rascal, and I shall take an opportunity of telling him so. But as I was saying, I will throw those
seventy acres together, and then I will try what will be the relative
effects of guano and the patent blood. But I must have real guano,
and so I shall go to Liverpool.'

' I think I would wait a little, Lucius. It is almost too late for
any change of that kind this year.'

' Wait ! Yes, and what has come of waiting ? We don't wait at
all in doubling our population every thirty-three years ; but when
we come to the feeding of them we are always for waiting. It is
that waiting which has reduced the intellectual development of one
half of the human race to its present terribly low state—or rather
prevented its rising in a degree proportionate to the increase of the
population. No more waiting for me, mother, if I can help it.'

' But, Lucius, should not such new attempts as that be made by
men with large capital ?' said the mother.

' Capital is a bugbear,' said the son, speaking on this matter quite
ex cathedrâ, as no doubt he was entitled to do by his extensive
reading at a German university—' capital is a bugbear. The capital
that is really wanting is thought, mind, combination, knowledge.'

' But, Lucius—'

' Yes, I know what you are going to say, mother. I don't boast that I possess all these things; but I do say that I will endeavour to obtain them.'

' I have no doubt you will; but should not that come first ?'

' That is waiting again. We all know as much as this, that good manure will give good crops if the sun be allowed full play upon the land, and nothing but the crop be allowed to grow. That is what I shall attempt at first, and there can be no great danger in that.' And so he went to Liverpool.

Lady Mason during his absence began to regret that she had not left him in the undisturbed and inexpensive possession of the Mongolidæ and the Iapetidæ. His rent from the estate, including that which she would have paid him as tenant of the smaller farm, would have enabled him to live with all comfort; and, if such had been his taste, he might have become a philosophical student, and lived respectably without adding anything to his income by the sweat of his brow. But now the matter was likely to become serious enough. For a gentleman farmer determined to wait no longer for the chemists, whatever might be the results, an immediate profitable return per acre could not be expected as one of them. Any rent from that smaller farm would now be out of the question, and it would be well if the payments made so punctually by old Mr. Greenwood were not also swallowed up in the search after un-adulterated guano. Who could tell whether in the pursuit of science he might not insist on chartering a vessel, himself, for the Peruvian coast?

CHAPTER III.

I HAVE said that Sir Peregrine Orme was not a rich man, meaning thereby that he was not a rich man considering his acknowledged position in the county. Such men not uncommonly have their tens, twelves, and twenty thousands a year; but Sir Peregrine's estate did not give him above three or four. He was lord of the manor of Hamworth, and possessed seignorial rights, or rather the skeleton and remembrance of such rights with reference to a very large district of country; but his actual property—that from which he still received the substantial benefits of ownership—was not so large as those of some of his neighbours. There was, however, no place within the county which was so beautifully situated as The Cleeve, or which had about it so many of the attractions of age. The house itself had been built at two periods,—a new set of rooms having been added to the remains of the old Elizabethan structure in the time of Charles II. It had not about it anything that was peculiarly grand or imposing, nor were the rooms large or even commodious; but everything was old, venerable, and picturesque. Both the dining-room and the library were panelled with black wainscoating; and though the drawing-rooms were papered, the tall, elaborately-worked wooden chimney-pieces still stood in them, and a wooden band or belt round the rooms showed that the panels were still there, although hidden by the modern paper.

But it was for the beauty and wildness of its grounds that The Cleeve was remarkable. The land fell here and there into narrow, wild ravines and woody crevices. The soil of the park was not rich, and could give but little assistance to the chemists in supplying the plentiful food expected by Mr. Mason for the coming multitudes of the world; it produced in some parts heather instead of grass, and was as wild and unprofitable as Cleeve Common, which stretched for miles outside the park palings; but it seemed admirably adapted for deer and for the maintenance of half-decayed venerable oaks. Young timber also throve well about the place, and in this respect Sir Peregrine was a careful landlord. There ran a river through the park,—the River Cleeve, from which the place and parish are said to have taken their names;—a river, or rather a stream, very narrow and inconsiderable as to its volume of water, but which passed for some two miles through so narrow a passage as to give to it the appearance of a cleft or fissure in the rocks.   The water tumbled over stones through this entire course, making it seem to be fordable almost everywhere without danger of wet feet; but in truth there was hardly a spot at which it could be crossed without a bold leap from rock to rock.   Narrow as was the aperture through which the water had cut its way, nevertheless a path had been contrived, now on one side of the stream and now on the other, crossing it here and there by slight hanging wooden bridges. The air here was always damp with spray, and the rocks on both sides were covered with long mosses, as were also the overhanging boughs of the old trees.   This place was the glory of The Cleeve, and as far as picturesque beauty goes it was very glorious. There was a spot in the river from whence a steep path led down from the park to the water, and at this spot the deer would come to drink.   I know nothing more beautiful than this sight, when three or four of them could be so seen from one of the wooden bridges towards the hour of sunset in the autumn.

Sir Peregrine himself at this time was an old man, having passed his seventieth year.   He was a fine, handsome English gentleman with white hair, keen gray eyes, a nose slightly aquiline, and lips now too closely pressed together in consequence of the havoc which time had made among his teeth.   He was tall, but had lost something of his height from stooping,—was slight in his form, but well made, and vain of the smallness of his feet and the whiteness of his hands.   He was generous, quick tempered, and opinionated; generally very mild to those who would agree with him and submit to him, but intolerant of contradiction, and conceited as to his experience of the world and the wisdom which he had thence derived.   To those who were manifestly his inferiors he was affable, to his recognized equals he was courteous, to women he was almost always gentle;—but to men who claimed an equality which he would not acknowledge, he could make himself particularly disagreeable.   In judging the position which a man should hold in the world, Sir Peregrine was very resolute in ignoring all claims made by wealth alone.   Even property in land could not in his eyes create a gentleman.   A gentleman, according to his ideas, should at any rate have great-grandfathers capable of being traced in the world's history ; and the greater the number of such, and the more easily traceable they might be on the world's surface, the more unquestionable would be the status of the claimant in question. Such being the case, it may be imagined that Joseph Mason, Esq., of Groby Park did not rank high in the estimation of Sir Peregrine Orme.

I have said that Sir Peregrine was fond of his own opinion;

but nevertheless he was a man whom it was by no means difficult
to lead. In the first place he was singularly devoid of suspicion.
The word of a man or of a woman was to him always credible,
until full proof had come home to him that it was utterly unworthy of credit. After that such a man or woman might as well
spare all speech as regards the hope of any effect on the mind of
Sir Peregrine Orme. He did not easily believe a fellow-creature to
be a liar, but a liar to him once was a liar always. And then he was
amenable to flattery, and few that are so are proof against the lead-
ing-strings of their flatterers. All this was well understood of Sir
Peregrine by those about him. His gardener, his groom, and his
woodman all knew his foibles. They all loved him, respected
him, and worked for him faithfully; but each of them had his own
way in his own branch.

And there was another person at The Cleeve who took into her
own hands a considerable share of the management and leading of
Sir Peregrine, though, in truth, she made no efforts in that direction. This was Mrs. Orme, the widow of his only child, and the
mother of his heir. Mrs. Orme was a younger woman than Mrs.
Mason of Orley Farm by nearly five years, though her son was but
twelve months junior to Lucius Mason. She had been the daughter
of a brother baronet, whose family was nearly as old as that of the
Ormes; and therefore, though she had come penniless to her
husband, Sir Peregrine had considered that his son had married
well. She had been a great beauty, very small in size and delicate
of limb, fair haired, with soft blue wondering eyes, and a dimpled
cheek. Such she had been when young Peregrine Orme brought
her home to The Cleeve, and the bride at once became the darling
of her father-in-law. One year she had owned of married joy, and
then all the happiness of the family had been utterly destroyed,
and for the few following years there had been no sadder household
in all the country-side than that of Sir Peregrine Orme. His son,
his only son, the pride of all who knew him, the hope of his political party in the county, the brightest among the bright ones of
the day for whom the world was just opening her richest treasures,
fell from his horse as he was crossing into a road, and his lifeless
body was brought home to The Cleeve.

All this happened now twenty years since, but the widow still
·wears the colours of mourning. Of her also the world of course
said that she would soon console herself with a second love; but
she too has given the world the lie. From that day to the present
she has never left the house of her father-in-law; she has been a
true child to him, and she has enjoyed all a child's privileges.
There has been but little favour for any one at The Cleeve who
has been considered by the baronet to disregard the wishes of
the mistress of the establishment. Any word from her has been

law to him, and he has of course expected also that her word
should be law to others. He has yielded to her in all things, and
attended to her will as though she were a little queen, recognizing in her feminine weakness a sovereign power, as some men
can and do ; and having thus for years indulged himself in a
quixotic gallantry to the lady of his household, he has demanded of
others that they also should bow the knee.

During the last twenty years The Cleeve has not been a gay
house. During the last ten those living there have been contented,
and in the main happy ; but there has seldom been many guests in
the old hall, and Sir Peregrine has not been fond of going to other
men's feasts. He inherited the property very early in life, and
then there were on it some few encumbrances. While yet a young
man he added something to these, and now, since his own son's
death, he has been setting his house in order, that his grandson
should receive the family acres intact. Every shilling due on the
property has been paid off; and it is well that this should be so,
for there is reason to fear that the heir will want a helping hand
out of some of youth's difficulties,—perhaps once or twice before his
passion for rats gives place to a good English gentlemanlike resolve
to hunt twice a week, look after his timber, and live well within
his means.

The chief fault in the character of young Peregrine Orme was
that he was so young. There are men who are old at one-and-
twenty,—are quite fit for Parliament, the magistrate's bench, the
care of a wife, and even for that much sterner duty, the care of a
balance at the bankers ; but there are others who at that age are still
boys,—whose inner persons and characters have not begun to clothe
themselves with the ' toga virilis.' I am not sure that those whose
boyhoods are so protracted have the worst of it, if in this hurrying and competitive age they can be saved from being absolutely
trampled in the dust before they are able to do a little trampling
on their own account. Fruit that grows ripe the quickest is not the
sweetest ; nor when housed and garnered will it keep the longest.
For young Peregrine there was no need of competitive struggles.
The days have not yet come, though they are no doubt coming,
when ' detur digniori' shall be the rule of succession to all titles,
honours, and privileges whatsoever. Only think what a lift it
would give to the education of the country in general, if any lad
from seventeen to twenty-one could go in for a vacant dukedom ;
and if a goodly inheritance could be made absolutely incompatible
with incorrect spelling and doubtful proficiency in rule of three !

Luckily for Peregrine junior these days are not yet at hand, or
I fear that there would be little chance for him. While Lucius
Mason was beginning to think that the chemists might be hurried,
and that agriculture might be beneficially added to philology, our

friend Peregrine had just been rusticated, and the head of his college had intimated to the baronet that it would be well to take the young man's name off the college books. This accordingly had been done, and the heir of The Cleeve was at present at home with his mother and grandfather. What special act of grace had led to this severity we need not inquire, but we may be sure that the frolics of which he had been guilty had been essentially young in their nature. He had assisted in driving a farmer's sow into the man's best parlour, or had daubed the top of the tutor's cap with white paint, or had perhaps given liberty to a bag full of rats in the college hall at dinner-time. Such were the youth's academical amusements, and as they were pursued with unremitting energy it was thought well that he should be removed from Oxford.

Then had come the terrible question of his university bills. One after another, half a score of them reached Sir Peregrine, and then took place that terrible interview,—such as most young men have had to undergo at least once,—in which he was asked how he intended to absolve himself from the pecuniary liabilities which he had incurred.

' I am sure I don't know,' said young Orme, sadly.

' But I shall be glad, sir, if you will favour me with your intentions,' said Sir Peregrine, with severity. ' A gentleman does not, I presume, send his orders to a tradesman without having some intention of paying him for his goods.'

' I intended that they should all be paid, of course.'

' And how, sir? by whom?'

' Well, sir,—I suppose I intended that you should pay them;' and the scapegrace as he spoke looked full up into the baronet's face with his bright blue eyes,—not impudently, as though defying his grandfather, but with a bold confidence which at once softened the old man's heart.

Sir Peregrine turned away and walked twice the length of the library; then, returning to the spot where the other stood, he put his hand on his grandson's shoulder. ' Well, Peregrine, I will pay them,' he said. ' I have no doubt that you did so intend when you incurred them;—and that was perhaps natural. I will pay them; but for your own sake, and for your dear mother's sake, I hope that they are not very heavy. Can you give me a list of all that you owe?'

Young Peregrine said that he thought he could, and sitting down at once he made a clean breast of it. With all his foibles, follies, and youthful ignorances, in two respects he stood on good ground. He was neither false nor a coward. He continued to scrawl down items as long as there were any of which he could think, and then handed over the list in order that his grandfather might add them up. It was the last he ever heard of the matter; and when he re-visited Oxford some twelve months afterwards, the tradesmen whom he had honoured with his custom bowed to him as low as though he had already inherited twenty thousand a year.

Peregrine Orme was short in stature as was his mother, and he also had his mother's wonderfully bright blue eyes; but in other respects he was very like his father and grandfather;—very like all the Ormes who had lived for ages past. His hair was light; his forehead was not large, but well formed and somewhat prominent; his nose had something, though not much, of the eagle's beak; his mouth was handsome in its curve, and his teeth were good, and his chin was divided by a deep dimple. His figure was not only short, but stouter than that of the Ormes in general. He was very strong on his legs; he could wrestle, and box, and use the single-stick with a quickness and precision that was the terror of all the freshmen who had come in his way.

Mrs. Orme, his mother, no doubt thought that he was perfect. Looking at the reflex of her own eyes in his, and seeing in his face so sweet a portraiture of the nose and mouth and forehead of him whom she had loved so dearly and lost so soon, she could not but think him perfect. When she was told that the master of Lazarus had desired that her son should be removed from his college, she had accused the tyrant of unrelenting, persecuting tyranny; and the gentle arguments of Sir Peregrine had no effect towards changing her ideas. On that disagreeable matter of the bills little or nothing was said to her. Indeed, money was a subject with which she was never troubled. Sir Peregrine conceived that money was a man's business, and that the softness of a woman's character should be preserved by a total absence of all pecuniary thoughts and cares.

And then there arose at The Cleeve a question as to what should immediately be done with the heir. He himself was by no means so well prepared with an answer as had been his friend Lucius Mason. When consulted by his grandfather, he said that he did not know. He would do anything that Sir Peregrine wished. Would Sir Peregrine think it well that he should prepare himself for the arduous duties of a master of hounds? Sir Peregrine did not think this at all well, but it did not appear that he himself was prepared with any immediate proposition. Then Peregrine discussed the matter with his mother, explaining that he had hoped at any rate to get the next winter's hunting with the H. H.;—which letters have represented the Hamworth Fox Hunt among sporting men for many years past. To this his mother made no objection, expressing a hope, however, that he would go abroad in the spring. ' Home-staying youths have ever homely wits,' she said to him, smiling on him ever so sweetly.

' That's quite true, mother,' he said. ' And that's why I should like to go to Leicestershire this winter.' But going to Leicestershire this winter was out of the question.

CHAPTER IV.

GOING to Leicestershire was quite out of the question for young Orme at this period of his life, but going to London unfortunately was not so. He had become acquainted at Oxford with a gentleman of great skill in his peculiar line of life, whose usual residence was in the metropolis; and so great had been the attraction found in the character and pursuits of this skilful gentleman, that our hero had not been long at The Cleeve, after his retirement from the university, before he visited his friend. Cowcross Street, Smithfield, was the site of this professor's residence, the destruction of rats in a barrel was his profession, and his name was Carroty Bob. It is not my intention to introduce the reader to Carroty Bob in person, as circumstances occurred about this time which brought his intimacy with Mr. Orme to an abrupt conclusion. It would be needless to tell how our hero was induced to back a certain terrier, presumed to be the pride of Smithfield; how a great match came off, second only in importance to a contest for the belt of England; how money was lost and quarrels arose, and how Peregrine Orme thrashed one sporting gent within an inch of his life, and fought his way out of Carroty Bob's house at twelve o'clock at night. The tale of the row got into the newspapers, and of course reached The Cleeve. Sir Peregrine sent for his grandson into his study, and insisted on knowing everything;—how much money there was to pay, and what chance there might be of an action and damages. Of an action and damages there did not seem to be any chance, and the amount of money claimed was not large. Rats have this advantage, that they usually come cheaper than race-horses; but then, as Sir Peregrine felt sorely, they do not sound so well.

' Do you know, sir, that you are breaking your mother's heart?' said Sir Peregrine, looking very sternly at the young man—as sternly as he was able to look, let him do his worst.

Peregrine the younger had a very strong idea that he was not doing anything of the kind. He had left her only a quarter of an hour since; and though she had wept during the interview, she had forgiven him with many caresses, and had expressed her opinion that the chief fault had lain with Carroty Bob and those other wretched people who had lured her dear child into their villainous den. She had altogether failed to conceal her pride at his having fought his way out from among them, and had ended by sup plying his pocket out of her own immediate resources. 'I hope not, sir,' said Peregrine the younger, thinking over some of these things.

'But you will, sir, if you go on with this shameless career. I do not speak of myself. I do not expect you to sacrifice your tastes for me; but I did think that you loved your mother!'

'So I do;—and you too.'

'I am not speaking about myself, sir. When I think what your father was at your age;—how nobly——' And then the baronet was stopped in his speech, and wiped his eyes with his handkerchief. 'Do you think that your father, sir, followed such pursuits as these? Do you think that he spent his time in the pursuit of—rats?'

'Well; I don't know; I don't think he did. But I have heard you say, sir, that you sometimes went to cockfights when you were young.'

'To cockfights! well, yes. But let me tell you, sir, that I always went in the company of gentlemen—that is, when I did go, which was very seldom.' The baronet in some after-dinner half-hour had allowed this secret of his youth to escape from him, imprudently.

'And I went to the house in Cowcross Street with Lord John Fitzjoly.'

'The last man in all London with whom you ought to associate! But I am not going to argue with you, sir. If you think, and will continue to think, that the slaughtering of vermin is a proper pursuit——'

'But, sir, foxes are vermin also.'

'Hold your tongue, sir, and listen to me. You know very well what I mean, sir. If you think that—rats are a proper pursuit for a gentleman in your sphere of life, and if all that I can say has no effect in changing your opinion,—I shall have done. I have not many years of life before me, and when I shall be no more, you can squander the property in any vile pursuits that may be pleasing to you. But, sir, you shall not do it while I am living; nor, if I can help it, shall you rob your mother of such peace of mind as is left for her in this world. I have only one alternative for you, sir ——.' Sir Peregrine did not stop to explain what might be the other branch of this alternative. 'Will you give me your word of honour as a gentleman that you will never again concern yourself in this disgusting pursuit?'

'Never, grandfather!' said Peregrine, solemnly.

Sir Peregrine before he answered bethought himself that any

pledge given for a whole life-time must be foolish; and he bethought himself also that if he could wean his heir from rats for a year or so, the taste would perish from lack of nourishment. ' I will say for two years,' said Sir Peregrine, still maintaining his austere look.

' For two years!' repeated Peregrine the younger; ' and this is the fourth of October.'

' Yes, sir; for two years,' said the baronet, more angry than ever at the young man's pertinacity, and yet almost amused at his grandson's already formed resolve to go back to his occupation at the first opportunity allowed.

' Couldn't you date it from the end of August, sir? The best of the matches always come off in September.'

' No, sir; I will not date it from any other time than the present. Will you give me your word of honour as a gentleman, for two years?'

Peregrine thought over the proposition for a minute or two in sad anticipation of all that he was to lose, and then slowly gave his adhesion to the terms. ' Very well, sir;—for two years.' And then he took out his pocket-book and wrote in it slowly.

It was at any rate manifest that he intended to keep his word, and that was much; so Sir Peregrine accepted the promise for what it was worth. ' And now,' said he, ' if you have got nothing better to do, we will ride down to Crutchley Wood.'

' I should like it of all things,' said his grandson.

' Samson wants me to cut a new bridle-path through from the larches at the top of the hill down to Crutchley Bottom; but I don't think I'll have it done. Tell Jacob to let us have the nags; I'll ride the gray pony. And ask your mother if she'll ride with us.'

It was the manner of Sir Peregrine to forgive altogether when he did forgive; and to commence his forgiveness in all its integrity from the first moment of the pardon. There was nothing he disliked so much as being on bad terms with those around him, and with none more so than with his grandson. Peregrine well knew how to make himself pleasant to the old man, and when duly encouraged would always do so. And thus the family party, as they rode on this occasion through the woods of The Cleeve, discussed oaks and larches, beech and birches, as though there were no such animal as a rat in existence, and no such place known as Cowcross Street.

' Well, Perry, as you and Samson are both of one mind, I suppose the path must be made,' said Sir Peregrine, as he got off his horse at the entrance of the stable-yard, and prepared to give his feeble aid to Mrs. Orme.

Shortly after this the following note was brought up to The Cleeve by a messenger from Orley Farm :—

' MY DEAR SIR PEREGRINE,

   ' IF you are quite disengaged at twelve o'clock to-morrow, I will walk over to The Cleeve at that hour. Or if it would suit you better to call here as you are riding, I would remain within till you come. I want your kind advice on a certain matter.

           ' Most sincerely yours,

' *Thursday.*'   ' MARY MASON.

 Lady Mason, when she wrote this note, was well aware that it would not be necessary for her to go to The Cleeve. Sir Peregrine's courtesy would not permit him to impose any trouble on a lady when the alternative of taking that trouble on himself was given to him. Moreover, he liked to have some object for his daily ride; he liked to be consulted ' on certain matters;' and he especially liked being so consulted by Lady Mason. So he sent word back that he would be at the farm at twelve on the following day, and exactly at that hour his gray pony or cob might have been seen slowly walking up the avenue to the farm-house.

 The Cleeve was not distant from Orley Farm more than two miles by the nearest walking-path, although it could not be driven much under five. With any sort of carriage one was obliged to come from The Cleeve House down to the lodge on the Hamworth and Alston road, and then to drive through the town of Hamworth, and so back to the farm. But in walking one would take the path along the river for nearly a mile, thence rise up the hill to the top of Crutchley Wood, descend through the wood to Crutchley Bottom, and, passing along the valley, come out at the foot of Cleeve Hill, just opposite to Orley Farm Gate. The distance for a horseman was somewhat greater, seeing that there was not as yet any bridle-way through Crutchley Wood. Under these circumstances the journey between the two houses was very frequently made on foot; and for those walking from The Cleeve House to Hamworth the nearest way was by Lady Mason's gate.

 Lady Mason's drawing-room was very pretty, though it was by no means fashionably furnished. Indeed, she eschewed fashion in all things, and made no pretence of coming out before the world as a great lady. She had never kept any kind of carriage, though her means, combined with her son's income, would certainly have justified her in a pony-chaise. Since Lucius had become master of the house he had presented her with such a vehicle, and also with the pony and harness complete; but as yet she had never used it, being afraid, as she said to him with a smile, of appearing ambitious before the stern citizens of Hamworth. ' Nonsense, mother,' he had replied, with a considerable amount of young dignity in his face. ' We are all entitled to those comforts for which we can afford to pay without injury to any one. I shall take it ill of you if I do not see you using it.'

' Oh, Sir Peregrine, this is so kind of you,' said Lady Mason, coming forward to meet her friend. She was plainly dressed, without any full exuberance of costume, and yet everything about her was neat and pretty, and everything had been the object of feminine care. A very plain dress may occasion as much study as the most elaborate,—and may be quite as worthy of the study it has caused. Lady Mason, I am inclined to think, was by no means indifferent to the subject, but then to her belonged the great art of hiding her artifice.

' Not at all; not at all,' said Sir Peregrine, taking her hand and pressing it, as he always did. ' What is the use of neighbours if they are not neighbourly?' This was all very well from Sir Peregrine in the existing case; but he was not a man who by any means recognized the necessity of being civil to all who lived near him. To the great and to the poor he was neighbourly; but it may be doubted whether he would have thought much of Lady Mason if she had been less good looking or less clever.

' Ah! I know how good you always are to me. But I'll tell you why I am troubling you now. Lucius went off two days since to Liverpool.'

' My grandson told me that he had left home.'

' He is an excellent young man, and I am sure that I have every reason to be thankful.' Sir Peregrine, remembering the affair in Cowcross Street, and certain other affairs of a somewhat similar nature, thought that she had; but for all that he would not have exchanged his own bright-eyed lad for Lucius Mason with all his virtues and all his learning.

' And indeed I am thankful,' continued the widow. ' Nothing can be better than his conduct and mode of life; but——'

' I hope he has no attraction at Liverpool, of which you disapprove.'

' No, no; there is nothing of that kind. His attraction is——; but perhaps I had better explain the whole matter. Lucius, you know, has taken to farming.'

' He has taken up the land which you held yourself, has he not?'

' Yes, and a little more; and he is anxious to add even to that. He is very energetic about it, Sir Peregrine.'

' Well; the life of a gentleman farmer is not a bad one; though in his special circumstances I would certainly have recommended a profession.'

' Acting upon your advice I did urge him to go to the bar. But he has a will of his own, and a mind altogether made up as to the line of life which he thinks will suit him best. What I fear now is, that he will spend more money upon experiments that he can afford.'

'Experimental farming is an expensive amusement,' said Sir Peregrine, with a very serious shake of his head.

'I am afraid it is; and now he has gone to Liverpool to buy —— guano,' said the widow, feeling some little shame in coming to so inconsiderable a conclusion after her somewhat stately prologue.

'To buy guano! Why could he not get his guano from Walker, as my man Symonds does?'

'He says it is not good. He analyzed it, and——'

'Fiddlestick! Why didn't he order it in London, if he didn't like Walker's. Gone to Liverpool for guano! I'll tell you what it is, Lady Mason; if he intends to farm his land in that way, he should have a very considerable capital at his back. It will be a long time before he sees his money again.' Sir Peregrine had been farming all his life, and had his own ideas on the subject. He knew very well that no gentleman, let him set to work as he might with his own land, could do as well with it as a farmer who must make a living out of his farming besides paying the rent; —who must do that or else have no living; and he knew also that such operations as those which his young friend was now about to attempt was an amusement fitted only for the rich. It may be also that he was a little old fashioned, and therefore prejudiced against new combinations between agriculture and chemistry. 'He must put a stop to that kind of work very soon, Lady Mason; he must indeed; or he will bring himself to ruin—and you with him.'

Lady Mason's face became very grave and serious. 'But what can I say to him, Sir Peregrine? In such a matter as that I am afraid that he would not mind me. If you would not object to speaking to him?'

Sir Peregrine was graciously pleased to say that he would not object. It was a disagreeable task, he said, that of giving advice to a young man who was bound by no tie either to take it or even to receive it with respect.

'You will not find him at all disrespectful; I think I can promise that,' said the frightened mother: and that matter was ended by a promise on the part of the baronet to take the case in hand, and to see Lucius immediately on his return from Liverpool. 'He had better come and dine at The Cleeve,' said Sir Peregrine, 'and we will have it out after dinner.' All of which made Lady Mason very grateful.

CHAPTER V.

WE left Lady Mason very grateful at the end of the last chapter for the promise made to her by Sir Peregrine with reference to her son; but there was still a weight on Lady Mason's mind. They say that the pith of a lady's letter is in the postscript, and it may be that that which remained for Lady Mason to say, was after all the matter as to which she was most anxious for assistance. ' As you are here,' she said to the baronet, ' would you let me mention another subject?'

' Surely,' said he, again putting down his hat and riding-stick.

Sir Peregrine was not given to close observation of those around him, or he might have seen by the heightened colour of the lady's face, and by the slight nervous hesitation with which she began to speak, that she was much in earnest as to this other matter. And had he been clever in his powers of observation he might have seen also that she was anxious to hide this feeling. ' You remember the circumstances of that terrible lawsuit?' she said, at last.

' What; as to Sir Joseph's will? Yes; I remember them well.'

' I know that I shall never forget all the kindness that you showed me,' said she. ' I don't know how I should have lived through it without you and dear Mrs. Orme.'

' But what about it now?'

' I fear I am going to have further trouble.'

' Do you mean that the man at Groby Park is going to try the case again? It is not possible after such a lapse of time. I am no lawyer, but I do not think that he can do it.'

' I do not know—I do not know what he intends, or whether he intends anything; but I am sure of this,—that he will give me trouble if he can. But I will tell you the whole story, Sir Peregrine. It is not much, and perhaps after all may not be worth attention. You know the attorney in Hamworth who married Miriam Usbech?'

' What, Samuel Dockwrath? Oh, yes; I know him well enough; and to tell the truth I do not think very well of him. Is he not a tenant of yours?'

' Not at present.' And then Lady Mason explained the manner in which the two fields had been taken out of the lawyer's hands by her son's order.

'Ah! he was wrong there,' said the baronet. 'When a man has held land so long it should not be taken away from him except under pressing circumstances; that is if he pays his rent.'

Mr. Dockwrath did pay his rent, certainly; and now, I fear, he is determined to do all he can to injure us.'

'But what injury can Mr. Dockwrath do you?'

'I do not know; but he has gone down to Yorkshire,—to Mr. Mason's place; I know that; and he was searching through some papers of old Mr. Usbech's before he went. Indeed, I may say that I know as a fact that he has gone to Mr. Mason with the hope that these law proceedings may be brought on again.'

'You know it as a fact?'

'I think I may say so.'

'But, dear Lady Mason, may I ask you how you know this as a fact?'

'His wife was with me yesterday,' she said, with some feeling of shame as she disclosed the source from whence she had obtained her information.

'And did she tell the tale against her own husband?'

'Not as meaning to say anything against him, Sir Peregrine; you must not think so badly of her as that; nor must you think that I would willingly obtain information in such a manner. But you must understand that I have always been her friend; and when she found that Mr. Dockwrath had left home on a matter in which I am so nearly concerned, I cannot but think it natural that she should let me know.'

To this Sir Peregrine made no direct answer. He could not quite say that he thought it was natural, nor could he give any expressed approval of any such intercourse between Lady Mason and the attorney's wife. He thought it would be better that Mr. Dockwrath should be allowed to do his worst, if he had any intention of doing evil, and that Lady Mason should pass it by without condescending to notice the circumstance. But he made allowances for her weakness, and did not give utterance to his disapproval in words.

'I know you think that I have done wrong,' she then said, appealing to him; and there was a tone of sorrow in her voice which went to his heart.

'No, not wrong; I cannot say that you have done wrong. It may be a question whether you have done wisely.'

'Ah! if you only condemn my folly, I will not despair. It is probable I may not have done wisely, seeing that I had not you to direct me. But what shall I do now? Oh, Sir Peregrine, say that you will not desert me if all this trouble is coming on me again!'

'No, I will not desert you, Lady Mason; you may be sure of that.'

'Dearest friend!'

'But I would advise you to take no notice whatever of Mr.

Dockwrath and his proceedings. I regard him as a person entirely beneath your notice, and if I were you I should not move at all in this matter unless I received some legal summons which made it necessary for me to do so. I have not the honour of any personal acquaintance with Mr. Mason of Groby Park.' It was in this way that Sir Peregrine always designated his friend's stepson—' but if I understand the motives by which he may probably be actuated in this or in any other matter, I do not think it likely that he will expend money on so very unpromising a case.'

' He would do anything for vengeance.'

' I doubt if he would throw away his money even for that, unless he were very sure of his prey. And in this matter, what can he possibly do? He has the decision of the jury against him, and at the time he was afraid to carry the case up to a court of appeal.'

' But, Sir Peregrine, it is impossible to know what documents he may have obtained since that.'

' What documents can do you any harm;—unless, indeed, there should turn out to be a will subsequent to that under which your son inherits the property?'

' Oh, no; there was no subsequent will.'

' Of course there was not; and therefore you need not frighten yourself. It is just possible that some attempt may be made now that your son is of age, but I regard even that as improbable.'

' And you would not advise me then to say anything to Mr. Furnival?'

' No; certainly not—unless you receive some legal notice which may make it necessary for you to consult a lawyer. Do nothing; and if Mrs. Dockwrath comes to you again, tell her that you are not disposed to take any notice of her information. Mrs. Dockwrath is, I am sure, a very good sort of woman. Indeed I have always heard so. But, if I were you, I don't think that I should feel inclined to have much conversation with her about my private affairs. What you tell her you tell also to her husband.' And then the baronet, having thus spoken words of wisdom, sat silent in his arm-chair; and Lady Mason, still looking into his face, remained silent also for a few minutes.

' I am so glad I asked you to come,' she then said.

' I am delighted, if I have been of any service to you.

' Of any service! oh, Sir Peregrine, you cannot understand what it is to live alone as I do,—for of course I cannot trouble Lucius with these matters; nor can a man, gifted as you are, comprehend how a woman can tremble at the very idea that those law proceedings may possibly be repeated.'

Sir Peregrine could not but remember as he looked at her that during all those law proceedings, when an attack was made, not only on her income but on her honesty, she had never seemed to tremble. She had always been constant to herself, even when things appeared to be going against her. But years passing over her head since that time had perhaps told upon her courage.

' But I will fear nothing now, as you have promised that you will still be my friend.'

' You may be very sure of that, Lady Mason. I believe that I may fairly boast that I do not easily abandon those whom I have once regarded with esteem and affection; among whom Lady Mason will, I am sure, allow me to say that she is reckoned as by no means the least.' And then taking her hand, the old gentleman bowed over it and kissed it.

' My dearest, dearest friend!' said she; and lifting Sir Peregrine's beautifully white hand to her lips she also kissed that. It will be remembered that the gentleman was over seventy, and that this pretty scene could therefore be enacted without impropriety on either side. Sir Peregrine then went, and as he passed out of the door Lady Mason smiled on him very sweetly. It is quite true that he was over seventy; but nevertheless the smile of a pretty woman still had charms for him, more especially if there was a tear in her eye the while;—for Sir Peregrine Orme had a soft heart.

As soon as the door was closed behind him Lady Mason seated herself in her accustomed chair, and all trace of the smile vanished from her face. She was alone now, and could allow her countenance to be a true index of her mind. If such was the case her heart surely was very sad. She sat there perfectly still for nearly an hour, and during the whole of that time there was the same look of agony on her brow. Once or twice she rubbed her hands across her forehead, brushing back her hair, and showing, had there been any one by to see it, that there was many a gray lock there mixed with the brown hairs. Had there been any one by, she would, it may be surmised, have been more careful.

There was no smile in her face now, neither was there any tear in her eye. The one and the other emblem were equally alien to her present mood.. But there was sorrow at her heart, and deep thought in her mind. She knew that her enemies were conspiring against her,—against her and against her son; and what steps might she best take in order that she might baffle them?

' I have got that woman on the hip now.' Those were the words which Mr. Dockwrath had uttered into his wife's ears, after two days spent in searching through her father's papers. The poor woman had once thought of burning all those papers—in old days before she had become Mrs. Dockwrath. Her friend, Lady Mason, had counselled her to do so, pointing out to her that they were troublesome, and could by no possibility lead to profit; but she had consulted her lover, and he had counselled her to burn nothing. ' Would that she had been guided by her friend!' she now said to

"There was sorrow in her heart, and deep thought in her mind."

herself with regard to that old trunk, and perhaps occasionally with regard to some other things.

' I have got that woman on the hip at last!' and there had been a gleam of satisfaction in Samuel's eye as he uttered the words which had convinced his wife that it was not an idle threat. She knew nothing of what the box had contained; and now, even if it had not been kept safe from her under Samuel's private key, the contents which were of interest had of course gone. ' I have business in the north, and shall be away for about a week,' Mr. Dockwrath had said to her on the following morning.

' Oh, very well; then I'll put up your things,' she had answered in her usual mild, sad, whining, household voice. Her voice at home was always sad and whining, for she was overworked, and had too many cares, and her lord was a tyrant to her rather than a husband.

' Yes, I must see Mr. Mason immediately. And look here, Miriam, I positively insist that you do not go to Orley Farm, or hold any intercourse whatever with Lady Mason. D'ye hear?'

Mrs. Dockwrath said that she did hear, and promised obedience. Mr. Dockwrath probably guessed that the moment his back was turned all would be told at the farm, and probably also had no real objection to her doing so. Had he in truth wished to keep his proceedings secret from Lady Mason he would not have divulged them to his wife. And then Mr. Dockwrath did start for the north, bearing certain documents with him; and soon after his departure Mrs. Dockwrath did pay a visit to Orley Farm.

Lady Mason sat there perfectly still for about an hour thinking what she would do. She had asked Sir Peregrine, and had the advantage of his advice; but that did not weigh much with her. What she wanted from Sir Peregrine was countenance and absolute assistance in the day of trouble,—not advice. She had desired to renew his interest in her favour, and to receive from him his assurance that he would not desert her; and that she had obtained. It was of course also necessary that she should consult him; but in turning over within her own mind this and that line of conduct, she did not, consciously, attach any weight to Sir Peregrine's opinion. The great question for her to decide was this;—should she put herself and her case into the hands of her friend Mr. Furnival now at once, or should she wait till she had received some certain symptom of hostile proceedings? If she did see Mr. Furnival, what could she tell him? only this, that Mr. Dockwrath had found some document among the papers of old Mr. Usbech, and had gone off with the same to Groby Park in Yorkshire. What that document might be she was as ignorant as the attorney's wife.

When the hour was ended she had made up her mind that she would do nothing more in the matter, at any rate on that day.

CHAPTER VI.

MR. SAMUEL DOCKWRATH was a little man, with sandy hair, a pale face, and stone-blue eyes. In judging of him by appearance only and not by the ear, one would be inclined to doubt that he could be a very sharp attorney abroad and a very persistent tyrant at home. But when Mr. Dockwrath began to talk, one's respect for him began to grow. He talked well and to the point, and with a tone of voice that could command where command was possible, persuade where persuasion was required, mystify when mystification was needed, and express with accuracy the tone of an obedient humble servant when servility was thought to be expedient. We will now accompany him on his little tour into Yorkshire.

Groby Park is about seven miles from Leeds, and as Mr. Dockwrath had in the first instance to travel from Hamworth up to London, he did not reach Leeds till late in the evening. It was a nasty cold, drizzling night, so that the beauties and marvels of the large manufacturing town offered him no attraction, and at nine o'clock he had seated himself before the fire in the commercial room at The Bull, had called for a pair of public slippers, and was about to solace all his cares with a glass of mahogany-coloured brandy and water and a cigar. The room had no present occupant but himself, and therefore he was able to make the most of all its comforts. He had taken the solitary arm-chair, and had so placed himself that the gas would fall direct from behind his head on to that day's Leeds and Halifax Chronicle, as soon as he should choose to devote himself to local politics.

The waiter had looked at him with doubtful eyes when he asked to be shown into the commercial room, feeling all but confident that such a guest had no right to be there. He had no bulky bundles of samples, nor any of those outward characteristics of a commercial 'gent' with which all men conversant with the rail and road are acquainted, and which the accustomed eye of a waiter recognizes at a glance. And here it may be well to explain that ordinary travellers are in this respect badly treated by the customs of England, or rather by the hotel-keepers. All inn-keepers have commercial rooms, as certainly as they have taps and bars, but all of them do not have commercial rooms in the properly exclusive sense. A stranger, therefore, who has asked for and obtained his mutton-chop in the commercial room of The Dolphin, The Bear, and The George, not unnaturally asks to be shown into the same chamber at the King's Head. But the King's Head does a business with real commercials, and the stranger finds himself— out of his element.

''Mercial, sir?' said the waiter at The Bull Inn, Leeds, to Mr. Dockwrath, in that tone of doubt which seemed to carry an answer to his own question. But Mr. Dockwrath was not a man to be put down by a waiter. 'Yes,' said he. 'Didn't you hear me say so?' And then the waiter gave way. None of those lords of the road were in the house at the moment, and it might be that none would come that night.

Mr. Dockwrath had arrived by the 8·22 P.M. down, but the 8·45 P.M. up from the north followed quick upon his heels, and he had hardly put his brandy and water to his mouth before a rush and a sound of many voices were heard in the hall. There is a great difference between the entrance into an inn of men who are not known there and of men who are known. The men who are not known are shy, diffident, doubtful, and anxious to propitiate the chambermaid by great courtesy. The men who are known are loud, jocular, and assured;—or else, in case of deficient accommodation, loud, angry, and full of threats. The guests who had now arrived were well known, and seemed at present to be in the former mood. ' Well, Mary, my dear, what's the time of day with you?' said a rough, bass voice, within the hearing of Mr. Dockwrath. 'Much about the old tune, Mr. Moulder,' said the girl at the bar. 'Time to look alive and keep moving. Will you have them boxes up stairs, Mr. Kantwise?' and then there were a few words about the luggage, and two real commercial gentlemen walked into the room.

Mr. Dockwrath resolved to stand upon his rights, so he did not move his chair, but looked up over his shoulder at the new comers. The first man who entered was short and very fat;—so fat that he could not have seen his own knees for some considerable time past. His face rolled with fat, as also did all his limbs. His eyes were large, and bloodshot. He wore no beard, and therefore showed plainly the triple bagging of his fat chin. In spite of his over-whelming fatness, there was something in his face that was masterful and almost vicious. His body had been overcome by eating, but not as yet his spirit,—one would be inclined to say. This was Mr. Moulder, well known on the road as being in the grocery and spirit line; a pushing man, who understood his business, and was well trusted by his firm in spite of his habitual intemperance. What did the firm care whether or no he killed himself by eating and drinking? He sold his goods, collected his money, and made his remittances. If he got drunk at night that was nothing to them, seeing that he always did his quota of work the next day. But Mr. Moulder did not get drunk. His brandy and water went into his blood, and into his eyes, and into his feet, and into his hands,—but not into his brain.

The other was a little spare man in the hardware line, of the name of Kantwise. He disposed of fire-irons, grates, ovens, and kettles, and was at the present moment heavily engaged in the sale of certain newly-invented metallic tables and chairs lately brought out by the Patent Steel Furniture Company, for which Mr. Kantwise did business. He looked as though a skin rather too small for the purpose had been drawn over his head and face, so that his forehead and cheeks and chin were tight and shiny. His eyes were small and green, always moving about in his head, and were seldom used by Mr. Kantwise in the ordinary way. At whatever he looked he looked sideways; it was not that he did not look you in the face, but he always looked at you with a sidelong glance, never choosing to have you straight in front of him. And the more eager he was in conversation—the more anxious he might be to gain his point, the more he averted his face and looked askance; so that sometimes he would prefer to have his antagonist almost behind his shoulder. And then as he did this, he would thrust forward his chin, and having looked at you round the corner till his eyes were nearly out of his head, he would close them both and suck in his lips, and shake his head with rapid little shakes, as though he were saying to himself, ' Ah, sir! you're a bad un, a very bad un.' His nose—for I should do Mr. Kantwise injustice if I did not mention this feature—seemed to have been compressed almost into nothing by that skin-squeezing operation. It was long enough, taking the measurement down the bridge, and projected sufficiently, counting the distance from the upper lip; but it had all the properties of a line; it possessed length without breadth. There was nothing in it from side to side. If you essayed to pull it, your fingers would meet. When I shall have also said that the hair on Mr. Kantwise's head stood up erect all round to the height of two inches, and that it was very red, I shall have been accurate enough in his personal description.

That Mr. Moulder represented a firm good business, doing tea, coffee, and British brandy on a well-established basis of capital and profit, the travelling commercial world in the north of England was well aware. No one entertained any doubt about his employers, Hubbles and Grease of Houndsditch. Hubbles and Grease were all right, as they had been any time for the last twenty years. But I cannot say that there was quite so strong a confidence felt in the Patent Steel Furniture Company generally, or in the individual operations of Mr. Kantwise in particular. The world in Yorkshire and Lancashire was doubtful about metallic tables, and it was thought that Mr. Kantwise was too eloquent in their praise.

Mr. Moulder when he had entered the room, stood still, to enable the waiter to peel off from him his greatcoat and the large shawl with which his neck was enveloped, and Mr. Kantwise performed the same operation for himself, carefully folding up the articles of clothing as he took them off. Then Mr. Moulder fixed his eyes on Mr. Dockwrath, and stared at him very hard. 'Who's the party, James?' he said to the waiter, speaking in a whisper that was plainly heard by the attorney.

'Gen'elman by the 8·22 down,' said James.

'Commercial?' asked Mr. Moulder, with angry frown.

'He says so himself, anyways,' said the waiter.

'Gammon!' replied Mr. Moulder, who knew all the bearings of a commercial man thoroughly, and could have put one together if he were only supplied with a little bit—say the mouth, as Professor Owen always does with the Dodoes. Mr. Moulder now began to be angry, for he was a stickler for the rights and privileges of his class, and had an idea that the world was not so conservative in that respect as it should be. Mr. Dockwrath, however, was not to be frightened, so he drew his chair a thought nearer to the fire, took a sup of brandy and water, and prepared himself for war if war should be necessary.

'Cold evening, sir, for the time of year,' said Mr. Moulder, walking up to the fireplace, and rolling the lumps of his forehead about in his attempt at a frown. In spite of his terrible burden of flesh, Mr. Moulder could look angry on occasions, but he could only do so when he was angry. He was not gifted with a command of his facial muscles.

'Yes,' said Mr. Dockwrath, not taking his eyes from off the Leeds and Halifax Chronicle. 'It is coldish. Waiter, bring me a cigar.'

This was very provoking, as must be confessed. Mr. Moulder had not been prepared to take any step towards turning the gentleman out, though doubtless he might have done so had he chosen to exercise his prerogative. But he did expect that the gentleman would have acknowledged the weakness of his footing, by moving himself a little towards one side of the fire, and he did not expect that he would have presumed to smoke without asking whether the practice was held to be objectionable by the legal possessors of the room. Mr. Dockwrath was free of any such pusillanimity. 'Waiter,' he said again, 'bring me a cigar, d'ye hear?'

The great heart of Moulder could not stand this unmoved. He had been an accustomed visitor to that room for fifteen years, and had always done his best to preserve the commercial code unsullied. He was now so well known, that no one else ever presumed to take

the chair at the four o'clock commercial dinner if he were present.
It was incumbent on him to stand forward and make a fight, more
especially in the presence of Kantwise, who was by no means
stanch to his order.   Kantwise would at all times have been glad
to have outsiders in the room, in order that he might puff his
tables, and if possible effect a sale ;—a mode of proceeding held in
much aversion by the upright, old-fashioned, commercial mind.

'Sir,' said Mr. Moulder, having become very red about the cheeks
and chin, 'I and this gentleman are going to have a bit of supper,
and it aint accustomed to smoke in commercial rooms during
meals.   You know the rules no doubt if you're commercial yourself;
—as I suppose you are, seeing you in this room.'

Now Mr. Moulder was wrong in his law, as he himself was very
well aware.   Smoking is allowed in all commercial rooms when
the dinner has been some hour or so off the table.   But then it was
necessary that he should hit the stranger in some way, and the
chances were that the stranger would know nothing about commercial law.   Nor did he; so he merely looked Mr. Moulder hard
in the face.   But Mr. Kantwise knew the laws well enough, and
as he saw before him a possible purchaser of metallic tables, he came
to the assistance of the attorney.

'I think you are a little wrong there, Mr. Moulder; eh; aint
you ?' said he.

'Wrong about what?' said Moulder, turning very sharply upon
his base-minded compatriot.

'Well, as to smoking.   It's nine o'clock, and if the gentleman——'

'I don't care a brass farthing about the clock,' said the other,
'but when I'm going to have a bit of steak with my tea, in my own
room, I chooses to have it comfortable.'

'Goodness me, Mr. Moulder, how many times have I seen you
sitting there with a pipe in your mouth, and half a dozen gents
eating their teas the while in this very room?   The rule of the case
I take it to be this; when ——'

'Bother your rules.'

'Well; it was you spoke of them.'

'The question I take to be this,' said Moulder, now emboldened
by the opposition he had received.   'Has the gentleman any right
to be in this room at all, or has he not?   Is he commercial, or is he
—— miscellaneous ?   That's the chat, as I take it.'

'You're on the square there, I must allow,' said Kantwise.

'James,' said Moulder, appealing with authority to the waiter,
who had remained in the room during the controversy ;—and now
Mr. Moulder was determined to do his duty and vindicate his profession, let the consequences be what they might.   'James, is that
gentleman commercial, or is he not ?'

It was clearly necessary now that Mr. Dockwrath himself should take his own part, and fight his own battle. 'Sir,' said he, turning to Mr. Moulder, 'I think you'll find it extremely difficult to define that word;—extremely difficult. In this enterprising country all men are more or less commercial.'

'Hear! hear!' said Mr. Kantwise.

'That's gammon,' said Mr. Moulder.

'Gammon it may be,' said Mr. Dockwrath, 'but nevertheless it's right in law. Taking the word in its broadest, strictest, and most intelligible sense, I am a commercial gentleman; and as such I do maintain that I have a full right to the accommodation of this public room.'

'That's very well put,' said Mr. Kantwise.

'Waiter,' thundered out Mr. Moulder, as though he imagined that that functionary was down the yard at the taproom instead of standing within three feet of his elbow. 'Is this gent a commercial, or is he not? Because if not,—then I'll trouble you to send Mr. Crump here. My compliments to Mr. Crump, and I wish to see him.' Now Mr. Crump was the landlord of the Bull Inn.

'Master's just stepped out, down the street,' said James.

'Why don't you answer my question, sir?' said Moulder, becoming redder and still more red about his shirt-collars.

'The gent said as how he was 'mercial,' said the poor man. 'Was I to go to contradict a gent and tell him he wasn't when he said as how he was?'

'If you please,' said Mr. Dockwrath, 'we will not bring the waiter into this discussion. I asked for the commercial room, and he did his duty in showing me to the door of it. The fact I take to be this; in the south of England the rules to which you refer are not kept so strictly as in these more mercantile localities.'

'I've always observed that,' said Kantwise.

'I travelled for three years in Devonshire, Somersetshire, and Wiltshire,' said Moulder, 'and the commercial rooms were as well kept there as any I ever see.'

'I alluded to Surrey and Kent,' said Mr. Dockwrath.

'They're uncommonly miscellaneous in Surrey and Kent,' said Kantwise. 'There's no doubt in the world about that.'

'If the gentleman means to say that he's come in here because he didn't know the custom of the country, I've no more to say, of course,' said Moulder. 'And in that case, I, for one, shall be very happy if the gentleman can make himself comfortable in this room as a stranger, and I may say guest;—paying his own shot, of course.'

'And as for me, I shall be delighted,' said Kantwise. 'I never did like too much exclusiveness. What's the use of bottling oneself up? that's what I always say. Besides, there's no charity in it. We gents as are always on the road should show a little charity to them as aint so well accustomed to the work.'

At this allusion to charity Mr. Moulder snuffled through his nose to show his great disgust, but he made no further answer. Mr. Dockwrath, who was determined not to yield, but who had nothing to gain by further fighting, bowed his head, and declared that he felt very much obliged. Whether or no there was any touch of irony in his tone, Mr. Moulder's ears were not fine enough to discover. So they now sat round the fire together, the attorney still keeping his seat in the middle. And then Mr. Moulder ordered his little bit of steak with his tea. ' With the gravy in it, James,' he said, solemnly. ' And a bit of fat, and a few slices of onion, thin mind, put on raw, not with all the taste fried out ; and tell the cook if she don't do it as it should be done, I'll be down into the kitchen and do it myself. You'll join me, Kantwise, eh ?'

' Well, I think not; I dined at three, you know.'

' Dined at three ! What of that ? a dinner at three won't last a man for ever. You might as well join me.'

' No, I think not. Have you got such a thing as a nice red herring in the house, James ?'

' Get one round the corner, sir.'

' Do, there's a good fellow; and I'll take it for a relish with my tea. I'm not so fond of your solids three times a day. They heat the blood too much.'

' Bother,' grunted Moulder ; and then they went to their evening meal, over which we will not disturb them. The steak, we may presume, was cooked aright, as Mr. Moulder did not visit the kitchen, and Mr. Kantwise no doubt made good play with his unsubstantial dainty, as he spoke no further till his meal was altogether finished.

' Did you ever hear anything of that Mr. Mason who lives near Bradford ?' asked Mr. Kantwise, addressing himself to Mr. Moulder, as soon as the things had been cleared from the table, and that latter gentleman had been furnished with a pipe and a supply of cold without.

' I remember his father when I was a boy,' said Moulder, not troubling himself to take his pipe from his mouth. ' Mason and Martock in the Old Jewry ; very good people they were too.'

' He's decently well off now, I suppose, isn't he ?' said Kantwise, turning away his face, and looking at his companion out of the corners of his eyes.

' I suppose he is. That place there by the road-side is all his own, I take it. Have you been at him with some of your rusty, rickety tables and chairs ?'

' Mr. Moulder, you forget that there is a gentleman here who won't understand that you're at your jokes. I was doing business at Groby Park, but I found the party uncommon hard to deal with.'

' Didn't complete the transaction ?'

' Well, no ; not exactly ; but I intend to call again. He's close enough himself, is Mr. Mason. But his lady, Mrs. M.! Lord love you, Mr. Moulder; that is a woman!'

' She is ; is she? As for me, I never have none of these private dealings. It don't suit my book at all; nor it aint what I've been accustomed to. If a man's wholesale, let him be wholesale.' And then, having enunciated this excellent opinion with much energy, he took a long pull at his brandy and water.

' Very old fashioned, Mr. Moulder,' said Kantwise, looking round the corner, then shutting his eyes and shaking his head.

' May be,' said Moulder, ' and yet none the worse for that. I call it hawking and peddling, that going round the country with your goods on your back. It aint trade.' And then there was a lull in the conversation, Mr. Kantwise, who was a very religious gentle man, having closed his eyes, and being occupied with some internal anathema against Mr. Moulder.

' Begging your pardon, sir, I think you were talking about one Mr. Mason who lives in these parts,' said Dockwrath.

' Exactly. Joseph Mason, Esq., of Groby Park,' said Mr. Kant- wise, now turning his face upon the attorney.

' I suppose I shall be likely to find him at home to-morrow, if I call ?'

' Certainly, sir ; certainly; leastwise I should say so. Any personal acquaintance with Mr. Mason, sir ? If so, I meant nothing offensive by my allusion to the lady, sir; nothing at all, I can assure you.'

' The lady's nothing to me, sir; nor the gentleman either ;—only that I have a little business with him.'

' Shall be very happy to join you in a gig, sir, to-morrow, as far as Groby Park ; or fly, if more convenient. I shall only take a few patterns with me, and they're no weight at all ;—none in the least, sir. They go on behind, and you wouldn't know it, sir.' To this, however, Mr. Dockwrath would not assent. As he wanted to see Mr. Mason very specially, he should go early, and preferred going by himself.

' No offence, I hope,' said Mr. Kantwise.

' None in the least,' said Mr. Dockwrath.

' And if you would allow me, sir, to have the pleasure of showing you a few of my patterns, I'm sure I should be delighted.' This he said observing that Mr. Moulder was sitting over his empty glass with the pipe in his hand, and his eyes fast closed. ' I think, sir, I could show you an article that would please you very much. You see, sir, that new ideas are coming in every day, and wood, sir, is altogether going out,—altogether going out as regards furniture. In another twenty years, sir, there won't be such a thing as a wooden table in the country, unless with some poor person that can't afford to refurnish. Believe me, sir, iron's the thing now-a-days.'

' And indian-rubber,' said Dockwrath.

' Yes; indian-rubber's wonderful too. Are you in that line, sir?'

' Well; no; not exactly.'

' It's not like iron, sir. You can't make a dinner-table for fourteen people out of indian-rubber, that will shut up into a box 3—6 by 2—4 deep, and 2—6 broad. Why, sir, I can let you have a set of drawing-room furniture for fifteen ten that you've never seen equalled in wood for three times the money;—ornamented in the tastiest way, sir, and fit for any lady's drawing-room or boodoor. The ladies of quality are all getting them now for their boodoors. There's three tables, eight chairs, easy rocking-chair, music-stand, stool to match, and pair of stand-up screens, all gilt in real Louey catorse; and it goes in three boxes 4—2 by 2—1 and 2—3. Think of that, sir. For fifteen ten and the boxes in.' Then there was a pause, after which Mr. Kantwise added—' If ready money, the carriage paid.' And then he turned his head very much away, and looked back very hard at his expected customer.

' I'm afraid the articles are not in my line,' said Mr. Dockwrath.

' It's the tastiest present for a gentleman to make to his lady that has come out since—since those sort of things have come out at all. You'll let me show you the articles, sir. It will give me the sincerest pleasure.' And Mr. Kantwise proposed to leave the room in order that he might introduce the three boxes in question.

' They would not be at all in my way,' said Mr. Dockwrath.

' The trouble would be nothing,' said Mr. Kantwise, ' and it gives me the greatest pleasure to make them known when I find any one who can appreciate such undoubted luxuries;' and so saying Mr. Kantwise skipped out of the room, and soon returned with James and Boots, each of the three bearing on his shoulder a deal box nearly as big as a coffin, all of which were deposited in different parts of the room. Mr. Moulder in the mean time snored heavily, his head falling on to his breast every now and again. But nevertheless he held fast by his pipe.

Mr. Kantwise skipped about the room with wonderful agility, unfastening the boxes, and taking out the contents, while Joe the boots and James the waiter stood by assisting. They had never yet seen the glories of these chairs and tables, and were therefore not unwilling to be present. It was singular to see how ready Mr. Kantwise was at the work, how recklessly he threw aside the whitey-brown paper in which the various pieces of painted iron were enveloped, and with what a practised hand he put together one article after another. First there was a round loo-table, not quite so large in its circumference as some people might think desirable, but, nevertheless, a round loo-table. The pedestal with

"There is nothing like iron, Sir; nothing."

its three claws was all together. With a knowing touch Mr. Kant-wise separated the bottom of what looked like a yellow stick, and, lo! there were three legs, which he placed carefully on the ground. Then a small bar was screwed on to the top, and over the bar was screwed the leaf, or table itself, which consisted of three pieces unfolding with hinges. These, when the screw had been duly fastened in the centre, opened out upon the bar, and there was the table complete.

It was certainly a 'tasty' article, and the pride with which Mr. Kantwise glanced back at it was quite delightful. The top of the table was blue, with a red bird of paradise in the middle; and the edges of the table, to the breadth of a couple of inches, were yellow. The pillar also was yellow, as were the three legs. 'It's the real Louey catorse,' said Mr. Kantwise, stooping down to go on with table number two, which was, as he described it, a 'chess,' having the proper number of blue and light-pink squares marked upon it; but this also had been made Louey catorse with reference to its legs and edges. The third table was a 'sofa,' of proper shape, but rather small in size. Then, one after another, he brought forth and screwed up the chairs, stools, and sundry screens, and within a quarter of an hour he had put up the whole set complete. The red bird of paradise and the blue ground appeared on all, as did also the yellow legs and edgings which gave to them their peculiarly fashionable character. 'There,' said Mr. Kantwise, looking at them with fond admiration, 'I don't mind giving a personal guarantee that there's nothing equal to that for the money either in England or in France.'

'They are very nice,' said Mr. Dockwrath. When a man has had produced before him for his own and sole delectation any article or articles, how can he avoid eulogium? Mr. Dockwrath found himself obliged to pause, and almost feared that he should find himself obliged to buy.

'Nice! I should rather think they are,' said Mr. Kantwise, becoming triumphant,—'and for fifteen ten, delivered, boxes in-cluded. There's nothing like iron, sir, nothing; you may take my word for that. They're so strong, you know. Look here, sir.' And then Mr. Kantwise, taking two of the pieces of whitey-brown paper which had been laid aside, carefully spread one on the centre of the round table, and the other on the seat of one of the chairs. Then lightly poising himself on his toe, he stepped on to the chair, and from thence on to the table. In that position he skilfully brought his feet together, so that his weight was directly on the leg, and gracefully waved his hands over his head. James and Boots stood by admiring, with open mouths, and Mr. Dockwrath, with his hands in his pockets, was meditating whether he could not give the order without complying with the terms as to ready money.

'Look at that for strength,' said Mr. Kantwise from his exalted position. 'I don't think any lady of your acquaintance, sir, would allow you to stand on her rosewood or mahogany loo table. And if she did, you would not like to adventure it yourself. But look at this for strength,' and he waved his arms abroad, still keeping his feet skilfully together in the same exact position.

At that moment Mr. Moulder awoke. 'So you've got your iron traps out, have you?' said he. 'What; you're there, are you? Upon my word I'd sooner you than me.'

'I certainly should not like to see you up here, Mr. Moulder. I doubt whether even this table would bear five-and-twenty stone. Joe, lend me your shoulder, there's a good fellow.' And then Mr. Kantwise, bearing very lightly on the chair, descended to the ground without accident.

'Now, that's what I call gammon,' said Moulder.

'What is gammon, Mr. Moulder?' said the other, beginning to be angry.

'It's all gammon. The chairs and tables is gammon, and so is the stools and the screens.'

'Mr. Moulder, I didn't call your tea and coffee and brandy gammon.'

'You can't; and you wouldn't do any harm if you did. Hubbles and Grease are too well known in Yorkshire for you to hurt them. But as for all that show-off and gimcrack-work, I tell you fairly it aint what I call trade, and it aint fit for a commercial room. It's gammon, gammon, gammon! James, give me a bedcandle.' And so Mr. Moulder took himself off to bed.

'I think I'll go too,' said Mr. Dockwrath.

'You'll let me put you up the set, eh?' said Mr. Kantwise.

'Well; I'll think about it,' said the attorney. 'I'll not just give you an answer to-night. Good night, sir; I'm very much obliged to you.' And he too went, leaving Mr. Kantwise to repack his chairs and tables with the assistance of James the waiter.

CHAPTER VII.

THE MASONS OF GROBY PARK.

GROBY Park is about seven miles from Leeds, in the direction of Bradford, and thither on the morning after the scene described in the last chapter Mr. Dockwrath was driven in one of the gigs belonging to the Bull Inn. The park itself is spacious, but is flat and uninteresting, being surrounded by a thin belt of new-looking fir-trees, and containing but very little old or handsome timber. There are on the high road two very important lodges, between which is a large ornamented gate, and from thence an excellent road leads to the mansion, situated in the very middle of the domain. The house is Greek in its style of architecture,—at least so the owner says; and if a portico with a pediment and seven Ionic columns makes a house Greek, the house in Groby Park undoubtedly is Greek.

Here lived Mr. and Mrs. Mason, the three Misses Mason, and occasionally the two young Messrs. Mason; for the master of Groby Park was blessed with five children. He himself was a big, broad, heavy-browed man, in whose composition there was nothing of tenderness, nothing of poetry, and nothing of taste; but I cannot say that he was on the whole a bad man. He was just in his dealings, or at any rate endeavoured to be so. He strove hard to do his duty as a county magistrate against very adverse circumstances. He endeavoured to enable his tenants and labourers to live. He was severe to his children, and was not loved by them; but nevertheless they were dear to him, and he endeavoured to do his duty by them. The wife of his bosom was not a pleasant woman, but nevertheless he did his duty by her; that is, he neither deserted her, nor beat her, nor locked her up. I am not sure that he would not have been justified in doing one of these three things, or even all the three; for Mrs. Mason of Groby Park was not a pleasant woman.

But yet he was a bad man in that he could never forget and never forgive. His mind and heart were equally harsh and hard and inflexible. He was a man who considered that it behoved him as a man to resent all injuries, and to have his pound of flesh in all cases. In his inner thoughts he had ever boasted to himself that he had paid all men all that he owed. He had, so he thought, injured no one in any of the relations of life. His tradesmen got their money regularly. He answered every man's letter. He exacted nothing from any man for which he did not pay. He never ill used a servant either by bad language or by over work. He never amused himself, but devoted his whole time to duties. He would fain even have been hospitable, could he have gotten his neighbours to come to him and have induced his wife to put upon the table sufficient food for them to eat.

Such being his virtues, what right had any one to injure him? When he got from his grocer adulterated coffee,—he analyzed the coffee, as his half-brother had done the guano,—he would have flayed the man alive if the law would have allowed him. Had he not paid the man monthly, giving him the best price as though for the best article? When he was taken in with a warranty for a horse, he pursued the culprit to the uttermost. Maid-servants who would not come from their bedrooms at six o'clock, he would himself disturb while enjoying their stolen slumbers. From his children he exacted all titles of respect, because he had a right to them. He wanted nothing that belonged to any one else, but he could not endure that aught should be kept from him which he believed to be his own. It may be imagined, therefore, in what light he esteemed Lady Mason and her son, and how he regarded their residence at Orley Farm, seeing that he firmly believed that Orley Farm was his own, if all the truth were known.

I have already hinted that Mrs. Mason was not a delightful woman. She had been a beauty, and still imagined that she had not lost all pretension to be so considered. She spent, therefore, a considerable portion of her day in her dressing-room, spent a great deal of money for clothes, and gave herself sundry airs. She was a little woman with long eyes, and regular eyelashes, with a straight nose, and thin lips and regular teeth. Her face was oval, and her hair was brown. It had at least once been all brown, and that which was now seen was brown also. But, nevertheless, although she was possessed of all these charms, you might look at her for ten days together, and on the eleventh you would not know her if you met her in the streets.

But the appearance of Mrs. Mason was not her forte. She had been a beauty; but if it had been her lot to be known in history, it was not as a beauty that she would have been famous. Parsimony was her great virtue, and a power of saving her strong point. I have said that she spent much money in dress, and some people will perhaps think that the two points of character are not compatible. Such people know nothing of a true spirit of parsimony. It is from the backs and bellies of other people that savings are made with the greatest constancy and the most satisfactory results.

The parsimony of a mistress of a household is best displayed on matters eatable ;—on matters eatable and drinkable; for there is a fine scope for domestic savings in tea, beer, and milk. And in such matters chiefly did Mrs. Mason operate, going as far as she dared towards starving even her husband. But nevertheless she would feed herself in the middle of the day, having a roast fowl with bread sauce in her own room. The miser who starves himself and dies without an ounce of flesh on his bones, while his skinny head lies on a bag of gold, is, after all, respectable. There has been a grand passion in his life, and that grandest work of man, self-denial. You cannot altogether despise one who has clothed himself with rags and fed himself with bone-scrapings, while broadcloth and ortolans were within his easy reach. But there are women, wives and mothers of families, who would give the bone-scrapings to their husbands and the bones to their servants, while they hide the ortolans for themselves; and would dress their children in rags, while they cram chests, drawers, and boxes with silks and satins for their own backs. Such a woman one can thoroughly despise, and even hate ; and such a woman was Mrs. Mason of Groby Park.

I shall not trouble the reader at present with much description of the young Masons. The eldest son was in the army, and the younger at Cambridge, both spending much more money than their father allowed them. Not that he, in this respect, was specially close-fisted. He ascertained what was sufficient,—amply sufficient as he was told by the colonel of the regiment and the tutor of the college,—and that amount he allowed, assuring both Joseph and John that if they spent more, they would themselves have to pay for it out of the moneys which should enrich them in future years. But how could the sons of such a mother be other than spend-thrifts ? Of course they were extravagant; of course they spent more than they should have done ; and their father resolved that he would keep his word with them religiously.

The daughters were much less fortunate, having no possible means of extravagance allowed to them. Both the father and mother decided that they should go out into the county society, and therefore their clothing was not absolutely of rags. But any young lady who does go into society, whether it be of county or town, will fully understand the difference between a liberal and a stingy wardrobe. Girls with slender provisions of millinery may be fit to go out,—quite fit in their father's eyes ; and yet all such going out may be matter of intense pain. It is all very well for the world to say that a girl should be happy without reference to her clothes. Show me such a girl, and I will show you one whom I should be very sorry that a boy of mine should choose as his sweetheart.

The three Misses Mason, as they always were called by the Groby Park people, had been christened Diana, Creusa, and Penelope, their mother having a passion for classic literature, which she indulged by a use of Lemprière's dictionary. They were not especially pretty, nor were they especially plain. They were well grown and healthy, and quite capable of enjoying themselves in any of the amusements customary to young ladies,—if only the opportunities were afforded them.

Mr. Dockwrath had thought it well to write to Mr. Mason, acquainting that gentleman with his intended visit. Mr. Mason, he said to himself, would recognize his name, and know whence he came, and under such circumstances would be sure to see him, although the express purpose of the proposed interview should not have been explained to him. Such in result was exactly the case. Mr. Mason did remember the name of Dockwrath, though he had never hitherto seen the bearer of it; and as the letter was dated from Hamworth, he felt sufficient interest in the matter to await at home the coming of his visitor.

'I know your name, Mr. Mason, sir, and have known it long,' said Mr. Dockwrath, seating himself in the chair which was offered to him in the magistrate's study; 'though I never had the pleasure of seeing you before,—to my knowledge. My name is Dockwrath, sir, and I am a solicitor. I live at Hamworth, and I married the daughter of old Mr. Usbech, sir, whom you will remember.'

Mr. Mason listened attentively as these details were uttered before him so clearly, but he said nothing, merely bowing his head at each separate statement. He knew all about old Usbech's daughter nearly as well as Mr. Dockwrath did himself, but he was a man who knew how to be silent upon occasions.

'I was too young, sir,' continued Dockwrath, 'when you had that trial about Orley Farm to have anything to do with the matter myself, but nevertheless I remember all the circumstances as though it was yesterday. I suppose, sir, you remember them also?'

'Yes, Mr. Dockwrath, I remember them very well.'

'Well, sir, my impression has always been that——' And then the attorney st'pped. It was quite his intention to speak out plainly before Mr. Mason, but he was anxious that that gentleman should speak out too. At any rate it might be well that he should be induced to express some little interest in the matter.

'Your impression, you say, has always been——' said Mr. Mason, repeating the words of his companion, and looking as ponderous and grave as ever. His countenance, however, expressed nothing but his usual ponderous solemnity.

'My impression always was——that there was something that had not been as yet found out.'

' What sort of thing, Mr. Dockwrath?'

' Well; some secret. I don't think that your lawyers managed the matter well, Mr. Mason.'

' You think you would have done it better, Mr. Dockwrath?'

' I don't say that, Mr. Mason. I was only a lad at the time, and could not have managed it at all. But they didn't ferret about enough. Mr. Mason, there's a deal better evidence than any that is given by word of mouth. A clever counsel can turn a witness pretty nearly any way he likes, but he can't do that with little facts. He hasn't the time, you see, to get round them. Your lawyers, sir, didn't get up the little facts as they should have done.'

' And you have got them up since, Mr. Dockwrath?'

' I don't say that, Mr. Mason. You see all my interest lies in maintaining the codicil. My wife's fortune came to her under that deed. To be sure that's gone and spent long since, and the Lord Chancellor with all the judges couldn't enforce restitution; but, nevertheless, I wouldn't wish that any one should have a claim against me on that account.'

' Perhaps you will not object to say what it is that you do wish?'

' I wish to see right done, Mr. Mason; that's all. I don't think that Lady Mason or her son have any right to the possession of that place. I don't think that that codicil was a correct instrument; and in that case of Mason versus Mason I don't think that you and your friends got to the bottom of it.' And then Mr. Dockwrath leaned back in his chair with an inward determination to say nothing more, until Mr. Mason should make some sign.

That gentleman, however, still remained ponderous and heavy, and therefore there was a short period of silence—' And have you got to the bottom of it since, Mr. Dockwrath?' at last he said.

' I don't say that I have,' said the attorney.

' Might I ask then what it is you purpose to effect by the visit with which you have honoured me? Of course you are aware that these are very private matters; and although I should feel myself under an obligation to you, or to any man who might assist me to arrive at any true facts which have hitherto been concealed, I am not disposed to discuss the affair with a stranger on grounds of mere suspicion.'

' I shouldn't have come here, Mr. Mason, at very great expense, and personal inconvenience to myself in my profession, if I had not some good reason for doing so. I don't think that you ever got to the bottom of that matter, and I can't say that I have done so now; I haven't even tried. But I tell you what, Mr. Mason; if you wish it, I think I could put you in the way of—trying.'

' My lawyers are Messrs. Round and Crook of Bedford Row. Will it not be better that you should go to them, Mr. Dockwrath?'

'No, Mr. Mason. I don't think it will be better that I should go to them. I know Round and Crook well, and don't mean to say a word against them ; but if I go any farther in this affair I must do it with the principal. I am not going to cut my own throat for the sake of mending any man's little finger. I have a family of sixteen children, Mr. Mason, and I have to look about very sharp,—very sharp indeed.' Then there was another pause, and Mr. Dockwrath began to perceive that Mr. Mason was not by nature an open, demonstrative, or communicative man. If anything further was to be done, he himself must open out a little. 'The fact is, Mr. Mason, that I have come across documents which you should have had at that trial. Round and Crook ought to have had them, only they weren't half sharp. Why, sir, Mr. Usbech had been your father's man of business for years upon years, and yet they didn't half go through his papers. They turned 'em over and looked at 'em ; but never thought of seeing what little facts might be proved.'

'And these documents are with you now, here ?'

'No, Mr. Mason, I am not so soft as that. I never carry about original documents unless when ordered to prove. Copies of one or two items I have made ; not regular copies, Mr. Mason, but just a line or two to refresh my memory.' And Mr. Dockwrath took a small letter-case out of his breast coat pocket.

By this time Mr. Mason's curiosity had been roused, and he began to think it possible that his visitor had discovered information which might be of importance to him. 'Are you going to show me any document ?' said he.

'That's as may be,' said the attorney. 'I don't know as yet whether you care to see it. I have come a long way to do you a service, and it seems to me you are rather shy of coming forward to meet me. As I said before, I've a very heavy family, and I'm not going to cut the nose off my own face to put money into any other man's pocket. What do you think my journey down here will cost me, including loss of time, and interruption to my business ?'

'Look here, Mr. Dockwrath ; if you are really able to put me into possession of any facts regarding the Orley Farm estate which I ought to know, I will see that you are compensated for your time and trouble. Messrs. Round and Crook——'

'I'll have nothing to do with Round and Crook. So that's settled, Mr. Mason.'

'Then, Mr. Dockwrath——'

'Half a minute, Mr. Mason. I'll have nothing to do with Round and Crook ; but as I know you to be a gentleman and a man of honour, I'll put you in possession of what I've discovered, and leave it to you afterwards to do what you think right about my expenses, time, and services. You won't forget that it is a long

way from Hamworth to Groby Park. And if you should succeed——'

'If I am to look at this document, I must do so without pledging
myself to anything,' said Mr. Mason, still with much solemnity.
He had great doubts as to his new acquaintance, and much feared
that he was derogating from his dignity as a county magistrate
and owner of Groby Park in holding any personal intercourse with
him; but nevertheless he could not resist the temptation. He
most firmly believed that that codicil had not expressed the genuine
last will and fair disposition of property made by his father, and it
might certainly be the case that proof of all that he believed was
to be found among the papers of the old lawyer. He hated Lady
Mason with all his power of hatred, and if there did, even yet,
exist for him a chance of upsetting her claims and ruining her before
the world, he was not the man to forego that chance.

'Well, sir, you shall see it,' said Mr. Dockwrath; 'or rather hear
it, for there is not much to see.' And so saying he extracted from
his pocket-book a very small bit of paper.

'I should prefer to read it, if it's all the same to you, Mr. Dockwrath. I shall understand it much better in that way.'

'As you like, Mr. Mason,' said the attorney, handing him the
small bit of paper. 'You will understand, sir, that it's no real
copy, but only a few dates and particulars, just jotted down to
assist my own memory.' The document, supported by which
Mr. Dockwrath had come down to Yorkshire, consisted of half a
sheet of note paper, and the writing upon this covered hardly the
half of it. The words which Mr. Mason read were as follows :—

'Date of codicil. 14th July 18—.

'Witnesses to the instrument. John Kenneby; Bridget Bolster;
Jonathan Usbech. N.B. Jonathan Usbech died before the testator.

'Mason and Martock. Deed of separation; dated 14th July 18—.

'Executed at Orley Farm.

'Witnesses John Kenneby; and Bridget Bolster. Deed was prepared in the office of Jonathan Usbech, and probably executed in
his presence.'

That was all that was written on the paper, and Mr. Mason read
the words to himself three times before he looked up, or said anything concerning them. He was not a man quick at receiving new
ideas into his mind, or of understanding new points; but that which
had once become intelligible to him and been made his own, remained so always. 'Well,' said he, when he read the above words
for the third time.

'You don't see it, sir ?' said Mr. Dockwrath.

'See what ?' said Mr. Mason, still looking at the scrap of paper.

'Why; the dates, to begin with.'

I see that the dates are the same;—the 14th of July in the same year.'

' Well,' said Mr. Dockwrath, looking very keenly into the magistrate's face.

' Well,' said Mr. Mason, looking over the paper at his boot.

' John Kenneby and Bridget Bolster were witnesses to both the instruments,' said the attorney.

' So I see,' said the magistrate.

' But I don't remember that it came out in evidence that either of them recollected having been called on for two signatures on the same day.'

' No; there was nothing of that came out;—or was even hinted at.'

' No; nothing even hinted at, Mr. Mason,—as you justly observe. That is what I mean by saying that Round and Crook's people didn't get up their little facts. Believe me, sir, there are men in the profession out of London who know quite as much as Round and Crook. They ought to have had those facts, seeing 'that the very copy of the document was turned over by their hands.' And Mr. Dockwrath hit the table heavily in the warmth of his indignation against his negligent professional brethren. Earlier in the interview Mr. Mason would have been made very angry by such freedom, but he was not angry now.

' Yes; they ought to have known it,' said he. But he did not even yet see the point. He merely saw that there was a point worth seeing.

' Known it! Of course they ought to have known it. Look here, Mr. Mason! If I had it on my mind that I'd thrown over a client of mine by such carelessness as that, I'd—I'd strike my own name off the rolls; I would indeed. I never could look a counsel in the face again, if I'd neglected to brief him with such facts as those. I suppose it was carelessness; eh, Mr. Mason?'

' Oh, yes; I'm afraid so,' said Mr. Mason, still rather in the dark.

' They could have had no object in keeping it back, I should say.'

' No; none in life. But let us see, Mr. Dockwrath; how does it bear upon us? The dates are the same, and the witnesses the same.'

' The deed of separation is genuine. There is no doubt about that.'

' Oh; you're sure of that?'

' Quite certain. I found it entered in the old office books. It was the last of a lot of such documents executed between Mason and Martock after the old man gave up the business. You see she was always with him, and knew all about it.'

' About the partnership deed ?'

' Of course she did. She's a clever woman, Mr. Mason ; very clever, and it's almost a pity that she should come to grief. She has carried it on so well ; hasn't she ?'

Mr. Mason's face now became very black. ' Why,' said he, ' if what you seem to allege be true, she must bo a—a—a—. What do you mean, sir, by pity ?'

Mr. Dockwrath shrugged his shoulders. ' It is very blue,' said he, ' uncommon blue.'

' She must be a swindler ; a common swindler. Nay, worse than that.'

' Oh, yes, a deal worse than that, Mr. Mason. And as for common ;—according to my way of thinking there's nothing at all common about it. I look upon it as about the best got-up plant I ever remember to have heard of. I do, indeed, Mr. Mason.' The attorney during the last ten minutes of the conversation had quite altered his tone, understanding that he had already achieved a great part of his object ; but Mr. Mason in his intense anxiety did not observe this. Had Mr. Dockwrath, in commencing the conversation, talked about ' plants ' and ' blue,' Mr. Mason would probably have rung his bell for the servant. ' If it's anything, it's forgery,' said Mr. Dockwrath, looking his companion full in the face.

' I always felt sure that my father never intended to sign such a codicil as that.'

' He never did sign it, Mr. Mason.'

' And,—and the witnesses !' said Mr. Mason, still not enlightened as to the true extent of the attorney's suspicion.

' They signed the other deed ; that is two of them did. There is no doubt about that ;—on that very day. They certainly did witness a signature made by the old gentleman in his own room on that 14th of July. The original of that document, with the date and their names, will be forthcoming soon enough.'

' Well,' said Mr. Mason.

' But they did not witness two signatures.'

' You think not, eh !'

' I'm sure of it. The girl Bolster would have remembered it, and would have said so. She was sharp enough.'

' Who wrote all the names then at the foot of the will ?' said Mr. Mason.

' Ah ! that's the question. Who did write them ? We know very well, Mr. Mason, you and I that is, who did not. And having come to that, I think we may give a very good guess who did.'

And then they both sat silent for some three or four minutes. Mr. Dockwrath was quite at his ease, rubbing his chin with his hand, playing with a paper-knife which he had taken from the study table, and waiting till it should please Mr. Mason to renew the conversation. Mr. Mason was not at his ease, though all idea of affecting any reserve before the attorney had left him. He was thinking how best he might confound and destroy the woman who had robbed him for so many years; who had defied him, got the better of him, and put him to terrible cost; who had vexed his spirit through his whole life, deprived him of content, and had been to him as a thorn ever present in a festering sore. He had always believed that she had defrauded him, but this belief had been qualified by the unbelief of others. It might have been, he had half thought, that the old man had signed the codicil in his dotage, having been cheated and bullied into it by the woman. There had been no day in her life on which he would not have ruined her, had it been in his power to do so. But now—now, new and grander ideas were breaking in upon his mind. Could it be possible that he might live to see her, not merely deprived of her ill-gained money, but standing in the dock as a felon to receive sentence for her terrible misdeeds? If that might be so, would he not receive great compensation for all that he had suffered? Would it not be sweet to his sense of justice that both of them should thus at last have their own? He did not even yet understand all that Mr. Dockwrath suspected. He did not fully perceive why the woman was supposed to have chosen as the date of her forgery, the date of that other genuine deed. But he did understand, he did perceive—at least so he thought,—that new and perhaps conclusive evidence of her villainy was at last within his reach.

'And what shall we do now, Mr. Dockwrath?' he said at last.

'Well; am I to understand that you do me the honour of asking my advice upon that question as being your lawyer?'

This question immediately brought Mr. Mason back to business that he did understand. 'A man in my position cannot very well change his legal advisers at a moment's notice. You must be very well aware of that, Mr. Dockwrath. Messrs. Round and Crook——'

'Messrs. Round and Crook, sir, have neglected your business in a most shameful manner. Let me tell you that, sir.'

'Well; that's as may be. I'll tell you what I'll do, Mr. Dockwrath; I'll think over this matter in quiet, and then I'll come up to town. Perhaps when there I may expect the honour of a further visit from you.'

'And you won't mention the matter to Round and Crook?'

'I can't undertake to say that, Mr. Dockwrath. I think it will perhaps be better that I should mention it, and then see you afterwards.'

'And how about my expenses down here?'

Just at this moment there came a light tap at the study door, and before the master of the house could give or withhold permission the mistress of the house entered the room. ' My dear,' she said, ' I didn't know that you were engaged.'

' Yes, I am engaged,' said the gentleman.

' Oh, I'm sure I beg pardon. Perhaps this is the gentleman from Hamworth ?'

' Yes, ma'am,' said Mr. Dockwrath. ' I am the gentleman from Hamworth. I hope I have the pleasure of seeing you very well, ma'am ?' And getting up from his chair he bowed politely.

' Mr. Dockwrath, Mrs. Mason,' said the lady's husband, introducing them; and then Mrs. Mason curtsied to the stranger. She too was very anxious to know what might be the news from Hamworth.

' Mr. Dockwrath will lunch with us, my dear,' said Mr. Mason. And then the lady, on hospitable cares intent, left them again to themselves.

CHAPTER VIII.

THOUGH Mr. Dockwrath was somewhat elated by this invitation to lunch, he was also somewhat abashed by it. He had been far from expecting that Mr. Mason of Groby Park would do him any such honour, and was made aware by it of the great hold which he must have made upon the attention of his host. But nevertheless he immediately felt that his hands were to a certain degree tied. He, having been invited to sit down at Mr. Mason's table, with Mrs. M. and the family,—having been treated as though he were a gentleman, and thus being for the time put on a footing of equality with the county magistrate, could not repeat that last important question: 'How about my expenses down here?' nor could he immediately go on with the grand subject in any frame of mind which would tend to further his own interests. Having been invited to lunch he could not haggle with due persistency for his share of the business in crushing Lady Mason, nor stipulate that the whole concern should not be trusted to the management of Round and Crook. As a source of pride this invitation to eat was pleasant to him, but he was forced to acknowledge to himself that it interfered with business.

Nor did Mr. Mason feel himself ready to go on with the conversation in the manner in which it had been hitherto conducted. His mind was full of Orley Farm and his wrongs, and he could bring himself to think of nothing else; but he could no longer talk about it to the attorney sitting there in his study. 'Will you take a turn about the place while the lunch is getting ready?' he said. So they took their hats and went out into the garden.

'It is dreadful to think of,' said Mr. Mason, after they had twice walked in silence the length of a broad gravel terrace.

'What; about her ladyship?' said the attorney.

'Quite dreadful!' and Mr. Mason shuddered. 'I don't think I ever heard of anything so shocking in my life. For twenty years, Mr. Dockwrath, think of that. Twenty years!' and his face as he spoke became almost black with horror.

'It is very shocking,' said Mr. Dockwrath; 'very shocking. What on earth will be her fate if it be proved against her? She has brought it on herself; that is all that one can say of her.'

'D—— her! d—— her!' exclaimed the other, gnashing his teeth with concentrated wrath. 'No punishment will be bad enough for her. Hanging would not be bad enough.'

'They can't hang her, Mr. Mason,' said Mr. Dockwrath, almost frightened by the violence of his companion.

'No; they have altered the laws, giving every encouragement to forgers, villains, and perjurers. But they can give her penal servitude for life. They must do it.'

'She is not convicted yet, you know.'

'D—— her!' repeated the owner of Groby Park again, as he thought of his twenty years of loss. Eight hundred a year for twenty years had been taken away from him; and he had been worsted before the world after a hard fight. 'D—— her!' he continued in a growl between his teeth. Mr. Dockwrath when he had first heard his companion say how horrid and dreadful the affair was, had thought that Mr. Mason was alluding to the condition in which the lady had placed herself by her assumed guilt. But it was of his own condition that he was speaking. The idea which shocked him was the thought of the treatment which he himself had undergone. The dreadful thing at which he shuddered was his own ill usage. As for her;—pity for her! Did a man ever pity a rat that had eaten into his choicest dainties?

'The lunch is on the table, sir,' said the Groby Park footman in the Groby Park livery. Under the present household arrangement of Groby Park all the servants lived on board wages. Mrs. Mason did not like this system, though it had about it certain circumstances of economy which recommended it to her; it interfered greatly with the stringent aptitudes of her character and the warmest passion of her heart; it took away from her the delicious power of serving out the servants' food, of locking up the scraps of meat, and of charging the maids with voracity. But, to tell the truth, Mr. Mason had been driven by sheer necessity to take this step, as it had been found impossible to induce his wife to give out sufficient food to enable the servants to live and work. She knew that in not doing so she injured herself; but she could not do it. The knife in passing through the loaf would make the portion to be parted with less by one third than the portion to be retained. Half a pound of salt butter would reduce itself to a quarter of a pound. Portions of meat would become infinitesimal. When standing with viands before her, she had not free will over her hands. She could not bring herself to part with victuals, though she might ruin herself by retaining them. Therefore, by the order of the master, were the servants placed on board wages.

Mr. Dockwrath soon found himself in the dining-room, where the
three young ladies with their mamma were already seated at the
table. It was a handsome room, and the furniture was handsome;
but nevertheless it was a heavy room, and the furniture was heavy.
The table was large enough for a party of twelve, and might have
borne a noble banquet; as it was the promise was not bad, for there
were three large plated covers concealing hot viands, and in some
houses lunch means only bread and cheese.

Mr. Mason went through a form of introduction between Mr.
Dockwrath and his daughters. ' That is Miss Mason, that Miss
Creusa Mason, and this Miss Penelope. John, remove the covers.'
And the covers were removed, John taking them from the table
with a magnificent action of his arm which I am inclined to think
was not innocent of irony. On the dish before the master of the
house,—a large dish which must I fancy have been selected by the
cook with some similar attempt at sarcasm,—there reposed three
scraps, as to the nature of which Mr. Dockwrath, though he looked
hard at them, was unable to enlighten himself. But Mr. Mason
knew them well, as he now placed his eyes on them for the third
time. They were old enemies of his, and his brow again became
black as he looked at them. The scraps in fact consisted of two
drumsticks of a fowl and some indescribable bone out of the back
of the same. The original bird had no doubt first revealed all its
glories to human eyes,—presuming the eyes of the cook to be in-
human—in Mrs. Mason's ' boodoor.' Then, on the dish before the
lady, there were three other morsels, black-looking and very
suspicious to the eye, which in the course of conversation were
proclaimed to be ham,—broiled ham. Mrs. Mason would never
allow a ham in its proper shape to come into the room, because it
is an article upon which the guests are themselves supposed to
operate with the carving-knife. Lastly, on the dish before
Miss Creusa there reposed three potatoes.

The face of Mr. Mason became very black as he looked at the
banquet which was spread upon his board, and Mrs. Mason, eyeing
him across the table, saw that it was so. She was not a lady who
despised such symptoms in her lord, or disregarded in her valour
the violence of marital storms. She had quailed more than once
or twice under rebuke occasioned by her great domestic virtue,
and knew that her husband, though he might put up with much as
regarded his own comfort and that of his children, could be very
angry at injuries done to his household honour and character as a
hospitable English country gentleman.

Consequently the lady smiled and tried to look self-satisfied as
she invited her guest to eat. ' This is ham,' said she with a little
simper, ' broiled ham, Mr. Dockwrath; and there is chicken at the
other; end I think they call it—devilled.'

'Shall I assist the young ladies to anything first?' said the attorney, wishing to be polite.

'Nothing, thank you,' said Miss Penelope, with a very stiff bow. She also knew that Mr. Dockwrath was an attorney from Hamworth, and considered herself by no means bound to hold any sort of conversation with him.

'My daughters only eat bread and butter in the middle of the day,' said the lady. 'Creusa, my dear, will you give Mr. Dockwrath a potato. Mr. Mason, Mr. Dockwrath will probably take a bit of that chicken.'

'I would recommend him to follow the girls' example, and confine himself to the bread and butter,' said the master of the house, pushing about the scraps with his knife and fork. 'There is nothing here for him to eat.'

'My dear!' exclaimed Mrs. Mason.

'There is nothing here for him to eat,' repeated Mr. Mason. 'And as far as I can see there is nothing there either. What is it you pretend to have in that dish?'

'My dear!' again exclaimed Mrs. Mason.

'What is it?' repeated the lord of the house in an angry tone.

'Broiled ham, Mr. Mason.'

'Then let the ham be brought in,' said he. 'Diana, ring the bell.'

'But the ham is not cooked, Mr. Mason,' said the lady. 'Broiled ham is always better when it has not been first boiled.'

'Is there no cold meat in the house?' he asked.

'I am afraid not,' she replied, now trembling a little in anticipation of what might be coming after the stranger should have gone. 'You never like large joints yourself, Mr. Mason; and for ourselves we don't eat meat at luncheon.'

'Nor anybody else either, here,' said Mr. Mason in his anger.

'Pray don't mind me, Mr. Mason,' said the attorney, 'pray don't, Mr. Mason. I am a very poor fist at lunch; I am indeed.'

'I am sure I am very sorry, very sorry, Mr. Mason,' continued the lady. 'If I had known that an early dinner was required, it should have been provided;—although the notice given was so very short.'

'I never dine early,' said Mr. Dockwrath, thinking that some imputation of a low way of living was conveyed in this supposition that he required a dinner under the pseudonym of a lunch. 'I never do, upon my word—we are quite regular at home at half-past five, and all I ever take in the middle of the day is a biscuit and a glass of sherry,—or perhaps a bite of bread and cheese. Don't be uneasy about me, Mrs. Mason.'

The three young ladies, having now finished their repast, got up from the table and retired, following each other out of the room in a line. Mrs. Mason remained for a minute or two longer, and then she also went. 'The carriage has been ordered at three, Mr. M.,' she said. ' Shall we have the pleasure of your company?' ' No,' growled the husband. And then the lady went, sweeping a low curtsy to Mr. Dockwrath as she passed out of the room.

There was again a silence between the host and his guest for some two or three minutes, during which Mr. Mason was endeavouring to get the lunch out of his head, and to redirect his whole mind to Lady Mason and his hopes of vengeance. There is nothing perhaps so generally consoling to a man as a well-established grievance; a feeling of having been injured, on which his mind can brood from hour to hour, allowing him to plead his own cause in his own court, within his own heart,—and always to plead it successfully. At last Mr. Mason succeeded, and he could think of his enemy's fraud and forget his wife's meanness. ' I suppose I may as well order my gig now,' said Mr. Dockwrath, as soon as his host had arrived at this happy frame of mind.

' Your gig? ah, well. Yes. I do not know that I need detain you any longer. I can assure you that I am much obliged to you, Mr. Dockwrath, and I shall hope to see you in London very shortly.'

' You are determined to go to Round and Crook, I suppose?'

' Oh, certainly.'

' You are wrong, sir. They'll throw you over again as sure as your name is Mason.'

' Mr. Dockwrath, you must if you please allow me to judge of that myself.'

' Oh, of course, sir, of course. But I'm sure that a gentleman like you, Mr. Mason, will understand——'

' I shall understand that I cannot expect your services, Mr. Dockwrath, — your valuable time and services,—without remunerating you for them. That shall be fully explained to Messrs. Round and Crook.'

' Very well, sir; very well. As long as I am paid for what I do, I am content. A professional gentleman of course expects that. How is he to get along else; particular with sixteen children?' And then Mr. Dockwrath got into the gig, and was driven back to the Bull at Leeds.

CHAPTER IX.

A CONVIVIAL MEETING.

On the whole Mr. Dockwrath was satisfied with the results of his trip to Groby Park, and was in a contented frame of mind as he was driven back to Leeds. No doubt it would have been better could he have persuaded Mr. Mason to throw over Messrs. Round and Crook, and put himself altogether into the hands of his new adviser; but this had been too much to expect. He had not expected it, and had made the suggestion as the surest means of getting the best terms in his power, rather than with a hope of securing the actual advantage named. He had done much towards impressing Mr. Mason with an idea of his own sharpness, and perhaps something also towards breaking the prestige which surrounded the names of the great London firm. He would now go to that firm and make his terms with them. They would probably be quite as ready to acquiesce in the importance of his information as had been Mr. Mason.

Before leaving the inn after breakfast he had agreed to join the dinner in the commercial room at five o'clock, and Mr. Mason's hot lunch had by no means induced him to alter his purpose. 'I shall dine here,' he had said when Mr. Moulder was discussing with the waiter the all-important subject of dinner. 'At the commercial table, sir?' the waiter had asked, doubtingly. Mr. Dockwrath had answered boldly in the affirmative, whereat Mr. Moulder had growled; but Mr. Kantwise had expressed his satisfaction. 'We shall be extremely happy to enjoy your company,' Mr. Kantwise had said, with a graceful bow, making up by his excessive courtesy for the want of any courtesy on the part of his brother-traveller. With reference to all this Mr. Moulder said nothing: the stranger had been admitted into the room, to a certain extent even with his own consent, and he could not now be turned out; but he resolved within his own mind that for the future he would be more firm in maintaining the ordinances and institutes of his profession.

On his road home Mr. Dockwrath had encountered Mr. Kantwise going to Groby Park, intent on his sale of a drawing-room set of the metallic furniture; and when he again met him in the commercial room he asked after his success. 'A wonderful woman that, Mr.

Dockwrath,' said Mr. Kantwise, ' a really wonderful woman; no particular friend of yours I think you say ?'

' None in the least, Mr. Kantwise.'

' Then I may make bold to assert that for persevering sharpness she beats all that I ever met, even in Yorkshire;' and Mr. Kantwise looked at his new friend over his shoulder, and shook his head as though lost in wonder and admiration. ' What do you think she's done now?'

' She didn't give you much to eat, I take it.'

' Much to eat!   I'll tell you what it is, Mr. Dockwrath ; my belief is that that woman would have an absolute pleasure in starving a Christian; I do indeed. I'll tell you what she has done; she has made me put her up a set of them things at twelve, seventeen, six! I needn't tell you that they were never made for the money.'

' Why, then, did you part with them at a loss ?'

'Well; that's the question. I was soft, I suppose. She got round me, badgering me, till I didn't know where I was. She wanted them as a present for the curate's wife, she said. Whatever should induce her to make a present !'

' She got them for twelve, seventeen, six; did she?' said Dockwrath, thinking that it might be as well to remember this, if he should feel inclined to make a purchase himself.

' But they was strained, Mr. Dockwrath; I must admit they was strained,—particularly the loo.'

' You had gone through your gymnastics on it a little too often?' asked the attorney. But this Mr. Kantwise would not acknowledge. The strength of that table was such that he could stand on it for ever without injury to it; but nevertheless, in some other way it had become strained, and therefore he had sold the set to Mrs. Mason for 12l. 17s. 6d., that lady being minded to make a costly present to the wife of the curate of Groby.

When dinner-time came Mr. Dockwrath found that the party was swelled to the number of eight, five other undoubted commercials having brought themselves to anchor at the Bull Inn during the day. To all of these Mr. Kantwise introduced him. ' Mr. Gape, Mr. Dockwrath,' said he, gracefully moving towards them the palm of his hand, and eyeing them over his shoulder. ' Mr. Gape is in the stationery line,' he added, in a whisper to the attorney, 'and does for Cumming and Jibber of St. Paul's Churchyard. Mr. Johnson, Mr. Dockwrath. Mr. J. is from Sheffield. Mr. Snengkeld, Mr. Dockwrath;' and then he imparted in another whisper the necessary information as to Mr. Snengkeld. ' Soft goods, for Brown Brothers, of Snow Hill,' and so on through the whole fraternity. Each member bowed as his name was mentioned; but they did not do so very graciously, as Mr. Kantwise was not a great man among them. Had the stranger been introduced to them by

Moulder,—Moulder the patriarch,—his reception among them would have been much warmer. And then they sat down to dinner, Mr. Moulder taking the chair as president, and Mr. Kantwise sitting opposite to him, as being the longest sojourner at the inn. Mr. Dockwrath sat at the right hand of Kantwise, discreetly avoiding the neighbourhood of Moulder, and the others ranged themselves according to fancy at the table. ' Come up along side of me, old fellow,' Moulder said to Snengkeld. ' It aint the first time that you and I have smacked our lips together over the same bit of roast beef.' ' Nor won't, I hope, be the last by a long chalk, Mr. Moulder,' said Snengkeld, speaking with a deep, hoarse voice which seemed to ascend from some region of his body far below his chest. Moulder and Snengkeld were congenial spirits; but the latter, though the older man, was not endowed with so large a volume of body or so highly dominant a spirit. Brown Brothers, of Snow Hill, were substantial people, and Mr. Snengkeld travelled in strict accordance with the good old rules of trade which Moulder loved so well.

The politeness and general good manners of the company were something very pretty to witness. Mr. Dockwrath, as a stranger, was helped first, and every courtesy was shown to him. Even Mr. Moulder carved the beef for him with a loving hand, and Mr. Kantwise was almost subservient in his attention. Mr. Dockwrath thought that he had certainly done right in coming to the commercial table, and resolved on doing so on all occasions of future journeys. So far all was good. The commercial dinner, as he had ascertained, would cost him only two shillings, and a much inferior repast eaten by himself elsewhere would have stood in his bill for three. So far all was good; but the test by which he was to be tried was now approaching him.

When the dinner was just half over,—Mr. Moulder well knew how to mark the time—that gentleman called for the waiter, and whispered an important order into that functionary's ears. The functionary bowed, retired from the room, and reappeared again in two minutes, bearing a bottle of sherry in each hand; one of these he deposited at the right hand of Mr. Moulder, and the other at the right hand of Mr. Kantwise.

' Sir,' said Mr. Moulder, addressing himself with great ceremony to Mr. Dockwrath, ' the honour of a glass of wine with you, sir,' and the president, to give more importance to the occasion, put down his knife and fork, leaned back in his chair, and put both his hands upon his waistcoat, looking intently at the attorney out of his little eyes.

Mr. Dockwrath was immediately aware that a crisis had come upon him which demanded an instant decision. If he complied with the president's invitation he would have to pay his proportion

of all the wine bill that might be incurred that evening by the
seven commercial gentlemen at the table, and he knew well
that commercial gentlemen do sometimes call for bottle after
bottle with a reckless disregard of expense. But to him, with his
sixteen children, wine at an hotel was terrible. A pint of beer and
a glass of brandy and water were the luxuries which he had promised himself, and with manly fortitude he resolved that he would
not be coerced into extravagance by any president or any Moulder.

' Sir,' said he, ' I'm obliged by the honour, but I don't drink wine
to my dinner.' Whereupon Mr. Moulder bowed his head very
solemnly, winked at Snengkeld, and then drank wine with that
gentleman.

' It's the rule of the room,' whispered Mr. Kantwise into Mr.
Dockwrath's ear; but Mr. Dockwrath pretended not to hear him,
and the matter was allowed to pass by for the time.

But Mr. Snengkeld asked him for the honour, as also did Mr.
Gape, who sat at Moulder's left hand; and then Mr. Dockwrath
began to wax angry. ' I think I remarked before that I don't drink
wine to my dinner,' he said; and then the three at the president's
end of the table all looked at each other very solemnly, and
they all winked; and after that there was very little conversation
during the remainder of the meal, for men knew that the goddess of
discord was in the air.

The cheese came, and with that a bottle of port wine, which was
handed round, Mr. Dockwrath of course refusing to join in the conviviality; and then the cloth was drawn, and the decanters were put
before the president. ' James, bring me a little brandy and water,'
said the attorney, striving to put a bold face on the matter, but yet
speaking with diminished voice.

' Half a moment, if you please, sir,' said Moulder; and then he
exclaimed with stentorian voice, 'James, the dinner bill.' ' Yes,
sir,' said the waiter, and disappeared without any thought towards
the requisition for brandy-and-water from Mr. Dockwrath.

For the next five minutes they all remained silent, except that
Mr. Moulder gave the Queen's health as he filled his glass and
pushed the bottles from him. ' Gentlemen, the Queen,' and then
he lifted his glass of port up to the light, shut one eye as he looked
at it, and immediately swallowed the contents as though he were
taking a dose of physic. ' I'm afraid they'll charge you for the
wine,' said Mr. Kantwise, again whispering to his neighbour. But
Mr. Dockwrath paid no apparent attention to what was said to him.
He was concentrating his energies with a view to the battle.

James, the waiter, soon returned. He also knew well what was
about to happen, and he trembled as he handed in the document to
the president. ' Let's have it, James,' said Moulder, with much
pleasantry, as he took the paper in his hand. ' The old ticket

I suppose; five bob a head.' And then he read out the bill, the total of which, wine and beer included, came to forty shillings. ' Five shillings a head, gentlemen, as I said. You and I can make a pretty good guess as to the figure; eh, Snengkeld?' And then he put down his two half-crowns on the waiter, as also did Mr. Snengkeld, and then Mr. Gape, and so on till it came to Mr. Kantwise.

' I think you and I will leave it, and settle at the bar,' said Kantwise, appealing to Dockwrath, and intending peace if peace were still possible.

' No,' shouted Moulder, from the other end of the table; ' let the man have his money now, and then his troubles will be over. If there's to be any fuss about it, let's have it out. I like to see the dinner bill settled as soon as the dinner is eaten. Then one gets an appetite for one's supper.'

' I don't think I have the change,' said Kantwise, still putting off the evil day.

' I'll lend it you,' said Moulder, putting his hand into his trousers-pockets. But the money was forthcoming out of Mr. Kantwise's own proper repositories, and with slow motion he put down the five shillings one after the other.

And then the waiter came to Mr. Dockwrath. ' What's this?' said the attorney, taking up the bill and looking at it. The whole matter had been sufficiently explained to him, but nevertheless Mr. Moulder explained it again. ' In commercial rooms, sir, as no doubt you must be well aware, seeing that you have done us the honour of joining us here, the dinner bill is divided equally among all the gentlemen as sit down. It's the rule of the room, sir. You has what you like, and you calls for what you like, and con-wiviality is thereby encouraged. The figure generally comes to five shillings, and you afterwards gives what you like to the waiter. That's about it, aint it, James?'

' That's the rule, sir, in all commercial rooms as I ever see,' said the waiter.

The matter had been so extremely well put by Mr. Moulder, and that gentleman's words had carried with them so much conviction, that Dockwrath felt himself almost tempted to put down the money : as far as his sixteen children and general ideas of economy were concerned he would have done so; but his legal mind could not bear to be beaten. The spirit of litigation within him told him that the point was to be carried. Moulder, Gape, and Snengkeld together could not make him pay for wine he had neither ordered nor swallowed. His pocket was guarded by the law of the land, and not by the laws of any special room in which he might chance to find himself. ' I shall pay two shillings for my dinner,' said he, ' and sixpence for my beer;' and then he deposited the half-crown.

' Do you mean us to understand,' said Moulder, ' that after forcing your way into this room, and sitting down along with gentlemen at this table, you refuse to abide by the rules of the room?' And Mr. Moulder spoke and looked as though he thought that such treachery must certainly lead to most disastrous results. The disastrous result which a stranger might have expected at the moment would be a fit of apoplexy on the part of the worthy president.

' I neither ordered that wine nor did I drink it,' said Mr. Dock-wrath, compressing his lips, leaning back in his chair, and looking up into one corner of the ceiling.

' The gentleman certainly did not drink the wine,' said Kant-wise, ' I must acknowledge that ; and as for ordering it, why that was done by the president, in course.'

' Gammon !' said Mr. Moulder, and he fixed his eyes steadfastly upon his Vice. ' Kantwise, that's gammon. The most of what you says is gammon.'

' Mr. Moulder, I don't exactly know what you mean by that word gammon, but it's objectionable. To my feelings it's very objectionable. I say that the gentleman did not drink the wine, and I appeal to the gentleman who sits at the gentleman's right, whether what I say is not correct. If what I say is correct, it can't be—gammon. Mr. Busby, did the gentleman drink the wine, or did he not?'

' Not as I see,' said Mr. Busby, somewhat nervous at being thus brought into the controversy. He was a young man just commencing his travels, and stood in awe of the great Moulder.

' Gammon !' shouted Moulder, with a very red face. ' Everybody at the table knows he didn't drink the wine. Everybody saw that he declined the honour when proposed, which I don't know that I ever saw a gentleman do at a commercial table till this day, barring that he was a teetotaller, which is gammon too. But its P. P. here, as every commercial gentleman knows, Kantwise as well as the best of us.'

' P. P., that's the rule,' growled Snengkeld, almost from under the table.

' In commercial rooms, as the gentleman must be aware, the rule is as stated by my friend on my right,' said Mr. Gape. ' The wine is ordered by the president or chairman, and is paid for in equal proportions by the company or guests,' and in his oratory Mr. Gape laid great stress on the word ' or.' ' The gentleman will easily perceive that such a rule as this is necessary in such a society ; and unless—'

But Mr. Gape was apt to make long speeches, and therefore Mr. Moulder interrupted him. ' You had better pay your five shillings, sir, and have no jaw about it. The man is standing idle there.'

' It's not the value of the money,' said Dockwrath, ' but I must decline to acknowledge that I am amenable to the jurisdiction.'

' There has clearly been a mistake,' said Johnson from Sheffield, ' and we had better settle it among us; anything is better than a row.' Johnson from Sheffield was a man somewhat inclined to dispute the supremacy of Moulder from Houndsditch.

' No, Johnson,' said the president. ' Anything is not better than a row. A premeditated infraction of our rules is not better than a row.'

' Did you say premeditated ?' said Kantwise. ' I think not premeditated.'

' I did say premeditated, and I say it again.'

' It looks uncommon like it,' said Snengkeld.

' When a gentleman,' said Gape, ' who does not belong to a society—'

' It's no good having more talk,' said Moulder, ' and we'll soon bring this to an end. Mr. —— ; I haven't the honour of knowing the gentleman's name.'

' My name is Dockwrath, and I am a solicitor.'

' Oh, a solicitor ; are you ? and you said last night you was commercial ! Will you be good enough to tell us, Mr. Solicitor—for I didn't just catch your name, except that it begins with a dock—and that's where most of your clients are to be found, I suppose—'

' Order, order, order !' said Kantwise, holding up both his hands.

' It's the chair as is speaking,' said Mr. Gape, who had a true Englishman's notion that the chair itself could not be called to order.

' You shouldn't insult the gentleman because he has his own ideas,' said Johnson.

' I don't want to insult no one,' continued Moulder; ' and those who know me best, among whom I can't as yet count Mr. Johnson, though hopes I shall some day, won't say it of me.' ' Hear—hear —hear !' from both Snengkeld and Gape ; to which Kantwise added a little ' hear—hear !' of his own, of which Mr. Moulder did not quite approve. ' Mr. Snengkeld and Mr. Gape, they're my old friends, and they knows me. And they knows the way of a commercial room—which some gentlemen don't seem as though they do. I don't want to insult no one ; but as chairman here at this conwivial meeting, I asks that gentleman who says he is a solicitor whether he means to pay his dinner bill according to the rules of the room, or whether he don't ?'

' I've paid for what I've had already,' said Dockwrath, ' and I don't mean to pay for what I've not had.'

' James,' exclaimed Moulder—and all the chairman was in his voice as he spoke,—' my compliments to Mr. Crump, and I will request his attendance for five minutes :' and then James left the

room, and there was silence for a while, during which the bottles
made their round of the table.

'Hadn't we better send back the pint of wine which Mr. Dockwrath hasn't used?' suggested Kantwise.

'I'm d—— if we do!' replied Moulder, with much energy; and
the general silence was not again broken till Mr. Crump made his
appearance; but the chairman whispered a private word or two to
his friend Snengkeld. 'I never sent back ordered liquor to the
bar yet, unless it was bad; and I'm not going to begin now.'

And then Mr. Crump came in. Mr. Crump was a very clean-
looking person, without any beard; and dressed from head to foot
in black. He was about fifty, with grizzly gray hair, which stood
upright on his head, and his face at the present moment wore on it
an innkeeper's smile. But it could also assume an innkeeper's
frown, and on occasions did so—when bills were disputed, or unreasonable strangers thought that they knew the distance in post-
ing miles round the neighbourhood of Leeds better than did he,
Mr. Crump, who had lived at the Bull Inn all his life. But
Mr. Crump rarely frowned on commercial gentleman, from whom
was derived the main stay of his business and the main prop of his
house.

'Mr. Crump,' began Moulder, 'here has occurred a very unpleasant transaction.'

'I know all about it, gentlemen,' said Mr. Crump. 'The waiter
has acquainted me, and I can assure you, gentlemen, that I am
extremely sorry that anything should have arisen to disturb the
harmony of your dinner-table.'

'We must now call upon you, Mr. Crump,' began Mr. Moulder,
who was about to demand that Dockwrath should be turned bodily
out of the room.

'If you'll allow me one moment, Mr. Moulder,' continued
Mr. Crump, 'and I'll tell you what is my suggestion. The
gentleman here, who I understand is a lawyer, does not wish to
comply with the rules of the commercial room.'

'I certainly don't wish or intend to pay for drink that I didn't
order and haven't had,' said Dockwrath.

'Exactly,' said Mr. Crump. 'And therefore, gentlemen, to get out
of the difficulty, we'll presume, if you please, that the bill is paid.'

'The lawyer, as you call him, will have to leave the room,' said
Moulder.

'Perhaps he will not object to step over to the coffee-room on
the other side,' suggested the landlord.

'I can't think of leaving my seat here under such circumstances,'
said Dockwrath.

'You can't,' said Moulder. 'Then you must be made, as I
take it.'

And then they all marched out of the room each with his own glass.

' Let me see the man that will make me,' said Dockwrath.

Mr. Crump looked very apologetic and not very comfortable. ' There is a difficulty, gentlemen ; there is a difficulty, indeed,' he said. ' The fact is, the gentleman should not have been showed into the room at all ;' and he looked very angrily at his own servant, James.

' He said he was 'mercial,' said James. ' So he did. Now he says as how he's a lawyer. What's a poor man to do ?'

' I'm a commercial lawyer,' said Dockwrath.

' He must leave the room, or I shall leave the house,' said Moulder.

' Gentlemen, gentlemen !' said Crump. ' This kind of thing does not happen often, and on this occasion I must try your kind patience. If Mr. Moulder would allow me to suggest that the commercial gentlemen should take their wine in the large drawing-room up stairs this evening, Mrs. C. will do her best to make it comfortable for them in five minutes. There of course they can be private.'

There was something in the idea of leaving Mr. Dockwrath alone in his glory which appeased the spirit of the great Moulder. He had known Crump, moreover, for many years, and was aware that it would be a dangerous, and probably an expensive proceeding to thrust out the attorney by violence. ' If the other gentlemen are agreeable, I am,' said he. The other gentlemen were agreeable, and, with the exception of Kantwise, they all rose from their chairs.

' I must say I think you ought to leave the room as you don't choose to abide by the rules,' said Johnson, addressing himself to Dockwrath.

' That's your opinion,' said Dockwrath.

' Yes, it is,' said Johnson. ' That's my opinion.'

' My own happens to be different,' said Dockwrath ; and so he kept his chair.

' There, Mr. Crump,' said Moulder, taking half a crown from his pocket, and throwing it on the table. ' I shan't see you at a loss.'

' Thank you, sir,' said Mr. Crump ; and he very humbly took up the money.

' I keep a little account for charity at home,' said Moulder.

' It don't run very high, do it ?' asked Snengkeld, jocosely.

' Not out of the way, it don't. But now I shall have the pleasure of writing down in it that I paid half a crown for a lawyer who couldn't afford to settle his own dinner bill. Sir, we have the pleasure of wishing you a good night.'

' I hope you'll find the large drawing-room up stairs quite comfortable,' said Dockwrath.

And then they all marched out of the room, each with his own glass. Mr. Moulder leading the way with stately step. It was pleasant to see them as they all followed their leader across the open passage of the gateway, in by the bar, and so up the chief staircase. Mr. Moulder walked slowly, bearing the bottle of port and his own glass, and Mr. Snengkeld and Mr. Gape followed in line, bearing also their own glasses, and maintaining the dignity of their profession under circumstances of some difficulty.

'Gentlemen, I really am sorry for this little accident,' said Mr. Crump, as they were passing the bar; 'but a lawyer, you know——'

'And such a lawyer, eh, Crump?' said Moulder.

'It might be five-and-twenty pound to me to lay a hand on him!' said the landlord.

When the time came for Mr. Kantwise to move, he considered the matter well. The chances, however, as he calculated them, were against any profitable business being done with the attorney, so he also left the room. 'Good night, sir,' he said as he went. 'I wish you a very good night.'

'Take care of yourself,' said Dockwrath; and then the attorney spent the rest of the evening alone.

CHAPTER X.

MR., MRS., AND MISS FURNIVAL.

I WILL now ask my readers to come with me up to London, in order that I may introduce them to the family of the Furnivals. We shall see much of the Furnivals before we reach the end of our present undertaking, and it will be well that we should commence our acquaintance with them as early as may be done.

Mr. Furnival was a lawyer—I mean a barrister—belonging to Lincoln's Inn, and living at the time at which our story is supposed to commence in Harley Street. But he had not been long a resident in Harley Street, having left the less fashionable neighbourhood of Russell Square only two or three years before that period. On his marriage he had located himself in a small house in Keppel Street, and had there remained till professional success, long waited for, enabled him to move further west, and indulge himself with the comforts of larger rooms and more servants. At the time of which I am now speaking Mr. Furnival was known, and well known, as a successful man; but he had struggled long and hard before that success had come to him, and during the earliest years of his married life had found the work of keeping the wolf from his door to be almost more than enough for his energies.

Mr. Furnival practised at the common law bar, and early in life had attached himself to the home circuit. I cannot say why he obtained no great success till he was nearer fifty than forty years of age. At that time I fancy that barristers did not come to their prime till a period of life at which other men are supposed to be in their decadence. Nevertheless, he had married on nothing, and had kept the wolf from the door. To do this he had been constant at his work in season and out of season, during the long hours of day and the long hours of night. Throughout his term times he had toiled in court, and during the vacations he had toiled out of court. He had reported volumes of cases, having been himself his own short-hand writer,—as it is well known to most young lawyers, who as a rule always fill an upper shelf in their law libraries with Furnival and Staples' seventeen volumes in calf. He had worked for the booksellers, and for the newspapers, and for the attorneys,—always working, however, with reference to the law ; and though he had worked for years with the lowest pay, no man had heard him complain. That no woman had heard him do so, I will not say ; as it is more than probable that into the sympathizing ears of Mrs. Furnival he did pour forth plaints as to the small wages which the legal world meted out to him in return for his labours. He was a constant, hard, patient man, and at last there came to him the full reward of all his industry. What was the special case by which Mr. Furnival obtained his great success no man could say. In all probability there was no special case. Gradually it began to be understood that he was a safe man, understanding his trade, true to his clients, and very damaging as an opponent. Legal gentlemen are, I believe, quite as often bought off as bought up. Sir Richard and Mr. Furnival could not both be required on the same side, seeing what a tower of strength each was in himself; but then Sir Richard would be absolutely neutralized if Mr. Furnival were employed on the other side. This is a system well understood by attorneys, and has been found to be extremely lucrative by gentlemen leading at the bar.

Mr. Furnival was now fifty-five years of age, and was beginning to show in his face some traces of his hard work. Not that he was becoming old, or weak, or worn ; but his eye had lost its fire— except the fire peculiar to his profession ; and there were wrinkles in his forehead and cheeks ; and his upper lip, except when he was speaking, hung heavily over the lower ; and the loose skin below his eye was forming itself into saucers; and his hair had become grizzled ; and on his shoulders, except when in court, there was a slight stoop. As seen in his wig and gown he was a man of commanding presence,—and for ten men in London who knew him in this garb, hardly one knew him without it. He was nearly six feet high, and stood forth prominently, with square,

broad shoulders and a large body. His head also was large; his
forehead was high, and marked strongly by signs of intellect; his
nose was long and straight, his eyes were very gray, and capable to
an extraordinary degree both of direct severity and of concealed
sarcasm. Witnesses have been heard to say that they could endure
all that Mr. Furnival could say to them, and continue in some sort
to answer all his questions, if only he would refrain from looking
at them. But he would never refrain; and therefore it was now
well understood how great a thing it was to secure the services of
Mr. Furnival. 'Sir,' an attorney would say to an unfortunate
client doubtful as to the expenditure, ' your witnesses will not be
able to stand in the box if we allow Mr. Furnival to be engaged on
the other side.' I am inclined to think that Mr. Furnival owed to
this power of his eyes his almost unequalled perfection in that
peculiar branch of his profession. His voice was powerful, and
not unpleasant when used within the precincts of a court, though
it grated somewhat harshly on the ears in the smaller compass of a
private room. His flow of words was free and good, and seemed to
come from him without the slightest effort. Such at least was
always the case with him when standing wigged and gowned before
a judge. Latterly, however, he had tried his eloquence on another
arena, and not altogether with equal success. He was now in
Parliament, sitting as member for the Essex Marshes, and he had
not as yet carried either the country or the House with him,
although he had been frequently on his legs. Some men said that
with a little practice he would yet become very serviceable as an
honourable and learned member; but others expressed a fear that
he had come too late in life to these new duties.

I have spoken of Mr. Furnival's great success in that branch of
his profession which required from him the examination of evidence,
but I would not have it thought that he was great only in this, or
even mainly in this. There are gentlemen at the bar, among whom
I may perhaps notice my old friend Mr. Chaffanbrass as the most
conspicuous, who have confined their talents to the browbeating of
witnesses,—greatly to their own profit, and no doubt to the advantage of society. But I would have it understood that Mr. Furnival
was by no means one of these. He had been no Old Bailey lawyer,
devoting himself to the manumission of murderers, or the security
of the swindling world in general. He had been employed on
abstruse points of law, had been great in will cases, very learned as
to the rights of railways, peculiarly apt in enforcing the dowries of
married women, and successful above all things in separating
husbands and wives whose lives had not been passed in accordance with the recognized rules of Hymen. Indeed there is no
branch of the Common Law in which he was not regarded as great
and powerful, though perhaps his proficiency in damaging the

general characters of his opponents has been recognized as his especial forte. Under these circumstances I should grieve to have him confounded with such men as Mr. Chaffanbrass, who is hardly known by the profession beyond the precincts of his own peculiar court in the City. Mr. Furnival's reputation has spread itself wherever stuff gowns and horsehair wigs are held in estimation.

Mr. Furnival when clothed in his forensic habiliments certainly possessed a solemn and severe dignity which had its weight even with the judges. Those who scrutinized his appearance critically might have said that it was in some respects pretentious; but the ordinary jurymen of this country are not critical scrutinizers of appearance, and by them he was never held in light estimation. When in his addresses to them, appealing to their intelligence, education, and enlightened justice, he would declare that the property of his clients was perfectly safe in their hands, he looked to be such an advocate as a litigant would fain possess when dreading the soundness of his own cause. Any cause was sound to him when once he had been feed for its support, and he carried in his countenance his assurance of this soundness,—and the assurance of unsoundness in the cause of his opponent. Even he did not always win; but on the occasion of his losing, those of the uninitiated who had heard the pleadings would express their astonishment that he should not have been successful.

When he was divested of his wig his appearance was not so perfect. There was then a hard, long straightness about his head and face, giving to his countenance the form of a parallelogram, to which there belonged a certain meanness of expression. He wanted the roundness of forehead, the short lines, and the graceful curves of face which are necessary to unadorned manly comeliness. His whiskers were small, grizzled, and ill grown, and required the ample relief of his wig. In no guise did he look other than a clever man; but in his dress as a simple citizen he would perhaps be taken as a clever man in whose tenderness of heart and cordiality of feeling one would not at first sight place implicit trust.

As a poor man Mr. Furnival had done his duty well by his wife and family,—for as a poor man he had been blessed with four children. Three of these had died as they were becoming men and women, and now, as a rich man, he was left with one daughter, an only child. As a poor man Mr. Furnival had been an excellent husband, going forth in the morning to his work, struggling through the day, and then returning to his meagre dinner and his long evenings of unremitting drudgery. The bodily strength which had supported him through his work in those days must have been immense, for he had allowed himself no holidays. And then success and money had come,—and Mrs. Furnival sometimes found

herself not quite so happy as she had been when watching beside
him in the days of their poverty.

The equal mind,—as mortal Delius was bidden to remember, and
as Mr. Furnival might also have remembered had time been allowed
him to cultivate the classics,—the equal mind should be as sedulously maintained when things run well, as well as when they run
hardly ; and perhaps the maintenance of such equal mind is more
difficult in the former than in the latter stage of life. Be that as it
may, Mr. Furnival could now be very cross on certain domestic
occasions, and could also be very unjust. And there was worse
than this,—much worse behind. He, who in the heyday of his
youth would spend night after night poring over his books, copy-
ing out reports, and never asking to see a female habiliment brighter
or more attractive than his wife's Sunday gown, he, at the age of
fifty-five, was now running after strange goddesses ! The member
for the Essex Marshes, in these his latter days, was obtaining for
himself among other successes the character of a Lothario ; and
Mrs. Furnival, sitting at home in her genteel drawing-room near
Cavendish Square, would remember with regret the small dingy
parlour in Keppel Street.

Mrs. Furnival in discussing her grievances would attribute them
mainly to port wine. In his early days Mr. Furnival had been
essentially an abstemious man. Young men who work fifteen hours
a day must be so. But now he had a strong opinion about certain
Portuguese vintages, was convinced that there was no port wine in
London equal to the contents of his own bin, saving always a certain
green cork appertaining to his own club, which was to be extracted
at the rate of thirty shillings a cork. And Mrs. Furnival attributed
to these latter studies not only a certain purple hue which was
suffusing his nose and cheeks, but also that unevenness of character
and those supposed domestic improprieties to which allusion has
been made. It may, however, be as well to explain that Mrs. Ball,
the old family cook and housekeeper, who had ascended with the
Furnivals in the world, opined that made-dishes did the mischief.
He dined out too often, and was a deal too particular about his
dinner when he dined at home. If Providence would see fit to
visit him with a sharp attack of the gout, it would—so thought
Mrs. Ball—be better for all parties.

Whether or no it may have been that Mrs. Furnival at fifty-five—
for she and her lord were of the same age—was not herself as
attractive in her husband's eyes as she had been at thirty, I will
not pretend to say. There can have been no just reason for any
such change in feeling, seeing that the two had grown old together.
She, poor woman, would still have been quite content with the
attentions of Mr. Furnival, though his hair was grizzled and his nose
was blue ; nor did she ever think of attracting to herself the admira-

tion of any swain whose general comeliness might be more free from all taint of age. Why then should he wander afield—at the age of fifty-five? That he did wander afield, poor Mrs. Furnival felt in her agony convinced; and among those ladies whom on this account she most thoroughly detested was our friend Lady Mason of Orley Farm. Lady Mason and the lawyer had first become acquainted in the days of the trial, now long gone by, on which occasion Mr. Furnival had been employed as the junior counsel; and that acquaintance had ripened into friendship, and now flourished in full vigour,—to Mrs. Furnival's great sorrow and disturbance.

Mrs. Furnival herself was a stout, solid woman, sensible on most points, but better adapted, perhaps, to the life in Keppel Street than that to which she had now been promoted. As Kitty Blacker she had possessed feminine charms which would have been famous had they been better known. Mr. Furnival had fetched her from farther East—from the region of Great Ormond-street and the neighbourhood of Southampton Buildings. Her cherry cheeks, and her round eye, and her full bust, and her fresh lip, had conquered the hard-tasked lawyer; and so they had gone forth to fight the world together. Her eye was still round, and her cheek red, and her bust full,—there had certainly been no falling off there; nor will I say that her lip had lost all its freshness. But the bloom of her charms had passed away, and she was now a solid, stout, motherly woman, not bright in converse, but by no means deficient in mother-wit, recognizing well the duties which she owed to others, but recognizing equally well those which others owed to her. All the charms of her youth—had they not been given to him, and also all her solicitude, all her anxious fighting with the hard world? When they had been poor together, had she not patched and turned and twisted, sitting silently by his side into the long nights, because she would not ask him for the price of a new dress? And yet now, now that they were rich—? Mrs. Furnival, when she put such questions within her own mind, could hardly answer this latter one with patience. Others might be afraid of the great Mr. Furnival in his wig and gown; others might be struck dumb by his power of eye and mouth; but she, she, the wife of his bosom, she could catch him without his armour. She would so catch him and let him know what she thought of all her wrongs. So she said to herself many a day, and yet the great deed, in all its explosive-ness, had never yet been done. Small attacks of words there had been many, but hitherto the courage to speak out her griefs openly had been wanting to her.

I can now allow myself but a small space to say a few words of Sophia Furnival, and yet in that small space must be confined all the direct description which can be given of one of the principal personages of this story. At nineteen Miss Furnival was in all respects a young woman. She was forward in acquirements, in manner, in general intelligence, and in powers of conversation. She was a handsome, tall girl, with expressive gray eyes and dark-brown hair. Her mouth, and hair, and a certain motion of her neck and turn of her head, had come to her from her mother, but her eyes were those of her father : they were less sharp perhaps, less eager after their prey ; but they were bright as his had been bright, and sometimes had in them more of absolute command than he was ever able to throw into his own.

Their golden days had come on them at a period of her life which enabled her to make a better use of them than her mother could do. She never felt herself to be struck dumb by rank or fashion, nor did she in the drawing-rooms of the great ever show signs of an Eastern origin. She could adapt herself without an effort to the manners of Cavendish Square ;—ay, and if need were, to the ways of more glorious squares even than that. Therefore was her father never ashamed to be seen with her on his arm in the houses of his new friends, though on such occasions he was willing enough to go out without disturbing the repose of his wife. No mother could have loved her children with a warmer affection than that which had warmed the heart of poor Mrs. Furnival ; but under such circumstances as these was it singular that she should occasionally become jealous of her own daughter?

Sophia Furnival was, as I have said, a clever, attractive girl, handsome, well-read, able to hold her own with the old as well as with the young, capable of hiding her vanity if she had any, mild and gentle to girls less gifted, animated in conversation, and yet possessing an eye that could fall softly to the ground, as a woman's eye always should fall upon occasions.

Nevertheless she was not altogether charming. ' I don't feel quite sure that she is real,' Mrs. Orme had said of her, when on a certain occasion Miss Furnival had spent a day and a night at The Cleeve.

CHAPTER XI.

Lucius Mason on his road to Liverpool had passed through London, and had found a moment to call in Harley Street. Since his return from Germany he had met Miss Furnival both at home at his mother's house—or rather his own—and at the Cleeve. Miss Furnival had been in the neighbourhood, and had spent two days with the great people at the Cleeve, and one day with the little people at Orley Farm. Lucius Mason had found that she was a sensible girl, capable of discussing great subjects with him; and had possibly found some other charms in her. Therefore he had called in Harley Street.

On that occasion he could only call as he passed through London without delay; but he received such encouragement as induced him to spend a night in town on his return, in order that he might accept an invitation to drink tea with the Furnivals. ' We shall be very happy to see you,' Mrs. Furnival had said, backing the proposition which had come from her daughter without any very great fervour; ' but I fear Mr. Furnival will not be at home. Mr. Furnival very seldom is at home now.' Young Mason did not much care for fervour on the part of Sophia's mother, and therefore had accepted the invitation, though he was obliged by so doing to curtail by some hours his sojourn among the guano stores of Liverpool.

It was the time of year at which few people are at home in London, being the middle of October; but Mrs. Furnival was a lady of whom at such periods it was not very easy to dispose. She could have made herself as happy as a queen even at Margate, if it could have suited Furnival and Sophia to be happy at Margate with her. But this did not suit Furnival or Sophia. As regards money, any or almost all other autumnal resorts were open to her, but she could be contented at none of them because Mr. Furnival always pleaded that business—law business or political business—took him elsewhere. Now Mrs. Furnival was a woman who did not like to be deserted, and who could not, in the absence of those social joys which Providence had vouchsafed to her as her own, make herself happy with the society of other women such as herself. Furnival was her husband, and

she wanted him to carve for her, to sit opposite to her at the breakfast table, to tell her the news of the day, and to walk to church
with her on Sundays. They had been made one flesh and one
bone, for better and worse, thirty years since; and now in her
latter days she could not put up with disseveration and dislocation.

She had gone down to Brighton in August, soon after the House
broke up, and there found that very handsome apartments had
been taken for her—rooms that would have made glad the heart
of many a lawyer's wife. She had, too, the command of a fly,
done up to look like a private brougham, a servant in livery, the
run of the public assembly-rooms, a sitting in the centre of the
most fashionable church in Brighton—all that the heart of woman
could desire. All but the one thing was there; but, that one thing
being absent, she came moodily back to town at the end of September. She would have exchanged them all with a happy heart for
very moderate accommodation at Margate, could she have seen
Mr. Furnival's blue nose on the other side of the table every morning
and evening as she sat over her shrimps and tea.

Men who had risen in the world as Mr. Furnival had done do
find it sometimes difficult to dispose of their wives. It is not that
the ladies are in themselves more unfit for rising than their lords,
or that if occasion demanded they would not as readily adapt them
selves to new spheres. But they do not rise, and occasion does
not demand it. A man elevates his wife to his own rank, and
when Mr. Brown, on becoming solicitor-general, becomes Sir Jacob,
Mrs. Brown also becomes my lady. But the whole set among whom
Brown must be more or less thrown do not want her ladyship. On
Brown's promotion she did not become part of the bargain. Brown
must henceforth have two existences—a public and a private existence; and it will be well for Lady Brown, and well also for Sir
Jacob, if the latter be not allowed to dwindle down to a minimum.

If Lady B. can raise herself also, if she can make her own
occasion—if she be handsome and can flirt, if she be impudent and
can force her way, if she have a daring mind and can commit great
expenditure, if she be clever and can make poetry, if she can in
any way create a separate glory for herself, then, indeed, Sir Jacob
with his blue nose may follow his own path, and all will be well.
Sir Jacob's blue nose seated opposite to her will not be her summum
bonum.

But worthy Mrs. Furnival—and she was worthy—had created for
herself no such separate glory, nor did she dream of creating it;
and therefore she had, as it were, no footing left to her. On this
occasion she had gone to Brighton, and had returned from it sulky
and wretched, bringing her daughter back to London at the period of
London's greatest desolation. Sophia had returned uncomplaining,
remembering that good things were in store for her. She had been

asked to spend her Christmas with the Staveleys at Noningsby —the family of Judge Staveley, who lives near Alston, at a very pretty country place so called. Mr. Furnival had been for many years acquainted with Judge Staveley—had known the judge when he was a leading counsel; and now that Mr. Furnival was a rising man, and now that he had a pretty daughter, it was natural that the young Staveleys and Sophia Furnival should know each other. But poor Mrs. Furnival was too ponderous for this mounting late in life, and she had not been asked to Noningsby. She was much too good a mother to repine at her daughter's promised gaiety. Sophia was welcome to go; but by all the laws of God and man it would behove her lord and husband to eat his mincepie at home.

'Mr. Furnival was to be back in town this evening,' the lady said, as though apologizing to young Mason for her husband's absence, when he entered the drawing-room, ' but he has not come, and I dare say will not come now.'

Mason did not care a straw for Mr. Furnival. 'Oh! won't he?' said he. 'I suppose business keeps him.'

'Papa is very busy about politics just at present,' said Sophia, wishing to make matters smooth in her mother's mind. ' He was obliged to be at Romford in the beginning of the week, and then he went down to Birmingham. There is some congress going on there, is there not?'

' All that must take a great deal of time,' said Lucius.

' Yes ; and it is a terrible bore,' said Sophia. ' I know papa finds it so.'

' Your papa likes it, I believe,' said Mrs. Furnival, who would not hide even her grievances under a bushel.

' I don't think he likes being so much from home, mamma. Of course he likes excitement, and success. All men do. Do they not, Mr. Mason?'

' They all ought to do so, and women also.'

' Ah! but women have no sphere, Mr. Mason.'

' They have minds equal to those of men,' said Lucius, gallantly, ' and ought to be able to make for themselves careers as brilliant.'

' Women ought not to have any spheres,' said Mrs. Furnival.

' I don't know that I quite agree with you there, mamma.'

' The world is becoming a great deal too fond of what you call excitement and success. Of course it is a good thing for a man to make money by his profession, and a very hard thing when he can't do it,' added Mrs. Furnival, thinking of the olden days. ' But if success in life means rampaging about, and never knowing what it is to sit quiet over his own fireside, I for one would as soon manage to do without it.'

' But, mamma, I don't see why success should always be rampageous.'

' Literary women who have achieved a name bear their honours quietly,' said Lucius.

' I don't know,' said Mrs. Furnival. ' I am told that some of them are as fond of gadding as the men. As regards the old maids, I don't care so much about it; people who are not married may do what they like with themselves, and nobody has anything to say to them. But it is very different for married people. They have no bus·ness to be enticed away from their homes by any success.'

' Mamma is all for a Darby and Joan life,' said Sophia, laughing.

' No I am not, my dear; and you should not say so. I don't advocate anything that is absurd. But I do say that life should be lived at home. That is the best part of it. What is the meaning of home if it isn't that?'

Poor Mrs. Furnival! she had no idea that she was complaining to a stranger of her husband. Had any one told her so she would have declared that she was discussing general world-wide topics; but Lucius Mason, young as he was, knew that the marital shoe was pinching the lady's domestic corn, and he made haste to change the subject.

' You know my mother, Mrs. Furnival?'

Mrs. Furnival said that she had the honour of acquaintance with Lady Mason; but on this occasion also she exhibited but little fervour.

' I shall meet her up in town to-morrow,' said Lucius. ' She is coming up for some shopping.'

' Oh! indeed,' said Mrs. Furnival.

' And then we go down home together. I am to meet her at the chymist's at the top of Chancery Lane.'

Now this was a very unnecessary communication on the part of young Mason, and also an unfortunate one. ' Oh! indeed,' said Mrs. Furnival again, throwing her head a little back. Poor woman! she could not conceal what was in her mind, and her daughter knew all about it immediately. The truth was this. Mr. Furnival had been for some days on the move, at Birmingham and elsewhere, and had now sent up sudden notice that he should probably be at home that very night. He should probably be at home that night, but in such case would be compelled to return to his friends at Birmingham on the following afternoon. Now if it were an ascertained fact that he was coming to London merely with the view of meeting Lady Mason, the wife of his bosom would not think it necessary to provide for him the warmest possible welcome. This of course was not an ascertained fact; but was there not terrible grounds of suspicion? Mr. Furnival's law chambers were in Old Square, Lincoln's Inn, close to Chancery Lane, and Lady Mason had made her appointment with her son within five minutes' walk of that locality. And was it not in itself a strange coincidence that

Lady Mason, who came to town so seldom, should now do so on the very day of Mr. Furnival's sudden return? She felt sure that they were to meet on the morrow, but yet she could not declare even to herself that it was an ascertained fact.

'Oh! indeed,' she said; and Sophia understood all about it, though Lucius did not.

Then Mrs. Furnival sank into silence; and we need not follow, word for word, the conversation between the young lady and the young gentleman. Mr. Mason thought that Miss Furnival was a very nice girl, and was not at all ill pleased to have an opportunity of passing an evening in her company; and Miss Furnival thought—. What she thought, or what young ladies may think generally about young gentlemen, is not to be spoken openly; but it seemed as though she also were employed to her own satisfaction, while her mother sat moody in her own arm-chair. In the course of the evening the footman in livery brought in tea, handing it round on a big silver salver, which also added to Mrs. Furnival's unhappiness. She would have liked to sit behind her tea-tray as she used to do in the good old hard-working days, with a small pile of buttered toast on the slop-bowl, kept warm by hot water below it. In those dear old hard-working days, buttered toast had been a much-loved delicacy with Furnival; and she, kind woman, had never begrudged her eyes, as she sat making it for him over the parlour fire. Nor would she have begrudged them now, neither her eyes nor the work of her hands, nor all the thoughts of her heart, if he would have consented to accept of her handiwork; but in these days Mr. Furnival had learned a relish for other delicacies.

She also had liked buttered toast, always, however, taking the pieces with the upper crust, in order that the more luscious morsels might be left for him; and she had liked to prepare her own tea leisurely, putting in slowly the sugar and cream—skimmed milk it had used to be, dropped for herself with a sparing hand, in order that his large breakfast-cup might be whitened to his liking; but though the milk had been skimmed and scanty, and though the tea itself had been put in with a sparing hand, she had then been mistress of the occasion. She had had her own way, and in stinting herself had found her own reward. But now—the tea had no flavour now that it was made in the kitchen and brought to her, cold and vapid, by a man in livery whom she half feared to keep waiting while she ministered to her own wants.

And so she sat moody in her arm-chair, cross and sulky, as her daughter thought. But yet there was a vein of poetry in her heart as she sat there, little like a sibyl as she looked. Dear old days, in which her cares and solicitude were valued; in which she could do something for the joint benefit of the firm into which she had been taken as a partner! How happy she had been in her struggles, how

piteously had her heart yearned towards him when she thought that
he was struggling too fiercely, how brave and constant he had
been; and how she had loved him as he sat steady as a rock at his
grinding work! Now had come the great success of which they had
both dreamed together, of which they had talked as arm in arm they
were taking the exercise that was so needful to him, walking quickly
round Russell Square, quickly round Bloomsbury Square and Bedford
Square, and so back to the grinding work in Keppel Street. It had
come now—all of which they had dreamed, and more than all they
had dared to hope. But of what good was it? Was he happy?
No; he was fretful, bilious, and worn with toil which was hard to
him because he ate and drank too much; he was ill at ease in
public, only half understanding the political life which he was
obliged to assume in his new ambition; and he was sick in his
conscience—she was sure that must be so: he could not thus neglect
her, his loving, constant wife, without some pang of remorse. And
was she happy? She might have revelled in silks and satins, if
silks and satins would have done her old heart good. But they
would do her no good. How she had joyed in a new dress, when it
had been so hard to come by, so slow in coming, and when he
would go with her to the choosing of it! But her gowns now were
hardly of more interest to her than the joints of meat which the
butcher brought to the door with the utmost regularity. It behoved
the butcher to send good beef and the milliner to send good silk,
and there was an end of it.

Not but what she could have been ecstatic about a full skirt on a
smart body if he would have cared to look at it. In truth she was
still soft and young enough within, though stout, and solid, and
somewhat aged without. Though she looked cross and surly that
night, there was soft poetry within her heart. If Providence, who
had bountifully given, would now by chance mercifully take away
those gifts, would she not then forgive everything and toil for him
again with the same happiness as before? Ah! yes; she could
forgive everything, anything, if he would only return and be contented to sit opposite to her once again. ' O mortal Delius, dearest
lord and husband!' she exclaimed within her own breast, in
language somewhat differing from that of the Roman poet, ' why
hast thou not remembered to maintain a mind equal in prosperity
as it was always equal and well poised in adversity? Oh! my
Delius, since prosperity has been too much for thee, may the Lord
bless thee once more with the adversity which thou canst bear—
which thou canst bear, and I with thee!' Thus did she sing sadly
within her own bosom—sadly, but with true poetic cadence; while
Sophia and Lucius Mason, sitting by, when for a moment they
turned their eyes upon her, gave her credit only for the cross
solemnity supposed to be incidental to obese and declining years.

Mr. Furnival's welcome home.

And then there came a ring at the bell and a knock at the door, and a rush along the nether passages, and the lady knew that he of whom she had been thinking had arrived. In olden days she had ever met him in the narrow passage, and, indifferent to the maid, she had hung about his neck and kissed him in the hall. But now she did not stir from her chair. She could forgive him all and run again at the sound of his footstep, but she must first know that such forgiveness and such running would be welcome.

'That's papa,' said Sophia.

'Don't forget that I have not met him since I have been home from Germany,' said Lucius. 'You must introduce me.'

In a minute or two Mr. Furnival opened the door and walked into the room. Men when they arrive from their travels now-a-days have no strippings of greatcoats, no deposits to make of thick shawls and double gloves, no absolutely necessary changes of raiment. Such had been the case when he had used to come back cold and weary from the circuits; but now he had left Birmingham since dinner by the late express, had enjoyed his nap in the train for two hours or so, and walked into his own drawing-room as he might have done had he dined in his own dining-room.

'How are you, Kitty?' he said to his wife, handing to her the forefinger of his right hand by way of greeting. 'Well, Sophy, my love;' and he kissed his daughter. 'Oh! Lucius Mason. I am very glad to see you. I can't say I should have remembered you unless I had been told. You are very welcome in Harley Street, and I hope you will often be here.'

'It's not very often he'd find you at home, Mr. Furnival,' said the aggrieved wife.

'Not so often as I could wish just at present; but things will be more settled, I hope, before very long. How's your mother, Lucius?'

'She's pretty well, thank you, sir. I've to meet her in town to-morrow, and go down home with her.'

There was then silence in the room for a few seconds, during which Mrs. Furnival looked very sharply at her husband. 'Oh! she's to be in town, is she?' said Mr. Furnival, after a moment's consideration. He was angry with Lady Mason at the moment for having put him into this position. Why had she told her son that she was to be up in London, thus producing conversation and tittle-tattle which made deceit on his part absolutely necessary? Lady Mason's business in London was of a nature which would not bear much open talking. She herself, in her earnest letter summoning Mr. Furnival up from Birmingham, had besought him that her visit to his chambers might not be made matter of discussion. New troubles might be coming on her, but also they might not; and she was very anxious that no one should know that she was seeking a lawyer's advice on the matter. To all this Mr. Furnival had given in his adhesion; and yet she had put it into her son's power to come to his drawing-room and chatter there of her whereabouts. For a moment or two he doubted; but at the expiration of those moments he saw that the deceit was necessary. 'She's to be in town, is she?' said he. The reader will of course observe that this deceit was practised, not as between husband and wife with reference to an assignation with a lady, but between the lawyer and the outer world with reference to a private meeting with a client. But then it is sometimes so difficult to make wives look at such matters in the right light.

'She's coming up for some shopping,' said Lucius.

'Oh! indeed,' said Mrs. Furnival. She would not have spoken if she could have helped it, but she could not help it; and then there was silence in the room for a minute or two, which Lucius vainly endeavoured to break by a few indifferent observations to Miss Furnival. The words, however, which he uttered would not take the guise of indifferent observations, but fell flatly on their ears, and at the same time solemnly, as though spoken with the sole purpose of creating sound.

'I hope you have been enjoying yourself at Birmingham,' said Mrs. Furnival.

'Enjoyed myself! I did not exactly go there for enjoyment.'

'Or at Romford, where you were before?'

'Women seem to think that men have no purpose but amusement when they go about their daily work,' said Mr. Furnival; and then he threw himself back in his arm-chair, and took up the last Quarterly.

Lucius Mason soon perceived that all the harmony of the evening had in some way been marred by the return of the master of the house, and that he might be in the way if he remained; he therefore took his leave.

'I shall want breakfast punctually at half-past eight to-morrow morning,' said Mr. Furnival, as soon as the stranger had withdrawn. 'I must be in chambers before ten;' and then he took his candle and withdrew to his own room.

Sophia rang the bell and gave the servant the order; but Mrs. Furnival took no trouble in the matter whatever. In the olden days she would have bustled down before she went to bed, and have seen herself that everything was ready, so that the master of the house might not be kept waiting. But all this was nothing to her now.

CHAPTER XII.

MR. FURNIVAL's chambers were on the first floor in a very dingy edifice in Old Square, Lincoln's Inn. This square was always dingy, even when it was comparatively open and served as the approach from Chancery Lane to the Lord Chancellor's Court; but now it has been built up with new shops for the Vice-Chancellor, and to my eyes it seems more dingy than ever.

He there occupied three rooms, all of them sufficiently spacious for the purposes required, but which were made oppressive by their general dinginess and by a smell of old leather which pervaded them. In one of them sat at his desk Mr. Crabwitz, a gentleman who had now been with Mr. Furnival for the last fifteen years, and who considered that no inconsiderable portion of the barrister's success had been attributable to his own energy and genius. Mr. Crabwitz was a genteel-looking man, somewhat over forty years of age, very careful as to his gloves, hat, and umbrella, and not a little particular as to his associates. As he was unmarried, fond of ladies' society, and presumed to be a warm man in money matters, he had his social successes, and looked down from a considerable altitude on some men who from their professional rank might have been considered as his superiors. He had a small bachelor's box down at Barnes, and not unfrequently went abroad in the vacations. The door opening into the room of Mr. Crabwitz was in the corner front-ing you on the left-hand side as you entered the chambers. Immediately on your left was a large waiting-room, in which an additional clerk usually sat at an ordinary table. He was not an authorized part of the establishment, being kept only from week to week; but nevertheless, for the last two or three years he had been always there, and Mr. Crabwitz intended that he should remain, for he acted as fag to Mr. Crabwitz. This waiting-room was very dingy, much more so than the clerk's room, and boasted of no furni-ture but eight old leathern chairs and two old tables. It was surrounded by shelves which were laden with books and dust, which by no chance were ever disturbed. But to my ideas the most dingy of the three rooms was that large one in which the great man him-self sat; the door of which directly fronted you as you entered.

The furniture was probably better than that in the other chambers, and the place had certainly the appearance of warmth and life which comes from frequent use; but nevertheless, of all the rooms in which I ever sat I think it was the most gloomy. There were heavy curtains to the windows, which had once been ruby but were now brown; and the ceiling was brown, and the thick carpet was brown, and the books which covered every portion of the wall were brown, and the painted wood-work of the doors and windows was of a dark brown. Here, on the morning with which we have now to deal, sat Mr. Furnival over his papers from ten to twelve, at which latter hour Lady Mason was to come to him. The holidays of Mr. Crabwitz had this year been cut short in consequence of his patron's attendance at the great congress which was now sitting, and although all London was a desert, as he had piteously complained to a lady of his acquaintance whom he had left at Boulogne, he was there in the midst of the desert, and on this morning was sitting in attendance at his usual desk.

Why Mr. Furnival should have breakfasted by himself at half-past eight in order that he might be at his chambers at ten, seeing that the engagement for which he had come to town was timed for twelve, I will not pretend to say. He did not ask his wife to join him, and consequently she did not come down till her usual time. Mr. Furnival breakfasted by himself, and at ten o'clock he was in his chambers. Though alone for two hours he was not idle, and exactly at twelve Mr. Crabwitz opened his door and announced Lady Mason.

When we last parted with her after her interview with Sir Peregrine Orme, she had resolved not to communicate with her friend the lawyer,—at any rate not to do so immediately. Thinking on that resolve she had tried to sleep that night; but her mind was altogether disturbed, and she could get no rest. What, if after twenty years of tranquillity all her troubles must now be recommenced? What if the battle were again to be fought,—with such termination as the chances of war might send to her? Why was it that she was so much greater a coward now than she had been then? Then she had expected defeat, for her friends had bade her not to be sanguine; but in spite of that she had borne up and gone gallantly through the ordeal. But now she felt that if Orley Farm were hers to give she would sooner abandon it than renew the contest. Then, at that former period of her life, she had prepared her mind to do or die in the cause. She had wrought herself up for the work, and had carried it through. But having done that work, having accomplished her terrible task, she had hoped that rest might be in store for her.

As she rose from her bed on the morning after her interview with Sir Peregrine, she determined that she would seek counsel from him

in whose counsel she could trust. Sir Peregrine's friendship was
more valuable to her than that of Mr. Furnival, but a word of advice
from Mr. Furnival was worth all the spoken wisdom of the baronet,
ten times over. Therefore she wrote her letter, and proposed an
appointment; and Mr. Furnival, tempted as I have said by some
evil spirit to stray after strange goddesses in these his blue-nosed
days, had left his learned brethren at their congress in Birmingham,
and had hurried up to town to assist the widow. He had left that
congress, though the wisest Rustums of the law from all the civilized countries of Europe were there assembled, with Boanerges at
their head, that great, old, valiant, learned, British Rustum, inquiring with energy, solemnity, and caution, with much shaking of
ponderous heads and many sarcasms from those which were not
ponderous, whether any and what changes might be made in the
modes of answering that great question, ' Guilty or not guilty ?' and
that other equally great question, ' Is it meum or is it tuum ?'
To answer which question justly should be the end and object
of every lawyer's work. There were great men there from Paris,
very capable, the Ulpians, Tribonians, and Papinians of the new
empire, armed with the purest sentiments expressed in antithetical
and magniloquent phrases, ravishing to the ears, and armed also
with a code which, taken in its integrity, would necessarily, as
the logical consequence of its clauses, drive all injustice from the
face of the earth. And there were great practitioners from Germany, men very skilled in the use of questions, who profess that
the tongue of man, if adequately skilful, may always prevail on
guilt to disclose itself; who believe in the power of their own
craft to produce truth, as our forefathers believed in torture; and
sometimes with the same result. And of course all that was great
on the British bench, and all that was famous at the British bar was
there,—men very unlike their German brethren, men who thought
that guilt never should be asked to tell of itself,—men who were
customarily but unconsciously shocked whenever unwary guilt did
tell of itself. Men these were, mostly of high and noble feeling, born
and bred to live with upright hearts and clean hands, but taught
by the peculiar tenets of their profession to think that that which
was high and noble in their private intercourse with the world need
not also be so esteemed in their legal practice. And there were Italians
there, good-humoured, joking, easy fellows, who would laugh their
clients in and out of their difficulties; and Spaniards, very grave
and serious, who doubted much in their minds whether justice might
not best be bought and sold; and our brethren from the United
States were present also, very eager to show that in this country
law, and justice also, were clouded and nearly buried beneath their
wig and gown.

All these and all this did Mr. Furnival desert for the space of

twenty-four hours in order that he might comply with the request
of Lady Mason. Had she known what it was that she was calling
on him to leave, no doubt she would have borne her troubles for
another week,—for another fortnight, till those Rustums at Birmingham had brought their labours to a close. She would not have
robbed the English bar of one of the warmest supporters of its
present mode of practice, even for a day, had she known how much
that support was needed at the present moment. But she had not
known; and Mr. Furnival, moved by her woman's plea, had not
been hard enough in his heart to refuse her.

When she entered the room she was dressed very plainly as was
her custom, and a thick veil covered her face; but still she was
dressed with care. There was nothing of the dowdiness of the
lone lorn woman about her, none of that lanky, washed-out appearance which sorrow and trouble so often give to females. Had she
given way to dowdiness, or suffered herself to be, as it were,
washed out, Mr. Furnival, we may say, would not have been
there to meet her;—of which fact Lady Mason was perhaps aware.

'I am so grateful to you for this trouble,' she said, as she raised
her veil, and while he pressed her hand between both his own.
'I can only ask you to believe that I would not have troubled you
unless I had been greatly troubled myself.'

Mr. Furnival, as he placed her in an arm-chair by the fireside,
declared his sorrow that she should be in grief, and then he took
the other arm-chair himself, opposite to her, or rather close to her,
—much closer to her than he ever now seated himself to Mrs. F.
'Don't speak of my trouble,' said he, 'it is nothing if I can do
anything to relieve you.' But though he was so tender, he did not
omit to tell her of her folly in having informed her son that she
was to be in London. 'And have you seen him?' asked Lady
Mason.

'He was in Harley Street with the ladies last night. But it does
not matter. It is only for your sake that I speak, as I know that
you wish to keep this matter private. And now let us hear what it
is. I cannot think that there can be anything which need really
cause you trouble.' And he again took her hand,—that he might
encourage her. Lady Mason let him keep her hand for a minute
or so, as though she did not notice it; and yet as she turned her
eyes to him it might appear that his tenderness had encouraged
her.

Sitting there thus, with her hand in his,—with her hand in his
during the first portion of the tale—she told him all that she wished
to tell. Something more she told now to him than she had done to
Sir Peregrine. 'I learned from her,' she said, speaking about
Mrs. Dockwrath and her husband, 'that he had found out something
about dates which the lawyers did not find out before.'

' Something about dates,' said Mr. Furnival, looking with all his
eyes into the fire.   ' You do not know what about dates ?'

' No;   only this;   that he said that the lawyers in Bedford
Row——'

' Round and Crook.'

' Yes; he said that they were idiots not to have found it out
before ; and then he went off to Groby Park.   He came back last
night; but of course I have not seen her since.'

By this time Mr. Furnival had dropped the hand, and was sitting
still, meditating, looking earnestly at the fire while Lady Mason was
looking earnestly at him.   She was trying to gather from his face
whether he had seen signs of danger, and he was trying to gather
from her words whether there might really be cause to apprehend
danger.   How was he to know what was really inside her mind;
what were her actual thoughts and inward reasonings on this
subject; what private knowledge she might have which was still
kept back from him ?   In the ordinary intercourse of the world
when one man seeks advice from another, he who is consulted
demands in the first place that he shall be put in possession of all
the circumstances of the case.   How else will it be possible that he
should give advice ?   But in matters of law it is different.   If I,
having committed a crime, were to confess my criminality to the
gentleman engaged to defend me, might he not be called on to say :
' Then, O my friend, confess it also to the judge; and so let justice
be done.   Ruat cœlum, and the rest of it ?'   But who would pay a
lawyer for counsel such as that?

In this case there was no question of payment.   The advice to be
given was to a widowed woman from an experienced man of the
world ; but, nevertheless, he could only make his calculations as
to her peculiar case in the way in which he ordinarily calculated.
Could it be possible that anything had been kept back from him ?
Were there facts unknown to him, but known to her, which would
be terrible, fatal, damning to his sweet friend if proved before all
the world ?   He could not bring himself to ask her, but yet it was
so material that he should know !   Twenty years ago, at the time
of the trial, he had at one time thought,—it hardly matters to tell
what, but those thoughts had not been favourable to her cause.   Then
his mind had altered, and he had learned,—as lawyers do learn—to
believe in his own case.   And when the day of triumph had come,
he had triumphed loudly, commiserating his dear friend for the
unjust suffering to which she had been subjected, and speaking in
no low or modified tone as to the grasping, greedy cruelty of that
man of Groby Park.   Nevertheless, through it all, he had felt that
Round and Crook had not made the most of their case.

And now he sat, thinking, not so much whether or no she had
been in any way guilty with reference to that will, as whether the

counsel he should give her ought in any way to be based on the possibility of her having been thus guilty. Nothing might be so damning to her cause as that he should make sure of her innocence, if she were not innocent ; and yet he would not ask her the question. If innocent, why was it that she was now so much moved, after twenty years of quiet possession ?

' It was a pity,' he said, at last, ' that Lucius should have disturbed that fellow in the possession of his fields.'

' It was; it was !' she said. ' But I did not think it possible that Miriam's husband should turn against me. Would it be wise, do you think, to let him have the land again ?'

' No, I do not think that. It would be telling him, and telling others also, that you are afraid of him. If he have obtained any information that may be considered of value by Joseph Mason, he can sell it at a higher price than the holding of these fields is worth.'

' Would it be well——?' She was asking a question and then checked herself.

' Would what be well ?'

' I am so harassed that I hardly know what I am saying. Would it be wise, do you think, if I were to pay him anything, so as to keep him quiet ?'

' What; buy him off, you mean ?'

' Well, yes ;—if you call it so. Give him some sum of money in compensation for his land ; and on the understanding, you know ——,' and then she paused.

' That depends on what he may have to sell,' said Mr. Furnival, hardly daring to look at her.

' Ah ; yes,' said the widow. And then there was another pause.

' I do not think that that would be at all discreet,' said Mr. Furnival. ' After all, the chances are that it is all moonshine.'

' You think so ?'

' Yes; I cannot but think so. What can that man possibly have found among the old attorney's papers that may be injurious to your interests ?'

' Ah! I do not know; I understand so little of these things. At the time they told me,—you told me that the law might possibly go against my boy's rights. It would have been bad then, but it would be ten times more dreadful now.'

' But there were many questions capable of doubt then, which were definitively settled at the trial. As to your husband's intellect on that day, for instance.'

' There could be no doubt as to that.'

' No ; so it has been proved ; and they will not raise that point again. Could he possibly have made a later will ?'

' No ; I am sure he did not. Had he done so it could not have been found among Mr. Usbech's papers; for, as far as I remember, the poor man never attended to any business after that day.'

' What day?'

' The 14th of July, the day on which he was with Sir Joseph.'

It was singular, thought the barrister, with how much precision she remembered the dates and circumstances. That the circumstances of the trial should be fresh on her memory was not wonderful; but how was it that she knew so accurately things which had occurred before the trial,—when no trial could have been expected? But as to this he said nothing.

' And you are sure he went to Groby Park?'

' Oh, yes; I have no doubt of it. I am quite sure.'

' I do not know that we can do anything but wait. Have you mentioned this to Sir Peregrine?' It immediately occurred to Lady Mason's mind that it would be by no means expedient, even if it were possible, to keep Mr. Furnival in ignorance of anything that she really did; and she therefore explained that she had seen Sir Peregrine. ' I was so troubled at the first moment that I hardly knew where to turn,' she said.

' You were quite right to go to Sir Peregrine.'

' I am so glad you are not angry with me as to that.'

' And did he say anything—anything particular?'

' He promised that he would not desert me, should there be any new difficulty.'

' That is well. It is always good to have the countenance of such a neighbour as he is.'

' And the advice of such a friend as you are.' And she again put out her hand to him.

' Well; yes. It is my trade, you know, to give advice,' and he smiled as he took it.

' How should I live through such troubles without you?'

' We lawyers are very much abused now-a-days,' said Mr. Furnival, thinking of what was going on down at Birmingham at that very moment; ' but I hardly know how the world would get on without us.'

' Ah! but all lawyers are not like you.'

' Some perhaps worse, and a great many much better. But, as I was saying, I do not think I would take any steps at present. The man Dockwrath is a vulgar, low-minded, revengeful fellow; and I would endeavour to forget him.'

' Ah, if I could!'

' And why not? What can he possibly have learned to your injury?' And then as it seemed to Lady Mason that Mr. Furnival expected some reply to this question, she forced herself to give him one. ' I suppose that he cannot know anything.'

' I tell you what I might do,' said Mr. Furnival, who was still

musing. ' Round himself is not a bad fellow, and I am acquainted
with him. He was the junior partner in that house at the time of
the trial, and I know that he persuaded Joseph Mason not to appeal
to the Lords. I will contrive, if possible, to see him. I shall be
able to learn from him at any rate whether anything is being done.'

' And then if I hear that there is not, I shall be comforted.'

' Of course ; of course.

' But if there is——'

' I think there will be nothing of the sort,' said Mr. Furnival,
leaving his seat as he spoke.

' But if there is—— I shall have your aid?' and she slowly rose
from her chair as she spoke.

Mr. Furnival gave her a promise of this, as Sir Peregrine had
done before; and then with her handkerchief to her eyes she
thanked him. Her tears were not false as Mr. Furnival well saw;
and seeing that she wept, and seeing that she was beautiful, and
feeling that in her grief and in her beauty she had come to him for
aid, his heart was softened towards her, and he put out his arms as
though he would take her to his heart—as a daughter. ' Dearest
friend,' he said, ' trust me that no harm shall come to you.'

' I will trust you,' she said, gently stopping the motion of his
arm. ' I will trust you, altogether. And when you have seen Mr.
Round, shall I hear from you ?'

At this moment, as they were standing close together, the door
opened, and Mr. Crabwitz introduced another lady—who indeed
had advanced so quickly towards the door of Mr. Furnival's room,
that the clerk had been hardly able to reach it before her.

' Mrs. Furnival, if you please, sir,' said Mr. Crabwitz.

CHAPTER XIII.

UNFORTUNATELY for Mr. Furnival, the intruder was Mrs. Furnival —whether he pleased or whether he did not please. There she was in his law chamber, present in the flesh, a sight pleasing neither to her husband nor to her husband's client. She had knocked at the outside door, which, in the absence of the fag, had been opened by Mr. Crabwitz, and had immediately walked across the passage towards her husband's room, expressing her knowledge that Mr. Furnival was within. Mr. Crabwitz had all the will in the world to stop her progress, but he found that he lacked the power to stay it for a moment.

The advantages of matrimony are many and great—so many and so great, that all men, doubtless, ought to marry. But even matrimony may have its drawbacks; among which unconcealed and undeserved jealousy on the part of the wife is perhaps as disagreeable as any. What is a man to do when he is accused before the world,—before any small fraction of the world, of making love to some lady of his acquaintance? What is he to say? What way is he to look? 'My love, I didn't. I never did, and wouldn't think of it for worlds. I say it with my hand on my heart. There is Mrs. Jones herself, and I appeal to her.' He is reduced to that! But should any innocent man be so reduced by the wife of his bosom?

I am speaking of undeserved jealousy, and it may therefore be thought that my remarks do not apply to Mrs. Furnival. They do apply to her as much as to any woman. That general idea as to the strange goddesses was on her part no more than a suspicion; and all women who so torment themselves and their husbands may plead as much as she could. And for this peculiar idea as to Lady Mason she had no ground whatever. Lady Mason may have had her faults, but a propensity to rob Mrs. Furnival of her husband's affections had not hitherto been one of them. Mr. Furnival was a clever lawyer, and she had great need of his assistance; therefore she had come to his chambers, and therefore she had placed her hand in his. That Mr. Furnival liked his client because she was good looking may be true. I like my horse, my picture. the view from my study window for the same reason. I am inclined to think that there was nothing more in it than that.

'My dear!' said Mr. Furnival, stepping a little back, and letting his hands fall to his sides. Lady Mason also took a step backwards, and then with considerable presence of mind recovered herself and put out her hand to greet Mrs. Furnival.

'How do you do, Lady Mason?' said Mrs. Furnival, without any presence of mind at all. 'I hope I have the pleasure of seeing you very well. I did hear that you were to be in town—shopping; but I did not for a moment expect the—gratification of finding you here.' And every word that the dear, good, heart-sore woman spoke, told the tale of her jealousy as plainly as though she had flown at Lady Mason's cap with all the bold demonstrative energy of Spitalfields or St. Giles.

'I came up on purpose to see Mr. Furnival about some unfortunate law business,' said Lady Mason.

'Oh, indeed! Your son Lucius did say—shopping.'

'Yes; I told him so. When a lady is unfortunate enough to be driven to a lawyer for advice, she does not wish to make it known. I should be very sorry if my dear boy were to guess that I had this new trouble; or, indeed, if any one were to know it. I am sure that I shall be as safe with you, dear Mrs. Furnival, as I am with your husband.' And she stepped up to the angry matron, looking earnestly into her face.

To a true tale of woman's sorrow Mrs. Furnival's heart could be as soft as snow under the noonday sun. Had Lady Mason gone to her and told her all her fears and all her troubles, sought counsel and aid from her, and appealed to her motherly feelings, Mrs. Furnival would have been urgent night and day in persuading her husband to take up the widow's case. She would have bade him work his very best without fee or reward, and would herself have shown Lady Mason the way to Old Square, Lincoln's Inn. She would have been discreet too, speaking no word of idle gossip to any one. When he, in their happy days, had told his legal secrets to her, she had never gossiped,—had never spoken an idle word concerning them. And she would have been constant to her friend, giving great consolation in the time of trouble, as one woman can console another. The thought that all this might be so did come across her for a moment, for there was innocence written in Lady Mason's eyes. But then she looked at her husband's face; and as she found no innocence there, her heart was again hardened. The woman's face could lie;—'the faces of such women are all lies,' Mrs. Furnival said to herself;—but in her presence his face had been compelled to speak the truth.

'Oh dear, no; I shall say nothing of course,' she said. 'I am quite sorry that I intruded. Mr. Furnival, as I happened to be in

"Your son Lucius did say—shopping."

Holborn—at Mudie's for some books—I thought I would come down and ask whether you intend to dine at home to-day. You said nothing about it either last night or this morning; and nowadays one really does not know how to manage in such matters.'

'I told you that I should return to Birmingham this afternoon; I shall dine there,' said Mr. Furnival, very sulkily.

'Oh, very well. I certainly knew that you were going out of town. I did not at all expect that you would remain at home; but I thought that you might, perhaps, like to have your dinner before you went. Good morning, Lady Mason; I hope you may be successful in your—lawsuit.' And then, curtsying to her husband's client, she prepared to withdraw.

'I believe I have said all that I need say, Mr. Furnival,' said Lady Mason; 'so that if Mrs. Furnival wishes—,' and she also gathered herself up as though she were ready to leave the room.

'I hardly know what Mrs. Furnival wishes,' said the husband.

'My wishes are nothing,' said the wife, 'and I really am quite sorry that I came in.' And then she did go, leaving her husband and the woman of whom she was jealous once more alone together. Upon the whole I think that Mr. Furnival was right in not going home that day to his dinner.

As the door closed somewhat loudly behind the angry lady— Mr. Crabwitz having rushed out hardly in time to moderate the violence of the slam—Lady Mason and her imputed lover were left looking at each other. It was certainly hard upon Lady Mason, and so she felt it. Mr. Furnival was fifty-five, and endowed with a bluish nose; and she was over forty, and had lived for twenty years as a widow without incurring a breath of scandal.

'I hope I have not been to blame,' said Lady Mason in a soft, sad voice; 'but perhaps Mrs. Furnival specially wished to find you alone.'

'No, no; not at all.'

'I shall be so unhappy if I think that I have been in the way. If Mrs. Furnival wished to speak to you on business I am not surprised that she should be angry, for I know that barristers do not usually allow themselves to be troubled by their clients in their own chambers.'

'Nor by their wives,' Mr. Furnival might have added, but he did not.

'Do not mind it,' he said; 'it is nothing. She is the best-tempered woman in the world; but at times it is impossible to answer even for the best tempered.'

'I will trust you to make my peace with her.'

'Yes, of course; she will not think of it after to-day; nor must you, Lady Mason.'

'Oh, no; except that I would not for the world be the cause of annoyance to my friends. Sometimes I am almost inclined to think that I will never trouble any one again with my sorrows, but let things come and go as they may. Were it not for poor Lucius I should do so.'

Mr. Furnival, looking into her face, perceived that her eyes were full of tears. There could be no doubt as to their reality. Her eyes were full of genuine tears, brimming over and running down; and the lawyer's heart was melted. ' I do not know why you should say so,' he said. ' I do not think your friends begrudge any little trouble they may take for you. I am sure at least that I may so say for myself.'

' You are too kind to me; but I do not on that account the less know how much it is I ask of you.'

' " The labour we delight in physics pain," ' said Mr. Furnival gallantly. ' But, to tell the truth, Lady Mason, I cannot understand why you should be so much out of heart. I remember well how brave and constant you were twenty years ago, when there really was cause for trembling.'

' Ah, I was younger then.'

' So the almanac tells us; but if the almanac did not tell us I should never know it. We are all older, of course. Twenty years does not go by without leaving its marks, as I can feel myself.'

' Men do not grow old as women do, who live alone and gather rust as they feed on their own thoughts.'

' I know no one whom time has touched so lightly as yourself, Lady Mason; but if I may speak to you as a friend——'

' If you may not, Mr. Furnival, who may?'

' I should tell you that you are weak to be so despondent, or rather so unhappy.'

' Another lawsuit would kill me, I think. You say that I was brave and constant before, but you cannot understand what I suffered. I nerved myself to bear it, telling myself that it was the first duty that I owed to the babe that was lying on my bosom. And when standing there in the Court, with that terrible array around me, with the eyes of all men on me, the eyes of men who thought that I had been guilty of so terrible a crime, for the sake of that child who was so weak I could be brave. But it nearly killed me. Mr. Furnival, I could not go through that again; no, not even for his sake. If you can save me from that, even though it be by the buying off of that ungrateful man——'

' You must not think of that.'

' Must I not? ah me!'

' Will you tell Lucius all this, and let him come to me?'

' No; not for worlds. He would defy every one, and glory in the fight; but after all it is I that must bear the brunt. No; he shall not know it;—unless it becomes so public that he must know it.'

And then, with some further pressing of the hand, and further words of encouragement which were partly tender as from the man, and partly forensic as from the lawyer, Mr. Furnival permitted her to go, and she found her son at the chemist's shop in Holborn as she had appointed. There were no traces of tears or of sorrow in her face as she smiled on Lucius while giving him her hand, and then when they were in a cab together she asked him as to his success at Liverpool.

' I am very glad that I went,' said he, ' very glad indeed. I saw the merchants there who are the real importers of the article, and I have made arrangements with them.'

' Will it be cheaper so, Lucius ?'

' Cheaper ! not what women generally call cheaper. If there be anything on earth that I hate, it is a bargain. A man who looks for bargains must be a dupe or a cheat, and is probably both.'

' Both, Lucius. Then he is doubly unfortunate.'

' He is a cheat because he wants things for less than their value ; and a dupe because, as a matter of course, he does not get what he wants. I made no bargain at Liverpool,—at least, no cheap bargain ; but I have made arrangements for a sufficient supply of a first-rate unadulterated article at its proper market price, and I do not fear but the results will be remunerative.' And then, as they went home in the railway carriage the mother talked to her son about his farming as though she had forgotten her other trouble, and she explained to him how he was to dine with Sir Peregrine.

' I shall be delighted to dine with Sir Peregrine,' said Lucius, ' and very well pleased to have an opportunity of talking to him about his own way of managing his land ; but, mother, I will not promise to be guided by so very old-fashioned a professor.'

Mr. Furnival, when he was left alone, sat thinking over the interview that had passed. At first, as was most natural, he bethought himself of his wife ; and I regret to say that the love which he bore to her, and the gratitude which he owed to her, and the memory of all that they had suffered and enjoyed together, did not fill his heart with thoughts towards her as tender as they should have done. A black frown came across his brow as he meditated on her late intrusion, and he made some sort of resolve that that kind of thing should be prevented for the future. He did not make up his mind how he would prevent it,—a point which husbands sometimes overlook in their marital resolutions. And then, instead of counting up her virtues, he counted up his own. Had he not given her everything ; a house such as she had not dreamed of in her younger days ? servants, carriages, money, comforts, and luxuries of all sorts ? He had begrudged her nothing, had let her have her full share of all his hard-earned gains ; and yet she could be ungrateful for all this, and allow her head to be filled with whims and fancies as though she were a young girl,—to his great annoyance and confusion. He would let her know that his chambers, his law chambers, should be private even from her. He would not allow himself to become a laughing-stock to his own clerks and his own brethren through the impertinent folly of a woman who owed to him everything;—and so on! I regret to say that he never once thought of those lonely evenings in Harley Street, of those long days which the poor woman was doomed to pass without the only companionship which was valuable to her. He never thought of that vow which they had both made at the altar, which she had kept so loyally, and which required of him a cherishing, comforting, enduring love. It never occurred to him that in denying her this he as much broke his promise to her as though he had taken to himself in very truth some strange goddess, leaving his wedded wife with a cold ceremony of alimony or such-like. He had been open-handed to her as regards money, and therefore she ought not to be troublesome! He had done his duty by her, and therefore he would not permit her to be troublesome! Such, I regret to say, were his thoughts and resolutions as he sat thinking and resolving about Mrs. Furnival.

And then, by degrees, his mind turned away to that other lady, and they became much more tender. Lady Mason was certainly both interesting and comely in her grief. Her colour could still come and go, her hand was still soft and small, her hair was still brown and smooth. There were no wrinkles in her brow though care had passed over it; her step could still fall lightly, though it had borne a heavy weight of sorrow. I fear that he made a wicked comparison—a comparison that was wicked although it was made unconsciously.

But by degrees he ceased to think of the woman and began to think of the client, as he was in duty bound to do. What was the real truth of all this? Was it possible that she should be alarmed in that way because a small country attorney had told his wife that he had found some old paper, and because the man had then gone off to Yorkshire? Nothing could be more natural than her anxiety, supposing her to be aware of some secret which would condemn her if discovered;—but nothing more unnatural if there were no such secret. And she must know! In her bosom, if in no other, must exist the knowledge whether or no that will were just. If that will were just, was it possible that she should now tremble so violently, seeing that its justice had been substantially proved in various courts of law? But if it were not just—if it were a forgery, a forgery made by her, or with her cognizance—and that now this truth was to be made known! How terrible would that be! But terrible is not the word which best describes the idea as it entered Mr. Furnival's mind. How wonderful would it be; how wonderful would it all have been! By whose hand in such case had those signatures been traced? Could it be possible that she, soft, beautiful, graceful as she was now, all but a girl as she had then been, could have done it, unaided,—by herself?—that she could have sat down in the still hour of the night, with that old man on one side and her baby in his cradle on the other, and forged that will, signatures and all, in such a manner as to have carried her point for twenty years, —so skilfully as to have baffled lawyers and jurymen and resisted the eager greed of her cheated kinsman? If so, was it not all wonderful! Had not she been a woman worthy of wonder!

And then Mr. Furnival's mind, keen and almost unerring at seizing legal points, went eagerly to work, considering what new evidence might now be forthcoming. He remembered at once the circumstances of those two chief witnesses, the clerk who had been so muddle-headed, and the servant-girl who had been so clear. They had certainly witnessed some deed, and they had done so on that special day. If there had been a fraud, if there had been a forgery, it had been so clever as almost to merit protection! But if there had been such fraud, the nature of the means by which it might be detected became plain to the mind of the barrister,—plainer to him without knowledge of any circumstances than it had done to Mr. Mason after many of such circumstances had been explained to him.

But it was impossible. So said Mr. Furnival to himself, out loud ;—speaking out loud in order that he might convince himself. It was impossible, he said again; but he did not convince himself. Should he ask her? No; it was not on the cards that he should do that. And perhaps, if a further trial were forthcoming, it might be better for her sake that he should be ignorant. And then, having declared again that it was impossible, he rang his bell. 'Crabwitz,' said he, without looking at the man, ' just step over to Bedford Row, with my compliments, and learn what is Mr. Round's present address ;—old Mr. Round, you know.'

Mr. Crabwitz stood for a moment or two with the door in his hand, and Mr. Furnival, going back to his own thoughts, was expecting the man's departure. ' Well,' he said, looking up and seeing that his myrmidon still stood there.

Mr. Crabwitz was not in a very good humour, and had almost made up his mind to let his master know that such was the case. Looking at his own general importance in the legal world, and the inestimable services which he had rendered to Mr. Furnival, he did not think that that gentleman was treating him well. He had been summoned back to his dingy chamber almost without an excuse, and now that he was in London was not permitted to join even for a day the other wise men of the law who were assembled at the great congress. For the last four days his heart had been yearning

to go to Birmingham, but had yearned in vain; and now his
master was sending him about town as though he were an errand-
lad.

'Shall I step across to the lodge and send the porter's boy to
Round and Crook's?' asked Mr. Crabwitz.

'The porter's boy! no; go yourself; you are not busy. Why
should I send the porter's boy on my business?' The fact probably
was, that Mr. Furnival forgot his clerk's age and standing. Crabwitz had been ready to run anywhere when his employer had first
known him, and Mr. Furnival did not perceive the change.

'Very well, sir; certainly I will go if you wish it;—on this
occasion that is. But I hope, sir, you will excuse my saying——'

'Saying what?'

'That I am not exactly a messenger, sir. Of course I'll go now,
as the other clerk is not in.'

'Oh, you're too great a man to walk across to Bedford Row, are
you? Give me my hat, and I'll go.'

'Oh, no, Mr. Furnival, I did not mean that. I'll step over to
Bedford Row, of course :—only I did think——'

'Think what?'

'That perhaps I was entitled to a little more respect, Mr. Furnival. It's for your sake as much as my own that I speak, sir; but
if the gentlemen in the Lane see me sent about like a lad of twenty,
sir, they'll think——'

'What will they think?'

'I hardly know what they'll think, but I know it will be very
disagreeable, sir;—very disagreeable to my feelings. I did think,
sir, that perhaps——'

'I'll tell you what it is, Crabwitz, if your situation here does not
suit you, you may leave it to-morrow. I shall have no difficulty
in finding another man to take your place.'

'I am sorry to hear you speak in that way, Mr. Furnival, very
sorry—after fifteen years, sir——.'

'You find yourself too grand to walk to Bedford Row!'

'Oh, no. I'll go now, of course, Mr. Furnival.' And then
Mr. Crabwitz did go, meditating as he went many things to himself.
He knew his own value, or thought that he knew it; and might it
not be possible to find some patron who would appreciate his services
more justly than did Mr. Furnival?

CHAPTER XIV.

DINNER AT THE CLEEVE.

LADY MASON on her return from London found a note from Mrs. Orme asking both her and her son to dine at The Cleeve on the following day. As it had been already settled between her and Sir Peregrine that Lucius should dine there in order that he might be talked to respecting his mania for guano, the invitation could not be refused; but, as for Lady Mason herself, she would much have preferred to remain at home.

Indeed, her uneasiness on that guano matter had been so out-weighed by worse uneasiness from another source, that she had become, if not indifferent, at any rate tranquil on the subject. It might be well that Sir Peregrine should preach his sermon, and well that Lucius should hear it; but for herself it would, she thought, have been more comfortable for her to eat her dinner alone. She felt, however, that she could not do so. Any amount of tedium would be better than the danger of offering a slight to Sir Peregrine, and therefore she wrote a pretty little note to say that both of them would be at The Cleeve at seven.

' Lucius, my dear, I want you to do me a great favour,' she said as she sat by her son in the Hamworth fly.

' A great favour, mother! of course I will do anything for you that I can.'

' It is that you will bear with Sir Peregrine to-night.'

' Bear with him! I do not know exactly what you mean. Of course I will remember that he is an old man, and not answer him as I would one of my own age.'

' I am sure of that, Lucius, because you are a gentleman. As much forbearance as that a young man, if he be a gentleman, will always show to an old man. But what I ask is something more that that. Sir Peregrine has been farming all his life.'

' Yes; and see what are the results! He has three or four hun-dred acres of uncultivated land on his estate, all of which would grow wheat.'

' I know nothing about that,' said Lady Mason.

' Ah, but that's the question. My trade is to be that of a farmer, and you are sending me to school. Then comes the question, Of what sort is the schoolmaster ?'

'I am not talking about farming now, Lucius.'

'But he will talk of it.'

'And cannot you listen to him without contradicting him—for my sake? It is of the greatest consequence to me,—of the very greatest, Lucius, that I should have the benefit of Sir Peregrine's friendship.'

'If he would quarrel with you because I chanced to disagree with him about the management of land, his friendship would not be worth having.'

'I do not say that he will do so; but I am sure you can understand that an old man may be tender on such points. At any rate I ask it from you as a favour. You cannot guess how important it is to me to be on good terms with such a neighbour.'

'It is always so in England,' said Lucius, after pausing for a while. 'Sir Peregrine is a man of family, and a baronet; of course all the world, the world of Hamworth that is, should bow down at his feet. And I too must worship the golden image which Nebuchadnezzar, the King of Fashion, has set up!'

'Lucius, you are unkind to me.'

'No, mother, not unkind; but like all men, I would fain act in such matters as my own judgment may direct me.'

'My friendship with Sir Peregrine Orme has nothing to do with his rank; but it is of importance to me that both you and I should stand well in his sight.' There was nothing more said on the matter; and then they got down at the front door, and were ushered through the low wide hall into the drawing-room.

The three generations of the family were there,—Sir Peregrine, his daughter-in-law, and the heir. Lucius Mason had been at The Cleeve two or three times since his return from Germany, and on going there had always declared to himself that it was the same to him as though he were going into the house of Mrs. Arkwright, the doctor's widow at Hamworth,—or even into the kitchen of Farmer Greenwood. He rejoiced to call himself a democrat, and would boast that rank could have no effect on him. But his boast was an untrue boast, and he could not carry himself at The Cleeve as he would have done and did in Mrs. Arkwright's little drawing-room. There was a majesty in the manner of Sir Peregrine which did awe him; there were tokens of birth and a certain grace of manner about Mrs. Orme which kept down his assumption; and even with young Peregrine he found that though he might be equal he could by no means be more than equal. He had learned more than Peregrine Orme, had ten times more knowledge in his head, had read books of which Peregrine did not even know the names and probably never would know them; but on his side also young Orme possessed

something which the other wanted. What that something might be
Lucius Mason did not at all understand.

Mrs. Orme got up from her corner on the sofa to greet her friend,
and with a soft smile and two or three all but whispered words
led her forward to the fire. Mrs. Orme was not a woman given to
much speech or endowed with outward warmth of manners, but she
could make her few words go very far; and then the pressure of
her hand, when it was given, told more than a whole embrace from
some other women. There are ladies who always kiss their female
friends, and always call them ' dear.' In such cases one cannot but
pity her who is so bekissed. Mrs. Orme did not kiss Lady Mason,
nor did she call her dear; but she smiled sweetly as she uttered
her greeting, and looked kindness out of her marvellously blue eyes ;
and Lucius Mason, looking on over his mother's shoulders, thought
that he would like to have her for his friend in spite of her rank.
If Mrs. Orme would give him a lecture on farming it might be
possible to listen to it without contradiction; but there was no
chance for him in that respect. Mrs. Orme never gave lectures to
any one on any subject.

' So, Master Lucius, you have been to Liverpool, I hear,' said Sir
Peregrine.

' Yes, sir—I returned yesterday.'

' And what is the world doing at Liverpool?'

' The world is wide awake there, sir.'

' Oh, no doubt; when the world has to make money it is always
wide awake. But men sometimes may be wide awake and yet
make no money;—may be wide awake, or at any rate think that
they are so.'

' Better that, Sir Peregrine, than wilfully go to sleep when there
is so much work to be done.'

' A man when he's asleep does no harm,' said Sir Peregrine.

' What a comfortable doctrine to think of when the servant comes
with the hot water at eight o'clock in the morning!' said his
grandson.

' It is one that you study very constantly, I fear,' said the old
man, who at this time was on excellent terms with his heir. There
had been no apparent hankering after rats since that last compact
had been made, and Peregrine had been doing great things with
the H. H.; winning golden opinions from all sorts of sportsmen,
and earning a great reputation for a certain young mare which had
been bred by Sir Peregrine himself. Foxes are vermin as well
as rats, as Perry in his wickedness had remarked; but a young man
who can break an old one's heart by a predilection for rat-catching
may win it as absolutely and irretrievably by prowess after a fox.
Sir Peregrine had told to four different neighbours how a fox had
been run into, in the open, near Alston, after twelve desperate miles,

and how on that occasion Peregrine had been in at the death
with the huntsman and only one other.   ' And the mare, you know,
is only four years old and hardly half trained,' said Sir Peregrine,
with great exultation.   ' The young scamp, to have ridden her in
that way!' It may be doubted whether he would have been a
prouder man or said more about it if his grandson had taken
honours.

And then the gong sounded, and Sir Peregrine led Lady Mason
into the dining-room.   Lucius, who as we know thought no more
of the Ormes than of the Joneses and Smiths, paused in his awe
before he gave his arm to Mrs. Orme; and when he did so he led
her away in perfect silence, though he would have given anything to
be able to talk to her as he went.   But he bethought himself that
unfortunately he could find nothing to say.   And when he sat down
it was not much better.   He had not dined at The Cleeve before,
and I am not sure whether the butler in plain clothes and the two
men in livery did not help to create his confusion,—in spite of his
well-digested democratic ideas.

The conversation during dinner was not very bright.   Sir Peregrine said a few words now and again to Lady Mason, and she
replied with a few others.   On subjects which did not absolutely
appertain to the dinner, she perhaps was the greatest talker; but
even she did not say much.   Mrs. Orme as a rule never spoke
unless she were spoken to in any company consisting of more than
herself and one other; and young Peregrine seemed to imagine that
carving at the top of the table, asking people if they would take
stewed beef, and eating his own dinner, were occupations quite sufficient for his energies.   ' Have a bit more beef, Mason; do.   If you
will, I will.'   So far he went in conversation, but no farther while
his work was still before him.

When the servants were gone it was a little better, but not
much.   ' Mason, do you mean to hunt this season?' Peregrine
asked.

' No,' said the other.

' Well, I would if I were you.   You will never know the fellows
about here unless you do.'

' In the first place I can't afford the time,' said Lucius, ' and in
the next place I can't afford the money.'   This was plucky on his
part, and it was felt to be so by everybody in the room; but perhaps
had he spoken all the truth, he would have said also that he was not
accustomed to horsemanship.

' To a fellow who has a place of his own as you have, it costs
nothing,' said Peregrine.

' Oh, does it not?' said the baronet; ' I used to think differently.'

' Well; not so much, I mean, as if you had everything to buy.
Besides, I look upon Mason as a sort of a Crœsus.   What on earth

has he got to do with his money? And then as to time ;—upon my word I don't understand what a man means when he says he has not got time for hunting.'

' Lucius intends to be a farmer,' said his mother.

' So do I,' said Peregrine. ' By Jove, I should think so. If I had two hundred acres of land in my own hand I should not want anything else in the world, and would never ask any one for a shilling.'

' If that be so, I might make the best bargain at once that ever a man made,' said the baronet. ' If I might take you at your word, Master Perry——.'

' Pray don't talk of it, sir,' said Mrs. Orme.

' You may be quite sure of this, my dear—that I shall not do more than talk of it.' Then Sir Peregrine asked Lady Mason if she would take any more wine ; after which the ladies withdrew, and the lecture commenced.

But we will in the first place accompany the ladies into the drawing-room for a few minutes. It was hinted in one of the first chapters of this story that Lady Mason might have become more intimate than she had done with Mrs. Orme, had she so pleased it ; and by this it will of course be presumed that she had not so pleased. All this is perfectly true. Mrs. Orme had now been living at The Cleeve the greater portion of her life, and had never while there made one really well-loved friend. She had a sister of her own, and dear old friends of her childhood, who lived far away from her in the northern counties. Occasionally she did see them, and was then very happy ; but this was not frequent with her. Her sister, who was married to a peer, might stay at The Cleeve for a fortnight, perhaps once in the year ; but Mrs. Orme herself seldom left her own home. She thought, and certainly not without cause, that Sir Peregrine was not happy in her absence, and therefore she never left him. Then, living there so much alone, was it not natural that her heart should desire a friend?

But Lady Mason had been living much more alone. She had no sister to come to her, even though it were but once a year. She had no intimate female friend, none to whom she could really speak with the full freedom of friendship, and it would have been de-lightful to have bound to her by ties of love so sweet a creature as Mrs. Orme, a widow like herself,—and like herself a widow with one only son. But she, warily picking her steps through life, had learned the necessity of being cautious in all things. The coun-tenance of Sir Peregrine had been invaluable to her, and might it not be possible that she should lose that countenance? A word or two spoken now and then again, a look not intended to be noticed, an altered tone, or perhaps a change in the pressure of the old man's hand, had taught Lady Mason to think that he might disapprove such intimacy. Probably at the moment she was right, for she was quick at reading such small signs. It behoved her to be very careful, and to indulge in no pleasure which might be costly ; and therefore she had denied herself in this matter,—as in so many others.

But now it had occurred to her that it might be well to change her conduct. Either she felt that Sir Peregrine's friendship for her was too confirmed to be shaken, or perhaps she fancied that she might strengthen it by means of his daughter-in-law. At any rate she resolved to accept the offer which had once been tacitly made to her, if it were still open to her to do so.

'How little changed your boy is!' she said when they were seated near to each other, with their coffee-cups between them.

'No ; he does not change quickly ; and, as you say, he is a boy still in many things. I do not know whether it may not be better that it should be so.'

'I did not mean to call him a boy in that sense,' said Lady Mason.

'But you might ; now your son is quite a man.'

'Poor Lucius! yes ; in his position it is necessary. His little bit of property is already his own; and then he has no one like Sir Peregrine to look out for him. Necessity makes him manly.'

'He will be marrying soon, I dare say,' suggested Mrs. Orme.

'Oh, I hope not. Do you think that early marriages are good for young men ?'

'Yes, I think so. Why not ?' said Mrs. Orme, thinking of her own year of married happiness. 'Would you not wish to see Lucius marry ?'

'I fancy not. I should be afraid lest I should become as nothing to him. And yet I would not have you think that I am selfish.'

'I am sure that you are not that. I am sure that you love him better than all the world besides. I can feel what that is myself.'

'But you are not alone with your boy as I am. If he were to send me from him, there would be nothing left for me in this world.'

'Send you from him! Ah, because Orley Farm belongs to him. But he would not do that; I am sure he would not.'

'He would do nothing unkind ; but how could he help it if his wife wished it ? But nevertheless I would not keep him single for that reason ;—no, nor for any reason if I knew that he wished to marry. But it would be a blow to me.'

'I sincerely trust that Peregrine may marry early,' said Mrs. Orme, perhaps thinking that babies were preferable either to rats or foxes.

'Yes, it would be well I am sure, because you have ample means, and the house is large'; and you would have his wife to love.'

Over their Wine.

' If she were nice it would be so sweet to have her for a daughter. I also am very much alone, though perhaps not so much as you are, Lady Mason.'

' I hope not—for I am sometimes very lonely.'

' I have often thought that.'

' But I should be wicked beyond everything if I were to complain, seeing that Providence has given me so much that I had no right to expect. What should I have done in my loneliness if Sir Peregrine's hand and door had never been opened to me?' And then for the next half-hour the two ladies held sweet converse together, during which we will go back to the gentlemen over their wine.

' Are you drinking claret?' said Sir Peregrine, arranging himself and his bottles in the way that was usual to him. He had ever been a moderate man himself, but nevertheless he had a business-like way of going to work after dinner, as though there was a good deal to be done before the drawing-room could be visited.

' No more wine for me, sir,' said Lucius.

' No wine!' said Sir Peregrine the elder.

' Why, Mason, you'll never get on if that's the way with you,' said Peregrine the younger.

' I'll try at any rate,' said the other.

' Water-drinker, moody thinker,' and Peregrine sang a word or two from an old drinking-song.

' I am not quite sure of that. We Englishmen I suppose are the moodiest thinkers in all the world, and yet we are not so much given to water-drinking as our lively neighbours across the Channel.'

Sir Peregrine said nothing more on the subject, but he probably thought that his young friend would not be a very comfortable neighbour. His present task, however, was by no means that of teaching him to drink, and he struck off at once upon the business he had undertaken. ' So your mother tells me that you are going to devote all your energies to farming.'

' Hardly that, I hope. There is the land, and I mean to see what I can do with it. It is not much, and I intend to combine some other occupation with it.'

' You will find that two hundred acres of land will give you a good deal to do ;—that is if you mean to make money by it.'

' I certainly hope to do that,—in the long run.'

' It seems to me the easiest thing in the world,' said Peregrine.

' You'll find out your mistake some day; but with Lucius Mason it is very important that he should make no mistake at the commencement. For a country gentleman I know no prettier amusement than experimental farming ;—but then a man must give up all idea of making his rent out of the land.'

' I can't afford that,' said Lucius.

' No; and that is why I take the liberty of speaking to you. I hope that the great friendship which I feel for your mother will be allowed to stand as my excuse.'

' I am very much obliged by your kindness, sir; I am indeed.'

' The truth is, I think you are beginning wrong. You have now been to Liverpool, to buy guano, I believe.'

' Yes, that and some few other things. There is a man there who has taken out a patent——'

' My dear fellow, if you lay out your money in that way, you will never see it back again. Have you considered in the first place what your journey to Liverpool has cost you?'

' Exactly nine and sixpence per cent. on the money that I laid out there. Now that is not much more than a penny in the pound on the sum expended, and is not for a moment to be taken into consideration in comparison with the advantage of an improved market.'

There was more in this than Sir Peregrine had expected to encounter. He did not for a moment doubt the truth of his own experience or the folly and danger of the young man's proceedings; but he did doubt his own power of proving either the one or the other to one who so accurately computed his expenses by percentages on his outlay. Peregrine opened his eyes and sat by, wondering in silence. What on earth did Mason mean by an improved market?

' I am afraid then,' said the baronet, ' that you must have laid out a large sum of money.'

' A man can't do any good, Sir Peregrine, by hoarding his capital. I don't think very much of capital myself—'

' Don't you?'

' Not of the theory of capital;—not so much as some people do; but if a man has got it, of course it should be expended on the trade to which it is to be applied.'

' But some little knowledge—some experience is perhaps desirable before any great outlay is made.'

' Yes; some little knowledge is necessary, — and some great knowledge would be desirable if it were accessible;—but it is not, as I take it.'

' Long years, perhaps, devoted to such pursuits——'

' Yes, Sir Peregrine; I know what you are going to say. Experience no doubt will teach something. A man who has walked thirty miles a day for thirty years will probably know what sort of shoes will best suit his feet, and perhaps also the kind of food that will best support him through such exertion; but there is very little chance of his inventing any quicker mode of travelling.'

' But he will have earned his wages honestly,' said Sir Peregrine,

almost angrily. In his heart he was very angry, for he did not love
to be interrupted.

'Oh, yes; and if that were sufficient we might all walk our
thirty miles a day. But some of us must earn wages for other
people, or the world will make no progress. Civilization, as I take
it, consists in efforts made not for oneself but for others.'

'If you won't take any more wine we will join the ladies,' said
the baronet.

'He has not taken any at all,' said Peregrine, filling his own
glass for the last time and emptying it.

'That young man is the most conceited puppy it was ever my
misfortune to meet,' said Sir Peregrine to Mrs. Orme, when she
came to kiss him and to take his blessing as she always did before
leaving him for the night.

'I am sorry for that,' said she, 'for I like his mother so much.'

'I also like her,' said Sir Peregrine; 'but I cannot say that I shall
ever be very fond of her son.'

'I'll tell you what, mamma,' said young Peregrine, the same
evening in his mother's dressing-room. 'Lucius Mason was too
many for the governor this evening.'

'I hope he did not tease your grandfather.'

'He talked him down regularly, and it was plain enough that
the governor did not like it.'

And then the day was over.

CHAPTER XV.

A MORNING CALL AT MOUNT PLEASANT VILLA.

ON the following day Lady Mason made two visits, using her new
vehicle for the first time. She would fain have walked had she
dared; but she would have given terrible offence to her son by doing
so. He had explained to her, and with some truth, that as their
joint income was now a thousand a year, she was quite entitled to
such a luxury; and then he went on to say that as he had bought
it for her, he should be much hurt if she would not use it. She had
put it off from day to day, and now she could put it off no longer.

Her first visit was by appointment at The Cleeve. She had promised Mrs. Orme that she would come up, some special purpose
having been named;—but with the real idea, at any rate on the part
of the latter, that they might both be more comfortable together
than alone. The walk across from Orley Farm to The Cleeve had
always been very dear to Lady Mason. Every step of it was over
beautiful ground, and a delight in scenery was one of the few plea-

sures which her lot in life had permitted her to enjoy. But to-day she could not allow herself the walk. Her pleasure and delight must be postponed to her son's wishes! But then she was used to that.

She found Mrs. Orme alone, and sat with her for an hour. I do not know that anything was said between them which deserves to be specially chronicled. Mrs. Orme, though she told her many things, did not tell her what Sir Peregrine had said as he was going up to his bedroom on the preceding evening, nor did Lady Mason say much about her son's farming. She had managed to gather from Lucius that he had not been deeply impressed by anything that had fallen from Sir Peregrine on the subject, and therefore thought it as well to hold her tongue. She soon perceived also, from the fact of Mrs. Orme saying nothing about Lucius, that he had not left behind him any very favourable impression. This was to her cause of additional sorrow, but she knew that it must be borne. Nothing that she could say would induce Lucius to make himself acceptable to Sir Peregrine.

When the hour was over she went down again to her little carriage, Mrs. Orme coming with her to look at it, and in the hall they met Sir Peregrine.

'Why does not Lady Mason stop for lunch?' said he. 'It is past half-past one. I never knew anything so inhospitable as turning her out at this moment.'

'I did ask her to stay,' said Mrs. Orme.

'But I command her to stay,' said Sir Peregrine, knocking his stick upon the stone floor of the hall. 'And let me see who will dare to disobey me. John, let Lady Mason's carriage and pony stand in the open coach-house till she is ready.' So Lady Mason went back and did remain for lunch. She was painfully anxious to maintain the best-possible footing in that house, but still more anxious not to have it thought that she was intruding. She had feared that Lucius by his offence might have estranged Sir Peregrine against herself; but that at any rate was not the case.

After lunch she drove herself to Hamworth and made her second visit. On this occasion she called on one Mrs. Arkwright, who was a very old acquaintance, though hardly to be called an intimate friend. The late Mr. Arkwright—Dr. Arkwright as he used to be styled in Hamworth—had been Sir Joseph's medical attendant for many years, and therefore there had been room for an intimacy. No real friendship, that is no friendship of confidence, had sprung up; but nevertheless the doctor's wife had known enough of Lady Mason in her younger days to justify her in speaking of things which would not have been mentioned between merely ordinary acquaintance. 'I am glad to see you have got promotion,' said the old lady, looking out at Lady Mason's little phaeton on the gravel sweep which divided Mrs. Arkwright's house from the street.   For Mrs. Arkwright's house was Mount Pleasant Villa, and therefore was entitled to a sweep.

'It was a present from Lucius,' said the other, 'and as such must be used.   But I shall never feel myself at home in my own carriage.'

'It is quite proper, my dear Lady Mason, quite proper.   With his income and with yours I do not wonder that he insists upon it.   It is quite proper, and just at the present moment peculiarly so.'

Lady Mason did not understand this; but she would probably have passed it by without understanding it, had she not thought that there was some expression more than ordinary in Mrs. Ark-wright's face.   'Why peculiarly so at the present moment?' she said.

'Because it shows that this foolish report which is going about has no foundation.   People won't believe it for a moment when they see you out and about, and happy-like.'

'What rumour, Mrs. Arkwright?'   And Lady Mason's heart sunk within her as she asked the question.   She felt at once to what it must allude, though she had conceived no idea as yet that there was any rumour on the subject.   Indeed, during the last forty-eight hours, since she had left the chambers of Mr. Furnival, she had been more at ease within herself than during the previous days which had elapsed subsequent to the ill-omened visit made to her by Miriam Dockwrath.   It had seemed to her that Mr. Furnival anti-cipated no danger, and his manner and words had almost given her confidence.   But now,—now that a public rumour was spoken of, her heart was as low again as ever.

'Sure, haven't you heard?' said Mrs. Arkwright.   'Well, I wouldn't be the first to tell you, only that I know that there is no truth in it.'

'You might as well tell me now, as I shall be apt to believe worse than the truth after what you have said.'

And then Mrs. Arkwright told her.   'People have been saying that Mr. Mason is again going to begin those law proceedings about the farm; but I for one don't believe it.'

'People have said so!'   Lady Mason repeated.   She meant nothing; it was nothing to her who the people were.   If one said it now, all would soon be saying it.   But she uttered the words because she felt herself forced to say something, and the power of thinking what she might best say was almost taken away from her.

'I am sure I don't know where it came from,' said Mrs. Ark-wright; 'but I would not have alluded to it if I had not thought that of course you had heard it.   I am very sorry if my saying it has vexed you.'

'Oh, no,' said Lady Mason, trying to smile.

'As I said before, we all know that there is nothing in it; and your having the pony chaise just at this time will make everybody see that you are quite comfortable yourself.'

'Thank you, yes; good-bye, Mrs. Arkwright.' And then she made a great effort, feeling aware that she was betraying herself, and that it behoved her to say something which might remove the suspicion which her emotion must have created. 'The very name of that lawsuit is so dreadful to me that I can hardly bear it. The memory of it is so terrible to me, that even my enemies would hardly wish that it should commence again.'

'Of course it is merely a report,' said Mrs. Arkwright, almost trembling at what she had done.

'That is all—at least I believe so. I had heard myself that some such threat had been made, but I did not think that any tidings of it had got abroad.'

'It was Mrs. Whiting told me. She is a great busybody, you know.' Mrs. Whiting was the wife of the present doctor.

'Dear Mrs. Arkwright, it does not matter in the least. Of course I do not expect that people should hold their tongue on my account. Good-bye, Mrs. Arkwright.' And then she got into the little carriage, and did contrive to drive herself home to Orley Farm.

'Dear, dear, dear, dear!' said Mrs. Arkwright to herself when she was left alone. 'Only to think of that; that she should be knocked in a heap by a few words—in a moment, as we may say.' And then she began to consider of the matter. 'I wonder what there is in it! There must be something, or she would never have looked so like a ghost. What will they do if Orley Farm is taken away from them after all!' And then Mrs. Arkwright hurried out on her daily little toddle through the town, that she might talk about this and be talked to on the same subject. She was by no means an ill-natured woman, nor was she at all inclined to direct against Lady Mason any slight amount of venom which might alloy her disposition. But then the matter was of such importance! The people of Hamworth had hardly yet ceased to talk of the last Orley Farm trial; and would it not be necessary that they should talk much more if a new trial were really pending? Looking at the matter in that light, would not such a trial be a godsend to the people of Hamworth? Therefore I beg that it may not be imputed to Mrs. Arkwright as a fault that she toddled out and sought eagerly for her gossips.

Lady Mason did manage to drive herself home; but her success in the matter was more owing to the good faith and propriety of her pony, than to any skilful workmanship on her own part. Her first desire had been to get away from Mrs. Arkwright, and having made that effort she was for a time hardly able to make any other. It was fast coming upon her now. Let Sir Peregrine say what comforting words he might, let Mr. Furnival assure her that she was safe with ever so much confidence, nevertheless she could not but believe, could not but feel inwardly convinced, that that which she so dreaded was to happen. It was written in the book of her destiny that there should be a new trial.

And now, from this very moment, the misery would again begin. People would point at her, and talk of her. Her success in obtaining Orley Farm for her own child would again be canvassed at every house in Hamworth; and not only her success, but the means also by which that success had been obtained. The old people would remember and the young people would inquire ; and, for her, tranquillity, repose, and that retirement of life which had been so valuable to her, were all gone.

There could be no doubt that Dockwrath had spread the report immediately on his return from Yorkshire; and had she well thought of the matter she might have taken some comfort from this. Of course he would tell the story which he did tell. His confidence in being able again to drag the case before the Courts would by no means argue that others believed as he believed. In fact the enemies now arraigned against her were only those whom she already knew to be so arraigned. But she had not sufficient command of her thoughts to be able at first to take comfort from such a reflection as this. She felt, as she was being carried home, that the world was going from her, and that it would be well for her, were it possible, that she should die.

But she was stronger when she reached her own door than she had been at Mrs. Arkwright's. There was still within her a great power of self-maintenance, if only time were allowed to her to look about and consider how best she might support herself. Many women are in this respect as she was. With forethought and summoned patience they can endure great agonies ; but a sudden pang, unexpected, overwhelms them. She got out of the pony carriage with her ordinary placid face, and walked up to her own room without having given any sign that she was uneasy ; and then she had to determine how she should bear herself before her son. It had been with her a great object that both Sir Peregrine and Mr. Furnival should first hear of the tidings from her, and that they should both promise her their aid when they had heard the story as she would tell it. In this she had been successful; and it now seemed to her that prudence would require her to act in the same way towards Lucius. Had it been possible to keep this matter from him altogether, she would have given much to do so ; but now it would not be possible. It was clear that Mr. Dockwrath had chosen to make the matter public, acting no doubt with forethought in doing so ; and Lucius would be sure to hear words which would become common in Hamworth. Difficult as the task would be to her, it would be best that she should prepare him. So she sat alone till dinner-time planning how she would do this. She had sat alone for hours in the same way planning how she would tell her story to Sir Peregrine; and again as to her second story for Mr. Furnival. Those whose withers are unwrung can hardly guess how absolutely a sore under the collar will embitter every hour for the poor jade who is so tormented!

But she met him at dinner with a smiling face. He loved to see her smile, and often told her so, almost upbraiding her when she would look sad. Why should she be sad, seeing that she had every-thing that a woman could desire? Her mind was burdened with no heavy thoughts as to feeding coming multitudes. She had no con-tests to wage with the desultory chemists of the age. His purpose was to work hard during the hours of the day,—hard also during many hours of the night; and it was becoming that his mother should greet him softly during his few intervals of idleness. He told her so, in some words not badly chosen for such telling; and she, loving mother that she was, strove valiantly to obey him.

During dinner she could not speak to him, nor immediately after dinner. The evil moment she put off from half-hour to half-hour, still looking as though all were quiet within her bosom as she sat beside him with her book in her hand. He was again at work before she began her story: he thought at least that he was at work, for he had before him on the table both Prichard and Latham, and was occupied in making copies from some drawings of skulls which purposed to represent the cerebral development of certain of our more distant Asiatic brethren.

'Is it not singular,' said he, 'that the jaws of men born and bred in a hunter state should be differently formed from those of the agricultural tribes?'

'Are they?' said Lady Mason.

'Oh yes; the maxillary profile is quite different. You will see this especially with the Mongolians, among the Tartar tribes. It seems to me to be very much the same difference as that between a man and a sheep, but Prichard makes no such remark. Look here at this fellow; he must have been intended to eat nothing but flesh; and that raw, and without any knife or fork.'

'I don't suppose they had many knives or forks.'

'By close observation I do not doubt that one could tell from a single tooth not only what food the owner of it had been accustomed to eat, but what language he had spoken. I say close observation, you know. It could not be done in a day.'

'I suppose not.' And then the student again bent over his drawing. 'You see it would have been impossible for the owner of such a jaw as that to have ground a grain of corn between his teeth, or to have masticated even a cabbage.'

' Lucius,' said Lady Mason, becoming courageous on the spur of the moment, ' I want you to leave that for a moment and speak to me.'

' Well,' said he, putting down his pencil and turning round. ' Here I am.'

' You have heard of the lawsuit which I had with your brother when you were an infant?'

' Of course I have heard of it; but I wish you would not call that man my brother. He would not own me as such, and I most certainly would not own him. As far as I can learn he is one of the most detestable human beings that ever existed.'

' You have heard of him from an unfavourable side, Lucius ; you should remember that. He is a hard man, I believe ; but I do not know that he would do anything which he thought to be unjust.'

' Why then did he try to rob me of my property ?'

' Because he thought that it should have been his own. I cannot see into his breast, but I presume that it was so.'

' I do not presume anything of the kind, and never shall. I was an infant and you were a woman,—a woman at that time without many friends, and he thought that he could rob us under cover of the law. Had he been commonly honest it would have been enough for him to know what had been my father's wishes, even if the will had not been rigidly formal. I look upon him as a robber and a thief.'

' I am sorry for that, Lucius, because I differ from you. What I wish to tell you now is this,—that he is thinking of trying the question again.'

' What !—thinking of another trial now ?' and Lucius Mason pushed his drawings and books from him with a vengeance.

' So I am told.'

' And who told you ? I cannot believe it. If he intended anything of the kind I must have been the first person to hear of it. It would be my business now, and you may be sure that he would have taken care to let me know his purpose.'

' And then by degrees she explained to him that the man himself, Mr. Mason of Groby, had as yet declared no such purpose. She had intended to omit all mention of the name of Mr. Dockwrath, but she was unable to do so without seeming to make a mystery with her son. When she came to explain how the rumour had arisen and why she had thought it necessary to tell him this, she was obliged to say that it had all arisen from the wrath of the attorney. ' He has been to Groby Park,' she said, ' and now that he has returned he is spreading this report.'

' I shall go to him to-morrow, said Lucius, very sternly.

' No, no ; you must not do that. You must promise me that you will not do that.'

' But I shall. You cannot suppose that I shall allow such a man as that to tamper with my name without noticing it! It is my business now.'

' No, Lucius. The attack will be against me rather than you ;— that is, if an attack be made. I have told you because I do not like to have a secret from you.'

' Of course you have told me. If you are attacked who should defend you, if I do not ?'

' The best defence, indeed the only defence till they take some active step, will be silence. Most probably they will not do any-thing, and then we can afford to live down such reports as these. You can understand, Lucius, that the matter is grievous enough to me ; and I am sure that for my sake you will not make it worse by a personal quarrel with such a man as that.'

' I shall go to Mr. Furnival,' said he, ' and ask his advice.'

' I have done that already, Lucius. I thought it best to do so, when first I heard that Mr. Dockwrath was moving in the matter. It was for that that I went up to town.'

' And why did you not tell me ?'

' I then thought that you might be spared the pain of knowing anything of the matter. I tell you now because I hear to-day in Hamworth that people are talking on the subject. You might be annoyed, as I was just now, if the first tidings had reached you from some stranger.'

He sat silent for a while, turning his pencil in his hand, and looking as though he were going to settle the matter off hand by his own thoughts. ' I tell you what it is, mother ; I shall not let the burden of this fall on your shoulders. You carried on the battle before, but I must do so now. If I can trace any word of scandal to that fellow Dockwrath, I shall indict him for a libel.'

' Oh, Lucius !'

' I shall, and no mistake !'

What would he have said had he known that his mother had absolutely proposed to Mr. Furnival to buy off Mr. Dockwrath's animosity, almost at any price ?

CHAPTER XVI.

MR. DOCKWRATH, as he left Leeds and proceeded to join the bosom of his family, was not discontented with what he had done. It might not improbably have been the case that Mr. Mason would altogether refuse to see him, and having seen him, Mr. Mason might altogether have declined his assistance. He might have been forced as a witness to disclose his secret, of which he could make so much better a profit as a legal adviser. As it was, Mr. Mason had promised to pay him for his services, and would no doubt be induced to go so far as to give him a legal claim for payment. Mr. Mason had promised to come up to town, and had instructed the Hamworth attorney to meet him there; and under such circumstances the Hamworth attorney had but little doubt that time would produce a considerable bill of costs in his favour.

And then he thought that he saw his way to a great success. I should be painting the Devil too black were I to say that revenge was his chief incentive in that which he was doing. All our motives are mixed; and his wicked desire to do evil to Lady Mason in return for the evil which she had done to him was mingled with professional energy, and an ambition to win a cause that ought to be won—especially a cause which others had failed to win. He said to himself, on finding those names and dates among old Mr. Usbech's papers, that there was still an opportunity of doing something considerable in this Orley Farm Case, and he had made up his mind to do it. Professional energy, revenge, and money considerations would work hand in hand in this matter; and therefore, as he left Leeds in the second-class railway carriage for London, he thought over the result of his visit with considerable satisfaction.

He had left Leeds at ten, and Mr. Moulder had come down in the same omnibus to the station, and was travelling in the same train in a first-class carriage. Mr. Moulder was a man who despised the second-class, and was not slow to say so before other commercials who travelled at a cheaper rate than he did. 'Hubbles and Grease,' he said, 'allowed him respectably, in order that he might go about their business respectable; and he wasn't going to give the firm a bad name by being seen in a second-class carriage, although the difference would go into his own pocket. That wasn't the way he had begun, and that wasn't the way he was going to end.' He said nothing to Mr. Dockwrath in the morning, merely bowing in answer to that gentleman's salutation. 'Hope you were comfortable last night in the back drawing-room,' said Mr. Dockwrath; but Mr. Moulder in reply only looked at him.

At the Mansfield station, Mr. Kantwise, with his huge wooden boxes, appeared on the platform, and he got into the same carriage with Mr. Dockwrath. He had come on by a night train, and had been doing a stroke of business that morning. 'Well, Kantwise,' Moulder holloaed out from his warm, well-padded seat, 'doing it cheap and nasty, eh?'

'Not at all nasty, Mr. Moulder,' said the other. 'And I find myself among as respectable a class of society in the second-class as you do in the first; quite so;—and perhaps a little better,' Mr. Kantwise added, as he took his seat immediately opposite to Mr. Dockwrath. 'I hope I have the pleasure of seeing you pretty bobbish this morning, sir.' And he shook hands cordially with the attorney.

'Tidy, thank you,' said Dockwrath. 'My company last night did not do me any harm; you may swear to that.'

'Ha! ha! ha! I was so delighted that you got the better of Moulder; a domineering party, isn't he? quite terrible! For myself, I can't put up with him sometimes.'

'I didn't have to put up with him last night.'

'No, no; it was very good, wasn't it now? very capital, indeed. All the same I wish you'd heard Busby give us "Beautiful Venice, City of Song!" A charming voice has Busby; quite charming.' And there was a pause for a minute or so, after which Mr. Kantwise resumed the conversation. 'You'll allow me to put you up one of those drawing-room sets?' he said.

'Well, I am afraid not. I don't think they are strong enough where there are children.'

'Dear, dear; dear, dear; to hear you say so, Mr. Dockwrath! Why, they are made for strength. They are the very things for children, because they don't break, you know.'

'But they'd bend terribly.'

'By no means. They're so elastic that they always recovers themselves. I didn't show you that; but you might turn the backs of them chairs nearly down to the ground, and they will come straight again. You let me send you a set for your wife to look at. If she's not charmed with them I'll—I'll—I'll eat them.'

'Women are charmed with anything,' said Mr. Dockwrath. 'A new bonnet does that.'

'They know what they are about pretty well, as I dare say you

have found out. I'll send express to Sheffield and have a completely new set put up for you.'

' For twelve seventeen six, of course ?'

' Oh! dear no, Mr. Dockwrath. The lowest figure for ready
money, delivered free, is fifteen ten.'

' I couldn't think of paying more than Mrs. Mason.'

' Ah! but that was a damaged set; it was, indeed. And she
merely wanted it as a present for the curate's wife. The table was
quite sprung, and the music-stool wouldn't twist.'

' But you'll send them to me new ?'

' New from the manufactory ; upon my word we will.'

' A table that you have never acted upon—have never shown off
on; standing in the middle, you know ?'

' Yes; upon my honour. You shall have them direct from the
workshop, and sent at once; you shall find them in your drawing-
room on Tuesday next.'

' We'll say thirteen ten.'

' I couldn't do it, Mr. Dockwrath—' And so they went on, bar-
gaining half the way up to town, till at last they came to terms for
fourteen eleven. ' And a very superior article your lady will find
them,' Mr. Kantwise said as he shook hands with his new friend
at parting.

One day Mr. Dockwrath remained at home in the bosom of his
family, saying all manner of spiteful things against Lady Mason,
and on the next day he went up to town and called on Round and
Crook. That one day he waited in order that Mr. Mason might
have time to write; but Mr. Mason had written on the very day
of the visit to Groby Park, and Mr. Round junior was quite ready
for Mr. Dockwrath when that gentleman called.

Mr. Dockwrath when at home had again cautioned his wife to
have no intercourse whatever ' with that swindler at Orley Farm,'
wishing thereby the more thoroughly to imbue poor Miriam with
a conviction that Lady Mason had committed some fraud with
reference to the will. ' You had better say nothing about the
matter anywhere ; d' you hear? People will talk; all the world
will be talking about it before long. But that is nothing to you.
If people ask you, say that you believe that I am engaged in the
case professionally, but that you know nothing further.' As to all
which Miriam of course promised the most exact obedience. But
Mr. Dockwrath, though he only remained one day in Hamworth
before he went to London, took care that the curiosity of his
neighbours should be sufficiently excited.

Mr. Dockwrath felt some little trepidation at the heart as he
walked into the office of Messrs. Round and Crook in Bedford Row.
Messrs. Round and Crook stood high in the profession, and were
men who in the ordinary way of business would have had no

personal dealings with such a man as Mr. Dockwrath. Had any such intercourse become necessary on commonplace subjects Messrs. Round and Crook's confidential clerk might have seen Mr. Dockwrath, but even he would have looked down upon the Hamworth attorney as from a great moral height. But now, in the matter of the Orley Farm Case, Mr. Dockwrath had determined that he would transact business only on equal terms with the Bedford Row people. The secret was his—of his finding; he knew the strength of his own position, and he would use it. But nevertheless he did tremble inwardly as he asked whether Mr. Round was within;— or if not Mr. Round, then Mr. Crook.

There were at present three members in the firm, though the old name remained unaltered. The Mr. Round and the Mr. Crook of former days were still working partners;—the very Round and the very Crook who had carried on the battle on the part of Mr. Mason of Groby twenty years ago; but to them had been added another Mr. Round, a son of old Round, who, though his name did not absolutely appear in the nomenclature of the firm, was, as a working man, the most important person in it. Old Mr. Round might now be said to be ornamental and communicative. He was a hale man of nearly seventy, who thought a great deal of his peaches up at Isleworth, who came to the office five times a week—not doing very much hard work, and who took the largest share in the profits. Mr. Round senior had enjoyed the reputation of being a sound, honourable man, but was now considered by some to be not quite sharp enough for the practice of the present day.

Mr. Crook had usually done the dirty work of the firm, having been originally a managing clerk; and he still did the same—in a small way. He had been the man to exact penalties, look after costs, and attend to any criminal business, or business partly criminal in its nature, which might chance find its way to them. But latterly in all great matters Mr. Round junior, Mr. Matthew Round —his father was Richard—was the member of the firm on whom the world in general placed the greatest dependence. Mr. Mason's letter had in the ordinary way of business come to him, although it had been addressed to his father, and he had resolved on acting on it himself.

When Mr. Dockwrath called Mr. Round senior was at Birmingham, Mr. Crook was taking his annual holiday, and Mr. Round junior was reigning alone in Bedford Row. Instructions had been given to the clerks that if Mr. Dockwrath called he was to be shown in, and therefore he found himself seated, with much less trouble than he had expected, in the private room of Mr. Round junior. He had expected to see an old man, and was therefore somewhat confused, not feeling quite sure that he was in company with one of the principals; but nevertheless, looking at the room, and especially at the arm-chair and carpet, he was aware that the legal gentleman who motioned him to a seat could be no ordinary clerk.

The manner of this legal gentleman was not, as Mr. Dockwrath thought, quite so ceremoniously civil as it might be, considering the important nature of the business to be transacted between them. Mr. Dockwrath intended to treat on equal terms, and so intending would have been glad to have shaken hands with his new ally at the commencement of their joint operations. But the man before him—a man younger than himself too—did not even rise from his chair. 'Ah! Mr. Dockwrath,' he said, taking up a letter from the table, 'will you have the goodness to sit down?' And Mr. Matthew Round wheeled his own arm-chair towards the fire, stretching out his legs comfortably, and pointing to a somewhat distant seat as that intended for the accommodation of his visitor. Mr. Dockwrath seated himself in the somewhat distant seat, and deposited his hat upon the floor, not being as yet quite at home in his position; but he made up his mind as he did so that he would be at home before he left the room.

'I find that you have been down in Yorkshire with a client of ours, Mr. Dockwrath,' said Mr. Matthew Round.

'Yes, I have,' said he of Hamworth.

'Ah! well—; you are in the profession yourself, I believe?'

'Yes; I am an attorney.'

'Would it not have been well to have come to us first?'

'No, I think not. I have not the pleasure of knowing your name, sir.'

'My name is Round—Matthew Round.'

'I beg your pardon, sir; I did not know,' said Mr. Dockwrath, bowing. It was a satisfaction to him to learn that he was closeted with a Mr. Round, even if it were not the Mr. Round. 'No, Mr. Round, I can't say that I should have thought of that. In the first place I didn't know whether Mr. Mason employed any lawyer, and in the next——'

'Well, well; it does not matter. It is usual among the profession; but it does not in the least signify. Mr. Mason has written to us, and he says that you have found out something about that Orley Farm business.'

'Yes; I have found out something. At least, I rather think so.'

'Well, what is it, Mr. Dockwrath?'

'Ah! that's the question. It's rather a ticklish business, Mr. Round; a family affair, as I may say.'

'Whose family?'

'To a certain extent my family, and to a certain extent Mr. Mason's family. I don't know how far I should be justified in laying all the facts before you—wonderful facts they are too—

in an off-hand way like that. These matters have to be considered a great deal. It is not only the extent of the property. There is much more than that in it, Mr. Round.'

' If you don't tell me what there is in it, I don't see what we are to do. I am sure you did not give yourself the trouble of coming up here from Hamworth merely with the object of telling us that you are going to hold your tongue.'

' Certainly not, Mr. Round.'

' Then what did you come to say ?'

' May I ask you, Mr. Round, what Mr. Mason has told you with reference to my interview with him ?'

' Yes ; I will read you a part of his letter—" Mr. Dockwrath is of opinion that the will under which the estate is now enjoyed is absolutely a forgery." I presume you mean the codicil, Mr. Dockwrath ?'

' Oh yes ! the codicil of course.'

' " And he has in his possession documents which I have not seen, but which seem to me, as described, to go far to prove that this certainly must have been the case." And then he goes on with a description of dates, although it is clear that he does not understand the matter himself—indeed he says as much. Now of course we must see these documents before we can give our client any advice.' A certain small portion of Mr. Mason's letter Mr. Round did then read, but he did not read those portions in which Mr. Mason expressed his firm determination to reopen the case against Lady Mason, and even to prosecute her for forgery if it were found that he had anything like a fair chance of success in doing so. ' I know that you were convinced,' he had said, addressing himself personally to Mr. Round senior, ' that Lady Mason was acting in good faith. I was always convinced of the contrary, and am more sure of it now than ever.' This last paragraph, Mr. Round junior had not thought it necessary to read to Mr. Dockwrath.

' The documents to which I allude are in reference to my confidential family matters ; and I certainly shall not produce them without knowing on what ground I am standing.'

' Of course you are aware, Mr. Dockwrath, that we could compel you.'

' There, Mr. Round, I must be allowed to differ.'

' It won't come to that, of course. If you have anything worth showing, you'll show it ; and if we make use of you as a witness, it must be as a willing witness.'

' I don't think it probable that I shall be a witness in the matter at all.'

' Ah, well ; perhaps not. My own impression is that no case will be made out ; that there will be nothing to take before a jury.'

' There again, I must differ from you, Mr. Round.'

'Oh, of course! I suppose the real fact is, that it is a matter of money. You want to be paid for what information you have got. That is about the long and the short of it; eh, Mr. Dockwrath?'

'I don't know what you call the long and the short of it, Mr. Round; or what may be your way of doing business. As a professional man, of course I expect to be paid for my work;—and I have no doubt that you expect the same.'

'No doubt, Mr. Dockwrath; but—as you have made the comparison, I hope you will excuse me for saying so—we always wait till our clients come to us.'

Mr. Dockwrath drew himself up with some intention of becoming angry; but he hardly knew how to carry it out; and then it might be a question whether anger would serve his turn. 'Do you mean to say, Mr. Round, if you had found documents such as these, you would have done nothing about them—that you would have passed them by as worthless?'

'I can't say that till I know what the documents are. If I found papers concerning the client of another firm, I should go to that firm if I thought that they demanded attention.'

'I didn't know anything about the firm;—how was I to know?'

'Well! you know now, Mr. Dockwrath. As I understand it, our client has referred you to us. If you have any anything to say, we are ready to hear it. If you have anything to show, we are ready to look at it. If you have nothing to say, and nothing to show—'

'Ah, but I have; only—'

'Only you want us to make it worth your while. We might as well have the truth at once. Is not that about it?'

'I want to see my way, of course.'

'Exactly. And now, Mr. Dockwrath, I must make you understand that we don't do business in that way.'

'Then I shall see Mr. Mason again myself.'

'That you can do. He will be in town next week, and, as I believe, wishes to see you. As regards your expenses, if you can show us that you have any communication to make that is worth our client's attention, we will see that you are paid what you are out of pocket, and some fair remuneration for the time you may have lost;—not as an attorney, remember, for in that light we cannot regard you.'

'I am every bit as much an attorney as you are.'

'No doubt; but you are not Mr. Mason's attorney; and as long as it suits him to honour us with his custom, you cannot be so regarded.'

'That's as he pleases.'

'No; it is not, Mr. Dockwrath. It is as he pleases whether he employs you or us; but it is not as he pleases whether he employs both on business of the same class. He may give us his confidence, or he may withdraw it.'

'Looking at the way the matter was managed before, perhaps the latter may be the better for him.'

'Excuse me, Mr. Dockwrath, for saying that that is a question I shall not discuss with you.'

Upon this Mr. Dockwrath jumped from his chair, and took up his hat. 'Good morning to you, sir,' said Mr. Round, without moving from his chair; 'I will tell Mr. Mason that you have declined making any communication to us. He will probably know your address—if he should want it.'

Mr. Dockwrath paused. Was he not about to sacrifice substantial advantage to momentary anger? Would it not be better that he should carry this impudent young London lawyer with him if it were possible? 'Sir,' said he, 'I am quite willing to tell you all that I know of this matter at present, if you will have the patience hear it.'

'Patience, Mr. Dockwrath! Why I am made of patience. Sit down again, Mr. Dockwrath, and think of it.'

Mr. Dockwrath did sit down again, and did think of it; and it ended in his telling to Mr. Round all that he had told to Mr. Mason. As he did so, he looked closely at Mr. Round's face, but there he could read nothing. 'Exactly,' said Mr. Round. 'The fourteenth of July is the date of both. I have taken a memorandum of that. A final deed for closing partnership, was it? I have got that down. John Kenneby and Bridget Bolster. I remember the names,—witnesses to both deeds, were they? I understand; nothing about this other deed was brought up at the trial? I see the point—such as it is. John Kennedy and Bridget Bolster;—both believed to be living. Oh, you can give their address, can you? Decline to do so now? Very well; it does not matter. I think I understand it all now, Mr. Dockwrath; and when we want you again, you shall hear from us. Samuel Dockwrath, is it? Thank you. Good morning. If Mr. Mason wishes to see you, he will write, of course. Good day, Mr. Dockwrath.'

And so Mr. Dockwrath went home, not quite contented with his day's work.

CHAPTER XVII.

It will be remembered that Mr. Crabwitz was sent across from Lincoln's Inn to Bedford Row to ascertain the present address of old Mr. Round. ' Mr. Round is at Birmingham,' he said, coming back. ' Every one connected with the profession is at Birmingham, except——'

' The more fools they,' said Mr. Furnival.

' I am thinking of going down myself this evening,' said Mr. Crabwitz. ' As you will be out of town, sir, I suppose I can be spared?'

' You too!'

' And why not me, Mr. Furnival? When all the profession is meeting together, why should not I be there as well as another? I hope you do not deny me my right to feel an interest in the great subjects which are being discussed.'

' Not in the least, Mr. Crabwitz. I do not deny you your right to be Lord Chief Justice, if you can accomplish it. But you cannot be Lord Chief Justice and my clerk at the same time. Nor can you be in my chambers if you are at Birmingham. I rather think I must trouble you to remain here, as I cannot tell at what moment I may be in town again.'

' Then, sir, I'm afraid——' Mr. Crabwitz began his speech and then faltered. He was going to tell Mr. Furnival that he must suit himself with another clerk, when he remembered his fees, and paused. It would be very pleasant to him to quit Mr. Furnival, but where could he get such another place? He knew that he himself was invaluable, but then he was invaluable only to Mr. Furnival. Mr. Furnival would be mad to part with him, Mr. Crabwitz thought; but then would he not be almost more mad to part with Mr. Furnival?

' Eh; well?' said Mr. Furnival.

' Oh! of course; if you desire it, Mr. Furnival, I will remain. But I must say I think it is rather hard.'

' Look here, Mr. Crabwitz; if you think my service is too hard upon you, you had better leave it. But if you take upon yourself to tell me so again, you must leave it. Remember that.' Mr. Furnival possessed the master mind of the two; and Mr. Crabwitz felt this as he slunk back to his own room.

So Mr. Round also was at Birmingham, and could be seen there. This was so far well; and Mr. Furnival, having again with ruthless malice sent Mr. Crabwitz for a cab, at once started for the Euston Square Station. He could master Mr. Crabwitz, and felt a certain pleasure in having done so; but could he master Mrs. F.? That lady had on one or two late occasions shown her anger at the existing state of her domestic affairs, and had once previously gone so far as to make her lord understand that she was jealous of his proceedings with reference to other goddesses. But she had never before done this in the presence of other people;—she had never allowed any special goddess to see that she was the special object of such jealousy. Now she had not only committed herself in this way, but had also committed him, making him feel himself to be ridiculous; and it was highly necessary that some steps should be taken;—if he only knew what step! All which kept his mind active as he journeyed in the cab.

At the station he found three or four other lawyers, all bound for Birmingham. Indeed, during this fortnight the whole line had been alive with learned gentlemen going to and fro, discussing weighty points as they rattled along the iron road, and shaking their ponderous heads at the new ideas which were being ventilated. Mr. Furnival, with many others—indeed, with most of those who were so far advanced in the world as to be making bread by their profession—was of opinion that all this palaver that was going on in the various tongues of Babel would end as it began—in words. 'Vox et præterea nihil.' To practical Englishmen most of these international congresses seem to arrive at nothing else. Men will not be talked out of the convictions of their lives. No living orator would convince a grocer that coffee should be sold without chicory; and no amount of eloquence will make an English lawyer think that loyalty to truth should come before loyalty to his client. And therefore our own pundits, though on this occasion they went to Birmingham, summoned by the greatness of the occasion, by the dignity of foreign names, by interest in the question, and by the influence of such men as Lord Boanerges, went there without any doubt on their minds as to the rectitude of their own practice, and fortified with strong resolves to resist all idea of change.

And indeed one cannot understand how the bent of any man's mind should be altered by the sayings and doings of such a congress.

'Well, Johnson, what have you all been doing to-day?' asked Mr. Furnival of a special friend whom he chanced to meet at the club which had been extemporized at Birmingham.

'We have had a paper read by Von Bauhr. It lasted three hours.'

'Three hours! heavens! Von Bauhr is, I think, from Berlin.'

'Yes; he and Dr. Slotacher. Slotacher is to read his paper the day after to-morrow.'

'Then I think I shall go to London again. But what did Von Bauhr say to you during those three hours?'

'Of course it was all in German, and I don't suppose that any one understood him,—unless it was Boanerges. But I believe it was the old story, going to show that the same man might be judge, advocate, and jury.'

'No doubt;—if men were machines, and if you could find such machines perfect at all points in their machinery.'

'And if the machines had no hearts?'

'Machines don't have hearts,' said Mr. Furnival; 'especially those in Germany. And what did Boanerges say? His answer did not take three hours more, I hope.'

'About twenty minutes; but what he did say was lost on Von Bauhr, who understands as much English as I do German. He said that the practice of the Prussian courts had always been to him a subject of intense interest, and that the general justice of their verdicts could not be impugned.'

'Nor ought it, seeing that a single trial for murder will occupy a court for three weeks. He should have asked Von Bauhr how much work he usually got through in the course of a sessions. I don't seem to have lost much by being away. By-the-by, do you happen to know whether Round is here?'

'What, old Round? I saw him in the hall to-day yawning as though he would burst.' And then Mr. Furnival strolled off to look for the attorney among the various purlieus frequented by the learned strangers.

'Furnival,' said another barrister, accosting him—an elderly man, small, with sharp eyes and bushy eyebrows, dirty in his attire and poor in his general appearance, 'have you seen Judge Staveley?' This was Mr. Chaffanbrass, great at the Old Bailey, a man well able to hold his own in spite of the meanness of his appearance. At such a meeting as this the English bar generally could have had no better representative than Mr. Chaffanbrass.

'No; is he here?'

'He must be here. He is the only man they could find who knows enough Italian to understand what that fat fellow from Florence will say to-morrow.'

'We're to have the Italian to-morrow, are we?'

'Yes; and Staveley afterwards. It's as good as a play; only, like all plays, it's three times too long. I wonder whether anybody here believes in it?'

'Yes, Felix Graham does.'

'He believes everything—unless it is the Bible. He is one of those young men who look for an instant millennium, and who regard themselves not only as the prophets who foretell it, but as the preachers who will produce it. For myself, I am too old for a new gospel, with Felix Graham as an apostle.'

' They say that Boanerges thinks a great deal of him.'

' That can't be true, for Boanerges never thought much of any one but himself. Well, I'm off to bed, for I find a day here ten times more fatiguing than the Old Bailey in July.'

On the whole the meeting was rather dull, as such meetings usually are. It must not be supposed that any lawyer could get up at will, as the spirit moved him, and utter his own ideas ; or that all members of the congress could speak if only they could catch the speaker's eye. Had this been so, a man might have been supported by the hope of having some finger in the pie, sooner or later. But in such case the congress would have lasted for ever. As it was, the names of those who were invited to address the meeting were arranged, and of course men from each country were selected who were best known in their own special walks of their profession. But then these best-known men took an unfair advantage of their position, and were ruthless in the lengthy cruelty of their addresses. Von Bauhr at Berlin was no doubt a great lawyer, but he should not have felt so confident that the legal proceedings of England and of the civilized world in general could be reformed by his reading that book of his from the rostrum in the hall at Birmingham! The civilized world in general, as there represented, had been disgusted, and it was surmised that poor Dr. Slotacher would find but a meagre audience when his turn came.

At last Mr. Furnival succeeded in hunting up Mr. Round, and found him recruiting outraged nature with a glass of brandy and water and a cigar. ' Looking for me, have you? Well, here I am ; that is to say, what is left of me. Were you in the hall to-day ?'

' No ; I was up in town.'

' Ah! that accounts for your being so fresh. I wish I had been there. Do you ever do anything in this way ?' and Mr. Round touched the outside of his glass of toddy with his spoon. Mr. Furnival said that he never did do anything in that way, which was true. Port wine was his way, and it may be doubted whether on the whole it is not the more dangerous way of the two. But Mr. Furnival, though he would not drink brandy and water or smoke cigars, sat down opposite to Mr. Round, and had soon broached the subject which was on his mind.

' Yes,' said the attorney, ' it is quite true that I had a letter on the subject from Mr. Mason. The lady is not wrong in supposing that some one is moving in the matter.'

' And your client wishes you to take up the case again ?'

' No doubt he does He was not a man that I ever greatly liked,

Mr. Furnival, though I believe he means well. He thinks that he has been ill used; and perhaps he was ill used—by his father.'

' But that can bo no possible reason for badgering the life out of his father's widow twenty years after his father's death !'

' Of course he thinks that he has some new evidence. I can't say I looked into the matter much myself. I did read the letter; but that was all, and then I handed it to my son. As far as I remember, Mr. Mason said that some attorney at Hamworth had been to him.'

' Exactly; a low fellow whom you would be ashamed to see in your office! He fancies that young Mason has injured him; and though he has received numberless benefits from Lady Mason, this is the way in which he chooses to be revenged on her son.'

' We should have nothing to do with such a matter as that, you know. It's not our line.'

' No, of course it is not; I am well aware of that. And I am equally well aware that nothing Mr. Mason can do can shake Lady Mason's title, or rather her son's title, to the property. But, Mr. Round, if he be encouraged to gratify his malice——'

' If who be encouraged?'

' Your client, Mr. Mason of Groby;—there can be no doubt that he might harass this unfortunate lady till he brought her nearly to the grave.'

' That would be a pity, for I believe she's still an uncommon pretty woman.' And the attorney indulged in a little fat inward chuckle; for in these days Mr. Furnival's taste with reference to strange goddesses was beginning to be understood by the profession.

' She is a very old friend of mine,' said Mr. Furnival, gravely, ' a very old friend indeed; and if I were to desert her now, she would have no one to whom she could look.'

' Oh, ah, yes; I'm sure you're very kind ;' and Mr. Round altered his face and tone, so that they might be in conformity with those of his companion. ' Anything I can do, of course I shall be very happy. I should be slow, myself, to advise my client to try the matter again, but to tell the truth anything of this kind would go to my son now. I did read Mr. Mason's letter, but I immediately handed it to Matthew.'

' I will tell you how you can oblige me, Mr. Round.'

' Do tell me ; I am sure I shall be very happy.'

' Look into this matter yourself, and talk it over with Mr. Mason before you allow anything to be done. It is not that I doubt your son's discretion. Indeed we all know what an exceedingly good man of business he is.'

' Matthew is sharp enough,' said the prosperous father.

' But then young men are apt to be too sharp. I don't know whether you remember the case about that Orley Farm, Mr. Round.'

' As well as if it were yesterday,' said the attorney.

' Then you must recollect how thoroughly you were convinced that your client had not a leg to stand upon.'

' It was I that insisted that he should not carry it before the Chancellor. Crook had the general management of those cases then, and would have gone on; but I said, no. I would not see my client's money wasted in such a wild-goose chase. In the first place the property was not worth it; and in the next place there was nothing to impugn the will. If I remember right it all turned on whether an old man who had signed as witness was well enough to write his name.'

' That was the point.'

' And I think it was shown that he had himself signed a receipt on that very day—or the day after, or the day before. It was something of that kind.'

' Exactly; those were the facts. As regards the result of a new trial, no sane man, I fancy, could have any doubt. You know as well as any one living how great is the strength of twenty years of possession——'

' It would be very strong on her side, certainly.'

' He would not have a chance; of course not. But, Mr. Round, he might make that poor woman so wretched that death would be a relief to her. Now it may be possible that something looking like fresh evidence may have been discovered; something of this kind probably has been found, or this man would not be moving; he would not have gone to the expense of a journey to Yorkshire had he not got hold of some new story.'

' He has something in his head; you may be sure of that.'

' Don't let your son be run away with by this, or advise your client to incur the terrible expense of a new trial, without knowing what you are about. I tell you fairly that I do dread such a trial on this poor lady's account. Reflect what it would be, Mr. Round, to any lady of your own family.'

' I don't think Mrs. Round would mind it much; that is, if she were sure of her case.'

' She is a strong-minded woman; but poor Lady Mason ——.'

' She was strong-minded enough too, if I remember right, at the last trial. I shall never forget how composed she was when old Bennett tried to shake her evidence. Do you remember how bothered he was?'

' He was an excellent lawyer,—was Bennett. There are few better men at the bar now-a-days.'

' You wouldn't have found him down here, Mr. Furnival, listening to a German lecture three hours' long. I don't know how it is, but I think we all used to work harder in those days than the young men do now.' And then these eulogists of past days went back to the memories of their youths, declaring how in the old glorious years, now gone, no congress such as this would have had a chance of success. Men had men's work to do then, and were not wont to play the fool, first at one provincial town and then at another, but stuck to their oars and made their fortunes. 'It seems to me, Mr. Furnival,' said Mr. Round, 'that this is all child's play, and to tell the truth I am half ashamed of myself for being here.'

'And you'll look into that matter yourself, Mr. Round?'

'Yes, I will, certainly.'

'I shall take it as a great favour. Of course you will advise your client in accordance with any new facts which may be brought before you; but as I feel certain that no case against young Mason can have any merits, I do hope that you will be able to suggest to Mr. Mason of Groby that the matter should be allowed to rest.' And then Mr. Furnival took his leave, still thinking how far it might be possible that the enemy's side of the question might be supported by real merits. Mr. Round was a good-natured old fellow, and if the case could be inveigled out of his son's hands and into his own, it might be possible that even real merits should avail nothing.

'I confess I am getting rather tired of it,' said Felix Graham that evening to his friend young Staveley, as he stood outside his bedroom door at the top of a narrow flight of stairs in the back part of a large hotel at Birmingham.

'Tired of it! I should think you are too.'

'But nevertheless I am as sure as ever that good will come from it. I am inclined to think that the same kind of thing must be endured before any improvement is made in anything.'

'That all reformers have to undergo Von Bauhr?'

'Yes, all of them that do any good. Von Bauhr's words were very dry, no doubt.'

'You don't mean to say that you understood them?'

'Not many of them. A few here and there, for the first half-hour, came trembling home to my dull comprehension, and then—'

'You went to sleep.'

'The sounds became too difficult for my ears; but dry and dull and hard as they were, they will not absolutely fall to the ground. He had a meaning in them, and that meaning will reproduce itself in some shape.'

'Heaven forbid that it should ever do so in my presence! All the iniquities of which the English bar may be guilty cannot be so intolerable to humanity as Von Bauhr.'

'Well, good-night, old fellow; your governor is to give us his ideas to-morrow, and perhaps he will be as bad to the Germans as your Von Bauhr was to us.'

'Then I can only say that my governor will be very cruel to the Germans.' And so they two went to their dreams.

In the mean time Von Bauhr was sitting alone looking back on
the past hours with ideas and views very different from those of the
many English lawyers who were at that time discussing his
demerits. To him the day had been one long triumph, for his
voice had sounded sweet in his own ears as, period after period, he
had poured forth in full flowing language the gathered wisdom and
experience of his life. Public men in England have so much to do,
that they cannot give time to the preparation of speeches for such
meetings as these, but Von Bauhr had been at work on his pamphlet
for months. Nay, taking it in the whole, had he not been at work
on it for years? And now a kind Providence had given him the
opportunity of pouring it forth before the assembled pundits
gathered from all the nations of the civilized world.

As he sat there, solitary in his bedroom, his hands dropped down
by his side, his pipe hung from his mouth on to his breast, and his
eyes, turned up to the ceiling, were lighted almost with inspiration.
Men there at the congress, Mr. Chaffanbrass, young Staveley, Felix
Graham, and others, had regarded him as an impersonation of dull-
ness; but through his mind and brain, as he sat there wrapped in
his old dressing-gown, there ran thoughts which seemed to lift him
lightly from the earth into an elysium of justice and mercy. And
at the end of this elysium, which was not wild in its beauty, but
trim and orderly in its gracefulness—as might be a beer-garden at
Munich—there stood among flowers and vases a pedestal, grand
above all other pedestals in that garden; and on this there was a
bust with an inscription :—' To Von Bauhr, who reformed the laws
of nations.'

It was a grand thought; and though there was in it much of
human conceit, there was in it also much of human philanthropy.
If a reign of justice could be restored through his efforts—through
those efforts in which on this hallowed day he had been enabled to
make so great a progress—how beautiful would it be! And then
as he sat there, while the smoke still curled from his unconscious
nostrils, he felt that he loved all Germans, all Englishmen, even
all Frenchmen, in his very heart of hearts, and especially those
who had travelled wearily to this English town that they might
listen to the results of his wisdom. He said to himself, and said
truly, that he loved the world, and that he would willingly spend
himself in these great endeavours for the amelioration of its laws
and the perfection of its judicial proceedings. And then he betook
himself to bed in a frame of mind that was not unenviable.

I am inclined, myself, to agree with Felix Graham that such
efforts are seldom absolutely wasted. A man who strives honestly
to do good will generally do good, though seldom perhaps as much
as he has himself anticipated. Let Von Bauhr have his pedestal
among the flowers, even though it be small and humble!

Von Bauhr's Dream.

CHAPTER XVIII.

On the following morning, before breakfast, Felix Graham and Augustus Staveley prepared themselves for the labours of the coming day by a walk into the country; for even at Birmingham, by perseverance, a walk into the country may be attained,—and very pretty country it is when reached. These congress meetings did not begin before eleven, so that for those who were active time for matutinal exercise was allowed.

Augustus Staveley was the only son of the judge who on that day was to defend the laws of England from such attacks as might be made on them by a very fat advocate from Florence. Of Judge Staveley himself much need not be said now, except that he lived at Noningsby near Alston, distant from The Cleeve about nine miles, and that at his house Sophia Furnival had been invited to pass the coming Christmas. His son was a handsome clever fellow, who had nearly succeeded in getting the Newdegate, and was now a member of the Middle Temple. He was destined to follow the steps of his father, and become a light at the Common Law bar; but hitherto he had not made much essential progress. The world had been too pleasant to him to allow of his giving many of his hours to work. His father was one of the best men in the world, revered on the bench, and loved by all men; but he had not sufficient parental sternness to admit of his driving his son well into harness. He himself had begun the world with little or nothing, and had therefore succeeded; but his son was already possessed of almost everything that he could want, and therefore his success seemed doubtful. His chambers were luxuriously furnished, he had his horse in Piccadilly, his father's house at Noningsby was always open to him, and the society of London spread out for him all its allurements. Under such circumstances how could it be expected that he should work? Nevertheless he did talk of working, and had some idea in his head of the manner in which he would do so. To a certain extent he had worked, and he could talk fluently of the little that he knew. The idea of a *far niente* life would have been intolerable to him; but there were many among his friends who began to think that such a life would nevertheless be his ultimate destiny. Nor did it much matter, they said, for the judge was known to have made money.

But his friend Felix Graham was rowing in a very different boat; and of him also many prophesied that he would hardly be able to push his craft up against the strength of the stream. Not that he was an idle man, but that he would not work at his oars in the only approved method of making progress for his boat. He also had been at Oxford; but he had done little there except talk at a debating society, and make himself notorious by certain ideas on religious subjects which were not popular at the University. He had left without taking a degree, in consequence, as it was believed, of some such notions, and had now been called to the bar with a fixed resolve to open that oyster with such weapons, offensive and defensive, as nature had given to him. But here, as at Oxford, he would not labour on the same terms with other men, or make himself subject to the same conventional rules; and therefore it seemed only too probable that he might win no prize. He had ideas of his own that men should pursue their labours without special conventional regulations, but should be guided in their work by the general great rules of the world,—such for instance as those given in the commandments:—Thou shalt not bear false witness; Thou shalt not steal; and others. His notions no doubt were great, and perhaps were good; but hitherto they had not led him to much pecuniary success in his profession. A sort of a name he had obtained, but it was not a name sweet in the ears of practising attorneys.

And yet it behoved Felix Graham to make money, for none was coming to him ready made from any father. Father or mother he had none, nor uncles and aunts likely to be of service to him. He had begun the world with some small sum, which had grown smaller and smaller, till now there was left to him hardly enough to create an infinitesimal dividend. But he was not a man to become down-hearted on that account. A living of some kind he could pick up, and did now procure for himself, from the press of the day. He wrote poetry for the periodicals, and politics for the penny papers with considerable success and sufficient pecuniary results. He would sooner do this, he often boasted, than abandon his great ideas or descend into the arena with other weapons than those which he regarded as fitting for an honest man's hand.

Augustus Staveley, who could be very prudent for his friend, declared that marriage would set him right. If Felix would marry he would quietly slip his neck into the collar and work along with the team, as useful a horse as ever was put at the wheel of a coach. But Felix did not seem inclined to marry. He had notions about that also, and was believed by one or two who knew him intimately to cherish an insane affection for some unknown damsel, whose parentage, education, and future were not likely to assist his views in the outer world. Some said that he was educating this damsel for his wife,—moulding her, so that she might be made fit to suit his taste; but Augustus, though he knew the secret of all this, was of opinion that it would come right at last. ' He'll meet some girl in the world with a hatful of money, a pretty face, and a sharp tongue; then he'll bestow his moulded bride on a neighbouring baker with two hundred pounds for her fortune;—and everybody will be happy.'

Felix Graham was by no means a handsome man. He was tall and thin, and his face had been slightly marked with the small-pox. He stooped in his gait as he walked, and was often awkward with his hands and legs. But he was full of enthusiasm, indomitable, as far as pluck would make him so, in contests of all kinds, and when he talked on subjects which were near his heart there was a radiance about him which certainly might win the love of the pretty girl with the sharp tongue and the hatful of money. Staveley, who really loved him, had already selected the prize, and she was no other than our friend, Sophia Furnival. The sharp tongue and the pretty face and the hatful of money would all be there; but then Sophia Furnival was a girl who might perhaps expect in return for these things more than an ugly face which could occasionally become radiant with enthusiasm.

The two men had got away from the thickness of the Birmingham smoke, and were seated on the top rung of a gate leading into a stubble field. So far they had gone with mutual consent, but further than this Staveley refused to go. He was seated with a cigar in his mouth. Graham also was smoking, but he was accommodated with a short pipe.

' A walk before breakfast is all very well,' said Staveley, ' but I am not going on a pilgrimage. We are four miles from the inn this minute.'

' And for your energies that is a good deal. Only think that you should have been doing anything for two hours before you begin to feed.'

' I wonder why matutinal labour should always be considered as so meritorious. Merely, I take it, because it is disagreeable.'

' It proves that the man can make an effort.'

' Every prig who wishes to have it believed that he does more than his neighbours either burns the midnight lamp or gets up at four in the morning. Good wholesome work between breakfast and dinner never seems to count for anything.'

' Have you ever tried?'

' Yes; I am trying now, here at Birmingham.'

'Not you.'

' That's so like you, Graham. You don't believe that anybody is attending to what is going on except yourself. I mean to-day to take in the whole theory of Italian jurisprudence.'

'I have no doubt that you may do so with advantage. I do not suppose that it is very good, but it must at any rate be better than our own. Come, let us go back to the town; my pipe is finished.'

'Fill another, there's a good fellow. I can't afford to throw away my cigar, and I hate walking and smoking. You mean to assert that our whole system is bad, and rotten, and unjust?'

'I mean to say that I think so.'

'And yet we consider ourselves the greatest people in the world, —or at any rate the honestest.'

'I think we are; but laws and their management have nothing to do with making people honest. Good laws won't make people honest, nor bad laws dishonest.'

'But a people who are dishonest in one trade will probably be dishonest in others. Now, you go so far as to say that all English lawyers are rogues.'

'I have never said so. I believe your father to be as honest a man as ever breathed.'

'Thank you, sir,' and Staveley lifted his hat.

'And I would fain hope that I am an honest man myself.'

'Ah, but you don't make money by it.'

'What I do mean is this, that from our love of precedent and ceremony and old usages, we have retained a system which contains many of the barbarities of the feudal times, and also many of its lies. We try our culprit as we did in the old days of the ordeal. If luck will carry him through the hot ploughshares, we let him escape though we know him to be guilty. We give him the advantage of every technicality, and teach him to lie in his own defence, if nature has not sufficiently so taught him already.'

'You mean as to his plea of not guilty.'

'No, I don't; that is little or nothing. We ask him whether or no he confesses his guilt in a foolish way, tending to induce him to deny it; but that is not much. Guilt seldom will confess as long as a chance remains. But we teach him to lie, or rather we lie for him during the whole ceremony of his trial. We think it merciful to give him chances of escape, and hunt him as we do a fox, in obedience to certain laws framed for his protection.'

'And should he have no protection?'

'None certainly, as a guilty man; none which may tend towards the concealing of his guilt. Till that be ascertained, proclaimed, and made apparent, every man's hand should be against him.'

'But if he is innocent?'

'Therefore let him be tried with every possible care. I know

The English Von Bauhr and his pupil.

you understand what I mean, though you look as though you did not. For the protection of his innocence let astute and good men work their best, but for the concealing of his guilt let no astute or good man work at all.'

‘And you would leave the poor victim in the dock without defence?’

‘By no means. Let the poor victim, as you call him,—who in ninety-nine cases out of a hundred is a rat who has been preying in our granaries,—let him, I say, have his defender,—the defender of his possible innocence, not the protector of his probable guilt. It all resolves itself into this. Let every lawyer go into court with a mind resolved to make conspicuous to the light of day that which seems to him to be the truth. A lawyer who does not do that—who does the reverse of that, has in my mind undertaken work which is unfit for a gentleman and impossible for an honest man.’

‘What a pity it is that you should not have an opportunity of rivalling Von Bauhr at the congress!’

‘I have no doubt that Von Bauhr said a great deal of the same nature; and what Von Bauhr said will not wholly be wasted, though it may not yet have reached our sublime understandings.’

‘Perhaps he will vouchsafe to us a translation.’

‘It would be useless at present, seeing that we cannot bring ourselves to believe it possible that a foreigner should in any respect be wiser than ourselves. If any such point out to us our follies, we at once claim those follies as the special evidences of our wisdom. We are so self-satisfied with our own customs, that we hold up our hands with surprise at the fatuity of men who presume to point out to us their defects. Those practices in which we most widely depart from the broad and recognized morality of all civilized ages and countries are to us the Palladiums of our jurisprudence. Modes of proceeding which, if now first proposed to us, would be thought to come direct from the devil, have been made so sacred by time that they have lost all the horror of their falseness in the holiness of their age. We cannot understand that other nations look upon such doings as we regard the human sacrifices of the Brahmins; but the fact is that we drive a Juggernaut's car through every assize town in the country, three times a year, and allow it to be dragged ruthlessly through the streets of the metropolis at all times and seasons. Now come back to breakfast, for I won't wait here any longer.’ Seeing that these were the ideas of Felix Graham, it is hardly a matter of wonder that such men as Mr. Furnival and Mr. Round should have regarded his success at the bar as doubtful.

‘Uncommon bad mutton chops these are,’ said Staveley, as they sat at their meal in the coffee-room of the Imperial Hotel.

‘Are they?’ said Graham. ‘They seem to me much the same as other mutton chops.’

' They are uneatable.　And look at this for coffee !　Waiter, take this away, and have·some made fresh.'

' Yes, sir,' said the waiter, striving to escape without further comment.

' And, waiter—'

' Yes, sir;' and the poor overdriven functionary returned.

' Ask them from me whether they know how to make coffee.　It does not consist of an unlimited supply of lukewarm water poured over an infinitesimal proportion of chicory.　That process, time-honoured in the hotel line, will not produce the beverage called coffee.　Will you have the goodness to explain that in the bar as coming from me?'

' Yes, sir,' said the waiter ; and then he was allowed to disappear.

' How can you give yourself so much trouble with no possible hope of an advantageous result?' said Felix Graham.

' That's what you weak men always say.　Perseverance in such a course will produce results.　It is because we put up with bad things that hotel-keepers continue to give them to us.　Three or four Frenchmen were dining with my father yesterday at the King's Head, and I had to sit at the bottom of the table.　I declare to you that I literally blushed for my country; I did indeed.　It was useless to say anything then, but it was quite clear that there was nothing that one of them could eat.　At any hotel in France you'll get a good dinner ; but we're so proud that we are ashamed to take lessons.'　And thus Augustus Staveley was quite as loud against his own country, and as laudatory with regard to others, as Felix Graham had been before breakfast.

And so the congress went on at Birmingham.　The fat Italian from Tuscany read his paper ; but as he, though judge in his own country and reformer here in England, was somewhat given to comedy, this morning was not so dull as that which had been devoted to Von Bauhr.　After him Judge Staveley made a very elegant, and some said, a very eloquent speech ; and so that day was done.　Many other days also wore themselves away in this process ; numerous addresses were read, and answers made to them, and the newspapers for the time were full of law.　The defence of our own system, which was supposed to be the most remarkable for its pertinacity, if not for its justice, came from Mr. Furnival, who roused himself to a divine wrath for the occasion.　And then the famous congress at Birmingham was brought to a close, and all the foreigners returned to their own countries.

CHAPTER XIX.

THE STAVELEY FAMILY.

THE next two months passed by without any events which deserve our special notice, unless it be that Mr. Joseph Mason and Mr. Dockwrath had a meeting in the room of Mr. Matthew Round, in Bedford Row. Mr. Dockwrath struggled hard to effect this without the presence of the London attorney; but he struggled in vain. Mr. Round was not the man to allow any stranger to tamper with his client, and Mr. Dockwrath was forced to lower his flag before him. The result was that the document or documents which had been discovered at Hamworth were brought up to Bedford Row; and Dockwrath at last made up his mind that as he could not supplant Matthew Round, he would consent to fight under him as his lieutenant—or even as his sergeant or corporal, if no higher position might be allowed to him.

'There is something in it, certainly, Mr. Mason,' said young Round; 'but I cannot undertake to say as yet that we are in a position to prove the point.'

'It will be proved,' said Mr. Dockwrath.

'I confess it seems to me very clear,' said Mr. Mason, who by this time had been made to understand the bearings of the question. 'It is evident that she chose that day for her date because those two persons had then been called upon to act as witnesses to that other deed.'

'That of course is our allegation. I only say that we may have some difficulty in proving it.

'The crafty, thieving swindler!' exclaimed Mr. Mason.

'She has been sharp enough if it is as we think,' said Round, laughing; and then there was nothing more done in the matter for some time, to the great disgust both of Mr. Dockwrath and Mr. Mason. Old Mr. Round had kept his promise to Mr. Furnival; or, at least, had done something towards keeping it. He had not himself taken the matter into his own hands, but he had begged his son to be cautious. 'It's not the sort of business that we care for, Mat.,' said he; 'and as for that fellow down in Yorkshire, I never liked him.' To this Mat. had answered that neither did he like Mr. Mason; but as the case had about it some very remarkable points, it was necessary to look into it; and then the matter was allowed to stand over till after Christmas.

We will now change the scene to Noningsby, the judge's country seat, near Alston, at which a party was assembled for the Christmas holidays. The judge was there of course,—without his wig; in which guise I am inclined to think that judges spend the more com fortable hours of their existence : and there also was Lady Staveley, her presence at home being altogether a matter of course, inasmuch as she had no other home than Noningsby. For many years past, ever since the happy day on which Noningsby had been acquired, she had repudiated London; and the poor judge, when called upon by his duties to reside there, was compelled to live like a bachelor, in lodgings. Lady Staveley was a good, motherly, warm-hearted woman, who thought a great deal about her flowers and fruit, believing that no one else had them so excellent,—much also about her butter and eggs, which in other houses were, in her opinion, generally unfit to be eaten; she thought also a great deal about her children, who were all swans,—though, as she often observed with a happy sigh, those of her neighbours were so uncommonly like geese. But she thought most of all of her husband, who in her eyes was the perfection of all manly virtues. She had made up her mind that the position of a puisne judge in England was the highest which could fall to the lot of any mere mortal. To become a Lord Chancellor, or a Lord Chief Justice, or a Chief Baron, a man must dabble with Parliament, politics, and dirt; but the bench-fellows of these politicians were selected for their wisdom, high conduct, knowledge, and discretion. Of all such selections, that made by the late king when he chose her husband, was the one which had done most honour to England, and had been in all its results most beneficial to Englishmen. Such was her creed with reference to domestic matters.

The Staveley young people at present were only two in number, Augustus, namely, and his sister Madeline. The eldest daughter was married, and therefore, though she spent these Christmas holidays at Noningsby, must not be regarded as one of the Noningsby family. Of Augustus we have said enough; but as I intend that Madeline Staveley shall, to many of my readers, be the most inte-resting personage in this story, I must pause to say something of her. I must say something of her; and as, with all women, the outward and visible signs of grace and beauty are those which are thought of the most, or at any rate spoken of the oftenest, I will begin with her exterior attributes. And that the muses may assist me in my endeavour, teaching my rough hands to draw with some accuracy the delicate lines of female beauty, I now make to them my humble but earnest prayer.

Madeline Staveley was at this time about nineteen years of age.

That she was perfect in her beauty I cannot ask the muses to say, but that she will some day become so, I think the goddesses may be requested to prophesy. At present she was very slight, and appeared to be almost too tall for her form. She was indeed above the average height of women, and from her brother encountered some ridicule on this head; but not the less were all her movements soft, graceful, and fawnlike as should be those of a young girl. She was still at this time a child in heart and spirit, and could have played as a child had not the instinct of a woman taught to her the expediency of a staid demeanour. There is nothing among the wonders of womanhood more wonderful than this, that the young mind and young heart—hearts and minds young as youth can make them, and in their natures as gay,—can assume the gravity and discretion of threescore years and maintain it successfully before all comers. And this is done, not as a lesson that has been taught, but as the result of an instinct implanted from the birth. Let us remember the mirth of our sisters in our homes, and their altered demeanours when those homes were opened to strangers; and remember also that this change had come from the inward working of their own feminine natures!

But I am altogether departing from Madeline Staveley's external graces. It was a pity almost that she should ever have become grave, because with her it was her smile that was so lovely. She smiled with her whole face. There was at such moments a peculiar laughing light in her gray eyes, which inspired one with an earnest desire to be in her confidence; she smiled with her soft cheek, the light tints of which would become a shade more pink from the excitement, as they softly rippled into dimples; she smiled with her forehead which would catch the light from her eyes and arch itself in its glory; but above all she smiled with her mouth, just showing, but hardly showing, the beauty of the pearls within. I never saw the face of a woman whose mouth was equal in pure beauty, in beauty that was expressive of feeling, to that of Madeline Staveley. Many have I seen with a richer lip, with a more luxurious curve, much more tempting as baits to the villainy and rudeness of man; but never one that told so much by its own mute eloquence of a woman's happy heart and a woman's happy beauty. It was lovely as I have said in its mirth, but if possible it was still more lovely in its woe; for then the lips would separate, and the breath would come, and in the emotion of her suffering the life of her beauty would be unrestrained.

Her face was oval, and some might say that it was almost too thin; they might say so till they knew it well, but would never say so when they did so know it. Her complexion was not clear, though it would be wrong to call her a brunette. Her face and forehead were never brown, but yet she could not boast the pure pink and the pearly white which go to the formation of a clear complexion. For myself I am not sure that I love a clear complexion. Pink and white alone will not give that hue which seems best to denote light and life, and to tell of a mind that thinks and of a heart that feels. I can name no colour in describing the soft changing tints of Madeline Staveley's face, but I will make bold to say that no man ever found it insipid or inexpressive.

And now what remains for me to tell? Her nose was Grecian, but perhaps a little too wide at the nostril to be considered perfect in its chiselling. Her hair was soft and brown,—that dark brown which by some lights is almost black; but she was not a girl whose loveliness depended much upon her hair. With some women it is their great charm,—Neæras who love to sit half sleeping in the shade,—but it is a charm that possesses no powerful eloquence. All beauty of a high order should speak, and Madeleine's beauty was ever speaking. And now that I have said that, I believe that I have told all that may be necessary to place her outward form before the inward eyes of my readers.

In commencing this description I said that I would begin with her exterior; but it seems to me now that in speaking of these I have sufficiently noted also that which was within. Of her actual thoughts and deeds up to this period it is not necessary for our purposes that anything should be told; but of that which she might probably think or might possibly do, a fair guess may, I hope, be made from that which has been already written.

Such was the Staveley family. Those of their guests whom it is necessary that I should now name, have been already introduced to us. Miss Furnival was there, as was also her father. He had not intended to make any prolonged stay at Noningsby,—at least so he had said in his own drawing-room : but nevertheless he had now been there for a week, and it seemed probable that he might stay over Christmas-day. And Felix Graham was there. He had been asked with a special purpose by his friend Augustus, as we already have heard; in order, namely, that he might fall in love with Sophia Furnival, and by the aid of her supposed hatful of money avoid the evils which would otherwise so probably be the consequence of his highly impracticable turn of mind. The judge was not averse to Felix Graham; but as he himself was a man essentially practical in all his views, it often occurred that, in his mild kindly way, he ridiculed the young barrister. And Sir Peregrine Orme was there, being absent from home as on a very rare occasion; and with him of course were Mrs. Orme and his grandson. Young Perry was making, or was prepared to make, somewhat of a prolonged stay at Noningsby. He had a horse there with him for the hunting, which was changed now and again; his groom going backwards and forwards between that place and The Cleeve.

Sir Peregrine, however, intended to return before Christmas, and Mrs. Orme would go with him. He had come for four days, which for him had been a long absence from home, and at the end of the four days he would be gone.

They were all sitting in the dining-room round the luncheon-table on a hopelessly wet morning, listening to a lecture from the judge on the abomination of eating meat in the middle of the day, when a servant came behind young Orme's chair and told him that Mr. Mason was in the breakfast-parlour and wished to see him.

'Who wishes to see you?' said the baronet in a tone of surprise. He had caught the name, and thought at the moment that it was the owner of Groby Park.

'Lucius Mason,' said Peregrine, getting up. 'I wonder what he can want me for?'

'Oh, Lucius Mason,' said the grandfather. Since the discourse about agriculture he was not personally much attached even to Lucius; but for his mother's sake he could be forgiven.

'Pray ask him into lunch,' said Lady Staveley. Something had been said about Lady Mason since the Ormes had been at No-ningsby, and the Staveley family were prepared to regard her with sympathy, and if necessary with the right hand of fellowship.

'He is the great agriculturist, is he not?' said Augustus. 'Bring him in by all means; there is no knowing how much we may not learn before dinner on such a day as this.'

'He is an ally of mine; and you must not laugh at him,' said Miss Furnival, who was sitting next to Augustus.

But Lucius Mason did not come in. Young Orme remained with him for about a quarter of an hour, and then returned to the room, declaring with rather a serious face, that he must ride to Hamworth and back before dinner.

'Are you going with young Mason?' asked his grandfather.

'Yes, sir; he wishes me to do something for him at Hamworth, and I cannot well refuse him.'

'You are not going to fight a duel!' said Lady Staveley, holding up her hands in horror as the idea came across her brain.

'A duel!' screamed Mrs. Orme. 'Oh, Peregrine!'

'There can be nothing of the sort,' said the judge. 'I should think that young Mason is not so foolish; and I am sure that Peregrine Orme is not.'

'I have not heard of anything of the kind,' said Peregrine, laughing.

'Promise me, Peregrine,' said his mother. 'Say that you promise me.'

'My dearest mother, I have no more thought of it than you have;—indeed I may say not so much.'

'You will be back to dinner?' said Lady Staveley.

'Oh yes, certainly.'

'And tell Mr. Mason,' said the judge, 'that if he will return with you we shall be delighted to see him.'

The errand which took Peregrine Orme off to Hamworth will be explained in the next chapter, but his going led to a discussion among the gentlemen after dinner as to the position in which Lady Mason was now placed. There was no longer any possibility of keeping the matter secret, seeing that Mr. Dockwrath had taken great care that every one in Hamworth should hear of it. He had openly declared that evidence would now be adduced to prove that Sir Joseph Mason's widow had herself forged the will, and had said to many people that Mr. Mason of Groby had determined to indict her for forgery. This had gone so far that Lucius had declared as openly that he would prosecute the attorney for a libel, and Dockwrath had sent him word that he was quite welcome to do so if he pleased.

'It is a scandalous state of things,' said Sir Peregrine, speaking with much enthusiasm, and no little temper, on the subject. 'Here is a question which was settled twenty years ago to the satisfaction of every one who knew anything of the case, and now it is brought up again that two men may wreak their vengeance on a poor widow. They are not men; they are brutes.'

'But why does she not bring an action against this attorney?' said young Staveley.

'Such actions do not easily lie,' said his father. 'It may be quite true that Dockwrath may have said all manner of evil things against this lady, and yet it may be very difficult to obtain evidence of a libel. It seems to me from what I have heard that the man himself wishes such an action to be brought.'

'And think of the state of poor Lady Mason!' said Mr. Furnival. 'Conceive the misery which it would occasion her if she were dragged forward to give evidence on such a matter!'

'I believe it would kill her,' said Sir Peregrine.

'The best means of assisting her would be to give her some countenance,' said the judge; 'and from all that I can hear of her, she deserves it.'

'She does deserve it,' said Sir Peregrine, 'and she shall have it. The people at Hamworth shall see at any rate that my daughter regards her as a fit associate. I am happy to say that she is coming to The Cleeve on my return home, and that she will remain there till after Christmas.'

'It is a very singular case,' said Felix Graham, who had been thinking over the position of the lady hitherto in silence.

'Indeed it is,' said the judge; 'and it shows how careful men should be in all matters relating to their wills. The will and the codicil, as it appears, are both in the handwriting of the widow, who acted as an amanuensis not only for her husband but for the attorney. That fact does not in my mind produce suspicion; but I do not doubt that it has produced all this suspicion in the mind of the claimant. The attorney who advised Sir Joseph should have known better.'

'It is one of those cases,' continued Graham, 'in which the sufferer should be protected by the very fact of her own innocence. No lawyer should consent to take up the cudgels against her.'

'I am afraid that she will not escape persecution from any such professional chivalry,' said the judge.

'All that is moonshine,' said Mr. Furnival.

'And moonshine is a very pretty thing if you were not too much afraid of the night air to go and look at it. If the matter be as you all say, I do think that any gentleman would disgrace himself by lending a hand against her.'

'Upon my word, sir, I fully agree with you,' said Sir Peregrine, bowing to Felix Graham over his glass.

'I will take permission to think, Sir Peregrine,' said Mr. Furnival, 'that you would not agree with Mr. Graham if you had given to the matter much deep consideration.'

'I have not had the advantage of a professional education,' said Sir Peregrine, again bowing, and on this occasion addressing himself to the lawyer; 'but I cannot see how any amount of learning should alter my views on such a subject.'

'Truth and honour cannot be altered by any professional arrangements,' said Graham; and then the conversation turned away from Lady Mason, and directed itself to those great corrections of legal reform which had been debated during the past autumn.

The Orley Farm Case, though in other forms and different language, was being discussed also in the drawing-room. 'I have not seen much of her,' said Sophia Furnival, who by some art had usurped the most prominent part in the conversation, 'but what I did see I liked much. She was at The Cleeve when I was staying there, if you remember, Mrs. Orme.' Mrs. Orme said that she did remember.

'And we went over to Orley Farm. Poor lady! I think everybody ought to notice her under such circumstances. Papa, I know, would move heaven and earth for her if he could.'

'I cannot move the heaven or the earth either,' said Lady Staveley; 'but if I thought that my calling on her would be any satisfaction to her——'

'It would, Lady Staveley,' said Mrs. Orme. 'It would be a great satisfaction to her. I cannot tell you how warmly I regard her, nor how perfectly Sir Peregrine esteems her.'

'We will drive over there next week, Madeline.'

'Do, mamma. Everybody says that she is very nice.'

'It will be so kind of you, Lady Staveley,' said Sophia Furnival.

'Next week she will be staying with us,' said Mrs. Orme. 'And that would save you three miles, you know, and we should be so glad to see you.'

Lady Staveley declared that she would do both. She would call at The Cleeve, and again at Orley Farm after Lady Mason's return home. She well understood, though she could not herself then say so, that the greater part of the advantage to be received from her kindness would be derived from its being known at Hamworth that the Staveley carriage had been driven up to Lady Mason's door.

'Her son is very clever, is he not?' said Madeline, addressing herself to Miss Furnival.

Sophia shrugged her shoulders and put her head on one side with a pretty grace. 'Yes, I believe so. People say so. But who is to tell whether a young man be clever or no?'

'But some are so much more clever than others. Don't you think so?'

'Oh yes, as some girls are so much prettier than others. But if Mr. Mason were to talk Greek to you, you would not think him clever.'

'I should not understand him, you know.'

'Of course not; but you would understand that he was a blockhead to show off his learning in that way. You don't want him to be clever, you see; you only want him to be agreeable.'

'I don't know that I want either the one or the other.'

'Do you not? I know I do. I think that young men in society are bound to be agreeable, and that they should not be there if they do not know how to talk pleasantly, and to give something in return for all the trouble we take for them.'

'I don't take any trouble for them,' said Madeline laughing.

'Surely you must, if you only think of it. All ladies do, and so they ought. But if in return for that a man merely talks Greek to me, I, for my part, do not think that the bargain is fairly carried out.'

'I declare you will make me quite afraid of Mr. Mason.'

'Oh, he never talks Greek:—at least he never has to me. I rather like him. But what I mean is this, that I do not think a man a bit more likely to be agreeable because he has the reputation of being very clever. For my part I rather think that I like stupid young men.'

'Oh, do you? Then now I shall know what you think of Augustus. We think he is very clever; but I do not know any man who makes himself more popular with young ladies.'

'Ah, then he is a gay deceiver.'

'He is gay enough, but I am sure he is no deceiver. A man may make himself nice to young ladies without deceiving any of them; may he not?'

' You must not take me " au pied de la lettre," Miss Staveley, or I shall be lost. Of course he may. But when young gentlemen are so very nice, young ladies are so apt to——'

' To what?'

' Not to fall in love with them exactly, but to be ready to be fallen in love with; and then if a man does do it he is a deceiver. I declare it seems to me that we don't allow them a chance of going right.'

' I think that Augustus manages to steer through such difficulties very cleverly.'

' He sails about in the open sea, touching at all the most lovely capes and promontories, and is never driven on shore by stress of weather! What a happy sailor he must be!'

' I think he is happy, and that he makes others so.'

' He ought to be made an admiral at once. But we shall hear some day of his coming to a terrible shipwreck.'

' Oh, I hope not!'

' He will return home in desperate plight, with only two planks left together, with all his glory and beauty broken and crumpled to pieces against some rock that he has despised in his pride.'

' Why do you prophesy such terrible things for him?'

' I mean that he will get married.'

' Get married! of course he will. That's just what we all want. You don't call that a shipwreck; do you?'

' It's the sort of shipwreck that these very gallant barks have to encounter.'

' You don't mean that he'll marry a disagreeable wife!'

' Oh, no; not in the least. I only mean to say that like other sons of Adam, he will have to strike his colours. I dare say, if the truth were known, he has done so already.'

' I am sure he has not.'

' I don't at all ask to know his secrets, and I should look upon you as a very bad sister if you told them.'

' But I am sure he has not got any,—of that kind.'

' Would he tell you if he had?'

' Oh, I hope so; any serious secret. I am sure he ought, for I am always thinking about him.'

' And would you tell him your secrets?'

' I have none.'

' But when you have, will you do so?'

' Will I? Well, yes; I think so. But a girl has no such secret,' she continued to say, after pausing for a moment. ' None, generally, at least, which she tells, even to herself, till the time comes in which she tells it to all whom she really loves.' And then there was another pause for a moment.

' I am not quite so sure of that,' said Miss Furnival. After which the gentlemen came into the drawing-room.

Augustus Staveley had gone to work in a manner which he conceived to be quite systematic, having before him the praiseworthy object of making a match between Felix Graham and Sophia Furnival. ' By George, Graham,' he had said, ' the finest girl in London is coming down to Noningsby; upon my word I think she is.'

' And brought there expressly for your delectation, I suppose.'

' Oh no, not at all; indeed, she is not exactly in my style; she is too,—too,—too— in point of fact, too much of a girl for me. She has lots of money, and is very clever, and all that kind of thing.'

' I never knew you so humble before.'

' I am not joking at all. She is a daughter of old Furnival's, whom by-the-by I hate as I do poison. Why my governor has him down at Noningsby I can't guess. But I tell you what, old fellow, he can give his daughter five-and-twenty thousand pounds. Think of that, Master Brook.' But Felix Graham was a man who could not bring himself to think much of such things on the spur of the moment, and when he was introduced to Sophia, he did not seem to be taken with her in any wonderful way.

Augustus had asked his mother to help him, but she had laughed at him. ' It would be a splendid arrangement,' he had said with energy. ' Nonsense, Gus,' she had answered. ' You should always let those things take their chance. All I will ask of you is that you don't fall in love with her yourself; I don't think her family would be nice enough for you.'

But Felix Graham certainly was ungrateful for the friendship spent upon him, and so his friend felt it. Augustus had contrived to whisper into the lady's ear that Mr. Graham was the cleverest young man now rising at the bar, and as far as she was concerned, some amount of intimacy might at any rate have been produced; but he, Graham himself, would not put himself forward. ' I will pique him into it,' said Augustus to himself, and therefore when on this occasion they came into the drawing-room, Staveley immediately took a vacant seat beside Miss Furnival, with the very friendly object which he had proposed to himself.

There was great danger in this, for Miss Furnival was certainly handsome, and Augustus Staveley was very susceptible. But what will not a man go through for his friend? ' I hope we are to have the honour of your company as far as Monkton Grange the day we meet there,' he said. The hounds were to meet at Monkton Grange, some seven miles from Noningsby, and all the sportsmen from the house were to be there.

' I shall be delighted,' said Sophia, ' that is to say if a seat in the carriage can be spared for me.'

'But we'll mount you. I know that you are a horsewoman.' In answer to which Miss Furnival confessed that she was a horse-woman, and owned also to having brought a habit and hat with her.

'That will be delightful. Madeline will ride also, and you will meet the Miss Tristrams. They are the famous horsewomen of this part of the country.'

'You don't mean that they go after the dogs, across the hedges.'

'Indeed they do.'

'And does Miss Staveley do that?'

'Oh, no—Madeline is not good at a five-barred gate, and would make but a very bad hand at a double ditch. If you are inclined to remain among the tame people, she will be true to your side.'

'I shall certainly be one of the tame people, Mr. Staveley.'

'I rather think I shall be with you myself; I have only one horse that will jump well, and Graham will ride him. By-the-by, Miss Furnival, what do you think of my friend Graham?'

'Think of him! Am I bound to have thought anything about him by this time?'

'Of course you are;—or at any rate of course you have. I have no doubt that you have composed in your own mind an essay on the character of everybody here. People who think at all always do.'

'Do they? My essay upon him then is a very short one.'

'But perhaps not the less correct on that account. You must allow me to read it.'

'Like all my other essays of that kind, Mr. Staveley, it has been composed solely for my own use, and will be kept quite private.'

'I am so sorry for that, for I intended to propose a bargain to you. If you would have shown me some of your essays, I would have been equally liberal with some of mine.' And in this way, before the evening was over, Augustus Staveley and Miss Furnival became very good friends.

'Upon my word she is a very clever girl,' he said afterwards, as young Orme and Graham were sitting with him in an outside room which had been fitted up for smoking.

'And uncommonly handsome,' said Peregrine.

'And they say she'll have lots of money,' said Graham. 'After all, Staveley, perhaps you could not do better.'

'She's not my style at all,' said he. 'But of course a man is obliged to be civil to girls in his own house.' And then they all went to bed.

CHAPTER XX.

MR. DOCKWRATH IN HIS OWN OFFICE.

In the conversation which had taken place after dinner at Noningsby with regard to the Masons Peregrine Orme took no part, but his silence had not arisen from any want of interest on the subject. He had been over to Hamworth that day on a very special mission regarding it, and as he was not inclined to speak of what he had then seen and done, he held his tongue altogether.

'I want you to do me a great favour,' Lucius had said to him, when the two were together in the breakfast-parlour of Noningsby; 'but I am afraid it will give you some trouble.'

'I sha'n't mind that,' said Peregrine, 'if that's all.'

'You have heard of this row about Joseph Mason and my mother? It has been so talked of that I fear you must have heard it.'

'About the lawsuit? Oh yes. It has certainly been spoken of at The Cleeve.'

'Of course it has. All the world is talking of it. Now there is a man named Dockwrath in Hamworth—;' and then he went on to explain how it had reached him from various quarters that Mr. Dockwrath was accusing his mother of the crime of forgery; how he had endeavoured to persuade his mother to indict the man for libel; how his mother had pleaded to him with tears in her eyes that she found it impossible to go through such an ordeal; and how he, therefore, had resolved to go himself to Mr. Dockwrath. 'But,' said he, 'I must have some one with me, some gentleman whom I can trust, and therefore I have ridden over to ask you to accompany me as far as Hamworth.'

'I suppose he is not a man that you can kick,' said Peregrine.

'I am afraid not,' said Lucius; 'he's over forty years old, and has dozens of children.'

'And then he is such a low beast,' said Peregrine.

'I have no idea of kicking him, but I think it would be wrong to allow him to go on saying these frightful things of my mother, without showing him that we are not afraid of him.' Upon this the two young men got on horseback, and riding into Hamworth, put their horses up at the inn.

' And now I suppose we might as well go at once,' said Peregrine,
with a very serious face.

' Yes,' said the other; ' there's nothing to delay us.   I cannot
tell you how much obliged I am to you for coming with me.'

' Oh, don't say anything about that; of course I'm only too
happy.'   But all the same he felt that his heart was beating, and
that he was a little nervous.   Had he been called upon to go in and
thrash somebody, he would have been quite at home; but he did
not feel at his ease in making an inimical visit to an attorney's
office.

It would have been wise, perhaps, if in this matter Lucius had
submitted himself to Lady Mason's wishes.   On the previous
evening they had talked the matter over with much serious energy.
Lucius had been told in the streets of Hamworth by an inter-
meddling little busybody of an apothecary that it behoved him to
do something, as Mr. Dockwrath was making grievous accusations
against his mother.   Lucius had replied haughtily, that he and his
mother would know how to protect themselves, and the apothecary
had retreated, resolving to spread the report everywhere.   Lucius
on his return home had declared to the unfortunate lady that she
had now no alternative left to her.   She must bring an action against
the man, or at any rate put the matter into the hands of a lawyer
with a view of ascertaining whether she could do so with any chance
of success.   If she could not, she must then make known her reason
for remaining quiet.   In answer to this, Lady Mason had begun by
praying her son to allow the matter to pass by.

' But it will not pass by,' Lucius had said.

' Yes, dearest, if we leave it, it will,—in a month or two.   We
can do nothing by interference.   Remember the old saying, You
cannot touch pitch without being defiled.'

But Lucius had replied, almost with anger, that the pitch had
already touched him, and that he was defiled.   ' I cannot consent
to hold the property,' he had said, ' unless something be done.'
And then his mother had bowed her head as she sat, and had covered
her face with her hands.

' I shall go to the man myself,' Lucius had declared with energy.

' As your mother, Lucius, I implore you not to do so,' she had said
to him through her tears.

' I must either do that or leave the country.   It is impossible
that I should live here, hearing such things said of you, and doing
nothing to clear your name.'   To this she had made no actual reply,
and now he was standing at the attorney's door about to do that
which he had threatened.

They found Mr. Dockwrath sitting at his desk at the other side
of which was seated his clerk.   He had not yet promoted himself to
the dignity of a private office, but generally used his parlour as

such when he was desirous of seeing his clients without disturbance. On this occasion, however, when he saw young Mason enter, he made no offer to withdraw. His hat was on his head as he sat on his stool, and he did not even take it off as he returned the stiff salutation of his visitor. 'Keep your hat on your head Mr. Orme,' he said, as Peregrine was about to take his off. 'Well, gentlemen, what can I do for you?'

Lucius looked at the clerk, and felt that there would be great difficulty in talking about his mother before such a witness. 'We wish to see you in private, Mr. Dockwrath, for a few minutes—if it be convenient.'

'Is not this private enough?' said Dockwrath. 'There is no one here but my confidential clerk.'

'If you could make it convenient——' began Lucius.

'Well, then, Mr. Mason, I cannot make it convenient, and there is the long and the short of it. You have brought Mr. Orme with you to hear what you've got to say, and I choose that my clerk shall remain by to hear it also. Seeing the position in which you stand there is no knowing what may come of such an interview as this.'

'In what position do I stand, sir?'

'If you don't know, Mr. Mason, I am not going to tell you. I feel for you, I do upon my word. I feel for you, and I pity you.' Mr. Dockwrath as he thus expressed his commiseration was sitting with his high chair tilted back, with his knees against the edge of his desk, with his hat almost down upon his nose as he looked at his visitors from under it, and he amused himself by cutting up a quill pen into small pieces with his penknife. It was not pleasant to be pitied by such a man as that, and so Peregrine Orme conceived.

'Sir, that is nonsense,' said Lucius. 'I require no pity from you or from any man.'

'I don't suppose there is one in all Hamworth that does not feel for you,' said Dockwrath.

'He means to be impudent,' said Peregrine. 'You had better come to the point with him at once.'

'No, I don't mean to be impudent, young gentleman. A man may speak his own mind in his own house I suppose without any impudence. You wouldn't stand cap in hand to me if I were to go down to you at The Cleeve.

'I have come here to ask of you,' said Lucius, 'whether it be true that you are spreading these reports about the town with reference to Lady Mason. If you are a man you will tell me the truth.'

'Well; I rather think I am a man.'

'It is necessary that Lady Mason should be protected from such

infamous falsehoods, and it may be necessary to bring the matter
into a court of law——'

'You may be quite easy about that, Mr. Mason. It will be
necessary.'

'As it may be necessary, I wish to know whether you will acknowledge that these reports have come from you?'

'You want me to give evidence against myself. Well, for once
in a way I don't mind if I do. The reports have come from me.
Now, is that manly?' And Mr. Dockwrath, as he spoke, pushed his
hat somewhat off his nose, and looked steadily across into the face
of his opponent.

Lucius Mason was too young for the task which he had undertaken, and allowed himself to be disconcerted. He had expected
that the lawyer would deny the charge, and was prepared for
what he would say and do in such a case; but now he was not
prepared.

'How on earth could you bring yourself to be guilty of such
villainy?' said young Orme.

'Highty-tighty! What are you talking about, young man? The
fact is, you do not know what you are talking about. But as I have
a respect for your grandfather and for your mother I will give you
and them a piece of advice, gratis. Don't let them be too thick
with Lady Mason till they see how this matter goes.'

'Mr. Dockwrath,' said Lucius, 'you are a mean, low, vile
scoundrel.'

'Very well, sir. Adams, just take a note of that. Don't mind
what Mr. Orme said. I can easily excuse him. He'll know the
truth before long, and then he'll beg my pardon.'

'I'll take my oath I look upon you as the greatest miscreant that
ever I met,' said Peregrine, who was of course bound to support his
friend.

'You'll change your mind, Mr. Orme, before long, and then you'll
find that you have met a worse miscreant than I am. Did you put
down those words, Adams?'

'Them as Mr. Mason spoke? Yes; I've got them down.'

'Read them,' said the master.

And the clerk read them, 'Mr. Dockwrath, you are a mean, low,
vile scoundrel.'

'And now, young gentlemen, if you have got nothing else to
observe, as I am rather busy, perhaps you will allow me to wish you
good morning.'

'Very well, Mr. Dockwrath,' said Mason; 'you may be sure that
you will hear further from me.'

'We shall be sure to hear of each other. There is no doubt in
the world about that,' said the attorney. And then the two young
men withdrew with an unexpressed feeling in the mind of each of

them, that they had not so completely got the better of their antagonist as the justice of their case demanded.

They then remounted their horses, and Orme accompanied his
friend as far as Orley Farm, from whence he got into the Alston
road through The Cleeve grounds. ' And what do you intend to do
now ?' said Peregrine as soon as they were mounted.

' I shall employ a lawyer,' said he, ' on my own footing; not my
mother's lawyer, but some one else. Then I suppose I shall be
guided by his advice.' Had he done this before he made his visit to
Mr. Dockwrath, perhaps it might have been better. All this sat
very heavily on poor Peregrine's mind; and therefore as the company
were talking about Lady Mason after dinner, he remained silent,
listening, but not joining in the conversation.

The whole of that evening Lucius and his mother sat together,
saying nothing. There was not absolutely any quarrel between
them, but on this terrible subject there was an utter want of accordance, and almost of sympathy. It was not that Lucius had ever
for a moment suspected his mother of aught that was wrong. Had
he done so he might perhaps have been more gentle towards her
in his thoughts and words. He not only fully trusted her, but he
was quite fixed in his confidence that nothing could shake either
her or him in their rights. But under these circumstances he could
not understand how she could consent to endure without resistance
the indignities which were put upon her. ' She should combat
them for my sake, if not for her own,' he said to himself over and
over again. And he had said so also to her, but his words had had
no effect.

She, on the other hand, felt that he was cruel to her. She was
weighed down almost to the ground by these sufferings which had
fallen on her, and yet he would not be gentle and soft to her. She
could have borne it all, she thought, if he would have borne with
her. She still hoped that if she remained quiet no further trial
would take place. At any rate this might be so. That it would be
so she had the assurance of Mr. Furnival. And yet all this evil
which she dreaded worse than death was to be precipitated on her
oy her son! So they sat through the long evening, speechless; each
seated with the pretence of reading, but neither of them capable of
the attention which a book requires.

He did not tell her then that he had been with Mr. Dockwrath,
but she knew by his manner that he had taken some terrible step.
She waited patiently the whole evening, hoping that he would tell
her, but when the hour came for her to go up to her room he had
told her nothing. If he now were to turn against her, that would
be worse than all! She went up to her room and sat herself down
to think. All that passed through her brain on that night I may
not now tell; but the grief which pressed on her at this moment

with peculiar weight was the self-will and obstinacy of her boy.
She said to herself that she would be willing now to die,—to give
back her life at once, if such might be God's pleasure; but that
her son should bring down her hairs with shame and sorrow to the
grave——! In that thought there was a bitterness of agony which
she knew not how to endure!

The next morning at breakfast he still remained silent, and his
brow was still black. ' Lucius,' she said, ' did you do anything in
that matter yesterday?'

' Yes, mother; I saw Mr. Dockwrath.'

' Well?'

' I took Peregrine Orme with me that I might have a witness,
and I then asked him whether he had spread these reports. He acknowledged that he had done so, and I told him that he was a
villain.'

Upon hearing this she uttered a long, low sigh, but she said
nothing. What use could there now be in her saying aught? Her
look of agony went to the young man's heart, but he still thought
that he had been right. ' Mother,' he continued to say, ' I am very
sorry to grieve you in this way;—very sorry. But I could not hold
up my head in Hamworth,—I could not hold up my head anywhere,
if I heard these things said of you and did not resent it.'

' Ah, Lucius, if you knew the weakness of a woman!'

' And therefore you should let me bear it all. There is nothing
I would not suffer; no cost I would not undergo rather than you
should endure all this. If you would only say that you would leave
it to me!'

' But it cannot be left to you. I have gone to a lawyer, to Mr.
Furnival. Why will you not permit that I should act in it as he
thinks best? Can you not believe that that will be the best for both
of us?'

' If you wish it, I will see Mr. Furnival?'

Lady Mason did not wish that, but she was obliged so far to yield
as to say that he might do so if he would. Her wish was that he
should bear it all and say nothing. It was not that she was indifferent to good repute among her neighbours, or that she was careless
as to what the apothecaries and attorneys said of her; but it was
easier for her to bear the evil than to combat it. The Ormes and
the Furnivals would support her. They and such-like persons
would acknowledge her weakness, and would know that from her
would not be expected such loud outbursting indignation as might
be expected from a man. She had calculated the strength of her
own weakness, and thought that she might still be supported by
that,—if only her son would so permit.

It was two days after this that Lucius was allowed the honour of
a conference by appointment with the great lawyer; and at the ex-

piration of an hour's delay he was shown into the room by Mr. Crabwitz. ' And, Crabwitz,' said the barrister, before he addressed himself to his young friend, ' just run your eye over those papers, and let Mr. Bideawhile have them to-morrow morning; and, Crabwitz——.'

' Yes, sir.'

' That opinion of Sir Richard's in the Ahatualpaca Mining Company—I have not seen it, have I ?'

' It's all ready, Mr. Furnival.'

' I will look at it in five minutes. And now, my young friend, what can I do for you ?'

It was quite clear from Mr. Furnival's tone and manner that he did not mean to devote much time to Lucius Mason, and that he was not generally anxious to hold any conversation with him on the subject in question. Such, indeed, was the case. Mr. Furnival was determined to pull Lady Mason out of the sea of trouble into which she had fallen, let the effort cost him what it might, but he did not wish to do so by the instrumentality, or even with the aid, of her son.

' Mr. Furnival,' began Mason, ' I want to ask your advice about these dreadful reports which are being spread on every side in Hamworth about my mother.'

' If you will allow me then to say so, I think that the course which you should pursue is very simple. Indeed there is, I think, only one course which you can pursue with proper deference to your mother's feelings.'

' And what is that, Mr. Furnival ?'

' Do nothing, and say nothing. I fear from what I have heard that you have already done and said much more than was prudent.'

' But how am I to hear such things as these spoken of my own mother ?'

' That depends on the people by whom the things are spoken. In this world, if we meet a chimney-sweep in the path we do not hustle with him for the right of way. Your mother is going next week to The Cleeve. It was only yesterday that I heard that the Noningsby people are going to call on her. You can hardly, I suppose, desire for your mother better friends than such as these. And can you not understand why such people gather to her at this moment? If you can understand it you will not trouble yourself to interfere much more with Mr. Dockwrath.'

There was a rebuke in this which Lucius Mason was forced to endure; but nevertheless as he retreated disconcerted from the barrister's chambers, he could not bring himself to think it right that such calumny should be borne without resistance. He knew but little as yet of the ordinary life of gentlemen in England; but he did know,—so at least he thought,—that it was the duty of a son to shield his mother from insult and libel.

CHAPTER XXI.

IT seems singular to me myself, considering the idea which I have in my own mind of the character of Lady Staveley, that I should be driven to declare that about this time she committed an unpardonable offence, not only against good nature, but also against the domestic proprieties. But I am driven so to say, although she herself was of all women the most good-natured and most domestic; for she asked Mr. Furnival to pass his Christmas-day at Noningsby, and I find it impossible to forgive her that offence against the poor wife whom in that case he must leave alone by her desolate hearth. She knew that he was a married man as well as I do. Sophia, who had a proper regard for the domestic peace of her parents, and who could have been happy at Noningsby without a father's care, not unfrequently spoke of her, so that her existence in Harley Street might not be forgotten by the Staveleys—explaining, however, as she did so, that her dear mother never left her own fireside in winter, so that no suspicion might be entertained that an invitation was desired for her also; nevertheless, in spite of all this, on two separate occasions did Lady Staveley say to Mr. Furnival that he might as well prolong his visit over Christmas.

And yet Lady Staveley was not attached to Mr. Furnival with any peculiar warmth of friendship; but she was one of those women whose foolish hearts will not allow themselves to be controlled in the exercise of their hospitality. Her nature demanded of her that she should ask a guest to stay. She would not have allowed a dog to depart from her house at this season of the year, without suggesting to him that he had better take his Christmas bone in her yard. It was for Mr. Furnival to adjust all matters between himself and his wife. He was not bound to accept the invitation because she gave it; but she, finding him there, already present in the house, did feel herself bound to give it;—for which offence, as I have said before, I cannot bring myself to forgive her.

At his sin in staying away from home, or rather—as far as the story has yet carried us—in thinking that he would do so, I am by no means so much surprised. An angry ill-pleased wife is no pleasant companion for a gentleman on a long evening. For those who

have managed that things shall run smoothly over the domestic rug
there is no happier time of life than these long candlelight hours of
home and silence. No spoken content or uttered satisfaction is
necessary. The fact that is felt is enough for peace. But when
the fact is not felt; when the fact is by no means there; when the
thoughts are running in a direction altogether different; when
bitter grievances from one to the other fill the heart, rather than
memories of mutual kindness; then, I say, those long candlelight
hours of home and silence are not easy of endurance. Mr. Furnival
was a man who chose to be the master of his own destiny, so at
least to himself he boasted; and therefore when he found himself
encountered by black looks and occasionally by sullen words, he
declared to himself that he was ill-used and that he would not bear
it. Since the domestic rose would no longer yield him honey, he
would seek his sweets from the stray honeysuckle on which there
grew no thorns.

Mr. Furnival was no coward. He was not one of those men who
wrong their wives by their absence, and then prolong their absence
because they are afraid to meet their wives. His resolve was to
be free himself, and to be free without complaint from her. He
would have it so, that he might remain out of his own house for a
month at the time and then return to it for a week—at any rate
without outward bickerings. I have known other men who have
dreamed of such a state of things, but at this moment I can remember
none who have brought their dream to bear.

Mr. Furnival had written to his wife,—not from Noningsby, but
from some provincial town, probably situated among the Essex
marshes,—saying various things, and among others that he should
not, as he thought, be at home at Christmas-day. Mrs. Furnival
had remarked about a fortnight since that Christmas-day was
nothing to her now; and the base man, for it was base, had hung
upon this poor, sore-hearted word an excuse for remaining away
from home. 'There are lawyers of repute staying at Noningsby,'
he had said, 'with whom it is very expedient that I should remain
at this present crisis.'—When yet has there been no crisis present to
a man who has wanted an excuse?—'And therefore I may probably
stay,'—and so on. Who does not know the false mixture of excuse
and defiance which such a letter is sure to maintain; the crafty words
which may be taken as adequate reason if the receiver be timid
enough so to receive them, or as a noisy gauntlet thrown to the
ground if there be spirit there for the picking of it up? Such letter
from his little borough in the Essex marshes did Mr. Furnival write
to the partner of his cares, and there was still sufficient spirit left for
the picking up of the gauntlet. 'I shall be home to-morrow,' the
letter had gone on to say, 'but I will not keep you waiting for
dinner, as my hours are always so uncertain. I shall be at my

chambers till late, and will be with you before tea. I will then return to Alston on the following morning.' There was at any rate good courage in this on the part of Mr. Furnival;—great courage; but with it coldness of heart, dishonesty of purpose, and black ingratitude. Had she not given everything to him?

Mrs. Furnival when she got the letter was not alone. 'There,' said she, throwing it over to a lady who sat on the other side of the fireplace handling a loose sprawling mass of not very clean crochet-work. 'I knew he would stay away on Christmas-day. I told you so.'

'I didn't think it possible,' said Miss Biggs, rolling up the big ball of soiled cotton, that she might read Mr. Furnival's letter at her leisure. 'I didn't really think it possible—on Christmas-day! Surely, Mrs. Furnival, he can't mean Christmas-day? Dear, dear, dear! and then to throw it in your face in that way that you said you didn't care about it.'

'Of course I said so,' answered Mrs. Furnival. 'I was not going to ask him to come home as a favour.'

'Not to make a favour of it, of course not.' This was Miss Biggs from ——. I am afraid if I tell the truth I must say that she came from Red Lion Square! And yet nothing could be more respectable than Miss Biggs. Her father had been a partner with an uncle of Mrs. Furnival's; and when Kitty Blacker had given herself and her young prettinesses to the hardworking lawyer, Martha Biggs had stood at the altar with her, then just seventeen years of age, and had promised to her all manner of success for her coming life. Martha Biggs had never, not even then, been pretty; but she had been very faithful. She had not been a favourite with Mr. Furnival, having neither wit nor grace to recommend her, and therefore in the old happy days of Keppel Street she had been kept in the background; but now, in this present time of her adversity, Mrs. Furnival found the benefit of having a trusty friend.

'If he likes better to be with these people down at Alston, I am sure it is the same to me,' said the injured wife.

'But there's nobody special at Alston, is there?' asked Miss Biggs, whose soul sighed for a tale more piquant than one of mere general neglect. She knew that her friend had dreadful suspicions, but Mrs. Furnival had never as yet committed herself by uttering the name of any woman as her rival. Miss Biggs thought that a time had now come in which the strength of their mutual confidence demanded that such name should be uttered. It could not be expected that she should sympathize with generalities for ever. She longed to hate, to reprobate, and to shudder at the actual name of the wretch who had robbed her friend of a husband's heart. And therefore she asked the question, 'There's nobody special at Alston, is there?'

Now Mrs. Furnival knew to a furlong the distance from Noningsby to Orley Farm, and knew also that the station at Hamworth was only twenty-five minutes from that at Alston. She gave no immediate answer, but threw up her head and shook her nostrils, as though she were preparing for war; and then Miss Martha Biggs knew that there was somebody special at Alston. Between such old friends why should not the name be mentioned?

On the following day the two ladies dined at six, and then waited tea patiently till ten. Had the thirst of a desert been raging within that drawing-room, and had tea been within immediate call, those ladies would have died ere they would have asked for it before his return. He had said he would be home to tea, and they would have waited for him, had it been till four o'clock in the morning! Let the female married victim ever make the most of such positive wrongs as Providence may vouchsafe to her. Had Mrs. Furnival ordered tea on this evening before her husband's return, she would have been a woman blind to the advantages of her own position. At ten the wheels of Mr. Furnival's cab were heard, and the faces of both the ladies prepared themselves for the encounter.

'Well, Kitty, how are you?' said Mr. Furnival, entering the room with his arms prepared for a premeditated embrace. 'What, Miss Biggs with you? I did not know. How do you do, Miss Biggs?' and Mr. Furnival extended his hand to the lady. They both looked at him, and they could tell from the brightness of his eye and from the colour of his nose that he had been dining at his club, and that the bin with the precious cork had been visited on his behalf.

'Yes, my dear; it's rather lonely being here in this big room all by oneself so long; so I asked Martha Biggs to come over to me. I suppose there's no harm in that.'

'Oh, if I'm in the way,' began Miss Biggs, 'or if Mr. Furnival is going to stay at home for long——'

'You are not in the way, and I am not going to stay at home for long,' said Mr. Furnival, speaking with a voice that was perhaps a little thick,—only a very little thick. No wife on good terms with her husband would have deigned to notice, even in her own mind, an amount of thickness of voice which was so very inconsiderable. But Mrs. Furnival at the present moment did notice it.

'Oh, I did not know,' said Miss Biggs.

'You know now,' said Mr. Furnival, whose ear at once appreciated the hostility of tone which had been assumed.

'You need not be rude to my friend after she has been waiting tea for you till near eleven o'clock,' said Mrs. Furnival. 'It is nothing to me, but you should remember that she is not used to it.'

'I wasn't rude to your friend, and who asked you to wait tea till near eleven o'clock? It is only just ten now, if that signifies.'

' You expressly desired me to wait tea, Mr. Furnival. I have got
your letter, and will show it you if you wish it.'

' Nonsense ; I just said I should be home——'

' Of course you just said you would be home, and so we waited ;
and it's not nonsense ; and I declare——! Never mind, Martha,
don't mind me, there's a good creature. I shall get over it soon ;'
and then fat, solid, good-humoured Mrs. Furnival burst out into
an hysterical fit of sobbing. There was a welcome for a man on
his return to his home after a day's labour !

Miss Biggs immediately got up and came round behind the
drawing-room table to her friend's head. ' Be calm, Mrs. Furnival,'
she said ; ' do be calm, and then you will be better soon. Here is
the hartshorn.'

' It doesn't matter, Martha : never mind : leave me alone,' sobbed
the poor woman.

' May I be excused for asking what is really the matter ?' said
Mr. Furnival, ' for I'll be whipped if I know.' Miss Biggs looked
at him as if she thought that he ought to be whipped.

' I wonder you ever come near the place at all, I do,' said
Mrs. Furnival.

' What place ?' asked Mr. Furnival.

' This house in which I am obliged to live by myself, without a
soul to speak to, unless when Martha Biggs comes here.'

' Which would be much more frequent, only that I know I am
not welcome to everybody.'

' I know that you hate it. How can I help knowing it ?—and
you hate me too ; I know you do ;—and I believe you would be
glad if you need never come back here at all ; I do. Don't,
Martha ; leave me alone. I don't want all that fuss. There ; I can
hear it now, whatever it is. Do you choose to have your tea,
Mr. Furnival ? or do you wish to keep the servants waiting out of
their beds all night ?'

' D—— the servants,' said Mr. Furnival.

' Oh laws !' exclaimed Miss Biggs, jumping up out of her chair
with her hands and fingers outstretched, as though never, never in
her life before, had her ears been wounded by such wicked words
as those.

' Mr. Furnival, I am ashamed of you,' said his wife with gathered
calmness of stern reproach.

Mr. Furnival was very wrong to swear ; doubly wrong to swear
before his wife ; trebly wrong to swear before a lady visitor ; but it
must be confessed that there was provocation. That he was at this
present period of his life behaving badly to his wife must be
allowed, but on this special evening he had intended to behave well.
The woman had sought a ground of quarrel against him, and had
driven him on till he had forgotten himself in his present after-

dinner humour. When a man is maintaining a whole household on his own shoulders, and working hard to maintain it well, it is not right that he should be brought to book because he keeps the servants up half an hour later than usual to wash the tea-things. It is very proper that the idle members of the establishment should conform to hours, but these hours must give way to his require-ments. In those old days of which we have spoken so often he might have had his tea at twelve, one, two, or three without a murmur. Though their staff of servants then was scanty enough, there was never a difficulty then in supplying any such want for him. If no other pair of hands could boil the kettle, there was one pair of hands there which no amount of such work on his behalf could tire. But now, because he had come in for his tea at ten o'clock, he was asked if he intended to keep the servants out of their beds all night!

' Oh laws!' said Miss Biggs, jumping up from her chair as though she had been electrified.

Mr. Furnival did not think it consistent with his dignity to keep up any dispute in the presence of Miss Biggs, and therefore sat himself down in his accustomed chair without further speech. 'Would you wish to have tea now, Mr. Furnival?' asked his wife again, putting considerable stress upon the word now.

' I don't care about it,' said he.

' And I am sure I don't at this late hour,' said Miss Biggs. ' But so tired as you are, dear—'

' Never mind me, Martha; as for myself, I shall take nothing now.' And then they all sat without a word for the space of some five minutes. ' If you like to go, Martha,' said Mrs. Furnival, ' don't mind waiting for me.'

' Oh, very well,' and then Miss Biggs took her bed-candle and left the room. Was it not hard upon her that she should be forced to absent herself at this moment, when the excitement of the battle was about to begin in earnest? Her footsteps lingered as she slowly re-treated from the drawing-room door, and for one instant she absolutely paused, standing still with eager ears. It was but for an instant, and then she went on up stairs, out of hearing, and sitting herself down by her bedside allowed the battle to rage in her imagination.

Mr. Furnival would have sat there silent till his wife had gone also, and so the matter would have terminated for that evening,—had she so willed it. But she had been thinking of her miseries; and, having come to some sort of resolution to speak of then openly, what time could she find more appropriate for doing so than the present? ' Tom,' she said,—and as she spoke there was still a twinkle of the old love in her eye, ' we are not going on together as well as we should do,—not lately. Would it not be well to make a change before it is too late?'

' What change?' he asked; not exactly in an ill humour, but with
a husky, thick voice. He would have preferred now that she
should have followed her friend to bed.

' I do not want to dictate to you, Tom, but—! Oh Tom, if you
knew how wretched I am!'

' What makes you wretched?'

' Because you leave me all alone; because you care more for
other people than you do for me; because you never like to be at
home, never if you can possibly help it. You know you don't.
You are always away now upon some excuse or other; you know
you are. I don't have you home to dinner not one day ,in the
week through the year. That can't be right, and you know it is
not. Oh Tom! you are breaking my heart, and deceiving me,—
you are. Why did I go down and find that woman in your
chamber with you, when you were ashamed to own to me that she
was coming to see you? If it had been in the proper way of law
business, you wouldn't have been ashamed. Oh Tom!'

The poor woman had begun her plaint in a manner that was not
altogether devoid of a discreet eloquence. If only she could have
maintained that tone, if she could have confined her words to the tale
of her own grievances, and have been contented to declare that she
was unhappy, only because he was not with her, it might have
been well. She might have touched his heart, or at any rate his
conscience, and there might have been some enduring result for
good. But her feelings had been too many for her, and as her
wrongs came to her mind, and the words heaped themselves upon
her tongue, she could not keep herself from the one subject which
she should have left untouched. Mr. Furnival was not the man to
bear any interference such as this, or to permit the privacy of
Lincoln's Inn to be invaded even by his wife. His brow grew
very black, and his eyes became almost bloodshot. The port wine
which might have worked him to softness, now worked him to
anger, and he thus burst forth with words of marital vigour:

' Let me tell you once for ever, Kitty, that I will admit of no
interference with what I do, or the people whom I may choose to
see in my chambers in Lincoln's Inn. If you are such an infatuated simpleton as to believe—'

' Yes; of course I am a simpleton; of course I am a fool; women
always are.'

' Listen to me, will you?'

' Listen, yes; it's my business to listen. Would you like that I
should give this house up for her, and go into lodgings somewhere?
I shall have very little objection as matters are going now. Oh
dear, oh dear, that things should ever have come to this!'

' Come to what?'

' Tom, I could put up with a great deal,—more I think than most

women; I could slave for you like a drudge, and think nothing
about it. And now that you have got among grand people, I could
see you go out by yourself without thinking much about that
either. I am very lonely sometimes,—very; but I could bear that.
Nobody has longed to see you rise in the world half so anxious as I
have done. But, Tom, when I know what your goings on are with
a nasty, sly, false woman like that, I won't bear it; and there's an
end.' In saying which final words Mrs. Furnival rose from her
seat, and thrice struck her hand by no means lightly on the loo
table in the middle of the room.

'I did not think it possible that you should be so silly. I did
not indeed.'

'Oh, yes, silly! very well. Women always are silly when they
mind that kind of thing. Have you got anything else to say, sir?'

'Yes, I have; I have this to say, that I will not endure this sort
of usage.'

'Nor I won't,' said Mrs. Furnival; 'so you may as well understand it at once. As long as there was nothing absolutely wrong,
I would put up with it for the sake of appearances, and because of
Sophia. For myself I don't mind what loneliness I may have to
bear. If you had been called on to go out to the East Indies or
even to China, I could have put up with it. But this sort of thing
I won't put up with;—nor I won't be blind to what I can't help
seeing. So now, Mr. Furnival, you may know that I have made up
my mind.' And then, without waiting further parley, having
wisked herself in her energy near to the door, she stalked out, and
went up with hurried steps to her own room.

Occurrences of a nature such as this are in all respects unpleasant in a household. Let the master be ever so much master, what
is he to do? Say that his wife is wrong from the beginning to the
end of the quarrel,—that in no way improves the matter. His
anxiety is that the world abroad shall not know he has ought amiss
at home; but she, with her hot sense of injury, and her loud revolt
against supposed wrongs, cares not who hears it. 'Hold your
tongue, madam,' the husband says. But the wife, bound though she
be by an oath of obedience, will not obey him, but only screams
the louder.

All which, as Mr. Furnival sat there thinking of it, disturbed his
mind much. That Martha Biggs would spread the tale through
all Bloomsbury and St. Pancras of course he was aware. 'If she
drives me to it, it must be so,' he said to himself at last. And then
he also betook himself to his rest. And so it was that preparations
for Christmas were made in Harley Street.

Christmas at Noningsby.—Morning.

CHAPTER XXII.

CHRISTMAS AT NONINGSBY.

THE house at Noningsby on Christmas-day was puite full, and yet it was by no means a small house. Mrs. Arbuthnot, the judge's married daughter, was there, with her three children; and Mr. Funival was there, having got over those domestic difficulties in which we lately saw him as best he might; and Lucius Mason was there, having been especially asked by Lady Staveley when she heard that his mother was to be at The Cleeve. There could be no more comfortable country-house than Noningsby; and it was, in its own way, pretty, though essentially different in all respects from The Cleeve. It was a new house from the cellar to the ceiling, and as a house was no doubt the better for being so. All the rooms were of the proper proportion, and all the newest appliances for comfort had been attached to it. But nevertheless it lacked that something, in appearance rather than in fact, which age alone can give to the residence of a gentleman in the country. The gardens also were new, and the grounds around them trim, and square, and orderly. Noningsby was a delightful house; no one with money and taste at command could have created for himself one more delightful; but then there are delights which cannot be created even by money and taste.

It was a pleasant sight to see, the long, broad, well-filled breakfast table, with all that company round it. There were some eighteen or twenty gathered now at the table, among whom the judge sat pre-eminent, looming large in an arm-chair and having a double space allotted to him;—some eighteen or twenty, children included. At the bottom of the table sat Lady Staveley, who still chose to preside among her own tea cups as a lady should do; and close to her, assisting in the toils of that presidency, sat her daughter Madeline. Nearest to them were gathered the children, and the rest had formed themselves into little parties, each of which already well knew its own place at the board. In how very short a time will come upon one that pleasant custom of sitting in an accustomed place! But here, at these Noningsby breakfasts, among other customs already established, there was one by which Augustus Staveley was always privileged to sit by the side of Sophia Furnival. No doubt his original object was still unchanged. A match between that lady and his friend Graham was still desirable, and by perseverance he might pique Felix Graham to arouse himself. But hitherto Felix Graham had not aroused himself in that direction, and one or two people among the party were inclined to mistake young Staveley's intentions.

'Gus,' his sister had said to him the night before, 'I declare I think you are going to make love to Sophia Furnival.'

'Do you?' he had replied. 'As a rule I do not think there is any one in the world for whose discernment I have so much respect as I have for yours. But in this respect even you are wrong.'

'Ah, of course you say so.'

'If you won't believe me, ask her. What more can I say?'

'I certainly shan't ask her, for I don't know her well enough.'

'She's a very clever girl; let me tell you that, whoever falls in love with her.'

'I'm sure she is, and she is handsome too, very; but for all that she is not good enough for our Gus.'

'Of course she is not, and therefore I am not thinking of her. And now go to bed and dream that you have got the Queen of the Fortunate Islands for your sister-in-law.'

But although Staveley was himself perfectly indifferent to all the charms of Miss Furnival, nevertheless he could hardly restrain his dislike to Lucius Mason, who, as he thought, was disposed to admire the lady in question. In talking of Lucius to his own family and to his special friend Graham, he had called him conceited, pedantic, uncouth, unenglish, and detestable. His own family, that is, his mother and sister, rarely contradicted him in anything; but Graham was by no means so cautious, and usually contradicted him in everything. Indeed, there was no sign of sterling worth so plainly marked in Staveley's character as the full conviction which he entertained of the superiority of his friend Felix.

'You are quite wrong about him,' Felix had said. 'He has not been at an English school, or English university, and therefore is not like other young men that you know; but he is, I think, well educated and clever. As for conceit, what man will do any good who is not conceited? Nobody holds a good opinion of a man who has a low opinion of himself.'

'All the same, my dear fellow, I do not like Lucius Mason.'

'And some one else, if you remember, did not like Dr. Fell.'

'And now, good people, what are you all going to do about church?' said Staveley, while they were still engaged with their rolls and eggs.

'I shall walk,' said the judge.

'And I shall go in the carriage,' said the judge's wife.

' That disposes of two; and now it will take half an hour to settle for the rest. Miss Furnival, you no doubt will accompany my mother. As I shall be among the walkers you will see how much I sacrifice by the suggestion.'

It was a mile to the church, and Miss Furnival knew the advantage of appearing in her seat unfatigued and without subjection to wind, mud, or rain. ' I must confess,' she said, ' that under all the circumstances, I shall prefer your mother's company to yours;' whereupon Staveley, in the completion of his arrangements, assigned the other places in the carriage to the married ladies of the company.

' But I have taken your sister Madeline's seat in the carriage,' protested Sophia with great dismay.

' My sister Madeline generally walks.'

' Then of course I shall walk with her;' but when the time came Miss Furnival did go in the carriage whereas Miss Staveley went on foot.

It so fell out, as they started, that Graham found himself walking at Miss Staveley's side, to the great disgust, no doubt, of half a dozen other aspirants for that honour. ' I cannot help thinking,' he said, as they stepped briskly over the crisp white frost, ' that this Christmas-day of ours is a great mistake.'

' Oh, Mr. Graham !' she exclaimed.

' You need not regard me with horror,—at least not with any special horror on this occasion.'

' But what you say is very horrid.'

' That, I flatter myself, seems so only because I have not yet said it. That part of our Christmas-day which is made to be in any degree sacred is by no means a mistake.'

' I am glad you think that.'

' Or rather, it is not a mistake in as far as it is in any degree made sacred. But the peculiar conviviality of the day is so ponderous! Its roast-beefiness oppresses one so thoroughly from the first moment of one's waking, to the last ineffectual effort at a bit of fried pudding for supper !'

' But you need not eat fried pudding for supper. Indeed, here, I am afraid, you will not have any supper offered you at all.'

' No; not to me individually, under that name. I might also manage to guard my ownself under any such offers. But there is always the flavour of the sweetmeat, in the air,—of all the sweetmeats, edible and non edible.'

' You begrudge the children their snap-dragon. That's what it all means, Mr. Graham.'

' No; I deny it; unpremeditated snap-dragon is dear to my soul; and I could expend myself in blindman's buff.'

' You shall then, after dinner; for of course you know that we all dine early.'

' But blindman's buff at three, with snap-dragon at a quarter to four—charades at five, with wine and sweet cake at half-past six, is ponderous. And that's our mistake. The big turkey would be very good ;—capital fun to see a turkey twice as big as it ought to be! But the big turkey, and the mountain of beef, and the pudding weighing a hundredweight, oppress one's spirits by their combined gravity. And then they impart a memory of indigestion, a halo as it were of apoplexy, even to the church services.'

' I do not agree with you the least in the world.'

' I ask you to answer me fairly. Is not additional eating an ordinary Englishman's ordinary idea of Christmas-day?'

' I am only an ordinary Englishwoman and therefore cannot say. It is not my idea.'

' I believe that the ceremony, as kept by us, is perpetuated by the butchers and beersellers, with a helping hand from the grocers. It is essentially a material festival; and I would not object to it even on that account if it were not so grievously overdone. How the sun is moistening the frost on the ground. As we come back the road will be quite wet.'

' We shall be going home then and it will not signify. Remember, Mr. Graham, I shall expect you to come forward in great strength for blindman's buff.' As he gave her the required promise, he thought that even the sports of Christmas-day would be bearable, if she also were to make one of the sportsmen; and then they entered the church.

I do not know anything more pleasant to the eye than a pretty country church, decorated for Christmas-day. The effect in a city is altogether different. I will not say that churches there should not be decorated, but comparatively it is a matter of indifference. No one knows who does it. The peculiar munificence of the squire who has sacrificed his holly bushes is not appreciated. The work of the fingers that have been employed is not recognized. The efforts made for hanging the pendent wreaths to each capital have been of no special interest to any large number of the worshippers. It has been done by contract, probably, and even if well done has none of the grace of association. But here at Noningsby church, the winter flowers had been cut by Madeline and the gardener, and the red berries had been grouped by her own hands. She and the vicar's wife had stood together with perilous audacity on the top of the clerk's desk while they fixed the branches beneath the cushion of the old-fashioned turret, from which the sermons were preached. And all this had of course been talked about at the house; and some of the party had gone over to see, including Sophia Furnival, who had declared that nothing could be so delightful, though she had omitted to endanger her fingers by any participation in the work. And the children had regarded the operation as a triumph of all that was wonderful in decoration; and thus many of them had been made happy.

On their return from church, Miss Furnival insisted on walking, in order, as she said, that Miss Staveley might not have all the fatigue; but Miss Staveley would walk also, and the carriage, after a certain amount of expostulation and delay, went off with its load incomplete.

' And now for the plum-pudding part of the arrangement,' said Felix Graham.

' Yes, Mr. Graham,' said Madeline, ' now for the plum-pudding —and the blindman's buff.'

' Did you ever see anything more perfect than the church, Mr. Mason?' said Sophia.

' Anything more perfect? no; in that sort of way, perhaps, never. I have seen the choir of Cologne.'

' Come, come; that's not fair,' said Graham. ' Don't import Cologne in order to crush us here down in our little English villages. You never saw the choir of Cologne bright with holly berries.'

' No; but I have with cardinal's stockings, and bishop's robes.'

' I think I should prefer the holly,' said Miss Furnival. ' And why should not our churches always look like that, only changing the flowers and the foliage with the season? It would make the service so attractive.'

' It would hardly do at Lent,' said Madeline, in a serious tone.

' No, perhaps not at Lent exactly.'

Peregrine and Augustus Staveley were walking on in front, not perhaps as well satisfied with the day as the rest of the party. Augustus, on leaving the church, had made a little effort to assume his place as usual by Miss Furnival's side, but by some accident of war, Mason was there before him. He had not cared to make one of a party of three, and therefore had gone on in advance with young Orme. Nor was Peregrine himself much more happy. He did not know why, but he felt within his breast a growing aversion to Felix Graham. Graham was a puppy, he thought, and a fellow that talked too much; and then he was such a confoundedly ugly dog, and—and—and—Peregrine Orme did not like him. He was not a man to analyze his own feelings in such matters. He did not ask himself why he should have been rejoiced to hear that instant business had taken Felix Graham off to Hong Kong; but he knew that he would have rejoiced. He knew also that Madeline Staveley was——. No; he did not know what she was; but when he was alone, he carried on with her all manner of imaginary conversations, though when he was in her company he had hardly a word to say to her. Under these circumstances he fraternized with her brother; but even in that he could not receive much satisfaction, seeing that he could not abuse Graham to Graham's special friend, nor could he breathe a sigh as to Madeline's perfections into the ear of Madeline's brother.

The children,—and there were three or four assembled there besides those belonging to Mrs. Arbuthnot, were by no means inclined to agree with Mr. Graham's strictures as to the amusements of Christmas-day. To them it appeared that they could not hurry fast enough into the vorvex of its dissipations. The dinner was a serious consideration, especially with reference to certain illuminated mince-pies which were the crowning glory of that banquet; but time for these was almost begrudged in order that the fast handkerchief might be tied over the eyes of the first blindman.

'And now we'll go into the schoolroom,' said Marian Arbuthnot, jumping up and leading the way. 'Come along, Mr. Felix;' and Felix Graham followed her.

Madeline had declared that Felix Graham should be blinded first, and such was his doom. 'Now mind you catch me, Mr. Felix; pray do,' said Marian, when she had got him seated in a corner of the room. She was a beautiful fair little thing, with long, soft curls, and lips red as a rose, and large, bright blue eyes, all soft and happy and laughing, loving the friends of her childhood with passionate love, and fully expecting an equal devotion from them. It is of such children that our wives and sweethearts should be made.

'But how am I to find you when my eyes are blinded?'

'Oh, you can feel, you know. You can put your hand on the top of my head. I mustn't speak, you know; but I'm sure I shall laugh; and then you must guess that it's Marian.' That was her idea of playing blindman's buff according to the strict rigour of the game.

'And you'll give me a big kiss?' said Felix.

'Yes, when we've done playing,' she promised with great seriousness.

And then a huge white silk handkerchief, as big as a small sail, was brought down from grandpapa's dressing-room, so that nobody should see the least bit 'in the world,' as Marian had observed with great energy; and the work of blinding was commenced. 'I ain't big enough to reach round,' said Marian, who had made an effort, but in vain. 'You do it, aunt Mad.,' and she tendered the handkerchief to Miss Staveley, who, however, did not appear very eager to undertake the task.

'I'll be the executioner,' said grandmamma, 'the more especially as I shall not take any other share in the ceremony. This shall be the chair of doom. Come here, Mr. Graham, and submit yourself to me.' And so the first victim was blinded. 'Mind you remember,' said Marian, whispering into his ear as he was led away. 'Green spirits and white; blue spirits and gray—,' and then he

Christmas at Noningsby.—Evening.

was twirled round in the room and left to commence his search as best he might.

Marian Arbuthnot was not the only soft little laughing darling that wished to be caught, and blinded, so that there was great pulling at the blindman's tails, and much grasping at his outstretched arms before the desired object was attained. And he wandered round the room skilfully, as though a thought were in his mind false to his treaty with Marian,—as though he imagined for a moment that some other prize might be caught. But if so, the other prize evaded him carefully, and in due progress of play, Marian's soft curls were within his grasp. ' I'm sure I didn't speak, or say a word,' said she, as she ran up to her grandmother to have the handkerchief put over her eyes. ' Did I, grandmamma ?'

' There are more ways of speaking than one,' said Lady Staveley. ' You and Mr. Graham understand each other, I think.

' Oh, I was caught quite fairly,' said Marian—' and now lead me round and round.' To her at any rate the festivities of Christmasday were not too ponderous for real enjoyment.

And then, at last, somebody caught the judge. I rather think it was Madeline; but his time in truth was come, and he had no chance of escape. The whole room was set upon his capture, and though he barricaded himself with chairs and children, he was duly apprehended and named. ' That's papa; I know by his watchchain, for I made it.'

' Nonsense, my dears,' said the judge. ' I will do no such thing. I should never catch anybody, and should remain blind for ever.'

' But grandpapa must,' said Marian. ' It's the game that he should be blinded when he's caught.'

' Suppose the game was that we should be whipped when we are caught, and I was to catch you,' said Augustus.

' But I would not play that game,' said Marian.

' Oh, papa, you must,' said Madeline. ' Do—and you shall catch Mr. Furnival.'

' That would be a temptation,' said the judge. ' I've never been able to do that yet, though I've been trying it for some years.'

' Justice is blind,' said Graham. ' Why should a judge be ashamed to follow the example of his own goddess ?' And so at last the owner of the ermine submitted, and the stern magistrate of the bench was led round with the due incantation of the spirits, and dismissed into chaos to seek for a new victim.

One of the rules of blindman's buff at Noningsby was this, that it should not be played by candlelight,—a rule that is in every way judicious, as thereby an end is secured for that which might otherwise be unending. And therefore when it became so dark in the schoolroom that there was not much difference between the blind man and the others, the handkerchief was smuggled away, and the game was at an end.

'And now for snap-dragon,' said Marian.

'Exactly as you predicted, Mr. Graham,' said Madeline: 'blind-man's buff at a quarter past three, and snap-dragon at five.'

'I revoke every word that I uttered, for I was never more amused in my life.'

'And you will be prepared to endure the wine and sweet cake when they come.'

'Prepared to endure anything, and go through everything. We shall be allowed candles now, I suppose.'

'Oh, no, by no means. Snap-dragon by candlelight! who ever heard of such a thing? It would wash all the dragon out of it, and leave nothing but the snap. It is a necessity of the game that it should be played in the dark,—or rather by its own lurid light.'

'Oh, there is a lurid light; is there?'

'You shall see;' and then she turned away to make her preparations.

To the game of snap-dragon, as played at Noningsby, a ghost was always necessary, and aunt Madeline had played the ghost ever since she had been an aunt, and there had been any necessity for such a part. But in previous years the spectators had been fewer in number and more closely connected with the family. 'I think we must drop the ghost on this occasion,' she said, coming up to her brother.

'You'll disgust them all dreadfully if you do,' said he. 'The young Sebrights have come specially to see the ghost.'

'Well, you can do ghost for them.'

'I! no; I can't act a ghost. Miss Furnival, you'd make a lovely ghost.'

'I shall be most happy to be useful,' said Sophia.

'Oh, aunt Mad., you must be ghost,' said Marian, following her.

'You foolish little thing, you; we are going to have a beautiful ghost—a divine ghost,' said uncle Gus.

'But we want Madeline to be the ghost,' said a big Miss Sebright, ten or eleven years old.

'She's always ghost,' said Marian.

'To be sure; it will be much better,' said Miss Furnival. 'I only offered my poor services hoping to be useful. No Banquo that ever lived could leave a worse ghost behind him that I should prove.'

It ended in there being two ghosts. It had become quite impossible to rob Miss Furnival of her promised part, and Madeline could not refuse to solve the difficulty in this way without making more of the matter than it deserved. The idea of two ghosts was delightful to the children, more especially as it entailed two large dishes full of raisins, and two blue fires blazing up from burnt brandy. So the girls went out, not without proffered assistance from the gentlemen, and after a painfully long interval of some fifteen or twenty minutes,—for Miss Furnival's back hair would not come down and adjust itself into ghostlike lengths with as much readiness as that of her friend—they returned bearing the dishes before them on large trays. In each of them the spirit was lighted as they entered the schoolroom door, and thus, as they walked in, they were illuminated by the dark-blue flames which they carried.

'Oh, is it not grand?' said Marian, appealing to Felix Graham.

'Uncommonly grand,' he replied.

'And which ghost do you think is the grandest? I'll tell you which ghost I like the best,—in a secret, you know; I like aunt Mad. the best, and I think she's the grandest too.'

'And I'll tell you in a secret that I think the same. To my mind she is the grandest ghost I ever saw in my life.'

'Is she indeed?' asked Marian, solemnly, thinking probably that her new friend's experience in ghosts must be extensive. However that might be, he thought that as far as his experience in women went, he had never seen anything more lovely than Madeleine Staveley dressed in a long white sheet, with a long bit of white cambric pinned round her face.

And it may be presumed that the dress altogether is not unbecoming when accompanied by blue flames, for Augustus Staveley and Lucius Mason thought the same thing of Miss Furnival, whereas Peregrine Orme did not know whether he was standing on his head or his feet as he looked at Miss Staveley. Miss Furnival may possibly have had some inkling of this when she offered to undertake the task, but I protest that such was not the case with Madeline. There was no second thought in her mind when she first declined the ghosting, and afterwards undertook the part. No wish to look beautiful in the eyes of Felix Graham had come to her—at any rate as yet; and as to Peregrine Orme, she had hardly thought of his existence. 'By heavens!' said Peregrine to himself, 'she is the most beautiful creature that I ever saw;' and then he began to speculate within his own mind how the idea might be received at The Cleeve.

But there was no such realized idea with Felix Graham. He saw that Madeline Staveley was very beautiful, and he felt in an unconscious manner that her character was very sweet. He may have thought that he might have loved such a girl, had such love been a thing permitted to him. But this was far from being the case. Felix Graham's lot in this life, as regarded that share which his heart might have in it, was already marked out for him;— marked out for himself and by himself. The future wife of his bosom had already been selected, and was now in course of preparation for the duties of her future life. He was one of those few wise men who have determined not to take a partner in life at hazard, but to mould a young mind and character to those pursuits and modes of thought which may best fit a woman for the duties she will have to perform. What little it may be necessary to know of the earlier years of Mary Snow shall be told hereafter. Here it will be only necessary to say that she was an orphan, that as yet she was little more than a child, and that she owed her maintenance and the advantage of her education to the charity and love of her destined husband. Therefore, as I have said, it was manifest that Felix Graham could not think of falling in love with Miss Staveley, even had not his very low position, in reference to worldly affairs, made any such passion on his part quite hopeless. But with Peregrine Orme the matter was different. There could be no possible reason why Peregrine Orme should not win and wear the beautiful girl whom he so much admired.

But the ghosts are kept standing over their flames, the spirit is becoming exhausted, and the raisins will be burnt. At snap-dragon, too, the ghosts here had something to do. The law of the game is this—a law on which Marian would have insisted had not the flames been so very hot—that the raisins shall become the prey of those audacious marauders only who dare to face the presence of the ghost, and to plunge their hands into the burning dish. As a rule the boys do this, clawing out the raisins, while the girls pick them up and eat them. But here at Noningsby the boys were too little to act thus as pioneers in the face of the enemy, and the raisins might have remained till the flames were burnt out, had not the beneficent ghost scattered abroad the richness of her own treasures.

' Now, Marian,' said Felix Graham, bringing her up in his arms.

' But it will burn, Mr. Felix. Look there; see; there are a great many at that end. You do it.'

' I must have another kiss then.'

' Very well, yes; if you get five.' And then Felix dashed his hand in among the flames and brought forth a fistful of fruit, which imparted to his fingers and wristband a smell of brandy for the rest of the evening.

' If you take so many at a time I shall rap your knuckles with the spoon,' said the ghost, as she stirred up the flames to keep them alive.

' But the ghost shouldn't speak,' said Marian, who was evidently unacquainted with the best ghosts of tragedy.

' But the ghost must speak when such large hands invade the caldron;' and then another raid was effected, and the threatened blow was given. Had any one told her in the morning that she would that day have rapped Mr. Graham's knuckles with a kitchen spoon, she would not have believed that person; but it is thus that hearts are lost and won.

And Peregrine Orme looked on from a distance, thinking of it all. That he should have been stricken dumb by the beauty of any girl was surprising even to himself; for though young and almost boyish in his manners, he had never yet feared to speak out in any presence. The tutor at his college had thought him insolent beyond parallel; and his grandfather, though he loved him for his open face and plain outspoken words, found them sometimes almost too much for him. But now he stood there looking and longing, and could not summons courage to go up and address a few words to this young girl even in the midst of their sports. Twice or thrice during the last few days he had essayed to speak to her, but his words had been dull and vapid, and to himself they had appeared childish. He was quite conscious of his own weakness. More than once during that period of the snap-dragon, did he say to himself that he would descend into the lists and break a lance in that tournay; but still he did not descend, and his lance remained inglorious in its rest.

At the other end of the long table the ghost also had two attendant knights, and neither of them refrained from the battle. Augustus Staveley, if he thought it worth his while to keep the lists at all, would not be allowed to ride through them unopposed from any backwardness on the part of his rival. Lucius Mason was not likely to become a timid, silent, longing lover. To him it was not possible that he should fear the girl whom he loved. He could not worship that which he wished to obtain for himself. It may be doubted whether he had much faculty of worshipping anything in the truest meaning of that word. One worships that which one feels, through the inner and unexpressed conviction of the mind, to be greater, better, higher than oneself; but it was not probable that Lucius Mason should so think of any woman that he might meet.

Nor, to give him his due, was it probable that he should be in any way afraid of any man that he might encounter. He would fear neither the talent, nor the rank, nor the money influence, nor the dexterity of any such rival. In any attempt that he might make on a woman's heart he would regard his own chance as good against that of any other possible he. Augustus Staveley was master here at Noningsby, and was a clever, dashing, handsome, fashionable young fellow; but Lucius Mason never dreamed of retreating before such forces as those. He had words with which to speak as fair as those of any man, and flattered himself that he as well knew how to use them.

It was pretty to see with what admirable tact and judicious management of her smiles Sophia received the homage of the two young men, answering the compliments of both with ease, and so conducting herself that neither could fairly accuse her of undue favour to the other. But unfairly, in his own mind, Augustus did so accuse her. And why should he have been so venomous, seeing that he entertained no regard for the lady himself? His object was still plain enough,—that, namely, of making a match between his needy friend and the heiress.

His needy friend in the mean time played on through the long evening in thoughtless happiness; and Peregrine Orme, looking at the game from a distance, saw that rap given to the favoured knuckles with a bitterness of heart and an inner groaning of the spirit that will not be incomprehensible to many.

' I do so love that Mr. Felix !' said Marian, as her aunt Madeline kissed her in her little bed on wishing her good night. 'Don't you, aunt Mad.——?'

And so it was that Christmas-day was passed at Noningsby.

CHAPTER XXIII.

CHRISTMAS AT GROBY PARK.

CHRISTMAS-DAY was always a time of very great trial to Mrs. Mason of Groby Park. It behoved her, as the wife of an old English country gentleman, to spread her board plenteously at that season, and in some sort to make an open house of it. But she could not bring herself to spread any board with plenty, and the idea of an open house would almost break her heart. Unlimited eating ! There was something in the very sounds of such words which was appalling to the inner woman.

And on this Christmas-day she was doomed to go through an ordeal of very peculiar severity. It so happened that the cure of souls in the parish of Groby had been intrusted for the last two or three years to a young, energetic, but not very opulent curate. Why the rector of Groby should be altogether absent, leaving the work in the hands of a curate, whom he paid by the lease of a cottage and garden and fifty-five pounds a year,—thereby behaving as he imagined with extensive liberality,—it is unnecessary here to inquire. Such was the case, and the Rev. Adolphus Green, with Mrs. A. Green and the four children, managed to live with some difficulty on the produce of the. garden and the allotted stipend ; but could not probably have lived at all in that position had not Mrs. Adolphus Green been blessed with some small fortune.

It had so happened that Mrs. Adolphus Green had been instrumental in imparting some knowledge of singing to two of the Miss

Masons, and had continued her instructions over the last three years. This had not been done in any preconcerted way, but the lessons had grown by chance. Mrs. Mason the while had looked on with a satisfied eye at an arrangement that was so much to her taste.

' There are no regular lessons you know,' she had said to her husband, when he suggested that some reward for so much work would be expedient. ' Mrs. Green finds it convenient to have the use of my drawing-room, and would never see an instrument from year's end to year's end if she were not allowed to come up here. Depend upon it she gets a great deal more than she gives.'

But after two years' of tuition Mr. Mason had spoken a second time. ' My dear,' he said, ' I cannot allow the girls to accept so great a favour from Mrs. Green without making her some compensation.'

' I don't see that it is at all necessary,' Mrs. Mason had answered; ' but if you think so, we could send her down a hamper of apples,— that is, a basketful.' Now it happened that apples were very plentiful that year, and that the curate and his wife were blessed with as many as they could judiciously consume.

' Apples! nonsense!' said Mr. Mason.

' If you mean money, my dear, I couldn't do it. I wouldn't so offend a lady for all the world.'

' You could buy them something handsome, in the way of furniture. That little room of theirs that they call the drawing-room has nothing in it at all. Get Jones from Leeds to send them some things that will do for them.' And hence, after many inner misgivings, had arisen that purchase of a drawing-room set from Mr. Kantwise,—that set of metallic ' Louey Catorse furniture,' containing three tables, eight chairs, &c. &c., as to which it may be remembered that Mrs. Mason made such an undoubted bargain, getting them for less than cost price. That they had been ' strained,' as Mr. Kantwise himself admitted in discoursing on the subject to Mr. Dockwrath, was not matter of much moment. They would do extremely well for a curate's wife.

And now on this Christmas-day the present was to be made over to the happy lady. Mr. and Mrs. Green were to dine at Groby Park,—leaving their more fortunate children to the fuller festivities of the cottage; and the intention was that before dinner the whole drawing-room set should be made over. It was with grievous pangs of heart that Mrs. Mason looked forward to such an operation. Her own house was plenteously furnished from the kitchens to the attics, but still she would have loved to keep that metallic set of painted trumpery. She knew that the table would not screw on; she knew that the pivot of the music stool was bent; she knew that there was no place in the house in which they could stand; she must have known that in no possible way could they be of use to her or hers,—and yet she could not part with them without an agony. Her husband was infatuated in this matter of compensation for the use of Mrs. Green's idle hours; no compensation could be necessary;—and then she paid another visit to the metallic furniture. She knew in her heart of hearts that they could never be of use to anybody, and yet she made up her mind to keep back two out of the eight chairs. Six chairs would be quite enough for Mrs. Green's small room.

As there was to be feasting at five, real roast beef, plum-pudding and mince-pies;—'Mince-pies and plum-pudding together are vulgar, my dear,' Mrs. Mason had said to her husband; but in spite of the vulgarity he had insisted;—the breakfast was of course scanty. Mr. Mason liked a slice of cold meat in the morning, or the leg of a fowl, or a couple of fresh eggs as well as any man; but the matter was not worth a continual fight. 'As we are to dine an hour earlier to-day I did not think you would eat meat,' his wife said to him. 'Then there would be less expense in putting it on the table,' he had answered; and after that there was nothing more said about it. He always put off till some future day that great contest which he intended to wage and to win, and by which he hoped to bring it about that plenty should henceforward be the law of the land at Groby Park. And then they all went to church. Mrs. Mason would not on any account have missed church on Christmas-day or a Sunday. It was a cheap duty, and therefore rigidly performed. As she walked from her carriage up to the church-door she encountered Mrs. Green, and smiled sweetly as she wished that lady all the compliments of the season.

'We shall see you immediately after church,' said Mrs. Mason.

'Oh yes, certainly,' said Mrs. Green.

'And Mr. Green with you?'

'He intends to do himself the pleasure,' said the curate's wife.

'Mind he comes, because we have a little ceremony to go through before we sit down to dinner;' and Mrs. Mason smiled again ever so graciously. Did she think, or did she not think, that she was going to do a kindness to her neighbour? Most women would have sunk into their shoes as the hour grew nigh at which they were to show themselves guilty of so much meanness.

She stayed for the sacrament, and it may here be remarked that on that afternoon she rated both the footman and housemaid because they omitted to do so. She thought, we must presume, that she was doing her duty, and must imagine her to have been ignorant that she was cheating her husband and cheating her friend. She took the sacrament with admirable propriety of demeanour, and then on her return home, withdrew another chair from the set. There would still be six, including the rocking chair, and six would be quite enough for that little hole of a room.

There was a large chamber up stairs at Groby Park which had been used for the children's lessons, but which now was generally deserted. There was in it an old worn-out pianoforte,—and though Mrs. Mason had talked somewhat grandly of the use of her drawing-room, it was here that the singing had been taught. Into this room the metallic furniture had been brought, and up to that Christmas morning it had remained here packed in its original boxes. Hither immediately after breakfast Mrs. Mason had taken herself, and had spent an hour in her efforts to set the things forth to view. Two of the chairs she then put aside into a cupboard, and a third she added to her private store on her return to her work after church.

But, alas, alas! let her do what she would, she could not get the top on to the table. 'It's all smashed, ma'am,' said the girl whom she at last summoned to her aid. 'Nonsense, you simpleton; how can it be smashed when it's new,' said the mistress. And then she tried again, and again, declaring as she did so, that she would have the law of the rogue who had sold her a damaged article. Nevertheless she had known that it was damaged, and had bought it cheap on that account, insisting in very urgent language that the table was in fact worth nothing because of its injuries.

At about four Mr. and Mrs. Green walked up to the house and were shown into the drawing-room. Here was Mrs. Mason supported by Penelope and Creusa. As Diana was not musical, and therefore under no compliment to Mrs. Green, she kept out of the way. Mr. Mason also was absent. He knew that something very mean was about to be done, and would not show his face till it was over. He ought to have taken the matter in hand himself, and would have done so had not his mind been full of other things. He himself was a man terribly wronged and wickedly injured, and could not therefore in these present months interfere much in the active doing of kindnesses. His hours were spent in thinking how he might best obtain justice,—how he might secure his pound of flesh. He only wanted his own, but that he would have;—his own, with due punishment on those who had for so many years robbed him of it. He therefore did not attend at the presentation of the furniture.

' And now we'll go up stairs, if you please,' said Mrs. Mason, with that gracious smile for which she was so famous. 'Mr. Green, you must come too. Dear Mrs. Green has been so very kind to my two girls; and now I have got a few articles,—they are of the very newest fashion, and I do hope that Mrs. Green will like them.' And so they all went up into the schoolroom.

' There's a new fashion come up lately,' said Mrs. Mason as she walked along the corridor, 'quite new :—of metallic furniture. I don't know whether you have seen any.' Mrs. Green said she had not seen any as yet.

' The Patent Steel Furniture Company makes it, and it has got very greatly into vogue for small rooms. I thought that perhaps you would allow me to present you with a set for your drawing-room.'

' I'm sure it is very kind of you to think of it,' said Mrs. Green.

' Uncommonly so,' said Mr. Green. But both Mr. Green and Mrs. Green knew the lady, and their hopes did not run high.

And then the door was opened and there stood the furniture to view. There stood the furniture, except the three subtracted chairs, and the loo table. The claw and leg of the table indeed were standing there, but the top was folded up and lying on the floor beside it. ' I hope you'll like the pattern,' began Mrs. Mason. ' I'm told that it is the prettiest that has yet been brought out. There has been some little accident about the screw of the table, but the smith in the village will put that to rights in five minutes. He lives so close to you that I didn't think it worth while to have him up here.'

' It's very nice,' said Mrs. Green, looking round her almost in dismay.

' Very nice indeed,' said Mr. Green, wondering in his mind for what purpose such utter trash could have been manufactured, and endeavouring to make up his mind as to what they might possibly do with it. Mr. Green knew what chairs and tables should be, and was well aware that the things before him were absolutely useless for any of the ordinary purposes of furniture.

' And they are the most convenient things in the world,' said Mrs. Mason, ' for when you are going to change house you pack them all up again in these boxes. Wooden furniture takes up so much room, and is so lumbersome.'

' Yes, it is,' said Mrs. Green.

' I'll have them all put up again and sent down in the cart to-morrow.'

' Thank you; that will be very kind,' said Mr. Green, and then the ceremony of the presentation was over. On the following day the boxes were sent down, and Mrs. Mason might have abstracted even another chair without detection, for the cases lay unheeded from month to month in the curate's still unfurnished room. ' The fact is they cannot afford a carpet,' Mrs. Mason afterwards said to one of her daughters, ' and with such things as those they are quite right to keep them up till they can be used with advantage. I always gave Mrs. Green credit for a good deal of prudence.'

And then, when the show was over, they descended again into the drawing-room,—Mr. Green and Mrs. Mason went first, and Creusa followed. Penelope was thus so far behind as to be able to speak to her friend without being heard by the others.

' You know mamma,' she said, with a shrug of her shoulders and a look of scorn in her eye.

' The things are very nice.'

' No, they are not, and you know they are not. They are worthless; perfectly worthless.'

' But we don't want anything.'

' No; and if there had been no pretence of a gift it would all have been very well. What will Mr. Green think?'

' I rather think he likes iron chairs;' and then they were in the drawing-room.

Mr. Mason did not appear till dinner-time, and came in only just in time to give his arm to Mrs. Green. He had had letters to write,—a letter to Messrs. Round and Crook, very determined in its tone; and a letter also to Mr. Dockwrath, for the little attorney had so crept on in the affair that he was now corresponding with the principal. ' I'll teach those fellows in Bedford Row to know who I am,' he had said to himself more than once, sitting on his high stool at Hamworth.

And then came the Groby Park Christmas dinner. To speak the truth Mr. Mason had himself gone to the neighbouring butcher, and ordered the surloin of beef, knowing that it would be useless to trust to orders conveyed through his wife. He had seen the piece of meat put on one side for him, and had afterwards traced it on to the kitchen dresser. But nevertheless when it appeared at table it had been sadly mutilated. A stake had been cut off the full breadth of it—a monstrous cantle from out its fair proportions. The lady had seen the jovial, thick, ample size of the goodly joint, and her heart had been unable to spare it. She had made an effort and turned away, saying to herself that the responsibility was all with him. But it was of no use. There was that within her which could not do it. ' Your master will never be able to carve such a mountain of meat as that,' she had said, turning back to the cook. ' 'Deed, an' it's he that will, ma'am,' said the Irish mistress of the spit; for Irish cooks are cheaper than those bred and born in England. But nevertheless the thing was done, and it was by her own fair hands that the envious knife was used. ' I couldn't do it, ma'am,' the cook had said; ' I couldn't railly.'

Mr. Mason's face became very black when he saw the raid that had been effected, and when he looked up across the table his wife's eye was on him. She knew what she had to expect, and she knew also that it would not come now. Her eye stealthily looked at his, quivering with fear; for Mr. Mason could be savage enough in his anger. And what had she gained? One may as well ask what does the miser gain who hides away his gold in an old pot, or what does that other madman gain who is locked up for long long years because he fancies himself the grandmother of the Queen of England?

But there was still enough beef on the table for all of them to eat, and as Mrs. Mason was not intrusted with the carving of it, their plates were filled. As far as a sufficiency of beef can make a good dinner Mr. and Mrs. Green did have a good dinner on that Christmas-day. Beyond that their comfort was limited, for no one was in a humour for happy conversation.

And over and beyond the beef there was a plum-pudding and three mince-pies. Four mince-pies had originally graced the dish, but before dinner one had been conveyed away to some upstairs receptacle for such spoils. The pudding also was small, nor was it black and rich, and laden with good things as a Christmas pudding should be laden. Let us hope that what the guests so lost was made up to them on the following day, by an absence of those ill effects which sometimes attend upon the consumption of rich viands.

' And now, my dear, we'll have a bit of bread and cheese and a glass of beer,' Mr. Green said when he arrived at his own cottage. And so it was that Christmas-day was passed at Groby Park.

<hr>

CHAPTER XXIV.

CHRISTMAS IN GREAT ST. HELENS.

WE will now look in for a moment at the Christmas doings of our fat friend, Mr. Moulder. Mr. Moulder was a married man living in lodgings over a wine-merchant's vaults in Great St. Helens. He was blessed—or troubled, with no children, and prided himself greatly on the material comfort with which his humble home was surrounded. ' His wife,' he often boasted, ' never wanted for plenty of the best of eating; and for linen and silks and such-like, she could show her drawers and her wardrobes with many a great lady from Russell Square, and not be ashamed, neither! And then, as for drink,—' tipple,' as Mr. Moulder sportively was accustomed to name it among his friends, he opined that he was not altogether behind the mark in that respect. ' He had got some brandy— he didn't care what anybody might say about Cognac and eau de vie; but the brandy which he had got from Betts' private establishment seventeen years ago, for richness of flavour and fullness of strength, would beat any French article that anybody in the city could show. That at least was his idea. If anybody didn't like it, they needn't take it. There was whisky that would make your hair stand on end.' So said Mr. Moulder, and I can believe him; for it has made my hair stand on end merely to see other people drinking it.

And if comforts of apparel, comforts of eating and drinking, and comforts of the feather-bed and easy-chair kind can make a woman happy, Mrs. Moulder was no doubt a happy woman. She had quite fallen in to the mode of life laid out for her. She had a little bit of hot kidney for breakfast at about ten; she dined at three, having seen herself to the accurate cooking of her roast fowl, or her bit of sweetbread, and always had her pint of Scotch ale. She turned over all her clothes almost every day. In the evening she read Reynolds's Miscellany, had her tea and buttered muffins, took a thimbleful of brandy and water at nine, and then went to bed. The work of her life consisted in sewing buttons on to Moulder's shirts, and seeing that his things were properly got up when he was at home. No doubt she would have done better as to the duties of the world, had the world's duties come to her. As it was, very few such had come in her direction. Her husband was away from home three-fourths of the year, and she had no children that required attention. As for society, some four or five times a year she would drink tea with Mrs. Hubbles at Clapham. Mrs. Hubbles was the wife of the senior partner in the firm, and on such occasions Mrs. Moulder dressed herself in her best, and having travelled to Clapham in an omnibus, spent the evening in dull propriety on one corner of Mrs. Hubbles's sofa. When I have added to this that Moulder every year took her to Broadstairs for a fortnight, I think that I have described with sufficient accuracy the course of Mrs. Moulder's life.

On the occasion of this present Christmas-day Mr. Moulder entertained a small party. And he delighted in such occasional entertainments, taking extraordinary pains that the eatables should be of the very best; and he would maintain an hospitable good humour to the last,—unless anything went wrong in the cookery, in which case he could make himself extremely unpleasant to Mrs. M. Indeed, proper cooking for Mr. M. and the proper starching of the bands of his shirts were almost the only trials that Mrs. Moulder was doomed to suffer. ' What the d— are you for?' he would say, almost throwing the displeasing viands at her head across the table, or tearing the rough linen from off his throat. ' It ain't much I ask of you in return for your keep;' and then he would scowl at her with bloodshot eyes till she shook in her shoes. But this did not happen often, as experiences had made her careful.

But on this present Christmas festival all went swimmingly to the end. ' Now, bear a hand, old girl,' was the harshest word he said to her; and he enjoyed himself like Duncan, shut up in measureless content. He had three guests with him on this auspicious day. There was his old friend Snengkeld, who had dined with him on every Christmas since his marriage ; there was his wife's brother, of whom we will say a word or two just now ;— and there was our old friend, Mr. Kantwise. Mr. Kantwise was not exactly the man whom Moulder would have chosen as his guest, for they were opposed to each other in all their modes of thought and action; but he had come across the travelling agent of the Patent Metallic Steel Furniture Company on the previous day, and finding that he was to be alone in London on this general holiday, he had asked him out of sheer good nature. Moulder could be very good natured, and full of pity when the sorrow to be pitied arose from some such source as the want of a Christmas dinner. So Mr. Kantwise had been asked, and precisely at four o'clock he made his appearance at Great St. Helens.

But now, as to this brother-in-law. He was no other than that John Kenneby whom Miriam Usbech did not marry,—whom Miriam Usbech might, perhaps, have done well to marry. John Kenneby, after one or two attempts in other spheres of life, had at last got into the house of Hubbles and Grease, and had risen to be their book-keeper. He had once been tried by them as a traveller, but in that line he had failed. He did not possess that rough, ready, self-confident tone of mind which is almost necessary for a man who is destined to move about quickly from one circle of persons to another. After a six months' trial he had given that up, but during the time, Mr. Moulder, the senior traveller of the house, had married his sister. John Kenneby was a good, honest, painstaking fellow, and was believed by his friends to have put a few pounds together in spite of the timidity of his character.

When Snengkeld and Kenneby were shown up into the room, they found nobody there but Kantwise. That Mrs. Moulder should be down stairs looking after the roast turkey was no more than natural; but why should not Moulder himself be there to receive his guests? He soon appeared, however, coming up without his coat.

' Well, Snengkeld, how are you, old fellow; many happy returns, and all that; the same to you, John. I'll tell you what, my lads; it's a prime 'un. I never saw such a bird in all my days.'

' What, the turkey?' said Snengkeld.

' You didn't think it'd be a ostrich, did you?'

' Ha, ha, ha!' laughed Snengkeld. ' No, I didn't expect nothing but a turkey here on Christmas-day.'

' And nothing but a turkey you'll have, my boys. Can you eat turkey, Kantwise?'

Mr. Kantwise declared that his only passion in the way of eating was for a turkey.

' As for John, I'm sure of him. I've seen him at the work before.' Whereupon John grinned but said nothing.

' I never see such a bird in my life, certainly.'

' From Norfolk, I suppose,' said Snengkeld, with a great appearance of interest.

' Oh, you may swear to that. It weighed twenty-four pounds, for I put it into the scales myself, and old Gibbetts let me have it for a guinea. The price marked on it was five-and-twenty, for I saw it. He's had it hanging for a fortnight, and I've been to see it wiped down with vinegar regular every morning. And now, my boys, it's done to a turn. I've been in the kitchen most of the time myself, and either I or Mrs. M. has never left it for a single moment.'

'How did you manage about divine service?' said Kantwise; and then, when he had spoken, closed his eyes and sucked his lips.

Mr. Moulder looked at him for a minute, and then said, 'Gammon.'

'Ha, ha, ha!' laughed Snengkeld. And then Mrs. Moulder appeared, bringing the turkey with her; for she would trust it to no hands less careful than her own.

'By George, it is a bird,' said Snengkeld, standing over it and eyeing it minutely.

'Uncommon nice it looks,' said Kantwise.

'All the same, I wouldn't eat none, if I were you,' said Moulder, 'seeing what sinners have been a basting it.' And then they all sat down to dinner, Moulder having first resumed his coat.

For the next three or four minutes Moulder did not speak a word. The turkey was on his mind, with the stuffing, the gravy, the liver, the breast, the wings, and the legs. He stood up to carve it, and while he was at the work he looked at it as though his two eyes were hardly sufficient. He did not help first one person and then another, so ending by himself; but he cut up artistically as much as might probably be consumed, and located the fragments in small heaps or shares in the hot gravy; and then, having made a partition of the spoils, he served it out with unerring impartiality. To have robbed any one of his or her fair slice of the breast would, in his mind, have been gross dishonesty. In his heart he did not love Kantwise, but he dealt by him with the utmost justice in the great affair of the turkey's breast. When he had done all this, and his own plate was laden, he gave a long sigh. 'I shall never cut up such another bird as that, the longest day that I have to live,' he said; and then he took out his large red silk handkerchief and wiped the perspiration from his brow.

'Deary me, M.; don't think of that now,' said the wife.

'What's the use?' said Snengkeld. 'Care killed a cat.'

'And perhaps you may,' said John Kenneby, trying to comfort him; 'who knows?'

'It's all in the hands of Providence,' said Kantwise, 'and we should look to him.'

'And how does it taste?' asked Moulder, shaking the gloomy thoughts from his mind.

'Uncommon,' said Snengkeld, with his mouth quite full. 'I never eat such a turkey in all my life.'

' Like melted diamonds,' said Mrs. Moulder, who was not without a touch of poetry.

' Ah, there's nothing like hanging of 'em long enough, and watching of 'em well. It's that vinegar as done it ;' and then they went seriously to work, and there was nothing more said of any importance until the eating was nearly over.

And now Mrs. M. had taken away the cloth, and they were sitting cozily over their port wine. The very apple of the eye of the evening had not arrived even yet. That would not come till the pipes were brought out, and the brandy was put on the table, and the whisky was there that made the people's hair stand on end. It was then that the floodgates of convivial eloquence would be unloosed. In the mean time it was necessary to sacrifice something to gentility, and therefore they sat over their port wine.

' Did you bring that letter with you, John ?' said his sister. John replied that he had done so, and that he had also received another letter that morning from another party on the same subject.

' Do show it to Moulder, and ask him,' said Mrs. M.

' I've got 'em both on purpose,' said John ; and then he brought forth two letters, and handed one of them to his brother-in-law. It contained a request, very civilly worded, from Messrs. Round and Crook, begging him to call at their office in Bedford Row on the earliest possible day, in order that they might have some conversation with him regarding the will of the late Sir Joseph Mason, who died in 18—.

' Why, this is law business,' said Moulder, who liked no business of that description. ' Don't you go near them, John, if you ain't obliged.'

And then Kenneby gave his explanation on the matter, telling how in former years,—many years ago, he had been a witness in a lawsuit. And then as he told it he sighed, remembering Miriam Usbech, for whose sake he had remained unmarried even to this day. And he went on to narrate how he had been bullied in the court, though he had valiantly striven to tell the truth with exactness ; and as he spoke, an opinion of his became manifest that old Usbech had not signed the document in his presence. ' The girl signed it certainly,' said he, ' for I handed her the pen. I recollect it, as though it were yesterday.'

' They are the very people we were talking of at Leeds,' said Moulder, turning to Kantwise. ' Mason and Martock; don't you remember how you went out to Groby Park to sell some of them iron gimcracks? That was old Mason's son. They are the same people.'

' Ah, I shouldn't wonder,' said Kantwise, who was listening all the while. He never allowed intelligence of this kind to pass by him idly.

' And who's the other letter from?' asked Moulder. ' But, dash my wigs, it's past six o'clock. Come, old girl, why don't you give us the tobacco and stuff?'

' It ain't far to fetch,' said Mrs. Moulder. And then she put the tobacco and ' stuff' upon the table.

' The other letter is from an enemy of mine,' said John Kenneby, speaking very solemnly; ' an enemy of mine, named Dockwrath, who lives at Hamworth. He's an attorney too.'

' Dockwrath!' said Moulder.

Mr. Kantwise said nothing, but he looked round over his shoulder at Kenneby, and then shut his eyes.

' That was the name of the man whom we left in the commercial room at the Bull,' said Snengkeld.

' He went out to Mason's at Groby Park that same day,' said Moulder.

' Then it's the same man,' said Kenneby; and there was as much solemnity in the tone of his voice as though the unravelment of all the mysteries of the iron mask was now about to take place. Mr. Kantwise still said nothing, but he also perceived that it was the same man.

' Let me tell you, John Kenneby,' said Moulder, with the air of one who understood well the subject that he was discussing, ' if they two be the same man, then the man who wrote that letter to you is as big a blackguard as there is from this to hisself.' And Mr. Moulder in the excitement of the moment puffed hard at his pipe, took a long pull at his drink, and dragged open his waistcoat. ' I don't know whether Kantwise has anything to say upon that subject,' added Moulder.

' Not a word at present,' said Kantwise. Mr. Kantwise was a very careful man, and usually calculated with accuracy the value which he might extract from any circumstance with reference to his own main chance. Mr. Dockwrath had not as yet paid him for the set of metallic furniture, and therefore he also might well have joined in that sweeping accusation; but it might be that by a judicious use of what he now heard he might obtain the payment of that little bill,—and perhaps other collateral advantages.

And then the letter from Dockwrath to Kenneby was brought forth and read. ' My dear John,' it began,—for the two had known each other when they were lads together,—and it went on to request Kenneby's attendance at Hamworth for the short space of a few hours,—' I want to have a little conversation with you about a matter of considerable interest to both of us; and as I cannot expect you to undertake expense I enclose a money order for thirty shillings.'

' He's in earnest at any rate,' said Mr. Moulder.

' No mistake about that,' said Snengkeld.

But Mr. Kantwise spoke never a word.

It was at last decided that John Kenneby should go both to Hamworth and to Bedford Row, but that he should go to Hamworth first. Moulder would have counselled him to have gone to neither, but Snengkeld remarked that there were too many at work to let the matter sleep, and John himself observed that ' anyways he hadn't done anything to be ashamed of.'

' Then go,' said Moulder at last, ' only don't say more than you are obliged to.'

' I does not like these business talkings on Christmas night,' said Mrs. Moulder, when the matter was arranged.

' What can one do?' asked Moulder.

' It's a tempting of Providence in my mind,' said Kantwise, as he replenished his glass, and turned his eyes up to the ceiling.

' Now that's gammon,' said Moulder. And then there arose among them a long and animated discussion on matters theological.

' I'll tell you what my idea of death is,' said Moulder, after a while. ' I aint a bit afeard of it. My father was an honest man as did his duty by his employers, and he died with a bottom of brandy before him and a pipe in his mouth. I sha'n't live long myself——'

' Gracious, Moulder, don't!' said Mrs. M.

' No, more I sha'n't, 'cause I'm fat as he was; and I hope I may die as he did. I've been honest to Hubbles and Grease. They've made thousands of pounds along of me, and have never lost none. Who can say more than that? When I took to the old girl there, I insured my life, so that she shouldn't want her wittles and drink——'

' Oh, M., don't!'

' And I aint afeard to die. Snengkeld, my old pal, hand us the brandy.'

Such is the modern philosophy of the Moulders, pigs out of the sty of Epicurus. And so it was they passed Christmas-day in Great St. Helens.

CHAPTER XXV.

The Christmas doings at the Cleeve were not very gay. There was no visitor there, except Lady Mason, and it was known that she was in trouble. It must not, however, be supposed that she constantly bewailed herself while there, or made her friends miserable by a succession of hysterical tears. By no means. She made an effort to be serene, and the effort was successful—as such efforts usually are. On the morning of Christmas-day they duly attended church, and Lady Mason was seen by all Hamworth sitting in the Cleeve pew. In no way could the baronet's friendship have been shown more plainly than in this, nor could a more significant mark of intimacy have been given;—all which Sir Peregrine well understood. The people of Hamworth had chosen to talk scandal about Lady Mason, but he at any rate would show how little attention he paid to the falsehoods that there were circulated. So he stood by her at the pew door as she entered, with as much deference as though she had been a duchess; and the people of Hamworth, looking on, wondered which would be right, Mr. Dockwrath or Sir Peregrine.

After dinner Sir Peregrine gave a toast. ' Lady Mason, we will drink the health of the absent boys. God bless them! I hope they are enjoying themselves.'

' God bless them!' said Mrs. Orme, putting her handkerchief to her eyes.

' God bless them both!' said Lady Mason, also putting her handkerchief to her eyes. Then the ladies left the room, and that was the extent of their special festivity. ' Robert,' said Sir Peregrine immediately afterwards to his butler, ' let them have what port wine they want in the servants' hall—within measure.'

' Yes, Sir Peregrine.'

' And, Robert, I shall not want you again.'

' Thank you, Sir Peregrine.'

From all which it may be imagined that the Christmas doings at the Cleeve were chiefly maintained below stairs.

' I do hope they are happy,' said Mrs. Orme, when the two ladies were together in the drawing-room. 'They have a very nice party at Noningsby.'

'Your boy will be happy, I'm sure,' said Lady Mason.

'And why not Lucius also?'

It was sweet in Lady Mason's ear to hear her son called by his Christian name. All these increasing signs of interest and intimacy were sweet, but especially any which signified some favour shown to her son. 'This trouble weighs heavy on him,' she replied. 'It is only natural that he should feel it.'

'Papa does not seem to think much of it,' said Mrs. Orme. 'If I were you, I would strive to forget it.'

'I do strive,' said the other; and then she took the hand which Mrs. Orme had stretched out to her, and that lady got up and kissed her.

'Dearest friend,' said Mrs. Orme, 'if we can comfort you we will.' And then they sobbed in each other's arms.

In the mean time Sir Peregrine was sitting alone, thinking. He sat thinking, with his glass of claret untouched by his side, and with the biscuit which he had taken lying untouched upon the table. As he sat he had raised one leg upon the other, placing his foot on his knee, and he held it there with his hand upon his instep. And so he sat without moving for some quarter of an hour, trying to use all his mind on the subject which occupied it. At last he roused himself, almost with a start, and leaving his chair, walked three or four times the length of the room. 'Why should I not?' at last he said to himself, stopping suddenly and placing his hand upon the table. 'Why should I not, if it pleases me? It shall not injure him—nor her.' And then he walked again. 'But I will ask Edith,' he said, still speaking to himself. 'If she says that she disapproves of it, I will not do it.' And then he left the room, while the wine still remained untasted on the table.

On the day following Christmas Mr. Furnival went up to town, and Mr. Round junior—Mat Round, as he was called in the profession—came to him at his chambers. A promise had been made to the barrister by Round and Crook that no active steps should be taken against Lady Mason on the part of Joseph Mason of Groby, without notice being given to Mr. Furnival. And this visit by appointment was made in consequence of that promise.

'You see,' said Matthew Round, when that visit was nearly brought to a close, 'that we are pressed very hard to go on with this, and if we do not, somebody else will.'

'Nevertheless, if I were you, I should decline,' said Mr. Furnival.

'You're looking to your client, not to ours, sir,' said the attorney. 'The fact is that the whole case is very queer. It was proved on the last trial that Bolster and Kenneby were witnesses to a deed on the 14th of July, and that was all that was proved. Now we can prove that they were on that day witnesses to another deed. Were they witnesses to two ?'

' Why should they not be ?'

' That is for us to see. We have written to them both to come up to us, and in order that we might be quite on the square I thought it right to tell you.'

' Thank you; yes; I cannot complain of you. And what form do you think that your proceedings will take ?'

' Joseph Mason talks of indicting her for—forgery,' said the attorney, pausing a moment before he dared to pronounce the dread word.

' Indict her for forgery !' said Furnival, with a start. And yet the idea was one which had been for some days present to his mind's eye.

' I do not say so,' said Round. ' I have as yet seen none of the witnesses myself. If they are prepared to prove that they did sign two separate dòcuments on that day, the thing must pass off.' It was clear to Mr. Furnival that even Mr. Round junior would be glad that it should pass off. And then he also sat thinking. Might it not be probable that, with a little judicious exercise of their memory, those two witnesses would remember that they had signed two documents ; or at any rate, looking to the lapse of the time, that they might be induced to forget altogether whether they had signed one, two, or three ? Or even if they could be mystified so that nothing could be proved, it would still be well with his client. Indeed no magistrate would commit such a person as Lady Mason, especially after so long an interval, and no grand jury would find a bill against her, except upon evidence that was clear, well defined, and almost indubitable. If any point of doubt could be shown, she might be brought off without a trial, if only she would be true to herself. At the former trial there was the existing codicil, and the fact also that the two surviving reputed witnesses would not deny their signatures. These signatures—if they were genuine signatures—had been attached with all proper formality, and the form used went to state that the testator had signed the instrument in the presence of them all, they all being present together at the same time. The survivors had both asserted that when they did affix their names the three were then present, as was also Sir Joseph ; but there had been a terrible doubt even then as to the identity of the document ; and a doubt also as to there having been any signature made by one of the reputed witnesses—by that one, namely, who at the time of that trial was dead. Now another document was forthcoming, purporting to have been witnessed, on the same day, by these two surviving witnesses ! If that document were genuine, and if these two survivors should be clear that they had written their names but once on that 14th of July, in such case could it be possible to quash further public inquiry ? The criminal

prosecution might not be possible as a first proceeding, but if the
estate were recovered at common law, would not the criminal prosecution follow as a matter of course? And then Mr. Furnival
thought it all over again and again.

If this document were genuine—this new document which the
man Dockwrath stated that he had found—this deed of separation
of partnership which purported to have been executed on that 14th
of July! That was now the one important question. If it were
genuine! And why should there not be as strong a question of the
honesty of that document as of the other? Mr. Furnival well knew
that no fraudulent deed would be forged and produced without a
motive; and that if he impugned this deed he must show the
motive. Motive enough there was, no doubt. Mason might have
had it forged in order to get the property, or Dockwrath to gratify
his revenge. But in such case it would be a forgery of the present
day. There could have been no motive for such a forgery twenty
years ago. The paper, the writing, the attested signature of
Martock, the other party to it, would prove that it had not been
got up and manufactured now. Dockwrath would not dare to bring
forward such a forgery as that. There was no hope of any such
result.

But might not he, Furnival, if the matter were pushed before a
jury, make them think that the two documents stood balanced
against each other? and that Lady Mason's respectability, her long
possession, together with the vile malignity of her antagonists, gave
the greater probability of honesty to the disputed codicil? Mr.
Furnival did think that he might induce a jury to acquit her; but
he terribly feared that he might not be able to induce the world to
acquit her also. As he thought of all the case, he seemed to put himself apart from the world at large. He did not question himself as
to his own belief, but seemed to feel that it would suffice for him
if he could so bring it about that her other friends should think her
innocent. It would by no means suffice for him to secure for her
son the property, and for her a simple acquittal. It was not that
he dreaded the idea of thinking her guilty himself; perhaps he did
so think her now—he half thought her so, at any rate; but he
greatly dreaded the idea of others thinking so. It might be well to
buy up Dockwrath, if it were possible. If it were possible! But
then it was not possible that he himself could have a hand in such
a matter. Could Crabwitz do it? No; he thought not. And then,
at this moment, he was not certain that he could depend on Crabwitz.

And why should he trouble himself in this way? Mr. Furnival
was a man loyal to his friends at heart. Had Lady Mason been a
man, and had he pulled that man through great difficulties in early
life, he would have been loyally desirous of carrying him through
the same or similar difficulties at any after period. In that cause

which he had once battled he was always ready to do battle, without reference to any professional consideration of triumph or profit. It was to this feeling of loyalty that he had owed much of his success in life. And in such a case as this it may be supposed that that feeling would be strong. But then such a feeling presumed a case in which he could sympathize—in which he could believe. Would it be well that he should allow himself to feel the same interest in this case, to maintain respecting it the same personal anxiety, if he ceased to believe in it? He did ask himself the question, and he finally answered it in the affirmative. He had beaten Joseph Mason once in a good stand-up fight; and having done so, having thus made the matter his own, it was necessary to his comfort that he should beat him again, if another fight were to be fought. Lady Mason was his client, and all the associations of his life taught him to be true to her as such.

And as we are thus searching into his innermost heart we must say more than this. Mrs. Furnival perhaps had no sufficient grounds for those terrible fears of hers; but nevertheless the mistress of Orley Farm was very comely in the eyes of the lawyer. Her eyes, when full of tears, were very bright, and her hand, as it lay in his, was very soft. He laid out for himself no scheme of wickedness with reference to her; he purposely entertained no thoughts which he knew to be wrong; but, nevertheless, he did feel that he liked to have her by him, that he liked to be her adviser and friend, that he liked to wipe the tears from those eyes—not by a material handkerchief from his pocket, but by immaterial manly sympathy from his bosom; and that he liked also to feel the pressure of that hand. Mrs. Furnival had become solid, and heavy, and red; and though he himself was solid, and heavy, and red also —more so, indeed, in proportion than his poor wife, for his redness, as I have said before, had almost reached a purple hue; nevertheless his eye loved to look upon the beauty of a lovely woman, his ear loved to hear the tone of her voice, and his hand loved to meet the soft ripeness of her touch. It was very wrong that it should have been so, but the case is not without a parallel.

And therefore he made up his mind that he would not desert Lady Mason. He would not desert her; but how would he set about the fighting that would be necessary in her behalf? He was well aware of this, that if he fought at all, he must fight now. It would not do to let the matter go on till she should be summoned to defend herself. Steps which might now be available would be altogether unavailable in two or three months' time—would be so, perhaps, if he allowed two or three weeks to pass idly by him. Mr. Round, luckily, was not disposed to hurry his proceedings; nor, as far as he was concerned, was there any bitterness of antagonism. But with both Mason and Dockwrath there would be hot haste, and hotter malice. From those who were really her enemies she could expect no quarter.

He was to return on that evening to Noningsby, and on the following day he would go over to The Cleeve. He knew that Lady Mason was staying there; but his object in making that visit would not be merely that he might see her, but also that he might speak to Sir Peregrine, and learn how far the baronet was inclined to support his neighbour in her coming tribulation. He would soon be able to ascertain what Sir Peregrine really thought—whether he suspected the possibility of any guilt; and he would ascertain also what was the general feeling in the neighbourhood of Hamworth. It would be a great thing if he could spread abroad a conviction that she was an injured woman. It would be a great thing even if he could make it known that the great people of the neighbourhood so thought. The jurymen of Alston would be mortal men; and it might be possible that they should be imbued with a favourable bias on the subject before they assembled in their box for its consideration.

He wished that he knew the truth in the matter; or rather he wished he could know whether or no she were innocent, without knowing whether or no she were guilty. The fight in his hands would be conducted on terms so much more glorious if he could feel sure of her innocence. But then if he attempted that, and she were not innocent, all might be sacrificed by the audacity of his proceedings. He could not venture that, unless he were sure of his ground. For a moment or two he thought that he would ask her the question. He said to himself that he could forgive the fault. That it had been repented ere this he did not doubt, and it would be sweet to say to her that it was very grievous, but that yet it might be forgiven. It would be sweet to feel that she was in his hands, and that he would treat her with mercy and kindness. But then a hundred other thoughts forbade him to think more of this. If she had been guilty—if she declared her guilt to him—would not restitution be necessary? In that case her son must know it, and all the world must know it. Such a confession would be incompatible with that innocence before the world which it was necessary that she should maintain. Moreover, he must be able to proclaim aloud his belief in her innocence; and how could he do that, knowing her to be guilty—knowing that she also knew that he had such knowledge? It was impossible that he should ask any such question, or admit of any such confidence.

It would be necessary, if the case did come to a trial, that she should employ some attorney. The matter must come into the barrister's hands in the usual way, through a solicitor's house, and it would be well that the person employed should have a firm faith in his client. What could he say—he, as a barrister—if the attorney suggested to him that the lady might possibly be guilty? As he thought of all these things he almost dreaded the difficulties before him.

He rang the bell for Crabwitz—the peculiar bell which Crabwitz was bound to answer—having first of all gone through a little ceremony with his cheque-book. Crabwitz entered, still sulky in his demeanour, for as yet the old anger had not been appeased, and it was still a doubtful matter in the clerk's mind whether or no it might not be better for him to seek a master who would better appreciate his services. A more lucrative position it might be difficult for him to find; but money is not everything, as Crabwitz said to himself more than once.

'Crabwitz,' said Mr. Furnival, looking with a pleasant face at his clerk, 'I am leaving town this evening, and I shall be absent for the next ten days. If you like you can go away for a holiday.'

'It's rather late in the season now, sir,' said Crabwitz, gloomily, as though he were determined not to be pleased.

'It is a little late, as you say; but I really could not manage it earlier. Come, Crabwitz, you and I should not quarrel. Your work has been a little hard, but then so has mine also.'

'I fancy you like it, sir.'

'Ha! ha! Like it, indeed! But so do you like it—in its way. Come, Crabwitz, you have been an excellent servant to me; and I don't think that, on the whole, I have been a bad master to you.'

'I am making no complaint, sir.'

'But you're cross because I've kept you in town a little too long. Come, Crabwitz, you must forget all that. You have worked very hard this year past. Here is a cheque for fifty pounds. Get out of town for a fortnight or so, and amuse yourself.'

'I'm sure I'm very much obliged, sir,' said Crabwitz, putting out his hand and taking the cheque. He felt that his master had got the better of him, and he was still a little melancholy on that account. He would have valued his grievance at that moment almost more than the fifty pounds, especially as by the acceptance of it he surrendered all right to complain for some considerable time to come.

'By-the-by, Crabwitz,' said Mr. Furnival, as the clerk was about to leave the room.

'Yes, sir,' said Crabwitz.

'You have never chanced to hear of an attorney named Dockwrath, I suppose?'

'What! in London, Mr. Furnival?'

'No; I fancy he has no place of business in town. He lives I know at Hamworth.'

'It's he you mean, sir, that is meddling in this affair of Lady Mason's.'

'What! you have heard of that; have you?'

'Oh! yes, sir. It's being a good deal talked about in the profession. Messrs. Round and Crook's leading young man was up here with me the other day, and he did say a good deal about it. He's a very decent young man, considering his position, is Smart.'

'And he knows Dockwrath, does he?'

'Well, sir, I can't say that he knows much of the man; but Dockwrath has been at their place of business pretty constant of late, and he and Mr. Matthew seem thick enough together.'

'Oh! they do; do they?'

'So Smart tells me. I don't know how it is myself, sir. I don't suppose this Dockwrath is a very——'

'No, no; exactly. I dare say not. You've never seen him yourself, Crabwitz?'

'Who, sir? I, sir? No, sir, I've never set eyes on the man, sir. From all I hear it's not very likely he should come here; and I'm sure it is not at all likely that I should go to him.'

Mr. Furnival sat thinking awhile, and the clerk stood waiting opposite to him, leaning with both his hands upon the table. 'You don't know any one in the neighbourhood of Hamworth, I suppose?' Mr. Furnival said at last.

'Who, sir? I, sir? Not a soul, sir. I never was there in my life.'

'I'll tell you why I ask. I strongly suspect that that man Dockwrath is at some very foul play.' And then he told to his clerk so much of the whole story of Lady Mason and her affairs as he chose that he should know. 'It is plain enough that he may give Lady Mason a great deal of annoyance,' he ended by saying.

'There's no doubting that, sir,' said Crabwitz. 'And, to tell the truth, I believe his mind is made up to do it.'

'You don't think that anything could be done by seeing him? Of course Lady Mason has got nothing to compromise. Her son's estate is as safe as my hat; but——'

'The people at Round's think it isn't quite so safe, sir.'

'Then the people at Round's know nothing about it. But Lady Mason is so averse to legal proceedings that it would be worth her while to have matters settled. You understand?'

'Yes, sir; I understand. Would not an attorney be the best person, sir?'

'Not just at present, Crabwitz. Lady Mason is a very dear friend of mine——'

'Yes, sir; we know that,' said Crabwitz.

'If you could make any pretence for running down to Hamworth —change of air, you know, for a week or so. It's a beautiful country; just the place you like. And you might find out whether anything could be done, eh?'

Mr. Crabwitz was well aware, from the first, that he did not get fifty pounds for nothing.

"Why should I not."

CHAPTER XXVI.

WHY SHOULD I NOT?

A DAY or two after his conversation with Crabwitz, as described in the last chapter, Mr. Furnival was driven up to the door of Sir Peregrine Orme's house in a Hamworth fly. He had come over by train from Alston on purpose to see the baronet, whom he found seated in his library. At that very moment he was again asking himself those questions which he had before asked as he was walking up and down his own dining-room. 'Why should I not?' he said to himself,—'unless, indeed, it will make her unhappy.' And then the barrister was shown into his room, muffled up to his eyes -in his winter clothing.

Sir Peregrine and Mr. Furnival were well known to each other, and had always met as friends. They had been interested on the same side in the first Orley Farm Case, and possessed a topic of sympathy in their mutual dislike to Joseph Mason of Groby Park. Sir Peregrine therefore was courteous, and when he learned the subject on which he was to be consulted he became almost more than courteous.

'Oh! yes; she's staying here, Mr. Furnival. Would you like to see her?'

'Before I leave I shall be glad to see her, Sir Peregrine; but if I am justified in regarding you as specially her friend, it may perhaps be well that I should first have some conversation with you.' Sir Peregrine in answer to this declared that Mr. Furnival certainly would be so justified; that he did regard himself as Lady Mason's special friend, and that he was ready to hear anything that the barrister might have to say to him.

Many of the points of this case have already been named so often, and will, I fear, be necessarily named so often again that I will spare the repetition when it is possible. Mr. Furnival on this occasion told Sir Peregrine—not all that he had heard, but all that he thought it necessary to tell, and soon became fully aware that in the baronet's mind there was not the slightest shadow of suspicion that Lady Mason could have been in any way to blame. He, the baronet, was thoroughly convinced that Mr. Mason was the great sinner in this matter, and that he was prepared to harass an innocent and excellent lady from motives of disappointed cupidity and long-sustained malice, which made him seem in Sir Peregrine's eyes a being almost too vile for humanity. And of Dockwrath he thought almost as badly—only that Dockwrath was below the level of his thinking. Of Lady Mason he spoke as an excellent and beautiful woman driven to misery by unworthy persecution; and so spoke with an enthusiasm that was surprising to Mr. Furnival. It was very manifest that she would not want for friendly countenance, if friendly countenance could carry her through her difficulties.

There was no suspicion against Lady Mason in the mind of Sir Peregrine, and Mr. Furnival was careful not to arouse any such feeling. When he found that the baronet spoke of her as being altogether pure and good, he also spoke of her in the same tone; but in doing so his game was very difficult. ' Let him do his worst, Mr. Furnival,' said Sir Peregrine; ' and let her remain tranquil; that is my advice to Lady Mason. It is not possible that he can really injure her.'

' It is possible that he can do nothing—very probable that he can do nothing; but nevertheless, Sir Peregrine——'

' I would have no dealing with him or his. I would utterly disregard them. If he, or they, or any of them choose to take steps to annoy her, let her attorney manage that in the usual way. I am no lawyer myself, Mr. Furnival, but that I think is the manner in which things of this kind should be arranged. I do not know whether they have still the power of disputing the will, but if so, let them do it.'

Gradually, by very slow degrees, Mr. Furnival made Sir Peregrine understand that the legal doings now threatened were not of that nature;—that Mr. Mason did not now talk of proceeding at law for the recovery of the property, but for the punishment of his father's widow as a criminal; and at last the dreadful word ' forgery' dropped from his lips.

' Who dares to make such a charge as that?' demanded the baronet, while fire literally flashed from his eyes in his anger. And when he was told that Mr. Mason did make such a charge he called him ' a mean, unmanly dastard.' ' I do not believe that he would dare to make it against a man,' said Sir Peregrine.

But there was the fact of the charge—the fact that it had been placed in the hands of respectable attorneys, with instructions to them to press it on—and the fact also that the evidence by which that charge was to be supported possessed at any rate a *primâ facie* appearance of strength. All this it was necessary to explain to Sir Peregrine, as it would also be necessary to explain it to Lady Mason.

' Am I to understand, then, that you also think——?' began Sir Peregrine.

' You are not to understand that I think anything injurious to the lady; but I do fear that she is in a position of much jeopardy, and that great care will be necessary.'

'Good heavens! Do you mean to say that an innocent person can under such circumstances be in danger in this country?'

'An innocent person, Sir Peregrine, may be in danger of very great annoyance, and also of very great delay in proving that innocence. Innocent people have died under the weight of such charges. We must remember that she is a woman, and therefore weaker than you or I.'

'Yes, yes; but still——. You do not say that you think she can be in any real danger?' It seemed, from the tone of the old man's voice, as though he were almost angry with Mr. Furnival for supposing that such could be the case. 'And you intend to tell her all this?' he asked.

'I fear that, as her friend, neither you nor I will be warranted in keeping her altogether in the dark. Think what her feelings would be if she were summoned before a magistrate without any preparation!'

'No magistrate would listen to such a charge,' said Sir Peregrine.

'In that he must be guided by the evidence.'

'I would sooner throw up my commission than lend myself in any way to a proceeding so iniquitous.'

This was all very well, and the existence of such a feeling showed great generosity, and perhaps also poetic chivalry on the part of Sir Peregrine Orme; but it was not the way of the world, and so Mr. Furnival was obliged to explain. Magistrates would listen to the charge—would be forced to listen to the charge,—if the evidence were apparently sound. A refusal on the part of a magistrate to do so would not be an act of friendship to Lady Mason, as Mr. Furnival endeavoured to explain. 'And you wish to see her?' Sir Peregrine asked at last.

'I think she should be told; but as she is in your house, I will, of course, do nothing in which you do not concur.' Upon which Sir Peregrine rang the bell and desired the servant to take his compliments to Lady Mason and beg her attendance in the library if it were quite convenient. 'Tell her,' said Sir Peregrine, 'that Mr. Furnival is here.'

When the message was given to her she was seated with Mrs. Orme, and at the moment she summoned strength to say that she would obey the invitation, without displaying any special emotion while the servant was in the room; but when the door was shut, her friend looked at her and saw that she was as pale as death. She was pale and her limbs quivered, and that look of agony, which now so often marked her face, was settled on her brow. Mrs. Orme had never yet seen her with such manifest signs of suffering as she wore at this instant.

'I suppose I must go to them,' she said, slowly rising from her seat; and it seemed to Mrs. Orme that she was forced to hold by the table to support herself.

'Mr. Furnival is a friend, is he not?'

'Oh, yes! a kind friend, but——'

'They shall come in here if you like it better, dear.'

'Oh, no! I will go to them. It would not do that I should seem so weak. What must you think of me to see me so?'

'I do not wonder at it, dear,' said Mrs. Orme, coming round to her; 'such cruelty would kill me. I wonder at your strength rather than your weakness.' And then she kissed her. What was there about the woman that had made all those fond of her that came near her?

Mrs. Orme walked with her across the hall, and left her only at the library door. There she pressed her hand and again kissed her, and then Lady Mason turned the handle of the door and entered the room. Mr. Furnival, when he looked at her, was startled by the pallor of her face, but nevertheless he thought that she had never looked so beautiful. 'Dear Lady Mason,' said he, 'I hope you are well.'

Sir Peregrine advanced to her and handed her over to his own arm-chair. Had she been a queen in distress she could not have been treated with more gentle deference. But she never seemed to count upon this, or in any way to assume it as her right. I should accuse her of what I regard as a sin against all good taste were I to say that she was humble in her demeanour; but there was a soft meekness about her, an air of feminine dependence, a proneness to lean and almost to cling as she leaned, which might have been felt as irresistible by any man. She was a woman to know in her deep sorrow rather than in her joy and happiness; one with whom one would love to weep rather than to rejoice. And, indeed, the present was a time with her for weeping, not for rejoicing.

Sir Peregrine looked as though he were her father as he took her hand, and the barrister immediately comforted himself with the remembrance of the baronet's great age. It was natural, too, that Lady Mason should hang on him in his own house. So Mr. Furnival contented himself at the first moment with touching her hand and hoping that she was well. She answered hardly a word to either of them, but she attempted to smile as she sat down, and murmured something about the trouble she was giving them.

'Mr. Furnival thinks it best that you should be made aware of the steps which are being taken by Mr. Mason of Groby Park,' began Sir Peregrine. 'I am no lawyer myself, and therefore of course I cannot put my advice against his.'

'I am sure that both of you will tell me for the best,' she said.

'In such a matter as this it is right that you should be guided by him. That he is as firmly your friend as I am there can be no doubt.'

'I believe Lady Mason trusts me in that,' said the lawyer.

'Indeed I do; I would trust you both in anything,' she said.

'And there can be no doubt that he must be able to direct you for the best. I say so much at the first, because I myself so thoroughly despise that man in Yorkshire,—I am so convinced that anything which his malice may prompt him to do must be futile, that I could not myself have thought it needful to pain you by what must now be said.'

This was a dreadful commencement, but she bore it, and even was relieved by it. Indeed, no tale that Mr. Furnival could have to tell after such an exordium would be so bad as that which she had feared as the possible result of his visit. He might have come there to let her know that she was at once to be carried away— immediately to be taken to her trial—perhaps to be locked up in gaol. In her ignorance of the law she could only imagine what might or might not happen to her at any moment, and therefore the words which Sir Peregrine had spoken relieved her rather than added to her fears.

And then Mr. Furnival began his tale, and gradually put before her the facts of the matter. This he did with a choice of language and a delicacy of phraseology which were admirable, for he made her clearly understand the nature of the accusation which was brought against her without using any word which was in itself harsh in its bearing. He said nothing about fraud, or forgery, or false evidence, but he made it manifest to her that Joseph Mason had now instructed his lawyer to institute a criminal proceeding against her for having forged a codicil to her husband's will.

'I must bear it as best I may,' she said. 'May the Lord give me strength to bear it!'

'It is terrible to think of,' said Sir Peregrine; 'but nobody can doubt how it will end. You are not to suppose that Mr. Furnival intends to express any doubt as to your ultimate triumph. What we fear for you is the pain you must endure before this triumph comes.'

Ah, if that were all! As the baronet finished speaking she looked furtively into the lawyer's face to see how far the meaning of these smooth words would be supported by what she might read there. Would he also think that a final triumph did certainly await her? Sir Peregrine's real opinion was easily to be learned, either from his countenance or from his words; but it was not so with Mr. Furnival. In Mr. Furnival's face, and from Mr. Furnival's words, could be learned only that which Mr. Furnival wished to declare. He saw that glance, and fully understood it; and he knew instinctively, on the spur of the moment, that he must now either assure her by a lie, or break down all her hopes by the truth. That final triumph was not certain to her—was very far from certain! Should he now be honest to his friend, or dishonest? One great object with him was to secure the support which Sir Peregrine could give by his weight in the county; and therefore, as Sir Peregrine was present, it was needful that he should be dishonest. Arguing thus he looked the lie, and Lady Mason derived more comfort from that look than from all Sir Peregrine's words.

And then those various details were explained to her which Mr. Furnival understood that Mr. Dockwrath had picked up. They went into that matter of the partnership deed, and questions were asked as to the man Kenneby and the woman Bolster. They might both, Lady Mason said, have been witnesses to half a dozen deeds on that same day, for aught she knew to the contrary. She had been present with Sir Joseph, as far as she could now remember, during the whole of that morning, 'in and out, Sir Peregrine, as you can understand.' Sir Peregrine said that he did understand perfectly. She did know that Mr. Usbech had been there for many hours that day, probably from ten to two or three, and no doubt therefore much business was transacted. She herself remembered nothing but the affair of the will; but then that was natural, seeing that there was no other affair in which she had specially interested herself.

'No doubt these people did witness both the deeds,' said Sir Peregrine. 'For myself, I cannot conceive how that wretched man can be so silly as to spend his money on such a case as this.'

'He would do anything for revenge,' said Mr. Furnival.

And then Lady Mason was allowed to go back to the drawing-room, and what remained to be said was said between the two gentlemen alone. Sir Peregrine was very anxious that his own attorneys should be employed, and he named Messrs. Slow and Bideawhile, than whom there were no more respectable men in the whole profession. But then Mr. Furnival feared that they were too respectable. They might look at the matter in so straight-forward a light as to fancy their client really guilty; and what might happen then? Old Slow would not conceal the truth for all the baronets in England—no, nor for all the pretty women. The touch of Lady Mason's hand and the tear in her eye would be nothing to old Slow. Mr. Furnival, therefore, was obliged to explain that Slow and Bideawhile did not undertake that sort of business.

'But I should wish it to be taken up through them. There must be some expenditure, Mr. Furnival, and I should prefer that they should arrange about that.'

Mr. Furnival made no further immediate objection, and consented at last to having an interview with one of the firm on the subject, provided, of course, that that member of the firm came to him at his chambers. And then he took his leave. Nothing positive had been done, or even settled to be done, on this morning; but the persons most interested in the matter had been made to understand that the affair was taking an absolute palpable substance, and that steps must be taken—indeed, would be taken almost immediately. Mr. Furnival, as he left the house, resolved to employ the attorneys whom he might think best adapted for the purpose. He would settle that matter with Slow and Bideawhile afterwards.

And then, as he returned to Noningsby, he wondered at his persistence in the matter. He believed that his client had been guilty; he believed that this codicil was no real instrument made by Sir Joseph Mason. And so believing, would it not be better for him to wash his hands of the whole affair? Others did not think so, and would it not be better that such others should be her advisers? Was he not taking up for himself endless trouble and annoyance that could have no useful purpose? So he argued with himself, and yet by the time that he had reached Noningsby he had determined that he would stand by Lady Mason to the last. He hated that man Mason, as he declared to himself when providing himself with reasons for his resolve, and regarded his bitter, malicious justice as more criminal than any crime of which Lady Mason might have been guilty. And then as he leaned back in the railway carriage he still saw her pale face before him, still heard the soft tone of her voice, and was still melted by the tear in her eye. Young man, young friend of mine, who art now filled to the overflowing of thy brain with poetry, with chivalry, and love, thou seest seated opposite to thee there that grim old man, with long snuffy nose, with sharp piercing eyes, with scanty frizzled hairs. He is rich and cross, has been three times married, and has often quarrelled with his children. He is fond of his wine, and snores dreadfully after dinner. To thy seeming he is a dry, withered stick, from which all the sap of sentiment has been squeezed by the rubbing and friction of years. Poetry, the feeling if not the words of poetry,—is he not dead to it, even as the pavement is dead over which his wheels trundle? Oh, my young friend! thou art ignorant in this—as in most other things. He may not twitter of sentiment, as thou doest; nor may I trundle my hoop along the high road as do the little boys. The fitness of things forbids it. But that old man's heart is as soft as thine, if thou couldst but read it. The body dries up and withers away, and the bones grow old; the brain, too, becomes decrepit, as do the sight, the hearing, and the soul. But the heart that is tender once remains tender to the last.

Lady Mason, when she left the library, walked across the hall towards the drawing-room, and then she paused. She would fain remain alone for a while if it were possible, and therefore she

turned aside into a small breakfast parlour, which was used every
morning, but which was rarely visited afterwards during the day.
Here she sat, leaving the door slightly open, so that she might
know when Mr. Furnival left the baronet. Here she sat for a full
hour, waiting—waiting—waiting. There was no sofa or lounging-
chair in the room, reclining in which she could remain there half
sleeping, sitting comfortably at her ease; but she placed herself near
the table, and leaning there with her face upon her hand, she
waited patiently till Mr. Furnival had gone. That her mind was
full of thoughts I need hardly say, but yet the hour seemed very
long to her. At last she heard the library door open, she heard
Sir Peregrine's voice as he stood in the hall and shook hands with
his departing visitor, she heard the sound of the wheels as the fly
moved upon the gravel, and then she heard Sir Peregrine again
shut the library door behind him.

She did not immediately get up from her chair; she still waited
awhile, perhaps for another period of ten minutes, and then she
noiselessly left the room, and moving quickly and silently across
the hall she knocked at Sir Peregrine's door. This she did so
gently that at first no answer was made to her. Then she knocked
again, hardly louder but with a repeated rap, and Sir Peregrine
summoned her to come in. 'May I trouble you once more—for one
moment?' she said.

'Certainly, certainly; it is no trouble. I am glad that you are
here in the house at this time, that you may see me at any moment
that you may wish.'

'I do not know why you should be so good to me.'

'Because you are in great grief, in undeserved grief, because——.
Lady Mason, my services are at your command. I will act for you
as I would for a—daughter.'

'You hear now of what it is that they accuse me.'

'Yes,' he said; 'I do hear:' and as he spoke he came round so
that he was standing near to her, but with his back to the fireplace. 'I do hear, and I blush to think that there is a man in
England, holding the position of a county magistrate, who can so
forget all that is due to honesty, to humanity, and to self-respect.'

'You do not then think that I have been guilty of this thing?'

'Guilty—I think you guilty! No, nor does he think so. It is
impossible that he should think so. I am no more sure of my own
innocence than of yours;' and as he spoke he took both her hands
and looked into her face, and his eyes also were full of tears. 'You
may be sure of this, that neither I nor Edith will ever think you
guilty.'

'Dearest Edith,' she said; she had never before called Sir
Peregrine's daughter-in-law by her Christian name, and as she now
did so she almost felt that she had sinned. But Sir Peregrine took

it in good part. 'She is dearest,' he said; 'and be sure of this, that she will be true to you through it all.'

And so they stood for a while without further speech. He still held both her hands, and the tears still stood in his eyes. Her eyes were turned to the ground, and from them the tears were running fast. At first they ran silently, without audible sobbing, and Sir Peregrine, with his own old eyes full of salt water, hardly knew that she was weeping. But gradually the drops fell upon his hand, one by one at first, and then faster and faster; and soon there came a low sob, a sob all but suppressed, but which at last forced itself forth, and then her head fell upon his shoulder. 'My dear,' he said, himself hardly able to speak; 'my poor dear, my ill-used dear!' and as she withdrew one hand from his, that she might press a handkerchief to her face, his vacant arm passed itself round her waist. 'My poor, ill-used dear!' he said again, as he pressed her to his old heart, and leaning over her he kissed her lips.

So she stood for some few seconds, feeling that she was pressed close by the feeble pressure of his arm, and then she gradually sank through from his embrace, and fell upon her knees at his feet. She knelt at his feet, supporting herself with one arm upon the table, and with the other hand she still held his hand over which her head was bowed. 'My friend,' she said, still sobbing, and sobbing loudly now; 'my friend, that God has sent me in my trouble.' And then, with words that were wholly inaudible, she murmured some prayer on his behalf.

'I am better now,' she said, raising herself quickly to her feet when a few seconds had passed. 'I am better now,' and she stood erect before him. 'By God's mercy I will endure it; I think I can endure it now.'

'If I can lighten the load—'

'You have lightened it—of half its weight; but, Sir Peregine, I will leave this—'

'Leave this! go away from The Cleeve!'

'Yes; I will not destroy the comfort of your home by the wretchedness of my position. I will not—'

'Lady Mason, my house is altogether at your service. If you will be led by me in this matter, you will not leave it till this cloud shall have passed by you. You will be better to be alone now;' and then before she could answer him further, he led her to the door. She felt that it was better for her to be alone, and she hastened up the stairs to her own chamber.

'And why should I not?' said Sir Peregrine to himself, as he again walked the length of the library.

CHAPTER XXVII.

COMMERCE.

Lucius Mason was still staying at Noningsby when Mr. Furnival made his visit to Sir Peregrine, and on that afternoon he received a note from his mother. Indeed, there were three notes passed between them on that afternoon, for he wrote an answer to his mother, and then received a reply to that answer. Lady Mason told him that she did not intend to return home to the Farm quite immediately, and explained that her reason for not doing so was the necessity that she should have assistance and advice at this period of her trouble. She did not say that she misdoubted the wisdom of her son's counsels; but it appeared to him that she intended to signify to him that she did so, and he answered her in words that were sore and almost bitter. ' I am sorry,' he said, ' that you and I cannot agree about a matter that is of such vital concern to both of us; but as it is so, we can only act as each thinks best, you for yourself and I for myself. I am sure, however, that you will believe that my only object is your happiness and your fair name, which is dearer to me than anything else in the world.' In answer to this, she had written again immediately, filling her letter with sweet words of motherly love, telling him that she was sure, quite sure, of his affection and kind spirit, and excusing herself for not putting the matter altogether in his hands by saying that she was forced to lean on those who had supported her from the beginning—through that former trial which had taken place when he, Lucius, was yet a baby. ' And, dearest Lucius, you must not be angry with me,' she went on to say; ' I am suffering much under this cruel persecution, but my sufferings would be more than doubled if my own boy quarrelled with me.' Lucius, when he received this, flung up his head. ' Quarrel with her,' he said to himself; ' nothing on earth would make me quarrel with her; but I cannot say that that is right which I think to be wrong.' His feelings were good and honest, and kindly too in their way; but tenderness of heart was not his weakness. I should wrong him if I were to say that he was hard-hearted, but he flattered himself that he was just-hearted, which sometimes is nearly the same—as had been the case with his father before him, and was now the case with his half-brother Joseph.

The day after this was his last at Noningsby. He had told Lady Staveley that he intended to go, and though she had pressed his further stay, remarking that none of the young people intended to move till after twelfth-night, nevertheless he persisted. With the young people of the house themselves he had not much advanced himself; and altogether he did not find himself thoroughly happy in the judge's house. They were more thoughtless than he—as he thought; they did not understand him, and therefore he would leave them. Besides, there was a great day of hunting coming on, at which everybody was to take a part, and as he did not hunt that gave him another reason for going. 'They have nothing to do but amuse themselves,' he said to himself; 'but I have a man's work before me, and a man's misfortunes. I will go home and face both.'

In all this there was much of conceit, much of pride, much of deficient education—deficiency in that special branch of education which England has imparted to the best of her sons, but which is now becoming out of fashion. He had never learned to measure himself against others,—I do not mean his knowledge or his book-acquirements, but the every-day conduct of his life,— and to perceive that that which is insignificant in others must be insignificant in himself also. To those around him at Noningsby his extensive reading respecting the Iapetidæ recommended him not at all, nor did his agricultural ambitions;—not even to Felix Graham, as a companion, though Felix Graham could see further into his character than did the others. He was not such as they were. He had not the unpretentious, self-controlling humour, perfectly free from all conceit, which was common to them. Life did not come easy to him, and the effort which he was ever making was always visible. All men should ever be making efforts, no doubt; but those efforts should not be conspicuous. But yet Lucius Mason was not a bad fellow, and young Staveley showed much want of discernment when he called him empty-headed and selfish. Those epithets were by no means applicable to him. That he was not empty-headed is certain; and he was moreover capable of a great self-sacrifice.

That his talents and good qualities were appreciated by one person in the house, seemed evident to Lady Staveley and the other married ladies of the party. Miss Furnival, as they all thought, had not found him empty-headed. And, indeed, it may be doubted whether Lady Staveley would have pressed his stay at Noningsby, had Miss Furnival been less gracious. Dear Lady Staveley was always living in a fever lest her only son, the light of her eyes, should fall irrevocably in love with some lady that was by no means good enough for him. Revocably in love he was daily falling; but some day he would go too deep, and the waters would close over his well-loved head. Now in her dear old favouring eyes Sophia Furnival was by no means good enough, and it had been quite clear that Augustus had become thoroughly lost in his attempts to bring about a match between Felix Graham and the barrister's daughter. In preparing the bath for his friend he had himself fallen bodily into the water. He was always at Miss Furnival's side, as long as Miss Furnival would permit it. But it seemed to Lady Staveley that Miss Furnival, luckily, was quite as fond of having Lucius Mason at her side;—that of the two she perhaps preferred Lucius Mason. That her taste and judgment should be so bad was wonderful to Lady Staveley; but this depravity though wonderful was useful; and therefore Lucius Mason might have been welcome to remain at Noningsby.

It may, however, be possible that Miss Furnival knew what she was doing quite as well as Lady Staveley could know for her. In the first place she may possibly have thought it indiscreet to admit Mr. Staveley's attentions with too much freedom. She may have doubted their sincerity, or feared to give offence to the family, or Mr. Mason may in her sight have been the preferable suitor. That his gifts of intellect were at any rate equal to those of the other there can be no doubt. Then his gifts of fortune were already his own, and, for ought that Miss Furnival knew, might be equal to any that would ever appertain to the other gentleman. That Lady Staveley should think her swan better looking than Lady Mason's goose was very natural; but then Lady Mason would no doubt have regarded the two birds in an exactly opposite light. It is only fair to conceive that Miss Furnival was a better judge than either of them.

On the evening before his departure the whole party had been playing commerce; for the rule of the house during these holidays was this, that all the amusements brought into vogue were to be adapted to the children. If the grown-up people could adapt themselves to them, so much the better for them; if not, so much the worse; they must in such case provide for themselves. On the whole, the grown-up people seemed to live nearly as jovial a life as did the children. Whether the judge himself was specially fond of commerce I cannot say; but he persisted in putting in the whole pool, and played through the entire game, rigidly fighting for the same pool on behalf of a very small grandchild, who sat during the whole time on his knee. There are those who call cards the devil's books, but we will presume that the judge was of a different way of thinking.

On this special evening Sophia had been sitting next to Augustus, —a young man can always arrange these matters in his own house,— but had nevertheless lost all her lives early in the game. 'I will not have any cheating to-night,' she had said to her neighbour; 'I will take my chance, and if I die, I die. One can die but once.' And so she had died, three times indeed instead of once only, and had left the table. Lucius Mason also had died. He generally did die the first, having no aptitude for a collection of kings or aces, and so they two came together over the fire in the second drawing-room, far away from the card-players. There was nothing at all remarkable in this, as Mr. Furnival and one or two others who did not play commerce were also there; but nevertheless they were separated from those of the party who were most inclined to criticise their conduct.

' So you are leaving to-morrow, Mr. Mason,' said Sophia.

' Yes. I go home to-morrow after breakfast; to my own house, where for some weeks to come I shall be absolutely alone.'

' Your mother is staying at The Cleeve, I think.'

' Yes,—and intends remaining there as she tells me. I wish with all my heart she were at Orley Farm.'

' Papa saw her yesterday. He went over to The Cleeve on purpose to see her; and this morning he has been talking to me about her. I cannot tell you how I grieve for her.'

' It is very sad; very sad. But I wish she were in her own house. Under the circumstances as they now are, I think it would be better for her to be there than elsewhere. Her name has been disgraced—'

' No, Mr. Mason; not disgraced.'

' Yes; disgraced. Mark you; I do not say that she has been disgraced; and pray do not suppose it possible that I should think so. But a great opprobrium has been thrown on her name, and it would be better, I think, that she should remain at home till she has cast it off from her. Even for myself, I feel it almost wrong to be here; nor would I have come had I known when I did come as much as I do know now.'

' But no one can for a moment think that your mother has done anything that she should not have done.'

' Then why do so many people talk of her as though she had committed a great crime? Miss Furnival, I know that she is innocent. I know it as surely as I know the fact of my own existence—'

' And we all feel the same thing.'

' But if you were in my place,—if it were your father whose name was so bandied about in people's mouths, you would think that it behoved him to do nothing, to go nowhere, till he had forced the world to confess his innocence. And this is ten times stronger with regard to a woman. I have given my mother my counsel, and I regret to say that she differs from me.'

' Why do you not speak to papa?'

' I did once. I went to him at his chambers, and he rebuked me.'

' Rebuked you, Mr. Mason! He did not do that intentionally I am sure. I have heard him say that you are an excellent son.'

'But nevertheless he did rebuke me. He considered that I was travelling beyond my own concerns, in wishing to interfere for the protection of my mother's name. He said that I should leave it to such people as the Staveleys and the Ormes to guard her from ignominy and disgrace.'

'Oh, he did not mean that!'

'But to me it seems that it should be a son's first duty. They are talking of trouble and of cost. I would give every hour I have in the day, and every shilling I own in the world to save her from one week of such suffering as she now endures; but it cuts me to the heart when she tells me that because she is suffering, therefore she must separate herself from me. I think it would be better for her, Miss Furnival, to be staying at home with me, than to be at The Cleeve.'

'The kindness of Mrs. Orme must be a great support to her.'

'And why should not my kindness be a support to her,—or rather my affection? We know from whom all these scandals come. My desire is to meet that man in a court of law and thrust these falsehoods down his throat.'

'Ah! but you are a man.'

'And therefore I would take the burden from her shoulders. But no; she will not trust to me. The truth, Miss Furnival, is this, that she has not yet learned to think of me as a man. To her I am still the boy for whom she is bound to provide, not the son who should bear for her all her cares. As it is I feel that I do not dare again to trouble her with my advice.'

'Grandmamma is dead,' shouted out a shrill small voice from the card-table. 'Oh, grandmamma, do have one of my lives. Look! I've got three,' said another.

'Thank you, my dears; but the natural term of my existence has come, and I will not rebel against fate.'

'Oh, grandmamma,—we'll let you have another grace.'

'By no means, Charley. Indeed I am not clear that I am entitled to Christian burial, as it is.'

'A case of felo de se, I rather think' said her son. 'About this time of the night suicide does become common among the elders. Unfortunately for me, the pistol that I have been snapping at my own head for the last half-hour always hangs fire.'

There was not much of love-making in the conversation which had taken place between young Mason and Sophia; not much at least up to this point; but a confidence had been established, and before he left her he did say a word or two that was more tender in its nature. 'You must not be in dudgeon with me,' he said, 'for speaking to you of all this. Hitherto I have kept it all to myself, and perhaps I should still have done so.'

'Oh no; do not say that.'

' I am in great grief. It is dreadful to me to hear these things said, and as yet I have found no sympathy.'

' I can assure you, Mr. Mason, that I do sympathize with you most sincerely. I only wish my sympathy could be of more value.'

' It will be invaluable,' he said, not looking at her, but fixing his eyes upon the fire, ' if it be given with constancy from the first to the last of this sad affair.'

' It shall be so given,' said Miss Furnival, also looking at the fire.

' It will be tolerably long, and men will say cruel things of us. I can foresee this, that it will be very hard to prove to the world with certainty that there is no foundation whatever for these charges. If those who are now most friendly to us turn away from us—'

' I will never turn away from you, Mr. Mason.'

' Then give me your hand on that, and remember that such a promise in my ears means much.' He in his excitement had forgotten that there were others in the room who might be looking at them, and that there was a long vista open upon them direct from all the eyes at the card-table ; but she did not forget it. Miss Furnival could be very enthusiastic, but she was one of those who in her enthusiasm rarely forgot anything. Nevertheless, after a moment's pause, she gave him her hand. ' There it is,' she said ; ' and you may be sure of this, that with me also such a promise does mean something. And now I will say good night.' And so, having received the pressure of her hand, she left him.

' I will get you your candle,' he said, and so he did.

' Good night, papa,' she said, kissing her father. And then, with a slight muttered word to Lady Staveley, she withdrew, having sacrificed the remainder of that evening for the sake of acceding to Mr. Mason's request respecting her pledge. It could not be accounted strange that she should give her hand to the gentleman with whom she was immediately talking as she bade him good night.

' And now grandpapa is dead too,' said Marian, ' and there's nobody left but us three.'

' And we'll divide,' said Fanny Sebright ; and so the game of commerce was brought to an end.

CHAPTER XXVIII.

DURING these days Peregrine Orme—though he was in love up to his very chin, seriously in love, acknowledging this matter to himself openly, pulling his hair in the retirement of his bedroom, and resolving that he would do that which he had hitherto in life always been successful in doing—ask, namely, boldly for that he wanted sorely—Peregrine Orme, I say, though he was in this condition, did not in these days neglect his hunting. A proper attendance upon the proceedings of the H. H. was the only duty which he had hitherto undertaken in return for all that his grandfather had done for him, and I have no doubt that he conceived that he was doing a duty in going hither and thither about the county to their most distant meets. At this period of the present season it happened that Noningsby was more central to the proceedings of the hunt than The Cleeve, and therefore he was enabled to think that he was remaining away from home chiefly on business. On one point, however, he had stoutly come to a resolution. That question should be asked of Madeline Staveley before he returned to his grandfather's house.

And now had arrived a special hunting morning—special, because the meet was in some degree a show meet, appropriate for ladies, at a comfortable distance from Noningsby, and affording a chance of amusement to those who sat in carriages as well as to those on horseback. Monkton Grange was the well-known name of the place, a name perhaps dearer to the ladies than to the gentlemen of the country, seeing that show meets do not always give the best sport. Monkton Grange is an old farm-house, now hardly used as such, having been left, as regards the habitation, in the hands of a head labourer; but it still possesses the marks of ancient respectability and even of grandeur. It is approached from the high road by a long double avenue of elms, which still stand in all their glory. The road itself has become narrow, and the space between the side row of trees is covered by soft turf, up which those coming to the meet love to gallop, trying the fresh metal of their horses. And the old house itself is surrounded by a moat, dry indeed now for the most part, but nevertheless an evident moat, deep and well preserved, with a bridge over it which Fancy tells us must once

" Monkton Grange."

have been a drawbridge. It is here, in front of the bridge, that the old hounds sit upon their haunches, resting quietly round the horses of the huntsmen, while the young dogs move about, and would wander if the whips allowed them—one of the fairest sights to my eyes that this fair country of ours can show. And here the sportsmen and ladies congregate by degrees, men from a distance in dog-carts generally arriving first, as being less able to calculate the time with accuracy. There is room here too in the open space for carriages, and there is one spot on which always stands old Lord Alston's chariot with the four posters; an ancient sportsman he, who still comes to some few favourite meets; and though Alston Court is but eight miles from the Grange, the post-horses always look as though they had been made to do their best, for his lordship likes to move fast even in his old age. He is a tall thin man, bent much with age, and apparently too weak for much walking; he is dressed from head to foot in a sportsman's garb, with a broad stiffly starched coloured handkerchief tied rigidly round his neck. One would say that old as he is he has sacrificed in no way to comfort. It is with difficulty that he gets into his saddle, his servant holding his rein and stirrup and giving him perhaps some other slight assistance; but when he is there, there he will remain all day, and when his old blood warms he will gallop along the road with as much hot fervour as his grandson. An old friend he of Sir Peregrine's. ' And why is not your grandfather here to-day?' he said on this occasion to young Orme. ' Tell him from me that if he fails us in this way, I shall think he is getting old.' Lord Alston was in truth five years older than Sir Peregrine, but Sir Peregrine at this time was thinking of other things.

And then a very tidy little modern carriage bustled up the road, a brougham made for a pair of horses, which was well known to all hunting men in these parts. It was very unpretending in its colour and harness; but no vehicle more appropriate to its purpose ever carried two thorough-going sportsmen day after day about the country. In this as it pulled up under the head tree of the avenue were seated the two Miss Tristrams. The two Miss Tristrams were well known to the Hamworth Hunt—I will not merely say as fearless riders,—of most girls who hunt as much can be said as that; but they were judicious horsewomen; they knew when to ride hard, and when hard riding, as regarded any necessary for the hunt, would be absolutely thrown away. They might be seen for half the day moving about the roads as leisurely, or standing as quietly at the covert's side as might the seniors of the field. But when the time for riding did come, when the hounds were really running—when other young ladies had begun to go home—then the Miss Tristrams were always there;—there or thereabouts, as their admirers would warmly boast.

Nor did they commence their day's work as did other girls who came out on hunting mornings. With most such it is clear to see that the object is pretty much the same here as in the ballroom. ' Spectatum veniunt; veniunt spectentur ut ipsæ,' as it is proper, natural, and desirable that they should do. By that word ' spec tatum ' I would wish to signify something more than the mere use of the eyes. Perhaps an occasional word dropped here and there into the ears of a cavalier may be included in it; and the 'spec- tentur' also may include a word so received. But the Miss Tristrams came for hunting. Perhaps there might be a slight shade of affectation in the manner by which they would appear to come for that and that only. They would talk of nothing else, at any rate during the earlier portion of the day, when many listeners were by. They were also well instructed as to the country to be drawn, and usually had a word of import to say to the huntsman. They were good-looking, fair-haired girls, short in size, with bright gray eyes, and a short decisive mode of speaking. It must not be imagined that they were altogether indifferent to such matters as are dear to the hearts of other girls. They were not careless as to admiration, and if report spoke truth of them were willing enough to establish themselves in the world; but all their doings of that kind had a reference to their favourite amusement, and they would as soon have thought of flirting with men who did not hunt as some other girls would with men who did not dance.

I do not know that this kind of life had been altogether successful with them, or that their father had been right to permit it. He himself had formerly been a hunting man, but he had become fat and lazy, and the thing had dropped away from him. Occasionally he did come out with them, and when he did not do so some other senior of the field would have them nominally under charge; but practically they were as independent when going across the country as the young men who accompanied them. I have expressed a doubt whether this life was successful with them, and indeed such doubt was expressed by many of their neighbours. It had been said of each of them for the last three years that she was engaged, now to this man, and then to that other; but neither this man nor that other had yet made good the assertion, and now people were begin- ning to say that no man was engaged to either of them. Hunting young ladies are very popular in the hunting-field; I know no place in which girls receive more worship and attention; but I am not sure but they may carry their enthusiasm too far for their own interests, let their horsemanship be as perfect as it may be.

The two girls on this occasion sat in their carriage till the groom brought up their horses, and then it was wonderful to see with what ease they placed themselves in their saddles. On such occasions they admitted no aid from the gentlemen around them, but each stepping for an instant on a servant's hand, settled herself in a moment on horseback. Nothing could be more perfect than the whole thing, but the wonder was that Mr. Tristram should have allowed it.

The party from Noningsby consisted of six or seven on horseback, besides those in the carriage. Among the former there were the two young ladies, Miss Furnival and Miss Staveley, and our friends Felix Graham, Augustus Staveley, and Peregrine Orme. Felix Graham was not by custom a hunting man, as he possessed neither time nor money for such a pursuit; but to-day he was mounted on his friend Staveley's second horse, having expressed his determination to ride him as long as they two, the man and the horse, could remain together.

' I give you fair warning,' Felix had said, ' if I do not spare my own neck, you cannot expect me to spare your horse's legs.'

' You may do your worst,' Staveley had answered. ' If you give him his head, and let him have his own way, he won't come to grief, whatever you may do.'

On their road to Monkton Grange, which was but three miles from Noningsby, Peregrine Orme had ridden by the side of Miss Staveley, thinking more of her than of the affairs of the hunt, prominent as they were generally in his thoughts. How should he do it, and when, and in what way should he commence the deed? He had an idea that it might be better for him if he could engender some closer intimacy between himself and Madeline before he absolutely asked the fatal question; but the closer intimacy did not seem to produce itself readily. He had, in truth, known Madeline Staveley for many years, almost since they were children together; but lately, during these Christmas holidays especially, there had not been between them that close conversational alliance which so often facilitates such an overture as that which Peregrine was now desirous of making. And, worse again, he had seen that there was such close conversational alliance between Madeline and Felix Graham. He did not on that account dislike the young barrister, or call him, even within his own breast, a snob or an ass. He knew well that he was neither the one nor the other; but he knew as well that he could be no fit match for Miss Staveley, and, to tell the truth, he did not suspect that either Graham or Miss Staveley would think of such a thing. It was not jealousy that tormented him, so much as a diffidence in his own resources. He made small attempts which did not succeed, and therefore he determined that he would at once make a grand attempt. He would create himself an opportunity before he left Noningsby, and would do it even to-day on horseback, if he could find sufficient opportunity. In taking a determined step like that, he knew that he would not lack the courage.

'Do you mean to ride to-day,' he said to Madeline, as they were approaching the bottom of the Grange avenue. For the last half-mile he had been thinking what he would say to her, and thinking in vain; and now, at the last moment, he could summon no words to his assistance more potent for his purpose than these.

'If you mean by riding, Mr. Orme, going across the fields with you and the Miss Tristrams, certainly not. I should come to grief, as you call it, at the first ditch.'

'And that is just what I shall do,' said Felix Graham, who was at her other side.

'Then, if you take my advice, you'll remain with us in the wood, and act as squire of dames. What on earth would Marian do if aught but good was to befall you?'

'Dear Marian! She gave me a special commission to bring her the fox's tail. Foxes' tails are just like ladies.'

'Thank you, Mr. Graham. I've heard you make some pretty compliments, and that is about the prettiest.'

'A faint heart will never win either the one or the other, Miss Staveley.'

'Oh, ah, yes. That will do very well. Under these circumstances I will accept the comparison.'

All of which very innocent conversation was overheard by Peregrine Orme, riding on the other side of Miss Staveley's horse. And why not? Neither Graham nor Miss Staveley had any objection. But how was it that he could not join in and take his share in it? He had made one little attempt at conversation, and that having failed he remained perfectly silent till they reached the large circle at the head of the avenue. 'It's no use, this sort of thing,' he said to himself. 'I must do it at a blow, if I do it at all;' and then he rode away to the master of the hounds.

As our party arrived at the open space the Miss Tristrams were stepping out of their carriage, and they came up to shake hands with Miss Staveley.

'I am so glad to see you,' said the eldest; 'it is so nice to have some ladies out besides ourselves.'

'Do keep up with us,' said the second. 'It's a very open country about here, and anybody can ride it.' And then Miss Furnival was introduced to them. 'Does your horse jump, Miss Furnival?'

'I really do not know,' said Sophia; 'but I sincerely trust that if he does, he will refrain to-day.'

'Don't say so,' said the eldest sportswoman. 'If you'll only begin it will come as easy to you as going along the road;' and then, not being able to spare more of these idle moments, they both went off to their horses, walking as though their habits were no impediments to them, and in half a minute they were seated.

'What is Harriet on to-day?' asked Staveley of a constant member of the hunt. Now Harriet was the eldest Miss Tristram.

'A little brown mare she got last week. That was a terrible brush we had on Friday. You weren't out, I think. We killed in the open, just at the edge of Rotherham Common. Harriet was one of the few that was up, and I don't think the chestnut horse will be the better of it this season.'

'That was the horse she got from Griggs?'

'Yes; she gave a hundred and fifty for him; and I'm told he was as nearly done on Friday as any animal you ever put your eyes on. They say Harriet cried when she got home.' Now the gentleman who was talking about Harriet on this occasion was one with whom she would no more have sat down to table than with her own groom.

But though Harriet may have cried when she got home on that fatal Friday evening, she was full of the triumph of the hunt on this morning. It is not often that the hounds run into a fox and absolutely surround and kill him on the open ground, and when this is done after a severe run there are seldom many there to see it. If a man can fairly take a fox's brush on such an occasion as that, let him do it; otherwise let him leave it to the huntsman. On the occasion in question it seems that Harriet Tristram might have done so, and some one coming second to her had been gallant enough to do it for her.

'Oh, my lord, you should have been out on Friday,' she said to Lord Alston. 'We had the prettiest thing I ever saw.'

'A great deal too pretty for me, my dear.'

'Oh, you who know the roads so well would certainly have been up. I suppose it was thirteen miles from Cobbleton's Bushes to Rotherham Common.'

'Not much less, indeed,' said his lordship, unwilling to diminish the lady's triumph. Had a gentleman made the boast his lordship would have demonstrated that it was hardly more than eleven.

'I timed it accurately from the moment he went away,' said the lady, 'and it was exactly fifty-seven minutes. The first part of it was awfully fast. Then we had a little check at Moseley Bottom. But for that, nobody could have lived through it. I never shall forget how deep it was coming up from there to Cringleton. I saw two men get off to ease their horses up the deep bit of plough; and I would have done so too, only my horse would not have stood for me to get up.'

'I hope he was none the worse for it,' said the sporting character who had been telling Staveley just now how she had cried when she got home that night.

'To tell the truth, I fear it has done him no good. He would not feed, you know, that night at all.'

'And broke out into cold sweats,' said the gentleman.

'Exactly,' said the lady, not quite liking it, but still enduring with patience.

'Rather groggy on his pins the next morning?' suggested her friend.

'Very groggy,' said Harriet, regarding the word as one belonging to fair sporting phraseology.

'And inclined to go very much on the points of his toes. I know all about it, Miss Tristram, as well as though I'd seen him.'

'There's nothing but rest for it, I suppose.'

'Rest and regular exercise—that's the chief thing; and I should give him a mash as often as three times a week. He'll be all right again in three or four weeks,—that is if he's sound, you know.'

'Oh, as sound as a bell,' said Miss Tristram.

'He'll never be the same horse on a road though,' said the sporting gentlemen, shaking his head and whispering to Staveley.

And now the time had come at which they were to move. They always met at eleven; and at ten minutes past, to the moment, Jacob the huntsman would summons the old hounds from off their haunches. 'I believe we may be moving, Jacob,' said Mr. Williams, the master.

'The time be up,' said Jacob, looking at a ponderous timekeeper that might with truth be called a hunting-watch; and then they all moved slowly away back from the Grange, down a farm-road which led to Monkton Wood, distant from the old house perhaps a quarter of a mile.

'May we go as far as the wood?' said Miss Furnival to Augustus. 'Without being made to ride over hedges, I mean.'

'Oh, dear, yes; and ride about the wood half the day. It will be an hour and a half before a fox will break—even if he ever breaks.'

'Dear me! how tired you will be of us. Now do say something pretty, Mr. Staveley.'

'It's not my *métier*. We shall be tired, not of you, but of the thing. Galloping up and down the same cuts in the wood for an hour and a half is not exciting; nor does it improve the matter much if we stand still, as one should do by rights.'

'That would be very slow.'

'You need not be afraid. They never do here. Everybody will be rushing about as though the very world depended on their galloping.'

'I'm so glad; that's just what I like.'

'Everybody except Lord Alston, Miss Tristram, and the other old stagers. They will husband their horses, and come out as fresh at two o'clock as though they were only just out. There is nothing so valuable as experience in hunting.'

' Do you think it nice seeing a young lady with so much hunting knowledge ?'

' Now you want me to talk slander, but I won't do it.   I admire the Miss Tristrams exceedingly, and especially Julia.'

' And which is Julia ?'

' The youngest; that one riding by herself.'

' And why don't you go and express your admiration ?'

' Ah, me ! why don't we all express the admiration that we feel, and pour sweet praises into the ears of the lady that excites it ? Because we are cowards, Miss Furnival, and are afraid even of such a weak thing as a woman.'

' Dear me ! I should hardly have thought that you would suffer from such terror as that.'

' Because you don't quite know me, Miss Furnival.'

' And Miss Julia Tristram is the lady that has excited it ?'

' If it be not she, it is some other fair votary of Diana at present riding into Monkton Wood.'

' Ah, now you are giving me a riddle to guess, and I never guess riddles.   I won't even try at it.   But they all seem to be stopping.'

' Yes, they are putting the hounds into covert.   Now if you want to show yourself a good sportsman, look at your watch.   You see that Julia Tristram has got hers in her hand.'

' What's that for ?'

' To time the hounds ; to see how long they'll be before they find. It's very pretty work in a small gorse, but in a great wood like this I don't care much for being so accurate.   But for heaven's sake don't tell Julia Tristram ; I should not have a chance if she thought I was so slack.'

And now the hounds were scattering themselves in the wood, and the party rode up the centre roadway towards a great circular opening in the middle of it.   Here it was the recognized practice of the horsemen to stand, and those who properly did their duty would stand there ; but very many lingered at the gate, knowing that there was but one other exit from the wood, without over-coming the difficulty of a very intricate and dangerous fence.

' There be a gap, baint there ?' said one farmer to another, as they were entering.

' Yes, there be a gap, and young Grubbles broke his 'orse's back a getting over of it last year,' said the second farmer.

' Did he though ?' said the first; and so they both remained at the gate.

And others, a numerous body, including most of the ladies, gal-loped up and down the cross ways, because the master of the hounds and the huntsman did so.   ' D —— those fellows riding up and down after me wherever I go,' said the master.   ' I believe they think I'm to be hunted.'   This seemed to be said more especially to Miss Tristram, who was always in the master's confidence; and I fear that the fellows alluded to included Miss Furnival and Miss Staveley.

And then there came the sharp, eager sound of a hound's voice; a single, sharp, happy opening bark, and Harriet Tristram was the first to declare that the game was found. 'Just five minutes and twenty seconds, my lord,' said Julia Tristram to Lord Alston. 'That's not bad in a large wood like this.'

'Uncommonly good,' said his lordship. 'And when are we to get out of it?'

'They'll be here for the next hour, I'm afraid,' said the lady, not moving her horse from the place where she stood, though many of the more impetuous of the men were already rushing away to the gates. 'I have seen a fox go away from here without resting a minute; but that was later in the season, at the end of February. Foxes are away from home then.' All which observations showed a wonderfully acute sporting observation on the part of Miss Tristram.

And then the music of the dogs became fast and frequent, as they drove the brute across and along from one part of the large wood to another. Sure there is no sound like it for filling a man's heart with an eager desire to be at work. What may be the trumpet in battle I do not know, but I can imagine that it has the same effect. And now a few of them were standing on that wide circular piece of grass, when a sound the most exciting of them all reached their ears. 'He's away!' shouted a whip from a corner of the wood. The goodnatured beast, though as yet it was hardly past Christmas-time, had consented to bless at once so many anxious sportsmen, and had left the back of the covert with the full pack at his heels.

'There is no gate that way, Miss Tristram,' said a gentleman.

'There's a double ditch and bank that will do as well,' said she, and away she went directly after the hounds, regardless altogether of the gates. Peregrine Orme and Felix Graham, who were with her, followed close upon her track.

CHAPTER XXIX.

BREAKING COVERT.

'THERE's a double ditch and bank that will do as well,' Miss Tristram had said when she was informed that there was no gate out of the wood at the side on which the fox had broken. The gentleman who had tendered the information might as well have held his tongue, for Miss Tristram knew the wood intimately, was acquainted with the locality of all its gates, and was acquainted also with the points at which it might be left, without the assistance of any gate at all, by those who were well mounted and could ride their horses. Therefore she had thus replied, 'There's a double ditch and bank that will do as well.' And for the double ditch and bank at the end of one of the grassy roadways Miss Tristram at once prepared herself.

'That's the gap where Grubbles broke his horse's back,' said a man in a red coat to Peregrine Orme, and so saying he made up his wavering mind and galloped away as fast as his nag could carry him. But Peregrine Orme would not avoid a fence at which a lady was not afraid to ride; and Felix Graham, knowing little but fearing nothing, followed Peregrine Orme.

At the end of the roadway, in the middle of the track, there was the gap. For a footman it was doubtless the easiest way over the fence, for the ditch on that side was half filled up, and there was space enough left of the half-broken bank for a man's scrambling feet; but Miss Tristram at once knew that it was a bad place for a horse. The second or further ditch was the really difficult obstacle, and there was no footing in the gap from which a horse could take his leap. To the right of this the fence was large and required a good horse, but Miss Tristram knew her animal and was accustomed to large fences. The trained beast went well across on to the bank, poised himself there for a moment, and taking a second spring carried his mistress across into the further field apparently with ease. In that field the dogs were now running, altogether, so that a sheet might have covered them; and Miss Tristram, exulting within her heart and holding in her horse, knew that she had got away uncommonly well.

Peregrine Orme followed,—a little to the right of the lady's passage, so that he might have room for himself, and do no mischief in the event of Miss Tristram or her horse making any mistake at

the leap.　He also got well over.　But, alas! in spite of such early
success he was destined to see nothing of the hunt that day!　Felix
Graham, thinking that he would obey instructions by letting his
horse do as he pleased, permitted the beast to come close upon
Orme's track, and to make his jump before Orme's horse had taken
his second spring.

'Have a care,' said Peregrine, feeling that the two were together
on the bank, 'or you'll shove me into the ditch.'　He however got
well over.

Felix, attempting to 'have a care' just when his doing so could
be of no avail, gave his horse a pull with the curb as he was preparing for his second spring.　The outside ditch was broad and
deep and well banked up, and required that an animal should have
all his power.　It was at such a moment as this that he should
have been left to do his work without injudicious impediment from
his rider.　But poor Graham was thinking only of Orme's caution,
and attempted to stop the beast when any positive and absolute
stop was out of the question.　The horse made his jump, and,
crippled as he was, jumped short.　He came with his knees against
the further bank, threw his rider, and then in his struggle to right
himself rolled over him.

Felix felt at once that he was much hurt—that he had indeed
come to grief; but still he was not stunned nor did he lose his
presence of mind.　The horse succeeded in gaining his feet, and
then Felix also jumped up and even walked a step or two towards
the head of the animal with the object of taking the reins.　But
he found that he could not raise his arm, and he found also that he
could hardly breathe.

Both Peregrine and Miss Tristram looked back.　'There's nothing
wreng I hope,' said the lady; and then she rode on.　And let it be
understood that in hunting those who are in advance generally do
ride on.　The lame and the halt and the wounded, if they cannot
pick themselves up, have to be picked up by those who come after
them.　But Peregrine saw that there was no one else coming that
way.　The memory of young Grubbles' fate had placed an interdict
on that pass out of the wood, which nothing short of the pluck and
science of Miss Tristram was able to disregard.　Two cavaliers she
had carried with her.　One she had led on to instant slaughter, and
the other remained to look after his fallen brother-in-arms.　Miss
Tristram in the mean time was in the next field and had settled well
down to her work.

'Are you hurt, old fellow?' said Peregrine, turning back his
horse, but still not dismounting.

'Not much, I think,' said Graham, smiling.　'There's something
wrong about my arm,—but don't you wait.'　And then he found
that he spoke with difficulty.

Felix Graham in trouble.

'Can you mount again?'

'I don't think I'll mind that. Perhaps I'd better sit down.' Then Peregrine Orme knew that Graham was hurt, and jumping off his own horse he gave up all hope of the hunt.

'Here, you fellow, come and hold these horses.' So invoked a boy who in following the sport had got as far as this ditch did as he was bid, and scrambled over. 'Sit down, Graham; there; I'm afraid you are hurt. Did he roll on you?' But Felix merely looked up into his face,—still smiling. He was now very pale, and for the moment could not speak. Peregrine came close to him, and gently attempted to raise the wounded limb; whereupon Graham shuddered, and shook his head.

'I fear it is broken,' said Peregrine. Graham nodded his head, and raised his left hand to his breast; and Peregrine then knew that something else was amiss also.

I don't know any feeling more disagreeable than that produced by being left alone in a field, when out hunting, with a man who has been very much hurt and who is incapable of riding or walking. The hurt man himself has the privilege of his infirmities and may remain quiescent; but you, as his only attendant, must do something. You must for the moment do all, and if you do wrong the whole responsibility lies on your shoulders. If you leave a wounded man on the damp ground, in the middle of winter, while you run away, five miles perhaps, to the next doctor, he may not improbably—as you then think—be dead before you come back. You don't know the way; you are heavy yourself, and your boots are very heavy. You must stay therefore; but as you are no doctor you don't in the least know what is the amount of the injury. In your great trouble you begin to roar for assistance; but the woods re-echo your words, and the distant sound of the huntsman's horn, as he summons his hounds at a check, only mocks your agony.

But Peregrine had a boy with him. 'Get upon that horse,' he said at last; 'ride round to Farmer Griggs, and tell them to send somebody here with a spring cart. He has got a spring cart I know;—and a mattress in it.'

'But I haint no gude at roiding like,' said the boy, looking with dismay at Orme's big horse.

'Then run; that will be better, for you can go through the wood. You know where Farmer Griggs lives. The first farm the other side of the Grange.'

'Ay, ay, I knows where Farmer Griggs lives well enough.'

'Run then; and if the cart is here in half an hour I'll give you a sovereign.'

Inspirited by the hopes of such wealth, golden wealth, wealth for a lifetime, the boy was quickly back over the fence, and Peregrine was left alone with Felix Graham. He was now sitting down, with his feet hanging into the ditch, and Peregrine was kneeling behind him. 'I am sorry I can do nothing more,' said he ; 'but I fear we must remain here till the cart comes.'

'I am—so—vexed—about your hunt,' said Felix, gasping as he spoke. He had in fact broken his right arm which had been twisted under him as the horse rolled, and two of his ribs had been staved in by the pommel of his saddle. Many men have been worse hurt and have hunted again before the end of the season, but the fracture of three bones does make a man uncomfortable for the time. 'Now the cart—is—sent for, couldn't you—go on?' But it was not likely that Peregrine Orme would do that. 'Never mind me,' he said. 'When a fellow is hurt he has always to do as he's told. You'd better have a drop of sherry. Look here : I've got a flask at my saddle. There ; you can support yourself with that arm a moment. Did you ever see horses stand so quiet. I've got hold of yours, and now I'll fasten them together. I say, Whitefoot, you don't kick, do you?' And then he contrived to picket the horses to two branches, and having got out his case of sherry, poured a small modicum into the silver mug which was attached to the apparatus, and again supported Graham while he drank. 'You'll be as right as a trivet by-and-by ; only you'll have to make Noningsby your head-quarters for the next six weeks.' And then the same idea passed through the mind of each of them ;—how little a man need be pitied for such a misfortune if Madeline Staveley would consent to be his nurse.

No man could have less surgical knowledge than Peregrine Orme, but nevertheless he was such a man as one would like to have with him if one came to grief in such a way. He was cheery and up-hearted, but at the same time gentle and even thoughtful. His voice was pleasant and his touch could be soft. For many years afterwards Felix remembered how that sherry had been held to his lips, and how the young heir of The Cleeve had knelt behind him in his red coat, supporting him as he became weary with waiting, and saying pleasant words to him through the whole. Felix Graham was a man who would remember such things.

In running through the wood the boy first encountered three horsemen. They were the judge, with his daughter Madeline and Miss Furnival. 'There be a mon there who be a'most dead,' said the boy, hardly able to speak from want of breath. 'I be agoing for Farmer Griggs' cart.' And then they stopped him a moment to ask for some description, but the boy could tell them nothing to indicate that the wounded man was one of their friends. It might however be Augustus, and so the three rode on quickly towards the fence, knowing nothing of the circumstances of the ditches which would make it out of their power to get to the fallen sportsman.

But Peregrine heard the sound of the horses and the voices of the horsemen. 'By Jove, there's a lot of them coming down here,' said he. 'It's the judge and two of the girls. Oh, Miss Staveley, I'm so glad you've come. Graham has had a bad fall and hurt himself. You haven't a shawl, have you? the ground is so wet under him.'

'It doesn't signify at all,' said Felix, looking round and seeing the faces of his friends on the other side of the bank.

Madeline Staveley gave a slight shriek which her father did not notice, but which Miss Furnival heard very plainly. 'Oh papa,' she said, 'cannot you get over to him?' And then she began to bethink herself whether it were possible that she should give up something of her dress to protect the man who was hurt from the damp muddy ground on which he lay.

'Can you hold my horse, dear,' said the judge, slowly dismounting; for the judge, though he rode every day on sanitary considerations, had not a sportsman's celerity in leaving and recovering his saddle. But he did get down, and burdened as he was with a greatcoat, he did succeed in crossing that accursed fence. Accursed it was from henceforward in the annals of the H. H., and none would ride it but dare-devils who professed themselves willing to go at anything. Miss Tristram, however, always declared that there was nothing in it—though she avoided it herself, whispering to her friends that she had led others to grief there, and might possibly do so again if she persevered.

'Could you hold the horse?' said Madeline to Miss Furnival; 'and I will go for a shawl to the carriage.' Miss Furnival declared that to the best of her belief she could not, but nevertheless the animal was left with her, and Madeline turned round and galloped back towards the carriage. She made her horse do his best though her eyes were nearly blinded with tears, and went straight on for the carriage, though she would have given much for a moment to hide those tears before she reached it.

'Oh, mamma! give me a thick shawl; Mr. Graham has hurt himself in the field, and is lying on the grass.' And then in some incoherent and quick manner she had to explain what she knew of the accident before she could get a carriage-cloak out of the carriage. This, however, she did succeed in doing, and in some manner, very unintelligible to herself afterwards, she did gallop back with her burden. She passed the cloak over to Peregrine, who clambered up the bank to get it, while the judge remained on the ground, supporting the young barrister. Felix Graham, though he was weak, was not stunned or senseless, and he knew well who it was that had procured for him that comfort.

And then the carriage followed Madeline, and there was quite a concourse of servants and horses and ladies on the inside of the fence. But the wounded man was still unfortunately on the other side. No cart from Farmer Griggs made its appearance, though it was now more than half an hour since the boy had gone. Carts, when they are wanted in such sudden haste, do not make their appearance. It was two miles through the wood to Mr. Griggs's farm-yard, and more than three miles back by any route which the cart could take. And then it might be more than probable that in Farmer Griggs's establishment there was not always a horse ready in harness, or a groom at hand prepared to yoke him. Peregrine had become very impatient, and had more than once invoked a silent anathema on the farmer's head; but nevertheless there was no appearance of the cart.

'We must get him across the ditches into the carriage,' said the judge.

'If Lady Staveley will let us do that,' said Peregrine.

'The difficulty is not with Lady Staveley but with these nasty ditches,' said the judge, for he had been up to his knees in one of them, and the water had penetrated his boots. But the task was at last done. Mrs. Arbuthnot stood up on the back seat of the carriage so that she might hold the horses, and the coachman and footman got across into the field. 'It would be better to let me lie here all day,' said Felix, as three of them struggled back with their burden, the judge bringing up the rear with two hunting-whips and Peregrine's cap. 'How on earth any one would think of riding over such a place as that!' said the judge. But then, when he had been a young man it had not been the custom for barristers to go out hunting.

Madeline, as she saw the wounded man carefully laid on the back seat of the carriage, almost wished that she could have her mother's place that she might support him. Would they be careful enough with him? Would they remember how terrible must be the pain of that motion to one so hurt as he was? And then she looked into his face as he was made to lean back, and she saw that he still smiled. Felix Graham was by no means a handsome man; I should hardly sin against the truth if I were to say that he was ugly. But Madeline, as she looked at him now, lying there utterly without colour but always with that smile on his countenance, thought that no face to her liking had ever been more gracious. She still rode close to them as they went down the grassy road, saying never a word. And Miss Furnival rode there also, somewhat in the rear, condoling with the judge as to his wet feet.

'Miss Furnival,' he said, 'when a judge forgets himself and goes out hunting he has no right to expect anything better. What would your father have said had he seen me clambering up the bank with young Orme's hunting-cap between my teeth? I positively did.'

'He would have rushed to assist you,' said Miss Furnival, with a little burst of enthusiasm which was hardly needed on the occasion. And then Peregrine came after them leading Graham's horse. He had been compelled to return to the field and ride both the horses back into the wood, one after the other, while the footman held them. That riding back over fences in cold blood is the work that really tries a man's nerve. And a man has to do it too when no one is looking on. How he does crane and falter and look about for an easy place at such a moment as that! But when the blood is cold no places are easy.

The procession got back to Noningsby without adventure, and Graham as a matter of course was taken up to his bed. One of the servants had been despatched to Alston for a surgeon, and in an hour or two the extent of the misfortune was known. The right arm was broken—'very favourably,' as the doctor observed. But two ribs were broken—'rather unfavourably.' There was some talk of hæmorrhage and inward wounds, and Sir Jacob from Saville Row was suggested by Lady Staveley. But the judge, knowing the extent of Graham's means, made some further preliminary inquiries, and it was considered that Sir Jacob would not be needed—at any rate not as yet.

'Why don't they send for him?' said Madeline to her mother with rather more than her wonted energy.

'Your papa does not think it necessary, my dear. It would be very expensive, you know.'

'But, mamma, would you let a man die because it would cost a few pounds to cure him?'

'My dear, we all hope that Mr. Graham won't die—at any rate not at present. If there be any danger you may be sure that your papa will send for the best advice.'

But Madeline was by no means satisfied. She could not understand economy in a matter of life and death. If Sir Jacob's coming would have cost fifty pounds, or a hundred, what would that have signified, weighed in such a balance? Such a sum would be nothing to her father. Had Augustus fallen and broken his arm all the Sir Jacobs in London would not have been considered too costly could their joint coming have mitigated any danger. She did not however dare to speak to her mother again, so she said a word or two to Peregrine Orme, who was constant in his attendance on Felix. Peregrine had been very kind, and she had seen it, and her heart therefore warmed towards him.

'Don't you think he ought to have more advice, Mr. Orme?'

'Well, no; I don't know. He's very jolly, you know; only he can't talk. One of the bones ran into him, but I believe he's all right.'

'Oh, but that is so frightful!' and the tears were again in her eyes.

'If I were him I should think one doctor enough. But it's easy enough having a fellow down from London, you know, if you like it.'

'If he should get worse, Mr. Orme——.' And then Peregrine made her a sort of promise, but in doing so an idea shot through his poor heart of what the truth might really be. He went back and looked at Felix who was sleeping. 'If it is so I must bear it,' he said to himself; 'but I'll fight it on;' and a quick thought ran through his brain of his own deficiencies. He knew that he was not clever and bright in talk like Felix Graham. He could not say the right thing at the right moment without forethought. How he wished that he could! But still he would fight it on, as he would have done any losing match,—to the last. And then he sat down by Felix's head, and resolved that he would be loyal to his new friend all the same—loyal in all things needful. But still he would fight it on.

CHAPTER XXX.

ANOTHER FALL.

FELIX GRAHAM had plenty of nurses, but Madeline was not one of them. Augustus Staveley came home while the Alston doctor was still busy at the broken bones, and of course he would not leave his friend. He was one of those who had succeeded in the hunt, and consequently had heard nothing of the accident till the end of it. Miss Tristram had been the first to tell him that Mr. Graham had fallen in leaving the covert, but having seen him rise to his legs she had not thought he was seriously hurt.

'I do not know much about your friend,' she had said; 'but I think I may comfort you by an assurance that your horse is none the worse. I could see as much as that.'

'Poor Felix!' said Staveley. 'He has lost a magnificent run. I suppose we are nine or ten miles from Monkton Grange now?'

'Eleven if we are a yard,' said the lady. 'It was an ugly country, but the pace was nothing wonderful.' And then others dropped in, and at last came tidings about Graham. At first there was a whisper that he was dead. He had ridden over Orme, it was said; had nearly killed him, and had quite killed himself. Then the report became less fatal. Both horses were dead, but Graham was still living though with most of his bones broken.

'Don't believe it,' said Miss Tristram. 'In what condition Mr. Graham may be I won't say; but that your horse was safe and sound after he got over the fence, of that you may take my word.'

And thus, in a state of uncertainty, obtaining fresh rumours from every person he passed, Staveley hurried home. ' Right arm and two ribs,' Peregrine said to him, as he met him in the hall. ' Is that all ?' said Augustus. It was clear therefore that he did not think so much about it as his sister.

' If you'd let her have her head she'd never have come down like that,' Augustus said, as he sat that evening by his friend's bedside.

' But he pulled off, I fancy, to avoid riding over me,' said Peregrine.

' Then he must have come too quick at his leap,' said Augustus. ' You should have steadied him as he came to it.' From all which Graham perceived that a man cannot learn how to ride any particular horse by two or three words of precept.

' If you talk any more about the horse, or the hunt, or the accident, neither of you shall stay in the room,' said Lady Staveley, who came in at that moment. But they both did stay in the room, and said a great deal more about the hunt, and the horse, and the accident before they left it; and even became so far reconciled to the circumstance that they had a hot glass of brandy and water each, sitting by Graham's fire.

' But, Augustus, do tell me how he is,' Madeline said to her brother, as she caught him going to his room. She had become ashamed of asking any more questions of her mother.

' He's all right; only he'll be as fretful as a porcupine, shut up there. At least I should be. Are there lots of novels in the house ? Mind you send for a batch to-morrow. Novels are the only chance a man has when he's laid up like that.' Before breakfast on the following morning Madeline had sent off to the Alston circulating library a list of all the best new novels of which she could remember the names.

No definite day had hitherto been fixed for Peregrine's return to The Cleeve, and under the present circumstances he still remained at Noningsby assisting to amuse Felix Graham. For two days after the accident such seemed to be his sole occupation; but in truth he was looking for an opportunity to say a word or two to Miss Staveley, and paving his way as best he might for that great speech which he was fully resolved that he would make before he left the house. Once or twice he bethought himself whether he would not endeavour to secure for himself some confidant in the family, and obtain the sanction and special friendship either of Madeline's mother, or her sister, or her brother. But what if after that she should reject him ? Would it not be worse for him then that any one should have known of his defeat ? He could, as he thought, endure to suffer alone; but on such a matter as that pity would be unendurable. So as he sat there by Graham's fireside, pretending to read one of poor Madeline's novels for the sake of companionship, he determined that he would tell no one of his intention;—no one till he could make the opportunity for telling her.

And when he did meet her, and find, now and again, some moment for saying a word alone to her, she was very gracious to him. He had been so kind and gentle with Felix, there was so much in him that was sweet and good and honest, so much that such an event as this brought forth and made manifest, that Madeline, and indeed the whole family, could not but be gracious to him. Augustus would declare that he was the greatest brick he had ever known, repeating all Graham's words as to the patience with which the embryo baronet had knelt behind him on the cold muddy ground, supporting him for an hour, till the carriage had come up. Under such circumstances how could Madeline refrain from being gracious to him?

' But it is all from favour to Graham!' Peregrine would say to himself with bitterness; and yet though he said so he did not quite believe it. Poor fellow! It was all from favour to Graham. And could he have thoroughly believed the truth of those words which he repeated to himself so often, he might have spared himself much pain. He might have spared himself much pain, and possibly some injury; for if aught could now tend to mature in Madeline's heart an affection which was but as yet nascent, it would be the offer of some other lover. But such reasoning on the matter was much too deep for Peregrine Orme. ' It may be,' he said to himself, ' that she only pities him because he is hurt. If so, is not this time better for me than any other? If it be that she loves him, let me know it, and be out of my pain.' It did not then occur to him that circumstances such as those in question could not readily be made explicit;—that Madeline might refuse his love, and yet leave him no wiser than he now was as to her reasons for so refusing;—perhaps, indeed, leave him less wise, with increased cause for doubt and hopeless hope, and the green melancholy of a rejected lover.

Madeline during these two days said no more about the London doctor; but it was plain to all who watched her that her anxiety as to the patient was much more keen than that of the other ladies of the house. ' She always thinks everybody is going to die,' Lady Staveley said to Miss Furnival, intending, not with any consummate prudence, to account to that acute young lady for her daughter's solicitude. ' We had a cook here, three months since, who was very ill, and Madeline would never be easy till the doctor assured her that the poor woman's danger was altogether past.'

' She is so very warm-hearted,' said Miss Furnival in reply. ' It is quite delightful to see her. And she will have such pleasure when she sees him come down from his room.'

Lady Staveley on this immediate occasion said nothing to her daughter, but Mrs. Arbuthnot considered that a sisterly word might perhaps be spoken in due season.

'The doctor says he is doing quite well now,' Mrs. Arbuthnot said to her, as they were sitting alone.

'But does he indeed? Did you hear him?' said Madeline, who was suspicious.

'He did so, indeed. I heard him myself. But he says also that he ought to remain here, at any rate for the next fortnight,—if mamma can permit it without inconvenience.'

'Of course she can permit it. No one would turn any person out of their house in such a condition as that!'

'Papa and mamma both will be very happy that he should stay here;—of course they would not do what you call turning him out. But, Mad, my darling,'—and then she came up close and put her arm round her sister's waist. 'I think mamma would be more comfortable in his remaining here if your charity towards him were—what shall I say?—less demonstrative.'

'What do you mean, Isabella?'

'Dearest, dearest; you must not be angry with me. Nobody has hinted to me a word on the subject, nor do I mean to hint anything that can possibly be hurtful to you.'

'But what do you mean?'

'Don't you know, darling? He is a young man—and—and—people see with such unkind eyes, and hear with such scandal-loving ears. There is that Miss Furnival——'

'If Miss Furnival can think such things, I for one do not care what she thinks.'

'No, nor do I;—not as regards any important result. But may it not be well to be careful? You know what I mean, dearest?'

'Yes—I know. At least I suppose so. And it makes me know also how very cold and shallow and heartless people are! I won't ask any more questions, Isabella; but I can't know that a fellow-creature is suffering in the house,—and a person like him too, so clever, whom we all regard as a friend,—the most intimate friend in the world that Augustus has,—and the best too, as I heard papa himself say—without caring whether he is going to live or die.'

'There is no danger now, you know.'

'Very well; I am glad to hear it. Though I know very well that there must be danger after such a terrible accident as that.'

'The doctor says there is none.'

'At any rate I will not——' And then instead of finishing her sentence she turned away her head and put up her handkerchief to wipe away a tear.

'You are not angry with me, dear?' said Mrs. Arbuthnot.

'Oh, no,' said Madeline; and then they parted.

For some days after that Madeline asked no question whatever

about Felix Graham, but it may be doubted whether this did not
make the matter worse. Even Sophia Furnival would ask how he
was at any rate twice a day, and Lady Staveley continued to pay
him regular visits at stated intervals. As he got better she would
sit with him, and brought back reports as to his sayings. But
Madeline never discussed any of these; and refrained alike from
the conversation, whether his broken bones or his unbroken wit
were to be the subject of it. And then Mrs. Arbuthnot, knowing
that she would still be anxious, gave her private bulletins as to the
state of the sick man's progress;—all which gave on air of secrecy
to the matter, and caused even Madeline to ask herself why this
should be so.

On the whole I think that Mrs. Arbuthnot was wrong. Mrs. Arbuthnot and the whole Staveley family would have regarded a
mutual attachment between Mr. Graham and Madeline as a great
family misfortune. The judge was a considerate father to his
children, holding that a father's control should never be brought to
bear unnecessarily. In looking forward to the future prospects of
his son and daughters it was his theory that they should be free to
choose their life's companions for themselves. But nevertheless
it could not be agreeable to him that his daughter should fall in
love with a man who had nothing, and whose future success at his
own profession seemed to be so very doubtful. On the whole I
think that Mrs. Arbuthnot was wrong, and that the feeling that did
exist in Madeline's bosom might more possibly have died away,
had no word been said about it—even by a sister.

And then another event happened which forced her to look into
her own heart. Peregrine Orme did make his proposal. He waited
patiently during those two or three days in which the doctor's visits
were frequent, feeling that he could not talk about himself while
any sense of danger pervaded the house. But then at last a
morning came on which the surgeon declared that he need not call
again till the morrow; and Felix himself, when the medical back
was turned, suggested that it might as well be to-morrow week.
He began also to scold his friends, and look bright about the eyes,
and drink his glass of sherry in a pleasant dinner-table fashion, not
as if he were swallowing his physic. And Peregrine, when he saw
all this, resolved that the moment had come for the doing of his
deed of danger. The time would soon come at which he must
leave Noningsby, and he would not leave Noningsby till he had
learned his fate.

Lady Staveley, who with a mother's eye, had seen her daughter's
solicitude for Felix Graham's recovery,—had seen it, and animad-
verted on it to herself—had seen also, or at any rate had suspected,
that Peregrine Orme looked on her daughter with favouring eyes.
Now Peregrine Orme would have satisfied Lady Staveley as a son-

in-law. She liked his ways and manners of thought—in spite of
those rumours as to the rat-catching which had reached her ears.
She regarded him as quite clever enough to be a good husband, and
no doubt appreciated the fact that he was to inherit his title and
The Cleeve from an old grandfather instead of a middle-aged father.
She therefore had no objection to leave Peregrine alone with her
one ewe-lamb, and therefore the opportunity which he sought was
at last found.

'I shall be leaving Noningsby to-morrow, Miss Staveley,' he said
one day, having secured an interview in the back drawing-room—in
that happy half-hour which occurs in winter before the world
betakes itself to dress. Now I here profess my belief, that out of
every ten set offers made by ten young lovers, nine of such offers
are commenced with an intimation that the lover is going away.
There is a dash of melancholy in such tidings well suited to the
occasion. If there be any spark of love on the other side it will be
elicited by the idea of a separation. And then, also, it is so frequently the actual fact. This making of an offer is in itself a hard
piece of business,—a job to be postponed from day to day. It is so
postponed, and thus that dash of melancholy, and that idea of
separation are brought in at the important moment with so much
appropriate truth.

'I shall be leaving Noningsby to-morrow, Miss Staveley,' Peregrine said.

'Oh dear! we shall be so sorry. But why are you going? What
will Mr. Graham and Augustus do without you? You ought to
stay at least till Mr. Graham can leave his room.'

'Poor Graham!—not that I think he is much to be pitied either;
but he won't be about for some weeks to come yet.'

'You do not think he is worse; do you?'

'Oh, dear, no; not at all.' And Peregrine was unconsciously
irritated against his friend by the regard which her tone evinced.
'He is quite well; only they will not let him be moved. But,
Miss Staveley, it was not of Mr. Graham that I was going to
speak.'

'No—only I thought he would miss you so much.' And then
she blushed, though the blush in the dark of the evening was lost
upon him. She remembered that she was not to speak about Felix
Graham's health, and it almost seemed as though Mr. Orme had
rebuked her for doing so in saying that he had not come there to
speak of him.

'Lady Staveley's house has been turned up side down since this
affair, and it is time now that some part of the trouble should cease.'

'Oh! mamma does not mind it at all.'

'I know how good she is; but nevertheless, Miss Staveley, I
must go to-morrow.' And then he paused a moment before he

spoke again. 'It will depend entirely upon you,' he said, ' whether I may have the happiness of returning soon to Noningsby.'

'On me, Mr. Orme !'

'Yes, on you. I do not know how to speak properly that which I have to say ; but I believe I may as well say it out at once. I have come here now to tell you that I love you and to ask you to be my wife.' And then he stopped as though there were nothing more for him to say upon the matter.

It would be hardly extravagant to declare that Madeline's breath was taken away by the very sudden manner in which young Orme had made his proposition. It had never entered her head that she had an admirer in him. Previously to Graham's accident she had thought nothing about him. Since that event she had thought about him a good deal; but altogether as of a friend of Graham's. He had been good and kind to Graham, and therefore she had liked him and had talked to him. He had never said a word to her that had taught her to regard him as a possible lover ; and now that he was an actual lover, a declared lover standing before her, waiting for an answer, she was so astonished that she did not know how to speak. All her ideas too, as to love,—such ideas as she had ever formed, were confounded by this abruptness. She would have thought, had she brought herself absolutely to think upon it, that all speech of love should be very delicate ; that love should grow slowly, and then be whispered softly, doubtingly, and with infinite care. Even had she loved him, or had she been in the way towards loving him, such violence as this would have frightened her and scared her love away. Poor Peregrine ! His intentions had been so good and honest ! He was so true and hearty, and free from all conceit in the matter ! It was a pity that he should have marred his cause by such ill judgment.

But there he stood waiting an answer,—and expecting it to be as open, definite, and plain as though he had asked her to take a walk with him. 'Madeline,' he said, stretching out his hand when he perceived that she did not speak to him at once. ' There is my hand. If it be possible give me yours.'

'Oh, Mr. Orme !'

'I know that I have not said what I had to say very,—very gracefully. But you will not regard that I think. You are too good, and too true.'

She had now seated herself, and he was standing before her. She had retreated to a sofa in order to avoid the hand which he had offered her ; but he followed her, and even yet did not know that he had no chance of success. 'Mr. Orme,' she said at last, speaking hardly above her breath, ' what has made you do this ?'

'What has made me do it ? What has made me tell you that I love you ?'

'You cannot be in earnest!'

'Not in earnest! By heavens, Miss Staveley, no man who has said the same words was ever more in earnest. Do you doubt me when I tell you that I love you?'

'Oh, I am so sorry!' And then she hid her face upon the arm of the sofa and burst into tears.

Peregrine stood there, like a prisoner on his trial, waiting for a verdict. He did not know how to plead his cause with any further language; and indeed no further language could have been of any avail. The judge and jury were clear against him, and he should have known the sentence without waiting to have it pronounced in set terms. But in plain words he had made his offer, and in plain words he required that an answer should be given to him. 'Well,' he said, 'will you not speak to me? Will you not tell me whether it shall be so?'

'No,—no,—no,' she said.

'You mean that you cannot love me.' And as he said this the agony of his tone struck her ear and made her feel that he was suffering. Hitherto she had thought only of herself, and had hardly recognized it as a fact that he could be thoroughly in earnest.

'Mr. Orme, I am very sorry. Do not speak as though you were angry with me. But——'

'But you cannot love me?' And then he stood again silent, for there was no reply. 'Is it that, Miss Staveley, that you mean to answer? If you say that with positive assurance, I will trouble you no longer.' Poor Peregrine! He was but an unskilled lover!

'No!' she sobbed forth through her tears; but he had so framed his question that he hardly knew what No meant.

'Do you mean that you cannot love me, or may I hope that a day will come——. May I speak to you again——?'

'Oh, no, no! I can answer you now. It grieves me to the heart. I know you are so good. But, Mr. Orme——'

'Well—'

'It can never, never be.'

'And I must take that as answer?'

'I can make no other.' He still stood before her,—with gloomy and almost angry brow, could she have seen him; and then he thought he would ask her whether there was any other love which had brought about her scorn for him. It did not occur to him, at the first moment, that in doing so he would insult and injure her.

'At any rate I am not flattered by a reply which is at once so decided,' he began by saying.

'Oh! Mr. Orme, do not make me more unhappy——'

'But perhaps I am too late. Perhaps——' Then he remembered himself and paused. 'Never mind,' he said, speaking to himself rather than to her. 'Good-bye, Miss Staveley. You will at any rate say good-bye to me. I shall go at once now.'

'Go at once! Go away, Mr. Orme?'

'Yes; why should I stay here? Do you think that I could sit down to table with you all after that? I will ask your brother to explain my going; I shall find him in his room. Good-bye.'

She took his hand mechanically, and then he left her. When she came down to dinner she looked furtively round to this place and saw that it was vacant.

CHAPTER XXXI.

FOOTSTEPS IN THE CORRIDOR.

'UPON my word I am very sorrow,' said the judge. 'But what made him go off so suddenly? I hope there's nobody ill at The Cleeve!' And then the judge took his first spoonful of soup.

'No, no; there is nothing of that sort,' said Augustus. 'His grandfather wants him, and Orme thought he might as well start at once. He was always a sudden harum-scarum fellow like that.'

'He's a very pleasant, nice young man,' said Lady Staveley; 'and never gives himself any airs. I like him exceedingly.'

Poor Madeline did not dare to look either at her mother or her brother, but she would have given much to know whether either of them were aware of the cause which had sent Peregrine Orme so suddenly away from the house. At first she thought that Augustus surely did know, and she was wretched as she thought that he might probably speak to her on the subject. But he went on talking about Orme and his abrupt departure till she became convinced that he knew nothing and suspected nothing of what had occurred.

But her mother said never a word after that eulogium which she had uttered, and Madeline read that eulogium altogether aright. It said to her ears that if ever young Orme should again come forward with his suit, her mother would be prepared to receive him as a suitor; and it said, moreover, that if that suitor had been already sent away by any harsh answer, she would not sympathize with that harshness.

The dinner went on much as usual, but Madeline could not bring herself to say a word. She sat between her brother-in-law, Mr. Arbuthnot, on one side, and an old friend of her father's, of thirty years' standing, on the other. The old friend talked exclusively to Lady Staveley, and Mr. Arbuthnot, though he now and then uttered a word or two, was chiefly occupied with his dinner. During the last three or four days she had sat at dinner next to Peregrine

Footsteps in the corridor.

Orme, and it seemed to her now that she always had been able to talk to him. She had liked him so much too! Was it not a pity that he should have been so mistaken! And then as she sat after dinner, eating five or six grapes, she felt that she was unable to recall her spirits and look and speak as she was wont to do : a thing had happened which had knocked the ground from under her—had thrown her from her equipoise, and now she lacked the strength to recover herself and hide her dismay.

After dinner, while the gentlemen were still in the dining-room, she got a book, and nobody disturbed her as she sat alone pretending to read it. There never had been any intimate friendship between her and Miss Furnival, and that young lady was now employed in taking the chief part in a general conversation about wools. Lady Staveley got through a good deal of wool in the course of the year, as also did the wife of the old thirty-years' friend ; but Miss Furnival, short as her experience had been, was able to give a few hints to them both, and did not throw away the occasion. There was another lady there, rather deaf, to whom Mrs. Arbuthnot devoted herself, and therefore Madeline was allowed to be alone.

Then the men came in, and she was obliged to come forward and officiate at the tea-table. The judge insisted on having the teapot and urn brought into the drawing-room, and liked to have his cup brought to him by one of his own daughters. So she went to work and made the tea, but still she felt that she scarcely knew how to go through her task. What had happened to her that she should be thus beside herself, and hardly capable of refraining from open tears ? She knew that her mother was looking at her, and that now and again little things were done to give her ease if any ease were possible.

'Is anything the matter with my Madeline ?' said her father, looking up into her face, and holding the hand from which he had taken his cup.

'No, papa ; only I have got a headache.'

'A headache, dear ; that's not usual with you.'

'I have seen that she has not been well all the evening,' said Lady Staveley ; 'but I thought that perhaps she might shake it off. You had better go, my dear, if you are suffering. Isabella, I'm sure, will pour out the tea for us.'

And so she got away, and skulked slowly up stairs to her own room. She felt that it was skulking. Why should she have been so weak as to have fled in that way ? She had no headache—nor was it heartache that had now upset her. But a man had spoken to her openly of love, and no man had ever so spoken to her before.

She did not go direct to her own chamber, but passed along the corridor towards her mother's dressing-room. It was always her custom to remain there some half-hour before she went to bed, doing little things for her mother, and chatting with any other girl who might be intimate enough to be admitted there. Now she might remain there for an hour alone without danger of being disturbed; and she thought to herself that she would remain there till her mother came, and then unburthen herself of the whole story.

As she went along the corridor she would have to pass the room which had been given up to Felix Graham. She saw that the door was ajar, and as she came close up to it, she found the nurse in the act of coming out from the room. Mrs. Baker had been a very old servant in the judge's family, and had known Madeline from the day of her birth. Her chief occupation for some years had been nursing when there was anybody to nurse, and taking a general care and surveillance of the family's health when there was no special invalid to whom she could devote herself. Since Graham's accident she had been fully employed, and had greatly enjoyed the opportunities it had given her.

Mrs. Baker was in the doorway as Madeline attempted to pass by on tiptoe. 'Oh, he's a deal better now, Miss Madeline, so that you needn't be afeard of disturbing;—ain't you, Mr. Graham?' So she was thus brought into absolute contact with her friend, for the first time since he had hurt himself.

'Indeed I am,' said Felix; 'I only wish they'd let me get up and go down stairs. Is that Miss Staveley, Mrs. Baker?'

'Yes, sure. Come, my dear, he's got his dressing-gown on, and you may just come to the door and ask him how he does.'

'I am very glad to hear that you are so much better, Mr. Graham,' said Madeline, standing in the doorway with averted eyes, and speaking with a voice so low that it only just reached his ears.

'Thank you, Miss Staveley; I shall never know how to express what I feel for you all.'

'And there's none of 'em have been more anxious about you than she, I can tell you; and none of 'em aint kinderhearteder,' said Mrs. Baker.

'I hope you will be up soon and be able to come down to the drawing-room,' said Madeline. And then she did glance round, and for a moment saw the light of his eye as he sat upright in the bed. He was still pale and thin, or at least she fancied so, and her heart trembled within her as she thought of the danger he had passed.

'I do so long to be able to talk to you again; all the others come and visit me, but I have only heard the sounds of your footsteps as you pass by.'

'And yet she always walks like a mouse,' said Mrs. Baker.

'But I have always heard them,' he said. 'I hope Marian

thanked you for the books. She told me how you had gotten them for me.'

'She should not have said anything about them; it was Augustus who thought of them,' said Madeline.

'Marian comes to me four or five times a day,' he continued; 'I do not know what I should do without her.'

'I hope she is not noisy,' said Madeline.

'Laws, miss, he don't care for noise now, only he aint good at moving yet, and won't be for some while.'

'Pray take care of yourself, Mr. Graham,' she said; 'I need not tell you how anxious we all are for your recovery. Good night, Mr. Graham.' And then she passed on to her mother's dressing-room, and sitting herself down in an arm-chair opposite to the fire began to think—to think, or else to try to think.

And what was to be the subject of her thoughts? Regarding Peregrine Orme there was very little room for thinking. He had made her an offer, and she had rejected it as a matter of course, seeing that she did not love him. She had no doubt on that head, and was well aware that she could never accept such an offer. On what subject then was it necessary that she should think?

How odd it was that Mr. Graham's room door should have been open on this especial evening, and that nurse should have been standing there, ready to give occasion for that conversation! That was the idea that first took possession of her brain. And then she recounted all those few words which had been spoken as though they had had some special value—as though each word had been laden with interest. She felt half ashamed of what she had done in standing there and speaking at his bedroom door, and yet she would not have lost the chance for worlds. There had been nothing in what had passed between her and the invalid. The very words, spoken elsewhere, or in the presence of her mother and sister, would have been insipid and valueless; and yet she sat there feeding on them as though they were of flavour so rich that she could not let the sweetness of them pass from her. She had been stunned at the idea of poor Peregrine's love, and yet she never asked herself what was this new feeling. She did not inquire—not yet at least—whether there might be danger in such feelings.

She remained there, with eyes fixed on the burning coals, till her mother came up. 'What, Madeline,' said Lady Staveley, 'are you here still? I was in hopes you would have been in bed before this.'

'My headache is gone now, mamma; and I waited because—'

'Well, dear; because what?' and her mother came and stood over her and smoothed her hair. 'I know very well that something has been the matter. There has been something; eh, Madeline?'

'Yes, mamma.'

'And you have remained up that we may talk about it. Is that it, dearest?'

'I did not quite mean that, but perhaps it will be best. I can't be doing wrong, mamma, in telling you.'

'Well; you shall judge of that yourself;' and Lady Staveley sat down on the sofa so that she was close to the chair which Madeline still occupied. 'As a general rule I suppose you could not be doing wrong; but you must decide. If you have any doubt, wait till to-morrow.'

'No, mamma; I will tell you now. Mr. Orme—'

'Well, dearest. Did Mr. Orme say anything specially to you before he went away?'

'He—he—'

'Come to me, Madeline, and sit here. We shall talk better then.' And the mother made room beside her on the sofa for her daughter, and Madeline, running over, leaned with her head upon her mother's shoulder. 'Well, darling; what did he say? Did he tell you that he loved you?'

'Yes, mamma.'

'And you answered him—'

'I could only tell him—'

'Yes, I know. Poor fellow! But, Madeline, is he not an excellent young man;—one, at any rate, that is lovable? Of course in such a matter the heart must answer for itself. But I, looking at the offer as a mother—I could have been well pleased—'

'But, mamma, I could not—'

'Well, love: there shall be an end of it; at least for the present. When I heard that he had gone suddenly away I thought that something had happened.'

'I am so sorry that he should be unhappy, for I know that he is good.'

'Yes, he is good; and your father likes him, and Augustus. In such a matter as this, Madeline, I would never say a word to persuade you. I should think it wrong to do so. But it may be, dearest, that he has flurried you by the suddenness of his offer; and that you have not yet thought much about it.'

'But, mamma, I know that I do not love him.'

'Of course. That is natural. It would have been a great misfortune if you had loved him before you had reason to know that he loved you;—a great misfortune. But now,—now that you cannot but think of him, now that you know what his wishes are, perhaps you may learn—'

'But I have refused him, and he has gone away.'

'Young gentlemen under such circumstances sometimes come back again.'

'He won't come back, mamma, because—because I told him

so plainly—I am sure he understands that it is all to be at an end.'

' But if he should, and if you should then think differently towards him—'

' Oh, no !'

' But if you should, it may be well that you should know how all your friends esteem him. In a worldly view the marriage would be in all respects prudent : and as to disposition and temper, which I admit are much more important, I confess I think that he has all the qualities best adapted to make a wife happy. But, as I said before, the heart must speak for itself.'

' Yes; of course. And I know that I shall never love him;—not in that way.'

' You may be sure, dearest, that there will be no constraint put upon you. It might be possible that I or your papa should forbid a daughter's marriage, if she had proposed to herself an imprudent match; but neither he nor I would ever use our influence with a child to bring about a marriage because we think it prudent in a worldly point of view.' And then Lady Staveley kissed her daughter.

' Dear mamma, I know how good you are to me.' And she answered her mother's embrace by the pressure of her arm. But nevertheless she did not feel herself to be quite comfortable. There was something in the words which her mother had spoken which grated against her most cherished feelings;—something, though she by no means knew what. Why had her mother cautioned her in that way, that there might be a case in which she would refuse her sanction to a proposed marriage? Isabella's marriage had been concluded with the full agreement of the whole family; and she, Madeline, had certainly never as yet given cause either to father or mother to suppose that she would be headstrong and imprudent. Might not the caution have been omitted?—or was it intended to apply in any way to circumstances as they now existed?

' You had better go now, dearest,' said Lady Staveley, ' and for the present we will not think any more about this gallant young knight.' And then Madeline, having said good night, went off rather crestfallen to her own room. In doing so she again had to pass Graham's door, and as she went by it, walking not quite on tiptoe, she could not help asking herself whether or no he would really recognize the sound of her footsteps.

It is hardly necessary to say that Lady Staveley had conceived to herself a recognized purpose in uttering that little caution to her daughter; and she would have been quite as well pleased had circumstances taken Felix Graham out of her house instead of Peregrine Orme. But Felix Graham must necessarily remain for the next fortnight, and there could be no possible benefit in Orme's return, at any rate till Graham should have gone.

CHAPTER XXXII.

WHAT BRIDGET BOLSTER HAD TO SAY.

IT has been said in the earlier pages of this story that there was no prettier scenery to be found within thirty miles of London than that by which the little town of Hamworth was surrounded. This was so truly the case that Hamworth was full of lodgings which in the autumn season were always full of lodgers. The middle of winter was certainly not the time for seeing the Hamworth hills to advantage; nevertheless it was soon after Christmas that two rooms were taken there by a single gentleman who had come down for a week, apparently with no other view than that of enjoying himself. He did say something about London confinement and change of air; but he was manifestly in good health, had an excellent appetite, said a great deal about fresh eggs,—which at that time of the year was hardly reasonable, and brought with him his own pale brandy. This gentleman was Mr. Crabwitz.

The house at which he was to lodge had been selected with considerable judgment. It was kept by a tidy old widow known as Mrs. Trump; but those who knew anything of Hamworth affairs were well aware that Mrs. Trump had been left without a shilling, and could not have taken that snug little house in Paradise Row and furnished it complete y, out of her own means. No. Mrs. Trump's lodging-house was one of the irons which Samuel Dockwrath ever kept heating in the fire, for the behoof of those fourteen children. He had taken a lease of the house in Paradise Row, having made a bargain and advanced a few pounds while it was yet being built; and he then had furnished it and put in Mrs. Trump. Mrs. Trump received from him wages and a percentage; but to him were paid over the quota of shillings per week in consideration for which the lodgers were accommodated. All of which Mr. Crabwitz had ascertained before he located himself in Paradise Row.

And when he had so located himself he soon began to talk to Mrs. Trump about Mr. Dockwrath. He himself, as he told her in confidence, was in the profession of the law; he had heard of Mr. Dockwrath, and should be very glad if that gentleman would come over and take a glass of brandy and water with him some evening.

' And a very clever sharp gentleman he is,' said Mrs. Trump.

' With a tolerably good business, I suppose ?' asked Crabwitz.

' Pretty fair for that, sir. But he do be turning his hand to everything. He's a mortal long family of his own, and he has need of it all, if it's ever so much. But he'll never be poor for the want of looking after it.'

But Mr. Dockwrath did not come near his lodger on the first evening, and Mr. Crabwitz made acquaintance with Mrs. Dockwrath before he saw her husband. The care of the fourteen children was not supposed to be so onerous but that she could find a moment now and then to see whether Mrs. Trump kept the furniture properly dusted, and did not infringe any of the Dockwrathian rules. These were very strict ; and whenever they were broken it was on the head of Mrs. Dockwrath that the anger of the ruler mainly fell.

' I hope you find everything comfortable, sir,' said poor Miriam, having knocked at the sitting-room door when Crabwitz had just finished his dinner.

' Yes, thank you ; very nice. Is that Mrs. Dockwrath ?'

' Yes, sir. I'm Mrs. Dockwrath. As it's we who own the room I looked in to see if anything's wanting.'

' You are very kind. No ; nothing is wanting. But I should be delighted to make your acquaintance if you would stay for a moment. Might I ask you to take a chair ?' and Mr. Crabwitz handed her one.

' Thank you ; no, sir. I won't intrude.'

' Not at all, Mrs. Dockwrath. But the fact is, I'm a lawyer myself, and I should be so glad to become known to your husband. I have heard a great deal of his name lately as to a rather famous case in which he is employed.'

' Not the Orley Farm case ?' said Mrs. Dockwrath immediately.

' Yes, yes ; exactly.'

' And is he going on with that, sir ?' asked Mrs. Dockwrath with great interest.

' Is he not ? I know nothing about it myself, but I always supposed that such was the case. If I had such a wife as you, Mrs. Dockwrath, I should not leave her in doubt as to what I was doing in my own profession.'

' I know nothing about it, Mr. Cooke ;'—for it was as Mr. Cooke that he now sojourned at Hamworth. Not that it should be supposed he had received instructions from Mr. Furnival to come down to that place under a false name. From Mr. Furnival he had received no further instructions on that matter than those conveyed at the end of a previous chapter. ' I know nothing about it, Mr. Cooke ; and don't want to know generally. But I am anxious about this Orley Farm case. I do hope that he's going to drop it.'

And then Mr. Crabwitz elicited her view of the case with great ease.

On that evening, about nine, Mr. Dockwrath did go over to Paradise Row, and did allow himself to be persuaded to mix a glass of brandy and water and light a cigar. ‘ My missus tells me, sir, that you belong to the profession as well as myself.’

‘ Oh yes ; I’m a lawyer, Mr. Dockwrath.’

‘ Practising in town as an attorney, sir ?’

Not as an attorney on my own hook exactly. I chiefly employ my time in getting up cases for barristers. There’s a good deal done in that way.’

‘ Oh, indeed,’ said Mr. Dockwrath, beginning to feel himself the bigger man of the two ; and from that moment he patronized his companion instead of allowing himself to be patronized.

This went against the grain with Mr. Crabwitz, but, having an object to gain, he bore it. ‘ We hear a great deal up in London just at present about this Orley Farm case, and I always hear your name as connected with it. I had no idea when I was taking these lodgings that I was coming into a house belonging to that Mr. Dockwrath.’

‘ The same party, sir,’ said Mr. Dockwrath, blowing the smoke out of his mouth as he looked up to the ceiling.

And then by degrees Mr. Crabwitz drew him into conversation. Dockwrath was by nature quite as clever a man as Crabwitz, and in such a matter as this was not one to be outwitted easily ; but in truth he had no objection to talk about the Orley Farm case. ‘ I have taken it up on public motives, Mr. Cooke,’ he said, ‘ and I mean to go through with it.’

‘ Oh, of course ; in such a case as that you will no doubt go through with it ?’

‘ That’s my intention, I assure you. And I tell you what ; young Mason,—that’s the son of the widow of the old man who made the will——’

‘ Or rather who did not make it, as you say.’

‘ Yes, yes ; he made the will ; but he did not make the codicil—and that young Mason has no more right to the property than you have.’

‘ Hasn’t he now ?’

‘ No ; and I can prove it too.’

‘ Well ; the general opinion in the profession is that Lady Mason will stand her ground and hold her own. I don’t know what the points are myself, but I have heard it discussed, and that is certainly what people think.’

‘ Then people will find that they are very much mistaken.’

‘ I was talking to one of Round’s young men about it, and I fancy they are not very sanguine.’

‘ I do not care a fig for Round or his young men. It would be quite as well for Joseph Mason if Round and Crook gave up the matter altogether.   It lies in a nutshell, and the truth must come out whatever Round and Crook may choose to say.   And I'll tell you more—old Furnival, big a man as he thinks himself, cannot save her.'

'Has he anything to do with it?' asked Mr. Cooke.

'Yes; the sly old fox.   My belief is that only for him she'd give up the battle, and be down on her marrow-bones asking for mercy.'

'She'd have little chance of mercy, from what I hear of Joseph Mason.'

'She'd have to give up the property of course.   And even then I don't know whether he'd let her off.   By heavens! he couldn't let her off unless I chose.'   And then by degrees he told Mr. Cooke some of the circumstances of the case.

But it was not till the fourth evening that Mr. Dockwrath spent with his lodger that the intimacy had so far progressed as to enable Mr. Crabwitz to proceed with his little scheme.   On that day Mr. Dockwrath had received a notice that at noon on the following morning Mr. Joseph Mason and Bridget Bolster would both be at the house of Messrs. Round and Crook in Bedford Row, and that he could attend at that hour if it so pleased him.   It certainly would so please him, he said to himself when he got that letter; and in the evening he mentioned to his new friend the business which was taking him to London.

'If I might advise you in the matter, Mr. Dockwrath,' said Crabwitz, 'I should stay away altogether.'

'And why so?'

'Because that's not your market.   This poor devil of a woman—for she is a poor devil of a woman——'

'She'll be poor enough before long.'

'It can't be any gratification to you running her down.'

'Ah, but the justice of the thing.'

'Bother.   You're talking now to a man of the world.   Who can say what is the justice or the injustice of anything after twenty years of possession?   I have no doubt the codicil did express the old man's wish,—even from your own story.   But of course you are looking for your market.   Now it seems to me that there's a thousand pounds in your way as clear as daylight.'

'I don't see it myself, Mr. Cooke.'

'No; but I do.   The sort of thing is done every day.   You have your father-in-law's office journal?'

'Safe enough.'

'Burn it;—or leave it about in these rooms like;—so that somebody else may burn it.'

'I'd like to see the thousand pounds first.'

'Of course you'd do nothing till you knew about that;—nothing except keeping away from Round and Crook to-morrow. The money would be forthcoming if the trial were notoriously dropped by next assizes.'

Dockwrath sat thinking for a minute or two, and every moment of thought made him feel more strongly that he could not now succeed in the manner pointed out by Mr. Cooke. 'But where would be the market you are talking of?' said he.

'I could manage that,' said Crabwitz.

'And go shares in the business?'

'No, no; nothing of the sort.' And then he added, remembering that he must show that he had some personal object, 'If I got a trifle in the matter it would not come out of your allowance.'

The attorney again sat silent for a while, and now he remained so for full five minutes, during which Mr. Crabwitz puffed the smoke from between his lips with a look of supreme satisfaction. 'May I ask,' at last Mr. Dockwrath said, 'whether you have any personal interest in this matter?'

'None in the least;—that is to say, none as yet.'

'You did not come down here with any view——'

'Oh dear no; nothing of the sort. But I see at a glance that it is one of those cases in which a compromise would be the most judicious solution of difficulties. I am well used to this kind of thing, Mr. Dockwrath.'

'It would not do, sir,' said Mr. Dockwrath, after some further slight period of consideration. 'It wouldn't do. Round and Crook have all the dates, and so has Mason too. And the original of that partnership deed is forthcoming; and they know what witnesses to depend on. No, sir; I've begun this on public grounds, and I mean to carry it on. I am in a manner bound to do so as the representative of the attorney of the late Sir Joseph Mason;—and by heavens, Mr. Cooke, I'll do my duty.'

'I dare say you're right,' said Mr. Crabwitz, mixing a quarter of a glass more brandy and water.

'I know I'm right, sir,' said Dockwrath. 'And when a man knows he's right, he has a deal of inward satisfaction in the feeling.' After that Mr. Crabwitz was aware that he could be of no use at Hamworth, but he stayed out his week in order to avoid suspicion.

On the following day Mr. Dockwrath did proceed to Bedford Row, determined to carry out his original plan, and armed with that inward satisfaction to which he had alluded. He dressed himself in his best, and endeavoured as far as was in his power to look as though he were equal to the Messrs. Round. Old Crook he had seen once, and him he already despised. He had endeavoured to obtain a private interview with Mrs. Bolster before she could be seen by Matthew Round; but in this he had not succeeded. Mrs. Bolster was a prudent woman, and, acting doubtless under advice, had written to him, saying that she had been summoned to the office of Messrs. Round and Crook, and would there declare all that she knew about the matter. At the same time she returned to him a money order which he had sent to her.

Punctually at twelve he was in Bedford Row, and there he saw a respectable-looking female sitting at the fire in the inner part of the outer office. This was Bridget Bolster, but he would by no means have recognized her. Bridget had risen in the world and was now head chambermaid at a large hotel in the west of England. In that capacity she had laid aside whatever diffidence may have afflicted her earlier years, and was now able to speak out her mind before any judge or jury in the land. Indeed she had never been much afflicted by such diffidence, and had spoken out her evidence on that former occasion, now twenty years since, very plainly. But as she now explained to the head clerk, she had at that time been only a poor ignorant slip of a girl, with no more than eight pounds a year wages.

Dockwrath bowed to the head clerk, and passed on to Mat Round's private room. ' Mr. Matthew is inside, I suppose,' said he, and hardly waiting for permission he knocked at the door, and then entered. There he saw Mr. Matthew Round, sitting in his comfortable arm-chair, and opposite to him sat Mr. Mason of Groby Park.

Mr. Mason got up and shook hands with the Hamworth attorney, but Round junior made his greeting without rising, and merely motioned his visitor to a chair.

' Mr. Mason and the young ladies are quite well, I hope?' said Mr. Dockwrath, with a smile.

' Quite well, I thank you,' said the county magistrate.

' This matter has progressed since I last had the pleasure of seeing them. You begin to think I was right; eh, Mr. Mason?'

' Don't let us triumph till we are out of the wood?' said Mr. Round. ' It is a deal easier to spend money in such an affair as this than it is to make money by it. However we shall hear to-day more about it.'

' I do not know about making money,' said Mr. Mason, very solemnly. ' But that I have been robbed by that woman out of my just rights in that estate for the last twenty years,—that I may say I do know.'

' Quite true, Mr. Mason; quite true,' said Mr. Dockwrath with considerable energy.

' And whether I make money or whether I lose money I intend to proceed in this matter. It is dreadful to think that in this free and enlightened country so abject an offender should have been able to hold her head up so long without punishment and without disgrace.'

' That is exactly what I feel,' said Dockwrath. ' The very stones and trees of Hamworth cry out against her.'

'Gentlemen,' said Mr. Round, 'we have first to see whether there has been any injustice or not. If you will allow me I will explain to you what I now propose to do.'

'Proceed, sir,' said Mr. Mason, who was by no means satisfied with his young attorney.

'Bridget Bolster is now in the next room, and as far as I can understand the case at present, she would be the witness on whom your case, Mr. Mason, would most depend. The man Kenneby I have not yet seen; but from what I understand he is less likely to prove a willing witness than Mrs. Bolster.'

'I cannot go along with you there, Mr. Round,' said Dockwrath.

'Excuse me, sir, but I am only stating my opinion. If I should find that this woman is unable to say that she did not sign two separate documents on that day—that is, to say so with a positive and point blank assurance, I shall recommend you, as my client, to drop the prosecution.'

'I will never drop it,' said Mr. Mason.

'You will do as you please,' continued Round; 'I can only say what under such circumstances will be the advice given to you by this firm. I have talked the matter over very carefully with my father and with our other partner, and we shall not think well of going on with it unless I shall now find that your view is strongly substantiated by this woman.'

Then outspoke Mr. Dockwrath, 'Under these circumstances, Mr. Mason, if I were you, I should withdraw from the house at once. I certainly would not have my case blown upon.'

'Mr. Mason, sir, will do as he pleases about that. As long as the business with which he honours us is straightforward, we will do it for him, as for an old client, although it is not exactly in our own line. But we can only do it in accordance with our own judgment. I will proceed to explain what I now propose to do. The woman Bolster is in the next room, and I, with the assistance of my head clerk, will take down the headings of what evidence she can give.'

'In our presence, sir,' said Mr. Dockwrath; 'or if Mr. Mason should decline, at any rate in mine.'

'By no means, Mr. Dockwrath,' said Round.

'I think Mr. Dockwrath should hear her story,' said Mr. Mason.

'He certainly will not do so in this house or in conjunction with me. In what capacity should he be present, Mr. Mason?'

'As one of Mr. Mason's legal advisers,' said Dockwrath.

'If you are to be one of them, Messrs. Round and Crook cannot be the others. I think I explained that to you before. It now remains for Mr. Mason to say whether he wishes to employ our firm in this matter or not. And I can tell him fairly,' Mr. Round added this after a slight pause, 'that we shall be rather pleased than otherwise if he will put the case into other hands.'

'Of course I wish you to conduct it,' said Mr. Mason, who, with all his bitterness against the present holders of Orley Farm, was afraid of throwing himself into the hands of Dockwrath. He was not an ignorant man, and he knew that the firm of Round and Crook bore a high reputation before the world.

'Then,' said Round, 'I must do my business in accordance with my own views of what is right. I have reason to believe that no one has yet tampered with this woman,' and as he spoke he looked hard at Dockwrath, 'though probably attempts may have been made.'

'I don't know who should tamper with her,' said Dockwrath, 'unless it be Lady Mason—whom I must say you seem very anxious to protect.'

'Another word like that, sir, and I shall be compelled to ask you to leave the house. I believe that this woman has been tampered with by no one. I will now learn from her what is her remembrance of the circumstances as they occurred twenty years since, and I will then read to you her deposition. I shall be sorry, gentlemen, to keep you here, perhaps for an hour or so, but you will find the morning papers on the table.' And then Mr. Round, gathering up certain documents, passed into the outer office, and Mr. Mason and Mr. Dockwrath were left alone.

'He is determined to get that woman off,' said Mr. Dockwrath, in a whisper.

'I believe him to be an honest man,' said Mr. Mason, with some sternness.

'Honesty, sir! It is hard to say what is honesty and what is dishonesty. Would you believe it, Mr. Mason, only last night I had a thousand pounds offered me to hold my tongue about this affair?'

Mr. Mason at the moment did not believe this, but he merely looked hard into his companion's face, and said nothing.

'By the heavens above us what I tell you is true! a thousand pounds, Mr. Mason! Only think how they are going it to get this thing stifled. And where should the offer come from but from those who know I have the power?'

'Do you mean to say that the offer came from this firm?'

'Hush—sh, Mr. Mason. The very walls hear and talk in such a place as this. I'm not to know who made the offer, and I don't know. But a man can give a very good guess sometimes. The party who was speaking to me is up to the whole transaction, and knows exactly what is going on here—here, in this house. He let it all out, using pretty nigh the same words as Round used just now. He was full about the doubt that Round and Crook felt—that they'd never pull it through. I'll tell you what it is, Mr. Mason, they don't mean to pull it through.'

'What answer did you make to the man?'

'What answer! why I just put my thumb this way over my

shoulder. No, Mr. Mason, if I can't carry on without bribery and corruption, I won't carry on at all. He'd called at the wrong house with that dodge, and so he soon found.'

'And you think he was an emissary from Messrs. Round and Crook?'

'Hush—sh—sh. For heaven's sake, Mr. Mason, do be a little lower. You can put two and two together as well as I can, Mr. Mason. I find they make four. I don't know whether your calculation will be the same. My belief is, that these people are determined to save that woman. Don't you see it in that young fellow's eye—that his heart is all on the other side. Now he's got hold of that woman Bolster, and he'll teach her to give such evidence as will upset us. But I'll be even with him yet, Mr. Mason. If you'll only trust me, we'll both be even with him yet.'

Mr. Mason at the present moment said nothing further, and when Dockwrath pressed him to continue the conversation in whispers, he distinctly said that he would rather say no more upon the subject just then. He would wait for Mr. Round's return. 'Am I at liberty,' he asked, 'to mention that offer of the thousand pounds?'

'What—to Mat Round?' said Dockwrath. 'Certainly not, Mr. Mason. It wouldn't be our game at all.'

'Very well, sir.' And then Mr. Mason took up a newspaper, and no further words were spoken till the door opened and Mr. Round re-entered the room.

This he did with slow, deliberate step, and stopping on the hearth-rug, he stood leaning with his back against the mantelpiece. It was clear from his face to see that he had much to tell, and clear also that he was not pleased at the turn which affairs were taking.

'Well, gentlemen, I have examined the woman,' he said, 'and here is her deposition.'

'And what does she say?' asked Mr. Mason.

'Come, out with it, sir,' said Dockwrath. 'Did she, or did she not sign two documents on that day?'

'Mr. Mason,' said Round, turning to that gentleman, and altogether ignoring Dockwrath and his question; 'I have to tell you that her statement, as far as it goes, fully corroborates your view of the case. As far as it goes, mind you.'

'Oh, it does; does it?' said Dockwrath.

'And she is the only important witness?' said Mr. Mason with great exultation.

'I have never said that; what I did say was this—that your case must break down unless her evidence supported it. It does support it—strongly; but you will want more than that.'

'And now if you please, Mr. Round, what is it that she has deposed?' asked Dockwrath.

'She remembers it all then?' said Mason.

'She is a remarkably clear-headed woman, and apparently does remember a great deal. But her remembrance chiefly and most strongly goes to this—that she witnessed only one deed.'

'She can prove that, can she?' said Mason, and the tone of his voice was loudly triumphant.

'She declares that she never signed but one deed in the whole of her life—either on that day or on any other; and over and beyond this she says now—now that I have explained to her what that other deed might have been—that old Mr. Usbech told her that it was about a partnership.'

'He did, did he?' said Dockwrath, rising from his chair and clapping his hands. 'Very well. I don't think we shall want more than that, Mr. Mason.'

There was a tone of triumph in the man's voice, and a look of gratified malice in his countenance which disgusted Mr. Round and irritated him almost beyond his power of endurance. It was quite true that he would much have preferred to find that the woman's evidence was in favour of Lady Mason. He would have been glad to learn that she actually had witnessed the two deeds on the same day. His tone would have been triumphant, and his face gratified, had he returned to the room with such tidings. His feelings were all on that side, though his duty lay on the other. He had almost expected that it would be so. As it was, he was prepared to go on with his duty, but he was not prepared to endure the insolence of Mr. Dockwrath. There was a look of joy also about Mr. Mason which added to his annoyance. It might be just and necessary to prosecute that unfortunate woman at Orley Farm, but he could not gloat over such work.

'Mr. Dockwrath,' he said, 'I will not put up with such conduct here. If you wish to rejoice about this, you must go elsewhere.'

'And what are we to do now?' said Mr. Mason. 'I presume there need be no further delay.'

'I must consult with my partner. If you can make it convenient to call this day week——'

'But she will escape.'

'No, she will not escape. I shall not be ready to say anything before that. If you are not in town, then I can write to you.' And so the meeting was broken up, and Mr. Mason and Mr. Dockwrath left the lawyer's office together.

Mr. Mason and Mr. Dockwrath left the office in Bedford Row together, and thus it was almost a necessity that they should walk together for some distance through the streets. Mr. Mason was going to his hotel in Soho Square, and Mr. Dockwrath turned with him through the passage leading into Red Lion Square, linking his own arm in that of his companion. The Yorkshire county magistrate did not quite like this, but what was he to do?

' Did you ever see anything like that, sir ?' said Mr. Dockwrath;
' for by heavens I never did.'

' Like what?' said Mr. Mason.

' Like that fellow there;—that Round. It is my opinion that he
deserves to have his name struck from the rolls. Is it not clear
that he is doing all in his power to bring that wretched woman off?
And I'll tell you what, Mr. Mason, if you let him play his own
game in that way, he will bring her off.'

' But he expressly admitted that this woman Bolster's evidence
is conclusive.'

' Yes; he was so driven into a corner that he could not help
admitting that. The woman had been too many for him, and he
found that he couldn't cushion her. But do you mind my words,
Mr. Mason. He intends that you shall be beaten. It's as plain as
the nose on your face. You can read it in the very look of him,
and in every tone of his voice. At any rate I can. I'll tell you
what it is '—and then he squeezed very close to Mr. Mason—' he
and old Furnival understand each other in this matter like two
brothers. Of course Round will have his bill against you. Win
or lose, he'll get his costs out of your pocket. But he can make a
deuced pretty thing out of the other side as well. Let me tell
you, Mr. Mason, that when notes for a thousand pounds are flying
here and there, it isn't every lawyer that will see them pass by
him without opening his hand.'

' I do not think that Mr. Round would take a bribe,' said Mr.
Mason very stiffly.

' Wouldn't he? Just as a hound would a pat of butter. It's
your own look-out, you know, Mr. Mason. I haven't got an estate
of twelve hundred a year depending on it. But remember this;—
if she escapes now, Orley Farm is gone for ever.'

All this was extremely disagreeable to Mr. Mason. In the first
place he did not at all like the tone of equality which the Hamworth
attorney had adopted; he did not like to acknowledge that his
affairs were in any degree dependent on a man of whom he thought
so badly as he did of Mr. Dockwrath; he did not like to be told that
Round and Crook were rogues,—Round and Crook whom he had
known all his life; but least of all did he like the feeling of suspicion with which, in spite of himself, this man had imbued him,
or the fear that his victim might at last escape him. Excellent,
therefore, as had been the evidence with which Bridget Bolster had
declared herself ready to give in his favour, Mr. Mason was not a
contented man when he sat down to his solitary beefsteak in Soho
Square.

The Angel of Light.

CHAPTER XXXIII.

In speaking of the character and antecedents of Felix Graham I have said that he was moulding a wife for himself. The idea of a wife thus moulded to fit a man's own grooves, and educated to suit matrimonial purposes according to the exact views of the future husband was by no means original with him. Other men have moulded their wives, but I do not know that as a rule the practice has been found to answer. It is open, in the first place, to this objection,—that the moulder does not generally conceive such idea very early in life, and the idea when conceived must necessarily be carried out on a young subject. Such a plan is the result of much deliberate thought, and has generally arisen from long observation, on the part of the thinker, of the unhappiness arising from marriages in which there has been no moulding. Such a frame of mind comes upon a bachelor, perhaps about his thirty-fifth year, and then he goes to work with a girl of fourteen. The operation takes some ten years, at the end of which the moulded bride regards her lord as an old man. On the whole I think that the ordinary plan is the better, and even the safer. Dance with a girl three times, and if you like the light of her eye and the tone of voice with which she, breathless, answers your little questions about horseflesh and music—about affairs masculine and feminine,—then take the leap in the dark. There is danger, no doubt; but the moulded wife is, I think, more dangerous.

With Felix Graham the matter was somewhat different, seeing that he was not yet thirty, and that the lady destined to be the mistress of his family had already passed through three or four years of her noviciate. He had begun to be prudent early in life; or had become prudent rather by force of sentiment than by force of thought. Mary Snow was the name of his bride-elect; and it is probable that, had not circumstances thrown Mary Snow in his way, he would not have gone out of his way to seek a subject for his experiment. Mary Snow was the daughter of an engraver,—not of an artist who receives four or five thousand pounds for engraving the chef-d'œuvre of a modern painter,—but of a man who executed flourishes on ornamental cards for tradespeople, and assisted in the illustration of circus playbills. With this man Graham had become acquainted through certain transactions of his with the press, and had found him to be a widower, drunken, dissolute, and generally drowned in poverty. One child the man had, and that child was Mary Snow.

How it came to pass that the young barrister first took upon himself the charge of maintaining and educating this poor child need not now be told. His motives had been thoroughly good, and in the matter he had endeavoured to act the part of a kind Samaritan. He had found her pretty, half starved, dirty, ignorant, and modest; and so finding her had made himself responsible for feeding, cleaning, and teaching her,—and ultimately for marrying her. One would have said that in undertaking a task of such undoubted charity as that comprised in the three first charges, he would have encountered no difficulty from the drunken, dissolute, impoverished engraver. But the man from the beginning was cunning; and before Graham had succeeded in obtaining the custody of the child, the father had obtained a written undertaking from him that he would marry her at a certain age if her conduct up to that age had been becoming. As to this latter stipulation no doubt had arisen; and indeed Graham had so acted by her that had she fallen away the fault would have been all her own. There wanted now but one year to the coming of that day on which he was bound to make himself a happy man, and hitherto he himself had never doubted as to the accomplishment of his under-taking.

He had told his friends,—those with whom he was really intimate, Augustus Staveley and one or two others,—what was to be his matrimonial lot in life ; and they had ridiculed him for his quixotic chivalry. Staveley especially had been strong in his conviction that no such marriage would ever take place, and had already gone so far as to plan another match for his friend.

'You know you do not love her,' he had said, since Felix had been staying on this occasion at Noningsby.

'I know no such thing,' Felix had answered, almost in anger. 'On the contrary I know that I do love her.'

'Yes, as I love my niece Maria, or old Aunt Bessy, who always supplied me with sugar-candy when I was a boy.'

'It is I that have supplied Mary with her sugar-candy, and the love thus engendered is the stronger.'

'Nevertheless you are not in love with her, and never will be, and if you marry her you will commit a great sin.'

'How moral you have grown!'

'No, I'm not. I'm not a bit moral. But I know very well when a man is in love with a girl, and I know very well that you're not in love with Mary Snow. And I tell you what, my friend, if you do marry her you are done for life. There will absolutely be an end of you.'

'You mean to say that your royal highness will drop me.'

'I mean to say nothing about myself. My dropping you or not dropping you won't alter your lot in life. I know very well what a poor man wants to give him a start; and a fellow like you who has such quaint ideas on so many things requires all the assistance he can get. You should look out for money and connection.'

'Sophia Furnival, for instance.'

'No; she would not suit you. I perceive that now.'

'So I supposed. Well, my dear fellow, we shall not come to loggerheads about that. She is a very fine girl, and you are welcome to the hatful of money—if you can get it.'

'That's nonsense. I'm not thinking of Sophia Furnival any more than you are. But if I did it would be a proper marriage. Now—' And then he went on with some further very sage remarks about Miss Snow.

All this was said as Felix Graham was lying with his broken bones in the comfortable room at Noningsby; and to tell the truth, when it was so said his heart was not quite at ease about Mary Snow. Up to this time, having long since made up his mind that Mary should be his wife, he had never allowed his thoughts to be diverted from that purpose. Nor did he so allow them now,—as long as he could prevent them from wandering.

But, lying there at Noningsby, thinking of those sweet Christmas evenings, how was it possible that they should not wander? His friend had told him that he did not love Mary Snow; and then, when alone, he asked himself whether in truth he did love her. He had pledged himself to marry her, and he must carry out that pledge. But nevertheless did he love her? And if not her, did he love any other?

Mary Snow knew very well what was to be her destiny, and indeed had known it for the last two years. She was now nineteen years old,—and Madeline Staveley was also nineteen; she was nineteen, and at twenty she was to become a wife, as by agreement between Felix Graham and Mr. Snow, the drunken engraver. They knew their destiny,—the future husband and the future wife,—and each relied with perfect faith on the good faith and affection of the other.

Graham, while he was thus being lectured by Staveley, had under his pillow a letter from Mary. He wrote to her regularly—on every Sunday, and on every Tuesday she answered him. Nothing could be more becoming than the way she obeyed all his behests on such matters; and it really did seem that in his case the moulded wife would turn out to have been well moulded. When Staveley left him he again read Mary's letter. Her letters

were always of the same length, filling completely the four sides
of a sheet of note paper. They were excellently well written;
and as no one word in them was ever altered or erased, it was
manifest enough to Felix that the original composition was made on
a rough draft. As he again read through the four sides of the little
sheet of paper, he could not refrain from conjecturing what sort of
a letter Madeline Staveley might write. Mary Snow's letter ran as
follows :—

'3 Bloomfield Terrace, Peckham,
'Tuesday, 10 January, 18—.

'MY DEAREST FELIX'—she had so called him for the last twelve-
month by common consent between Graham and the very discreet
lady under whose charge she at present lived. Previously to that
she had written to him as, My dear Mr. Graham.

'MY DEAREST FELIX,

    'I am very glad to hear that your arm and your two ribs are
getting so much better. I received your letter yesterday, and was
glad to hear that you are so comfortable in the house of the very
kind people ,with whom you are staying. If I knew them I would
send them my respectful remembrances, but as I do not know them
I suppose it would not be proper. But I remember them in my
prayers.'—This last assurance was inserted under the express
instruction of Mrs. Thomas, who however did not read Mary's
letters, but occasionally, on some subjects, gave her hints as to
what she ought to say. Nor was there hypocrisy in this, for under
the instruction of her excellent mentor she had prayed for the kind
people.—'I hope you will be well enough to come and pay me a
visit before long, but pray do not come before you are well enough
to do so without giving yourself any pain. I am glad to hear that
you do not mean to go hunting any more, for it seems to me to be a
dangerous amusement.' And then the first paragraph came to an end.
    'My papa called here yesterday. He said he was very badly off
indeed, and so he looked. I did not know what to say at first, but
he asked me so much to give him some money, that I did give him
at last all that I had. It was nineteen shillings and sixpence.
Mrs. Thomas was angry, and told me I had no right to give
away your money, and that I should not have given more than
half a crown. I hope you will not be angry with me. I do not
want any more at present. But indeed he was very bad, especially
about his shoes.
    'I do not know that I have any more to say except that I put
back thirty lines of Télémaque into French every morning before
breakfast. It never comes near right, but nevertheless M. Grigaud
says it is well done He says that if it came quite right I should

compose French as well as M. Fénelon, which of course I cannot expect.

'I will now say good-bye, and I am yours most affectionately,

'MARY SNOW.'

There was nothing in this letter to give any offence to Felix Graham, and so he acknowledged to himself. He made himself so acknowledge, because on the first reading of it he had felt that he was half angry with the writer. It was clear that there was nothing in the letter which would justify censure;—nothing which did not, almost, demand praise. He would have been angry with her had she limited her filial donation to the half-crown which Mrs. Thomas had thought appropriate. He was obliged to her for that attention to her French which he had specially enjoined. Nothing could be more proper than her allusion to the Staveleys; —and altogether the letter was just what it ought to be. Nevertheless it made him unhappy and irritated him. Was it well that he should marry a girl whose father was ' indeed very bad, but especially about his shoes?' Staveley had told him that connection would be necessary for him, and what sort of a connection would this be? And was there one word in the whole letter that showed a spark of true love? Did not the footfall of Madeline Staveley's step as she passed along the passage go nearer to his heart than all the outspoken assurance of Mary Snow's letter?

Nevertheless he had undertaken to do this thing, and he would do it,—let the footfall of Madeline Staveley's step be ever so sweet in his ear. And then, lying back in his bed, he began to think whether it would have been as well that he should have broken his neck instead of his ribs in getting out of Monkton Grange covert.

Mrs. Thomas was a lady who kept a school consisting of three little girls and Mary Snow. She had in fact not been altogether successful in the line of life she had chosen for herself, and had hardly been able to keep her modest door-plate on her door, till Graham, in search of some home for his bride, then in the first noviciate of her moulding, had come across her. Her means were now far from plentiful; but as an average number of three children still clung to her, and as Mary Snow's seventy pounds per annum— to include clothes — were punctually paid, the small house at Peckham was maintained. Under these circumstances Mary Snow was somebody in the eyes of Mrs. Thomas, and Felix Graham was a very great person indeed.

Graham had received his letter on a Wednesday, and on the following Monday Mary, as usual, received one from him. These letters always came to her in the evening, as she was sitting over her tea with Mrs. Thomas, the three children having been duly put to bed. Graham's letters were very short, as a man with a

broken right arm and two broken ribs is not fluent with his pen.
But still a word or two did come to her. ' Dearest Mary, I am
doing better and better, and I hope I shall see you in about a
fortnight. Quite right in giving the money. Stick to the French.
Your own F. G.' But as he signed himself her own, his mind
misgave him that he was lying.

' It is very good of him to write to you while he is in such a
state,' said Mrs. Thomas.

' Indeed it is,' said Mary—very good indeed.' And then she
went on with the history of '' Rasselas '' in his happy valley, by
which study Mrs. Thomas intended to initiate her into that course
of novel-reading which has become necessary for a British lady.
But Mrs. Thomas had a mind to improve the present occasion. It
was her duty to inculcate in her pupil love and gratitude towards
the beneficent man who was doing so much for her. Gratitude for
favours past and love for favours to come ; and now, while that
scrap of a letter was lying on the table, the occasion for doing so
was opportune.

' Mary, I do hope you love Mr. Graham with all your heart and
all your strength.' She would have thought it wicked to say
more ; but so far she thought she might go, considering the sacred tie
which was to exist between her pupil and the gentleman in question.

' Oh, yes, indeed I do ;' and then Mary's eyes fell wishfully on the
cover of the book which lay in her lap while her finger kept the
place. Rasselas is not very exciting, but it was more so than
Mrs. Thomas.

' You would be very wicked if you did not. And I hope you
think sometimes of the very responsible duties which a wife owes
to her husband. And this will be more especially so with you than
with any other woman—almost that I ever heard of.'

There was something in this that was almost depressing to
poor Mary's spirit, but nevertheless she endeavoured to bear up
against it and do her duty. ' I shall do all I can to please him,
Mrs. Thomas ;—and indeed I do try about the French. And he says
I was right to give papa that money.'

' But there will be many more things than that when you've
stood at the altar with him and become his wife ;—bone of his bone,
Mary.' And she spoke these last words in a very solemn tone,
shaking her head, and the solemn tone almost ossified poor Mary's
heart as she heard it.

' Yes ; I know there will. But I shall endeavour to find out
what he likes.'

' I don't think he is so particular about his eating and drinking
as some other gentlemen ; though no doubt he will like his things
nice.'

' I know he is fond of strong tea, and I sha'n't forget that.'

'And about dress. He is not very rich you know, Mary; but it will make him unhappy if you are not always tidy. And his own shirts—I fancy he has no one to look after them now, for I so often see the buttons off. You should never let one of them go into his drawers without feeling them all to see that they're on tight.'

'I'll remember that,' said Mary, and then she made another little furtive attempt to open the book.

'And about your own stockings, Mary. Nothing is so useful to a young woman in your position as a habit of darning neat. I'm sometimes almost afraid that you don't like darning.'

'Oh, yes I do.' That was a fib; but what could she do, poor girl, when so pressed?

'Because I thought you would look at Jane Robinson's and Julia Wright's which are lying there in the basket. I did Rebecca's myself before tea, till my old eyes were sore.'

'Oh, I didn't know,' said Mary, with some slight offence in her tone. 'Why didn't you ask me to do them downright if you wanted?'

'It's only for the practice it will give you.'

'Practice! I'm always practising something.' But nevertheless she laid down the book, and dragged the basket of work up on to the table. 'Why, Mrs. Thomas, it's impossible to mend these; they're all darn.'

'Give them to me,' said Mrs. Thomas. And then there was silence between them for a quarter of an hour during which Mary's thoughts wandered away to the events of her future life. Would his stockings be so troublesome as these?

But Mrs. Thomas was at heart an honest woman, and as a rule was honest also in practice. Her conscience told her that Mr. Graham might probably not approve of this sort of practice for conjugal duties, and in spite of her failing eyes she resolved to do her duty. 'Never mind them, Mary,' said she. 'I remember now that you were doing your own before dinner.'

'Of course I was,' said Mary sulkily. 'And as for practice, I don't suppose he'll want me to do more of that than anything else.'

'Well, dear, put them by.' And Miss Snow did put them by, resuming Rasselas as she did so. Who darned the stockings of Rasselas and felt that the buttons were tight on his shirts? What a happy valley must it have been if a bride expectant were free from all such cares as these!

'I suppose, Mary, it will be some time in the spring of next year.' Mrs. Thomas was not reading, and therefore a little conversation from time to time was to her a solace.

'What will be, Mrs. Thomas?'

'Why, the marriage.'

'I suppose it will. He told father it should be early in 18—, and I shall be past twenty then.'

' I wonder where you'll go to live.'

' I don't know. He has never said anything about that.'

' I suppose not ; but I'm sure it will be a long way away from Peckham.' In answer to this Mary said nothing, but could not help wishing that it might be so. Peckham to her had not been a place bright with happiness, although she had become in so marked a way a child of good fortune. And then, moreover, she had a deep care on her mind with which the streets and houses and pathways of Peckham were closely connected. It would be very expedient that she should go far, far away from Peckham when she had become, in actual fact, the very wife of Felix Graham.

' Miss Mary,' whispered the red-armed maid of all work, creeping up to Mary's bedroom door, when they had all retired for the night, and whispering through the chink. ' Miss Mary. I've somethink to say.' And Mary opened the door. ' I've got a letter from him :' and the maid of all work absolutely produced a little note enclosed in a green envelope.

' Sarah, I told you not,' said Mary, looking very stern and hesitating with her finger whether or no she would take the letter.

' But he did so beg and pray. Besides, miss, as he says hisself he must have his answer. Any gen'leman, he says, 'as a right to a answer. And if you'd a seed him yourself I'm sure you'd have took it. He did look so nice with a blue and gold hankercher round his neck. He was a-going to the the-a-tre he said.'

' And who was going with him, Sarah ?'

' Oh, no one. Only his mamma and sister, and them sort. He's all right—he is.' And then Mary Snow did take the letter.

' And I'll come for the answer when you're settling the room after breakfast to-morrow ?' said the girl.

' No ; I don't know. I sha'n't send any answer at all. But, Sarah, for heaven's sake, do not say a word about it !'

' Who, I ? Laws love you, miss. I wouldn't ;—not for worlds of gold.' And then Mary was left alone to read a second letter from a second suitor.

' Angel of light !' it began, ' but cold as your own fair name.' Poor Mary thought it was very nice and very sweet, and though she was so much afraid of it that she almost wished it away, yet she read it a score of times. Stolen pleasures always are sweet. She had not cared to read those two lines from her own betrothed lord above once, or at the most twice ; and yet they had been written by a good man,—a man superlatively good to her, and written too with considerable pain.

She sat down all trembling to think of what she was doing ; and then, as she thought, she read the letter again. ' Angel of light ! but cold as your own fair name.' Alas, alas ! it was very sweet to her !

CHAPTER XXXIV.

MR. FURNIVAL LOOKS FOR ASSISTANCE.

'AND you think that nothing can be done down there?' said Mr. Furnival to his clerk, immediately after the return of Mr. Crabwitz from Hamworth to London.

'Nothing at all, sir,' said Mr. Crabwitz, with laconic significance.

'Well; I dare say not. If the matter could have been arranged at a reasonable cost, without annoyance to my friend Lady Mason, I should have been glad; but, on the whole, it will perhaps be better that the law should take its course. She will suffer a good deal, but she will be the safer for it afterwards.'

'Mr. Furnival, I went so far as to offer a thousand pounds!'

'A thousand pounds! Then they'll think we're afraid of them.'

'Not a bit more than they did before. Though I offered the money, he doesn't know the least that the offer came from our side. But I'll tell you what it is, Mr. Furnival—. I suppose I may speak my mind.'

'Oh, yes! But remember this, Crabwitz; Lady Mason is no more in danger of losing the property than you are. It is a most vexatious thing, but there can be no doubt as to what the result will be.'

'Well, Mr. Furnival,—I don't know.'

'In such matters, I am tolerably well able to form an opinion.'

'Oh, certainly!'

'And that's my opinion. Now I shall be very glad to hear yours.'

'My opinion is this, Mr. Furnival, that Sir Joseph never made that codicil.'

'And what makes you think so?'

'The whole course of the evidence. It's quite clear there was another deed executed that day, and witnessed by Bolster and Kenneby. Had there been two documents for them to witness, they would have remembered it so soon after the occurrence.'

'Well, Crabwitz, I differ from you,—differ from you in toto But keep your opinion to yourself, that's all. I've no doubt you did the best for us you could down at Hamworth, and I'm much obliged to you. You'll find we've got our hands quite full again,—

almost too full.' Then he turned round to his table, and to the papers upon it; whereupon, Crabwitz took the hint, and left the room.

But when he had gone, Mr. Furnival again raised his eyes from the papers on the table, and leaning back in his chair, gave himself up to further consideration of the Orley Farm case. Crabwitz he knew was a sharp, clever man, and now the opinion formed by Crabwitz, after having seen this Hamworth attorney, tallied with his own opinion. Yes; it was his own opinion. He had never said as much, even to himself, with those inward words which a man uses when he assures himself of the result of his own thoughts; but he was aware that it was his own opinion. In his heart of hearts, he did believe that that codicil had been fraudulently manufactured by his friend and client, Lady Mason.

Under these circumstances, what should he do? He had the handle of his pen between his teeth, as was his habit when he was thinking, and tried to bring himself to some permanent resolution.

How beautiful had she looked while she stood in Sir Peregrine's library, leaning on the old man's arm—how beautiful and how innocent! That was the form which his thoughts chiefly took. And then she had given him her hand, and he still felt the soft silken touch of her cool fingers. He would not be a man if he could desert a woman in such a strait. And such a woman! If even guilty, had she not expiated her guilt by deep sorrow? And then he thought of Mr. Mason of Groby Park; and he thought of Sir Peregrine's strong conviction, and of Judge Staveley's belief; and he thought also of the strong hold which public opinion and twenty years of possession would still give to the cause he favoured. He would still bring her through! Yes; in spite of her guilt, if she were guilty; on the strength of her innocency, if she were innocent; but on account of her beauty, and soft hand, and deep liquid eye. So at least he would have owned, could he have been honest enough to tell himself the whole truth.

But he must prepare himself for the battle in earnest. It was not as though he had been briefed in this case, and had merely to perform the duty for which he had been hired. He was to undertake the whole legal management of the affair. He must settle what attorney should have the matter in hand, and instruct that attorney how to reinstruct him, and how to reinstruct those other barristers who must necessarily be employed on the defence, in a case of such magnitude. He did not yet know under what form the attack would be made; but he was nearly certain that it would be done in the shape of a criminal charge. He hoped that it might take the direct form of an accusation of forgery. The stronger and more venomous the charge made, the stronger also would be public

opinion in favour of the accused, and the greater the chance of
an acquittal. But if she were to be found guilty on any charge, it
would matter little on what. Any such verdict of guilty would be
utter ruin and obliteration of her existence.

He must consult with some one, and at last he made up his mind to
go to his very old friend, Mr. Chaffanbrass. Mr. Chaffanbrass was
safe, and he might speak out his mind to him without fear of
damaging the cause. Not that he could bring himself to speak out
his real mind, even to Mr. Chaffanbrass. He would so speak that
Mr. Chaffanbrass should clearly understand him ; but still, not even
to his ears, would be say that he really believed Lady Mason to
have been guilty. How would it be possible that he should feign
before a jury his assured, nay, his indignant conviction of his
client's innocence, if he had ever whispered to any one his conviction of her guilt ?

On that same afternoon he sent to make an appointment with
Mr. Chaffanbrass, and immediately after breakfast, on the following
morning, had himself taken to that gentleman's chambers. The
chambers of this great guardian of the innocence—or rather not-
guiltiness of the public—were not in any so-named inn, but consisted of two gloomy, dark, panelled rooms in Ely Place. The
course of our story, however, will not cause us to make many visits
to Ely Place, and any closer description of them may be spared. I
have said that Mr. Chaffanbrass and Mr. Furnival were very old
friends. So they were. They had known each other for more than
thirty years, and each knew the whole history of the other's rise
and progress in the profession ; but any results of their friendship
at present were but scanty. They might meet each other in the
streets, perhaps, once in the year ; and occasionally—but very
seldom—might be brought together on subjects connected with
their profession ; as was the case when they travelled together
down to Birmingham. As to meeting in each other's houses, or
coming together for the sake of the friendship which existed,—the
idea of doing so never entered the head of either of them.

All the world knows Mr. Chaffanbrass—either by sight or by
reputation. Those who have been happy enough to see the face
and gait of the man as, in years now gone, he used to lord it at the
Old Bailey, may not have thought much of the privilege which was
theirs. But to those who have only read of him, and know of his
deeds simply by their triumphs, he was a man very famous and
worthy to be seen. 'Look; that's Chaffanbrass. It was he who
cross-examined —— at the Old Bailey, and sent him howling out of
London, banished for ever into the wilderness.' 'Where, where ?
Is that Chaffanbrass ? What a dirty little man !'

To this dirty little man in Ely Place, Mr. Furnival now went in
his difficulty. Mr. Furnival might feel himself sufficient to secure

the acquittal of an innocent person, or even of a guilty person, under ordinary circumstances; but if any man in England could secure the acquittal of a guilty person under extraordinary circumstances, it would be Mr. Chaffanbrass. This had been his special line of work for the last thirty years.

Mr. Chaffanbrass was a dirty little man; and when seen without his gown and wig, might at a first glance be thought insignificant. But he knew well how to hold his own in the world, and could maintain his opinion, unshaken, against all the judges in the land. ‘Well, Furnival, and what can I do for you?’ he said, as soon as the member for the Essex Marshes was seated opposite to him. ‘It isn’t often that the light of your countenance shines so far east as this. Somebody must be in trouble, I suppose?’

‘Somebody is in trouble,’ said Mr. Furnival; and then he began to tell his story. Mr. Chaffanbrass listened almost in silence throughout. Now and then he asked a question by a word or two, expressing no opinion whatever as he did so; but he was satisfied to leave the talking altogether in the hands of his visitor till the whole tale was told. ‘Ah,’ he said then, ‘a clever woman!’

‘An uncommonly sweet creature too,’ said Mr. Furnival.

‘I dare say,’ said Mr. Chaffanbrass; and then there was a pause.

‘And what can I do for you?’ said Mr. Chaffanbrass.

‘In the first place I should be very glad to have your advice; and then—. Of course I must lead in defending her,—unless it were well that I should put the case altogether in your hands.’

‘Oh no! don’t think of that. I couldn’t give the time to it. My heart is not in it, as yours is. Where will it be?’

‘At Alston, I suppose.’

‘At the Spring assizes. That will be—. Let me see; about the 10th of March.’

‘I should think we might get it postponed till the summer. Round is not at all hot about it.’

‘Should we gain anything by that? If a prisoner be innocent why torment him by delay. He is tolerably sure of escape. If he be guilty, extension of time only brings out the facts the clearer. As far as my experience goes, the sooner a man is tried the better, —always.’

‘And you would consent to hold a brief?’

‘Under you? Well; yes. I don’t mind it at Alston. Anything to oblige an old friend. I never was proud, you know.’

‘And what do you think about it, Chaffanbrass?’

‘Ah! that’s the question.’

‘She must be pulled through. Twenty years of possession! Think of that.’

‘That’s what Mason, the man down in Yorkshire, is thinking of. There’s no doubt of course about that partnership deed?’

'I fear not. Round would not go on with it if that were not all true.'

'It depends on those two witnesses, Furnival. I remember the case of old, though it was twenty years ago, and I had nothing to do with it. I remember thinking that Lady Mason was a very clever woman, and that Round and Crook were rather slow.'

'He's a brute; is that fellow, Mason of Groby Park.'

'A brute; is he? We'll get him into the box and make him say as much for himself. She's uncommonly pretty, isn't she?'

'She is a pretty woman.'

'And interesting? It will all tell, you know. A widow with one son, isn't she?'

'Yes, and she has done her duty admirably since her husband's death. You will find too that she has the sympathies of all the best people in her neighbourhood. She is staying now at the house of Sir Peregrine Orme, who would do anything for her.'

'Anything, would he?'

'And the Staveleys know her. The judge is convinced of her innocence.'

'Is he? He'll probably have the Home Circuit in the summer. His conviction expressed from the bench would be more useful to her. You can make Staveley believe everything in a drawing-room or over a glass of wine; but I'll be hanged if I can ever get him to believe anything when he's on the bench.'

'But, Chaffanbrass, the countenance of such people will be of great use to her down there. Everybody will know that she's been staying with Sir Peregrine.'

'I've no doubt she's a clever woman.'

'But this new trouble has half killed her.'

'I don't wonder at that either. These sort of troubles do vex people. A pretty woman like that should have everything smooth; shouldn't she? Well, we'll do the best we can. You'll see that I'm properly instructed. By-the-by, who is her attorney? In such a case as that you couldn't have a better man than old Solomon Aram. But Solomon Aram is too far east from you, I suppose?'

'Isn't he a Jew?'

'Upon my word I don't know. He's an attorney, and that's enough for me.'

And then the matter was again discussed between them, and it was agreed that a third counsel would be wanting. 'Felix Graham is very much interested in the case,' said Mr. Furnival, 'and is as firmly convinced of her innocence as—as I am.' And he managed to look his ally in the face and to keep his countenance firmly.

'Ah,' said Mr. Chaffanbrass. 'But what if he should happen to change his opinion about his own client?'

'We could prevent that, I think.'

' I'm not so sure. And then he'd throw her over as sure as your name's Furnival.'

' I hardly think he'd do that.'

' I believe he'd do anything.' And Mr. Chaffanbrass was quite moved to enthusiasm. ' I've heard that man talk more nonsense about the profession in one hour, than I ever heard before since I first put a cotton gown on my back. He does not understand the nature of the duty which a professional man owes to his client.'

' But he'd work well if he had a case at heart himself. I don't like him, but he is clever.'

' You can do as you like, of course. I shall be out of my ground down at Alston, and of course I don't care who takes the fag of the work. But I tell you this fairly;—if he does go into the case and then turns against us or drops it,—I shall turn against him and drop into him.'

' Heaven help him in such a case as that!' And then these two great luminaries of the law shook hands and parted.

One thing was quite clear to Mr. Furnival as he had himself carried in a cab from Ely Place to his own chambers in Lincoln's Inn. Mr. Chaffanbrass was fully convinced of Lady Mason's guilt. He had not actually said so, but he had not even troubled himself to go through the little ceremony of expressing a belief in her innocence. Mr. Furnival was well aware that Mr. Chaffanbrass would not on this account be less likely to come out strongly with such assurances before a jury, or to be less severe in his cross-examination of a witness whose evidence went to prove that guilt; but nevertheless the conviction was disheartening. Mr. Chaffanbrass would know, almost by instinct, whether an accused person was or was not guilty; and he had already perceived, by instinct, that Lady Mason was guilty. Mr. Furnival sighed as he stepped out of his cab, and again wished that he could wash his hands of the whole affair. He wished it very much;—but he knew that his wish could not be gratified.

' Solomon Aram!' he said to himself, as he again sat down in his arm-chair. ' It will sound badly to those people down at Alston. At the Old Bailey they don't mind that kind of thing.' And then he made up his mind that Solomon Aram would not do. It would be a disgrace to him to take a case out of Solomon Aram's hands. Mr. Chaffanbrass did not understand all this. Mr. Chaffanbrass had been dealing with Solomon Arams all his life. Mr. Chaffanbrass could not see the effect which such an alliance would have on the character of a barrister holding Mr. Furnival's position. Solomon Aram was a good man in his way no doubt;—perhaps the best man going. In taking every dodge to prevent a conviction no man could be better than Solomon Aram. All this Mr. Furnival felt;—but he felt also that he could not afford it. ' It would be tantamount to a confession of guilt to take such a man as that down into the country,' he said to himself, trying to excuse himself.

And then he also made up his mind that he would sound Felix Graham. If Felix Graham could be induced to take up the case thoroughly believing in the innocence of his client, no man would be more useful as a junior. Felix Graham went the Home Circuit on which Alston was one of the assize towns.

CHAPTER XXXV.

LOVE WAS STILL THE LORD OF ALL.

WHY should I not? Such had been the question which Sir Peregrine Orme had asked himself over and over again, in these latter days, since Lady Mason had been staying at his house; and the purport of the question was this:—Why should he not make Lady Mason his wife?

I and my readers can probably see very many reasons why he should not do so; but then we are not in love with Lady Mason. Her charms and her sorrows,—her soft, sad smile and her more lovely tears have not operated upon us. We are not chivalrous old gentlemen, past seventy years of age, but still alive, keenly alive, to a strong feeling of romance. That visit will perhaps be remembered which Mr. Furnival made at The Cleeve, and the subsequent interview between Lady Mason and the baronet. On that day he merely asked himself the question, and took no further step. On the subsequent day and the day after, it was the same. He still asked himself the question, sitting alone in his library; but he did not ask it as yet of any one else. When he met Lady Mason in these days his manner to her was full of the deference due to a lady and of the affection due to a dear friend; but that was all. Mrs. Orme, seeing this, and cordially concurring in this love for her guest, followed the lead which her father-in-law gave, and threw herself into Lady Mason's arms. They two were fast and bosom friends.

And what did Lady Mason think of all this? In truth there was much in it that was sweet to her, but there was something also that increased that idea of danger which now seemed to envelop her whole existence. Why had Sir Peregrine so treated her in the library, behaving towards her with such tokens of close affection? He had put his arm round her waist and kissed her lips and pressed her to his old bosom. Why had this been so? He had assured her that he would be to her as a father, but her woman's instinct had told her that the pressure of his hand had been warmer than that

which a father accords to his adopted daughter. No idea of anger
had come upon her for a moment; but she had thought about it
much, and had thought about it almost in dismay. What if the old
man did mean more than a father's love? It seemed to her as
though it must be a dream that he should do so; but what if he
did? How should she answer him? In such circumstances what
should she do or say? Could she afford to buy his friendship,—
even his warmest love at the cost of the enmity of so many others?
Would not Mrs. Orme hate her, Mrs. Orme, whom she truly, dearly,
eagerly loved? Mrs. Orme's affection was, of all personal gratifica-
tions, the sweetest to her. And the young heir,—would not he
hate her? Nay, would he not interfere and with some strong hand
prevent so mean a deed on the part of his grandfather? And if so,
would she not thus have lost them altogether? And then she
thought of that other friend whose aid would be so indispensable
to her in this dreadful time of tribulation. How would Mr. Furnival receive such tidings, if it should come to pass that such tidings
were to be told?

Lady Mason was rich with female charms, and she used them
partly with the innocence of the dove, but partly also with the wisdom of the serpent. But in such use as she did make of these only
weapons which Providence had given to her, I do not think that she
can be regarded as very culpable. During those long years of her
young widowhood in which nothing had been wanting to her, her
conduct had been free from any hint of reproach. She had been
content to find all her joy in her duties and in her love as a mother.
Now a great necessity for assistance had come upon her. It was
necessary that she should bind men to her cause, men powerful in
the world and able to fight her battle with strong arms. She did so
bind them with the only chains at her command,—but she had no
thought, nay, no suspicion of evil in so doing. It was very painful
to her when she found that she had caused unhappiness to Mrs.
Furnival; and it caused her pain now, also, when she thought of
Sir Peregrine's new love. She did wish to bind these men to her
by a strong attachment; but she would have stayed this feeling at
a certain point had it been possible for her so to manage it.

In the mean time Sir Peregrine still asked himself that question.
He had declared to himself when first the idea had come to him,
that none of those whom he loved should be injured. He would
even ask his daughter-in-law's consent, condescending to plead his
cause before her, making her understand his motives, and asking her
acquiescence as a favour. He would be so careful of his grandson
that this second marriage—if such event did come to pass—should
not put a pound out of his pocket, or at any rate should not hamper
the succession of the estate with a pound of debt. And then he
made excuses to himself as to the step which he proposed to take,

thinking how he would meet his friends, and how he would carry himself before his old servants.

Old men have made more silly marriages than this which he then desired. Gentlemen such as Sir Peregrine in age and station have married their housemaids,—have married young girls of eighteen years of age,—have done so and faced their friends and servants afterwards. The bride that he proposed to himself was a lady, an old friend, a woman over forty, and one whom by such a marriage he could greatly assist in her deep sorrow. Why should he not do it?

After much of such thoughts as these, extended over nearly a week, he resolved to speak his mind to Mrs. Orme. If it were to be done it should be done at once. The incredulous unromantic readers of this age would hardly believe me if I said that his main object was to render assistance to Lady Mason in her difficulty; but so he assured himself, and so he believed. This assistance to be of true service must be given at once;—and having so resolved he sent for Mrs. Orme into the library.

' Edith, my darling,' he said, taking her hand and pressing it between both his own as was often the wont with him in his more affectionate moods. 'I want to speak to you—on business that concerns me nearly ; may perhaps concern us all nearly. Can you give me half an hour?'

' Of course I can—what is it, sir ? I am a bad hand at business ; but you know that.'

' Sit down, dear ; there ; sit there, and I will sit here. As to this business, no one can counsel me as well as you.'

' Dearest father, I should be a poor councillor in anything.'

' Not in this, Edith. It is about Lady Mason that I would speak to you. We both love her dearly ; do we not ?'

' I do.'

' And are glad to have her here ?'

' Oh, so glad. When this trial is only over, it will be so sweet, to have her for a neighbour. We really know her now. And it will be so pleasant to see much of her.'

There was nothing discouraging in this, but still the words in some slight degree grated against Sir Peregrine's feelings. At the present moment he did not wish to think of Lady Mason as living at Orley Farm, and would have preferred that his daughter-in-law should have spoken of her as being there, at The Cleeve.

' Yes ; we know her now,' he said. ' And believe me in this, Edith ; no knowledge obtained of a friend in happiness is at all equal to that which is obtained in sorrow. Had Lady Mason been prosperous, had she never become subject to the malice and avarice of wicked people, I should never have loved her as I do love her.'

' Nor should I, father.'

' She is a cruelly ill-used woman, and a woman worthy of the kindest usage. I am an old man now, but it has never before been my lot to be so anxious for a fellow-creature as I am for her. It is dreadful to think that innocence in this country should be subject to such attacks.'

' Indeed it is; but you do not think that there is any danger?'

This was all very well, and showed that Mrs. Orme's mind was well disposed towards the woman whom he loved. But he had known that before, and he began to feel that he was not approaching the object which he had in view. ' Edith,' at last he said abruptly, ' I love her with my whole heart. I would fain make her—my wife.' Sir Peregrine Orme had never in his course through life failed in anything for lack of courage; and when the idea came home to him that he was trembling at the task which he had imposed on himself, he dashed at it at once. It is so that forlorn hopes are led, and become not forlorn; it is so that breaches are taken.

' Your wife!' said Mrs. Orme. She would not have breathed a syllable to pain him if she could have helped it, but the suddenness of the announcement overcame her for a moment.

' Yes, Edith, my wife. Let us discuss the matter before you condemn it. But in the first place I would have you to understand this—I will not marry her if you say that it will make you unhappy. I have not spoken to her as yet, and she knows nothing of this project.' Sir Peregrine, it may be presumed, had not himself thought much of that kiss which he had given her. ' You,' he continued to say, ' have given up your whole life to me. You are my angel. If this thing will make you unhappy it shall not be done.'

Sir Peregrine had not so considered it, but with such a woman as Mrs. Orme this was, of course, the surest way to overcome opposition. On her own behalf, thinking only of herself, she would stand in the way of nothing that could add to Sir Peregrine's happiness. But nevertheless the idea was strong in her mind that such a marriage would be imprudent. Sir Peregrine at present stood high before the world. Would he stand so high if he did this thing? His gray hair and old manly bearing were honoured and revered by all who knew him. Would this still be so if he made himself the husband of Lady Mason?' She loved so dearly, she valued so highly the honour that was paid to him! She was so proud of her own boy in that he was the grandson of so perfect a gentleman! Would not this be a sad ending to such a career? Such were the thoughts which ran through her mind at the moment.

' Make me unhappy!' she said getting up and going over to him. ' It is your happiness of which I would think. Will it make you more happy?'

'It will enable me to befriend her more effectually.'

'But, dearest father, you must be the first consideration to us,—to me and Peregrine.   Will it make you more happy?'

'I think it will,' he answered slowly.

'Then I, for one, will say nothing against it,' she answered. She was very weak, it will be said.   Yes, she was weak.   Many of the sweetest, kindest, best of women are weak in this way.   It is not every woman that can bring herself to say hard useful, wise words in opposition to the follies of those they love best.   A woman to be useful and wise no doubt should have such power. For myself I am not so sure that I like useful and wise women. 'Then I for one will say nothing against it,' said Mrs. Orme, deficient in utility, wanting in wisdom, but full of the sweetest affection.

'You are sure that you will not love her the less yourself?' said Sir Peregrine.

'Yes; I am sure of that.   If it were to be so, I should endeavour to love her the more.'

'Dearest Edith.   I have only one other person to tell.'

'Do you mean Peregrine?' she said in her softest voice.

'Yes.   Of course he must be told.   But as it would not be well to ask his consent,—as I have asked yours—' and then as he said this he kissed his brow.

'But you will let him know it?'

'Yes; that is if she accepts my proposition.   Then he shall know it immediately.   And, Edith, my dear, you may be sure of this; nothing that I do shall be allowed in any way to injure his prospects or to hamper him as regards money when I am gone.   If this marriage takes place I cannot do very much for her in the way of money; she will understand that.   Something I can of course.'

And then Mrs. Orme stood over the fire, looking at the hot coals, and thinking what Lady Mason's answer would be.   She esteemed Lady Mason very highly, regarding her as a woman sensible and conscientious at all points, and she felt by no means certain that the offer would be accepted.   What if Lady Mason should say that such an arrangement would not be possible for her.   Mrs. Orme felt that under such circumstances she at any rate would not withdraw her love from Lady Mason.

'And now I may as well speak to her at once,' said Sir Peregrine. 'Is she in the drawing-room?'

'I left her there.'

'Will you ask her to come to me—with my love?'

'I had better not say anything I suppose?'

Sir Peregrine in his heart of hearts wished that his daughter-in-law could say it all, but he would not give her such a commission. 'No; perhaps not.'   And then Mrs. Orme was going to leave him.

' One word more, Edith. You and I, darling, have known each other so long and loved each other so well, that I should be unhappy if I were to fall in your estimation.'

' There is no fear of that, father.'

' Will you believe me when I assure you that my great object in doing this is to befriend a good and worthy woman whom I regard as ill used—beyond all ill usage of which I have hitherto known anything ?'

She then assured him that she did so believe, and she assured him truly; after that she left him and went away to send in Lady Mason for her interview. In the mean time Sir Peregrine got up and stood with his back to the fire. He would have been glad that the coming scene could be over, and yet I should be wronging him to say that he was afraid of it. There would be a pleasure to him in telling her that he loved her so dearly and trusted her with such absolute confidence. There would be a sort of pleasure to him in speaking even of her sorrow, and in repeating his assurance that he would fight the battle for her with all the means at his command. And perhaps also there would be some pleasure in the downcast look of her eye, as she accepted the tender of his love. Something of that pleasure he had known already. And then he remembered the other alternative. It was quite upon the cards that she should decline his offer. He did not by any means shut his eyes to that. Did she do so, his friendship should by no means be withdrawn from her. He would be very careful from the onset that she should understand so much as that. And then he heard the light footsteps in the hall; the gentle hand was raised to the door, and Lady Mason was standing in the room.

' Dear Lady Mason,' he said, meeting her half way across the room, ' it is very kind of you to come to me when I send for you in this way.'

' It would be my duty to come to you, if it were half across the kingdom ;—and my pleasure also.'

' Would it ?' said he, looking into her face with all the wishfulness of a young lover. From that moment she knew what was coming. Strange as was the destiny which was to be offered to her at this period of her life, yet she foresaw clearly that the offer was to be made. What she did not foresee, what she could not foretell, was the answer which she might make to it!

' It would certainly be my sweetest pleasure to send for you if you were away from us,—to send for you or to follow you,' said he.

' I do not know how to make return for all your kind regard to me ;—to you and to dear Mrs. Orme.'

' Call her Edith, will you not? You did so call her once.'

' I call her so often when we are alone together, now ; and yet I feel that I have no right.'

' You have every right. You shall have every right if you will accept it. Lady Mason, I am an old man,—some would say a very old man. But I am not too old to love you. Can you accept the love of an old man like me?'

Lady Mason was, as we are aware, not taken in the least by surprise; but it was quite necessary that she should seem to be so taken. This is a little artifice which is excusable in almost any lady at such a period. ' Sir Peregrine,' she said, ' you do not mean more than the love of a most valued friend?'

' Yes, much more. I mean the love of a husband for his wife; of a wife for her husband.'

' Sir Peregrine! Ah me! You have not thought of this, my friend. You have not remembered the position in which I am placed. Dearest, dearest friend; dearest of all friends,'—and then she knelt before him, leaning on his knees, 'as he sat in his accustomed large arm-chair. ' It may not be so. Think of the sorrow that would come to you and yours, if my enemies should prevail.'

' By —— they shall not prevail!' swore Sir Peregrine, roundly; and as he swore the oath he put his two hands upon her shoulders.

' No; we will hope not. I should die here at your feet if I thought that they could prevail. But I should die twenty deaths were I to drag you with me into disgrace. There will be disgrace even in standing at that bar.'

' Who will dare to say so, when I shall stand there with you?' said Sir Peregrine.

There was a feeling expressed in his face as he spoke these words, which made it glorious, and bright, and beautiful. She, with her eyes laden with tears, could not see it; but nevertheless, she knew that it was bright and beautiful. And his voice was full of hot eager assurance,—that assurance which had the power to convey itself from one breast to another. Would it not be so? If he stood there with her as her husband and lord, would it not be the case that no one would dare to impute disgrace to her?

And yet she did not wish it. Even yet, thinking of all this as she did think of it, according to the truth of the argument which he himself put before her, she would still have preferred that it should not be so. If she only knew with what words to tell him so;—to tell him so and yet give no offence! For herself, she would have married him willingly. Why should she not? Nay, she could and would have loved him, and been to him a wife, such as he could have found in no other woman. But she said within her heart that she owed him kindness and gratitude—that she owed them all kindness, and that it would be bad to repay them in such a way as this. She also thought of Sir Peregrine's gray hairs, and of his proud standing in the county, and the respect in which men held him. Would it be well in her to drag him down in his last days from the noble pedestal on which he stood, and repay him thus for all that he was doing for her?

'Well,' said he, stroking her soft hair with his hands—the hair which appeared in front of the quiet prim cap she wore, 'shall it be so? Will you give me the right to stand there with you and defend you against the tongues of wicked men? We each have our own weakness, and we also have each our own strength. There I may boast that I should be strong.'

She thought again for a moment or two without rising from her knees, and also without speaking. Would such strength suffice? And if it did suffice, would it then be well with him? As for herself, she did love him. If she had not loved him before, she loved him now. Who had ever been to her so noble, so loving, so gracious as he? In her ears no young lover's vows had ever sounded. In her heart such love as all the world knows had never been known. Her former husband had been kind to her in his way, and she had done her duty by him carefully, painfully, and with full acceptance of her position. But there had been nothing there that was bright, and grand, and noble. She would have served Sir Peregrine on her knees in the smallest offices, and delighted in such services. It was not for lack of love that she must refuse him. But still she did not answer him, and still he stroked her hair.

'It would be better that you had never seen me,' at last she said; and she spoke with truth the thought of her mind. That she must do his bidding, whatever that bidding might be, she had in a certain way acknowledged to herself. If he would have it so, so it must be. How could she refuse him anything, or be disobedient in aught to one to whom she owed so much? But still it would be wiser otherwise; wiser for all—unless it were for herself alone. 'It would be better that you had never seen me,' she said.

'Nay, not so, dearest. That it would not be better for me,—for me and Edith I am quite sure. And I would fain hope that for you——'

'Oh, Sir Peregrine! you know what I mean. You know how I value your kindness. What should I be if it were withdrawn from me?'

'It shall not be withdrawn. Do not let that feeling actuate you. Answer me out of your heart, and however your heart may answer, remember this, that my friendship and support shall be the same. If you will take me for your husband, as your husband will I stand by you. If you cannot,—then I will stand by you as your father.'

What could she say? A word or two she did speak as to Mrs. Orme and her feelings, delaying her absolute reply—and as to Peregrine Orme and his prospects; but on both, as on all other points, the baronet was armed with his answer. He had spoken to his darling Edith, and she had gladly given her consent. To her it would be everything to have so sweet a friend. And then as to his heir, every care should be taken that no injury should be done to him; and speaking of this, Sir Peregrine began to say a few words, plaintively, about money. But then Lady Mason stopped him. 'No,' she said, 'she could not, and would not, listen to that. She would have no settlement. No consideration as to money should be made to weigh with her. It was in no degree for that ——' And then she wept there till she would have fallen had he not supported her.

What more is there to be told. Of course she accepted him. As far as I can see into such affairs no alternative was allowed to her. She also was not a wise woman at all points. She was one whose feelings were sometimes too many for her, and whose feelings on this occasion had been much too many for her. Had she been able to throw aside from her his offer, she would have done so; but she had felt that she was not able. 'If you wish it, Sir Peregrine,' she said at last.

'And can you love an old man?' he had asked. Old men sometimes will ask questions such as these. She did not answer him, but stood by his side; and then again he kissed her, and was happy.

He resolved from that moment that Lady Mason should no longer be regarded as the widow of a city knight, but as the wife elect of a country baronet. Whatever ridicule he might incur in this matter, he would incur at once. Men and women had dared to speak of her cruelly, and they should now learn that any such future speech would be spoken of one who was exclusively his property. Let any who chose to be speakers under such circumstances look to it. He had devoted himself to her that he might be her knight and bear her scathless through the fury of this battle. With God's help he would put on his armour at once for that fight. Let them who would now injure her look to it. As soon as might be she should bear his name; but all the world should know at once what was her right to claim his protection. He had never been a coward, and he would not now be guilty of the cowardice of hiding his intentions. If there were those who chose to smile at the old man's fancy, let them smile. There would be many, he knew, who would not understand an old man's honour and an old man's chivalry.

'My own one,' he then said, pressing her again to his side, 'will you tell Edith, or shall I? She expects it.' But Lady Mason begged that he would tell the tale. It was necessary, she said, that she should be alone for a while. And then, escaping, she went to her own chamber.

'Ask Mrs. Orme if she will kindly step to me,' said Sir Peregrine, having rang his bell for the servant.

Lady Mason escaped across the hall to the stairs, and succeeded in reaching her room without being seen by any one. Then she sat herself down, and began to look her future world in the face. Two questions she had to ask. Would it be well for her that this marriage should take place? and would it be well for him? In an off-hand way she had already answered both questions; but she had done so by feeling rather than by thought.

No doubt she would gain much in the coming struggle by such a position as Sir Peregrine would give her. It did seem to her that Mr. Dockwrath and Joseph Mason would hardly dare to bring such a charge as that threatened against the wife of Sir Peregrine Orme. And then, too, what evidence as to character would be so substantial as the evidence of such a marriage? But how would Mr. Furnival bear it, and if he were offended would it be possible that the fight should be fought without him? No; that would be impossible. The lawyer's knowledge, experience, and skill were as necessary to her as the baronet's position and character. But why should Mr. Furnival be offended by such a marriage? 'She did not know,' she said to herself. 'She could not see that there should be cause of offence.' But yet some inner whisper of her conscience told her that there would be offence. Must Mr. Furnival be told; and must he be told at once?

And then what would Lucius say and think, and how should she answer the strong words which her son would use to her? He would use strong words she knew, and would greatly dislike this second marriage of his mother. What grown-up son is ever pleased to hear that his mother is about to marry? The Cleeve must be her home now—that is, if she did this deed. The Cleeve must be her home, and she must be separated in all things from Orley Farm. As she thought of this her mind went back, and back to those long gone days in which she had been racked with anxiety that Orley Farm should be the inheritance of the little baby that was lying at her feet. She remembered how she had pleaded to the father, pointing out the rights of her son—declaring, and with justice, that for herself she had asked for nothing; but that for him —instead of asking might she not demand? Was not that other son provided for, and those grown-up women with their rich husbands? 'Is he not your child as well as they?' she had pleaded. 'Is he not your own, and as well worthy of your love?' She had succeeded in getting the inheritance for the baby at her feet;—but had his having it made her happy, or him? Then her child had been all in all to her; but now she felt that that child was half estranged from her about this very property, and would become wholly estranged by the method she was taking to secure it! 'I have toiled for him,' she said to herself, 'rising up early, and going to bed late; but the thief cometh in the night and despoileth it.' Who can guess the bitterness of her thoughts as she said this?

But her last thoughts, as she sat there thinking, were of him— Sir Peregrine. Would it be well for him that he should do this? And in thus considering she did not turn her mind chiefly to the usual view in which such a marriage would be regarded. Men might call Sir Peregrine an old fool and laugh at him; but for that she would, with God's help, make him amends. In those matters, he could judge for himself; and should he judge it right thus to link his life to hers, she would be true and leal to him in all things.

But then, about this trial. If there came disgrace and ruin, and an utter overthrow? If —— ? Would it not be well at any rate that no marriage should take place till that had been decided? She could not find it in her heart to bring down his old gray hairs with utter sorrow to the grave.

CHAPTER XXXVI.

WHAT THE YOUNG MEN THOUGHT ABOUT IT.

Lucius Mason at this time was living at home at Orley Farm, not by any means in a happy frame of mind. It will be perhaps remembered that he had at one time had an interview with Mr. Furnival in that lawyer's chambers, which was by no means consoling to him, seeing that Mr. Furnival had pooh-poohed him and his pretensions in a very off-hand way; and he had since paid a very memorable visit to Mr. Dockwrath in which he had hardly been more successful. Nevertheless, he had gone to another lawyer. He had felt it impossible to remain tranquil, pursuing the ordinary avocations of his life, while such dreadful charges were being made openly again his mother, and being so made without any authorized contradiction. He knew that she was innocent. No doubt on that matter ever perplexed his mind for a moment. But why was she such a coward that she would not allow him to protect her innocence in the only way which the law permitted? He could hardly believe that he had no power of doing so even without her sanction; and therefore he went to another lawyer.

The other lawyer did him no good. It was not practicable that he, the son, should bring an action for defamatory character on the part of the mother, without that mother's sanction. Moreover, as this new lawyer saw in a moment, any such interference on the part of Lucius, and any interposition of fresh and new legal proceedings would cripple and impede the advisers to whom Lady Mason had herself confided her own case. The new lawyer could do nothing, and thus Lucius, again repulsed, betook himself to Orley Farm in no happy frame of mind.

For some day or two after this he did not see his mother. He would not go down to The Cleeve, though they sent up and asked him; and she was almost afraid to go across to the house and visit him. ' He will be in church on Sunday,' she had said to Mrs. Orme. But he was not in church on Sunday, and then on Sunday afternoon she did go to him. This, it will be understood, was before Sir Peregrine had made his offer, and therefore as to that, there was as yet no embarrassment on the widow's mind.

' I cannot help feeling, mother,' he said, after she had sat there with him for a short time, ' that for the present there is a division between you and me.'

' Oh, Lucius !'

' It is no use our denying it to ourselves. It is so. You are in trouble, and you will not listen to my advice. You leave my house and take to the roof of a new and an untried friend.'

' No, Lucius ; not that.'

' Yes. I say a new friend. Twelve months ago, though you might call there, you never did more than that—and even that but seldom. They are new friends; and yet, now that you are in trouble, you choose to live with them.'

' Dear Lucius, is there any reason why I should not visit at The Cleeve ?'

' Yes ; if you ask me—yes ;' and now he spoke very sternly. ' There is a cloud upon you, and you should know nothing of visitings and of new friendships till that cloud has been dispersed. While these things are being said of you, you should set at no other table than this, and drink of no man's cup but mine. I know your innocence,' and as he went on to speak, he stood up before her and looked down fully into her face, ' but others do not. I know how unworthy are these falsehoods with which wicked men strive to crush you, but others believe that they are true accusations. They cannot be disregarded, and now it seems,—now that you have allowed them to gather to a head, they will result in a trial, during which you will have to stand at the bar charged with a dreadful crime.'

' Oh, Lucius !' and she hid her eyes in her hands. ' I could not have helped it. How could I have helped it ?'

' Well ; it must be so now. And till that trial is over, here should be your place. Here, at my right hand ; I am he who am bound to stand by you. It is I whose duty it is to see that your name be made white again, though I spend all I have, ay, and my life in doing it. I am the one man on whose arm you have a right to

Lucius Mason in his Study.

lean. And yet, in such days as these, you leave my house and go to that of a stranger.'

'He is not a stranger, Lucius.'

'He cannot be to you as a son should be. However, it is for you to judge. I have no control in this matter, but I think it right that you should know what are my thoughts.'

And then she had crept back again to The Cleeve. Let Lucius say what he might, let this additional sorrow be ever so bitter, she could not obey her son's behests. If she did so in one thing she must do so in all. She had chosen her advisers with her best discretion, and by that choice she must abide—even though it separated her from her son. She could not abandon Sir Peregrine Orme and Mr. Furnival. So she crept back and told all this to Mrs. Orme. Her heart would have utterly sunk within her could she not have spoken openly to some one of this sorrow.

'But he loves you,' Mrs. Orme had said, comforting her. 'It is not that he does not love you.'

'But he is so stern to me.' And then Mrs. Orme had kissed her, and promised that none should be stern to her, there, in that house. On the morning after this Sir Peregrine had made his offer, and then she felt that the division between her and her boy would be wider than ever. And all this had come of that inheritance which she had demanded so eagerly for her child.

And now Lucius was sitting alone in his room at Orley Farm, having, for the present, given up all idea of attempting anything himself by means of the law. He had made his way into Mr. Dockwrath's office, and had there insulted the attorney in the presence of witnesses. His hope now was that the attorney might bring an action against him. If that were done he would thus have the means of bringing out all the facts of the case before a jury and a judge. It was fixed in his mind that if he could once drag that reptile before a public tribunal, and with loud voice declare the wrong that was being done, all might be well. The public would understand and would speak out, and the reptile would be scorned and trodden under foot. Poor Lucius! It is not always so easy to catch public sympathy, and it will occur sometimes that the wrong reptile is crushed by the great public heel.

He had his books before him as he sat there—his Latham and his Pritchard, and he had the jawbone of one savage and the skull of another. His Liverpool bills for unadulterated guano were lying on the table, and a philosophical German treatise on agriculture which he had resolved to study. It became a man, he said to himself, to do a man's work in spite of any sorrow. But, nevertheless, as he sat there, his studies were but of little service to him. How many men have declared to themselves the same thing, but have failed when the trial came! Who can command the temper and the mind? At ten I will strike the lyre and begin my poem. But at ten the poetic spirit is under a dark cloud—because the water for the tea had not boiled when it was brought in at nine. And so the lyre remains unstricken.

And Lucius found that he could not strike his lyre. For days he had sat there and no good note had been produced. And then he had walked over his land, having a farming man at his heels, thinking that he could turn his mind to the actual and practical working of his land. But little good had come of that either. It was January, and the land was sloppy and half frozen. There was no useful work to be done on it. And then what farmer Greenwood had once said of him was true enough, 'The young maister's spry and active surely; but he can't let unself down to stable doong and the loik o' that.' He had some grand idea of farming—a conviction that the agricultural world in general was very backward, and that he would set it right. Even now in his sorrow, as he walked through his splashy, frozen fields, he was tormented by a desire to do something, he knew not what, that might be great.

He had no such success on the present occasion and returned disconsolate to the house. This happened about noon on the day after that on which Sir Peregrine had declared himself. He returned as I have said to the house, and there at the kitchen door he met a little girl whom he knew well as belonging to The Cleeve. She was a favourite of Mrs. Orme's, was educated and clothed by her, and ran on her messages. Now she had brought a letter up to Lucius from his mother. Curtsying low she so told him, and he at once went into the sitting-room where he found it lying on his table. His hand was nervous as he opened it; but if he could have seen how tremulous had been the hand that wrote it! The letter was as follows :—

' DEAREST LUCIUS,

' I know you will be very much surprised at what I am going to tell you, but I hope you will not judge me harshly. If I know myself at all I would take no step of any kind for my own advantage which could possibly injure you. At the present moment we unfortunately do not agree about a subject which is troubling us both, and I cannot therefore consult you as I should otherwise have done. I trust that by God's mercy these troubles may come to an end, and that there may be no further differences between you and me.

' Sir Peregrine Orme has made me an offer of marriage and I have accepted it——' Lucius Mason when he had read so far threw down the letter upon the table, and rising suddenly from his chair walked rapidly up and down the room. ' Marry him!' he said out loud, ' marry him!' The idea that their fathers and mothers should marry and enjoy themselves is always a thing horrible to be thought of in the minds of the rising generation. Lucius Mason now began to feel against his mother the same sort of anger which Joseph Mason had felt when his father had married again. ' Marry him !' And then he walked rapidly about the room, as though some great injury had been threatened to him.

And so it had, in his estimation. Was it not her position in life to be his mother ? Had she not had her young days ? But it did not occur to him to think what those young days had been. And this then was the meaning of her receding from his advice and from his roof ! She had been preparing for herself in the world new hopes, a new home, and a new ambition. And she had so prevailed upon the old man that he was about to do this foolish thing ! Then again he walked up and down the room, injuring his mother much in his thoughts. He gave her credit for none of those circumstances which had truly actuated her in accepting the hand which Sir Peregrine had offered her. In that matter touching the Orley Farm estate he could acquit his mother instantly,—with acclamation. But in this other matter he had pronounced her guilty before she had been allowed to plead. Then he took up the letter and finished it.

' Sir Peregrine Orme has made me an offer of marriage and I have accepted it. It is very difficult to explain in a letter all the causes that have induced me to do so. The first perhaps is this, that I feel myself so bound to him by love and gratitude, that I think it my duty to fall in with all his wishes. He has pointed out to me that as my husband he can do more for me than would be possible for him without that name. I have explained to him that I would rather perish than that he should sacrifice himself; but he is pleased to say that it is no sacrifice. At any rate he so wishes it, and as Mrs. Orme has cordially assented, I feel myself bound to fall in with his views. It was only yesterday that Sir Peregrine made his offer. I mention this that you may know that I have lost no time in telling you.

' Dearest Lucius, believe that I shall be as ever

' Your most affectionate mother,

' MARY MASON.'

' The little girl will wait for an answer if she finds that you are at the farm.'

' No,' he said to himself, still walking about the room. ' She can never be to me the same mother that she was. I would have sacrificed everything for her. She should have been the mistress of my house, at any rate till she herself should have wished it otherwise. But now——' And then his mind turned away suddenly to Sophia Furnival.

I cannot myself but think that had that affair of the trial been set at rest Lady Mason would have been prudent to look for another home. The fact that Orley Farm was his house and not hers occurred almost too frequently to Lucius Mason; and I am not certain that it would have been altogether comfortable as a permanent residence for his mother after he should have brought home to it some such bride as her he now proposed to himself.

It was necessary that he should write an answer to his mother, which he did at once.

'Orley Farm, — January.

' Dear Mother,

' It is I fear too late for me to offer any counsel on the subject of your letter. I cannot say that I think you are right.

'Your affectionate son,

' Lucius Mason.'

And then, having finished this, he again walked the room. 'It is all up between me and her,' he said, 'as real friends in life and heart. She shall still have the respect of a son, and I shall have the regard of a mother. But how can I trim my course to suit the welfare of the wife of Sir Peregrine Orme?' And then he lashed himself into anger at the idea that his mother should have looked for other solace than that which he could have given.

Nothing more from The Cleeve reached him that day; but early on the following morning he had a visitor whom he certainly had not expected. Before he sat down to his breakfast he heard the sound of a horse's feet before the door, and immediately afterwards Peregrine Orme entered the sitting-room. He was duly shown in by the servant, and in his ordinary way came forward quickly and shook hands. Then he waited till the door was closed, and at once began upon the subject which had brought him there,

' Mason, he said, ' you have heard of this that is being done at The Cleeve?'

Lucius immediately fell back a step or two, and considered for a moment how he should answer. He had pressed very heavily on his mother in his own thoughts, but he was not prepared to hear her harshly spoken of by another.

' Yes,' said he, ' I have heard.'

' And I understand from your mother that you do not approve of it.'

' Approve of it! No; I do not approve of it.'

' Nor by heavens do I!'

' I do not approve of it,' said Mason, speaking with deliberation; ' but I do not know that I can take any steps towards preventing it.'

' Cannot you see her, and talk to her, and tell her how wrong it is?'

' Wrong! I do not know that she is wrong in that sense. I do not know that you have any right to blame her. Why do not you speak to your grandfather ?'

' So I have—as far as it was possible for me. But you do not know Sir Peregrine. No one has any influence over him, but my mother ;—and now also your mother.'

' And what does Mrs. Orme say ?'

' She will say nothing. I know well that she disapproves of it. She must disapprove of it, though she will not say so. She would rather burn off both her hands than displease my grandfather. She says that he asked her and that she consented.'

' It seems to me that it is for her and you to prevent this.'

' No; it is for your mother to prevent it. Only think of it, Mason. He is over seventy, and, as he says himself, he will not burden the estate with a new jointure. Why should she do it ?'

' You are wronging her there. It is no affair of money. She is not going to marry him for what she can get.'

' Then why should she do it ?'

' Because he tells her. These troubles about the lawsuit have turned her head, and she has put herself entirely into his hands. I think she is wrong. I could have protected her from all this evil, and would have done so. I could have done more, I think, than Sir Peregrine can do. But she has thought otherwise, and I do not know that I can help it.'

' But will you speak to her ? Will make her perceive that she is injuring a family that is treating her with kindness ?'

' If she will come here I will speak to her. I cannot do it there. I cannot go down to your grandfather's house with such an object as that.'

' All the world will turn against her if she marries him,' said Peregrine. And then there was silence between them for a moment or two.

' It seems to me,' said Lucius at last, ' that you wrong my mother very much in this matter, and lay all the blame where but the smallest part of the blame is deserved. She has no idea of money in her mind, or any thought of pecuniary advantage. She is moved solely by what your grandfather has said to her,—and by an insane dread of some coming evil which she thinks may be lessened by his assistance. You are in the house with them, and can speak to him, —and if you please to her also. I do not see that I can do either.'

' And you will not help me to break it off ?'

' Certainly,—if I can see my way.'

' Will you write to her ?'

' Well ; I will think about it.'

' Whether she be to blame or not it must be your duty as well as mine to prevent such a marriage if it be possible. Think what people will say of it ?'

After some further discussion Peregrine remounted his horse, and rode back to The Cleeve, not quite satisfied with young Mason.

'If you do speak to her,—to my mother, do it gently.' Those were the last words whispered by Lucius as Peregrine Orme had his foot in the stirrup.

Young Peregrine Orme, as he rode home, felt that the world was using him very unkindly. Everything was going wrong with him, and an idea entered his head that he might as well go and look for Sir John Franklin at the North Pole, or join some energetic traveller in the middle of Central Africa. He had proposed to Madeline Staveley and had been refused. That in itself caused a load to lie on his heart which was almost unendurable;—and now his grandfather was going to disgrace himself. He had made his little effort to be respectable and discreet, devoting himself to the county hunt and county drawing-rooms, giving up the pleasures of London and the glories of dissipation. And for what?

Then Peregrine began to argue within himself as some others have done before him—

'Were it not better done as others use——' he said to himself, in that or other language; and as he rode slowly into the courtyard of The Cleeve, he thought almost with regret of his old friend Carroty Bob.

Peregrine's Eloquence.

CHAPTER XXXVII.

In the last chapter Peregrine Mason called at Orley Farm with the view of discussing with Lucius Mason the conduct of their respective progenitors; and, as will be remembered, the young men agreed in a general way that their progenitors were about to make fools of themselves. Poor Peregrine, however, had other troubles on his mind. Not only had his grandfather been successful in love, but he had been unsuccessful. As he had journeyed home from Noningsby to The Cleeve in a high-wheeled vehicle which he called his trap, he had determined, being then in a frame of mind somewhat softer than was usual with him, to tell all his troubles to his mother. It sounds as though it were lack-a-daisical—such a resolve as this on the part of a dashing young man, who had been given to the pursuit of rats, and was now a leader among the sons of Nimrod in the pursuit of foxes. Young men of the present day, when got up for the eyes of the world, look and talk as though they could never tell their mothers anything,—as though they were harder than flint, and as little in want of a woman's counsel and a woman's help as a colonel of horse on the morning of a battle. But the rigid virility of his outward accoutrements does in no way alter the man of flesh and blood who wears them; the young hero, so stern to the eye, is, I believe, as often tempted by stress of sentiment to lay bare the sorrow of his heart as is his sister. On this occasion Peregrine said to himself that he would lay bare the sorrow of his heart. He would find out what others thought of that marriage which he had proposed to himself; and then, if his mother encouraged him, and his grandfather approved, he would make another attack, beginning on the side of the judge, or perhaps on that of Lady Staveley.

But he found that others, as well as he, were labouring under a stress of sentiment; and when about to tell his own tale, he had learned that a tale was to be told to him. He had dined with Lady Mason, his mother, and his grandfather, and the dinner had been very silent. Three of the party were in love, and the fourth was burdened with the telling of the tale. The baronet himself said nothing on the subject as he and his grandson sat over their wine;

but later in the evening Peregrine was summoned to his mother's room, and she, with considerable hesitation and much diffidence, informed him of the coming nuptials.

' Marry Lady Mason !' he had said.

' Yes, Peregrine. Why should he not do so if they both wish it ?'

Peregrine thought that there were many causes and impediments sufficiently just why no such marriage should take place, but he had not his arguments ready at his fingers' ends. He was so stunned by the intelligence that he could say but little about it on that occasion. By the few words that he did say, and by the darkness of his countenance, he showed plainly enough that he disapproved. And then his mother said all that she could in the baronet's favour, pointing out that in a pecuniary way Peregrine would receive benefit rather than injury.

' I'm not thinking of the money, mother.'

' No, my dear ; but it is right that I should tell you how considerate your grandfather is.'

' All the same, I wish he would not marry this woman.'

' Woman, Peregrine ! You should not speak in that way of a friend whom I dearly love.'

' She is a woman all the same.' And then he sat sulkily, looking at the fire. His own stress of sentiment did not admit of free discussion at the present moment, and was necessarily postponed. On that other affair he was told that his grandfather would be glad to see him on the following morning ; and then he left his mother.

' Your grandfather, Peregrine, asked for my assent,' said Mrs. Orme ; ' and I thought it right to give it.' This she said to make him understand that it was no longer in her power to oppose the match. And she was thoroughly glad that this was so, for she would have lacked the courage to oppose Sir Peregrine in anything.

On the next morning Peregrine saw his grandfather before breakfast. His mother came to his room door while he was dressing to whisper a word of caution to him. ' Pray, be courteous to him,' she said. ' Remember how good he is to you—to us both ! Say that you congratulate him.'

' But I don't,' said Peregrine.

' Ah, but, Peregrine——'

' I'll tell you what I'll do, mother. I'll leave the house altogether and go away, if you wish it.'

' Oh, Peregrine ! How can you speak in that way ? But he's waiting now. Pray, pray, be kind in your manner to him.'

He descended with the same sort of feeling which had oppressed him on his return home after his encounter with Carroty Bob in Smithfield. Since then he had been on enduring good terms with his grandfather, but now again all the discomforts of war were imminent.

'Good morning, sir,' he said, on going into his grandfather's dressing-room.

'Good morning, Peregrine.' And then there was silence for a moment or two.

'Did you see your mother last night?'

'Yes; I did see her.'

'And she told you what it is that I propose to do?'

'Yes, sir; she told me.'

'I hope you understand, my boy, that it will not in any way affect your own interests injuriously.'

'I don't care about that, sir—one way or the other.'

'But I do, Peregrine. Having seen to that I think that I have a right to please myself in this matter.'

'Oh, yes, sir; I know you have the right.'

'Especially as I can benefit others. Are you aware that your mother has cordially given her consent to the marriage?'

'She told me that you had asked her, and that she had agreed to it. She would agree to anything.'

'Peregrine, that is not the way in which you should speak of your mother.'

And then the young man stood silent, as though there was nothing more to be said. Indeed, he had nothing more to say. He did not dare to bring forward in words all the arguments against the marriage which were now crowding themselves into his memory, but he could not induce himself to wish the old man joy, or to say any of those civil things which are customary on such occasions. The baronet sat for a while, silent also, and a cloud of anger was coming across his brow; but he checked that before he spoke. 'Well, my boy,' he said, and his voice was almost more than usually kind, 'I can understand your thoughts, and we will say nothing of them at present. All I will ask of you is to treat Lady Mason in a manner befitting the position in which I intend to place her.'

'If you think it will be more comfortable, sir, I will leave The Cleeve for a time.'

'I hope that may not be necessary—Why should it? Or at any-rate, not as yet,' he added, as a thought as to his wedding day occurred to him. And then the interview was over, and in another half-hour they met again at breakfast.

In the breakfast-room Lady Mason was also present. Peregrine was the last to enter, and as he did so his grandfather was already standing in his usual place, with the book of Prayers in his hand, waiting that the servants should arrange themselves at their chairs before he knelt down. There was no time then for much greeting, but Peregrine did shake hands with her as he stept across to his accustomed corner. He shook hands with her, and felt that her hand was very cold; but he did not look at her, nor did he hear any answer given to his few muttered words. When they all got up she remained close to Mrs. Orme, as though she might thus be protected from the anger which she feared from Sir Peregrine's other friends. And at breakfast also she sat close to her, far away from the baronet, and almost hidden by the urn from his grandson. Sitting there she said nothing; neither in truth did she eat anything. It was a time of great suffering to her, for she knew that her coming could not be welcomed by the young heir. ' It must not be,' she said to herself over and over again. ' Though he turn me out of the house, I must tell him that it cannot be so.'

After breakfast Peregrine had ridden over to Orley Farm, and there held his consultation with the other heir. On his returning to The Cleeve, he did not go into the house, but having given up his horse to a groom, wandered away among the woods. Lucius Mason had suggested that he, Peregrine Orme, should himself speak to Lady Mason on this matter. He felt that his grandfather would be very angry, should he do so. But he did not regard that much. He had filled himself full with the theory of his duties, and he would act up to it. He would see her, without telling any one what was his purpose, and put it to her whether she would bring down this destruction on so noble a gentleman. Having thus resolved, he returned to the house, when it was already dark, and making his way into the drawing-room, sat himself down before the fire, still thinking of his plan. The room was dark, as such rooms are dark for the last hour or two before dinner in January, and he sat himself in an arm-chair before the fire, intending to sit there till it would be necessary that he should go to dress. It was an unaccustomed thing with him so to place himself at such a time, or to remain in the drawing-room at all till he came down for a few minutes before dinner; but he did so now, having been thrown out of his usual habits by the cares upon his mind. He had been so seated about a quarter of an hour, and was already nearly asleep, when he heard the rustle of a woman's garment, and looking round, with such light as the fire gave him, perceived that Lady Mason was in the room. She had entered very quietly, and was making her way in the dark to a chair which she frequently occupied, between the fire and one of the windows, and in doing so she passed so near Peregrine as to touch him with her dress.

' Lady Mason,' he said, speaking, in the first place, in order that she might know that she was not alone, ' it is almost dark; shall I ring for candles for you ?'

She started at hearing his voice, begged his pardon for disturbing him, declined his offer of light, and declared that she was going up again to her own room immediately. But it occurred to him that if it would be well that he should speak to her, it would be well that he should do so at once; and what opportunity could be more fitting than the present? 'If you are not in a hurry about anything,' he said, 'would you mind staying here for a few minutes?'

'Oh no, certainly not.' But he could perceive that her voice trembled in uttering even these few words.

'I think I'd better light a candle,' he said; and then he did light one of those which stood on the corner of the mantelpiece,—a solitary candle, which only seemed to make the gloom of the large room visible. She, however, was standing close to it, and would have much preferred that the room should have been left to its darkness.

'Won't you sit down for a few minutes?' and then she sat down. 'I'll just shut the door, if you don't mind.' And then, having done so, he returned to his own chair and again faced the fire. He saw that she was pale and nervous, and he did not like to look at her as he spoke. He began to reflect also that they might probably be interrupted by his mother, and he wished that they could adjourn to some other room. That, however, seemed to be impossible; so he summoned up all his courage, and began his task.

'I hope you won't think me uncivil, Lady Mason, for speaking to you about this affair.'

'Oh no, Mr. Orme; I am sure that you will not be uncivil to me.'

'Of course I cannot help feeling a great concern in it, for it's very nearly the same, you know, as if he were my father. Indeed, if you come to that, it's almost worse; and I can assure you it is nothing about money that I mind. Many fellows in my place would be afraid about that, but I don't care twopence what he does in that respect. He is so honest and so noble-hearted, that I am sure he won't do me a wrong.'

'I hope not, Mr. Orme; and certainly not in respect to me.'

'I only mention it for fear you should misunderstand me. But there are other reasons, Lady Mason, why this marriage will make me—make me very unhappy.'

'Are there? I shall be so unhappy if I make others unhappy.'

'You will then,—I can assure you of that. It is not only me, but your own son. I was up with him to-day, and he thinks of it the same as I do.'

'What did he say, Mr. Orme?'

'What did he say? Well, I don't exactly remember his words; but he made me understand that your marriage with Sir Peregrine would make him very unhappy. He did indeed. Why do you not see him yourself, and talk to him?'

'I thought it best to write to him in the first place.'

'Well, now you have written; and don't you think it would be well that you should go up and see him? You will find that he is quite as strong against it as I am,—quite.'

Peregrine, had he known it, was using the arguments which were of all the least likely to induce Lady Mason to pay a visit to Orley Farm. She dreaded the idea of a quarrel with her son, and would have made almost any sacrifice to prevent such a misfortune; but at the present moment she feared the anger of his words almost more than the anger implied by his absence. If this trial could be got over, she would return to him and almost throw herself at his feet; but till that time, might it not be well that they should be apart? At any rate, these tidings of his discontent could not be efficacious in inducing her to seek him.

'Dear Lucius!' she said, not addressing herself to her companion, but speaking her thoughts. 'I would not willingly give him cause to be discontented with me.'

'He is, then, very discontented. I can assure you of that.'

'Yes; he and I think differently about all this.'

'Ah, but don't you think you had better speak to him before you quite make up your mind? He is your son, you know; and an uncommon clever fellow too. He'll know how to say all this much better than I do.'

'Say what, Mr. Orme?'

'Why, of course you can't expect that anybody will like such a marriage as this;—that is, anybody except you and Sir Peregrine.'

'Your mother does not object to it.'

'My mother! But you don't know my mother yet. She would not object to have her head cut off if anybody wanted it that she cared about. I do not know how it has all been managed, but I suppose Sir Peregrine asked her. Then of course she would not object. But look at the common sense of it, Lady Mason. What does the world always say when an old man like my grandfather marries a young woman?'

'But I am not ——.' So far she got, and then she stopped herself.

'We have all liked you very much. I'm sure I have for one; and I'll go in for you, heart and soul, in this shameful law business. When Lucius asked me, I didn't think anything of going to that scoundrel in Hamworth; and all along I've been delighted that Sir Peregrine took it up. By heavens! I'd be glad to go down to Yorkshire myself, and walk into that fellow that wants to do you this injury. I would indeed; and I'll stand by you as strong as anybody. But, Lady Mason, when it comes to one's grandfather marrying, it——it——it——. Think what people in the county will say of him. If it was your father, and if he had been at the top of the tree all his life, how would you like to see him get a fall, and be laughed at as though he were in the mud just when he was too old ever to get up again ?'

I am not sure whether Lucius Mason, with all his cleverness, could have put the matter much better, or have used a style of oratory more efficacious to the end in view. Peregrine had drawn his picture with a coarse pencil, but he had drawn it strongly, and with graphic effect. And then he paused; not with self-confidence, or as giving his companion time to see how great had been his art, but in want of words, and somewhat confused by the strength of his own thoughts. So he got up and poked the fire, turned his back to it, and then sat down again. 'It is such a deuce of a thing, Lady Mason,' he said, ' that you must not be angry with me for speaking out.'

' Oh, Mr. Orme, I am not angry, and I do not know what to say to you.'

' Why don't you speak to Lucius ?'

' What could he say more than you have said ? Dear Mr. Orme, I would not injure him,—your grandfather, I mean,—for all that the world holds.'

' You will injure him ;—in the eyes of all his friends.'

' Then I will not do it. I will go to him, and beg him that it may not be so. I will tell him that I cannot. Anything will be better than bringing him to sorrow or disgrace.'

' By Jove ! but will you really ?' Peregrine was startled and almost frightened at the effect of his own eloquence. What would the baronet say when he learned that he had been talked out of his wife by his grandson ?

' Mr. Orme,' continued Lady Mason, ' I am sure you do not understand how this matter has been brought about. If you did, however much it might grieve you, you would not blame me, even in your thoughts. From the first to the last my only desire has been to obey your grandfather in everything.'

' But you would not marry him out of obedience ?'

' I would—and did so intend. I would, certainly; if in doing so I did him no injury. You say that your mother would give her life for him. So would I;—that or anything else that I could give, without hurting him or others. It was not I that sought for this marriage ; nor did I think of it. If you were in my place, Mr. Orme, you would know how difficult it is to refuse.'

Peregrine again got up, and standing with his back to the fire, thought over it all again. His soft heart almost relented towards the woman who had borne his rough words with so much patient kindness. Had Sir Peregrine been there then, and could he have condescended so far, he might have won his grandson's consent without much trouble. Peregrine, like some other generals, had expended his energy in gaining his victory, and was more ready now to come to easy terms than he would have been had he suffered in the combat.

'Well,' he said after a while, 'I'm sure I'm very much obliged to you for the manner in which you have taken what I said to you. Nobody knows about it yet, I suppose; and perhaps, if you will talk to the governor——'

'I will talk to him, Mr. Orme.'

'Thank you; and then perhaps all things may turn out right. I'll go and dress now.' And so saying he took his departure, leaving her to consider how best she might act at this crisis of her life, so that things might go right, if such were possible. The more she thought of it, the less possible it seemed that her affairs should be made to go right.

CHAPTER XXXVIII.

OH, INDEED!

THE dinner on that day at The Cleeve was not very dull. Peregrine had some hopes that the idea of the marriage might be abandoned, and was at any rate much better disposed towards Lady Mason than he had been. He spoke to her, asking her whether she had been out, and suggesting roast mutton or some such creature comfort. This was lost neither on Sir Peregrine nor on Mrs. Orme, and they both exerted themselves to say a few words in a more cheery tone than had been customary in the house for the last day or two. Lady Mason herself did not say much; but she had sufficient tact to see the effort which was being made; and though she spoke but little she smiled and accepted graciously the courtesies that were tendered to her.

Then the two ladies went away, and Peregrine was again left with his grandfather. 'That was a nasty accident that Graham had going out of Monkton Grange,' said he, speaking on the moment of his closing the dining-room door after his mother. 'I suppose you heard all about it, sir?' Having fought his battle so well before dinner, he was determined to give some little rest to his half-vanquished enemy.

'The first tidings we heard were that he was dead,' said Sir Peregrine, filling his glass.

'No; he wasn't dead. But of course you know that now. He broke an arm and two ribs, and got rather a bad squeeze. He was just behind me, you know, and I had to wait for him. I lost the run, and had to see Harriet Tristram go away with the best lead any one has had to a fast thing this year. That's an uncommon nasty place at the back of Monkton Grange.'

' I hope, Peregrine, you don't think too much about Harriet Tristram.'

' Think of her! who? I? Think of her in what sort of a way? I think she goes uncommonly well to hounds.'

' That may be, but I should not wish to see you pin your happiness on any lady that was celebrated chiefly for going well to hounds.'

' Do you mean marry her?' and Peregrine immediately made a strong comparison in his mind between Miss Tristram and Madeline Staveley.

' Yes ; that's what I did mean.'

' I wouldn't have her if she owned every fox-cover in the county. No, by Jove! I know a trick worth two of that. It's jolly enough to see them going, but as to being in love with them—in that sort of way—'

' You are quite right, my boy; quite right. It is not that that a man wants in a wife.'

' No,' said Peregrine, with a melancholy cadence in his voice, thinking of what it was that he did want. And so they sat sipping their wine. The turn which the conversation had taken had for the moment nearly put Lady Mason out of the young man's head.

' You would be very young to marry yet,' said the baronet.

' Yes, I should be young ; but I don't know that there is any harm in that.'

' Quite the contrary, if a young man feels himself to be sufficiently settled. Your mother I know would be very glad that you should marry early ;—and so should I, if you married well.'

What on earth could all this mean? It could not be that his grandfather knew that he was in love with Miss Staveley ; and had this been known his grandfather would not have talked of Harriet Tristram. ' Oh yes; of course a fellow should marry well. I don't think much of marrying for money.'

' Nor do I, Peregrine ;—I think very little of it.'

' Nor about being of very high birth.'

' Well; it would make me unhappy—very unhappy if you were to marry below your own rank.'

' What do you call my own rank?'

' I mean any girl whose father is not a gentleman, and whose mother is not a lady; and of whose education among ladies you could not feel certain.'

' I could be quite certain about her,' said Peregrine, very innocently.

' Her! what her?'

' Oh, I forgot that we were talking about nobody.'

' You don't mean Harriet Tristram?'

' No, certainly not.'

' Of whom were you thinking, Peregrine? May I ask—if it be
not too close a secret?' And then again there was a pause, during
which Peregrine emptied his glass and filled it again. He had no
objection to talk to his grandfather about Miss Staveley, but he
felt ashamed of having allowed the matter to escape him in this sort
of way. ' I will tell you why I ask, my boy,' continued the baronet.
' I am going to do that which many people will call a very foolish
thing.'

' You mean about Lady Mason.'

' Yes; I mean my own marriage with Lady Mason. We will not
talk about that just at present, and I only mention it to explain
that before I do so, I shall settle the property permanently. If you
were married I should at once divide it with you. I should like to
keep the old house myself, till I die——'

' Oh, sir!'

' But sooner than give you cause of offence I would give that up.'

' I would not consent to live in it unless I did so as your guest.'

' Until your marriage I think of settling on you a thousand a
year;—but it would add to my happiness if I thought it likely that
you would marry soon. Now may I ask of whom were you thinking?'

Peregrine paused for a second or two before he made any reply,
and then he brought it out boldly. ' I was thinking of Madeline
Staveley.'

' Then, my boy, you were thinking of the prettiest girl and the
best-bred lady in the county. Here's her health;' and he filled
for himself a bumper of claret. ' You couldn't have named a woman
whom I should be more proud to see you bring home. And your
mother's opinion of her is the same as mine. I happen to know
that;' and with a look of triumph he drank his glass of wine, as
though much that was very joyful to him had been already settled.

' Yes,' said Peregrine mournfully, ' she is a very nice girl; at
least I think so.'

' The man who can win her, Peregrine, may consider himself to
be a lucky fellow. You were quite right in what you were saying
about money. No man feels more sure of that than I do. But if I
am not mistaken Miss Staveley will have something of her own. I
rather think that Arbuthnot got ten thousand pounds.'

' I'm sure I don't know, sir,' said Peregrine; and his voice was
by no means as much elated as that of his grandfather.

' I think he did; or if he didn't get it all, the remainder is settled
on him. And the judge is not a man to behave better to one child
than to another.'

' I suppose not.'

And then the conversation flagged a little, for the enthusiasm was
all one side. It was moreover on that side which naturally would
have been the least enthusiastic. Poor Peregrine had only told

half his secret as yet, and that not the most important half. To Sir Peregrine the tidings, as far as he had heard them, were very pleasant. He did not say to himself that he would purchase his grandson's assent to his own marriage by giving his consent to his grandson's marriage. But it did seem to him that the two affairs, acting upon each other, might both be made to run smooth. His heir could have made no better choice in selecting the lady of his love. Sir Peregrine had feared much that some Miss Tristram or the like might have been tendered to him as the future Lady Orme, and he was agreeably surprised to find that a new mistress for The Cleeve had been so well chosen. He would be all kindness to his grandson and win from him, if it might be possible, reciprocal courtesy and complaisance. ' Your mother will be very pleased when she hears this,' he said.

' I meant to tell my mother,' said Peregrine, still very dolefully, ' but I do not know that there is anything in it to please her. I only said that I—I admired Miss Staveley.'

' My dear boy, if you'll take my advice you'll propose to her at once. You have been staying in the same house with her, and ——'

' But I have.'

' Have what ?'

' I have proposed to her.'

' Well ?'

' And she has refused me. You know all about it now, and there's no such great cause for joy.'

' Oh, you have proposed to her. Have you spoken to her father or mother ?'

' What was the use when she told me plainly that she did not care for me ? Of course I should have asked her father. As to Lady Staveley, she and I got on uncommonly well. I'm almost inclined to think that she would not have objected.'

' It would be a very nice match for them, and I dare say she would not have objected.' And then for some ten minutes they sat looking at the fire. Peregrine had nothing more to say about it, and the baronet was thinking how best he might encourage his grandson.

' You must try again, you know,' at last he said.

' Well ; I fear not. I do not think it would be any good. I'm not quite sure she does not care for some one else ?'

' Who is he ?'

' Oh, a fellow that's there. The man who broke his arm. I don't say she does, you know, and of course you won't mention it.'

Sir Peregrine gave the necessary promises, and then endeavoured to give encouragement to the lover. He would himself see the judge, if it were thought expedient, and explain what liberal settlement would be made on the lady in the event of her altering her mind. ' Young ladies, you know, are very prone to alter their minds on such matters,' said the old man. In answer to which Peregrine declared his conviction that Madeline Staveley would not alter her mind. But then do not all despondent lovers hold that opinion of their own mistresses?

Sir Peregrine had been a great gainer by what had occurred, and so he felt it. At any rate all the novelty of the question of his own marriage was over, as between him and Peregrine; and then he had acquired a means of being gracious which must almost disarm his grandson of all power of criticism. When he, an old man, was ready to do so much to forward the views of a young man, could it be possible that the young man should oppose his wishes? And Peregrine was aware that his power of opposition was thus lessened.

In the evening nothing remarkable occurred between them. Each had his or her own plans; but these plans could not be furthered by anything to be said in a general assembly. Lady Mason had already told to Mrs. Orme all that had passed in the drawing-room before dinner, and Sir Peregrine had determined that he would consult Mrs. Orme as to that matter regarding Miss Staveley. He did not think much of her refusal. Young ladies always do refuse —at first.

On the day but one following this there came another visit from Mr. Furnival, and he was for a long time closeted with Sir Peregrine. Matthew Round had, he said, been with him, and had felt himself obliged in the performance of his duty to submit a case to counsel on behalf of his client Joseph Mason. He had not as yet received the written opinion of Sir Richard Leatheram, to whom he had applied; but nevertheless, as he wished to give every possible notice, he had called to say that his firm were of opinion that an action must be brought either for forgery or for perjury.

' For perjury!' Mr. Furnival had said.

' Well; yes. We would wish to be as little harsh as possible. But if we convict her of having sworn falsely when she gave evidence as to having copied the codicil herself, and having seen it witnessed by the pretended witnesses;—why in that case of course the property would go back.'

' I can't give any opinion as to what might be the result in such a case,' said Mr. Furnival.

Mr. Round had gone on to say that he thought it improbable that the action could be tried before the summer assizes.

' The sooner the better as far as we are concerned,' said Mr. Furnival.

' If you really mean that, I will see that there shall be no unnecessary delay.' Mr. Furnival had declared that he did really mean it, and so the interview had ended.

Mr. Furnival had really meant it, fully concurring in the opinion which Mr. Chaffanbrass had expressed on this matter; but nevertheless the increasing urgency of the case had almost made him tremble. He still carried himself with a brave outside before Mat Round, protesting as to the utter absurdity as well as cruelty of the whole proceeding; but his conscience told him that it was not absurd. 'Perjury!' he said to himself, and then he rang the bell for Crabwitz. The upshot of that interview was that Mr. Crabwitz received a commission to arrange a meeting between that great barrister, the member for the Essex Marshes, and Mr. Solomon Aram.

'Won't it look rather, rather—rather— ; you know what I mean, sir ?' Crabwitz had asked.

'We must fight these people with their own weapons,' said Mr. Furnival;—not exactly with justice, seeing that Messrs. Round and Crook were not at all of the same calibre in the profession as Mr. Solomon Aram.

Mr. Furnival had already at this time seen Mr. Slow, of the firm of Slow and Bideawhile, who were Sir Peregrine's solicitors. This he had done chiefly that he might be able to tell Sir Peregrine that he had seen him. Mr. Slow had declared that the case was one which his firm would not be prepared to conduct, and he named a firm to which he should recommend his client to apply. But Mr. Furnival, carefully considering the whole matter, had resolved to take the advice and benefit by the experience of Mr. Chaffanbrass.

And then he went down once more to The Cleeve. Poor Mr. Furnival ! In these days he was dreadfully buffeted about both as regards his outer man and his inner conscience by this unfortunate case, giving up to it time that would otherwise have turned itself into heaps of gold ; giving up domestic conscience— for Mrs. Furnival was still hot in her anger against poor Lady Mason ; and giving up also much peace of mind, for he felt that he was soiling his hands by dirty work. But he thought of the lady's pale sweet face, of her tear-laden eye, of her soft beseeching tones, and gentle touch ; he thought of these things—as he should not have thought of them ;—and he persevered.

On this occasion he was closeted with Sir Peregrine for a couple of hours, and each heard much from the other that surprised him very much. Sir Peregrine, when he was told that Mr. Solomon Aram from Bucklersbury, and Mr. Chaffanbrass from the Old Bailey, were to be retained for the defence of his future wife, drew himself up and said that he could hardly approve of it. The gentlemen named were no doubt very clever in criminal concerns ; he could understand as much as that, though he had not had great opportunity of looking into affairs of that sort. But surely, in Lady Mason's case, assistance of such a description would hardly be needed. Would it not be better to consult Messrs. Slow and Bideawhile?

And then it turned out that Messrs. Slow and Bideawhile had been consulted; and Mr. Furnival, not altogether successfully, endeavoured to throw dust into the baronet's eyes, declaring that in a combat with the devil one must use the devil's weapons. He assured Sir Peregrine that he had given the matter his most matured and indeed most painful professional consideration; there were unfortunate circumstances which required peculiar care; it was a matter which would depend entirely on the evidence of one or two persons who might be suborned; and in such a case it would be well to trust to those who knew how to break down and crush a lying witness. In such work as that Slow and Bideawhile would be innocent and ignorant as babes. As to breaking down and crushing a witness anxious to speak the truth, Mr. Furnival at that time said nothing.

'I will not think that falsehood and fraud can prevail,' said Sir Peregrine proudly.

'But they do prevail sometimes,' said Mr. Furnival. And then with much outer dignity of demeanour, but with some shame-faced tremblings of the inner man hidden under the guise of that outer dignity, Sir Peregrine informed the lawyer of his great purpose.

'Indeed!' said Mr. Furnival, throwing himself back into his chair with a start.

'Yes, Mr. Furnival. I should not have taken the liberty to trouble you with a matter so private in its nature, but for your close professional intimacy and great friendship with Lady Mason.'

'Oh, indeed!' said Mr. Furnival; and the baronet could understand from the lawyer's tone that even he did not approve.

CHAPTER XXXIX.

WHY SHOULD HE GO?

'I AM well aware, Mr. Staveley, that you are one of those gentlemen who amuse themselves by frequently saying such things to girls. I had learned your character in that respect before I had been in the house two days.'

'Then, Miss Furnival, you learned what was very false. May I ask who has blackened me in this way in your estimation?' It will be easily seen from this that Mr. Augustus Staveley and Miss Furnival were at the present moment alone together in one of the rooms at Noningsby.

'My informant,' she replied, 'has been no one especial sinner whom you can take by the throat and punish. Indeed, if you must shoot anybody, it should be chiefly yourself, and after that your father, and mother, and sisters. But you need not talk of being black. Such sins are venial now-a-days, and convey nothing deeper than a light shade of brown.'

'I regard a man who can act in such a way as very base.'

'Such a way as what, Mr. Staveley?'

'A man who can win a girl's heart for his own amusement.'

'I said nothing about the winning of hearts. That is treachery of the worst dye; but I acquit you of any such attempt. When there is a question of the winning of hearts men look so different.'

'I don't know how they look,' said Augustus, not altogether satisfied as to the manner in which he was being treated—'but such has been my audacity,—my too great audacity on the present occasion.'

'You are the most audacious of men, for your audacity would carry you to the feet of another lady to-morrow without the slightest check.'

'And that is the only answer I am to receive from you?'

'It is quite answer enough. What would you have me do? Get up and decline the honour of being Mrs. Augustus Staveley with a curtsy?'

'No—I would have you do nothing of the kind. I would have you get up and accept the honour,—with a kiss.'

'So that you might have the kiss, and I might have the—; I was going to say disappointment, only that would be untrue. Let me assure you that I am not so demonstrative in my tokens of regard.'

'I wonder whether you mean that you are not so honest?'

'No, Mr. Staveley; I mean nothing of the kind; and you are very impertinent to express such a supposition. What have I done or said to make you suppose that I have lost my heart to you?'

'As you have mine, it is at any rate human nature in me to hope that I might have yours.'

'Psha! your heart! You have been making a shuttlecock of it till it is doubtful whether you have not banged it to pieces. I know two ladies who carry in their caps two feathers out of it. It is so easy to see when a man is in love. They all go cross-gartered like Malvolio;—cross-gartered in their looks and words and doings.'

'And there is no touch of all this in me?'

'You cross-gartered! You have never got so far yet as a lack-a-daisical twist to the corner of your mouth. Did you watch Mr. Orme before he went away?'

'Why; was he cross-gartered?'

'But you men have no eyes; you never see anything. And your idea of love-making is to sit under a tree wishing, wondering whether the ripe fruit will fall down into your mouth. Ripe fruit does sometimes fall, and then it is all well with you. But if it won't, you pass on and say that it is sour. As for climbing—'

'The fruit generally falls too fast to admit of such exercise,' said Staveley, who did not choose that all the sharp things should be said on the other side.

'And that is the result of your very extended experience? The orchards which have been opened to you have not, I fear, been of the first quality. Mr. Staveley, my hand will do very well by itself. Such is not the sort of climbing that is required. That is what I call stooping to pick up the fruit that has fallen.' And as she spoke, she moved a little away from him on the sofa.

'And how is a man to climb?'

'Do you really mean that you want a lesson? But if I were to tell you, my words would be thrown away. Men will not labour who have gotten all that they require without work. Why strive to deserve any woman, when women are plenty who do not care to be deserved? That plan of picking up the fallen apples is so much the easier.'

The lesson might perhaps have been given, and Miss Furnival might have imparted to Mr. Staveley her idea of 'excelsior' in the matter of love-making, had not Mr. Staveley's mother come into the room at that moment. Mrs. Staveley was beginning to fear that the results of her Christmas hospitality would not be satisfactory. Peregrine Orme, whom she would have been so happy to welcome to the warmest corner of her household temple as a son, had been sent away in wretchedness and disappointment. Madeline was moping about the house, hardly making an effort to look like herself; attributing, in her mother's ears, all her complaint to that unexpected interview with Peregrine Orme, but not so attributing it—as her mother fancied—with correctness. And there was Felix Graham still in the room upstairs, the doctor having said that he might be moved in a day or two;—that is, such movement might possibly be effected without detriment;—but having said also that another ten days of uninterrupted rest would be very desirable. And now, in addition to this, her son Augustus was to be found on every wet morning closeted somewhere with Sophia Furnival;—on every wet morning, and sometimes on dry mornings also!

And then, on this very day, Lady Staveley had discovered that Felix Graham's door in the corridor was habitually left open. She knew her child too well, and was too clear and pure in her own mind, to suppose that there was anything wrong in this;—that clandestine talkings were arranged, or anything planned in secret. What she feared was that which really occurred. The door was left open, and as Madeline passed Felix would say a word, and then

Madeline would pause and answer him. Such words as they were might have been spoken before all the household, and if so spoken would have been free from danger. But they were not free from danger when spoken in that way, in the passage of a half-closed doorway;—all which Lady Staveley understood perfectly.

'Baker,' she had said, with more of anger in her voice than was usual with her, 'why do you leave that door open?'

'I think it sweetens the room, my lady;' and, indeed, Felix Graham sometimes thought so too.

'Nonsense; every sound in the house must be heard. Keep it shut, if you please.'

'Yes, my lady,' said Mrs. Baker—who also understood perfectly.

'He is better, my darling,' said Mrs. Baker to Madeline, the same day; 'and, indeed, for that he is well enough as regards eating and drinking. But it would be cruelty to move him yet. I heard what the doctor said.'

'Who talks of moving him?'

'Well, he talks of it himself; and the doctor said it might be possible. But I know what that means.'

'What does it mean?'

'Why, just this: that if we want to get rid of him, it won't quite be the death of him.'

'But who wants to get rid of him?'

'I'm sure I don't. I don't mind my trouble the least in life. He's as nice a young gentleman as ever I sat beside the bed of; and he's full of spirit—he is.'

And then Madeline appealed to her mother. Surely her mother would not let Mr. Graham be sent out of the house in his present state, merely because the doctor said it might be possible to move him without causing his instant death! And tears stood in poor Madeline's eyes as she thus pleaded the cause of the sick and wounded. This again tormented Lady Staveley, who found it necessary to give further caution to Mrs. Baker. 'Baker,' she said, 'how can you be so foolish as to be talking to Miss Madeline about Mr. Graham's arm?'

'Who, my lady? I, my lady?'

'Yes, you; when you know that the least thing frightens her. Don't you remember how ill it made her when Roger'—Roger was an old family groom—'when Roger had that accident?' Lady Staveley might have saved herself the trouble of the reminiscence as to Roger, for Baker knew more about it than that. When Roger's scalp had been laid bare by a fall, Miss Madeline had chanced to see it, and had fainted; but Miss Madeline was not fainting now. Baker knew all about it, almost better than Lady Staveley herself. It was of very little use talking to Baker about Roger the groom. Baker thought that Mr. Felix Graham was a very nice young man,

in spite of his 'not being exactly handsomelike about the phys-
gognomy,' as she remarked to one of the younger maids, who much
preferred Peregrine Orme.

Coming away from this last interview with Mrs. Baker, Lady
Staveley interrupted her son and Sophia Furnival in the back
drawing-room, and began to feel that her solicitude for her children
would be almost too much for her. Why had she asked that nasty
girl to her house, and why would not the nasty girl go away? As
for her going away, there was no present hope, for it had been
arranged that she should stay for another fortnight. Why could
not the Fates have been kind, and have allowed Felix Graham and
Miss Furnival to fall in love with each other? ' I can never make
a daughter of her if he does marry her,' Lady Staveley said to herself, as she looked at them.

Augustus looked as though he were detected, and stammered out
some question about his mother and the carriage; but Miss Furnival
did not for a moment lose her easy presence of mind. ' Lady Staveley,'
said she, ' why does not your son go and hunt, or shoot, or fish,
instead of staying in the house all day? It seems to me that his
time is so heavy on his hands that he will almost have to hang
himself.'

' I'm sure I can't tell,' said Lady Staveley, who was not so perfect
an actor as her guest.

' I do think gentlemen in the house in the morning always look
so unfortunate. You have been endeavouring to make yourself
agreeable, but you know you've been yawning.'

' Do you suppose then that men never sit still in the morning?'
said Augustus.

' Oh, in their chambers, yes; or on the bench, and perhaps also
behind counters; but they very seldom do so in a drawing-room.
You have been fidgeting about with the poker till you have
destroyed the look of the fireplace.'

' Well, I'll go and fidget up stairs with Graham,' said he; and so
he left the room.

' Nasty, sly girl,' said Lady Staveley to herself as she took up
her work and sat herself down in her own chair.

Augustus did go up to his friend and found him reading letters.
There was no one else in the room, and the door when Augustus
reached it was properly closed. ' I think I shall be off to-morrow,
old boy,' said Felix.

' Then I think you'll do no such thing,' said Augustus. ' What's
in the wind now?'

' The doctor said this morning that I could be moved without
danger.'

' He said that it might possibly be done in two or three days—
that was all. What on earth makes you so impatient? You've

Lady Staveley interrupting her Son and Sophia Furnival.

nothing to do. Nobody else wants to see you; and nobody here wants to get rid of you.'

'You're wrong in all your three statements.'

'The deuce I am! Who wants to get rid of you?'

'That shall come last. I have something to do, and somebody else does want to see me. I've got a letter from Mary here, and another from Mrs. Thomas;' and he held up to view two letters which he had received, and which had, in truth, startled him.

'Mary's duenna;—the artist who is supposed to be moulding the wife.'

'Yes; Mary's duenna, or Mary's artist, whichever you please.'

'And which of them wants to see you? It's just like a woman, to require a man's attendance exactly when he is unable to move.'

Then Felix, though he did not give up the letters to be read, described to a certain extent their contents. 'I don't know what on earth has happened,' he said. 'Mary is praying to be forgiven, and saying that it is not her fault; and Mrs. Thomas is full of apologies, declaring that her conscience forces her to tell everything; and yet, between them both, I do not know what has happened.'

'Miss Snow has probably lost the key of the workbox you gave her.'

'I have not given her a workbox.'

'Then the writing-desk. That's what a man has to endure when he will make himself head schoolmaster to a young lady. And so you're going to look after your charge with your limbs still in bandages?'

'Just so;' and then he took up the two letters and read them again, while Staveley still sat on the foot of the bed. 'I wish I knew what to think about it,' said Felix.

'About what?' said the other. And then there was another pause, and another reading of a portion of the letters.

'There seems something—something almost frightful to me,' said Felix gravely, 'in the idea of marrying a girl in a few months' time, who now, at so late a period of our engagement, writes to me in that sort of cold, formal way.'

'It's the proper moulded-wife style, you may depend,' said Augustus.

'I'll tell you what, Staveley, if you can talk to me seriously for five minutes, I shall be obliged to you. If that is impossible to you, say so, and I will drop the matter.'

'Well, go on; I am serious enough in what I intend to express, even though I may not be so in my words.'

'I'm beginning to have my doubts about this dear girl.'

'I've had my doubts for some time.'

'Not, mark you, with regard to myself. The question is not now whether I can love her sufficiently for my own happiness. On that side I have no longer the right to a doubt.'

'But you wouldn't marry her if you did not love her.'

'We need not discuss that. But what if she does not love me? What, if she would think it a release to be freed from this engagement? How am I find that out?'

Augustus sat for a while silent, for he did feel that the matter was serious. The case as he looked at it stood thus:—His friend Graham had made a very foolish bargain, from which he would probably be glad to escape, though he could not now bring himself to say as much. But this bargain, bad for him, would probably be very good for the young lady. The young lady, having no shilling of her own, and no merits of birth or early breeding to assist her outlook in the world, might probably regard her ready-made engagement to a clever, kind-hearted, high-spirited man, as an advantage not readily to be abandoned. Staveley, as a sincere friend, was very anxious that the match should be broken off; but he could not bring himself to tell Graham that he thought that the young lady would so wish. According to his idea the young lady must undergo a certain amount of disappointment, and receive a certain amount of compensation. Graham had been very foolish, and must pay for his folly. But in preparing to do so, it would be better that he should see and acknowledge the whole truth of the matter.

'Are you sure that you have found out your own feelings?' Staveley said at last; and his tone was then serious enough even for his friend.

'It hardly matters whether I have or have not,' said Felix.

'It matters above all things;—above all things, because as to them you may come to something like certainty. Of the inside of her heart you cannot know so much. The fact I take it is this—that you would wish to escape from this bondage.'

'No; not unless I thought she regarded it as bondage also. It may be that she does. As for myself, I believe that at the present moment such a marriage would be for me the safest step that I could take.'

'Safe as against what danger?'

'All dangers. How, if I should learn to love another woman,—some one utterly out of my reach,—while I am still betrothed to her?'

'I rarely flatter you, Graham, and don't mean to do it now; but no girl ought to be out of your reach. You have talent, position, birth, and gifts of nature, which should make you equal to any lady. As for money, the less you have the more you should look to get. But if you would cease to be mad, two years would give you command of an income.'

'But I shall never cease to be mad.'

'Who is it that cannot be serious, now?'

'Well, I will be serious—serious enough. I can afford to be so, as I have received my medical passport for to-morrow. No girl, you say, ought to be ought of my reach. If the girl were one Miss Staveley, should she be regarded as out of my reach?'

'A man doesn't talk about his own sister,' said Staveley, having got up from the bed and walked to the window, 'and I know you don't mean anything.'

'But, by heavens! I do mean a great deal.'

'What is it you mean, then?'

'I mean this—What would you say if you learned that I was a suitor for her hand?'

Staveley had been right in saying that a man does not talk about his own sister. When he had declared, with so much affectionate admiration for his friend's prowess, that he might aspire to the hand of any lady, that one retiring, modest-browed girl had not been thought of by him. A man in talking to another man about women is always supposed to consider those belonging to himself as exempt from the incidents of the conversation. The dearest friends do not talk to each other about their sisters when they have once left school; and a man in such a position as that now taken by Graham has to make fight for his ground as closely as though there had been no former intimacies. My friend Smith in such a matter as that, though I have been hail fellow with him for the last ten years, has very little advantage over Jones, who was introduced to the house for the first time last week. And therefore Staveley felt himself almost injured when Felix Graham spoke to him about Madeline.

'What would I say? Well—that is a question one does not understand, unless—unless you really meant to state it as a fact that it was your intention to propose to her.'

'But I mean rather to state it as a fact that it is not my intention to propose to her.'

'Then we had better not speak of her.'

'Listen to me a moment. In order that I may not do so, it will be better for me—better for us all, that I should leave the house.'

'Do you mean to say——?'

'Yes, I do mean to say! I mean to say all that your mind is now suggesting to you. I quite understand your feelings when you declare that a man does not like to talk of his own sister, and therefore we will talk of your sister no more. Old fellow, don't look at me as though you meant to drop me.'

Augustus came back to the bedside, and again seating himself, put his hand almost caressingly over his friend's shoulder. 'I did not think of this,' he said.

' No ; one never does think of it,' Graham replied.

' And she ?'

' She knows no more of it than that bed-post,' said Graham. ' The injury, such as there is, is all on one side. But I'll tell you who suspects it.'

' Baker ?'

' Your mother. I am much mistaken if you will not find that she, with all her hospitality, would prefer that I should recover my strength elsewhere.'

' But you have done nothing to betray yourself.'

' A mother's ears are very sharp. I know that it is so. I cannot explain to you how. Do you tell her that I think of getting up to London to-morrow, and see how she will take it. And, Staveley, do not for a moment suppose that I am reproaching her. She is quite right. I believe that I have in no way committed myself— that I have said no word to your sister with which Lady Staveley has a right to feel herself aggrieved ; but if she has had the wit to read the thoughts of my bosom, she is quite right to wish that I were out of the house.'

Poor Lady Staveley had been possessed of no such wit at all. The sphynx which she had read had been one much more in her own line. She had simply read the thoughts in her daughter's bosom—or rather, the feelings in her daughter's heart.

Augustus Staveley hardly knew what he ought to say. He was not prepared to tell his friend that he was the very brother-in-law for whose connection he would be desirous. Such a marriage for Madeline, even should Madeline desire it, would not be advantageous. When Augustus told Graham that he had gifts of nature which made him equal to any lady, he did not include his own sister. And yet the idea of acquiescing in his friend's sudden departure was very painful to him. ' There can be no reason why you should not stay up here, you know,' at last he said ;—and in so saying he pronounced an absolute verdict against poor Felix.

On few matters of moment to a man's own heart can he speak out plainly the whole truth that is in him. Graham had intended so to do, but had deceived himself. He had not absolutely hoped that his friend would say, ' Come among us, and be one of us ; take her, and be my brother.' But yet there came upon his heart a black load of disappointment, in that the words which were said were the exact opposite of these. Graham had spoken of himself as unfit to match with Madeline Staveley, and Madeline Staveley's brother had taken him at his word. The question which Augustus asked him-self was this—Was it, or was it not practicable that Graham should remain there without danger of intercourse with his sister ? To Felix the question came in a very different shape. After having spoken as he had spoken—might he be allowed to remain there, enjoying such intercourse, or might he not? That was the question to which he had unconsciously demanded an answer;—and unconsciously he had still hoped that the question might be answered in his favour. He had so hoped, although he was burdened with Mary Snow, and although he had spoken of his engagement with that lady in so rigid a spirit of self-martyrdom. But the question had been answered against him. The offer of a further asylum in the seclusion of that bedroom had been made to him by his friend with a sort of proviso that it would not be well that he should go further than the bedroom, and his inner feelings at once grated against each other, making him wretched and almost angry.

'Thank you, no; I understand how kind you are, but I will not do that. I will write up to-night, and shall certainly start to-morrow.'

'My dear fellow——'

'I should get into a fever, if I were to remain in this house after what I have told you. I could not endure to see you, or your mother, or Baker, or Marian, or any one else. Don't talk about it. Indeed, you ought to feel that it is not possible. I have made a confounded ass of myself, and the sooner I get away the better. I say—perhaps you would not be angry if I was to ask you to let me sleep for an hour or so now. After that I'll get up and write my letters.'

He was very sore. He knew that he was sick at heart, and ill at ease, and cross with his friend; and knew also that he was unreasonable in being so. Staveley's words and manner had been full of kindness. Graham was aware of this, and was therefore the more irritated with himself. But this did not prevent his being angry and cross with his friend.

'Graham,' said the other, 'I see clearly enough that I have annoyed you.'

'Not in the least. A man falls into the mud, and then calls to another man to come and see him. The man in the mud of course is not comfortable.'

'But you have called to me, and I have not been able to help you.'

'I did not suppose you would, so there has been no disappointment. Indeed, there was no possibility for help. I shall follow out the line of life which I have long since chalked out for myself, and I do not expect that I shall be more wretched than other poor devils around me. As far as my idea goes, it all makes very little difference. Now leave me; there's a good fellow.'

'Dear old fellow, I would give my right hand if it would make you happy!'

'But it won't. Your right hand will make somebody else happy, I hope.'

'I'll come up to you again before dinner.'

'Very well. And, Staveley, what we have now said cannot be forgotten between us ; but when we next meet, and ever after, let it be as though it were forgotten.' Then he settled himself down on the bed, and Augustus left the room.

It will not be supposed that Graham did go to sleep, or that he had any thought of doing so. When he was alone those words of his friend rang over and over again in his ears, ' No girl ought to be out of your reach.' Why should Madeline Staveley be out of his reach, simply because she was his friend's sister ? He had been made welcome to that house, and therefore he was bound to do nothing unhandsome by the family. But then he was bound by other laws, equally clear, to do nothing unhandsome by any other family—or by any other lady. If there was anything in Staveley's words, they applied as strongly to Staveley's sister as to any other girl. And why should not he, a lawyer, marry a lawyer's daughter ? Sophia Furnival, with her hatful of money, would not be considered too high for him ; and in what respect was Madeline Staveley above Sophia Furnival ? That the one was immeasurably above the other in all those respects which in his estimation tended towards female perfection, he knew to be true enough ; but the fruit which he had been forbidden to gather hung no higher on the social tree than that other fruit which he had been specially invited to pluck and garner.

And then Graham was not a man to think any fruit too high for him. He had no overweening idea of his own deserts, either socially or professionally, nor had he taught himself to expect great things from his own genius ; but he had that audacity of spirit which bids a man hope to compass that which he wishes to compass,—that audacity which is both the father and mother of success,—that audacity which seldom exists without the inner capability on which it ought to rest.

But then there was Mary Snow ! Augustus Staveley thought but little of Mary Snow. According to his theory of his friend's future life, Mary Snow might be laid aside without much difficulty. If this were so, why should not Madeline be within his reach ? But then was it so ? Had he not betrothed himself to Mary Snow in the presence of the girl's father, with every solemnity and assurance, in a manner fixed beyond that of all other betrothals ? Alas, yes ; and for this reason it was right that he should hurry away from Noningsby.

Then he thought of Mary's letter, and of Mrs. Thomas's letter. What was it that had been done ? Mary had written as though she had been charged with some childish offence ; but Mrs. Thomas talked solemnly of acquitting her own conscience. What could have happened that had touched Mrs. Thomas in the conscience ?

But his thoughts soon ran away from the little house at Peckham,

and settled themselves again at Noningsby.   Should he hear more
of Madeline's footsteps?—and if not, why should they have been
banished from the corridor?   Should he hear her voice again at the
door,—and if not, why should it have been hushed?   There is a
silence which may be more eloquent than the sounds which it follows.   Had no one in that house guessed the feelings in his bosom,
she would have walked along the corridor as usual, and spoken a
word with her sweet voice in answer to his word.   He felt sure
that this would be so no more; but who had stopped it, and why
should such sounds be no more heard?

At last he did go to sleep, not in pursuance of any plan formed
for doing so; for had he been asked he would have said that sleep
was impossible for him.   But he did go to sleep, and when he
awoke it was dark.   He had intended to have got up and dressed
on that afternoon, or to have gone through such ceremony of
dressing as was possible for him,—in preparation of his next day's
exercise; and now he rose up in his bed with a start, angry with
himself in having allowed the time to pass by him.

'Lord love you, Mr. Graham, why how you have slept!' said
Mrs. Baker.   'If I haven't just sent your dinner down again to
keep hot.   Such a beautiful pheasant, and the bread sauce'll be
lumpy now, for all the world like pap.'

'Never mind the bread sauce, Mrs. Baker;—the pheasant's the
thing.'

'And her ladyship's been here, Mr. Graham, only she wouldn't
have you woke.   She won't hear of your being moved to-morrow,
nor yet won't the judge.   There was a rumpus down stairs when
Mr. Augustus as much as mentioned it.   I know one who—'

'You know one who—you were saying?'

'Never mind.—It aint one more than another, but it's all.   You
aint to leave this to-morrow, so you may just give it over.   And
indeed your things is all at the wash, so you can't;—and now I'll
go down for the pheasant.'

Felix still declared very positively that he should go, but his
doing so did not shake Mrs. Baker.   The letter-bag he knew did
not leave till eight, and as yet it was not much past five.   He
would see Staveley again after his dinner, and then he would write.

When Augustus left the room in the middle of the day he encountered Madeline wandering about the house.   In these days
she did wander about the house, as though there were something
always to be done in some place apart from that in which she then
was.   And yet the things which she did were but few.   She neither
worked nor read, and as for household duties, her share in them
was confined almost entirely to the morning and evening teapot.

'It isn't true that he's to go to-morrow morning, Augustus, is
it?' said she.

'Who, Graham? Well; he says that he will. He is very anxious to get to London; and no doubt he finds it stupid enough lying there and doing nothing.'

'But he can do as much there as he can lying by himself in his own chambers, where I don't suppose he would have anybody to look after him. He thinks he's a trouble and all that, and therefore he wants to go. But you know mamma doesn't mind about trouble of that kind; and what should we think of it afterwards if anything bad was to happen to your friend because we allowed him to leave the house before he was in a fit state to be moved? Of course Mr. Pottinger says so—' Mr. Pottinger was the doctor. 'Of course Mr. Pottinger says so, because he thinks he has been so long here, and he doesn't understand.'

'But Mr. Pottinger would like to keep a patient.'

'Oh no; he's not at all that sort of man. He'd think of mamma, —the trouble I mean of having a stranger in the house. But you know mamma would think nothing of that, especially for such an intimate friend of yours.'

Augustus turned slightly round so as to look more fully into his sister's face, and he saw that a tear was gathered in the corner of her eye. She perceived his glance and partly shrank under it, but she soon recovered herself and answered it. 'I know what you mean,' she said, 'and if you choose to think so, I can't help it. But it is horrible—horrible—' and then she stopped herself, finding that a little sob would become audible if she trusted herself to further words.

'You know what I mean, Mad?' he said, putting his arm affectionately round her waist. 'And what is it that I mean? Come; you and I never have any secrets;—you always say so when you want to get at mine. Tell me what it is that I mean.'

'I haven't got any secret.'

'But what did I mean?'

'You looked at me, because I don't want you to let them send Mr. Graham away. If it was old Mr. Furnival I shouldn't like them to turn him out of this house when he was in such a state as that.'

'Poor Mr. Furnival; no; I think he would bear it worse than Felix.'

'Then why should he go? And why—should you look at me in that way?'

'Did I look at you, Mad? Well, I believe I did. We are to have no secrets; are we?'

'No,' said she. But she did not say it in the same eager voice with which hitherto she had declared that they would always tell each other everything.

'Felix Graham is my friend,' said he, 'my special friend; and I hope you will always like my friends. But——'

'Well?' she said.

'You know what I mean, Mad.'

'Yes,' she said.

'That is all, dearest.' And then she knew that he also had cautioned her not to fall in love with Felix Graham, and she felt angry with him for the caution. 'Why—why—why——?' But she hardly knew as yet how to frame the question which she desired to ask herself.

CHAPTER XL.

I CALL IT AWFUL.

'Oh indeed!' Those had been the words with which Mr. Furnival had received the announcement made by Sir Peregrine as to his proposed nuptials. And as he uttered them the lawyer drew himself up stiffly in his chair, looking much more like a lawyer and much less like an old family friend than he had done the moment before.

Whereupon Sir Peregrine drew himself up also. 'Yes,' he said. 'I should be intrusive if I were to trouble you with my motives, and therefore I need only say further as regards the lady, that I trust that my support, standing as I shall do in the position of her husband, will be more serviceable to her than it could otherwise have been in this trial which she will, I presume, be forced to undergo.'

'No doubt; no doubt,' said Mr. Furnival; and then the interview had ended. The lawyer had been anxious to see his client, and had intended to ask permission to do so; but he had felt on hearing Sir Peregrine's tidings that it would be useless now to make any attempt to see her alone, and that he could speak to her with no freedom in Sir Peregrine's presence. So he left The Cleeve, having merely intimated to the baronet the fact of his having engaged the services of Mr. Chaffanbrass and Mr. Solomon Aram. 'You will not see Lady Mason?' Sir Peregrine had asked. 'Thank you: I do not know that I need trouble her,' Mr. Furnival had answered. 'You of course will explain to her how the case at present stands. I fear she must reconcile herself to the fact of a trial. You are aware, Sir Peregrine, that the offence imputed is one for which bail will be taken. I should propose yourself and her son. Of course I should be happy to lend my own name, but as I shall be on the trial, perhaps it may be as well that this should be avoided.'

Bail will be taken! These words were dreadful in the ears of the expectant bridegroom. Had it come to this; that there was a question whether or no she should be locked up in a prison, like a felon? But nevertheless his heart did not misgive him. Seeing how terribly she was injured by others, he felt himself bound by the stronger law to cling to her himself. Such was the special chivalry of the man.

Mr. Furnival on his return to London thought almost more of Sir Peregrine than he did either of Lady Mason or of himself. Was it not a pity? Was it not a thousand pities that that aged noble gentleman should be sacrificed? He had felt angry with Sir Peregrine when the tidings were first communicated to him; but now, as he journeyed up to London this feeling of anger was transferred to his own client. This must be her doing, and such doing on her part, while she was in her present circumstances, was very wicked. And then he remembered her guilt,—her probable guilt, and his brow became very black. Her supposed guilt had not been horrible to him while he had regarded it as affecting herself alone, and in point of property affecting Joseph Mason and her son Lucius. He could look forward, sometimes almost trium-phantly, to the idea of washing her—so far as this world's washing goes—from that guilt, and setting her up again clear before the world, even though in doing so he should lend a hand in robbing Joseph Mason of his estate. But this dragging down of another—and such another—head into the vortex of ruin and misery was horrible to him. He was not straitlaced, or mealy-mouthed, or overburthened with scruples. In the way of his profession he could do many a thing at which—I express a single opinion with much anxious deference—at which an honest man might be scan-dalized if it became beneath his judgment unprofessionally. But this he could not stand. Something must be done in the matter. The marriage must be stayed till after the trial,—or else he must himself retire from the defence and explain both to Lady Mason and to Sir Peregrine why he did so.

And then he thought of the woman herself, and his spirit within him became very bitter. Had any one told him that he was jealous of the preference shown by his client to Sir Peregrine, he would have fumed with anger, and thought that he was fuming justly. But such was in truth the case. Though he believed her to have been guilty of this thing, though he believed her to be now guilty of the worse offence of dragging the baronet to his ruin, still he was jealous of her regard. Had she been content to lean upon him, to trust to him as her great and only necessary friend, he could have forgiven all else, and placed at her service the full force of his professional power,—even though by doing so he might have lowered himself in men's minds. And what reward did he expect? None. He had formed no idea that the woman would become his mistress. All that was as obscure before his mind's eye, as though she had been nineteen and he five-and-twenty.

He was to dine at home on this day, that being the first occasion of his doing so for—as Mrs. Furnival declared—the last six months. In truth, however, the interval had been long, though not so long as that. He had a hope that having announced his intention, he might find the coast clear and hear Martha Biggs spoken of as a dear one lately gone. But when he arrived at home Martha Biggs was still there. Under circumstances as they now existed Mrs. Furnival had determined to keep Martha Biggs by her, unless any special edict for her banishment should come forth. Then, in case of such special edict, Martha Biggs should go, and thence should arise the new casus belli. Mrs. Furnival had made up her mind that war was expedient,—nay, absolutely necessary. She had an idea, formed no doubt from the reading of history, that some allies require a smart brush now and again to blow away the clouds of distrust which become engendered by time between them; and that they may become better allies than ever afterwards. If the appropriate time for such a brush might ever come, it had come now. All the world,—so she said to herself,—was talking of Mr. Furnival and Lady Mason. All the world knew of her injuries.

Martha Biggs was second cousin to Mr. Crook's brother's wife— I speak of that Mr. Crook who had been professionally known for the last thirty years as the partner of Mr. Round. It had been whispered in the office in Bedford Row—such whisper I fear originating with old Round—that Mr. Furnival admired his fair client. Hence light had fallen upon the eyes of Martha Biggs, and the secret of her friend was known to her. Need I trace the course of the tale with closer accuracy?

' Oh, Kitty,' she had said to her friend with tears that evening— ' I cannot bear to keep it to myself any more! I cannot when I see you suffering so. It's awful.'

' Cannot bear to keep what, Martha?'

' Oh, I know. Indeed all the town knows it now.'

' Knows what? You know how I hate that kind of thing. If you have anything to say, speak out.'

This was not kind to such a faithful friend as Martha Biggs; but Martha knew what sacrifices friendship such as hers demanded, and she did not resent it.

' Well then;—if I am to speak out, it's—Lady Mason. And I do say that it's shameful, quite shameful;—and awful; I call it awful.'

Mrs. Furnival had not said much at the time to encourage the fidelity of her friend, but she was thus justified in declaring to herself that her husband's goings on had become the talk of all the world ;—and his goings on especially in that quarter in which she had long regarded them with so much dismay. She was not

therefore prepared to welcome him on this occasion of his coming
home to dinner by such tokens of friendly feeling as the dismissal
of her friend to Red Lion Square. When the moment for absolute
war should come Martha Biggs should be made to depart.

Mr. Furnival when he arrived at his own house was in a thoughtful mood, and disposed for quiet and domestic meditation. Had
Miss Biggs not been there he could have found it in his heart to
tell everything about Lady Mason to his wife, asking her counsel
as to what he should do with reference to that marriage. Could
he have done so, all would have been well; but this was not
possible while that red-faced lump of a woman from Red Lion
Square sat in his drawing-room, making everything uncomfortable.

The three sat down to dinner together, and very little was said
between them. Mr. Furnival did try to be civil to his wife, but
wives sometimes have a mode of declining such civilities without
committing themselves to overt acts of war. To Miss Biggs Mr.
Furnival could not bring himself to say anything civil, seeing that
he hated her; but such words as he did speak to her she received
with grim griffin-like austerity, as though she were ever meditating
on the awfulness of his conduct. And so in truth she was. Why his
conduct was more awful in her estimation since she had heard
Lady Mason's name mentioned, than when her mind had been
simply filled with general ideas of vague conjugal infidelity, I
cannot say; but such was the case. ' I call it awful,' were the first
words she again spoke when she found herself once more alone
with Mrs. Furnival in the drawing-room. And then she sat down
over the fire, thinking neither of her novel nor her knitting, with
her mind deliciously filled with the anticipation of coming
catastrophes.

' If I sit up after half-past ten would you mind going to bed?'
said Mrs. Furnival, when they had been in the drawing-room about
ten minutes.

' Oh no, not in the least,' said Miss Biggs. ' I'll be sure to go.'
But she thought it very unkind, and she felt as a child does who is
deceived in a matter of being taken to the play. If no one goes
the child can bear it. But to see others go, and to be left behind,
is too much for the feelings of any child,—or of Martha Biggs.

Mr. Furnival had no inclination for sitting alone over his wine
on this occasion. Had it been possible for him he would have preferred to have gone quickly up stairs, and to have taken his cup of
coffee from his wife's hand with some appreciation of domestic
comfort. But there could be no such comfort to him while Martha
Biggs was there, so he sat down stairs, sipping his port according
to his custom, and looking into the fire for a solution of his difficulties about Lady Mason. He began to wish that he had never
seen Lady Mason, and to reflect that the intimate friendship of

pretty women often brings with it much trouble. He was resolved on one thing. He would not go down into court and fight that battle for Lady Orme. Were he to do so the matter would have taken quite a different phase,—one that he had not at all anticipated. In case that his present client should then have become Lady Orme, Mr. Chaffanbrass and Mr. Solomon Aram might carry on the battle between them, with such assistance as they might be able to get from Messrs. Slow and Bideawhile. He became angry as he drank his port, and in his anger he swore that it should be so. And then as his anger became hot at the close of his libations, he remembered that Martha Biggs was up stairs, and became more angry still. And thus when he did go into the drawing-room at some time in the evening not much before ten, he was not in a frame of mind likely to bring about domestic comfort.

He walked across the drawing-room, sat down in an arm-chair by the table, and took up the last number of a review, without speaking to either of them. Whereupon Mrs. Furnival began to ply her needle which had been lying idly enough upon her work, and Martha Biggs fixed her eyes intently upon her book. So they sat twenty minutes without a word being spoken, and then Mrs. Furnival inquired of her lord whether he chose to have tea.

' Of course I shall,—when you have it,' said he.

' Don't mind us,' said Mrs. Furnival.

' Pray don't mind me,' said Martha Biggs. ' Don't let me be in the way.'

' No, I won't,' said Mr. Furnival. Whereupon Miss Biggs again jumped up in her chair as though she had been electrified. It may be remembered that on a former occasion Mr. Furnival had sworn at her—or at least in her presence.

' You need not be rude to a lady in your own house, because she is my friend,' said Mrs. Furnival.

' Bother,' said Mr. Furnival. ' And now if we are going to have any tea, let us have it.'

' I don't think I'll mind about tea to-night, Mrs. Furnival,' said Miss Biggs, having received a notice from her friend's eye that it might be well for her to depart. ' My head aches dreadful, and I shall be better in bed. Good-night, Mrs. Furnival.' And then she took her candle and went away.

For the next five minutes there was not a word said. No tea had been ordered, although it had been mentioned. Mrs. Furnival had forgotten it among the hot thoughts that were running through her mind, and Mr. Furnival was indifferent upon the subject. He knew that something was coming, and he resolved that he would have the upper hand let that something be what it might. He was being ill used,—so he said to himself—and would not put up with it.

At last the battle began. He was not looking, but he heard her first movement as she prepared herself. ' Tom!' she said, and then the voice of the war goddess was again silent. He did not choose to answer her at the instant, and then the war goddess rose from her seat and again spoke. ' Tom!' she said, standing over him and looking at him.

' What is it you mean?' said he, allowing his eyes to rise to her face over the top of his book.

' Tom!' she said for the third time.

' I'll have no nonsense, Kitty,' said he. ' If you have anything to say, say it.'

Even then she had intended to be affectionate,—had so intended at the first commencement of her address. She had no wish to be a war goddess. But he had assisted her attempt at love by no gentle word, by no gentle look, by no gentle motion. ' I have this to say,' she replied; ' you are disgracing both yourself and me, and I will not remain in this house to be a witness to it.'

' Then you may go out of the house.' These words, be it re- membered, were uttered not by the man himself, but by the spirit of port wine within the man.

' Tom, do you say that;—after all?'

' By heavens I do say it! I'll not be told in my own drawing- room, even by you, that I am disgracing myself.'

' Then why do you go after that woman down to Hamworth? All the world is talking of you. At your age too! You ought to be ashamed of yourself.'

' I can't stand this,' said he, getting up and throwing the book from him right across the drawing-room floor; 'and, by heavens! I won't stand it.'

' Then why do you do it, sir?'

' Kitty, I believe the devil must have entered into you to drive you mad.'

' Oh, oh, oh! very well, sir. The devil in the shape of drink and lust has entered into you. But you may understand this; I—will—not—consent to live with you while such deeds as these are being done.' And then without waiting for another word, she stormed out of the room.

END OF VOL. I.

ORLEY FARM

VOLUME II

Lady Mason leaving the Court.

VOLUME II

CONTENTS.

CONTENTS.

ILLUSTRATIONS TO VOLUME II.

ILLUSTRATIONS.

ORLEY FARM.

CHAPTER I.

HOW CAN I SAVE HIM?

'I WILL not consent to live with you while such deeds as these are being done.' Such were the last words which Mrs. Furnival spoke as she walked out of her own drawing-room, leaving her husband still seated in his arm-chair.

What was he to do? Those who would hang by the letter of the law in such matters may say that he should have rung the bell, sent for his wife, explained to her that obedience was a necessary duty on her part, and have finished by making her understand that she must and would continue to live wherever he chose that she should live. There be those who say that if a man be anything of a man, he can always insure obedience in his own household. He has the power of the purse and the power of the law; and if, having these, he goes to the wall, it must be because he is a poor creature. Those who so say have probably never tried the position.

Mr. Furnival did not wish to send for his wife, because by doing so he would have laid bare his sore before his servants. He could not follow her, because he knew that he should not find her alone in her room. Nor did he wish for any further parley, because he knew that she would speak loud, and probably sob—nay, very possibly proceed to a fainting fit. And, moreover, he much doubted whether he would have the power to keep her in the house if it should be her pleasure to leave it. And then what should he do? The doing of something in such a catastrophe, was, he thought, indispensable.

Was ever a man so ill treated? Was ever jealousy so groundless? Here was a woman, with whom he was on the point of quarrelling, who was engaged to be married to another man, whom for months past he had only seen as a client; and on her account he was to be told by his wife that she would not consent to live with him! Yes; it was quite indispensable that he should do something.

At last he went to bed, and slept upon it; not sharing the marital couch, but occupying his own dressing-room. In the morning, however, as he sat down to his solitary breakfast, he was as far as ever from having made up his mind what that something should be. A message was brought to him by an elderly female servant with a grave face,—the elderly servant who had lived with them since their poorer days,—saying that ' Missus would not come down to breakfast this morning.' There was no love sent, no excuse as to illness, no semblance of a peaceable reason, assumed even to deceive the servant. It was clear to Mr. Furnival that the servant was intended to know all about it. ' And Miss Biggs says, sir, that if you please you're not to wait for her.'

' Very well, that'll do,' said Mr. Furnival, who had not the slightest intention of waiting for Miss Biggs ; and then he sat himself down to eat his bacon, and bethink himself what step he would take with this recreant and troublesome spouse.

While he was thus employed the post came. The bulk of his letters as a matter of course went to his chambers ; but there were those among his correspondents who wrote to him at Harley Street. To-day he received three or four letters, but our concern will be with one only. This one bore the Hamworth post-mark, and he opened it the first, knowing that it came from Lady Mason. It was as follows :—

' *Private.*   ' THE CLEEVE, 23rd *January*, 18—.
' MY DEAR MR. FURNIVAL,
        ' I am so very sorry that I did not see you to-day ! Indeed, your leaving without seeing me has made me unhappy, for I cannot but think that it shows that you are displeased. Under these circumstances I must write to you and explain to you how that came to pass which Sir Peregrine told you. I have not let him know that I am writing to you, and I think for his sake that I had better not. But he is so good, and has shown to me such nobleness and affection, that I can hardly bring myself to have any secret from him.

' You may conceive what was my surprise when I first understood that he wished to make me his wife. It is hardly six months since I thought that I was almost exceeding my station in visiting at his house. Then by degrees I began to be received as a friend, and at last I found myself treated with the warmest love. But still I had no thought of this, and I knew that it was because of my great trouble that Sir Peregrine and Mrs. Orme were so good to me.

' When he sent for me into his library and told me what he wished, I could not refuse him anything. I promised obedience to him as though I were a child ; and in this way I found myself engaged to be his wife. When he told me that he would have it so, how could I refuse him, knowing as I do all that he has done for me, and

thinking of it as I do every minute ? As for loving him, of course
I love him. Who that knows him does not love him? He is made
to be loved. No one is so good and so noble as he. But of love of
that sort I had never dreamed.. Ah me, no !—a woman burdened
as I am does not think of love.

'He told me that he would have it so, and I said that I would
obey him; and he tried to prove to me that in this dreadful trial it
would be better for me. But I would not wish it on that account.
He has done enough for me without my causing him such injury.
When I argued it with him, trying to say that others would not
like it, he declared that Mrs. Orme would be well pleased, and,
indeed, so she told me afterwards herself. And thus I yielded to
him, and agreed that I would be his wife. But I was not happy,
thinking that I should injure him; and I promised only because I
could not deny him.

'But the day before yesterday young Mr. Orme, his grandson,
came to me and told me that such a marriage would be very wrong.
And I do believe him. He said that old family friends would look
down upon his grandfather and ridicule him if he were to make this
marriage. And I can see that it would be so. I would not have
such injury come upon him for the gain of all the world to myself.
So I have made up my mind to tell him that it cannot be, even
though I should anger him. And I fear that it will anger him, for
he loves to have his own way,—especially in doing good; and he
thinks that our marriage would rescue me altogether from the
danger of this trial.

'So I have made up my mind to tell him, but I have not found
courage to do it yet; and I do wish, dear Mr. Furnival, that I might
see you first. I fear that I may have lost your friendship by what
has already been done. If so, what will become of me ? When I
heard that you had gone without asking for me, my heart sank
within me. I have two friends whom I so dearly love, and I would
fain do as both direct me, if that may be possible. And now I
propose to go up to London to-morrow, and to be at your chambers
about one o'clock. I have told Sir Peregrine and Mrs. Orme that I
am going; but he is too noble-minded to ask questions now that he
thinks I may feel myself constrained to tell him. So I will call in
Lincoln's Inn at one o'clock, and I trust that if possible you will
see me. I am greatly in want of your advice, for in truth I hardly
know what to do.

'Pray believe me to be always your attached friend,
                                                'MARY MASON.'

There was hardly a word,—I believe not a word in that letter that
was not true. Her acceptance of Sir Peregrine had been given
exactly in the manner and for the reasons there explained; and

since she had accepted him she had been sorry for having done
so, exactly in the way now described. She was quite willing to
give up her husband if it was thought best,—but she was not
willing to give up her friend. She was not willing to give up
either friend, and her great anxiety was so to turn her conduct that
she might keep them both.

Mr. Furnival was gratified as he read the letter—gratified in spite
of his present frame of mind. Of course he would see her ;—and of
course, as he himself well knew, would take her again into favour.
But he must insist on her carrying out her purpose of abandoning
the marriage project. If, arising from this abandonment, there
should be any coolness on the part of Sir Peregrine, Mr. Furnival
would not regret it. Mr. Furnival did not feel quite sure whether
in the conduct of this case he was not somewhat hampered by the
—energetic zeal of Sir Peregrine's line of defence.

When he had finished the perusal of his letter and the consideration which it required, he put it carefully into his breast coat pocket,
envelope and all. What might not happen if he left that envelope
about in that house ? And then he took it out again, and observed
upon the cover the Hamworth post-mark, very clear. Post-marks
now-a-days are very clear, and everybody may know whence a letter
comes. His letters had been brought to him by the butler ; but was
it not probable that that ancient female servant might have seen
them first, and have conveyed to her mistress intelligence as to this
post-mark? If so—; and Mr. Furnival almost felt himself to be
guilty as he thought of it.

While he was putting on his greatcoat in the hall, the butler
assisting him, the ancient female servant came to him again. There
was a look about her face which told of war, and declared her to be,
if not the chief lieutenant of his wife, at any rate her colour-
serjeant. Martha Biggs no doubt was chief lieutenant. 'Missus
desires me to ask,' said she, with her grim face and austere voice,
'whether you will be pleased to dine at home to-day ?' And yet the
grim, austere woman could be affectionate and almost motherly in
her ministrations to him when things were going well, and had
eaten his salt and broken his bread for more than twenty years.
All this was very hard ! 'Because,' continued the woman, 'missus
says she thinks she shall be out this evening herself.'

'Where is she going ?'

'Missus didn't tell me, sir.'

He almost determined to go up-stairs and call upon her to tell
him what she was going to do, but he remembered that if he did it
would surely make a row in the house. Miss Biggs would put her
head out of some adjacent door and scream, 'Oh laws !' and he
would have to descend his own stairs with the consciousness that all
his household were regarding him as a brute. So he gave up that

project. 'No,' he said, 'I shall not dine at home;' and then he went his way.

'Missus is very aggravating,' said the butler, as soon as the door was closed.

'You don't know what cause she has, Spooner,' said the house-keeper very solemnly.

'Is it at his age? I believe it's all nonsense, I do;—feminine fancies, and vagaries of the weaker sex.'

'Yes, I dare say; that's what you men always say. But if he don't look out he'll find missus'll be too much for him. What'd he do if she were to go away from him?'

'Do?—why live twice as jolly. It would only be the first rumpus of the thing.'

I am afraid that there was some truth in what Spooner said. It is the first rumpus of the thing, or rather the fear of that, which keeps together many a couple.

At one o'clock there came a timid female rap at Mr. Furnival's chamber door, and the juvenile clerk gave admittance to Lady Mason. Crabwitz, since the affair of that mission down at Ham-worth, had so far carried a point of his, that a junior satellite was now permanently installed ; and for the future the indignity of opening doors, and 'just stepping out' into Chancery Lane, would not await him. Lady Mason was dressed all in black,—but this was usual with her when she left home. To-day, however, there was about her something blacker and more sombre than usual. The veil which she wore was thick, and completely hid her face; and her voice, as she asked for Mr. Furnival, was low and plaintive. But, nevertheless, she had by no means laid aside the charm of womanhood; or it might be more just to say that the charm of womanhood had not laid aside her. There was that in her figure, step, and gait of going which compelled men to turn round and look at her. We all know that she had a son some two or three and twenty years of age, and that she had not been quite a girl when she married. But, notwithstanding this, she was yet young; and though she made no effort—no apparent effort—to maintain the power and influence which beauty gives, yet she did maintain it.

He came forward and took her by the hand with all his old affec-tionate regard, and, muttering some words of ordinary salutation, led her to a chair. It may be that she muttered something also, but if so the sound was too low to reach his ears. She sat down where he placed her, and as she put her hand on the table near her arm, he saw that she was trembling.

'I got your letter this morning,' he said, by way of beginning the conversation.

'Yes,' she said; and then, finding that it was not possible that he should hear her through her veil, she raised it. She was very pale, and there was a look of painful care, almost of agony, round her mouth. He had never seen her look so pale,—but he said to himself at the same time that he had never seen her look so beautiful.

'And to tell you the truth, Lady Mason, I was very glad to get it. You and I had better speak openly to each other about this;—had we not?'

'Oh, yes,' she said. And then there was a struggle within her not to tremble—a struggle that was only too evident. She was aware of this, and took her hand off the table.

'I vexed you because I did not see you at The Cleeve the other day.'

'Because I thought that you were angry with me.'

'And I was so.'

'Oh, Mr. Furnival!'

'Wait a moment, Lady Mason. I was angry;—or rather sorry and vexed to hear of that which I did not approve. But your letter has removed that feeling. I can now understand the manner in which this engagement was forced upon you; and I understand also —do I not?—that the engagement will not be carried out?'

She did not answer him immediately, and he began to fear that she repented of her purpose. 'Because,' said he, 'under no other circumstances could I——'

'Stop, Mr. Furnival. Pray do not be severe with me.' And she looked at him with eyes which would almost have melted his wife, —and which he was quite unable to withstand. Had it been her wish, she might have made him promise to stand by her, even though she had persisted in her engagement.

'No, no; I will not be severe.'

'I do not wish to marry him,' she went on to say. 'I have re-solved to tell him so. That was what I said in my letter.'

'Yes, yes.'

'I do not wish to marry him. I would not bring his gray hairs with sorrow to the grave—no, not to save myself from——' And then, as she thought of that from which she desired to save herself, she trembled again, and was silent.

'It would create in men's minds such a strong impression against you, were you to marry him at this moment!'

'It is of him I am thinking;—of him and Lucius. Mr. Furnival, they might do their worst with me, if it were not for that thought. My boy!' And then she rose from her chair, and stood upright before him, as though she were going to do or say some terrible thing. He still kept his chair, for he was startled, and hardly knew what he would be about. That last exclamation had come from her almost with a shriek, and now her bosom was heaving as though her heart would burst with the violence of her sobbing. 'I will go,' she said. 'I had better go.' And she hurried away towards the door.

'No, no; do not go yet.' And he rose to stop her, but she was quite passive. 'I do not know why you should be so much moved now.' But he did know. He did understand the very essence and core of her feelings ;—as probably may the reader also. But it was impossible that he should allow her to leave him in her present state.

She sat down again, and leaning both her arms upon the table, hid her face within her hands. He was now standing, and for the moment did not speak to her. Indeed he could not bring himself to break the silence, for he saw her tears, and could still hear the violence of her sobs. And then she was the first to speak. 'If it were not for him,' she said, raising her head, 'I could bear it all. What will he do? what will he do?'

'You mean,' said Mr. Furnival, speaking very slowly, 'if the —verdict—should go against us.'

'It will go against us,' she said. 'Will it not?—tell me the truth. You are so clever, you must know. Tell me how it will go. Is there anything I can do to save him?' And she took hold of his arm with both her hands, and looked up eagerly—oh, with such terrible eagerness!—into his face.

Would it not have been natural now that he should have asked her to tell him the truth? And yet he did not dare to ask her. He thought that he knew it. He felt sure,—almost sure, that he could look into her very heart, and read there the whole of her secret. But still there was a doubt,—enough of doubt to make him wish to ask the question. Nevertheless he did not ask it.

'Mr. Furnival,' she said; and as she spoke there was a hardness came over the soft lines of her feminine face; a look of courage which amounted almost to ferocity, a look which at the moment recalled to his mind, as though it were but yesterday, the attitude and countenance she had borne as she stood in the witness-box at that other trial, now so many years since,—that attitude and countenance which had impressed the whole court with so high an idea of her courage. 'Mr. Furnival, weak as I am, I could bear to die here on the spot,—now—if I could only save him from this agony. It is not for myself I suffer.' And then the terrible idea occurred to him that she might attempt to compass her escape by death. But he did not know her. That would have been no escape for her son.

'And you too think that I must not marry him?' she said, putting up her hands to her brows as though to collect her thoughts.

'No; certainly not, Lady Mason.'

'No, no. It would be wrong. But, Mr. Furnival, I am so

driven that I know not how I should act. What if I should lose
my mind?' And as she looked at him there was that about her
eyes which did tell him that such an ending might be possible.

'Do not speak in such a way,' he said.

'No, I will not. I know that it is wrong. I will go down there,
and tell him that it must not,—must not be so. But I may stay at
The Cleeve;—may I not?'

'Oh, certainly—if he wishes it,—after your understanding with
him.'

'Ah; he may turn me out, may he not? And they are so kind
to me, so gentle and so good. And Lucius is so stern. But I will
go back. Sternness will perhaps be better for me now than love
and kindness.'

In spite of everything, in the teeth of his almost certain conviction of her guilt, he would now, even now, have asked her to come
to his own house, and have begged her to remain there till the trial
was over,—if only he had had the power to do so. What would it
be to him what the world might say, if she should be proved
guilty? Why should not he have been mistaken as well as others?
And he had an idea that if he could get her into his own hands he
might still bring her through triumphantly,—with assistance from
Solomon Aram and Chaffanbrass. He was strongly convinced of
her guilt, but by no means strongly convinced that her guilt could
be proved. But then he had no house at the present moment that
he could call his own. His Kitty, the Kitty of whom he still
sometimes thought with affection,—that Kitty whose soft motherly
heart would have melted at such a story of a woman's sorrows, if
only it had been rightly approached,—that Kitty was now vehe-
mently hostile, hostile both to him and to this very woman for
whom he would have asked her care.

'May God help me!' said the poor woman. 'I do not know
where else to turn for aid. Well; I may go now then. And, indeed, why should I take up your time further?'

But before she did go, Mr. Furnival gave her much counsel. He
did not ask as to her guilt, but he did give her that advice which
he would have thought most expedient had her guilt been declared
and owned. He told her that very much would depend on her
maintaining her present position and standing; that she was so to
carry herself as not to let people think that she was doubtful about
the trial; and that above all things she was to maintain a composed
and steadfast manner before her son. As to the Ormes, he bade
her not to think of leaving The Cleeve, unless she found that her
remaining there would be disagreeable to Sir Peregrine after her
explanation with him. That she was to decline the marriage
engagement, he was very positive; on that subject there was to be
no doubt.

And then she went; and as she passed down the dark passage into the new square by the old gate of the Chancellor's court, she met a stout lady. The stout lady eyed her savagely, but was not quite sure as to her identity. Lady Mason in her trouble passed the stout lady without taking any notice of her.

CHAPTER II.

JOHN KENNEBY GOES TO HAMWORTH.

WHEN John Kenneby dined with his sister and brother-in-law on Christmas-day he agreed, at the joint advice of the whole party there assembled, that he would go down and see Mr. Dockwrath at Hamworth, in accordance with the invitation received from that gentleman;—his enemy, Dockwrath, who had carried off Miriam Usbech, for whom John Kenneby still sighed,—in a gentle easy manner indeed,—but still sighed as though it were an affair but of yesterday. But though he had so agreed, and though he had never stirred from that resolve, he by no means did it immediately. He was a slow man, whose life had offered him but little excitement; and the little which came to him was husbanded well and made to go a long way. He thought about this journey for nearly a month before he took it, often going to his sister and discussing it with her, and once or twice seeing the great Moulder himself. At last he fixed a day and did go down to Hamworth.

He had, moreover, been invited to the offices of Messrs. Round and Crook, and that visit also was as yet unpaid. A clerk from the house in Bedford Row had found him out at Hubbles and Grease's, and had discovered that he would be forthcoming as a witness. On the special subject of his evidence not much had then passed, the clerk having had no discretion given him to sift the matter. But Kenneby had promised to go to Bedford Row, merely stipulating for a day at some little distance of time. That day was now near at hand; but he was to see Dockwrath first, and hence it occurred that he now made his journey to Hamworth.

But another member of that Christmas party at Great St. Helen's had not been so slow in carrying out his little project. Mr. Kantwise had at once made up his mind that it would be as well that he should see Dockwrath. It would not suit him to incur the expense of a journey to Hamworth, even with the additional view of extracting payment for that set of metallic furniture; but he wrote to the attorney telling him that he should be in London in the way of trade on such and such a day, and that he had tidings of importance to give with reference to the great Orley Farm case.

Dockwrath did see him, and the result was that Mr. Kantwise got his money, fourteen eleven;—at least he got fourteen seven six, and had a very hard fight for the three odd half-crowns,—and Dockwrath learned that John Kenneby, if duly used, would give evidence on his side of the question.

And then Kenneby did go down to Hamworth. He had not seen Miriam Usbech since the days of her marriage. He had remained hanging about the neighbourhood long enough to feast his eyes with the agony of looking at the bride, and then he had torn himself away. Circumstances since that had carried him one way and Miriam another, and they had never met. Time had changed him very little, and what change time had made was perhaps for the better. He hesitated less when he spoke, he was less straggling and undecided in his appearance, and had about him more of manhood than in former days. But poor Miriam had certainly not been altered for the better by years and circumstances as far as outward appearance went.

Kenneby as he walked up from the station to the house,—and from old remembrances he knew well where the house stood,—gave up his mind entirely to the thought of seeing Miriam, and in his memories of old love passages almost forgot the actual business which now brought him to the place. To him it seemed as though he was going to meet the same Miriam he had left,—the Miriam to whom in former days he had hardly ventured to speak of love, and to whom he must not now venture so to speak at all. He almost blushed as he remembered that he would have to take her hand.

There are men of this sort, men slow in their thoughts but very keen in their memories; men who will look for the glance of a certain bright eye from a window-pane, though years have rolled on since last they saw it,—since last they passed that window. Such men will bethink themselves, after an interval of weeks, how they might have brought up wit to their use and improved an occasion which chance had given them. But when the bright eyes do glance, such men pass by abashed; and when the occasion offers, their wit is never at hand. Nevertheless they are not the least happy of mankind, these never-readies; they do not pick up sudden prizes, but they hold fast by such good things as the ordinary run of life bestows upon them. There was a lady even now, a friend of Mrs. Moulder, ready to bestow herself and her fortune on John Kenneby,—a larger fortune than Miriam had possessed, and one which would not now probably be neutralized by so large a family as poor Miriam had bestowed upon her husband.

How would Miriam meet him? It was of this he thought, as he approached the door. Of course he must call her Mrs. Dockwrath, though the other name was so often on his tongue. He had made up

John Kennedy and Miriam Dockwrath.

his mind, for the last week past, that he would call at the private door
of the house, passing by the door of the office. Otherwise the chances
were that he would not see Miriam at all. His enemy, Dockwrath,
would be sure to keep him from her presence. Dockwrath had
ever been inordinately jealous. But when he came to the office-
door he hardly had the courage to pass on to that of the private
dwelling. His heart beat too quickly, and the idea of seeing
Miriam was almost too much for him. But, nevertheless, he did
carry out his plan, and did knock at the door of the house.

And it was opened by Miriam herself. He knew her instantly
in spite of all the change. He knew her, but the whole course of
his feelings were altered at the moment, and his blood was made
to run the other way. And she knew him too. ' La, John,' she
said, ' who'd have thought ot seeing you?' And she shifted the
baby whom she carried from one arm to the other as she gave him
her hand in token of welcome.

' It is a long time since we met,' he said. He felt hardly any
temptation now to call her Miriam. Indeed it would have seemed
altogether in opposition to the common order of things to do so.
She was no longer Miriam, but the maternal Dockwrath;—the
mother of that long string of dirty children whom he saw gathered
in the passage behind her. He had known as a fact that she had
all the children, but the fact had not made the proper impression
on his mind till he had seen them.

' A long time! 'Deed then it is. Why we've hardly seen each
other since you used to be a courting of me; have we? But, my!
John; why haven't you got a wife for yourself these many years?
But come in. I'm glad to see every bit of you, so I am ; though
I've hardly a place to put you to sit down in.' And then she
opened a door and took him into a little sitting-room on the left-
hand side of the passage.

His feeling of intense enmity to Dockwrath was beginning to
wear away, and one of modified friendship for the whole family
was supervening. It was much better that it should be so. He
could not understand before how Dockwrath had had the heart to
write to him and call him John, but now he did understand it.
He felt that he could himself be friendly with Dockwrath now,
and forgive him all the injury ; he felt also that it would not go
so much against the grain with him to marry that friend as to
whom his sister would so often solicit him.

' I think you may venture to sit down upon them,' said Miriam,
' though I can't say that I have ever tried myself.' This speech
referred to the chairs with which her room was supplied, and
which Kenneby seemed to regard with suspicion.

' They are very nice I'm sure,' said he, ' but I don't think I ever
saw any like them.'

'Nor nobody else either. But don't you tell him so,' and she nodded with her head to the side of the house on which the office stood. 'I had as nice a set of mahoganys as ever a woman could want, and bought with my own money too, John; but he's took them away to furnish some of his lodgings opposite, and put them things here in their place. Don't, Sam; you'll have 'em all twisted about nohows in no time if you go to use 'em in that way.'

'I wants to see the pictur' on the table,' said Sam.

'Drat the picture,' said Mrs. Dockwrath. 'It was hard, wasn't it, John, to see my own mahoganys, as I had rubbed with my own hands till they was ever so bright, and as was bought with my own money too, took away and them things brought here? Sam, if you twist that round any more, I'll box your ears. One can't hear oneself speak with the noise.'

'They don't seem to be very useful,' said Kenneby.

'Useful! They're got up for cheatery;—that's what they're got up for. And that Dockwrath should be took in with 'em—he that's so sharp at everything,—that's what surprises me. But laws, John, it isn't the sharp ones that gets the best off. You was never sharp, but you're as smirk and smooth as though you came out of a band-box. I am glad to see you, John, so I am.' And she put her apron up to her eyes and wiped away a tear.

'Is Mr. Dockwrath at home?' said John.

'Sam, run round and see if your father's in the office. He'll be home to dinner, I know. Molly, do be quiet with your sister. I never see such a girl as you are for bothering. You didn't come down about business, did you, John?' And then Kenneby explained to her that he had been summoned by Dockwrath as to the matter of this Orley Farm trial. While he was doing so, Sam returned to say that his father had stepped out, but would be back in half an hour, and Mrs. Dockwrath, finding it impossible to make use of her company sitting-room, took her old lover into the family apartment which they all ordinarily occupied.

'You can sit down there at any rate without it all crunching under you, up to nothing.' And she emptied for him as she spoke the seat of an old well-worn horse-hair bottomed arm-chair. 'As to them tin things I wouldn't trust myself on one of them; and so I told him, angry as it made him. But now about poor Lady Mason——. Sam and Molly, you go into the garden, there's good children. They is so ready with their ears, John; and he contrives to get everything out of 'em. Now do tell me about this.'

Kenneby could not help thinking that the love match between Miriam and her husband had not turned out in all respects well, and I fear that he derived from the thought a certain feeling of consolation. 'He' was spoken about in a manner that did not betoken unfailing love and perfect confidence. Perhaps Miriam was at this moment thinking that she might have done better with her youth and her money! She was thinking of nothing of the kind. Her mind was one that dwelt on the present, not on the past. She was unhappy about her furniture, unhappy about the frocks of those four younger children, unhappy that the loaves of bread went faster and faster every day, very unhappy now at the savageness with which her husband prosecuted his anger against Lady Mason. But it did not occur to her to be unhappy because she had not become Mrs. Kenneby.

Mrs. Dockwrath had more to tell in the matter than had Kenneby, and when the elder of the children who were at home had been disposed of she was not slow to tell it. ' Isn't it dreadful, John, to think that they should come against her now, and the will all settled as it was twenty year ago? But you won't say anything against her; will you now, John? She was always a good friend to you; wasn't she? Though it wasn't much use; was it?' It was thus that she referred to the business before them, and to the love passages of her early youth at the same time.

' It's a very dreadful affair,' said Kenneby, very solemnly; ' and the more I think of it the more dreadful it becomes.'

' But you won't say anything against her, will you? You won't go over to his side; eh, John?'

' I don't know much about sides,' said he.

' He'll get himself into trouble with it; I know he will. I do so wish you'd tell him, for he can't hurt you if you stand up to him. If I speak,—Lord bless you, I don't dare to call my soul my own for a week afterwards.'

' Is he so very——'

' Oh, dreadful, John. He's bid me never speak a word to her. But for all that I used till she went away down to The Cleeve yonder. And what do you think they say now? And I do believe it too. They say that Sir Peregrine is going to make her his lady. If he does that it stands to reason that Dockwrath and Joseph Mason will get the worst of it. I'm sure I hope they will; only he'll be twice as hard if he don't make money by it in some way.'

' Will he, now?'

' Indeed he will. You never knew anything like him for hardness if things go wrong awhile. I know he's got lots of money, because he's always buying up bits of houses; besides, what has he done with mine? but yet sometimes you'd hardly think he'd let me have bread enough for the children—and as for clothes——!' Poor Miriam! It seemed that her husband shared with her but few of the spoils or triumphs of his profession.

Tidings now came in from the office that Dockwrath was there. ' You'll come round and eat a bit of dinner with us?' said she,

hesitatingly. He felt that she hesitated, and hesitated himself in his
reply. 'He must say something in the way of asking you, you
know, and then say you'll come. His manner's nothing to you,
you know. Do now. It does me good to look at you, John; it
does indeed.' And then, without making any promise, he left her
and went round to the office.

Kenneby had made up his mind, talking over the matter with
Moulder and his sister, that he would be very reserved in any communication which he might make to Dockwrath as to his possible
evidence at the coming trial; but nevertheless when Dockwrath
had got him into his office, the attorney made him give a succinct
account of everything he knew, taking down his deposition in a
regular manner. 'And now if you'll just sign that,' Dockwrath
said to him when he had done.

'I don't know about signing,' said Kenneby. 'A man should
never write his own name unless he knows why.'

'You must sign your own deposition;' and the attorney frowned
at him and looked savage. 'What would a judge say to you in
court if you had made such a statement as this, affecting the character of a woman like Lady Mason, and then had refused to sign
it? You'd never be able to hold up your head again.'

'Wouldn't I?' said Kenneby gloomily; and he did sign it. This
was a great triumph to Dockwrath. Mat Round had succeeded in
getting the deposition of Bridget Bolster, but he had got that of
John Kenneby.

'And now,' said Dockwrath, 'I'll tell you what we'll do;—we'll
go to the Blue Posts—you remember the Blue Posts?—and I'll
stand a beef steak and a glass of brandy and water. I suppose
you'll go back to London by the 3 P.M. train. We shall have lots
of time.'

Kenneby said that he should go back by the 3 P.M. train, but he
declined, with considerable hesitation, the beef steak and brandy
and water. After what had passed between him and Miriam he
could not go to the Blue Posts with her husband.

'Nonsense, man,' said Dockwrath. 'You must dine somewhere.'

But Kenneby said that he should dine in London. He always
preferred dining late. Besides, it was a long time since he had
been at Hamworth, and he was desirous of taking a walk that he
might renew his associations.

'Associations!' said Dockwrath with a sneer. According to his
ideas a man could have no pleasant associations with a place unless
he had made money there or been in some way successful. Now
John Kenneby had enjoyed no success at Hamworth. 'Well then,
if you prefer associations to the Blue Posts I'll say good-bye to you.
I don't understand it myself. We shall see each other at the trial
you know.' Kenneby with a sigh said that he supposed they should.

' Are you going into the house,' said Dockwrath, ' to see her again?' and he indicated with his head the side on which his wife was, as she before had indicated his side.

' Well, yes; I think I'll say good-bye.'

' Don't be talking to her about this affair. She understands nothing about it, and everything goes up to that woman at Orley Farm.' And so they parted.

' And he wanted you to go to the Blue Posts, did he?' said Miriam when she heard of the proposition. ' It's like him. If there is to be any money spent it's anywhere but at home.'

' But I aint going,' said John.

' He'll go before the day's out, though he mayn't get his dinner there. And he'll be ever so free when he's there. He'll stand brandy and water to half Hamworth when he thinks he can get anything by it; but if you'll believe me, John, though I've all the fag of the house on me, and all them children, I can't get a pint of beer—not regular—betwixt breakfast and bedtime.' Poor Miriam! Why had she not taken advice when she was younger? John Kenneby would have given her what beer was good for her, quite regularly.

Then he went out and took his walk, sauntering away to the gate of Orley Farm, and looking up the avenue. He ventured up some way, and there at a distance before him he saw Lucius Mason walking up and down, from the house towards the road and back again, swinging a heavy stick in his hand, with his hat pressed down over his brows. Kenneby had no desire to speak to him; so he returned to the gate, and thence went back to the station, escaping the town by a side lane; and in this way he got back to London without holding further communication with the people of Hamworth.

CHAPTER III.

JOHN KENNEBY'S COURTSHIP.

' She's as sweet a temper, John, as ever stirred a lump of sugar in her tea,' said Mrs. Moulder to her brother, as they sat together over the fire in Great St. Helen's on that same evening,—after his return from Hamworth. ' That she is,—and so Smiley always found her. "She's always the same," Smiley said to me many a day. And what can a man want more than that?'

' That's quite true,' said John.

' And then as to her habits—I never knew her take a drop too much since first I set eyes on her, and that's nigh twenty years ago.'

She likes things comfortable ;—and why shouldn't she, with two
hundred a year of her own coming out of the Kingsland Road brick-
fields ? As for dress, her things is beautiful, and she is the woman
that takes care of 'em ! Why, I remember an Irish tabinet as
Smiley gave her when first that venture in the brick-fields came up
money ; if that tabinet is as much as turned yet, why, I'll eat it.
And then, the best of it is, she'll have you to-morrow. Indeed she
will ; or to-night, if you'll ask her. Goodness gracious ! if there
aint Moulder !' And the excellent wife jumped up from her seat,
poked the fire, emptied the most comfortable arm-chair, and hurried
out to the landing at the top of the stairs. Presently the noise of
a loudly wheezing pair of lungs was heard, and the commercial
traveller, enveloped from head to foot in coats and comforters, made
his appearance. He had just returned from a journey, and having
deposited his parcels and packages at the house of business of
Hubbles and Grease in Houndsditch, had now returned to the
bosom of his family. It was a way he had, not to let his wife know
exactly the period of his return. Whether he thought that by so
doing he might keep her always on the alert and ready for marital
inspection, or whether he disliked to tie himself down by the obligation of a fixed time for his return, Mrs. Moulder had never made
herself quite sure. But on neither view of the subject did she
admire this practice of her lord. She had on many occasions
pointed out to him how much more snug she could make him if he
would only let her know when he was coming. But he had never
taken the hint, and in these latter days she ceased to give it.

' Why, I'm uncommon cold,' he said in answer to his wife's inquiries after his welfare. ' And so would you be too, if you'd come
up from Leeds since you'd had your dinner. What, John, are you
there ? The two of you are making yourself snug enough, I suppose, with something hot ?'

' Not a drop he's had yet since he's been in the house,' said
Mrs. Moulder. ' And he's hardly as much as darkened the door
since you left it.' And Mrs. Moulder added, with some little hesitation in her voice, ' Mrs. Smiley is coming in to-night, Moulder.'

' The d—— she is ! There's always something of that kind when
I gets home tired out, and wants to be comfortable. I mean to
have my supper to myself, as I likes it, if all the Mother Smileys in
London choose to come the way. What on earth is she coming
here for this time of night ?'

' Why, Moulder, you know.'

' No ; I don't know. I only know this, that when a man's used
up with business he don't want to have any of that nonsense under
his nose.'

' If you mean me——' began John Kenneby.

' I don't mean you ; of course not ; and I don't mean anybody.

Here, take my coats, will you? and let me have a pair of slippers. If Mrs. Smiley thinks that I'm going to change my pants, or put myself about for her——'

'Laws, Moulder, she don't expect that.'

'She won't get it any way. Here's John dressed up as if he was going to a box in the the-atre. And you—why should you be going to expense, and knocking out things that costs money, because Mother Smiley's coming? I'll Smiley her.'

'Now, Moulder—' But Mrs. Moulder knew that it was of no use speaking to him at the present moment. Her task should be this,—to feed and cosset him if possible into good humour before her guest should arrive. Her praises of Mrs. Smiley had been very fairly true. But nevertheless she was a lady who had a mind and voice of her own, as any lady has a right to possess who draws in her own right two hundred a year out of a brick-field in the Kingsland Road. Such a one knows that she is above being snubbed, and Mrs. Smiley knew this of herself as well as any lady; and if Moulder, in his wrath, should call her Mother Smiley, or give her to understand that he regarded her as an old woman, that lady would probably walk herself off in great dudgeon,—herself and her share in the brick-field. To tell the truth, Mrs. Smiley required that considerable deference should be paid to her.

Mrs. Moulder knew well what was her husband's present ailment. He had dined as early as one, and on his journey up from Leeds to London had refreshed himself with drink only. That last glass of brandy which he had taken at the Peterborough station had made him cross. If she could get him to swallow some hot food before Mrs. Smiley came, all might yet be well.

'And what's it to be, M.?' she said in her most insinuating voice —'there's a lovely chop down stairs, and there's nothing so quick as that.'

'Chop!' he said, and it was all he did say at the moment.

'There's a 'am in beautiful cut,' she went on, showing by the urgency of her voice how anxious she was on the subject.

For the moment he did not answer her at all, but sat facing the fire, and running his fat fingers through his uncombed hair. 'Mrs. Smiley!' he said; 'I remember when she was kitchen-maid at old Pott's.'

'She aint nobody's kitchen-maid now,' said Mrs. Moulder, almost prepared to be angry in the defence of her friend.

'And I never could make out when it was that Smiley married her,—that is, if he ever did.'

'Now, Moulder, that's shocking of you. Of course he married her. She and I is nearly an age as possible, though I think she is a year over me. She says not, and it aint nothing to me. But I remember the wedding as if it was yesterday. You and I had never

set eyes on each other then, M.' This last she added in a plaintive
tone, hoping to soften him.

'Are you going to keep me here all night without anything?' he
then said. 'Let me have some whisky,—hot, with;—and don't
stand there looking at nothing.'

'But you'll take some solids with it, Moulder? Why it stands
to reason you'll be famished.'

'Do as you're bid, will you, and give me the whisky. Are you
going to tell me when I'm to eat and when I'm to drink, like a
child?' This he said in that tone of voice which made Mrs. Moulder
know that he meant to be obeyed; and though she was sure that he
would make himself drunk, she was compelled to minister to his
desires. She got the whisky and hot water, the lemon and sugar,
and set the things beside him; and then she retired to the sofa.
John Kenneby the while sat perfectly silent looking on. Perhaps
he was considering whether he would be able to emulate the
domestic management of Dockwrath or of Moulder when he should
have taken to himself Mrs. Smiley and the Kingsland brick-field.

'If you've a mind to help yourself, John, I suppose you'll do it,'
said Moulder.

'None for me just at present, thank'ee,' said Kenneby.

'I suppose you wouldn't swallow nothing less than wine in them
togs?' said the other, raising his glass to his lips. 'Well, here's
better luck, and I'm blessed if it's not wanting. I'm pretty well
tired of this go, and so I mean to let 'em know pretty plainly.'

All this was understood by Mrs. Moulder, who knew that it only
signified that her husband was half tipsy, and that in all probability he would be whole tipsy before long. There was no help
for it. Were she to remonstrate with him in his present mood, he
would very probably fling the bottle at her head. Indeed, remon-
strances were never of avail with him. So she sat herself down,
thinking how she would run down when she heard Mrs. Smiley's
step, and beg that lady to postpone her visit. Indeed it would be
well to send John to convey her home again.

Moulder swallowed his glass of hot toddy fast, and then mixed
another. His eyes were very bloodshot, and he sat staring at the
fire. His hands were thrust into his pockets between the periods
of his drinking, and he no longer spoke to any one. 'I'm —— if
I stand it,' he growled forth, addressing himself. 'I've stood it a
—— deal too long.' And then he finished the second glass. There
was a sort of understanding on the part of his wife that such inter-
jections as these referred to Hubbles and Grease, and indicated a
painfully advanced state of drink. There was one hope; the double
heat, that of the fire and of the whisky, might make him sleep;
and if so, he would be safe for two or three hours.

'I'm blessed if I do, and that's all,' said Moulder, grasping the whisky-bottle for the third time. His wife sat behind him very anxious, but not daring to interfere. 'It's going over the table, M.,' she then said.

'D—— the table!' he answered; and then his head fell forward on his breast, and he was fast asleep with the bottle in his hand.

'Put your hand to it, John,' said Mrs. Moulder in a whisper. But John hesitated. The lion might rouse himself if his prey were touched.

'He'll let it go easy if you put your hand to it. 'He's safe enough now. There. If we could only get him back from the fire a little, or his face'll be burnt off of him.'

'But you wouldn't move him?'

'Well, yes; we'll try. I've done it before, and he's never stirred. Come here, just behind. The casters is good, I know. Laws! aint he heavy?' And then they slowly dragged him back. He grunted out some half-pronounced threat as they moved him; but he did not stir, and his wife knew that she was again mistress of the room for the next two hours. It was true that he snored horribly, but then she was used to that.

'You won't let her come up, will you?' said John.

'Why not? She knows what men is as well I do. Smiley wasn't that way often, I believe; but he was awful when he was. He wouldn't sleep it off, quite innocent, like that; but would break everything about the place, and then cry like a child after it. Now Moulder's got none of that about him. The worst of it is, how am I ever to get him into bed when he wakes?'

While the anticipation of this great trouble was still on her mind, the ring at the bell was heard, and John Kenneby went down to the outer door that he might pay to Mrs. Smiley the attention of waiting upon her up stairs. And up stairs she came, bristling with silk— the identical Irish tabinet, perhaps, which had never been turned— and conscious of the business which had brought her.

'What—Moulder's asleep is he?' she said as she entered the room. 'I suppose that's as good as a pair of gloves, any way.'

'He aint just very well,' said Mrs. Moulder, winking at her friend; 'he's tired after a long journey.'

'Oh—h! ah—h!' said Mrs. Smiley, looking down upon the sleeping beauty, and understanding everything at a glance. 'It's uncommon bad for him, you know, because he's so given to flesh.'

'It's as much fatigue as anything,' said the wife.

'Yes, I dare say;' and Mrs. Smiley shook her head. 'If he fatigues himself so much as that often he'll soon be off the hooks.'

Much was undoubtedly to be borne from two hundred a year in a brick-field, especially when that two hundred a year was coming so very near home; but there is an amount of impertinent familiarity which must be put down even in two hundred a year. 'I've known worse cases than him, my dear; and that ended worse.'

'Oh, I dare say. But you're mistook if you mean Smiley. It was 'sepilus as took him off, as everybody knows.'

'Well, my dear, I'm sure I'm not going to say anything against that. And now, John, do help her off with her bonnet and shawl, while I get the tea-things.'

Mrs. Smiley was a firm set, healthy-looking woman of—about forty. She had large, dark, glassy eyes, which were bright without sparkling. Her cheeks were very red, having a fixed settled colour that never altered with circumstances. Her black wiry hair was ended in short crisp curls, which sat close to her head. It almost collected like a wig, but the hair was in truth her own. Her mouth was small, and her lips thin, and they gave to her face a look of sharpness that was not quite agreeable. Nevertheless she was not a bad-looking woman, and with such advantages as two hundred a year and the wardrobe which Mrs. Moulder had described, was no doubt entitled to look for a second husband.

'Well, Mr. Kenneby, and how do you find yourself this cold weather? Dear, how he do snore; don't he?'

'Yes,' said Kenneby, very thoughtfully, 'he does rather.' He was thinking of Miriam Usbech as she was twenty years ago, and of Mrs. Smiley as she appeared at present. Not that he felt inclined to grumble at the lot prepared for him, but that he would like to take a few more years to think about it.

And then they sat down to tea. The lovely chops which Moulder had despised, and the ham in beautiful cut which had failed to tempt him, now met with due appreciation. Mrs. Smiley, though she had never been known to take a drop too much, did like to have things comfortable; and on this occasion she made an excellent meal, with a large pocket-handkerchief of Moulder's—brought in for the occasion—stretched across the broad expanse of the Irish tabinet. 'We sha'n't wake him, shall we?' said she, as she took her last bit of muffin.

'Not till he wakes natural, of hisself,' said Mrs. Moulder. 'When he's worked it off, he'll rouse himself, and I shall have to get him to bed.'

'He'll be a bit patchy then, won't he?'

'Well, just for a while of course he will,' said Mrs. Moulder. 'But there's worse than him. To-morrow morning, maybe, he'll be just as sweet as sweet. It don't hang about him, sullen like. That' what I hate, when it hangs about 'em.' Then the tea-things were taken away, Mrs. Smiley in her familiarity assisting in the removal, and—in spite of the example now before them—some more sugar and some more spirits, and some more hot water were put upon the table. 'Well, I don't mind just the least taste in life, Mrs. Moulder, as we're quite between friends; and I'm sure you'll want it to-night to keep yourself up.' Mrs. Moulder would have answered these last words with some severity had she not felt that good humour now might be of great value to her brother.

'Well, John, and what is it you've got to say to her?' said Mrs. Moulder, as she put down her empty glass. Between friends who understood each other so well, and at their time of life, what was the use of ceremony?

'La, Mrs. Moulder, what should he have got to say? Nothing I'm sure as I'd think of listening to.'

'You try her, John.'

'Not but what I've the greatest respect in life for Mr. Kenneby, and always did have. If you must have anything to do with men, I've always said, recommend me to them as is quiet and steady, and hasn't got too much of the gab;—a quiet man is the man for me any day.'

'Well, John?' said Mrs. Moulder.

'Now, Mrs. Moulder, can't you keep yourself to yourself, and we shall do very well. Laws, how he do snore! When his head goes bobbling that way I do so fear he'll have a fit.'

'No he won't; he's coming to, all right. Well, John?'

'I'm sure I shall be very happy,' said John, 'if she likes it. She says that she respects me, and I'm sure I've a great respect for her. I always had—even when Mr. Smiley was alive.'

'It's very good of you to say so,' said she; not speaking however as though she were quite satisfied. What was the use of his remembering Smiley just at present?

'Enough's enough between friends any day,' said Mrs. Moulder. 'So give her your hand, John.'

'I think it'll be right to say one thing first,' said Kenneby, with a solemn and deliberate tone.

'And what's that?' said Mrs. Smiley, eagerly.

'In such a matter as this,' continued Kenneby, 'where the hearts are concerned——'

'You didn't say anything about hearts yet,' said Mrs. Smiley, with some measure of approbation in her voice.

'Didn't I,' said Kenneby. 'Then it was an omission on my part, and I beg leave to apologize. But what I was going to say is this: when the hearts are concerned, everything should be honest and above-board.'

'Oh of course,' said Mrs. Moulder; 'and I'm sure she don't suspect nothing else.'

'You'd better let him go on,' said Mrs. Smiley.

'My heart has not been free from woman's lovely image.'

'And isn't free now, is it, John?' said Mrs. Moulder.

'I've had my object, and though she's been another's, still I've kept her image on my heart.'

'But it aint there any longer, John? He's speaking of twenty years ago, Mrs. Smiley.'

'It's quite beautiful to hear him,' said Mrs. Smiley. 'Go on, Mr. Kenneby.'

'The years are gone by as though they was nothing, and still I've had her image on my heart. I've seen her to-day.'

'Her gentleman's still alive, aint he?' asked Mrs. Smiley.

'And likely to live,' said Mrs. Moulder.

'I've seen her to-day,' Kenneby continued; 'and now the Adriatic's free to wed another.'

Neither of the ladies present exactly understood the force of the quotation; but as it contained an appropriate reference to marriage, and apparently to a second marriage, it was taken by both of them in good part. He was considered to have made his offer, and Mrs. Smiley thereupon formally accepted him. 'He's spoke quite handsome, I'm sure,' said Mrs. Smiley to his sister; 'and I don't know that any woman has a right to expect more. As to the brick-fields——.' And then there was a slight reference to business, with which it will not be necessary that the readers of this story should embarrass themselves.

Soon after that Mr. Kenneby saw Mrs. Smiley home in a cab, and poor Mrs. Moulder sat by her lord till he roused himself from his sleep. Let us hope that her troubles with him were as little vexatious as possible; and console ourselves with the reflection that at twelve o'clock the next morning, after the second bottle of soda and brandy, he was ' as sweet as sweet.'

CHAPTER IV.

SHOWING HOW LADY MASON COULD BE VERY NOBLE.

LADY MASON returned to The Cleeve after her visit to Mr. Furnival's chambers, and nobody asked her why she had been to London or whom she had seen. Nothing could be more gracious than the deference which was shown to her, and the perfect freedom of action which was accorded to her. On that very day Lady Staveley had called at The Cleeve, explaining to Sir Peregrine and Mrs. Orme that her visit was made expressly to Lady Mason. 'I should have called at Orley Farm, of course,' said Lady Staveley, 'only that I hear that Lady Mason is likely to prolong her visit with you. I must trust to you, Mrs. Orme, to make all that understood.' Sir Peregrine took upon himself to say that it all should be understood, and then drawing Lady Staveley aside, told her of his own intended marriage. 'I cannot but be aware,' he said, 'that I have no business to trouble you with an affair that is so exclusively our own; but I have a wish, which perhaps you may understand, that there should be no secret about it. I think it better, for her sake,

that it should be known. If the connection can be of any service to
her, she should reap that benefit now, when some people are treating
her name with a barbarity which I believe to be almost unparalleled
in this country.' In answer to this Lady Staveley was of course
obliged to congratulate him, and she did so with the best grace in
her power ; but it was not easy to say much that was cordial, and
as she drove back with Mrs. Arbuthnot to Noningsby the words
which were said between them as to Lady Mason were not so kindly
meant towards that lady as their remarks on their journey to The
Cleeve.

Lady Staveley had hoped,—though she had hardly expressed her
hope even to herself, and certainly had not spoken of it to any one
else,—that she might have been able to say a word or two to Mrs.
Orme about young Peregrine, a word or two that would have shown
her own good feeling towards the young man,—her own regard, and
almost affection for him, even though this might have been done
without any mention of Madeline's name. She might have learned
in this way whether young Orme had made known at home what
had been his hopes and what his disappointments, and might have
formed some opinion whether or no he would renew his suit. She
would not have been the first to mention her daughter's name ; but
if Mrs. Orme should speak of it, then the subject would be free for
her, and she could let it be known that the heir of The Cleeve
should at any rate have her sanction and good will. What happiness could be so great for her as that of having a daughter so settled,
within eight miles of her ? And then it was not only that a marriage
between her daughter and Peregrine Orme would be an event so
fortunate, but also that those feelings with reference to Felix
Graham were so unfortunate ! That young heart, she thought, could
not as yet be heavy laden, and it might be possible that the whole
affair should be made to run in the proper course,—if only it could
be done at once. But now, that tale which Sir Peregrine had told
her respecting himself and Lady Mason had made it quite impossible
that anything should be said on the other subject. And then again,
if it was decreed that the Noningsby family and the family of The
Cleeve should be connected, would not such a marriage as this
between the baronet and Lady Mason be very injurious ? So that
Lady Staveley was not quite happy as she returned to her own house.

Lady Staveley's message, however, for Lady Mason was given
with all its full force. Sir Peregrine had felt grateful for what had
been done, and Mrs. Orme, in talking of it, made quite the most of
it. Civility from the Staveleys to the Ormes would not, in the ordinary course of things, be accounted of any special value. The two
families might, and naturally would, know each other on intimate
terms. But the Ormes would as a matter of course stand the
highest in general estimation. Now, however, the Ormes had to

bear up Lady Mason with them. Sir Peregrine had so willed it, and Mrs. Orme had not for a moment thought of contesting the wish of one whose wishes she had never contested. No words were spoken on the subject; but still with both of them there was a feeling that Lady Staveley's countenance and open friendship would be of value. When it had come to this with Sir Peregrine Orme, he was already disgraced in his own estimation,—already disgraced, although he declared to himself a thousand times that he was only doing his duty as a gentleman.

On that evening Lady Mason said no word of her new purpose. She had pledged herself both to Peregrine Orme and to Mr. Furnival. To both she had made a distinct promise that she would break off her engagement, and she knew well that the deed should be done at once. But how was she to do it? With what words was she to tell him that she had changed her mind and would not take the hand that he had offered to her? She feared to be a moment alone with Peregrine lest he should tax her with the non-fulfilment of her promise. But in truth Peregrine at the present moment was thinking more of another matter. It had almost come home to him that his grandfather's marriage might facilitate his own; and though he still was far from reconciling himself to the connection with Lady Mason, he was almost disposed to put up with it.

On the following day, at about noon, a chariot with a pair of post-horses was brought up to the door of The Cleeve at a very fast pace, and the two ladies soon afterwards learned that Lord Alston was closeted with Sir Peregrine. Lord Alston was one of Sir Peregrine's oldest friends. He was a man senior both in age and standing to the baronet; and, moreover, he was a friend who came but seldom to The Cleeve, although his friendship was close and intimate. Nothing was said between Mrs. Orme and Lady Mason, but each dreaded that Lord Alston had come to remonstrate about the marriage. And so in truth he had. The two old men were together for about an hour, and then Lord Alston took his departure without asking for, or seeing any other one of the family. Lord Alston had remonstrated about the marriage, using at last very strong language to dissuade the baronet from a step which he thought so unfortunate; but he had remonstrated altogether in vain. Every word he had used was not only fruitless, but injurious; for Sir Peregrine was a man whom it was very difficult to rescue by opposition, though no man might be more easily led by assumed acquiescence.

' Orme, my dear fellow,' said his lordship, towards the end of the interview, ' it is my duty, as an old friend, to tell you this.'

' Then, Lord Alston, you have done your duty.'

' Not while a hope remains that I may prevent this marriage.'

' There is ground for no such hope on your part; and permit me to say that the expression of such a hope to me is greatly wanting in courtesy.'

'You and I,' continued Lord Alston, without apparent attention to the last words which Sir Peregrine had spoken, 'have nearly come to the end of our tether here. Our careers have been run; and I think I may say as regards both, but I may certainly say as regards you, that they have been so run that we have not disgraced those who preceded us. Our dearest hopes should be that our names may never be held as a reproach by those who come after us.'

'With God's blessing I will do nothing to disgrace my family.'

'But, Orme, you and I cannot act as may those whose names in the world are altogether unnoticed. I know that you are doing this from a feeling of charity to that lady.'

'I am doing it, Lord Alston, because it so pleases me.'

'But your first charity is due to your grandson. Suppose that he was making an offer of his hand to the daughter of some nobleman,—as he is so well entitled to do,—how would it affect his hopes if it were known that you at the time had married a lady whose misfortune made it necessary that she should stand at the bar in a criminal court?'

'Lord Alston,' said Sir Peregrine, rising from his chair, 'I trust that my grandson may never rest his hopes on any woman whose heart could be hardened against him by such a thought as that.'

'But what if she should be guilty?' said Lord Alston.

'Permit me to say,' said Sir Peregrine, still standing, and standing now bolt upright, as though his years did not weigh on him a feather, 'that this conversation has gone far enough. There are some surmises to which I cannot listen, even from Lord Alston.'

Then his lordship shrugged his shoulders, declared that in speaking as he had spoken he had endeavoured to do a friendly duty by an old friend,—certainly the oldest, and almost the dearest friend he had,—and so he took his leave. The wheels of the chariot were heard grating over the gravel, as he was carried away from the door at a gallop, and the two ladies looked into each other's faces, saying nothing. Sir Peregrine was not seen from that time till dinner; but when he did come into the drawing-room his manner to Lady Mason was, if possible, more gracious and more affectionate than ever.

'So Lord Alston was here to-day,' Peregrine said to his mother that night before he went to bed.

'Yes, he was here.'

'It was about this marriage, mother, as sure as I am standing here.'

'I don't think Lord Alston would interfere about that, Perry.'

'Wouldn't he? He would interfere about anything he did not

like; that is, as far as the pluck of it goes. Of course he can't like
it. Who can?'

'Perry, your grandfather likes it; and surely he has a right to
please himself.'

'I don't know about that. You might say the same thing if he
wanted to kill all the foxes about the place, or do any other out-
landish thing. Of course he might kill them, as far as the law goes,
but where would he be afterwards? She hasn't said anything to
him, has she?'

'I think not.'

'Nor to you?'

'No; she has not spoken to me; not about that.'

'She promised me positively that she would break it off.'

'You must not be hard on her, Perry.'

Just as these words were spoken, there came a low knock at
Mrs. Orme's dressing-room door. This room, in which Mrs. Orme
was wont to sit for an hour or so every night before she went to
bed, was the scene of all the meetings of affection which took place
between the mother and the son. It was a pretty little apartment,
opening from Mrs. Orme's bed-room, which had at one time been
the exclusive property of Peregrine's father. But by degrees it had
altogether assumed feminine attributes; had been furnished with
soft chairs, a sofa, and a lady's table; and though called by the
name of Mrs. Orme's dressing-room, was in fact a separate sitting-
room devoted to her exclusive use. Sir Peregrine would not for
worlds have entered it without sending up his name beforehand,
and this he did on only very rare occasions. But Lady Mason had
of late been admitted here, and Mrs. Orme now knew that it was
her knock.

'Open the door, Perry,' she said; 'it is Lady Mason.' He did
open the door, and Lady Mason entered.

'Oh, Mr. Orme, I did not know that you were here.'

'I am just off. Good night, mother.'

'But I am disturbing you.'

'No, we had done;' and he stooped down and kissed his mother.
'Good night, Lady Mason. Hadn't I better put some coals on for
you, or the fire will be out?' He did put on the coals, and then
he went his way.

Lady Mason while he was doing this had sat down on the sofa,
close to Mrs. Orme; but when the door was closed Mrs. Orme was
the first to speak. 'Well, dear,' she said, putting her hand caressingly on the other's arm. I am inclined to think that had there
been no one whom Mrs. Orme was bound to consult but herself,
she would have wished that this marriage should have gone on. To
her it would have been altogether pleasant to have had Lady Mason
ever with her in the house; and she had none of those fears as

to future family retrospections respecting which Lord Alston had spoken with so much knowledge of the world.   As it was, her manner was so caressing and affectionate to her guest, that she did much more to promote Sir Peregrine's wishes than to oppose them. ' Well, dear,' she said, with her sweetest smile.

' I am so sorry that I have driven your son away.'

' He was going.   Besides, it would make no matter; he would stay here all night sometimes, if I didn't drive him away myself. He comes here and writes his letters at the most unconscionable hours, and uses up all my note-paper in telling some horsekeeper what is to be done with his mare.'

' Ah, how happy you must be to have him ! '

' Well, I suppose I am,' she said, as a tear came into her eyes. ' We are so hard to please.   I am all anxiety now that he should be married ; and if he were married, then I suppose I should grumble because I did not see so much of him.   He would be more settled if he would marry, I think.   For myself I approve of early marriages for young men.'   And then she thought of her own husband whom she had loved so well and lost so soon.   And so they sat silent for a while, each thinking of her own lot in life.

' But I must not keep you up all night,' said Lady Mason.

' Oh, I do so like you to be here,' said the other.   Then again she took hold of her arm, and the two women kissed each other.

' But, Edith,' said the other, ' I came in here to-night with a purpose.   I have something that I wish to say to you.   Can you listen to me ?'

' Oh yes,' said Mrs. Orme ; ' surely.'

' Has your son been talking to you about—about what was said between him and me the other day ?   I am sure he has, for I know he tells you everything,—as he ought to do.'

' Yes, he did speak to me,' said Mrs. Orme, almost trembling with anxiety.

' I am so glad, for now it will be easier for me to tell you.   And since that I have seen Mr. Furnival, and he says the same.   I tell you because you are so good and so loving to me.   I will keep nothing from you ; but you must not tell Sir Peregrine that I talked to Mr. Furnival about this.'

Mrs. Orme gave the required promise, hardly thinking at the moment whether or no she would be guilty of any treason against Sir Peregrine in doing so.

' I think I should have said nothing to him, though he is so very old a friend, had not Mr. Orme——'

' You mean Peregrine ?'

' Yes ; had not he been so—so earnest about it.   He told me that if I married Sir Peregrine I should be doing a cruel injury to him —to his grandfather.'

' He should not have said that.'

' Yes, Edith,—if he thinks it. He told me that I should be turning all his friends against him. So I promised him that I would speak to Sir Peregrine, and break it off if it be possible.'

' He told me that.'

' And then I spoke to Mr. Furnival, and he told me that I should be blamed by all the world if I were to marry him. I cannot tell you all he said, but he said this : that if—if——'

' If what, dear ?'

' If in the court they should say——'

' Say what ?'

' Say that I did this thing,—then Sir Peregrine would be crushed, and would die with a broken heart.'

' But they cannot say that ;—it is impossible. You do not think it possible that they can do so ?' And then again she took hold of Lady Mason's arm, and looked up anxiously into her face. She looked up anxiously, not suspecting anything, not for a moment presuming it possible that such a verdict could be justly given, but in order that she might see how far the fear of a fate so horrible was operating on her friend. Lady Mason's face was pale and woeworn, but not more so than was now customary with her.

' One cannot say what may be possible,' she answered slowly. ' I suppose they would not go on with it if they did not think they had some chance of success.'

' You mean as to the property ?'

' Yes; as to the property.'

' But why should they not try that, if they must try it, without dragging you there ?'

' Ah, I do not understand ; or at least I cannot explain it. Mr. Furnival says that it must be so; and therefore I shall tell Sir Peregrine to-morrow that all this must be given up.' And then they sat together silently, holding each other by the hand.

' Good night, Edith,' Lady Mason said at last, getting up from her seat.

' Good night, dearest.'

' You will let me be your friend still, will you not ?' said Lady Mason.

' My friend! Oh yes; always my friend. Why should this interfere between you and me ?'

' But he will be very angry—at least I fear that he will. Not that—not that he will have anything to regret. But the very strength of his generosity and nobleness will make him angry. He will be indignant because I do not let him make this sacrifice for me. And then—and then—I fear I must leave this house.'

' Oh no, not that; I will speak to him. He will do anything for me.'

' It will be better perhaps that I should go. People will think that I am estranged from Lucius. But if I go, you will come to me? He will let you do that; will he not?'

And then there were warm, close promises given, and embraces interchanged. The women did love each other with a hearty, true love, and each longed that they might be left together. And yet how different they were, and how different had been their lives !

The prominent thought in Lady Mason's mind as she returned to her own room was this :—that Mrs. Orme had said no word to dissuade her from the line of conduct which she had proposed to herself. Mrs. Orme had never spoken against the marriage as Peregrine had spoken, and Mr. Furnival. Her heart had not been stern enough to allow her to do that. But was it not clear that her opinion was the same as theirs? Lady Mason acknowledged to herself that it was clear, and acknowledged to herself also that no one was in favour of the marriage. ' I will do it immediately after breakfast,' she said to herself. And then she sat down,—and sat through the half the night thinking of it.

Mrs. Orme, when she was left alone, almost rebuked herself in that she had said no word of counsel against the undertaking which Lady Mason proposed for herself. For Mr. Furnival and his opinion she did not care much. Indeed, she would have been angry with Lady Mason for speaking to Mr. Furnival on the subject, were it not that her pity was too deep to admit of any anger. That the truth must be established at the trial Mrs. Orme felt all but confident. When alone she would feel quite sure on this point, though a doubt would always creep in on her when Lady Mason was with her. But now, as she sat alone, she could not realize the idea that the fear of a verdict against her friend should offer any valid reason against the marriage. The valid reasons, if there were such, must be looked for elsewhere. And were these other reasons so strong in their validity? Sir Peregrine desired the marriage ; and so did Lady Mason herself, as regarded her own individual wishes. Mrs. Orme was sure that this was so. And then for her own self, she— Sir Peregrine's daughter-in-law, the only lady concerned in the matter—she also would have liked it. But her son disliked it, and she had yielded so far to the wishes of her son. Well ; was it not right that with her those wishes should be all but paramount ? And thus she endeavoured to satisfy her conscience as she retired to rest.

On the following morning the four assembled at breakfast. Lady Mason hardly spoke at all to any one. Mrs. Orme, who knew what was about to take place, was almost as silent; but Sir Peregrine had almost more to say than usual to his grandson. He was in good spirits, having firmly made up his mind on a certain point ; and he showed this by telling Peregrine that he would ride with him

immediately after breakfast. 'What has made you so slack about
your hunting during the last two or three days ?' he asked.

'I shall hunt to-morrow,' said Peregrine.

'Then you can afford time to ride with me through the woods
after breakfast.' And so it would have been arranged had not Lady
Mason immediately said that she hoped to be able to say a few words
to Sir Peregrine in the library after breakfast. *Place aux dames,*
said he. 'Peregrine, the horses can wait.' And so the matter was
arranged while they were still sitting over their toast.

Peregrine, as this was said, had looked at his mother, but she had
not ventured to take her eyes for a moment from the teapot. Then
he had looked at Lady Mason, and saw that she was, as it were,
going through a fashion of eating her breakfast. In order to break
the absolute silence of the room he muttered something about the
weather, and then his grandfather, with the same object, answered
him. After that no words were spoken till Sir Peregrine, rising
from his chair, declared that he was ready.

He got up and opened the door for his guest, and then hurrying
across the hall, opened the library door for her also, holding it till
she had passed in. Then he took her left hand in his, and passing
his right arm round her waist, asked her if anything disturbed
her.

'Oh yes,' she said, 'yes; there is much that disturbs me. I have
done very wrong.'

'How done wrong, Mary?' She could not recollect that he had
called her Mary before, and the sound she thought was very sweet;
—was very sweet, although she was over forty, and he over seventy
years of age.

'I have done very wrong, and I have now come here that I may
undo it. Dear Sir Peregrine, you must not be angry with me.'

'I do not think that I shall be angry with you; but what is it,
dearest ?'

But she did not know how to find words to declare her purpose.
It was comparatively an easy task to tell Mrs. Orme that she had
made up her mind not to marry Sir Peregrine, but it was by no
means easy to tell the baronet himself. And now she stood there
leaning over the fireplace, with his arm round her waist,—as it
behoved her to stand no longer, seeing the resolution to which she
had come. But still she did not speak.

'Well, Mary, what is it? I know there is something on your
mind or you would not have summoned me in here. Is it about
the trial ? Have you seen Mr. Furnival again ?'

'No ; it is not about the trial,' she said, avoiding the other
question.

'What is it then ?'

'Sir Peregrine, it is impossible that we should be married.' And thus she brought forth her tidings, as it were at a gasp, speaking at the moment with a voice that was almost indicative of anger.

'And why not?' said he, releasing her from his arm and looking at her.

'It cannot be,' she said.

'And why not, Lady Mason?'

'It cannot be,' she said again, speaking with more emphasis, and with a stronger tone.

'And is that all that you intend to tell me? Have I done anything that has offended you?'

'Offended me! No. I do not think that would be possible. The offence is on the other side——'

'Then, my dear,——'

'But listen to me now. It cannot be. I know that it is wrong. Everything tells me that such a marriage on your part would be a sacrifice,—a terrible sacrifice. You would be throwing away your great rank——'

'No,' shouted Sir Peregrine; 'not though I married a kitchen-maid,—instead of a lady who in social life is my equal.'

'Ah, no; I should not have said rank. You cannot lose that;—but your station in the world, the respect of all around you, the—the—the——'

'Who has been telling you all this?'

'I have wanted no one to tell me. Thinking of it has told it me all. My own heart which is full of gratitude and love for you has told me.'

'You have not seen Lord Alston?'

'Lord Alston! oh, no.'

'Has Peregrine been speaking to you?'

'Peregrine!'

'Yes; Peregrine; my grandson?'

'He has spoken to me.'

'Telling you to say this to me. Then he is an ungrateful boy; —a very ungrateful boy. I would have done anything to guard him from wrong in this matter.'

'Ah; now I see the evil that I have done. Why did I ever come into the house to make quarrels between you?'

'There shall be no quarrel. I will forgive him even that if you will be guided by me. And, dearest Mary, you must be guided by me now. This matter has gone too far for you to go back—unless, indeed, you will say that personally you have an aversion to the marriage.'

'Oh, no; no; it is not that,' she said eagerly. She could not help saying it with eagerness. She could not inflict the wound on his feelings which her silence would then have given.

'Under those circumstances, I have a right to say that the marriage must go on.'

'No; no.'

'But I say it must. Sit down, Mary.' And she did sit down, while he stood leaning over her and thus spoke. 'You speak of sacrificing me. I am an old man with not many more years before me. If I did sacrifice what little is left to me of life with the object of befriending one whom I really love, there would be no more in it than what a man might do, and still feel that the balance was on the right side. But here there will be no sacrifice. My life will be happier, and so will Edith's. And so indeed will that boy's, if he did but know it. For the world's talk, which will last some month or two, I care nothing. This I will confess, that if I were prompted to this only by my own inclination, only by love for you——' and as he spoke he held out his hand to her, and she could not refuse him hers—'in such a case I should doubt and hesitate and probably keep aloof from such a step. But it is not so. In doing this I shall gratify my own heart, and also serve you in your great troubles. Believe me, I have thought of that.'

'I know you have, Sir Peregrine,—and therefore it cannot be.'

'But therefore it shall be. The world knows it now; and were we to be separated after what has past, the world would say that I—I had thought you guilty of this crime.'

'I must bear all that.' And now she stood before him, not looking him in the face, but with her face turned down towards the ground, and speaking hardly above her breath.

'By heavens, no; not whilst I can stand by your side. Not whilst I have strength left to support you and thrust the lie down the throat of such a wretch as Joseph Mason. No, Mary, go back to Edith and tell her that you have tried it, but that there is no escape for you.' And then he smiled at her. His smile at times could be very pleasant!

But she did not smile as she answered him. 'Sir Peregrine,' she said; and she endeavoured to raise her face to his but failed.

'Well, my love.'

'Sir Peregrine, I am guilty.'

'Guilty! Guilty of what?' he said, startled rather than instructed by her words.

'Guilty of all this with which they charge me.' And then she threw herself at his feet, and wound her arms round his knees.

Guilty.

CHAPTER V.

I VENTURE to think, I may almost say to hope, that Lady Mason's confession at the end of the last chapter will not have taken anybody by surprise. If such surprise be felt I must have told my tale badly. I do not like such revulsions of feeling with regard to my characters as surprises of this nature must generate. That Lady Mason had committed the terrible deed for which she was about to be tried, that Mr. Furnival's suspicion of her guilt was only too well founded, that Mr. Dockwrath with his wicked ingenuity had discovered no more than the truth, will, in its open revelation, have caused no surprise to the reader;—but it did cause terrible surprise to Sir Peregrine Orme.

And now we must go back a little and endeavour to explain how it was that Lady Mason had made this avowal of her guilt. That she had not intended to do so when she entered Sir Peregrine's library is very certain. Had such been her purpose she would not have asked Mrs. Orme to visit her at Orley Farm. Had such a course of events been in her mind she would not have spoken of her departure from The Cleeve as doubtful. No. She had intended still to keep her terrible secret to herself; still to have leaned upon Sir Peregrine's arm as on the arm of a trusting friend. But he had overcome her by his generosity; and in her fixed resolve that he should not be dragged down into this abyss of misery the sudden determination to tell the truth at least to him had come upon her. She did tell him all; and then, as soon as the words were out of her mouth, the strength which had enabled her to do so deserted her, and she fell at his feet overcome by weakness of body as well as spirit.

But the words which she spoke did not at first convey to his mind their full meaning. Though she had twice repeated the assertion that she was guilty, the fact of her guilt did not come home to his understanding as a thing that he could credit. There was something, he doubted not, to surprise and harass him,—something which when revealed and made clear might, or might not, affect his purpose of marrying,—something which it behoved this woman to tell before she could honestly become his wife, something which was destined to give his heart a blow. But he was very far as yet from understanding the whole truth. Let us think of those we love best, and ask ourselves how much it would take to convince us of their guilt in such a matter. That thrusting of the lie down the throat of Joseph Mason had become to him so earnest a duty, that the task of believing the lie to be on the other side was no easy one. The blow which he had to suffer was a cruel blow. Lady Mason, however, was merciful, for she might have enhanced the cruelty tenfold.

He stood there wondering and bewildered for some minutes of time, while she, with her face hidden, still clung round his knees. 'What is it?' at last he said. 'I do not understand.' But she had no answer to make to him. Her great resolve had been quickly made and quickly carried out, but now the reaction left her powerless. He stooped down to raise her; but when he moved she fell prone upon the ground; he could hear her sobs as though her bosom would burst with them.

And then by degrees the meaning of her words began to break upon him. 'I am guilty of all this with which they charge me.' Could that be possible? Could it be that she had forged that will; that with base, premeditated contrivance she had stolen that property; stolen it and kept it from that day to this;—through all these long years? And then he thought of her pure life, of her womanly, dignified repose, of her devotion to her son,—such devotion indeed!—of her sweet pale face and soft voice! He thought of all this, and of his own love and friendship for her,—of Edith's love for her! He thought of it all, and he could not believe that she was guilty. There was some other fault, some much lesser fault than that, with which she charged herself. But there she lay at his feet, and it was necessary that he should do something towards lifting her to a seat.

He stooped and took her by the hand, but his feeble strength was not sufficient to raise her. 'Lady Mason,' he said, 'speak to me. I do not understand you. Will you not let me seat you on the sofa?'

But she, at least, had realized the full force of the revelation she had made, and lay there covered with shame, broken-hearted, and unable to raise her eyes from the ground. With what inward struggles she had played her part during the last few months, no one might ever know! But those struggles had been kept to herself. The world, her world, that world for which she had cared, in which she had lived, had treated her with honour and respect, and had looked upon her as an ill-used innocent woman. But now all that would be over. Every one now must know what she was. And then, as she lay there, that thought came to her. Must every one know it? Was there no longer any hope for her? Must Lucius be told? She could bear all the rest, if only he might be ignorant of his mother's disgrace;—he, for whom all had been done! But no. He, and every one must know it. Oh! if the beneficent Spirit that sees all and pities all would but take her that moment from the world!

When Sir Peregrine asked her whether he should seat her on the sofa, she slowly picked herself up, and with her head still crouching towards the ground, placed herself where she before had been sitting. He had been afraid that she would have fainted, but she was not one of those women whose nature easily admits of such relief as that. Though she was always pale in colour and frail looking, there was within her a great power of self-sustenance. She was a woman who with a good cause might have dared anything. With the worst cause that a woman could well have, she had dared and endured very much. She did not faint, nor gasp as though she were choking, nor become hysteric in her agony; but she lay there, huddled up in the corner of the sofa, with her face hidden, and all those feminine graces forgotten which had long stood her in truth so royally. The inner, true, living woman was there at last,—that and nothing else.

But he,—what was he to do? It went against his heart to harass her at that moment; but then it was essential that he should know the truth. The truth, or a suspicion of the truth was now breaking upon him; and if that suspicion should be confirmed, what was he to do? It was at any rate necessary that everything should be put beyond a doubt.

'Lady Mason,' he said, 'if you are able to speak to me——'

'Yes,' she said, gradually straightening herself, and raising her head though she did not look at him. 'Yes. I am able.' But there was something terrible in the sound of her voice. It was such a sound of agony that he felt himself unable to persist.

'If you wish it I will leave you, and come back,—say in an hour.'

'No, no; do not leave me.' And her whole body was shaken with a tremour, as though of an ague fit. 'Do not go away, and I will tell you everything. I did it.'

'Did what?'

'I—forged the will. I did it all.—I am guilty.'

There was the whole truth now, declared openly and in the most simple words, and there was no longer any possibility that he should doubt. It was very terrible,—a terrible tragedy. But to him at this present moment the part most frightful was his and her present position. What should he do for her? How should he counsel her? In what way so act that he might best assist her without compromising that high sense of right and wrong which in him was a second nature. He felt at the moment that he would still give his last shilling to rescue her,—only that there was the property! Let the heavens fall, justice must be done there. Even a wretch such as Joseph Mason must have that which was clearly his own.

As she spoke those last words, she had risen from the sofa, and was now standing before him resting with her hands upon the table, like a prisoner in the dock.

'What!' he said; 'with your own hands?'

'Yes; with my own hands. When he would not do justice to my baby, when he talked of that other being the head of his house, I did it, with my own hands,—during the night.'

'And you wrote the names,—yourself?'

'Yes; I wrote them all.' And then there was again silence in the room; but she still stood, leaning on the table, waiting for him to speak her doom.

He turned away from the spot in which he had confronted her and walked to the window. What was he to do? How was he to help her? And how was he to be rid of her? How was he to save his daughter from further contact with a woman such as this? And how was he to bid his daughter behave to this woman as one woman should behave to another in her misery? Then too he had learned to love her himself,—had yearned to call her his own; and though this in truth was a minor sorrow, it was one which at the moment added bitterness to the others. But there she stood, still waiting her doom, and it was necessary that that doom should be spoken by him.

'If this can really be true——'

'It is true. You do not think that a woman would falsely tell such a tale as that against herself!'

'Then I fear—that this must be over between you and me.'

There was a relief to her, a sort of relief, in those words. The doom as so far spoken was so much a matter of course that it conveyed no penalty. Her story had been told in order that that result might be attained with certainty. There was almost a tone of scorn in her voice as she said, 'Oh yes; all that must be over.'

'And what next would you have me do?' he asked.

'I have nothing to request,' she said. 'If you must tell it to all the world, do so.'

'Tell it; no. It will not be my business to be an informer.'

'But you must tell it. There is Mrs. Orme.'

'Yes: to Edith!'

'And I must leave the house. Oh, where shall I go when he knows it? And where will he go?'. Wretched miserable woman, but yet so worthy of pity! What a terrible retribution for that night's work was now coming on her!

He again walked to the window to think how he might answer

these questions. Must he tell his daughter? Must he banish this
criminal at once from his house?   Every one now had been told of
his intended marriage; every one had been told through Lord
Alston, Mr. Furnival, and such as they. That at any rate must
now be untold. And would it be possible that she should remain
there, living with them at The Cleeve, while all this was being
done? In truth he did not know how to speak. He had not hardness of heart to pronounce her doom.

'Of course I shall leave the house,' she said, with something
almost of pride in her voice. 'If there be no place open to me but
a gaol I will do that. Perhaps I had better go now and get my
things removed at once. Say a word of love for me to her;—a
word of respectful love.' And she moved as though she were going
to the door.

But he would not permit her to leave him thus. He could not
let the poor, crushed, broken creature wander forth in her agony to
bruise herself at every turn, and to be alone in her despair. She
was still the woman whom he had loved; and, over and beyond
that, was she not the woman who had saved him from a terrible
downfall by rushing herself into utter ruin for his sake? He must
take some steps in her behalf—if he could only resolve what those
steps should be. She was moving to the door, but stopping her, he
took her by the hand. 'You did it,' he said, 'and he, your husband, knew nothing of it?' The fact itself was so wonderful, that he
had hardly as yet made even that all his own.

'I did it, and he knew nothing of it. I will go now, Sir Peregrine; I am strong enough.'

'But where will you go?'

'Ah me, where shall I go?' And she put the hand which was at
liberty up to her temple, brushing back her hair as though she
might thus collect her thoughts. 'Where shall I go? But he does
not know it yet. I will go now to Orley Farm. When must he be
told? Tell me that. When must he know it?'

'No, Lady Mason; you cannot go there to-day. It's very hard
to say what you had better do.'

'Very hard,' she echoed, shaking her head.

'But you must remain here at present;—at The Cleeve I mean;
at any rate for to-day. I will think about it. I will endeavour to
think what may be the best.'

'But—we cannot meet now. She and I;—Mrs. Orme?' And
then again he was silent; for in truth the difficulties were too
many for him. Might it not be best that she should counterfeit
illness and be confined to her own room? But then he was averse
to recommend any counterfeit; and if Mrs. Orme did not go to her
in her assumed illness, the counterfeit would utterly fail of effect in
the household. And then, should he tell Mrs. Orme? The weight

of these tidings would be too much for him; if he did not share them with some one. So he made up his mind that he must tell them to her—though to no other one.

' I must tell her,' he said.

' Oh yes,' she replied; and he felt her hand tremble in his, and dropped it. He had forgotten that he thus held her as all these thought pressed upon his brain.

' I will tell it to her, but to no one else. If I might advise you, I would say that it will be well for you now to take some rest. You are agitated, and——'

' Agitated! yes. But you are right, Sir Peregrine. I will go at once to my room. And then——'

' Then, perhaps,—in the course of the morning, you will see me again.'

' Where?—will you come to me there?'

' I will see you in her room, in her dressing-room. She will be down stairs, you know.' From which last words the tidings were conveyed to Lady Mason that she was not to see Mrs. Orme again.

And then she went, and as she slowly made her way across the hall she felt that all of evil, all of punishment that she had ever anticipated, had now fallen upon her. There are periods in the lives of some of us—-I trust but of few—when, with the silent inner voice of suffering, we call on the mountains to fall and crush us, and on the earth to gape open and take us in. When, with an agony of intensity, we wish that our mothers had been barren. In those moments the poorest and most desolate are objects to us of envy, for their sufferings can be as nothing to our own. Lady Mason, as she crept silently across the hall, saw a servant girl pass down towards the entrance to the kitchen, and would have given all, all that she had in the world, to have changed places with that girl. But no change was possible to her. Neither would the mountains crush her, nor would the earth take her in. There was her burden, and she must bear it to the end. There was the bed which she had made for herself, and she must lie upon it. No escape was possible to her. She had herself mixed the cup, and she must now drink of it to the dregs.

Slowly and very silently she made her way up to her own room, and having closed the door behind her sat herself down upon the bed. It was as yet early in the morning, and the servant had not been in the chamber. There was no fire there although it was still mid-winter. Of such details as these Sir Peregrine had remembered nothing when he recommended her to go to her own room. Nor did she think of them at first as she placed herself on the bed-side. But soon the bitter air pierced her through and through, and she shivered with the cold as she sat there. After a while she got herself a shawl, wrapped it close around her, and then sat down

again. She bethought herself that she might have to remain in
this way for hours, so she rose again and locked the door. It would
add greatly to her immediate misery if the servants were to come
while she was there, and see her in her wretchedness. Presently
the girls did come, and being unable to obtain entrance were told
by Lady Mason that she wanted the chamber for the present.
Whereupon they offered to light the fire, but she declared that she
was not cold. Her teeth were shaking in her head, but any suffering was better than the suffering of being seen.

  She did not lie down, or cover herself further than she was
covered with that shawl, nor did she move from her place for more
than an hour. By degrees she became used to the cold. She was
numbed, and, as it were, half dead in all her limbs, but she had
ceased to shake as she sat there, and her mind had gone back to the
misery of her position. There was so much for her behind that was
worse! What should she do when even this retirement should not
be allowed to her? Instead of longing for the time when she should
be summoned to meet Sir Peregrine, she dreaded its coming. It
would bring her nearer to that other meeting when she would have
to bow her head and crouch before her son.

  She had been there above an hour and was in truth ill with the
cold when she heard,—and scarcely heard,—a light step come
quickly along the passage towards her door. Her woman's ear
instantly told her who owned that step, and her heart once more
rose with hope. Was she coming there to comfort her, to speak to
the poor bruised sinner one word of feminine sympathy? The
quick light step stopped at the door, there was a pause, and then a
low, low knock was heard. Lady Mason asked no question, but
dropping from the bed hurried to the door and turned the key.
She turned the key, and as the door was opened half hid herself
behind it ;—and then Mrs. Orme was in the room.

  ' What! you have no fire ?' she said, feeling that the air struck her
with a sudden chill. ' Oh, this is dreadful! My poor, poor dear!'
And then she took hold of both Lady Mason's hands. Had she
possessed the wisdom of the serpent as well as the innocence of the
dove she could not have been wiser in her first mode of addressing
the sufferer. For she knew it all. During that dreadful hour
Sir Peregrine had told her the whole story; and very dreadful
that hour had been to her. He, when he attempted to give
counsel in the matter, had utterly failed. He had not known what
to suggest, nor could she say what it might be wisest for them all
to do ; but on one point her mind had been at once resolved. The
woman who had once been her friend, whom she had learned to
love, should not leave the house without some sympathy and
womanly care. The guilt was very bad ; yes, it was terrible ; she
acknowledged that it was a thing to be thought of only with shud-

dering. But the guilt of twenty years ago did not strike her senses
so vividly as the abject misery of the present day. There was no
pity in her bosom for Mr. Joseph Mason when she heard the story,
but she was full of pity for her who had committed the crime. It
was twenty years ago, and had not the sinner repented? Besides,
was she to be the judge? ' Judge not, and ye shall not be judged,'
she said, when she thought that Sir Peregrine spoke somewhat
harshly in the matter. So she said, altogether misinterpreting the
Scripture in her desire to say something in favour of the poor
woman.

But when it was hinted to her that Lady Mason might return to
Orley Farm without being again seen by her, her woman's heart at
once rebelled. ' If she has done wrong,' said Mrs. Orme——

' She has done great wrong—fearful wrong,' said Sir Peregrine.

' It will not hurt me to see her because she has done wrong.
Not see her while she is in the house ! If she were in the prison,
would I not go to see her ?' And then Sir Peregrine had said no
more, but he loved his daughter-in-law all the better for her un-
wonted vehemence.

' You will do what is right,' he said—' as you always do.' Then
he left her; and she, after standing for a few moments while she
shaped her thoughts, went straight away to Lady Mason's room.

She took Lady Mason by both her hands and found that they
were icy cold. ' Oh, this is dreadful,' she said. ' Come with me,
dear.' But Lady Mason still stood, up by the bed-head, whither
she had retreated from the door. Her eyes were still cast upon the
ground and she leaned back as Mrs. Orme held her, as though by her
weight she would hinder her friend from leading her from the room.

' You are frighfully cold,' said Mrs. Orme.

' Has he told you ?' said Lady Mason, asking the question in the
lowest possible whisper, and still holding back as she spoke.

' Yes; he has told me ;—but no one else—no one else.' And then
for a few moments nothing was spoken between them.

' Oh, that I could die !' said the poor wretch, expressing in words
that terrible wish that the mountains might fall upon her and
crush her.

' You must not say that. That would be wicked, you know. He
can comfort you. Do you not know that He will comfort you, if
you are sorry for your sins and go to Him ?'

But the woman in her intense suffering could not acknowledge
to herself any idea of comfort. ' Ah, me !' she exclaimed, with a
deep bursting sob which went straight to Mrs. Orme's heart. And
then a convulsive fit of trembling seized her so strongly that Mrs.
Orme could hardly continue to hold her hands.

' You are ill with the cold,' she said. ' Come with me, Lady
Mason, you shall not stay here longer.'

Lady Mason after her Confession.

Lady Mason then permitted herself to be led out of the room, and the two went quickly down the passage to the head of the front stairs, and from thence to Mrs. Orme's room.   In crossing the house they had seen no one and been seen by no one; and Lady Mason when she came to the door hurried in, that she might again hide herself in security for the moment.   As soon as the door was closed Mrs. Orme placed her in an arm-chair which she wheeled up to the front of the fire, and seating herself on a stool at the poor sinner's feet, chafed her hands within her own.   She took away the shawl and made her stretch out her feet towards the fire, and thus seated close to her, she spoke no word for the next half-hour as to the terrible fact that had become known to her.   Then, on a sudden, as though the ice of her heart had thawed from the warmth of the other's kindness, Lady Mason burst into a flood of tears, and flinging herself upon her friend's neck and bosom begged with earnest piteousness to be forgiven.

And Mrs. Orme did forgive her.   Many will think that she was wrong to do so, and I fear it must be acknowledged that she was not strong minded.   By forgiving her I do not mean that she pronounced absolution for the sin of past years, or that she endeavoured to make the sinner think that she was no worse for her sin.   Mrs. Orme was a good churchwoman but not strong, individually, in points of doctrine.   All that she left mainly to the woman's conscience and her own dealings with her Saviour,—merely saying a word of salutary counsel as to a certain spiritual pastor who might be of aid.   But Mrs. Orme forgave her,—as regarded herself.   She had already, while all this was unknown, taken this woman to her heart as pure and good.   It now appeared that the woman had not been pure, had not been good!—And then she took her to her heart again!   Criminal as the woman was, disgraced and debased, subject almost to the heaviest penalties of outraged law and justice, a felon against whom the actual hands of the law's myrmidons would probably soon prevail, a creature doomed to bear the scorn of the lowest of her fellow-creatures,—such as she was, this other woman, pure and high, so shielded from the world's impurity that nothing ignoble might touch her,—this lady took her to her heart again and promised in her ear with low sweet words of consolation that they should still be friends.   I cannot say that Mrs. Orme was right.   That she was weak minded I feel nearly certain.   But, perhaps, this weakness of mind may never be brought against her to her injury, either in this world or in the next.

I will not pretend to give the words which passed between them at that interview.   After a while Lady Mason allowed herself to be guided all in all by her friend's advice as though she herself had been a child.   It was decided that for the present,—that is for the next day or two—Lady Mason should keep her room at The Cleeve as an invalid. Counterfeit in this there would be none certainly, for indeed she was hardly fit for any place but her own bed. If inclined and able to leave her room, she should be made welcome to the use of Mrs. Orme's dressing-room. It would only be necessary to warn Peregrine that for the present he must abstain from coming there. The servants, Mrs. Orme said, had heard of their master's intended marriage. They would now hear that this intention had been abandoned. On this they would put their own construction, and would account in their own fashion for the fact that Sir Peregrine and his guest no longer saw each other. But no suspicion of the truth would get abroad when it was seen that Lady Mason was still treated as a guest at The Cleeve. As to such future steps as might be necessary to be taken, Mrs. Orme would consult with Sir Peregrine, and tell Lady Mason from time to time. And as for the sad truth, the terrible truth,—that, at any rate for the present, should be told to no other ears. And so the whole morning was spent, and Mrs. Orme saw neither Sir Peregrine nor her son till she went down to the library in the first gloom of the winter evening.

CHAPTER VI.

A WOMAN'S IDEA OF FRIENDSHIP.

SIR PEREGRINE after the hour that he had spent with his daughter-in-law,—that terrible hour during which Lady Mason had sat alone on the bed-side—returned to the library and remained there during the whole of the afternoon. It may be remembered that he had agreed to ride through the woods with his grandson; but that purpose had been abandoned early in the day, and Peregrine had in consequence been hanging about the house. He soon perceived that something was amiss, but he did not know what. He had looked for his mother, and had indeed seen her for a moment at her door; but she had told him that she could not then speak to him. Sir Peregrine also had shut himself up, but about the hour of dusk he sent for his grandson; and when Mrs. Orme, on leaving Lady Mason, went down to the library, she found them both together.

They were standing with their backs to the fire, and the gloom in the room was too dark to allow of their faces being seen, but she felt that the conversation between them was of a serious nature. Indeed what conversation in that house could be other than serious on that day? 'I see that I am disturbing you,' she said, preparing to retreat. 'I did not know that you were together.'

'Do not go, Edith,' said the old man. 'Peregrine, put a chair for your mother. I have told him that all this is over now between me and Lady Mason.'

She trembled as she heard the words, for it seemed to her that there must be danger now in even speaking of Lady Mason,— danger with reference to that dreadful secret, the divulging of which would be so fatal.

'I have told him,' continued Sir Peregrine, 'that for a few minutes I was angry with him when I heard from Lady Mason that he had spoken to her; but I believe that on the whole it is better that it should have been so.'

'He would be very unhappy if anything that he had done had distressed you,' said Mrs. Orme, hardly knowing what words to use, or how to speak. Nor did she feel quite certain as yet how much had been told to her son, and how much was concealed from him.

'No, no, no,' said the old man, laying his arm affectionately on the young man's shoulder. 'He has done nothing to distress me. There is nothing wrong—nothing wrong between him and me. Thank God for that. But, Perry, we will think now of that other matter. Have you told your mother anything about it?' And he strove to look away from the wretchedness of his morning's work to something in his family that still admitted of a bright hope.

'No, sir; not yet. We won't mind that just now.' And then they all remained silent, Mrs. Orme sitting, and the two men still standing with their backs towards the fire. Her mind was too intent on the unfortunate lady upstairs to admit of her feeling interest in that other unknown matter to which Sir Peregrine had alluded.

'If you have done with Perry,' she said at last, 'I would be glad to speak to you for a minute or two.'

'Oh yes,' said Peregrine ;—'we have done.' And then he went.

'You have told him,' said she, as soon as they were left together.

'Told him; what, of her? Oh no. I have told him that that,— that idea of mine has been abandoned.' From this time forth Sir Peregrine could never endure to speak of his proposed marriage, nor to hear it spoken of. 'He conceives that this has been done at her instance,' he continued.

'And so it has,' said Mrs. Orme, with much more of decision in her voice than was customary with her.

'And so it has,' he repeated after her.

'Nobody must know of this,'—said she very solemnly, standing up and looking into his face with eager eyes. 'Nobody but you and I.'

'All the world, I fear, will know it soon,' said Sir Peregrine.

'No; no. Why should all the world know it? Had she not told us we should not have known it. We should not have suspected it. Mr. Furnival, who understands these things;—he does not think her guilty.'

'But, Edith—the property!'

'Let her give that up—after a while; when all this has passed by. That man is not in want. It will not hurt him to be without it a little longer. It will be enough for her to do that when this trial shall be over.'

'But it is not hers. She cannot give it up. It belongs to her son,—or is thought to belong to him. It is not for us to be informers, Edith——'

'No, no; it is not for us to be informers. We must remember that.'

'Certainly. It is not for us to tell the story of her guilt; but her guilt will remain the same, will be acted over and over again every day, while the proceeds of the property go into the hands of Lucius Mason. It is that which is so terrible, Edith;—that her conscience should have been able to bear that load for the last twenty years! A deed done,—that admits of no restitution, may admit of repentance. We may leave that to the sinner and his conscience, hoping that he stands right with his Maker. But here, with her, there has been a continual theft going on from year to year,—which is still going on. While Lucius Mason holds a sod of Orley Farm, true repentance with her must be impossible. It seems so to me.' And Sir Peregrine shuddered at the doom which his own rectitude of mind and purpose forced him to pronounce.

'It is not she that has it,' said Mrs. Orme. 'It was not done for herself.'

'There is no difference in that,' said he sharply. 'All sin is selfish, and so was her sin in this. Her object was the aggrandizement of her own child; and when she could not accomplish that honestly, she did it by fraud, and—and—and——. Edith, my dear, you and I must look at this thing as it is. You must not let your kind heart make your eyes blind in a matter of such moment.'

'No, father; nor must the truth make our hearts cruel. You talk of restitution and repentance. Repentance is not the work of a day. How are we to say by what struggles her poor heart has been torn?'

'I do not judge her.'

'No, no; that is it. We may not judge her; may we? But we may assist her in her wretchedness. I have promised that I will do all I can to aid her. You will allow me to do so;—you will; will you not?' And she pressed his arm and looked up into his face, entreating him. Since first they two had known each other,

he had never yet denied her a request.   It was a law of his life
that he would never do so.   But now he hesitated, not thinking
that he would refuse her, but feeling that on such an occasion it
would be necessary to point out to her how far she might go without
risk of bringing censure on her own name.   But in this case,
though the mind of Sir Peregrine might be the more logical, the
purpose of his daughter-in law was the stronger.   She had resolved
that such communication with crime would not stain her, and she
already knew to what length she would go in her charity.   Indeed,
her mind was fully resolved to go far enough.

'I hardly know as yet what she intends to do; any assistance
that you can give her must, I should say, depend on her own line
of conduct.'

'But I want your advice as to that.   I tell you what I purpose.
It is clear that Mr. Furnival thinks she will gain the day at this
trial.'

'But Mr. Furnival does not know the truth.'

'Nor will the judge and the lawyers, and all the rest.   As you
say so properly, it is not for us to be the informers.   If they can
prove it, let them.   But you would not have her tell them all
against herself?'   And then she paused, waiting for his answer.

'I do not know.   I do not know what to say.   It is not for me to
advise her.'

'Ah, but it is for you,' she said; and as she spoke she put her
little hand down on the table with an energy which startled him.
'She is here—a wretched woman, in your house.   And why do you
know the truth?   Why has it been told to you and me?   Because
without telling it she could not turn you from that purpose of yours.
It was generous, father—confess that; it was very generous.'

'Yes, it was generous,' said Sir Peregrine.

'It was very generous.   It would be base in us if we allowed
ourselves to forget that.   But I was telling you my plan.   She
must go to this trial.'

'Oh yes; there will be no doubt as to that.'

'Then—if she can escape, let the property be given up afterwards.'

'I do not see how it is to be arranged.   The property will belong
to Lucius, and she cannot give it up then.   It is not so easy to put
matters right when guilt and fraud have set them wrong.'

'We will do the best we can.   Even suppose that you were to
tell Lucius afterwards;—you yourself! if that were necessary, you
know.'

And so by degrees she talked him over; but yet he would come
to no decision as to what steps he himself must take.   What if he
himself should go to Mr. Round, and pledge himself that the whole
estate should be restored to Mr. Mason of Groby, on condition that

the trial were abandoned? The world would probably guess the truth after that; but the terrible trial and the more terrible punishment which would follow it might be thus escaped. Poor Sir Peregrine! Even when he argued thus within himself, his conscience told him that in taking such a line of conduct, he himself would be guilty of some outrage against the law by aiding a criminal in her escape. He had heard of misprision of felony; but nevertheless, he allowed his daughter-in-law to prevail. Before such a step as this could be taken the consent of Lady Mason must of course be obtained; but as to that Mrs. Orme had no doubt. If Lucius could be induced to abandon the property without hearing the whole story, it would be well. But if that could not be achieved,— then the whole story must be told to him. 'And you will tell it,' Mrs. Orme said to him. 'It would be easier for me to cut off my right arm,' he answered; 'but I will do my best.'

And then came the question as to the place of Lady Mason's immediate residence. It was evident to Mrs. Orme that Sir Peregrine expected that she would at once go back to Orley Farm; —not exactly on that day, nor did he say on the day following. But his words made it very manifest that he did not think it right that she should under existing circumstances remain at the Cleeve. Sir Peregrine, however, as quickly understood that Mrs. Orme did not wish her to go away for some days.

'It would injure the cause if she were to leave us quite at once,' said Mrs. Orme.

'But how can she stay here, my dear,—with no one to see her; with none but the servants to wait upon her?'

'I should see her,' said Mrs. Orme, boldly.

'Do you mean constantly—in your old, friendly way?'

'Yes, constantly; and,' she added after a pause, 'not only here, but at Orley Farm also.' And then there was another pause between them.

Sir Peregrine certainly was not a cruel man, nor was his heart by any means hardened against the lady with whom circumstances had lately joined him so closely. Indeed, since the knowledge of her guilt had fully come upon him, he had undertaken the conduct of her perilous affairs in a manner more confidential even than that which had existed while he expected to make her his wife. But, nevertheless, it went sorely against the grain with him when it was proposed that there should still exist a close intimacy between the one cherished lady of his household and the woman who had been guilty of so base a crime. It seemed to him that he might touch pitch and not be defiled;—he or any man belonging to him. But he could not reconcile it to himself that the widow of his son should run such risk. In his estimation there was something almost more than human about the purity of the only woman that blessed his hearth. It seemed to him as though she were a sacred thing, to be guarded by a shrine,—to be protected from all contact with the pollutions of the outer world. And now it was proposed to him that she should take a felon to her bosom as her friend!

'But will that be necessary, Edith?' he said; 'and after all that has been revealed to us now, will it be wise?'

'I think so,' she said, speaking again with a very low voice. 'Why should I not?'

'Because she has shown herself unworthy of such friendship ;— unfit for it I should say.'

'Unworthy! Dear father, is she not as worthy and as fit as she was yesterday? If we saw clearly into each other's bosoms, whom should we think worthy?'

'But you would not choose for your friend one—one who could do such a deed as that?'

'No; I would not choose her because she had so acted; nor perhaps if I knew all beforehand would I open my heart to one who had so done. But it is different now. What are love and friendship worth if they cannot stand against such trials as these?'

'Do you mean, Edith, that no crime would separate you from a friend?'

'I have not said that. There are circumstances always. But if she repents,—as I am sure she does, I cannot bring myself to desert her. Who else is there that can stand by her now; what other woman? At any rate I have promised her, and you would not have me break my word.'

Thus she again gained her point, and it was settled that for the present Lady Mason should be allowed to occupy her own room,— her own room, and occasionally Mrs. Orme's sitting-room, if it pleased her to do so. No day was named for her removal, but Mrs. Orme perfectly understood that the sooner such a day could be fixed the better Sir Peregrine would be pleased. And, indeed, his household as at present arranged was not a pleasant one. The servants had all heard of his intended marriage, and now they must also hear that that intention was abandoned. And yet the lady would remain up stairs as a guest of his! There was much in this that was inconvenient; but under circumstances as they now existed, what could he do?

When all this was arranged and Mrs. Orme had dressed for dinner, she again went to Lady Mason. She found her in bed, and told her that at night she would come to her and tell her all. And then she instructed her own servant as to attending upon the invalid. In doing this she was cunning in letting a word fall here and there, that might teach the woman that that marriage purpose was all over; but nevertheless there was so much care and apparent affection in her mode of speaking, and she gave her orders for Lady

Mason's comfort with so much earnestness, that no idea could get abroad in the household that there had been any cause for absolute quarrel.

Late at night, when her son had left her, she did go again to her guest's room, and sitting down by the bedside she told her all that had been planned, pointing out however with much care that, as a part of those plans, Orley Farm was to be surrendered to Joseph Mason. 'You think that is right; do you not?' said Mrs. Orme, almost trembling as she asked a question so pertinent to the deed which the other had done, and to that repentance for the deed which was now so much to be desired.

'Yes,' said the other, ' of course it will be right.' And then the thought that it was not in her power to abandon the property occurred to her also. If the estate must be voluntarily surrendered, no one could so surrender it but Lucius Mason. She knew this, and felt at the moment that of all men he would be the least likely to do so, unless an adequate reason was made clearly plain to him. The same thought at the same moment was passing through the minds of them both; but Lady Mason could not speak out her thought, and Mrs. Orme would not say more on that terrible day to trouble the mind of the poor creature whose sufferings she was so anxious to assuage.

And then Lady Mason was left alone, and having now a partner in her secret, slept sounder than she had done since the tidings first reached her of Mr. Dockwrath's vengeance.

CHAPTER VII.

THE GEM OF THE FOUR FAMILIES.

AND now we will go back to Noningsby. On that evening Graham ate his pheasant with a relish although so many cares sat heavy on his mind, and declared, to Mrs. Baker's great satisfaction, that the cook had managed to preserve the bread sauce uninjured through all the perils of delay which it had encountered.

' Bread sauce is so ticklish ; a simmer too much and it's clean done for,' Mrs. Baker said with a voice of great solicitude. But she had been accustomed perhaps to patients whose appetites were fastidious. The pheasant and the bread sauce and the mashed potatoes, all prepared by Mrs. Baker's own hands to be eaten as spoon meat, disappeared with great celerity; and then, as Graham sat sipping the solitary glass of sherry that was allowed to him, meditating that he would begin his letter the moment the glass was empty, Augustus Staveley again made his appearance.

Bread Sauce is so ticklish.

' Well, old fellow,' said he, ' how are you now?' and he was particularly careful so to speak as to show by his voice that his affection for his friend was as strong as ever. But in doing so he showed also that there was some special thought still present in his mind,—some feeling which was serious in its nature if not absolutely painful.

' Staveley,' said the other, gravely, ' I have acquired knowledge to-day which I trust I may carry with me to my grave.'

' And what is that?' said Augustus, looking round to Mrs. Baker as though he thought it well that she should be out of the room before the expected communication was made. But Mrs. Baker's attention was so riveted by her patient's earnestness, that she made no attempt to go.

' It is a wasting of the best gifts of Providence,' said Graham, ' to eat a pheasant after one has really done one's dinner.'

' Oh, that's it, is it?' said Augustus.

' So it is, sir,' said Mrs. Baker, thinking that the subject quite justified the manner.

' And of no use whatsoever to eat only a little bit of one as a man does then. To know what a pheasant is you should have it all to yourself.'

' So you should, sir,' said Mrs. Baker, quite delighted and very much in earnest.

' And you should have nothing else. Then, if the bird be good to begin with, and has been well hung——'

' There's a deal it that,' said Mrs. Baker.

' Then, I say, you'll know what a pheasant is. That's the lesson which I have learned to-day, and I give it you as an adequate return for the pheasant itself.'

' I was almost afeard it would be spoilt by being brought up the second time,' said Mrs. Baker. ' And so I said to my lady ; but she wouldn't have you woke, nohow.' And then Mrs. Baker, having heard the last of the lecture, took away the empty wine-glass and shut the door behind her.

' And now I'll write those two letters,' said Graham. ' What I've written hitherto I wrote in bed, and I feel almost more awkward now I am up than I did then.'

' But what letters are they?'

' Well, one to my laundress to tell her I shall be there to-morrow, and one to Mary Snow to say that I'll see her the day after.'

' Then, Felix, don't trouble yourself to write either. You positively won't go to-morrow——'

' Who says so?'

' The governor. He has heard from my mother exactly what the doctor said, and declares that he won't allow it. He means to see the doctor himself before you stir. And he wants to see

you also. I am to tell you he'll come to you directly after breakfast.'

' I shall be delighted to see your father, and am very much gratified
by his kindness, but——'

' But what——'

' I'm a free agent, I suppose,—to go when I please ?'

' Not exactly. The law is unwritten ; but by traditional law a
man laid up in his bedroom is not free to go and come. No action
for false imprisonment would lie if Mrs. Baker kept all your clothes
away from you.'

' I should like to try the question.'

' You will have the opportunity, for you may be sure that you'll
not leave this to-morrow.'

' It would depend altogether on the evidence of the doctor.'

' Exactly so. And as the doctor in this case would clearly be on
the side of the defendants, a verdict on behalf of the plaintiff would
not be by any means attainable.' After that the matter was presumed to be settled, and Graham said no more as to leaving
Noningsby on the next day. As things turned out afterwards he
remained there for another week.

' I must at any rate write a letter to Mary Snow,' he said. And
to Mary Snow he did write some three or four lines, Augustus
sitting by the while. Augustus Staveley would have been very
glad to know the contents, or rather the spirit of those lines; but
nothing was said about them, and the letter was at last sealed up
and intrusted to his care for the post-bag. There was very little in it
that could have interested Augustus Staveley or any one else. It
contained the ordinary, but no more than the ordinary terms of
affection. He told her that he found it impracticable to move
himself quite immediately. And then as to that cause of displeasure,—that cause of supposed displeasure as to which both Mary
and Mrs. Thomas had written, he declared that he did not believe
that anything had been done that he should not find it easy to
forgive after so long an absence.

Augustus then remained there for another hour, but not a word
was said between the young men on that subject which was nearest,
at the moment, to the hearts of both of them. Each was thinking
of Madeline, but neither of them spoke as though any such subject
were in their thoughts.

' Heaven and earth !' said Augustus at last, pulling out his watch.
' It only wants three minutes to seven. I shall have a dozen
messages from the judge before I get down, to know whether he
shall come and help me change my boots. I'll see you again before
I go to bed. Good-bye, old fellow.' And then Graham was again
alone.

If Lady Staveley were really angry with him for loving her

daughter,—if his friend Staveley were in very truth determined that such love must under no circumstances be sanctioned,—would they treat him as they were treating him? Would they under such circumstances make his prolonged stay in the house an imperative necessity? He could not help asking himself this question, and answering it with some gleam of hope. And then he acknowledged to himself that it was ungenerous in him to do so. His remaining there,—the liberty to remain there which had been conceded to him,—had arisen solely from the belief that a removal in his present state would be injudicious. He assured himself of this over and over again, so that no false hope might linger in his heart. And yet hope did linger there whether false or true. Why might he not aspire to the hand of Madeline Staveley,—he who had been assured that he need regard no woman as too high for his aspirations?

'Mrs. Baker,' he said that evening, as that excellent woman was taking away his tea-things, 'I have not heard Miss Staveley's voice these two days.'

'Well, no; no more you have,' said she. 'There's two ways, you know, Mr. Graham, of going to her part of the house. There's the door that opens at the end of the passage by her mamma's room. She's been that way, and that's the reason, I suppose. There aint no other, I'm sure.'

'One likes to hear one's friends if one can't see them; that's all.'

'To be sure one does. I remember as how when I had the measles—I was living with my lady's mother, as maid to the young ladies. There was four of 'em, and I dressed 'em all—God bless 'em. They've all got husbands now and grown families—only there aint one among 'em equal to our Miss Madeline, though there's some of 'em much richer. When my lady married him,—the judge, you know,—he was the poorest of the lot. They didn't think so much of him when he came a-courting in those days.'

'He was only a practising barrister then.'

'Oh yes; he knew well how to practise, for Miss Isabella—as she was then—very soon made up her mind about him. Laws, Mr. Graham, she used to tell me everything in them days. They didn't want her to have nothing to say to Mr. Staveley at first; but she made up her mind, and though she wasn't one of them as has many words, like Miss Furnival down there, there was no turning her.'

'Did she marry at last against their wish?'

'Oh dear, no; nothing of that sort. She wasn't one of them flighty ones neither. She just made up her own mind and bided. And now I don't know whether she hasn't done about the best of 'em all. Them Oliphants is full of money, they do say—full of money. That was Miss Louisa, who came next. But, Lord love you, Mr. Graham, he's so crammed with gout as he can't ever put a foot to the ground; and as cross;—as cross as cross. We goes there sometimes, you know. Then the girls is all plain; and young Mr. Oliphant, the son,—why he never so much as speaks to his own father; and though they're rolling in money, they say he can't pay for the coat on his back. Now our Mr. Augustus, unless it is that he won't come down to morning prayers and always keeps the dinner waiting, I don't think there's ever a black look between him and his papa. And as for Miss Madeline,—she's the gem of the four families. Everybody gives that up to her.'

If Madeline's mother married a barrister in opposition to the wishes of her family—a barrister who then possessed nothing but his wits—why should not Madeline do so also? That was of course the line which his thoughts took? But then, as he said to himself, Madeline's father had been one of the handsomest men of his day, whereas he was one of the ugliest; and Madeline's father had been encumbered with no Mary Snow. A man who had been such a fool as he, who had gone so far out of the regular course, thinking to be wiser than other men, but being in truth much more silly, could not look for that success and happiness in life which men enjoy who have not been so lamentably deficient in discretion! 'Twas thus that he lectured himself; but still he went on thinking of Madeline Staveley.

There had been some disagreeable confusion in the house that afternoon after Augustus had spoken to his sister. Madeline had gone up to her own room, and had remained there, chewing the cud of her thoughts. Both her sister and her brother had warned her about this man. She could moreover divine that her mother was suffering under some anxiety on the same subject. Why was all this? Why should these things be said and thought? Why should there be uneasiness in the house on her account in this matter of Mr. Graham? She acknowledged to herself that there was such uneasiness;—and she almost acknowledged to herself the cause.

But while she was still sitting over her own fire, with her needle untouched beside her, her father had come home, and Lady Staveley had mentioned to him that Mr. Graham thought of going on the next day.

'Nonsense, my dear,' said the judge. 'He must not think of such a thing. He can hardly be fit to leave his room yet.'

'Pottinger does say that it has gone on very favourably,' pleaded Lady Staveley.

'But that's no reason he should destroy the advantages of his healthy constitution by insane imprudence. He's got nothing to do. He wants to go merely because he thinks he is in your way.'

Lady Staveley looked wishfully up in her husband's face, longing to tell him all her suspicions. But as yet her grounds for them were so slight that even to him she hesitated to mention them.

' His being here is no trouble to me, of course,' she said.

' Of course not. You tell him so, and he'll stay,' said the judge.
' I want to see him to-morrow myself ;—about this business of poor
Lady Mason's.'

Immediately after that he met his son. And Augustus also told
him that Graham was going.

' Oh no ; he's not going at all,' said the judge. ' I've settled that
with your mother.'

' He's very anxious to be off,' said Augustus gravely.

' And why ? Is there any reason ?'

' Well ; I don't know.' For a moment he thought he would tell
his father the whole story ; but he reflected that his doing so would
be hardly fair towards his friend. ' I don't know that there is any
absolute reason ; but I'm quite sure that he is very anxious to go.'

The judge at once perceived that there was something in the
wind, and during that hour in which the pheasant was being discussed up in Graham's room, he succeeded in learning the whole
from his wife. Dear, good, loving wife ! A secret of any kind
from him was an impossibility to her, although that secret went
no further than her thoughts.

' The darling girl is so anxious about him, that—that I'm afraid,'
said she.

' He's by no means a bad sort of man, my love,' said the judge.

' But he's got nothing—literally nothing,' said the mother.

' Neither had I, when I went a wooing,' said the judge. ' But,
nevertheless, I managed to have it all my own way.'

' You don't mean really to make a comparison ?' said Lady
Staveley. ' In the first place you were at the top of your profession.'

' Was I ? If so I must have achieved that distinction at a very
early age.' And then he kissed his wife very affectionately.
Nobody was there to see, and under such circumstances a man may
kiss his wife even though he be a judge, and between fifty and
sixty years old. After that he again spoke to his son, and in spite
of the resolves which Augustus had made as to what friendship
required of him, succeeded in learning the whole truth.

Late in the evening, when all the party had drunk their cups
of tea, when Lady Staveley was beginning her nap, and Augustus
was making himself agreeable to Miss Furnival—to the great
annoyance of his mother, who half rousing herself every now and
then, looked sorrowfully at what was going on with her winking
eyes,—the judge contrived to withdraw with Madeline into the
small drawing-room, telling her as he put his arm round her waist,
that he had a few words to say to her.

' Well, papa,' said she, as at his bidding she sat herself down
beside him on the sofa. She was frightened, because such sum-

monses were very unusual; but nevertheless her father's manner
towards her was always so full of love that even in her fear she
felt a comfort in being with him.

'My darling,' he said, 'I want to ask you one or two questions
—about our guest here who has hurt himself,—Mr. Graham.'

'Yes, papa.' And now she knew that she was trembling with
nervous dread.

'You need not think that I am in the least angry with you, or
that I suspect you of having done or said, or even thought anything
that is wrong. I feel quite confident that I have no cause to do so.'

'Oh, thank you, papa.'

'But I want to know whether Mr. Graham has ever spoken to
you—as a lover.'

'Never, papa.'

'Because under the circumstances of his present stay here, his
doing so would, I think, have been ungenerous.'

'He never has, papa, in any way—not a single word.'

'And you have no reason to regard him in that light.'

'No, papa.' But in the speaking of these last two words there
was a slight hesitation,—the least possible shade of doubt conveyed,
which made itself immediately intelligible to the practised ear of
the judge.

'Tell me all, my darling;—everything that there is in your
heart, so that we may help each other if that may be possible.'

'He has never said anything to me, papa.'

'Because your mamma thinks that you are more anxious about
him than you would be about an ordinary visitor.'

'Does she?'

'Has any one else spoken to you about Mr. Graham?'

'Augustus did, papa; and Isabella, some time ago.'

'Then I suppose they thought the same.'

'Yes; I suppose they did.'

'And now, dear, is there anything else you would like to say to
me about it?'

'No, papa, I don't think there is.'

'But remember this always;—that my only wishes respecting
you, and your mother's wishes also, are to see you happy and good.'

'I am very happy, papa.'

'And very good also to the best of my belief.' And then he
kissed her, and they went back again into the large drawing-room.

Many of my readers, and especially those who are old and wise,—
if I chance to have any such—will be inclined to think that the
judge behaved foolishly in thus cross-questioning his daughter on
a matter, which, if it were expedient that it should die away,
would die away the more easily the less it were talked about.
But the judge was an odd man in many of the theories of his life.

One of them, with reference to his children, was very odd, and altogether opposed to the usual practice of the world. It was this,—that they should be allowed, as far as was practicable, to do what they liked. Now the general opinion of the world is certainly quite the reverse—namely this, that children, as long as they are under the control of their parents, should be hindered and prevented in those things to which they are most inclined. Of course the world in general, in carrying out this practice, excuses it by an assertion,—made to themselves or others—that children customarily like those things which they ought not to like. But the judge had an idea quite opposed to this. Children, he said, if properly trained would like those things which were good for them. Now it may be that he thought his daughter had been properly trained.

'He is a very clever young man, my dear; you may be sure of that,' were the last words which the judge said to his wife that night.

'But then he has got nothing,' she replied; 'and he is so uncommonly plain.'

The judge would not say a word more, but he could not help thinking that this last point was one which might certainly be left to the young lady.

CHAPTER VIII.

THE ANGEL OF LIGHT UNDER A CLOUD.

On the following morning, according to appointment, the judge visited Felix Graham in his room. It was only the second occasion on which he had done so since the accident, and he was therefore more inclined to regard him as an invalid than those who had seen him from day to day.

'I am delighted to hear that your bones have been so amenable,' said the judge. 'But you must not try them too far. We'll get you down stairs into the drawing-room, and see how you get on there by the next few days.'

'I don't want to trouble you more than I can help,' said Felix, sheepishly. He knew that there were reasons why he should not go into that drawing-room, but of course he could not guess that those reasons were as well known to the judge as they were to himself.

'You sha'n't trouble us—more than you can help. I am not one of those men who tell my friends that nothing is a trouble. Of course you give trouble.'

' I am so sorry !'

' There's your bed to make, my dear fellow, and your gruel to warm. You know Shakspeare pretty well by heart I believe, and he puts that matter,—as he did every other matter,—in the best and truest point of view. Lady Macbeth didn't say she had no labour in receiving the king. "The labour we delight in physics pain," she said. Those were her words, and now they are mine.'

' With a more honest purpose behind,' said Felix.

' Well, yes ; I've no murder in my thoughts at present. So that is all settled, and Lady Staveley will be delighted to see you down stairs to-morrow.'

' I shall be only too happy,' Felix answered, thinking within his own mind that he must settle it all in the course of the day with Augustus.

' And now perhaps you will be strong enough to say a few words about business.'

' Certainly,' said Graham.

' You have heard of this Orley Farm case, in which our neigh-bour Lady Mason is concerned.'

' Oh yes ; we were all talking of it at your table ;—I think it was the night, or a night or two, before my accident.'

' Very well ; then you know all about it. At least as much as the public knows generally. It has now been decided on the part of Joseph Mason,—the husband's eldest son, who is endeavouring to get the property—that she shall be indicted for perjury.'

' For perjury !'

' Yes ; and in doing that, regarding the matter from his point of view, they are not deficient in judgment.'

' But how could she have been guilty of perjury ?'

' In swearing that she had been present when her husband and the three witnesses executed the deed. If they have any ground to stand on—and I believe they have none whatever, but if they have, they would much more easily get a verdict against her on that point than on a charge of forgery. Supposing it to be the fact that her husband never executed such a deed, it would be manifest that she must have sworn falsely in swearing that she saw him do so.'

' Why, yes ; one would say so.'

' But that would afford by no means conclusive evidence that she had forged the surreptitious deed herself.'

' It would be strong presumptive evidence that she was cognizant of the forgery.'

' Perhaps so,—but uncorroborated would hardly bring a verdict after such a lapse of years. And then moreover a prosecution for forgery, if unsuccessful, would produce more painful feeling. Whether successful or unsuccessful it would do so. Bail could not

be taken in the first instance, and such a prosecution would create
a stronger feeling that the poor lady was being persecuted.'

' Those who really understand the matter will hardly thank
them for their mercy.'

' But then so few will really understand it. The fact however
is that she will be indicted for perjury. I do not know whether
the indictment has not been already laid. Mr. Furnival was with
me in town yesterday, and at his very urgent request, I discussed
the whole subject with him. I shall be on the Home Circuit
myself on these next spring assizes, but I shall not take the
criminal business at Alston. Indeed I should not choose that this
matter should be tried before me under any circumstances, seeing
that the lady is my near neighbour. Now Furnival wants you to
be engaged on the defence as junior counsel.'

' With himself ?'

' Yes; with himself,—and with Mr. Chaffanbrass.'

' With Mr. Chaffanbrass !' said Graham, in a tone almost of
horror—as though he had been asked to league himself with all that
was most disgraceful in the profession;—as indeed perhaps he had
been.

' Yes—with Mr. Chaffanbrass.'

' Will that be well, judge, do you think ?'

' Mr. Chaffanbrass no doubt is a very clever man, and it may be
wise in such a case as this to have the services of a barrister
who is perhaps unequalled in his power of cross-examining a
witness.'

' Does his power consist in making a witness speak the truth, or
in making him conceal it ?'

' Perhaps in both. But here, if it be the case as Mr. Furnival
suspects, that witnesses will be suborned to give false evidence——'

' But surely the Rounds would have nothing to do with such a
matter as that ?'

' No, probably not. I am sure that old Richard Round would
abhor any such work as you or I would do. They take the evidence
as it is brought to them. I believe there is no doubt that at any
rate one of the witnesses to the codicil in question will now swear
that the signature to the document is not her signature.'

' A woman—is it ?'

' Yes; a woman. In such a case it may perhaps be allowable to
employ such a man as Mr. Chaffanbrass; and I should tell you also,
such another man as Mr. Solomon Aram.'

' Solomon Aram, too ! Why, judge, the Old Bailey will be left
bare.'

' The shining lights will certainly be down at Alston. Now
under those circumstances will you undertake the case ?'

' Would you;—in my place ?'

' Yes; if I were fully convinced of the innocence of my client at the beginning.'

' But what if I were driven to change my opinion as the thing progressed ?'

' You must go on, in such a case, as a matter of course.'

' I suppose I can have a day or two to think of it ?'

' Oh yes. I should not myself be the bearer to you of Mr. Furnival's message, were it not that I think that Lady Mason is being very cruelly used in the matter. If I were a young man in your position, I should take up the case *con amore*, for the sake of beauty and womanhood. I don't say that that Quixotism is very wise ; but still I don't think it can be wrong to join yourself even with such men as Chaffanbrass and Mr. Solomon Aram, if you can feel confident that you have justice and truth on your side.' Then after a few more words the interview was over, and the judge left the room making some further observation as to his hope of seeing Graham in the drawing-room on the next day.

On the following morning there came from Peckham two more letters for Graham, one of course from Mary Snow, and one from Mrs. Thomas. We will first give attention to that from the elder lady. She commenced with much awe, declaring that her pen trembled within her fingers, but that nevertheless she felt bound by her conscience and that duty which she owed to Mr. Graham, to tell him everything that had occurred,—' word by word,' as she expressed it. And then Felix, looking at the letter, saw that he held in his hand two sheets of letter paper, quite full of small writing, the latter of which was crossed. She went on to say that her care had been unremitting, and her solicitude almost maternal ; that Mary's conduct had on the whole been such as to inspire her with ' undeviating confidence ;' but that the guile of the present age was such, especially in respect to female servants—who seemed, in Mrs. Thomas's opinion to be sent in these days express from a very bad place for the express assistance of a very bad gentleman—that it was impossible for any woman, let her be ever so circumspect, to say ' what was what, or who was who.' From all which Graham learned that Mrs. Thomas had been ' done ;' but by the middle of the third page he had as yet learned nothing as to the manner of the doing.

But by degrees the long reel unwinded itself ;—angel of light, and all. Mary Snow had not only received but had answered a lover's letter. She had answered that lover's letter by making an appointment with him ; and she had kept that appointment,—with the assistance of the agent sent express from that very bad gentleman. All this Mrs. Thomas had only discovered afterwards by finding the lover's letter, and the answer which the angel of light had written. Both of these she copied verbatim, thinking probably that the original documents were too precious to be intrusted to the post; and then ended by saying that an additional year of celibacy, passed under a closer espionage, and with more severe moral training, might still perhaps make Mary Snow fit for the high destiny which had been promised to her.

The only part of this letter which Felix read twice was that which contained the answer from the angel of light to her lover. 'You have been very wicked to address me,' the angel of light said severely. 'And it is almost impossible that I should ever forgive you!' If only she could have brought herself to end there! But her nature, which the lover had greatly belied in likening it to her name, was not cold enough for this. So she added a few more words very indiscreetly. 'As I want to explain to you why I can never see you again, I will meet you on Thursday afternoon, at half-past four, a little way up Clapham Lane, at the corner of the doctor's wall, just beyond the third lamp.' It was the first letter she had ever written to a lover, and the poor girl had betrayed herself by keeping a copy of it.

And then Graham came to Mary Snow's letter to himself, which, as it was short, the reader shall have entire.

'MY DEAR MR. GRAHAM,

'I never was so unhappy in my life, and I am sure I don't know how to write to you. Of course I do not think you will ever see me again unless it be to upbraid me for my perfidy, and I almost hope you won't, for I should sink into the ground before your eyes. And yet I didn't mean to do anything very wrong, and when I did meet him I wouldn't as much as let him take me by the hand;— not of my own accord. I don't know what she has said to you, and I think she ought to have let me read it; but she speaks to me now in such a way that I don't know how to bear it. She has rummaged among everything I have got, but I am sure she could find nothing except those two letters. It wasn't my fault that he wrote to me, though I know now I ought not to have met him. He is quite a genteel young man, and very respectable in the medical line; only I know that makes no difference now, seeing how good you have been to me. I don't ask you to forgive me, but it nearly kills me when I think of poor papa.

'Yours always, most unhappy, and very sorry for what I have done,   MARY SNOW.'

Poor Mary Snow! Could any man under such circumstances have been angry with her? In the first place if men will mould their wives, they must expect that kind of thing; and then, after all, was there any harm done? If ultimately he did marry Mary Snow, would she make a worse wife because she had met the apothecary's assistant at the corner of the doctor's wall, under the third lamp-post? Graham, as he sat with the letters before him, made all manner of excuses for her; and this he did the more eagerly, because he felt that he would have willingly made this affair a cause for breaking off his engagement, if his conscience had not told him that it would be unhandsome in him to do so.

When Augustus came he could not show the letters to him. Had he done so it would have been as much as to declare that now the coast was clear as far as he was concerned. He could not now discuss with his friend the question of Mary Snow, without also discussing the other question of Madeline Staveley. So he swept the letters away, and talked almost entirely about the Orley Farm case.

'I only wish I were thought good enough for the chance,' said Augustus. 'By heavens! I would work for that woman as I never could work again for any fee that could be offered me.'

'So would I; but I don't like my fellow-labourers.'

'I should not mind that.'

'I suppose,' said Graham, 'there can be no possible doubt as to her absolute innocence?'

'None whatever. My father has no doubt. Furnival has no doubt. Sir Peregrine has no doubt,—who, by-the-by, is going to marry her.'

'Nonsense!'

'Oh, but he is though. He has taken up her case *con amore* with a vengeance.'

'I should be sorry for that. It makes me think him a fool, and her—a very clever woman.'

And so that matter was discussed, but not a word was said between them about Mary Snow, or as to that former conversation respecting Madeline Staveley. Each felt then there was a reserve between them; but each felt also that there was no way of avoiding this. 'The governor seems determined that you sha'n't stir yet awhile,' Augustus said as he was preparing to take his leave.

'I shall be off in a day or two at the furthest all the same,' said Graham.

'And you are to drink tea down stairs to-night. I'll come and fetch you as soon as we're out of the dining-room. I can assure you that your first appearance after your accident has been duly announced to the public, and that you are anxiously expected.' And then Staveley left him.

So he was to meet Madeline that evening. His first feeling at the thought was one of joy, but he soon brought himself almost to wish that he could leave Noningsby without any such meeting. There would have been nothing in it,—nothing that need have called for observation or remark,—had he not told his secret to Augustus. But his secret had been told to one, and might be known to others in the house. Indeed he felt sure that it was suspected by Lady Staveley. It could not, as he said to himself, have been suspected by the judge, or the judge would not have treated him in so friendly a manner, or have insisted so urgently on his coming down among them.

And then, how should he carry himself in her presence? If he were to say nothing to her, his saying nothing would be remarked; and yet he felt that all his powers of self-control would not enable him to speak to her in the same manner that he would speak to her sister. He had to ask himself, moreover, what line of conduct he did intend to follow. If he was still resolved to marry Mary Snow, would it not be better that he should take this bull by the horns and upset it at once? In such case, Madeline Staveley must be no more to him than her sister. But then he had two intentions. In accordance with one he would make Mary Snow his wife; and in following the other he would marry Miss Staveley. It must be admitted that the two brides which he proposed to himself were very different. The one that he had moulded for his own purposes was not, as he admitted, quite equal to her of whom nature, education, and birth had had the handling.

Again he dined alone; but on this occasion Mrs. Baker was able to elicit from him no enthusiasm as to his dinner. And yet she had done her best, and placed before him a sweetbread and dish of sea-kale that ought to have made him enthusiastic. 'I had to fight with the gardener for that like anything,' she said, singing her own praises when he declined to sing them.

'Dear me! They'll think that I am a dreadful person to have in the house.'

'Not a bit. Only they sha'n't think as how I'm going to be said "no" to in that way when I've set my mind on a thing. I know what's going and I know what's proper. Why, laws, Mr. Graham, there's heaps of things there and yet there's no getting of 'em;—unless there's a party or the like of that. What's the use of a garden I say,—or of a gardener neither, if you don't have garden stuff? It's not to look at. Do finish it now;—after all the trouble I had, standing over him in the cold while he cut it.'

'Oh dear, oh dear, Mrs. Baker, why did you do that?'

'He thought to perish me, making believe it took him so long to get at it; but I'm not so easy perished; I can tell him that! I'd have stood there till now but what I had it. Miss Madeline see'd me as I was coming in, and asked me what I'd been doing.'

'I hope you didn't tell her that I couldn't live without sea-kale?'

'I told her that I meant to give you your dinner comfortable as long as you had it up here; and she said——; but laws, Mr. Graham, you don't care what a young lady says to an old woman like me. You'll see her yourself this evening, and then you can tell her

whether or no the sea-kale was worth the eating! It's not so badly
biled; I will say that for Hannah Cook, though she is rampagious
sometimes.' He longed to ask her what words Madeline had used,
even in speaking on such a subject as this; but he did not dare to
do so. Mrs. Baker was very fond of talking about Miss Madeline,
but Graham was by no means assured that he should find an ally in
Mrs. Baker if he told her all the truth.

At last the hour arrived, and Augustus came to convoy him
down to the drawing-room. It was now many days since he had
been out of that room, and the very fact of moving was an excitement to him. He hardly knew how he might feel in walking down
stairs, and could not quite separate the nervousness arising from his
shattered bones from that other nervousness which came from his
—shattered heart. The word is undoubtedly a little too strong,
but as it is there, there let it stay. When he reached the drawing-
room, he almost felt that he had better decline to enter it. The
door however was opened, and he was in the room' before he could
make up his mind to any such step, and he found himself being
walked across the floor to some especial seat, while a dozen kindly
anxious faces were crowding round him.

'Here's an arm-chair, Mr. Graham, kept expressly for you, near
the fire,' said Lady Staveley. 'And I am extremely glad to see
you well enough to fill it.'

'Welcome out of your room, sir,' said the judge. ' I compliment you, and Pottinger also, upon your quick recovery; but allow
me to tell you that you don't yet look like a man fit to rough it
alone in London.'

'I feel very well, sir,' said Graham.

And then Mrs. Arbuthnot greeted him, and Miss Furnival, and
four or five others who were of the party, and he was introduced to
one or two whom he had not seen before. Marian too came up to
him,—very gently, as though he were as brittle as glass, having
been warned by her mother. 'Oh, Mr. Felix,' she said, 'I was so
unhappy when your bones were broken. I do hope they won't
break again.'

And then he perceived that Madeline was in the room and was
coming up to him. She had in truth not been there when he first
entered, having thought it better, as a matter of strategy, to follow
upon his footsteps. He was getting up to meet her, when Lady
Staveley spoke to him.

'Don't move, Mr. Graham. Invalids, you know, are chartered.'

I am very glad to see you once more downstairs,' said Madeline,
as she frankly gave him her hand,—not merely touching his—
' very, very glad. But I do hope you will get stronger before you
venture to leave Noningsby. You have frightened us all very
much by your terrible accident.'

All this she said in her peculiarly sweet silver voice, not speaking as though she were dismayed and beside herself, or in a hurry to get through a lesson which she had taught herself. She had her secret to hide, and had schooled herself how to hide it. But in so schooling herself she had been compelled to acknowledge to herself that the secret did exist. She had told herself that she must meet him, and that in meeting him she must hide it. This she had done with absolute success. Such is the peculiar power of women; and her mother, who had listened not only to every word, but to every tone of her voice, gave her exceeding credit.

'There's more in her than I thought there was,' said Sophia Furnival to herself, who had also listened and watched.

'It has not gone very deep with her,' said the judge, who on this matter was not so good a judge as Miss Furnival.

'She cares about me just as Mrs. Baker does,' said Graham to himself, who was the worst judge of them all. He muttered something quite unintelligible in answer to the kindness of her words; and then Madeline, having gone through her task, retired to the further side of the round table, and went to work among the teacups.

And then the conversation became general, turning altogether on the affairs of Lady Mason. It was declared as a fact by Lady Staveley that there was to be a marriage between Sir Peregrine Orme and his guest, and all in the room expressed their sorrow. The women were especially indignant. 'I have no patience with her,' said Mrs. Arbuthnot. 'She must know that such a marriage at his time of life must be ridiculous, and injurious to the whole family.'

The women were very indignant,—all except Miss Furnival, who did not say much, but endeavoured to palliate the crimes of Lady Mason in that which she did say. 'I do not know that she is more to blame than any other lady who marries a gentleman thirty years older than herself.'

'I do then,' said Lady Staveley, who delighted in contradicting Miss Furnival. 'And so would you too, my dear, if you had known Sir Peregrine as long as I have. And if—if—if—but it does not matter. I am very sorry for Lady Mason,—very. I think she is a woman cruelly used by her own connections; but my sympathies with her would be warmer if she had refrained from using her power over an old gentleman like Sir Peregrine, in the way she has done.' In all which expression of sentiment the reader will know that poor dear Lady Staveley was wrong from the beginning to the end.

'For my part,' said the judge, 'I don't see what else she was to do. If Sir Peregrine asked her, how could she refuse?'

'My dear!' said Lady Staveley.

'According to that, papa, every lady must marry any gentleman that asks her,' said Mrs. Arbuthnot.

'When a lady is under so deep a weight of obligation I don't know how she is to refuse. My idea is that Sir Peregrine should not have asked her.'

'And mine too,' said Felix. 'Unless indeed he did it under an impression that he could fight for her better as her husband than simply as a friend.'

'And I feel sure that that is what he did think,' said Madeline, from the further side of the table. And her voice sounded in Graham's ears as the voice of Eve may have sounded to Adam. No; let him do what he might in the world;—whatever might be the form in which his future career should be fashioned, one thing was clearly impossible to him. He could not marry Mary Snow. Had he never learned to know what were the true charms of feminine grace and loveliness, it might have been possible for him to do so, and to have enjoyed afterwards a fair amount of contentment. But now even contentment would be impossible to him under such a lot as that. Not only would he be miserable, but the woman whom he married would be wretched also. It may be said that he made up his mind definitely, while sitting in that arm-chair, that he would not marry Mary Snow. Poor Mary Snow! Her fault in the matter had not been great.

When Graham was again in his room, and the servant who was obliged to undress him had left him, he sat over his fire, wrapped in his dressing-gown, bethinking himself what he would do   'I will tell the judge everything,' he said at last. 'Then, if he will let me into his house after that, I must fight my own battle.' And so he betook himself to bed.

CHAPTER IX.

MRS. FURNIVAL CAN'T PUT UP WITH IT.

WHEN Lady Mason last left the chambers of her lawyer in Lincoln's Inn, she was watched by a stout lady as she passed through the narrow passage leading from the Old to the New Square. That fact will I trust be remembered, and I need hardly say that the stout lady was Mrs. Furnival. She had heard betimes of the arrival of that letter with the Hamworth postmark, had felt assured that it was written by the hands of her hated rival, and had at once prepared for action.

'I shall leave this house to-day,—immediately after breakfast,' she said to Miss Biggs, as they sat disconsolately at the table with the urn between them.

'And I think you will be quite right, my dear,' replied Miss Biggs. 'It is your bounden duty to put down such wicked iniquity as this;—not only for your own sake, but for that of morals in general. What in the world is there so beautiful and so lovely as a high tone of moral sentiment?' To this somewhat transcendental question Mrs. Furnival made no reply. That a high tone of moral sentiment as a thing in general, for the world's use, is very good, she was no doubt aware; but her mind at the present moment was fixed exclusively on her own peculiar case. That Tom Furnival should be made to give up seeing that nasty woman who lived at Hamworth, and to give up also having letters from her,—that at present was the extent of her moral sentiment. His wicked iniquity she could forgive with a facility not at all gratifying to Miss Biggs, if only she could bring about such a result as that. So she merely grunted in answer to the above proposition.

'And will you sleep away from this?' asked Miss Biggs.

'Certainly I will. I will neither eat here, nor sleep here, nor stay here till I know that all this is at an end. I have made up my mind what I will do.'

'Well?' asked the anxious Martha.

'Oh, never mind. I am not exactly prepared to talk about it. There are things one can't talk about,—not to anybody. One feels as though one would burst in mentioning it. I do, I know.'

Martha Biggs could not but feel that this was hard, but she knew that friendship is nothing if it be not long enduring. 'Dearest Kitty!' she exclaimed. 'If true sympathy can be of service to you——'

'I wonder whether I could get respectable lodgings in the neighbourhood of Red Lion Square for a week?' said Mrs. Furnival, once more bringing the conversation back from the abstract to the concrete.

In answer to this Miss Biggs of course offered the use of her own bedroom and of her father's house; but her father was an old man, and Mrs. Furnival positively refused to agree to any such arrangement. At last it was decided that Martha should at once go off and look for lodgings in the vicinity of her own home, that Mrs. Furnival should proceed to carry on her own business in her own way,—the cruelty being this, that she would not give the least hint as to what that way might be,—and that the two ladies should meet together in the Red Lion Square drawing-room at the close of the day.

'And about dinner, dear?' asked Miss Biggs.

'I will get something at a pastrycook's,' said Mrs. Furnival.

'And your clothes, dear?'

'Rachel will see about them; she knows.' Now Rachel was the old female servant of twenty years' standing; and the disappointment experienced by poor Miss Biggs at the ignorance in which she was left was greatly enhanced by a belief that Rachel knew more than she did. Mrs. Furnival would tell Rachel but would not tell her. This was very, very hard, as Miss Biggs felt. But, nevertheless, friendship, sincere friendship is long enduring, and true patient merit will generally receive at last its appropriate reward.

Then Mrs. Furnival had sat down, Martha Biggs having been duly sent forth on the mission after the lodgings, and had written a letter to her husband. This she intrusted to Rachel, whom she did not purpose to remove from that abode of iniquity from which she herself was fleeing, and having completed her letter she went out upon her own work. The letter ran as follows:—

'Harley Street—Friday.

'MY DEAREST TOM,

'I cannot stand this any longer, so I have thought it best to leave the house and go away. I am very sorry to be forced to such a step as this, and would have put up with a good deal first; but there are some things which I cannot put up with,—and won't. I know that a woman has to obey her husband, and I have always obeyed you, and thought it no hardship even when I was left so much alone; but a woman is not to see a slut brought in under her

very nose,—and I won't put up with it. We've been married now
going on over twenty-five years, and it's terrible to think of being
driven to this. I almost believe it will drive me mad, and then,
when I'm a lunatic, of course you can do as you please.

'I don't want to have any secrets from you. Where I shall go
I don't yet know, but I've asked Martha Biggs to take lodgings for
me somewhere near her. I must have somebody to speak to now
and again, so you can write to 23 Red Lion Square till you hear
further. It's no use sending for me, for I *won't come ;*—not till I
know that you think better of your present ways of going on. I
don't know whether you have the power to get the police to come
after me, but I advise you not. If you do anything of that sort
the people about shall hear of it.

'And now, Tom, I want to say one word to you. You can't
think it's a happiness to me going away from my own home where
I have lived respectable so many years, or leaving you whom I've
loved with all my whole heart. It makes me very very unhappy, so
that I could sit and cry all day if it weren't for pride and because
the servants shouldn't see me. To think that it has come to this
after all! Oh, Tom, I wonder whether you ever think of the old
days when we used to be so happy in Keppel Street! There wasn't
anybody then that you cared to see, except me ;—I do believe that.
And you'd always come home then, and I never thought bad of
it though you wouldn't have a word to speak to me for hours.
Because you were doing your duty. But you aint doing your duty
now, Tom. You know you aint doing your duty when you never
dine at home, and come home so cross with wine that you curse
and swear, and have that nasty woman coming to see you at your
chambers. Don't tell me it's about law business. Ladies don't
go to barristers' chambers about law business. All that is done by
attorneys. I've heard you say scores of times that you never would
see people themselves, and yet you see her.

'Oh, Tom, you have made me so wretched! But I can forgive
it all, and will never say another word about it to fret you, if you'll
only promise me to have nothing more to say to that woman. Of
course I'd like you to come home to dinner, but I'd put up with that.
You've made your own way in the world, and perhaps it's only
right you should enjoy it. I don't think so much dining at the
club can be good for you, and I'm afraid you'll have gout, but I
don't want to bother you about that.· Send me a line to say that
you won't see her any more, and I'll come back to Harley Street
at once. If you can't bring yourself to do that, you—and—I—
must—part. I can put up with a great deal, but I can't put up
with that ;—*and won't.*

'Your affectionate loving wife,
'C. FURNIVAL.'

'I wonder whether you ever think of the old days when we used to be so happy in Keppel Street?' Ah me, how often in after life, in those successful days when the battle has been fought and won, when all seems outwardly to go well,—how often is this reference made to the happy days in Keppel Street! It is not the prize that can make us happy: it is not even the winning of the prize, though for the one short half-hour of triumph that is pleasant enough. The struggle, the long hot hour of the honest fight, the grinding work—when the teeth are set, and the skin moist with sweat and rough with dust, when all is doubtful and sometimes desperate, when a man must trust to his own manhood knowing that those around him trust to it not at all,—that is the happy time of life. There is no human bliss equal to twelve hours of work with only six hours in which to do it. And when the expected pay for that work is worse than doubtful, the inner satisfaction is so much the greater. Oh, those happy days in Keppel Street, or it may be over in dirty lodgings in the Borough, or somewhere near the Marylebone workhouse;—anywhere for a moderate weekly stipend. Those were to us, and now are to others, and always will be to many, the happy days of life. How bright was love, and how full of poetry! Flashes of wit glanced here and there, and how they came home and warmed the cockles of the heart. And the unfrequent bottle! Methinks that wine has utterly lost its flavour since those days. There is nothing like it; long work, grinding weary work, work without pay, hopeless work; but work in which the worker trusts himself, believing it to be good. Let him, like Mahomet, have one other to believe in him, and surely nothing else is needed. 'Ah me! I wonder whether you ever think of the old days when we used to be so happy in Keppel Street?'

Nothing makes a man so cross as success, or so soon turns a pleasant friend into a captious acquaintance. Your successful man eats too much and his stomach troubles him; he drinks too much and his nose becomes blue. He wants pleasure and excitement, and roams about looking for satisfaction in places where no man ever found it. He frets himself with his banker's book, and everything tastes amiss to him that has not on it the flavour of gold. The straw of an omnibus always stinks; the linings of the cabs are filthy. There are but three houses round London at which an eatable dinner may be obtained. And yet a few years since how delicious was that cut of roast goose to be had for a shilling at the eating-house near Golden Square. Mrs. Jones and Mrs. Green, Mrs. Walker and all the other mistresses, are too vapid and stupid and humdrum for endurance. The theatres are dull as Lethe, and politics have lost their salt. Success is the necessary misfortune of life, but it is only to the very unfortunate that it comes early.

Mrs. Furnival, when she had finished her letter and fastened it,

drew one of the heavy dining-room arm-chairs over against the fire, and
sat herself down to consider her past life, still holding the letter in
her lap. She had not on that morning been very careful with her
toilet, as was perhaps natural enough. The cares of the world
were heavy on her, and he would not be there to see her. Her
hair was rough, and her face was red, and she had hardly had the
patience to make straight the collar round her neck. To the eye
she was an untidy, angry, cross-looking woman. But her heart
was full of tenderness,—full to overflowing. She loved him now
as well as ever she had loved him :—almost more as the thought
of parting from him pressed upon her! Was he not all in all to
her? Had she not worshipped him during her whole life? Could
she not forgive him?

Forgive him! Yes. Forgive him with the fullest, frankest,
freest pardon, if he would only take forgiveness. Should she burn
that letter in the fire, send to Biggs saying that the lodgings were
not wanted, and then throw herself at Tom's feet, imploring him
to have mercy upon her. All that she could do within her heart,
and make her words as passionate, as soft, and as poetical as might
be those of a young wife of twenty. But she felt that such words,
—though she could frame the sentence while sitting there—could
never get themselves spoken. She had tried it, and it had been of
no avail. Not only should she be prepared for softness, but he also
must be so prepared and at the same moment. If he should push
her from him and call her a fool when she attempted that throwing
of herself at his feet, how would it be with her spirit then? No.
She must go forth and the letter must be left. If there were any
hope of union for the future it must come from a parting for the
present. So she went upstairs and summoned Rachel, remaining
with her in consultation for some half-hour. Then she descended
with her bonnet and shawl, got into a cab while Spooner stood at
the door looking very serious, and was driven away,—whither,
no one knew in Harley Street except Mrs. Furnival herself, and
that cabman.

'She'll never put her foot inside this hall door again. That's my
idea of the matter,' said Spooner.

'Indeed and she will,' said Rachel, ' and be a happier woman
than ever she's been since the house was took.'

'If I know master,' said Spooner, ' he's not the man to get rid of
an old woman, easy like that, and then 'ave her back agin.'
Upon hearing which words, so very injurious to the sex in general,
Rachel walked into the house not deigning any further reply.

And then, as we have seen, Mrs. Furnival was there, standing
in the dark shadow of the Lincoln's Inn passage, when Lady
Mason left the lawyer's chambers. She felt sure that it was Lady
Mason, but she could not be quite sure. The woman, though she

came out from the entry which led to her husband's chambers, might have come down from some other set of rooms. Had she been quite certain she would have attacked her rival there, laying bodily hands upon her in the purlieus of the Lord Chancellor's Court. As it was, the poor bruised creature was allowed to pass by, and as she emerged out into the light at the other end of the passage Mrs. Furnival became quite certain of her identity.

'Never mind,' she said to herself. 'She sha'n't escape me long. Him I could forgive, if he would only give it up; but as for her—! Let what come of it, come may, I will tell that woman what I think of her conduct before I am many hours older.' Then, giving one look up to the windows of her husband's chambers, she walked forth through the dusty old gate into Chancery Lane, and made her way on foot up to No. 23 Red Lion Square. 'I'm glad I've done it,' she said to herself as she went; 'very glad. There's nothing else for it, when things come to such a head as that.' And in this frame of mind she knocked at her friend's door.

'Well!' said Martha Biggs, with her eyes, and mouth, and arms, and heart all open.

'Have you got me the lodgings?' said Mrs. Furnival.

'Yes, close by;—in Orange Street. I'm afraid you'll find them very dull. And what have you done?'

'I have done nothing, and I don't at all mind their being dull. They can't possibly be more dull than Harley Street.'

'And I shall be near you; sha'n't I?' said Martha Biggs.

'Umph,' said Mrs. Furnival. 'I might as well go there at once and get myself settled.' So she did, the affectionate Martha of course accompanying her; and thus the affairs of that day were over.

Her intention was to go down to Hamworth at once, and make her way up to Orley Farm, at which place she believed that Lady Mason was living. Up to this time she had heard no word of the coming trial beyond what Mr. Furnival had told her as to his client's 'law business.' And whatever he had so told her, she had scrupulously disbelieved. In her mind all that went for nothing. Law business! she was not so blind, so soft, so green, as to be hoodwinked by such stuff as that. Beautiful widows don't have personal interviews with barristers in their chambers over and over again, let them have what law business they may. At any rate Mrs. Furnival took upon herself to say that they ought not to have such interviews. She would go down to Orley Farm and she would have an interview with Lady Mason. Perhaps the thing might be stopped in that way.

On the following morning she received a note from her husband the consideration of which delayed her proceedings for that day.

' DEAR KITTY,' the note ran.

'I think you are very foolish. If regard for me had not kept you at home, some consideration with reference to Sophia should have done so. What you say about that poor lady at Orley Farm is too absurd for me to answer. If you would have spoken to me about her, I would have told you that which would have set your mind at rest, at any rate as regards her. I cannot do this in a letter, nor could I do it in the presence of your friend, Miss Biggs.

'I hope you will come back at once; but I shall not add to the absurdity of your leaving your own house by any attempt to bring you back again by force. As you must want money I enclose a check for fifty pounds. I hope you will be back before you want more; but if not I will send it as soon as you ask for it.

' Yours affectionately as always,

' T. FURNIVAL.'

There was about this letter an absence of sentiment, and an absence of threat, and an absence of fuss, which almost overset her. Could it be possible that she was wrong about Lady Mason? Should she go to him and hear his own account before she absolutely declared war by breaking into the enemy's camp at Orley Farm? Then, moreover, she was touched and almost overcome about the money. She wished he had not sent it to her. That money difficulty had occurred to her, and been much discussed in her own thoughts. Of course she could not live away from him if he refused to make her any allowance,—at least not for any considerable time. He had always been liberal as regards money since money had been plenty with him, and therefore she had some supply with her. She had jewels too which were her own; and though, as she had already determined, she would not part with them without telling him what she was about to do, yet she could, if pressed, live in this way for the next twelve months;—perhaps, with close economy, even for a longer time than that. In her present frame of mind she had looked forward almost with gratification to being pinched and made uncomfortable. She would wear her ordinary and more dowdy dresses; she would spend much of her time in reading sermons; she would get up very early and not care what she ate or drank. In short, she would make herself as uncomfortable as circumstances would admit, and thoroughly enjoy her grievances.

But then this check of fifty pounds, and this offer of as much more as she wanted when that was gone, rather took the ground from under her feet. Unless she herself chose to give way she might go on living in Orange Street to the end of the chapter, with every material comfort about her,—keeping her own brougham if she

liked, for the checks she now knew would come without stint.
And he would go on living in Harley Street, seeing Lady Mason as
often as he pleased. Sophia would be the mistress of the house;
and as long as this was so, Lady Mason would not show her face
there. Now this was not a course of events to which Mrs. Furnival
could bring herself to look forward with satisfaction.

All this delayed her during that day, but before she went to bed
she made up her mind that she would at any rate go down to Hamworth. Tom, she knew, was deceiving her; of that she felt morally
sure. She would at any rate go down to Hamworth, and trust to
her own wit for finding out the truth when there.

CHAPTER X.

IT IS QUITE IMPOSSIBLE.

ALL was now sadness at The Cleeve. It was soon understood
among the servants that there was to be no marriage, and the tidings
spread from the house, out among the neighbours and into Hamworth. But no one knew the reason of this change;—none except
those three, the woman herself who had committed the crime and
the two to whom she had told it. On that same night, the night of
the day on which the tale had been told, Lady Mason wrote a
line,—almost a single line to her son.

'DEAREST LUCIUS.

'All is over between me and Sir Peregrine. It is better
that it should be so. I write to tell you this without losing an
hour. For the present I remain here with my dear—dearest friends.
'Your own affectionate mother,
'M. MASON.'

This note she had written in obedience to the behests of Mrs.
Orme, and even under her dictation—with the exception of one or
two words, 'I remain here with my friends,' Mrs. Orme had said;
but Lady Mason had put in the two epithets, and had then declared
her own conviction that she had now no right to use such language.

'Yes, of me you may, certainly,' said Mrs. Orme, keeping close
to her shoulder.

'Then I will alter it,' said Lady Mason. 'I will write it again
and say I am staying with you.'

But this Mrs. Orme had forbidden. 'No; it will be better so,'
she said. 'Sir Peregrine would wish it. I am sure he would.
He quite agrees that——' Mrs. Orme did not finish her sentence,
but the letter was despatched, written as above. The answer

which Lucius sent down before breakfast the next morning was still shorter.

' DEAREST MOTHER,
    ' I am greatly rejoiced that it is so.
                        ' Your affectionate son,
                                ' L. M.'

He sent this note, but he did not go down to her, nor was there any other immediate communication between them.

All was now sadness at The Cleeve. Peregrine knew that that marriage project was over, and he knew also that his grandfather and Lady Mason did not now meet each other; but he knew nothing of the cause, though he could not but remark that he did not see her. On that day she did not come down either to dinner or during the evening; nor was she seen on the following morning. He, Peregrine, felt aware that something had occurred at that interview in the library after breakfast, but was lost in surmising what that something had been. That Lady Mason should have told his grandfather that the marriage must be given up would have been only in accordance with the promise made by her to him; but he did not think that that alone would have occasioned such utter sadness, such deathlike silence in the household. Had there been a quarrel Lady Mason would have gone home;—but she did not go home. Had the match been broken off without a quarrel, why should she mysteriously banish herself to two rooms so that no one but his mother should see her?

And he too had his own peculiar sorrow. On that morning Sir Peregrine had asked him to ride through the grounds, and it had been the baronet's intention to propose during that ride that he should go over to Noningsby and speak to the judge about Madeline. We all know how that proposition had been frustrated. And now Peregrine, thinking over the matter, saw that his grandfather was not in a position at the present moment to engage himself ardently in any such work. By whatever means or whatever words he had been induced to agree to the abandonment of that marriage engagement, that abandonment weighed very heavily on his spirits. It was plain to see that he was a broken man, broken in heart and in spirit. He shut himself up alone in his library all that afternoon, and had hardly a word to say when he came out to dinner in the evening. He was very pale too, and slow and weak in his step. He tried to smile as he came up to his daughter-in-law in the drawing-room; but his smile was the saddest thing of all. And then Peregrine could see that he ate nothing. He was very gentle in his demeanour to the servants, very courteous and attentive to Mrs. Orme, very kind to his grandson. But yet his mind was heavy,—brooding over some sorrow that oppressed it. On the following morning it was the same, and the grandson knew that he could look to his grandfather for no assistance at Noningsby.

Immediately after breakfast Peregrine got on his horse, without speaking to any one of his intention,—almost without having formed an intention, and rode off in the direction of Alston. He did not take the road, but went out through The Cleeve woods, on to the common, by which, had he turned to the left, he might have gone to Orley Farm; but when on the top of the rise from Crutchley Bottom he turned to the right, and putting his horse into a gallop, rode along the open ground till he came to an enclosure into which he leaped. From thence he made his way through a farm gate into a green country lane, along which he still pressed his horse, till he found himself divided from the end of a large wood by but one field. He knew the ground well, and the direction in which he was going. He could pass through that wood, and then down by an old farm-house at the other end of it, and so on to the Alston road, within a mile of Noningsby. He knew the ground well, for he had ridden over every field of it. When a man does so after thirty he forgets the spots which he passes in his hurry, but when he does so before twenty he never forgets. That field and that wood Peregrine Orme would never forget. There was the double ditch and bank over which Harriet Tristram had ridden with so much skill and courage. There was the spot on which he had knelt so long, while Felix Graham lay back against him, feeble and almost speechless. And there, on the other side, had sat Madeline on her horse, pale with anxiety but yet eager with hope, as she asked question after question as to him who had been hurt.

Peregrine rode up to the ditch, and made his horse stand while he looked at it. It was there, then, on that spot, that he had felt the first pang of jealousy. The idea had occurred to him that he for whom he had been doing a friend's offices with such zealous kindness was his worst enemy. Had he,—he, Peregrine Orme— broken his arms and legs, or even broken his neck, would she have ridden up, all thoughtless of herself, and thrown her very life into her voice as she had done when she knew that Felix Graham had fallen from his horse? And then he had gone on with his work, aiding the hurt man as zealously as before, but still feeling that he was bound to hate him. And afterwards, at Noningsby, he had continued to minister to him as to his friend,—zealously doing a friend's offices, but still feeling that the man was his enemy. Not that he was insincere. There was no place for insincerity or treachery within his heart. The man had done no ill,—was a good fellow—was entitled to his kindness by all the social laws which he knew. They two had gone together from the same table to the same spot, and had been close together when the one had come to sorrow. It was his duty to act as Graham's friend; and yet how could he not feel that he must hate him?

And now he sat looking at the fence, wishing,—wishing;—no, certainly not wishing that Graham's hurt had been more serious; but wishing that in falling from his horse he might utterly have fallen out of favour with that sweet young female heart; or rather wishing, could he so have expressed it, that he himself might have had the fall, and the broken bones, and all the danger,—so that he might also have had the interest which those eyes and that voice had shown.

And then quickly he turned his horse, and without giving the beast time to steady himself he rammed him at the fence. The leap out of the wood into the field was difficult, but that back into the wood was still worse. The up-jump was higher, and the ditch which must be first cleared was broader. Nor did he take it at the easiest part as he had done on that day when he rode his own horse and then Graham's back into the wood. But he pressed his animal exactly at the spot from which his rival had fallen. There were still the marks of the beast's struggle, as he endeavoured to save himself before he came down, head foremost, into the ditch. The bank had been somewhat narrowèd and paired away, and it was clearly the last place in the face of the whole opening into the wood, which a rider with his senses about him would have selected for his jump.

The horse knowing his master's humour, and knowing also,— which is so vitally important,—the nature of his master's courage, jumped at the bank, without pausing. As I have said, no time had been given him to steady himself,—not a moment to see where his feet should go, to understand and make the most of the ground that he was to use. He jumped and jumped well, but only half gained the top of the bank. The poor brute, urged beyond his power, could not get his hind feet up so near the surface as to give him a fulcrum for a second spring. For a moment he strove to make good his footing, still clinging with his fore feet, and then slowly came down backwards into the ditch, then regained his feet, and dragging himself with an effort from the mud, made his way back into the field. Peregrine Orme had kept his seat throughout. His legs were accustomed to the saddle and knew how to cling to it, while there was a hope that he might struggle through. And now that he was again in the field he wheeled his horse to a greater distance, striking him with his whip, and once more pushed him at the fence, The gallant beast went at it bravely, slightly swerving from the fatal spot to which Peregrine had endeavoured once more to guide him, leaped with a full spring from the unworn turf, and, barely touching the bank, landed himself and his master lightly within the precincts of the wood.

'Ah-h!' said Peregrine, shouting angrily at the horse, as though the brute had done badly instead of well. And then he rode down slowly through the wood, and out by Monkton Grange farm, round the moat, and down the avenue, and before long he was standing at Noningsby gate.

He had not made up his mind to any plan of action, nor indeed had he determined that he would ask to see any of the family or even enter the place. The woman at the lodge opened the gate, and he rode in mechanically, asking if any of them were at home. The judge and Mr. Augustus were gone up to London, but my lady and the other ladies were in the house. Mr. Graham had not gone, the woman said in answer to his question; nor did she know when he was going. And then, armed with this information, Peregrine Orme rode round to the stables, and gave up his horse to a groom.

'Yes, Lady Staveley was at home,' the servant said at the door. 'Would Mr. Orme walk into the drawing-room, where he would find the young ladies?' But Mr. Orme would not do this. He would go into a small book-room with which he was well acquainted, and have his name taken up to Lady Staveley. 'He did not,' he said, 'mean to stay very long; but particularly wished to see Lady Staveley.' In a few minutes Lady Staveley came to him, radiant with her sweetest smile, and with both her hands held out to greet him.

'My dear Mr. Orme,' she said, 'I am delighted to see you; but what made you run away from us so suddenly?' She had considered her words in that moment as she came across the hall, and had thought that in this way she might best enable him to speak.

'Lady Staveley,' he said, 'I have come here on purpose to tell you. Has your daughter told you anything?'

'Who—Madeline?'

'Yes, Madeline. I mean Miss Staveley. Has she said anything to you about me?'

'Well; yes, she has. Will you not sit down, Mr. Orme, and then we shall be more comfortable.' Hitherto he had stood up, and had blurted out his words with a sudden, determined, and almost ferocious air,—as though he were going to demand the girl's hand, and challenge all the household if it were refused him. But Lady Staveley understood his manner and his nature, and liked him almost the better for his abruptness.

'She has spoken to me, Mr. Orme; she has told me of what passed between you on the last day that you were with us.'

'And yet you are surprised that I should have gone! I wonder at that, Lady Staveley. You must have known——'

'Well; perhaps I did know; but sit down, Mr. Orme. I won't let you get up in that restless way, if we are to talk together. Tell me frankly; what is it you think that I can do for you?'

Never is a very long word.

' I don't suppose you can do anything ;—but I thought I would come over and speak to you. I don't suppose I've any chance ?' He had seated himself far back on a sofa, and was holding his hat between his knees, with his eyes fixed on the ground ; but as he spoke the last words he looked round into her face with an anxious inquiring glance which went direct to her heart.

' What can I say, Mr. Orme ?'

' Ah, no. Of course nothing. Good-bye, Lady Staveley. I might as well go. I know that I was a fool for coming here. I knew it as I was coming. Indeed I hardly meant to come in when I found myself at the gate.'

' But you must not go from us like that.'

' I must though. Do you think that I could go in and see her ? If I did I should make such a fool of myself that I could never again hold up my head. And I am a fool. I ought to have known that a fellow like me could have no chance with her. I could knock my own head off, if I only knew how, for having made such an ass of myself.'

' No one here thinks so of you, Mr. Orme.'

' No one here thinks what ?'

' That it was—unreasonable in you to propose to Madeline. We all know that you did her much honour.'

' Psha !' said he, turning away from her.

' Ah ! but you must listen to me. That is what we all think—Madeline herself, and I, and her father. No one who knows you could think otherwise. We all like you, and know how good and excellent you are. And as to worldly station, of course you stand above her.'

' Psha !' he said again angrily. How could any one presume to talk of the worldly station of his goddess ? For just then Madeline Staveley to him was a goddess !

' That is what we think, indeed, Mr. Orme. As for myself, had my girl come to me telling me that you had proposed to her, and telling me also that—that—that she felt that she might probably like you, I should have been very happy to hear it.' And Lady Staveley as she spoke, put out her hand to him.

' But what did she say ?' asked Peregrine, altogether disregarding the hand.

' Ah, she did not say that. She told me that she had declined the honour that you had offered her ;—that she did not regard you as she must regard the man to whom she would pledge her heart.'

' But did she say that she could never love me ?' And now as he asked the question he stood up again, looking down with all his eyes into Lady Staveley's face,—that face which would have been so friendly to him, so kind and so encouraging, had it been possible.

' Never is a long word, Mr. Orme.'

'Ah, but did she say it? Come, Lady Staveley; I know I have been a fool, but I am not a cowardly fool. If it be so;—if I have no hope, tell me at once, that I may go away. In that case I shall be better anywhere out of the county.'

'I cannot say that you should have no hope.'

'You think then that there is a chance?' and for a moment he looked as though all his troubles were nearly over.

'If you are so impetuous, Mr. Orme, I cannot speak to you. If you will sit down for a minute or two I will tell you exactly what I think about it.' And then he sat down, trying to look as though he were not impetuous. 'I should be deceiving you if I were not to tell you that she speaks of the matter as though it were all over, —as though her answer to you was a final one.'

'Ah; I knew it was so.'

'But then, Mr. Orme, many young ladies who have been at the first moment quite as sure of their decision have married the gentlemen whom they refused, and have learned to love them with all their hearts.'

'But she isn't like other girls,' said Peregrine.

'I believe she is a great deal better than many, but nevertheless she may be like others in that respect. I do not say that it will be so, Mr. Orme. I would not on any account give you hopes which I believed to be false. But if you are anxious in the matter——'

'I am as anxious about it as I am about my soul!'

'Oh fie, Mr. Orme! You should not speak in that way. But if you are anxious, I would advise you to wait.'

'And see her become the wife of some one else.'

'Listen to me, Mr. Orme. Madeline is very young. And so indeed are you too;—almost too young to marry as yet, even if my girl were willing that it should be so. But we all like you very much; and as you both are so very young, I think that you might wait with patience,—say for a year. Then come to Noningsby again, and try your fortune once more. That is my advice.'

'Will you tell me one thing, Lady Staveley?'

'What is that, Mr. Orme?'

'Does she care for any one else?'

Lady Staveley was prepared to do anything she could for her young friend except to answer that question. She did believe that Madeline cared for somebody else,—cared very much. But she did not think that any way would be opened by which that caring would be made manifest; and she thought also that if wholly ungratified by any word of intercourse that feeling would die away. Could she have told everything to Peregrine Orme she would have explained to him that his best chance lay in that liking for Felix Graham; or, rather, that as his rejection had been caused by that liking, his chance would be good again when that liking should have perished from starvation. But all this Lady Staveley could not explain to him; nor would it have been satisfactory to her feelings had it been in her power to do so. Still there remained the question, 'Does she care for any one else?'

'Mr. Orme,' she said, 'I will do all for you that a mother can do or ought to do; but I must not admit that you have a right to ask such a question as that. If I were to answer that now, you would feel yourself justified in asking it again when perhaps it might not be so easy to answer.'

'I beg your pardon, Lady Staveley;' and Peregrine blushed up to his eyes. 'I did not intend——'

'No; do not beg my pardon, seeing that you have given me no offence. As I said just now, all that a mother can and ought to do I will do for you. I am very frank, and tell you that I should be rejoiced to have you for my son-in-law.'

'I'm sure I'm very much obliged to you.'

'But neither by me nor by her father will any constraint ever be put on the inclinations of our child. At any rate as to whom she will not accept she will always be allowed to judge for herself. I have told you that to us you would be acceptable as a suitor; and after that I think it will be best to leave the matter for the present without any further words. Let it be understood that you will spend next Christmas at Noningsby, and then you will both be older and perhaps know your own minds better.'

'That's a year, you know.'

'A year is not so very long—at your time of life.' By which latter remark Lady Staveley did not show her knowledge of human nature.

'And I suppose I had better go now?' said Peregrine sheepishly.

'If you like to go into the drawing-room, I'm sure they will all be very glad to see you.'

But Peregrine declared that he would not do this on any account. 'You do not know, Lady Staveley, what a fool I should make myself. It would be all over with me then.'

'You should be more moderate in your feelings, Mr. Orme.'

'It's all very well saying that; but you wouldn't be moderate if Noningsby were on fire, or if you thought the judge was going to die.'

'Good gracious, Mr. Orme!'

'It's the same sort of thing to me, I can tell you. A man can't be moderate when he feels that he should like to break his own neck. I declare I almost tried to do it to-day.'

'Oh, Mr. Orme!'

'Well; I did. But don't suppose I say that as a sort of threat. I'm safe enough to live for the next sixty years. It's only the happy people and those that are some good in the world that die. Good-bye, Lady Staveley. I'll come back next Christmas;—that is

if it isn't all settled before then; but I know it will be no good.'
Then he got on his horse and rode very slowly home, along the
high road to The Cleeve.

Lady Staveley did not go in among the other ladies till luncheon
was announced, and when she did so, she said no word about her
visitor. Nevertheless it was known by them all that Peregrine
Orme had been there. 'Ah, that's Mr. Orme's roan-coloured horse,'
Sophia Furnival had said, getting up and thrusting her face close to
the drawing-room window. It was barely possible to see a portion
of the road from the drawing-room, but Sophia's eyes had been sharp
enough to see that portion.

'A groom has probably come over with a note,' said Mrs.
Arbuthnot.

'Very likely,' said Sophia. But they all knew from her voice
that the rider was no groom, and that she did not intend it to be
thought that he was a groom. Madeline said not a word, and kept
her countenance marvellously; but she knew well enough that
Peregrine had been with her mother; and guessed also why he had
been there.

Madeline had asked herself some serious questions, and had
answered them also, since that conversation which she had had with
her father. He had assured her that he desired only her happiness;
and though in so saying he had spoken nothing of marriage, she
had well understood that he had referred to her future happiness,—
at that time when by her own choice she should be leaving her
father's house. And now she asked herself boldly in what way
might that happiness be best secured. Hitherto she had refrained
from any such home questions. Latterly, within the last week or
two, ideas of what love meant had forced themselves upon her
mind. How could it have been otherwise? But she had never
dared to tell herself either that she did love, or that she did not.
Mr. Orme had come to her with his offer, plainly asking her for the
gift of her heart, and she had immediately been aware that any
such gift on her part was impossible,—any such gift in his favour.
She had known without a moment's thought that there was no
room for hesitation. Had he asked her to take wings and fly away
with him over the woods, the feat would not have been to her more
impossible than that of loving him as his wife. Yet she liked
him,—liked him much in these latter days, because he had been so
good to Felix Graham. When she felt that she liked him as she
refused him, she felt also that it was for this reason that she liked
him. On the day of Graham's accident she had thought nothing of
him,—had hardly spoken to him. But now she loved him—with a
sort of love, because he had been so good to Graham. Though in
her heart she knew all this, she asked herself no questions till her
father had spoken to her of her future happiness.

Then, as she wandered about the house alone,—for she still went on wandering,—she did ask herself a question or two. What was it that had changed her thus, and made her gay quick step so slow? what had altered the happy silver tone of her voice? what had created that load within her which seemed to weigh her down during every hour of the day? She knew that there had been a change; that she was not as she had been; and now she asked herself the question. Not on the first asking nor on the second did the answer come; not perhaps on the twentieth. But the answer did come at last, and she told herself that her heart was no longer her own. She knew and acknowledged to herself that Felix Graham was its master and owner.

And then came the second question. Under those circumstances what had she better do? Her mother had told her,—and the words had fallen deep into her ears,—that it would be a great misfortune if she loved any man before she had reason to know that that man loved her. She had no such knowledge as regarded Felix Graham. A suspicion that it might be so she did feel,—a suspicion which would grow into a hope let her struggle against it as she might. Baker, that injudicious Baker, had dropped in her hearing a word or two, which assisted this suspicion. And then the open frank question put to her by her father when he demanded whether Graham had addressed her as a lover, had tended towards the same result. What had she better do? Of one thing she now felt perfectly certain. Let the world go as it might in other respects, she could never leave her father's house as a bride unless the bridegroom were Felix Graham. A marriage with him might probably be impracticable, but any other marriage would be absolutely impossible. If her father or her mother told her not to think of Felix Graham, as a matter of course she would obey them; but not even in obedience to father or mother could she say that she loved any one else.

And now, all these matters having been considered, what should she do? Her father had invited her to tell everything to him, and she was possessed by a feeling that in this matter she might possibly find more indulgence with her father than with her mother; but yet it was more natural that her mother should be her confidante and adviser. She could speak to her mother, also, with a better courage, even though she felt less certain of sympathy. Peregrine Orme had now been there again, and had been closeted with Lady Staveley. On that ground she would speak, and having so resolved she lost no time in carrying out her purpose.

'Mamma, Mr. Orme was here to-day: was he not?'

'Yes, my love.' Lady Staveley was sorry rather than otherwise that her daughter had asked her, but would have been puzzled to explain why such should have been the case.

' I thought so,' said Madeline.

' He rode over, and told me among other things that the match between his grandfather and Lady Mason is at an end. I was very glad to hear it, for I thought that Sir Peregrine was going to do a very foolish thing.' And then there were a few further remarks on that subject, made probably by Lady Staveley with some undefined intention of inducing her daughter to think that Peregrine Orme had come over chiefly on that matter.

' But, mamma——'

' Well, my love.'

' Did he say anything about—about what he was speaking to me about?'

' Well, Madeline: he did. He did say something on that subject; but I had not intended to tell you unless you had asked.'

' I hope, mamma, he understands that what he wants can never happen;—that is if he does want it now?'

' He does want it certainly, my dear.'

' Then I hope you told him that it can never be? I hope you did, mamma!'

' But why should you be so certain about it, my love? He does not intend to trouble you with his suit,—nor do I. Why not leave that to time? There can be no reason why you should not see him again on a friendly footing when this embarrassment between you shall have passed away.'

' There would be no reason, mamma, if he were quite sure that there could never be any other footing.'

' Never is a very long word.'

' But it is the only true word, mamma. It would be wrong in you, it would indeed, if you were to tell him to come again. I like Mr. Orme very much as a friend, and I should be very glad to know him,—that is if he chose to know me.' And Madeline as she made this little proviso was thinking what her own worldly position might be as the wife of Felix Graham. ' But as it is quite impossible that he and I should ever be anything else to each other, he should not be asked to come here with any other intention.'

' But, Madeline, I do not see that it is so impossible.'

' Mamma, it is impossible; quite impossible!' To this assertion Lady Staveley made no answer in words, but there was that in her countenance which made her daughter understand that she did not quite agree in this assertion, or understand this impossibility.

' Mamma, it is quite, quite impossible!' Madeline repeated.

' But why so?' said Lady Staveley, frightened by her daughter's manner, and almost fearing that something further was to come which had by far better be left unsaid.

' Because, mamma, I have no love to give him. Oh, mamma, do not be angry with me; do not push me away. You know who

it is that I love.   You knew it before.'   And then she threw herself
on her knees, and hid her face on her mother's lap.

Lady Staveley had known it, but up to that moment she had
hoped that that knowledge might have remained hidden as though
it were unknown.

CHAPTER XI.

MRS. FURNIVAL'S JOURNEY TO HAMWORTH.

WHEN Peregrine got back to The Cleeve he learned that there was
a lady with his mother.   He had by this time partially succeeded
in reasoning himself out of his despondency.   He had learned at
any rate that his proposition to marry into the Staveley family had
been regarded with favour by all that family except the one whose
views on that subject were by far the most important to him ; and
he had learned, as he thought, that Lady Staveley had no suspicion
that her daughter's heart was preoccupied.   But in this respect
Lady Staveley had been too cunning for him.   ' Wait !' he said to
himself as he went slowly along the road.   ' It's all very well to
say wait, but there are some things which won't bear waiting for.
A man who waits never gets well away with the hounds.'   Nevertheless as he rode into the court-yard his hopes were somewhat
higher than they had been when he rode out of it.

' A lady ! what lady ?   You don't mean Lady Mason ?'

No.   The servant did not mean Lady Mason.   It was an elderly
stout lady who had come in a fly, and the elderly stout lady was
now in the drawing-room with his mother.   Lady Mason was still
upstairs.   We all know who was that elderly stout lady, and we
must now go back and say a few words as to her journey from
Orange Street to Hamworth.

On the preceding evening Mrs. Furnival had told Martha Biggs
what was her intention; or perhaps it would be more just to say
that Martha Biggs had worked it out of her.   Now that Mrs. Furnival had left the fashionable neighbourhood of Cavendish Square,
and located herself in that eastern homely district to which Miss
Biggs had been so long accustomed, Miss Biggs had been almost
tyrannical.   It was not that she was less attentive to her friend,
or less willing to slave for her with a view to any possible or
impossible result.   But the friend of Mrs. Furnival's bosom could
not help feeling her opportunity.   Mrs. Furnival had now thrown
herself very much upon her friend, and of course the friend now
expected unlimited privileges ;—as is always the case with friends
in such a position.   It is very well to have friends to lean upon,
but it is not always well to lean upon one's friends.

'I will be with you before you start in the morning,' said Martha.

'It will not be at all necessary,' said Mrs. Furnival.

'Oh, but I shall indeed. And, Kitty, I should think nothing of going with you, if you would wish it. Indeed I think you should have a female friend alongside of you in such a trouble. You have only to say the word and I'll go in a minute.'

Mrs. Furnival however did not say the word, and Miss Biggs was obliged to deny herself the pleasure of the journey. But true to her word she came in the morning in ample time to catch Mrs. Furnival before she started, and for half an hour poured out sweet counsel into her friend's ear. If one's friends would as a rule refrain from action how much more strongly would real friendship flourish in the world!

'Now, Kitty, I do trust you will persist in seeing her.'

'That's why I'm going there.'

'Yes; but she might put you off it, if you're not firm. Of course she'll deny herself if you send in your name first. What I should do would be this;—to ask to be shown in to her and then follow the servant. When the happiness of a life is at stake—the happinesses of two lives I may say, and perhaps the immortal welfare of one of them in another world,—one must not stand too much upon etiquette. You would never forgive yourself if you did. Your object is to save him and to shame her out of her vile conduct. To shame her and frighten her out of it if that be possible. Follow the servant in and don't give them a moment to think. That's my advice.'

In answer to all this Mrs. Furnival did not say much, and what little she did say was neither in the affirmative nor in the negative. Martha knew that she was being ill treated, but not on that account did she relax her friendly efforts. The time would soon come, if all things went well, when Mrs. Furnival would be driven by the loneliness of her position to open her heart in a truly loving and confidential manner. Miss Biggs hoped sincerely that her friend and her friend's husband might be brought together again;— perhaps by her own efforts: but she did not anticipate,—or perhaps desire any speedy termination of the present arrangements. It would be well that Mr. Furnival should be punished by a separation of some months. Then, when he had learned to know what it was to have a home without a 'presiding genius,' he might, if duly penitent and open in his confession, be forgiven. That was Miss Biggs's programme, and she thought it probable that Mrs. Furnival might want a good deal of consolation before that day of open confession arrived.

'I shall go with you as far as the station, Kitty,' she said in a very decided voice.

'It will not be at all necessary,' Mrs. Furnival replied.

'Oh, but I shall. You must want support at such a moment as this, and as far as I can give it you shall have it.'

'But it won't be any support to have you in the cab with me. If you will believe me, I had rather go alone. It is so necessary that I should think about all this.'

But Martha would not believe her: and as for thinking, she was quite ready to take that part of the work herself. 'Don't say another word,' she said, as she thrust herself in at the cab-door after her friend. Mrs. Furnival hardly did say another word, but Martha Biggs said many. She knew that Mrs. Furnival was cross, ill pleased, and not disposed to confidence. But what of that? Her duty as a friend was not altered by Mrs. Furnival's ill humour. She would persevere, and having in her hands so great an opportunity, did not despair but what the time might come when both Mr. and Mrs. Furnival would with united voices hail her as their preserver. Poor Martha Biggs! She did not mean amiss, but she was troublesome.

It was very necessary that Mrs. Furnival should think over the step which she was taking. What was it that she intended to do when she arrived at Hamworth? That plan of forcing her way into Lady Mason's house did not recommend itself to her the more in that it was recommended by Martha Biggs. 'I suppose you will come up to us this evening?' Martha said, when she left her friend in the railway carriage. 'Not this evening, I think. I shall be so tired,' Mrs. Furnival had replied. 'Then I shall come down to you,' said Martha, almost holloaing after her friend, as the train started. Mr. Furnival would not have been displeased had he known the state of his wife's mind at that moment towards her late visitor. During the whole of her journey down to Hamworth she tried to think what she would say to Lady Mason, but instead of so thinking her mind would revert to the unpleasantness of Miss Biggs's friendship.

When she left the train at the Hamworth station she was solicited by the driver of a public vehicle to use his fly, and having ascertained from the man that he well knew the position of Orley Farm, she got into the carriage and had herself driven to the residence of her hated rival. She had often heard of Orley Farm, but she had never as yet seen it, and now felt considerable anxiety both as regards the house and its occupant.

'This is Orley Farm, ma'am,' said the man, stopping at the gate. 'Shall I drive up?'

But at this moment the gate was opened by a decent, respectable woman,—Mrs. Furnival would not quite have called her a lady,—who looked hard at the fly as it turned on to the private road.

'Perhaps this lady could tell me,' said Mrs. Furnival, putting out her hand. 'Is this where Lady Mason lives?'

The woman was Mrs. Dockwrath. On that day Samuel Dockwrath had gone to London, but before starting he had made known
to his wife with fiendish glee that it had been at last decided by all
the persons concerned that Lady Mason should be charged with
perjury, and tried for that offence.

'You don't mean to say that the judges have said so?' asked poor
Miriam.

'I do mean to say that all the judges in England could not save
her from having to stand her trial, and it is my belief that all the
lawyers in the land cannot save her from conviction. I wonder
whether she ever thinks now of those fields which she took away
from me!'

Then, when her master's back was turned, she put on her bonnet
and walked up to Orley Farm. She knew well that Lady Mason
was at The Cleeve, and believed that she was about to become the
wife of Sir Peregrine; but she knew also that Lucius was at home,
and it might be well to let him know what was going on. She had
just seen Lucius Mason; when she was met by Mrs. Furnival's fly.
She had seen Lucius Mason, and the angry manner in which he
declared that he could in no way interfere in his mother's affairs
had frightened her. 'But, Mr. Lucius,' she had said, 'she ought
to be doing something, you know. There is no believing how bitter
Samuel is about it.'

'He may be as bitter as he likes, Mrs. Dockwrath,' young Mason
had answered with considerable dignity in his manner. 'It will
not in the least affect my mother's interests. In the present
instance, however, I am not her adviser.' Whereupon Mrs. Dockwrath had retired, and as she was afraid to go to Lady Mason at
The Cleeve, she was about to return home when she opened the
gate for Mrs. Furnival. She then explained that Lady Mason was
not at home and had not been at home for some weeks; that she
was staying with her friends at The Cleeve, and that in order to get
there Mrs. Furnival must go back through Hamworth and round by
the high road.

'I knows the way well enough, Mrs. Dockwrath,' said the driver.
'I've been at The Cleeve before now, I guess.'

So Mrs. Furnival was driven back to Hamworth, and on going
over that piece of ground she resolved that she would follow Lady
Mason to The Cleeve. Why should she be afraid of Sir Peregrine
Orme or of all the Ormes? Why should she fear any one while
engaged in the performance of so sacred a duty? I must confess
that in truth she was very much afraid, but nevertheless she had
herself taken on to The Cleeve. When she arrived at the door,
she asked of course for Lady Mason, but did not feel at all inclined
to follow the servant uninvited into the house as recommended by
Miss Biggs. Lady Mason, the man said, was not very well, and

after a certain amount of parley at the door the matter ended in her
being shown into the drawing-room, where she was soon joined by
Mrs. Orme.

'I am Mrs. Furnival,' she began, and then Mrs. Orme begged her
to sit down. 'I have come here to see Lady Mason—on some
business—some business not of a very pleasant nature. I'm sure I
don't know how to trouble you with it, and yet—' And then even
Mrs. Orme could see that her visitor was somewhat confused.

'Is it about the trial?' asked Mrs. Orme.

'Then there is really a lawsuit going on?'

'A lawsuit!' said Mrs. Orme, rather puzzled.

'You said something about a trial. Now, Mrs. Orme, pray do
not deceive me. I'm a very unhappy woman; I am indeed.'

'Deceive you! Why should I deceive you?'

'No, indeed. Why should you? And now I look at you I do
not think you will.'

'Indeed I will not, Mrs. Furnival.'

'And there is really a lawsuit then?' Mrs. Furnival persisted in
asking.

'I thought you would know all about it,' said Mrs. Orme, 'as
Mr. Furnival manages Lady Mason's law business. I thought that
perhaps it was about that that you had come.'

Then Mrs. Furnival explained that she knew nothing whatever
about Lady Mason's affairs, that hitherto she had not believed that
there was any trial or any lawsuit, and gradually explained the
cause of all her trouble. She did not do this without sundry interruptions, caused both by her own feelings and by Mrs. Orme's
exclamations. But at last it all came forth; and before she had
done she was calling her husband Tom, and appealing to her
listener for sympathy.

'But indeed it's a mistake, Mrs. Furnival. It is indeed. There
are reasons which make me quite sure of it.' So spoke Mrs. Orme.
How could Lady Mason have been in love with Mr. Furnival,—if such
a state of things could be possible under any circumstances,—seeing
that she had been engaged to marry Sir Peregrine? Mrs. Orme did
not declare her reasons, but repeated with very positive assurances
her knowledge that Mrs. Furnival was labouring under some very
grievous error.

'But why should she always be at his chambers? I have seen
her there twice, Mrs. Orme. I have indeed;—with my own eyes.'

Mrs. Orme would have thought nothing of it if Lady Mason had
been seen there every day for a week together, and regarded
Mrs. Furnival's suspicions as an hallucination bordering on in-
sanity. A woman be in love with Mr. Furnival! A very pretty
woman endeavour to entice away from his wife the affection of
such a man as that! As these ideas passed through Mrs. Orme's

mind she did not perhaps remember that Sir Peregrine, who was
more than ten years Mr. Furnival's senior, had been engaged to
marry the same lady. But then she herself loved Sir Peregrine
dearly, and she had no such feeling with reference to Mr. Furnival.
She however did what was most within her power to do to allay the
suffering under which her visitor laboured, and explained to her
the position in which Lady Mason was placed. ' I do not think
she can see you,' she ended by saying, ' for she is in very great
trouble.'

' To be tried for perjury !' said Mrs. Furnival, out of whose heart
all hatred towards Lady Mason was quickly departing. Had she
heard that she was to be tried for murder,—that she had been convicted of murder,—it would have altogether softened her heart
towards her supposed enemy. She could forgive her any offence
but the one.

' Yes indeed,' said Mrs. Orme, wiping a tear away from her eye
as she thought of all the troubles present and to come. ' It is the
saddest thing. Poor lady ! It would almost break your heart if
you were to see her. Since first she heard of this, which was before
Christmas, she has not had one quiet moment.'

' Poor creature !' said Mrs. Furnival.

' Ah, you would say so, if you knew all. She has had to depend
a great deal upon Mr. Furnival for advice, and without that I don't
know what she would do.' This Mrs. Orme said, not wishing to
revert to the charge against Lady Mason which had brought Mrs.
Furnival down to Hamworth, but still desirous of emancipating her
poor friend completely from that charge. ' And Sir Peregrine also
is very kind to her,—very.' This she added, feeling that up to that
moment Mrs. Furnival could have heard nothing of the intended
marriage, but thinking it probable that she must do so before
long. ' Indeed anybody would be kind to her who saw her in her
suffering. I am sure you would, Mrs. Furnival.'

' Dear, dear !' said Mrs. Furnival who was beginning to entertain
almost a kindly feeling towards Mrs. Orme.

' It is such a dreadful position for a lady. Sometimes I think
that her mind will fail her before the day comes.'

' But what a very wicked man that other Mr. Mason must be !'
said Mrs. Furnival.

That was a view of the matter on which Mrs. Orme could not say
much. She disliked that Mr. Mason as much as she could dislike a
man whom she had never seen, but it was not open to her now to
say that he was very wicked in this matter. ' I suppose he thinks
the property ought to belong to him,' she answered.

' That was settled years ago,' said Mrs. Furnival. ' Horrid, cruel
man ! But after all I don't see why she should mind it so much.'

' Oh, Mrs. Furnival !—to stand in a court and be tried.'

"Tom," she said, "I have come back."

' But if one is innocent! For my part, if I knew myself innocent I could brave them all. It is the feeling that one is wrong that cows one.' And Mrs. Furnival thought of the little confession which she would be called upon to make at home.

And then feeling some difficulty as to her last words in such an interview, Mrs. Furnival got up to go. ' Perhaps, Mrs. Orme,' she said, ' I have been foolish in this.'

' You have been mistaken, Mrs. Furnival. I am sure of that.'

' I begin to think I have. But, Mrs. Orme, will you let me ask you a favour? Perhaps you will not say anything about my coming here. I have been very unhappy ; I have indeed; and—' Mrs. Furnival's handkerchief was now up at her eyes, and Mrs. Orme's heart was again full of pity. Of course she gave the required promise ; and, looking to the character of the woman, we may say that, of course, she kept it.

' Mrs. Furnival! What was she here about?' Peregrine asked of his mother.

' I would rather not tell you, Perry,' said his mother, kissing him; and then there were no more words spoken on the subject.

Mrs. Furnival as she made her journey back to London began to dislike Martha Biggs more and more, and most unjustly attributed to that lady in her thoughts the folly of this journey to Hamworth. The journey to Hamworth had been her own doing, and had the idea originated with Miss Biggs the journey would never have been made. As it was, while she was yet in the train, she came to the strong resolution of returning direct from the London station to her own house in Harley Street. It would be best to cut the knot at once, and thus by a bold stroke of the knife rid herself of the Orange Street rooms and Miss Biggs at the same time. She did drive to Harley Street, and on her arrival at her own door was informed by the astonished Spooner that, ' Master was at home,— all alone in the dining-room. He was going to dine at home, and seemed very lonely like.' There, as she stood in the hall, there was nothing but the door between her and her husband, and she conceived that the sound of her arrival must have been heard by him. For a moment her courage was weak, and she thought of hurrying up stairs. Had she done so her trouble would still have been all before her. Some idea of this came upon her mind, and after a moment's pause, she opened the dining-room door and found herself in her husband's presence. He was sitting over the fire in his arm-chair, very gloomily, and had not heard the arrival. He too had some tenderness left in his heart, and this going away of his wife had distressed him.

' Tom,' she said, going up to him, and speaking in a low voice, ' I have come back again.' And she stood before him as a suppliant.

CHAPTER XII.

YES, Lady Staveley had known it before. She had given a fairly correct guess at the state of her daughter's affections, though she had not perhaps acknowledged to herself the intensity of her daughter's feelings. But the fact might not have mattered if it had never been told. Madeline might have overcome this love for Mr. Graham, and all might have been well if she had never mentioned it. But now the mischief was done. She had acknowledged to her mother,—and, which was perhaps worse, she had acknowledged to herself,—that her heart was gone, and Lady Staveley saw no cure for the evil. Had this happened but a few hours earlier she would have spoken with much less of encouragement to Peregrine Orme.

And Felix Graham was not only in the house, but was to remain there for yet a while longer, spending a very considerable portion of his time in the drawing-room. He was to come down on this very day at three o'clock, after an early dinner, and on the next day he was to be promoted to the dining-room. As a son-in-law he was quite ineligible. He had, as Lady Staveley understood, no private fortune, and he belonged to a profession which he would not follow in the only way by which it was possible to earn an income by it. Such being the case, her daughter, whom of all girls she knew to be the most retiring, the least likely to speak of such feelings unless driven to it by great stress,—her daughter had positively declared to her that she was in love with this man! Could anything be more hopeless? Could any position be more trying?

' Oh dear, oh dear, oh dear!' she said, almost wringing her hands in her vexation,—' No, my darling I am not angry,' and she kissed her child and smoothed her hair. ' I am not angry; but I must say I think it very unfortunate. He has not a shilling in the world.'

' I will do nothing that you and papa do not approve,' said Madeline, holding down her head.

' And then you know he doesn't think of such a thing himself— of course he does not. Indeed, I don't think he's a marrying man at all.'

' Oh, mamma, do not talk in that way;—as if I expected anything. I could not but tell you the truth when you spoke of Mr. Orme as you did.'

' Poor Mr. Orme! he is such an excellent young man.'

' I don't suppose he's better than Mr. Graham, mamma, if you speak of goodness.'

' I'm sure I don't know,' said Lady Staveley, very much put beside herself. ' I wish there were no such things as young men at all. There's Augustus making a fool of himself.' And she walked twice the length of the room in an agony of maternal anxiety. Peregrine Orme had suggested to her what she would feel if Noningsby were on fire; but could any such fire be worse than these pernicious love flames? He had also suggested another calamity, and as Lady Staveley remembered that, she acknowledged to herself that the Fates were not so cruel to her as they might have been. So she kissed her daughter, again assured her that she was by no means angry with her, and then they parted.

This trouble had now come to such a head that no course was any longer open to poor Lady Staveley, but that one which she had adopted in all the troubles of her married life. She would tell the judge everything, and throw all the responsibility upon his back. Let him decide whether a cold shoulder or a paternal blessing should be administered to the ugly young man up stairs, who had tumbled off his horse the first day he went out hunting, and who would not earn his bread as others did, but thought himself cleverer than all the world. The feelings in Lady Staveley's breast towards Mr. Graham at this especial time were not of a kindly nature. She could not make comparisons between him and Peregrine Orme without wondering at her daughter's choice. Peregrine was fair and handsome, one of the curled darlings of the nation, bright of eye and smooth of skin, good-natured, of a sweet disposition, a young man to be loved by all the world, and—incidentally—the heir to a baronetcy and a good estate. All his people were nice, and he lived close in the neighbourhood! Had Lady Staveley been set to choose a husband for her daughter she could have chosen none better. And then she counted up Felix Graham. His eyes no doubt were bright enough, but taken altogether he was,—at least so she said to herself—hideously ugly. He was by no means a curled darling. And then he was masterful in mind, and not soft and pleasant as was young Orme. He was heir to nothing, and as to people of his own he had none in particular. Who could say where he must live? As likely as not in Patagonia, having been forced to accept a judgeship in that new colony for the sake of bread. But her daughter should not go to Patagonia with him if she could help it! So when the judge came home that evening, she told him all before she would allow him to dress for dinner.

' He certainly is not very handsome,' the judge said, when Lady Staveley insisted somewhat strongly on that special feature of the case.

' I think he is the ugliest young man I know,' said her ladyship.

' He looks very well in his wig,' said the judge.

' Wig! Madeline would not see him in his wig; nor anybody else very often, seeing the way he is going on about his profession. What are we to do about it?'

' Well. I should say, do nothing.'

' And let him propose to the dear girl if he chooses to take the fancy into his head?'

' I don't see how we are to hinder him. But I have that impression of Mr. Graham that I do not think he will do anything unhandsome by us. He has some singular ideas of his own about law, and I grant you that he is plain——'

' The plainest young man I ever saw,' said Lady Staveley.

' But, if I know him, he is a man of high character and much more than ordinary acquirement.'

' I cannot understand Madeline,' Lady Staveley went on, not caring overmuch about Felix Graham's acquirements.

' Well, my dear, I think the key to her choice is this, that she has judged not with her eyes, but with her ears, or rather with her understanding. Had she accepted Mr. Orme, I as a father should of course have been well satisfied. He is, I have no doubt, a fine young fellow, and will make a good husband some day.'

' Oh, excellent!' said her ladyship; ' and The Cleeve is only seven miles.'

' But I must acknowledge that I cannot feel angry with Madeline.'

' Angry! no, not angry. Who would be angry with the poor child?'

' Indeed, I am somewhat proud of her. It seems to me that she prefers mind to matter, which is a great deal to say for a young lady.'

' Matter!' exclaimed Lady Staveley, who could not but feel that the term, as applied to such a young man as Peregrine Orme, was very opprobrious.

' Wit and intellect and power of expression have gone further with her than good looks and rank and worldly prosperity. If that be so, and I believe it is, I cannot but love her the better for it.'

' So do I love her, as much as any mother can love her daughter.'

' Of course you do.' And the judge kissed his wife.

' And I like wit and genius and all that sort of thing.'

' Otherwise you would have not taken me, my dear.'

' You were the handsomest man of your day. That's why I fell in love with you.'

' The compliment is a very poor one,' said the judge.

' Never mind that.   I like wit and genius too ; but wit and genius
are none the better for being ugly : and wit and genius should know
how to butter their own bread before they think of taking a wife.'

' You forget, my dear, that for aught we know wit and genius may
be perfectly free from any such thought.'   And then the judge made it
understood that if he were left to himself he would dress for dinner.

When the ladies left the parlour that evening they found Graham
in the drawing-room, but there was no longer any necessity for
embarrassment on Madeline's part at meeting him.   They had been
in the room together on three or four occasions, and therefore she
could give him her hand, and ask after his arm without feeling that
every one was watching her.   But she hardly spoke to him beyond
this, nor indeed did she speak much to anybody.   The conversation,
till the gentlemen joined them, was chiefly kept up by Sophia
Furnival and Mrs. Arbuthnot, and even after that the evening did
not pass very briskly.

One little scene there was, during which poor Lady Staveley's
eyes were anxiously fixed upon her son, though most of those in the
room supposed that she was sleeping.   Miss Furnival was to return
to London on the following day, and it therefore behoved Augustus
to be very sad.   In truth he had been rather given to a melancholy
humour during the last day or two.   Had Miss Furnival accepted
all his civil speeches, making him answers equally civil, the matter
might very probably have passed by without giving special trouble
to any one.   But she had not done this, and therefore Augustus
Staveley had fancied himself to be really in love with her.   What
the lady's intentions were I will not pretend to say ; but if she was
in truth desirous of becoming Mrs. Staveley, she certainly went
about her business in a discreet and wise manner.

' So you leave us to-morrow, immediately after breakfast,' said
he, having dressed his face with that romantic sobriety which he
had been practising for the last three days.

' I am sorry to say that such is the fact,' said Sophia.

' To tell you the truth I am not sorry,' said Augustus ; and he
turned away his face for a moment, giving a long sigh.

' I dare say not, Mr. Staveley ; but you need not have said so
to me,' said Sophia, pretending to take him literally at his word.

' Because I cannot stand this kind of thing any longer.   I suppose
I must not see you in the morning,—alone ?'

' Well, I suppose not.   If I can get down to prayers after having
all my things packed up, it will be as much as I can do.'

' And if I begged for half an hour as a last kindness——'

' I certainly should not grant it.   Go and ask your mother
whether such a request would be reasonable.'

' Psha !'

'Ah, but it's not psha! Half-hours between young ladies and young gentlemen before breakfast are very serious things.'

'And I mean to be serious,' said Augustus.

'But I don't,' said Sophia.

'I am to understand then that under no possible circumstances ——'

'Bless me, Mr. Staveley, how solemn you are.'

'There are occasions in a man's life when he is bound to be solemn. You are going away from us, Miss Furnival——'

'One would think I was going to Jeddo, whereas I am going to Harley Street.'

'And I may come and see you there!'

'Of course you may if you like it. According to the usages of the world you would be reckoned very uncivil if you did not. For myself I do not much care about such usages, and therefore if you omit it I will forgive you.'

'Very well; then I will say good-night,—and good-bye.' These last words he uttered in a strain which should have melted her heart, and as he took leave of her he squeezed her hand with an affection that was almost painful.

It may be remarked that if Augustus Staveley was quite in earnest with Sophia Furnival, he would have asked her that all-important question in a straightforward manner as Peregrine Orme had asked it of Madeline. Perhaps Miss Furnival was aware of this, and, being so aware, considered that a serious half-hour before breakfast might not as yet be safe. If he were really in love he would find his way to Harley Street. On the whole I am inclined to think that Miss Furnival did understand her business.

On the following morning Miss Furnival went her way without any further scenes of tenderness, and Lady Staveley was thoroughly glad that she was gone. 'A nasty, sly thing,' she said to Baker. 'Sly enough, my lady,' said Baker; 'but our Mr. Augustus will be one too many for her. Deary me, to think of her having the imperance to think of him.' In all which Miss Furnival was I think somewhat ill used. If young gentlemen, such as Augustus Staveley, are allowed to amuse themselves with young ladies, surely young ladies such as Miss Furnival should be allowed to play their own cards accordingly.

On that day, early in the morning, Felix Graham sought and obtained an interview with his host in the judge's own study. 'I have come about two things,' he said, taking the easy chair to which he was invited.

'Two or ten, I shall be very happy,' said the judge cheerily.

'I will take business first,' said Graham.

'And then pleasure will be the sweeter afterwards,' said the judge.

'I have been thinking a great deal about this case of Lady Mason's, and I have read all the papers, old and new, which Mr. Furnival has sent me. I cannot bring myself to suppose it possible that she can have been guilty of any fraud or deception.'

'I believe her to be free from all guilt in the matter—as I told you before. But then of course you will take that as a private opinion, not as one legally formed. I have never gone into the matter as you have done.'

'I confess that I do not like having dealings with Mr. Chaffanbrass and Mr. Aram.'

'Mr. Chaffanbrass and Mr. Aram may not be so bad as you, perhaps in ignorance, suppose them to be. Does it not occur to you that we should be very badly off without such men as Chaffanbrass and Aram?'

'So we should without chimney-sweepers and scavengers.'

'Graham, my dear fellow, judge not that you be not judged. I am older than you, and have seen more of these men. Believe me that as you grow older and also see more of them, your opinion will be more lenient,—and more just. Do not be angry with me for taking this liberty with you.'

'My dear judge, if you knew how I value it;—how I should value any mark of such kindness that you can show me! However I have decided that I will know something more of these gentlemen at once. If I have your approbation I will let Mr. Furnival know that I will undertake the case.'

The judge signified his approbation, and thus the first of those two matters was soon settled between them.

'And now for the pleasure,' said the judge.

'I don't know much about pleasure,' said Graham, fidgeting in his chair, rather uneasily. 'I'm afraid there is not much pleasure for either of us, or for anybody else, in what I'm going to say.'

'Then there is so much more reason for having it said quickly. Unpleasant things should always be got over without delay.'

'Nothing on earth can exceed Lady Staveley's kindness to me, and yours, and that of the whole family since my unfortunate accident.'

'Don't think of it. It has been nothing. We like you, but we should have done as much as that even if we had not.'

'And now I'm going to tell you that I have fallen in love with your daughter Madeline.' As the judge wished to have the tale told quickly, I think he had reason to be satisfied with the very succinct terms used by Felix Graham.

'Indeed!' said the judge.

'And that was the reason why I wished to go away at the earliest possible time—and still wish it.'

'You are right there, Mr. Graham. I must say you are right

there. Under all the circumstances of the case I think you were right to wish to leave us.'

'And therefore I shall go the first thing to-morrow morning'—in saying which last words poor Felix could not refrain from showing a certain unevenness of temper, and some disappointment.

'Gently, gently, Mr. Graham. Let us have a few more words before we accede to the necessity of anything so sudden. Have you spoken to Madeline on this subject?'

'Not a word.'

'And I may presume that you do not intend to do so.'

For a moment or so Felix Graham sat without speaking, and then, getting up from his chair, he walked twice the length of the room. 'Upon my word, judge, I will not answer for myself if I remain here,' he said at last.

A softer-hearted man than Judge Staveley, or one who could make himself more happy in making others happy, never sat on the English bench. Was not this a gallant young fellow before him,—gallant and clever, of good honest principles, and a true manly heart? Was he not a gentleman by birth, education, and tastes? What more should a man want for a son-in-law? And then his daughter had had the wit to love this man so endowed. It was almost on his tongue to tell Graham that he might go and seek the girl and plead his own cause to her.

But bread is bread, and butcher's bills are bills! The man and the father, and the successful possessor of some thousands a year, was too strong at last for the soft-hearted philanthropist. Therefore, having collected his thoughts, he thus expressed himself upon the occasion :—

'Mr. Graham, I think you have behaved very well in this matter, and it is exactly what I should have expected from you.' The judge at the time knew nothing about Mary Snow. 'As regards yourself personally I should be proud to own you as my son-in-law, but I am of course bound to regard the welfare of my daughter. Your means I fear are but small.'

'Very small indeed,' said Graham.

'And though you have all those gifts which should bring you on in your profession, you have learned to entertain ideas, which hitherto have barred you from success. Now I tell you what you shall do. Remain here two or three days longer, till you are fit to travel, and abstain from saying anything to my daughter. Come to me again in three months, if you still hold the same mind, and I will pledge myself to tell you then whether or no you have my leave to address my child as a suitor.'

Felix Graham silently took the judge's hand, feeling that a strong hope had been given to him, and so the interview was ended.

Lady Mason going before the Magistrates.

CHAPTER XIII.

LADY MASON remained at The Cleeve for something more than a week after that day on which she made her confession, during which time she was fully committed to take her trial at the next assizes at Alston on an indictment for perjury. This was done in a manner that astonished even herself by the absence of all publicity or outward scandal. The matter was arranged between Mr. Matthew Round and Mr. Solomon Aram, and was so arranged in accordance with Mr. Furnival's wishes. Mr. Furnival wrote to say that at such a time he would call at The Cleeve with a post-chaise. This he did, and took Lady Mason with him before two magistrates for the county who were sitting at Doddinghurst, a village five miles distant from Sir Peregrine's house. Here by agreement they were met by Lucius Mason who was to act as one of the bailsmen for his mother's appearance at the trial. Sir Peregrine was the other, but it was brought about by amicable management between the lawyers that his appearance before the magistrates was not required. There were also there the two attorneys, Bridget Bolster the witness, one Torrington from London who brought with him the absolute deed executed on that 14th of July with reference to the then dissolved partnership of Mason and Martock; and there was Mr. Samuel Dockwrath. I must not forget to say that there was also a reporter for the press, provided by the special care of the latter-named gentleman.

The arrival in the village of four different vehicles, and the sight of such gentlemen as Mr. Furnival, Mr. Round, and Mr. Aram, of course aroused some excitement there; but this feeling was kept down as much as possible, and Lady Mason was very quickly allowed to return to the carriage. Mr. Dockwrath made one or two attempts to get up a scene, and to rouse a feeling of public anger against the lady who was to be tried; but the magistrates put him down. They also seemed to be fully impressed with a sense of Lady Mason's innocence in the teeth of the evidence which was given against her. This was the general feeling on the minds of all people,—except of those who knew most about it. There was an idea that affairs had so been managed by Mr. Joseph Mason and Mr. Dockwrath that another trial was necessary, but that the unfortunate victim of Mr. Mason's cupidity and Mr. Dockwrath's malice would be washed white as snow when the day of that trial came. The chief performers on the present occasion were Round and Aram, and a stranger to such proceedings would have said that they were acting in concert. Mr. Round pressed for the indictment, and brought forward in a very short way the evidence of Bolster and Torrington. Mr. Aram said that his client was advised to reserve her defence, and was prepared with bail to any amount. Mr. Round advised the magistrates that reasonable bail should be taken, and then the matter was settled. Mr. Furnival sat on a chair close to the elder of those two gentlemen, and whispered a word to him now and then. Lady Mason was provided with an arm-chair close to Mr. Furnival's right hand, and close to her right hand stood her son. Her face was covered by a deep veil, and she was not called upon during the whole proceeding to utter one audible word. A single question was put to her by the presiding magistrate before the committal was signed, and it was understood that some answer was made to it; but this answer reached the ears of those in the room by means of Mr. Furnival's voice.

It was observed by most of those there that during the whole of the sitting Lady Mason held her son's hand; but it was observed also that though Lucius permitted this he did not seem to return the pressure. He stood there during the entire proceedings without motion or speech, looking very stern. He signed the bail-bond, but even that he did without saying a word. Mr. Dockwrath demanded that Lady Mason should be kept in custody till the bond should also have been signed by Sir Peregrine; but upon this Mr. Round remarked that he believed Mr. Joseph Mason had intrusted to him the conduct of the case, and the elder magistrate desired Mr. Dockwrath to abstain from further interference. 'All right,' said he to a person standing close to him. 'But I'll be too many for them yet, as you will see when she is brought before a judge and jury.' And then Lady Mason stood committed to take her trial at the next Alston assizes.

When Lucius had come forward to hand her from the post-chaise in which she arrived Lady Mason had kissed him, but this was all the intercourse that then passed between the mother and son. Mr. Furnival, however, informed him that his mother would return to Orley Farm on the next day but one.

'She thinks it better that she should be at home from this time to the day of the trial,' said Mr. Furnival; 'and on the whole Sir Peregrine is inclined to agree with her.'

'I have thought so all through,' said Lucius.

'But you are to understand that there is no disagreement between your mother and the family at The Cleeve. The idea of the marriage has, as I think very properly, been laid aside.'

' Of course it was proper that it should be laid aside.'

' Yes; but I must beg you to understand that there has been no quarrel. Indeed you will, I have no doubt, perceive that, as Mrs. Orme has assured me that she will see your mother constantly till the time comes.'

' She is very kind,' said Lucius. But it was evident from the tone of his voice that he would have preferred that all the Ormes should have remained away. In his mind this time of suffering to his mother and to him was a period of trial and probation,—a period, if not of actual disgrace, yet of disgrace before the world ; and he thought that it would have best become his mother to have abstained from all friendship out of her own family, and even from all expressed sympathy, till she had vindicated her own purity and innocence. And as he thought of this he declared to himself that he would have sacrificed everything to her comfort and assistance if she would only have permitted it. He would have loved her, and been tender to her, receiving on his own shoulders all those blows which now fell so hardly upon hers. Every word should have been a word of kindness ; every look should have been soft and full of affection. He would have treated her not only with all the love which a son could show to a mother, but with all the respect and sympathy which a gentleman could feel for a lady in distress. But then, in order that such a state of things as this should have existed, it would have been necessary that she should have trusted him. She should have leaned upon him, and,—though he did not exactly say so in talking over the matter with himself, still he thought it,—on him and on him only. But she had declined to lean upon him at all. She had gone away to strangers,—she, who should hardly have spoken to a stranger during these sad months! She would not have his care ; and under those circumstances he could only stand aloof, hold up his head, and look sternly. As for her innocence, that was a matter of course. He knew that she was innocent. He wanted no one to tell him that his own mother was not a thief, a forger, a castaway among the world's worst wretches. He thanked no one for such an assurance. Every honest man must sympathize with a woman so injured. It would be a necessity of his manhood and of his honesty ! But he would have valued most a sympathy which would have abstained from all expression till after that trial should be over. It should have been for him to act and for him to speak during this terrible period. But his mother who was a free agent had willed it otherwise.

And there had been one other scene. Mr. Furnival had introduced Lady Mason to Mr. Solomon Aram, having explained to her that it would be indispensable that Mr. Aram should see her, probably once or twice before the trial came on.

'But cannot it be done through you?' said Lady Mason. 'Though of course I should not expect that you can so sacrifice your valuable time.'

'Pray believe me that that is not the consideration,' said Mr. Furnival. 'We have engaged the services of Mr. Aram because he is supposed to understand difficulties of this sort better than any other man in the profession, and his chance of rescuing you from this trouble will be much better if you can bring yourself to have confidence in him—full confidence.' And Mr. Furnival looked into her face as he spoke with an expression of countenance that was very eloquent. 'You must not suppose that I shall not do all in my power. In my proper capacity I shall be acting for you with all the energy that I can use; but the case has now assumed an aspect which requires that it should be in an attorney's hands.' And then Mr. Furnival introduced her to Mr. Solomon Aram.

Mr. Solomon Aram was not, in outward appearance, such a man as Lady Mason, Sir Peregrine Orme, or others quite ignorant in such matters would have expected. He was not a dirty old Jew with a hooked nose and an imperfect pronunciation of English consonants. Mr. Chaffanbrass, the barrister, bore more resemblance to a Jew of that ancient type. Mr. Solomon Aram was a good-looking man about forty, perhaps rather over-dressed, but bearing about him no other sign of vulgarity. Nor at first sight would it probably have been discerned that he was of the Hebrew persuasion. He had black hair and a well-formed face; but his eyes were closer than is common with most of us, and his nose seemed to be somewhat swollen about the bridge. When one knew that he was a Jew one saw that he was a Jew; but in the absence of such previous knowledge he might have been taken for as good a Christian as any other attorney.

Mr. Aram raised his hat and bowed as Mr. Furnival performed the ceremony of introduction. This was done while she was still seated in the carriage, and as Lucius was waiting at the door to hand her down into the house where the magistrates were sitting. 'I am delighted to have the honour of making your acquaintance,' said Mr. Aram.

Lady Mason essayed to mutter some word; but no word was audible, nor was any necessary. 'I have no doubt,' continued the attorney, 'that we shall pull through this little difficulty without any ultimate damage whatsoever. In the mean time it is of course disagreeable to a lady of your distinction.' And then he made another bow. 'We are peculiarly happy in having such a tower of strength as Mr. Furnival,' and then he bowed to the barrister. And my old friend Mr. Chaffanbrass is another tower of strength. Eh, Mr. Furnival?' And so the introduction was over.

Lady Mason had quite understood Mr. Furnival;—had understood both his words and his face, when he told her how indispensable it was that she should have full confidence in this attorney. He had meant that she should tell him all. She must bring herself to confess everything to this absolute stranger. And then—for the first time—she felt sure that Mr. Furnival had guessed her secret. He also knew it, but it would not suit him that any one should know that he knew it! Alas, alas! would it not be better that all the world should know it and that there might be an end? Had not her doom been told to her? Even if the paraphernalia of justice,—the judge, and the jury, and the lawyers, could be induced to declare her innocent before all men, must she not confess her guilt to him,—to that one,—for whose verdict alone she cared? If he knew her to be guilty what matter who might think her innocent? And she had been told that all must be declared to him. That property was his,—but his only through her guilt; and that property must be restored to its owner! So much Sir Peregrine Orme had declared to be indispensable,—Sir Peregrine Orme, who in other matters concerning this case was now dark enough in his judgment. On that point, however, there need be no darkness. Though the heaven should fall on her devoted head, that tardy justice must be done!

When this piece of business had been completed at Doddinghurst, Lady Mason returned to The Cleeve, whither Mr. Furnival accompanied her. He had offered his seat in the post-chaise to Lucius, but the young man had declared that he was unwilling to go to The Cleeve, and consequently there was no opportunity for conversation between Lady Mason and her son. On her arrival she went at once to her room, and there she continued to live as she had done for the last few days till the morning of her departure came. To Mrs. Orme she told all that had occurred, as Mr. Furnival did also to Sir Peregrine. On that occasion Sir Peregrine said very little to the barrister, merely bowing his head courteously as each different point was explained, in intimation of his having heard and understood what was said to him. Mr. Furnival could not but see that his manner was entirely altered. There was no enthusiasm now, no violence of invective against that wretch at Groby Park, no positive assurance that his guest's innocence must come out at the trial bright as the day! He showed no inclination to desert Lady Mason's cause, and indeed insisted on hearing the particulars of all that had been done; but he said very little, and those few words adverted to the terrible sadness of the subject. He seemed too to be older than he had been, and less firm in his gait. That terrible sadness had already told greatly upon him. Those about him had observed that he had not once crossed the threshold of his hall door since the morning on which Lady Mason had taken to her own room.

'He has altered his mind,' said the lawyer to himself as he was driven back to the Hamworth station. 'He also now believes her to be guilty.' As to his own belief, Mr. Furnival held no argument within his own breast, but we may say that he was no longer perplexed by much doubt upon the matter.

And then the morning came for Lady Mason's departure. Sir Peregrine had not seen her since she had left him in the library after her confession, although, as may be remembered, he had undertaken to do so. But he had not then known how Mrs. Orme might act when she heard the story. As matters had turned out Mrs. Orme had taken upon herself the care of their guest, and all intercourse between Lady Mason and Sir Peregrine had passed through his daughter-in-law. But now, on this morning, he declared that he would go to her upstairs in Mrs. Orme's room, and himself hand her down through the hall into the carriage. Against this Lady Mason had expostulated, but in vain.

'It will be better so, dear,' Mrs. Orme had said. 'It will teach the servants and people to think that he still respects and esteems you.'

'But he does not!' said she, speaking almost sharply. 'How would it be possible? Ah, me—respect and esteem are gone from me for ever!'

'No, not for ever,' replied Mrs. Orme. 'You have much to bear, but no evil lasts for ever.'

'Will not sin last for ever;—sin such as mine?'

'Not if you repent;—repent and make such restitution as is possible. Lady Mason, say that you have repented. Tell me that you have asked Him to pardon you!' And then, as had been so often the case during these last days, Lady Mason sat silent, with hard, fixed eyes, with her hands clasped, and her lips compressed. Never as yet had Mrs. Orme induced her to say that she had asked for pardon at the cost of telling her son that the property which he called his own had been procured for him by his mother's fraud. That punishment, and that only, was too heavy for her neck to bear. Her acquittal in the law court would be as nothing to her if it must be followed by an avowal of her guilt to her own son!

Sir Peregrine did come upstairs and handed her down through the hall as he had proposed. When he came into the room she did not look at him, but stood leaning against the table, with her eyes fixed upon the ground.

'I hope you find yourself better,' he said, as he put out his hand to her. She did not even attempt to make a reply, but allowed him just to touch her fingers.

'Perhaps I had better not come down,' said Mrs. Orme. 'It will be easier to say good-bye here.'

'Good-bye,' said Lady Mason, and her voice sounded in Sir Peregrine's ears like a voice from the dead.

'God bless you and preserve you,' said Mrs. Orme, 'and restore you to your son. God will bless you if you will ask Him. No; you shall not go without a kiss.' And she put out her arms that Lady Mason might come to her.

The poor broken wretch stood for a moment as though trying to determine what she would do; and then, almost with a shriek, she threw herself on to the bosom of the other woman, and burst into a flood of tears. She had intended to abstain from that embrace; she had resolved that she would do so, declaring to herself that she was not fit to be held against that pure heart; but the tenderness of the offer had overcome her, and now she pressed her friend convulsively in her arms, as though there might yet be comfort for her as long as she could remain close to one who was so good to her.

'I shall come and see you very often,' said Mrs. Orme,—'almost daily.'

'No, no, no,' exclaimed the other, hardly knowing the meaning of her own words.

'But I shall. My father is waiting now, dear, and you had better go.'

Sir Peregrine had turned to the window, where he stood shading his eyes with his hand. When he heard his daughter-in-law's last words he again came forward, and offered Lady Mason his arm. 'Edith is right,' he said. 'You had better go now. When you are at home you will be more composed.' And then he led her forth, and down the stairs, and across the hall, and with infinite courtesy put her into the carriage. It was a moment dreadful to Lady Mason; but to Sir Peregrine, also, it was not pleasant. The servants were standing round, officiously offering their aid,—those very servants who had been told about ten days since that this lady was to become their master's wife and their mistress. They had been told so with no injunction as to secrecy, and the tidings had gone quickly through the whole country. Now it was known that the match was broken off, that the lady had been living upstairs secluded for the last week, and that she was to leave the house this morning, having been committed during the last day or two to stand her trial at the assizes for some terrible offence! He succeeded in his task. He handed her into the carriage, and then walked back through his own servants to the library without betraying to them the depth of his sorrow; but he knew that the last task had been too heavy for him. When it was done he shut himself up and sat there for hours without moving. He also declared to himself that the world was too hard for him, and that it would be well for him that he should die. Never till now had he come into close contact with crime, and now the criminal was one whom as a woman he had learned to love, and whom he had proposed to the world as his wife! The criminal was one who had declared her crime in order to protect him, and whom therefore he was still bound in honour to protect!

When Lady Mason arrived at Orley Farm her son was waiting at the door to receive her. It should have been said that during the last two days,—that is ever since the committal,—Mrs. Orme had urged upon her very strongly that it would be well for her to tell everything to her son. 'What! now, at once?' the poor woman had said. 'Yes, dear, at once,' Mrs. Orme had answered. 'He will forgive you, for I know he is good. He will forgive you, and then the worst of your sorrow will be over.' But towards doing this Lady Mason had made no progress even in her mind. In the violence of her own resolution she had brought herself to tell her guilt to Sir Peregrine. That effort had nearly destroyed her, and now she knew that she could not frame the words which should declare the truth to Lucius. What; tell him that tale; whereas her whole life had been spent in an effort to conceal it from him? No. She knew that she could not do it. But the idea of doing so made her tremble at the prospect of meeting him.

'I am very glad you have come home, mother,' said Lucius, as he received her. 'Believe me that for the present this will be the best place for both of us,' and then he led her into the house.

'Dear Lucius, it would always be best for me to be with you, if it were possible.'

He did not accuse her of hypocrisy in saying this; but he could not but think that had she really thought and felt as she now spoke nothing need have prevented her remaining with him. Had not his house ever been open to her? Had he not been willing to make her defence the first object of his life? Had he not longed to prove himself a good son? But she had gone from him directly that troubles came upon her, and now she said that she would fain be with him always—if it were possible! Where had been the impediment? In what way had it been not possible? He thought of this with bitterness as he followed her into the house, but he said not a word of it. He had resolved that he would be a pattern son, and even now he would not rebuke her.

She had lived in this house for some four-and-twenty years, but it seemed to her in no way like her home. Was it not the property of her enemy, Joseph Mason? and did she not know that it must go back into that enemy's hands? How then could it be to her like a home? The room in which her bed was laid was that very room in which her sin had been committed? There in the silent hours of the night, while the old man lay near his death in the adjoining chamber, had she with infinite care and much slow preparation done that deed, to undo which, were it possible, she would now give away her existence,—ay, her very body and soul. And yet for years she had slept in that room, if not happily at least tranquilly. It was matter of wonder to her now, as she looked back at her past life, that her guilt had sat so lightly on her shoulders. The black unwelcome guest, the spectre of coming evil, had ever been present to her; but she had seen it indistinctly, and now and then the power had been hers to close her eyes. Never again could she close them. Nearer to her, and still nearer, the spectre came; and now it sat upon her pillow, and put its claw upon her plate; it pressed upon her bosom with its fiendish strength, telling her that all was over for her in this world;—ay, and telling her worse even than that. Her return to her old home brought with it but little comfort.

And yet she was forced to make an effort at seeming glad that she had come there,—a terrible effort! He, her son, was not gay or disposed to receive from her a show of happiness; but he did think that she should compose herself and be tranquil, and that she should resume the ordinary duties of her life in her ordinarily quiet way. In all this she was obliged to conform herself to his wishes, —or to attempt so to conform herself, though her heart should break in the struggle. If he did but know it all, then he would suffer her to be quiet,—suffer her to lie motionless in her misery! Once or twice she almost said to herself that she would make the effort; but then she thought of him and his suffering, of his pride, of the respect which he claimed from all the world as the honest son of an honest mother, of his stubborn will and stiff neck, which would not bend, but would break beneath the blow. She had done all for him,—to raise him in the world; and now she could not bring herself to undo the work that had cost her so dearly!

That evening she went through the ceremony of dinner with him, and he was punctilious in waiting upon her as though bread and meat could comfort her or wine could warm her heart. There was no warmth for her in all the vintages of the south, no comfort though gods should bring to her their banquets. She was heavy laden,—laden to the breaking of her back, and did not know where to lay her burden down.

'Mother,' he said to her that night, lifting his head from the books over which he had been poring, 'There must be a few words between us about this affair. They might as well be spoken now.'

'Yes, Lucius; of course—if you desire it.'

'There can be no doubt now that this trial will take place.'

'No doubt?' she said. 'There can be no doubt.'

'Is it your wish that I should take any part in it?'

She remained silent for some moments before she answered him, thinking,—striving to think, how best she might do him pleasure. 'What part?' she said at last.

' A man's part, and a son's part. Shall I see these lawyers and
learn from them what they are at? Have I your leave to tell them that
you want no subterfuge, no legal quibbles,—that you stand firmly
on your own clear innocence, and that you defy your enemies to
sully it? Mother, those who have sent you to such men as that
cunning attorney have sent you wrong,—have counselled you
wrong.'

'It cannot be changed now, Lucius.'

' It can be changed, if you will tell me to change it.'

And then again she paused. Ah, think of her anguish as she
sought for words to answer him! 'No, Lucius,' she said, 'it
cannot be changed now.'

' So be it, mother; I will not ask again,' and then he moodily
returned to his books, while she returned to her thoughts. Ah,
think of her misery!

CHAPTER XIV.

TELLING ALL THAT HAPPENED BENEATH THE LAMP-POST.

WHEN Felix Graham left Noningsby and made his way up to
London, he came at least to one resolution which he intended to be
an abiding one. That idea of a marriage with a moulded wife
should at any rate be abandoned. Whether it might be his great
destiny to be the husband of Madeline Staveley, or whether he
might fail in achieving this purpose, he declared to himself that
it would be impossible that he should ever now become the husband
of Mary Snow. And the ease with which his conscience settled
itself on this matter as soon as he had received from the judge that
gleam of hope astonished even himself. He immediately declared
to himself that he could not marry Mary Snow without perjury!
How could he stand with her before the altar and swear that he
would love her, seeing that he did not love her at all,—seeing that
he altogether loved some one else? He acknowledged that he had
made an ass of himself in this affair of Mary Snow. This moulding
of a wife had failed with him, he said, as it always must fail with
every man. But he would not carry his folly further. He would
go to Mary Snow, tell her the truth, and then bear whatever injury
her angry father might be able to inflict on him. Independently
of that angry father he would of course do for Mary Snow all that
his circumstances would admit.

Perhaps the gentleman of a poetic turn of mind whom Mary had
consented to meet beneath the lamp-post might assist him in his
views; but whether this might be so or not, he would not throw

that meeting ungenerously in her teeth. He would not have allowed that offence to turn him from his proposed marriage had there been nothing else to turn him, and therefore he would not plead that offence as the excuse for his broken troth. That the breaking of that troth would not deeply wound poor Mary's heart— so much he did permit himself to believe on the evidence of that lamp-post.

He had written to Mrs. Thomas telling her when he would be at Peckham, but in his letter he had not said a word as to those terrible tidings which she had communicated to him. He had written also to Mary, assuring her that he accused her of no injury against him, and almost promising her forgiveness; but this letter Mary had not shown to Mrs. Thomas. In these days Mary's anger against Mrs. Thomas was very strong. That Mrs. Thomas should have used all her vigilance to detect such goings on as those of the lamp-post was only natural. What woman in Mrs. Thomas's position,—or in any other position,—would not have done so? Mary Snow knew that had she herself been the duenna she would have left no corner of a box unturned but she would have found those letters. And having found them she would have used her power over the poor girl. She knew that. But she would not have betrayed her to the man. Truth between woman and woman should have prevented that. Were not the stockings which she had darned for Mrs. Thomas legion in number? Had she not consented to eat the veriest scraps of food in order that those three brats might be fed into sleekness to satisfy their mother's eyes? Had she not reported well of Mrs. Thomas to her lord, though that house of Peckham was nauseous to her? Had she ever told to Mr. Graham any one of those little tricks which were carried on to allure him into a belief that things at Peckham were prosperous? Had she ever exposed the borrowing of those teacups when he came, and the fact that those knobs of white sugar were kept expressly on his behoof? No; she would have scorned to betray any woman; and that woman whom she had not betrayed should have shown the same feeling towards her. Therefore there was enmity at Peckham, and the stockings of those infants lay unmended in the basket.

'Mary, I have done it all for the best,' said Mrs. Thomas, driven to defend herself by the obdurate silence of her pupil.

'No, Mrs. Thomas, you didn't. You did it for the worst,' said Mary. And then there was again silence between them.

It was on the morning following this that Felix Graham was driven to the door in a cab. He still carried his arm in a sling, and was obliged to be somewhat slow in his movements, but otherwise he was again well. His accident however was so far a godsend to both the women at Peckham that it gave them a subject on

which they were called upon to speak, before that other subject
was introduced. Mary was very tender in her inquiries,—but
tender in a bashful retiring way. To look at her one would have
said that she was afraid to touch the wounded man lest he should
be again broken.

'Oh, I'm all right,' said he, trying to assume a look of good-
humour. 'I sha'n't go hunting again in a hurry; you may be
sure of that.'

'We have all great reason to be thankful that Providence interposed to save you,' said Mrs. Thomas, in her most serious tone.
Had Providence interposed to break Mrs. Thomas's collar-bone,
or at least to do her some serious outward injury, what a comfort
it would be, thought Mary Snow.

'Have you seen your father lately?' asked Graham.

'Not since I wrote to you about the money that he—borrowed,'
said Mary.

'I told her that she should not have given it to him,' said Mrs.
Thomas.

'She was quite right,' said Graham. 'Who could refuse assistance to a father in distress?' Whereupon Mary put her handkerchief up to her eyes and began to cry.

'That's true of course,' said Mrs. Thomas; 'but it would never
do that he should be a drain in that way. He should feel that if he
had any feeling.'

'So he has,' said Mary. 'And you are driven close enough yourself sometimes, Mrs. Thomas. There's days when you'd like to
borrow nineteen and sixpence if anybody would lend it you.'

'Very well,' said Mrs. Thomas, crossing her hands over each
other in her lap and assuming a look of resignation; 'I suppose
all this will be changed now. I have endeavoured to do my duty,
and very hard it has been.'

Felix felt that the sooner he rushed into the middle of the subject which brought him there, the better it would be for all parties.
That the two ladies were not very happy together was evident, and
then he made a little comparison between Madeline and Mary.
Was it really the case that for the last three years he had contemplated making that poor child his wife? Would it not be
better for him to tie a millstone round his neck and cast himself
into the sea? That was now his thought respecting Mary Snow.

'Mrs. Thomas,' he said, 'I should like to speak to Mary alone
for a few minutes if you could allow it.'

'Oh certainly; by all means. It will be quite proper.' And
gathering up a bundle of the unfortunate stockings she took herself
out of the room.

Mary, as soon as Graham had spoken, became almost pale, and
sat perfectly still with her eyes fixed on her betrothed husband.

While Mrs. Thomas was there she was prepared for war and her spirit was hot within her, but all that heat fled in a moment when she found herself alone with the man to whom it belonged to speak her doom. He had almost said that he would forgive her, but yet she had a feeling that that had been done which could not altogether be forgiven. If he asked her whether she loved the hero of the lamp-post what would she say? Had he asked her whether she loved him, Felix Graham, she would have sworn that she did, and have thought that she was swearing truly; but in answer to that other question if it were asked, she felt that her answer must be false. She had no idea of giving up Felix of her own accord, if he were still willing to take her. She did not even wish that he would not take her. It had been the lesson of her life that she was to be his wife, and, by becoming so, provide for herself and for her wretched father. Nevertheless a dream of something different from that had come across her young heart, and the dream had been so pleasant! How painfully, but yet with what a rapture, had her heart palpitated as she stood for those ten wicked minutes beneath the lamp-post!

'Mary,' said Felix, as soon as they were alone,—and as he spoke he came up to her and took her hand, 'I trust that I may never be the cause to you of any unhappiness;—that I may never be the means of making you sad.'

'Oh, Mr. Graham, I am sure that you never will. It is I that have been bad to you.'

'No, Mary, I do not think you have been bad at all. I should have been sorry that that had happened, and that I should not have known it.'

'I suppose she was right to tell, only——' In truth Mary did not at all understand what might be the nature of Graham's thoughts and feelings on such a subject. She had a strong woman's idea that the man whom she ought to love would not be gratified by her meeting another man at a private assignation, especially when that other man had written to her a love-letter; but she did not at all know how far such a sin might be regarded as pardonable according to the rules of the world recognized on such subjects. At first, when the letters were discovered and the copies of them sent off to Noningsby, she thought that all was over. According to her ideas, as existing at that moment, the crime was conceived to be one admitting of no pardon; and in the hours spent under that conviction all her consolation came from the feeling that there was still one who regarded her as an angel of light. But then she had received Graham's letter, and as she began to understand that pardon was possible, that other consolation waxed feeble and dim. If Felix Graham chose to take her, of course she was there for him to take. It never for a moment occurred to her that she could rebel against such taking, even though she did shine as an angel of light to one dear pair of eyes.

' I suppose she was right to tell you, only——'

' Do not think, Mary, that I am going to scold you, or even that I am angry with you.'

' Oh, but I know you must be angry.'

' Indeed I am not. If I pledge myself to tell you the truth in everything, will you be equally frank with me?'

' Yes,' said Mary. But it was much easier for Felix to tell the truth than for Mary to be frank. I believe that schoolmasters often tell fibs to schoolboys, although it would be so easy for them to tell the truth. But how difficult it is for the schoolboy always to tell the truth to his master! Mary Snow was now as a schoolboy before her tutor, and it may almost be said that the telling of the truth was to her impossible. But of course she made the promise. Who ever said that she would not tell the truth when so asked?

' Have you ever thought, Mary, that you and I would not make each other happy if we were married?'

' No; I have never thought that,' said Mary innocently. She meant to say exactly that which she thought Graham would wish her to say, but she was slow in following his lead.

' It has never occurred to you that though we might love each other very warmly as friends—and so I am sure we always shall—yet we might not suit each other in all respects as man and wife?'

' I mean to do the very best I can; that is, if—if—if you are not too much offended with me now.'

' But, Mary, it should not be a question of doing the best you can. Between man and wife there should be no need of such effort. It should be a labour of love.'

' So it will;—and I'm sure I'll labour as hard as I can.'

Felix began to perceive that the line he had taken would not answer the required purpose, and that he must be somewhat more abrupt with her,—perhaps a little less delicate, in coming to the desired point. ' Mary,' he said, ' what is the name of that gentleman whom—whom you met out of doors you know?'

' Albert Fitzallen,' said Mary, hesitating very much as she pronounced the name, but nevertheless rather proud of the sound.

' And you are—fond of him?' asked Graham.

Poor girl! What was she to say? ' No; I'm not very fond of him.'

' Are you not? Then why did you consent to that secret meeting?'

' Oh, Mr. Graham—I didn't mean ·it; indeed I didn't. And I didn't tell him to write to me, nor yet to come looking after me. Upon my word I didn't. But then I thought when he sent me that letter that he didn't know;—about you I mean; and so I thought

I'd better tell him; and that's why I went.   Indeed that was the reason.'

'Mrs. Thomas could have told him that.'

'But I don't like Mrs. Thomas, and I wouldn't for worlds that she should have had anything to do with it.   I think Mrs. Thomas has behaved very bad to me; so I do.   And you don't half know her; —that you don't.'

'I will ask you one more question, Mary, and before answering it I want to make you believe that my only object in asking it is to ascertain how I may make you happy.   When you did meet Mr. — this gentleman——'

'Albert Fitzallen.'

'When you did meet Mr. Fitzallen, did you tell him nothing else except that you were engaged to me?   Did you say nothing to him as to your feelings towards himself?'

'I told him it was very wrong of him to write me that letter.'

'And what more did you tell him?'

'Oh, Mr. Graham, I won't see him any more; indeed I won't.   I give you my most solemn promise.   Indeed I won't.   And I will never write a line to him,—or look at him.   And if he sends anything I'll send it to you.   Indeed I will.   There was never anything of the kind before; upon my word there wasn't.   I did let him take my hand, but I didn't know how to help it when I was there.   And he kissed me—only once.   There; I've told it all now, as though you were looking at me.   And I aint a bad girl, whatever she may say of me.   Indeed I aint.'   And then poor Mary Snow burst out into an agony of tears.

Felix began to perceive that he had been too hard upon her.   He had wished that the first overtures of a separation should come from her, and in wishing this he had been unreasonable.   He walked for a while about the room, and then going up to her he stood close by her and took her hand.   'Mary,' he said, 'I'm sure you're not a bad girl.

'No;' she said, 'no, I aint;' still sobbing convulsively.   'I didn't mean anything wrong, and I couldn't help it.'

'I am sure you did not, and nobody has said you did.'

'Yes, they have.   She has said so.   She said that I was a bad girl.   She told me so, up to my face.'

'She was very wrong if she said so.'

'She did then, and I couldn't bear it.'

'I have not said so, and I don't think so.   Indeed in all this matter I believe that I have been more to blame than you.'

'No;—I know I was wrong.   I know I shouldn't have gone to see him.'

'I won't even say as much as that, Mary.   What you should have done;—only the task would have been too hard for any young girl

—was to have told me openly that you—liked this young gentleman.'

'But I don't want ever to see him again.'

'Look here, Mary,' he said. But now he had dropped her hand and taken a chair opposite to her. He had begun to find that the task which he had proposed to himself was not so easy even for him. 'Look here, Mary. I take it that you do like this young gentleman. Don't answer me till I have finished what I am going to say. I suppose you do like him,—and if so it would be very wicked in you to marry me.'

'Oh, Mr. Graham——'

'Wait a moment, Mary. But there is nothing wicked in your liking him.' It may be presumed that Mr. Graham would hold such an opinion as this, seeing that he had allowed himself the same latitude of liking. 'It was perhaps only natural that you should learn to do so. You have been taught to regard me rather as a master than as a lover.'

'Oh, Mr. Graham, I'm sure I've loved you. I have indeed. And I will. I won't even think of Al——'

'But I want you to think of him,—that is if he be worth thinking of.'

'He's a very good young man, and always lives with his mother.'

'It shall be my business to find out that. And now Mary, tell me truly. If he be a good young man, and if he loves you well enough to marry you, would you not be happier as his wife than you would as mine?'

There! The question that he wished to ask her had got itself asked at last. But if the asking had been difficult, how much more difficult must have been the answer! He had been thinking over all this for the last fortnight, and had hardly known how to come to a resolution. Now he put the matter before her without a moment's notice and expected an instant decision. 'Speak the truth, Mary;—what you think about it;—without minding what anybody may say of you.' But Mary could not say anything, so she again burst into tears.

'Surely you know the state of your own heart, Mary?'

'I don't know,' she answered.

'My only object is to secure your happiness;—the happiness of both of us, that is.'

'I'll do anything you please,' said Mary.

'Well then, I'll tell you what I think. I fear that a marriage between us would not make either of us contented with our lives. I'm too old and too grave for you.' Yet Mary Snow was not younger than Madeline Staveley. 'You have been told to love me; and you think that you do love me because you wish to do what you think to be your duty. But I believe that people can never really love each other merely because they are told to do so. Of course I cannot say what sort of a young man Mr. Fitzallen may be; but if I find that he is fit to take care of you, and that he has means to support you,—with such little help as I can give,—I shall be very happy to promote such an arrangement.'

Everybody will of course say that Felix Graham was base in not telling her that all this arose, not from her love affair with Albert Fitzallen, but from his own love affair with Madeline Staveley. But I am inclined to think that everybody will be wrong. Had he told her openly that he did not care for her, but did care for some one else, he would have left her no alternative. As it was, he did not mean that she should have any alternative. But he probably consulted her feelings best in allowing her to think that she had a choice. And then, though he owed much to her, he owed nothing to her father; and had he openly declared his intention of breaking off the match because he had attached himself to some one else, he would have put himself terribly into her father's power. He was willing to submit to such pecuniary burden in the matter as his conscience told him that he ought to bear; but Mr. Snow's ideas on the subject of recompense might be extravagant; and therefore,—as regarded Snow the father,—he thought that he might make some slight and delicate use of the meeting under the lamp-post. In doing so he would be very careful to guard Mary from her father's anger. Indeed Mary would be surrendered, out of his own care, not to that of her father, but to the fostering love of the gentleman in the medical line of life.

'I'll do anything that you please,' said Mary, upon whose mind and heart all these changes had come with a suddenness which prevented her from thinking,—much less speaking her thoughts.

'Perhaps you had better mention it to Mrs. Thomas.'

'Oh, Mr. Graham, I'd rather not talk to her. I don't love her a bit.'

'Well, I will not press it on you if you do not wish it. And have I your permission to speak to Mr. Fitzallen;—and if he approves to speak to his mother?'

'I'll do anything you think best, Mr. Graham,' said poor Mary. She was poor Mary; for though she had consented to meet a lover beneath the lamp-post, she had not been without ambition, and had looked forward to the glory of being wife to such a man as Felix Graham. She did not however, for one moment, entertain any idea of resistance to his will.

And then Felix left her, having of course an interview with Mrs. Thomas before he quitted the house. To her, however, he said nothing. 'When anything is settled, Mrs. Thomas, I will let you know.' The words were so lacking in confidence that Mrs.

Thomas when she heard them knew that the verdict had gone against her.

Felix for many months had been accustomed to take leave of Mary Snow with a kiss. But on this day he omitted to kiss her, and then Mary knew that it was all over with her ambition. But love still remained to her. 'There is some one else who will be proud to kiss me,' she said to herself, as she stood alone in the room when he closed the door behind him.

CHAPTER XV.

WHAT TOOK PLACE IN HARLEY STREET.

'Tom, I've come back again,' said Mrs. Furnival, as soon as the dining-room door was closed behind her back.

'I'm very glad to see you; I am indeed,' said he, getting up and putting out his hand to her. 'But I really never knew why you went away.'

'Oh yes, you know. I'm sure you know why I went. But——'

'I'll be shot if I did then.'

'I went away because I did not like Lady Mason going to your chambers.'

'Psha!'

'Yes; I know I was wrong, Tom. That is I was wrong—about that.'

'Of course you were, Kitty.'

'Well; don't I say I was? And I've come back again, and I beg your pardon;—that is about the lady.'

'Very well. Then there's an end of it.'

'But Tom; you know I've been provoked. Haven't I now? How often have you been home to dinner since you have been member of Parliament for that place?'

'I shall be more at home now, Kitty.'

'Shall you indeed? Then I'll not say another word to vex you. What on earth can I want, Tom, except just that you should sit at home with me sometimes on evenings, as you used to do always in the old days? And as for Martha Biggs——'

'Is she come back too?'

'Oh dear no. She's in Red Lion Square. And I'm sure, Tom, I never had her here except when you wouldn't dine at home. I wonder whether you know how lonely it is to sit down to dinner all by oneself!'

'Why; I do it every other day of my life. And I never think of sending for Martha Biggs; I promise you that.'

' She isn't very nice, I know,' said Mrs. Furnival—' that is, for gentlemen.'

' I should say not,' said Mr. Furnival.   Then the reconciliation had been effected, and Mrs. Furnival went upstairs to prepare for dinner, knowing that her husband would be present, and that Martha Biggs would not.   And just as she was taking her accustomed place at the head of the table, almost ashamed to look up lest she should catch Spooner's eye who was standing behind his master, Rachel went off in a cab to Orange Street, commissioned to pay what might be due for the lodgings, to bring back her mistress's boxes, and to convey the necessary tidings to Miss Biggs.

' Well I never!' said Martha, as she listened to Rachel's story.

' And they're quite loving I can assure you,' said Rachel.

' It'll never last,' said Miss Biggs triumphantly—' never.   It's been done too sudden to last.'

' So I'll say good-night if you please, Miss Biggs,' said Rachel, who was in a hurry to get back to Harley Street.

' I think she might have come here before she went there; especially as it wasn't anything out of her way.   She couldn't have gone shorter than Bloomsbury Square, and Russell Square, and over Tottenham Court Road.'

' Missus didn't think of that, I dare say.'

' She used to know the way about these parts well enough.   But give her my love, Rachel.'   Then Martha Biggs was again alone, and she sighed deeply.

It was well that Mrs. Furnival came back so quickly to her own house, as it saved the scandal of any domestic quarrel before her daughter.   On the following day Sophia returned, and as harmony was at that time reigning in Harley Street, there was no necessity that she should be presumed to know anything of what had occurred. That she did know,—know exactly what her mother had done, and why she had done it, and how she had come back, leaving Martha Biggs dumfounded by her return, is very probable, for Sophia Furnival was a clever girl, and one who professed to understand the inns and outs of her own family,—and perhaps of some other families.   But she behaved very prettily to her papa and mamma on the occasion, never dropping a word which could lead either of them to suppose that she had interrogated Rachel, been confidential with the housemaid, conversed on the subject—even with Spooner, and made a morning call on Martha Biggs herself.

There arose not unnaturally some conversation between the mother and daughter as to Lady Mason ;—not as to Lady Mason's visits to Lincoln's Inn and their impropriety as formerly presumed; —not at all as to that ; but in respect to her present lamentable position and that engagement which had for a time existed between her and Sir Peregrine Orme.   On this latter subject Mrs. Furnival

had of course heard nothing during her interview with Mrs. Orme
at Noningsby.   At that time Lady Mason had formed the sole
subject of conversation; but in explaining to Mrs. Furnival that
there certainly could be no unhallowed feeling between her husband
and the lady, Mrs. Orme had not thought it necessary to allude to
Sir Peregrine's past intentions.   Mrs. Furnival, however, had heard
the whole matter discussed in the railway carriage, had since
interrogated her husband,—learning, however, not very much from
him,—and now inquired into all the details from her daughter.

'And she and Sir Peregrine were really to be married?' Mrs.
Furnival, as she asked the question, thought with confusion of her
own unjust accusations against the poor woman.   Under such
circumstances as those Lady Mason must of course have been innocent as touching Mr. Furnival.

'Yes,' said Sophia.   'There is no doubt whatsoever that they
were engaged.   Sir Peregrine told Lady Staveley so himself.'

'And now it's all broken off again?'

'Oh yes; it is all broken off now.   I believe the fact to be this.
Lord Alston, who lives near Noningsby, is a very old friend of
Sir Peregrine's.   When he heard of it he went to The Cleeve—
I know that for certain;—and I think he talked Sir Peregrine out
of it.'

'But, my conscience, Sophia——after he had made her the
offer!'

'I fancy that Mrs. Orme arranged it all.   Whether Lord Alston
saw her or not I don't know.   My belief is that Lady Mason behaved very well all through, though they say very bitter things
against her at Noningsby.'

'Poor thing!' said Mrs. Furnival, the feelings of whose heart
were quite changed as regarded Lady Mason.

'I never knew a woman so badly treated.'   Sophia had her own
reasons for wishing to make the best of Lady Mason's case.   'And
for myself I do not see why Sir Peregrine should not have married
her if he pleased.'

'He is rather old, my dear.'

'People don't think so much about that now-a-days as they used.
If he liked it, and she too, who had a right to say anything?   My
idea is that a man with any spirit would have turned Lord Alston
out of the house.   What business had he to interfere?'

'But about the trial, Sophia?'

'That will go on.   There's no doubt about that.   But they all
say that it's the most unjust thing in the world, and that she must
be proved innocent.   I heard the judge say so myself.'

'But why are they allowed to try her then?'

'Oh, papa will tell you that.'

'I never like to bother your papa about law business.'   Particularly not, Mrs. Furnival, when he has a pretty woman for his client!

'My wonder is that she should make herself so unhappy about it,' continued Sophia. 'It seems that she is quite broken down.'

'But won't she have to go and sit in the court,—with all the people staring at her?'

'That won't kill her,' said Sophia, who felt that she herself would not perish under any such process. 'If I was sure that I was in the right, I think that I could hold up my head against all that. But they say that she is crushed to the earth.'

'Poor thing!' said Lady Mason. 'I wish that I could do anything for her.' And in this way they talked the matter over very comfortably.

Two or three days after this Sophia Furnival was sitting alone in the drawing-room in Harley Street, when Spooner answered a double knock at the door, and Lucius Mason was shown upstairs. Mrs. Furnival had gone to make her peace in Red Lion Square, and there may perhaps be ground for supposing that Lucius had cause to expect that Miss Furnival might be seen at this hour without interruption. Be that as it may, she was found alone, and he was permitted to declare his purpose unmolested by father, mother, or family friends.

'You remember how we parted at Noningsby,' said he, when their first greetings were well over.

'Oh, yes; I remember it very well. I do not easily forget words such as were spoken then.'

'You said that you would never turn away from me.'

'Nor will I;—that is with reference to the matter as to which we were speaking.'

'Is our friendship then to be confined to one subject?'

'By no means. Friendship cannot be so confined, Mr. Mason. Friendship between true friends must extend to all the affairs of life. What I meant to say was this—— But I am quite sure that you understand me without any explanation.'

He did understand her. She meant to say that she had promised to him her sympathy and friendship, but nothing more. But then he had asked for nothing more. The matter of doubt within his own heart was this. Should he or should he not ask for more; and if he resolved on answering this question in the affirmative, should he ask for it now? He had determined that morning that he would come to some fixed purpose on this matter before he reached Harley Street. As he crossed out of Oxford Street from the omnibus he had determined that the present was no time for love-making;— walking up Regent Street, he had told himself that if he had one faithful heart to bear him company he could bear his troubles better;—as he made his way along the north side of Cavendish

Square he pictured to himself what would be the wound to his pride if he were rejected;—and in passing the ten or twelve houses which intervened in Harley Street between the corner of the square and the abode of his mistress, he told himself that the question must be answered by circumstances.

'Yes, I understand you,' he said. 'And believe me in this—I would not for worlds encroach on your kindness. I knew that when I pressed your hand that night, I pressed the hand of a friend, —and nothing more.'

'Quite so,' said Sophia. Sophia's wit was usually ready enough, but at that moment she could not resolve with what words she might make the most appropriate reply to her—friend. What she did say was rather lame, but it was not dangerous.

'Since that I have suffered a great deal,' said Lucius. 'Of course you know that my mother has been staying at The Cleeve?'

'Oh yes. I believe she left it only a day or two since.'

'And you heard perhaps of her—. I hardly know how to tell you, if you have not heard it.'

'If you mean about Sir Peregrine, I have heard of that.'

'Of course you have. All the world has heard of it.' And Lucius Mason got up and walked about the room holding his hand to his brow. 'All the world are talking about it. Miss Furnival, you have never known what it is to blush for a parent.'

Miss Furnival at the moment felt a sincere hope that Mr. Mason might never hear of Mrs. Furnival's visit to the neighbourhood of Orange Street and of the causes which led to it, and by no means thought it necessary to ask for her friend's sympathy on that subject. 'No,' said she, 'I never have; nor need you do so for yours. Why should not Lady Mason have married Sir Peregrine Orme, if they both thought such a marriage fitting?'

'What; at such a time as this; with these dreadful accusations running in her ears? Surely this was no time for marrying! And what has come of it? People now say that he has rejected her and sent her away.'

'Oh no. They cannot say that.'

'But they do. It is reported that Sir Peregrine has sent her away because he thinks her to be guilty. That I do not believe. No honest man, no gentleman, could think her guilty. But is it not dreadful that such things should be said?'

'Will not the trial take place very shortly now? When that is once over all these troubles will be at an end.'

'Miss Furnival, I sometimes think that my mother will hardly have strength to sustain the trial. She is so depressed that I almost fear her mind will give way; and the worst of it is that I am altogether unable to comfort her.'

'Surely that at present should specially be your task

' I cannot do it. What should I say to her? I think that she is wrong in what she is doing; thoroughly, absolutely wrong. She has got about her a parcel of lawyers. I beg your pardon, Miss Furnival, but you know I do not mean such as your father.'

' But has not he advised it?'

' If so I cannot but think he is wrong. They are the very scum of the gaols; men who live by rescuing felons from the punishment they deserve. What can my mother require of such services as theirs? It is they that frighten her and make her dread all manner of evils. Why should a woman who knows herself to be good and just fear anything that the law can do to her?'

' I can easily understand that such a position as hers must be very dreadful. You must not be hard upon her, Mr. Mason, because she is not as strong as you might be.'

' Hard upon her! Ah, Miss Furnival, you do not know me. If she would only accept my love I would wait upon her as a mother does upon her infant. No labour would be too much for me; no care would be too close. But her desire is that this affair should never be mentioned between us. We are living now in the same house, and though I see that this is killing her yet I may not speak of it.' Then he got up from his chair, and as he walked about the room he took his handkerchief from his pocket and wiped his eyes.

' I wish I could comfort you,' said she. And in saying so she spoke the truth. By nature she was not tender hearted, but now she did sympathize with him. By nature, too, she was not given to any deep affection, but she did feel some spark of love for Lucius Mason. ' I wish I could comfort you.' And as she spoke she also got up from her chair.

' And you can,' said he, suddenly stopping himself and coming close to her. ' You can comfort me,—in some degree. You and you only can do so. I know this is no time for declarations of love. Were it not that we are already so much to each other, I would not indulge myself at such a moment with such a wish. But I have no one whom I can love; and—it is very hard to bear.' And then he stood, waiting for her answer, as though he conceived that he had offered her his hand.

But Miss Furnival well knew that she had received no offer. ' If my warmest sympathy can be of service to you——'

' It is your love I want,' he said, taking her hand as he spoke. ' Your love, so that I may look on you as my wife;—your acceptance of my love, so that we may be all in all to each other. There is my hand. I stand before you now as sad a man as there is in all London. But there is my hand—will you take it and give me yours in pledge of your love.'

I should be unjust to Lucius Mason were I to omit to say that he played his part with a becoming air. Unhappiness and a melancholy mood suited him perhaps better than the world's ordinary good-humour. He was a man who looked his best when under a cloud, and shone the brightest when everything about him was dark. And Sophia also was not unequal to the occasion. There was, however, this difference between them. Lucius was quite honest in all that he said and did upon the occasion; whereas Miss Furnival was only half honest. Perhaps she was not capable of a higher pitch of honesty than that.

' There is my hand,' said she; and they stood holding each other, palm to palm.

' And with it your heart?' said Lucius.

' And with it my heart,' answered Sophia. Nor as she spoke did she hesitate for a moment, or become embarrassed, or lose her command of feature. Had Augustus Staveley gone through the same ceremony at Noningsby in the same way I am inclined to think that she would have made the same answer. Had neither done so, she would not on that account have been unhappy. What a blessed woman would Lady Staveley have been had she known what was being done in Harley Street at this moment!

In some short rhapsody of love it may be presumed that Lucius indulged himself when he found that the affair which he had in hand had so far satisfactorily arranged itself. But he was in truth too wretched at heart for any true enjoyment of the delights of a favoured suitor. They were soon engaged again on that terrible subject, seated side by side indeed and somewhat close, but the tone of their voices and their very words were hardly different from what they might have been had no troth been plighted between them. His present plan was that Sophia should visit Orley Farm for a time, and take that place of dear and bosom friend which a woman circumstanced as was his mother must so urgently need. We, my readers, know well who was now that loving friend, and we know also which was best fitted for such a task, Sophia Furnival or Mrs. Orme. But we have had, I trust, better means of reading the characters of those ladies than had fallen to the lot of Lucius Mason, and should not be angry with him because his eyes were dark.

Sophia hesitated a moment before she answered this proposition, —not as though she were slack in her love, or begrudged her services to his mother; but it behoved her to look carefully at the circumstances before she would pledge herself to such an arrangement as that. If she went to Orley Farm on such a mission would it not be necessary to tell her father and mother,—nay, to tell all the world that she was engaged to Lucius Mason; and would it be wise to make such a communication at the present moment? Lucius said a word to her of going into court with his mother, and sitting with her, hand in hand, while that ordeal was passing by.

In the publicity of such sympathy there was something that suited the bearings of Miss Furnival's mind. The idea that Lady Mason was guilty had never entered her head, and therefore, on this she thought there could be no disgrace in such a proceeding. But nevertheless—might it not be prudent to wait till that trial were over?

' If you are my wife you must be her daughter; and how can you better take a daughter's part?' pleaded Lucius.

'No, no; and I would do it with my whole heart. But, Lucius, does she know me well enough? It is of her that we must think. After all that you have told me, can we think that she would wish me to be there?'

It was his desire that his mother should learn to have such a wish, and this he explained to her. He himself could do but little at home because he could not yield his opinion on those matters of importance as to which he and his mother differed so vitally; but if she had a woman with her in the house,—such a woman as his own Sophia—then he thought her heart would be softened and part of her sorrow might be assuaged.

Sophia at last said that she would think about it. It would be improper, she said, to pledge herself to anything rashly. It might be that as her father was to defend Lady Mason, he might on that account object to his daughter being in the court. Lucius declared that this would be unreasonable,—unless indeed Mr. Furnival should object to his daughter's engagement. And might he not do so? Sophia thought it very probable that he might. It would make no difference in her, she said. Her engagement would be equally binding,—as permanently binding, let who would object to it. And as she made this declaration, there was of course a little love scene. But, for the present, it might be best that in this matter she should obey her father. And then she pointed out how fatal it might be to avert her father from the cause while the trial was still pending. Upon the whole she acted her part very prudently, and when Lucius left her she was pledged to nothing but that one simple fact of a marriage engagement.

CHAPTER XVI.

In the mean time Sir Peregrine was sitting at home trying to deter mine in what way he should act under the present emergency, actuated as he was on one side by friendship and on the other by duty. For the first day or two—nay for the first week after the confession had been made to him,—he had been so astounded, had been so knocked to the earth, and had remained in such a state of bewilder ment, that it had been impossible for him to form for himself any line of conduct. His only counsellor had been Mrs. Orme ; and, though he could not analyze the matter, he felt that her woman's ideas of honour and honesty were in some way different from his ideas as a man. To her the sorrows and utter misery of Lady Mason seemed of greater weight than her guilt. At least such was the impression which her words left. Mrs. Orme's chief anxiety in the matter still was that Lady Mason should be acquitted ;—as strongly so now as when they both believed her to be as guiltless as themselves. But Sir Peregrine could not look at in this light. He did not say that he wished that she might be found guilty ;—nor did he wish it. But he did announce his opinion to his daughter-in-law that the ends of justice would so be best promoted, and that if the matter were driven to a trial it would not be for the honour of the court that a false verdict should be given. Nor would he believe that such a false verdict could be obtained. An English judge and an English jury were to him the Palladium of discerning truth. In an English court of law such a matter could not remain dark ;—nor ought it, let whatever misery betide. It was strange how that old man should have lived so near the world for seventy years, should have taken his place in Parliament and on the bench, should have rubbed his shoulders so constantly against those of his neighbours, and yet have retained so strong a reliance on the purity of the world in general. Here and there such a man may still be found, but the number is becoming very few.

As for the property, that must of necessity be abandoned. Lady Mason had signified her agreement to this ; and therefore he was so far willing that she should be saved from further outward punish ment, if that were still possible. His plan was this ; and to his thinking it was the only plan that was feasible. Let the estate be at once given up to the proper owner,—even now, before the day of trial should come; and then let them trust, not to Joseph Mason, but to Joseph Mason's advisers to abstain from prosecuting the offender. Even this course he knew to be surrounded by a thousand difficulties; but it might be possible. Of Mr. Round, old Mr. Round, he had heard a good report. He was a kind man, and even in this very matter had behaved in a way that had shamed his client. Might it not be possible that Mr. Round would engage to drop the prosecution if the immediate return of the property were secured? But to effect this must he not tell Mr. Round of the woman's guilt? And could he manage it himself? Must he not tell Mr. Furnival? And by so doing, would he not rob Lady Mason of her sole remaining tower of strength?—for if Mr. Furnival knew that she was guilty, Mr. Furnival must of course abandon her cause. And then Sir Peregrine did not know how to turn himself, as he thus argued the matter within his own bosom.

And then too his own disgrace sat very heavy on him. Whether or no the law might pronounce Lady Mason to have been guilty, all the world would know her guilt. When that property should be abandoned, and her wretched son turned out to earn his bread, it would be well understood that she had been guilty. And this was the woman, this midnight forger, whom he had taken to his bosom, and asked to be his wife! He had asked her, and she had consented, and then he had proclaimed the triumph of his love to all the world. When he stood there holding her to his breast he had been proud of her affection. When Lord Alston had come to him with his caution he had scorned his old friend and almost driven him from his door. When his grandson had spoken a word, not to him but to another, he had been full of wrath. He had let it be known widely that he would feel no shame in showing her to the world as Lady Orme. And now she was a forger, and a perjurer, and a thief;—a thief who for long years had lived on the proceeds of her dexterous theft. And yet was he not under a deep obligation to her—under the very deepest? Had she not saved him from a worse disgrace;—saved him at the cost of all that was left to herself? Was he not still bound to stand by her? And did he not still love her?

Poor Sir Peregrine! May we not say that it would have been well for him if the world and all its trouble could have now been ended so that he might have done with it?

Mrs. Orme was his only counsellor, and though she could not be brought to agree with him in all his feelings, yet she was of infinite comfort to him. Had she not shared with him this terrible secret his mind would have given way beneath the burden. On the day after Lady Mason's departure from The Cleeve, he sat for an hour in the library considering what he would do, and then he sent for his daughter-in-law. If it behoved him to take any step to stay the trial, he must take it at once. The matter had been pressed on by each side, and now the days might be counted up to that day on which the judges would arrive in Alston. That trial would be very terrible to him in every way. He had promised, during those pleasant hours of his love and sympathy in which he had felt no doubt as to his friend's acquittal, that he would stand by her when she was arraigned. That was now impossible, and though he had not dared to mention it to Lady Mason, he knew that she would not expect that he should do so. But to Mrs. Orme he had spoken on the matter, and she had declared her purpose of taking the place which it would not now become him to fill! Sir Peregrine had started from his chair when she had so spoken. What! his daughter! She, the purest of the pure, to whom the very air of a court of law would be a contamination;—she, whose whiteness had never been sullied by contact with the world's dust; she set by the side of that terrible criminal, hand in hand with her, present to all the world as her bosom friend! There had been but few words between them on the matter; but Sir Peregrine had felt strongly that that might not be permitted. Far better than that it would be that he should humble his gray hairs and sit there to be gazed at by the crowd. But on all accounts how much was it to be desired that there should be no trial!

'Sit down, Edith,' he said, as with her soft step she came up to him. 'I find that the assizes will be here, in Alston, at the end of next month.'

'So soon as that, father?'

'Yes; look here : the judges will come in on the 25th of March.'

'Ah me—that is very sudden. But, father, will it not be best for her that it should be over?'

Mrs. Orme still thought, had always thought that the trial itself was unavoidable. Indeed she had thought and she did think that it afforded to Lady Mason the only possible means of escape. Her mind on the subject, if it could have been analyzed, would probably have been this. As to the property, that question must for the present stand in abeyance. It is quite right that it should go to its detestable owners,—that it should be made over to them at some day not very distant. But for the present, the trial for that old, long-distant crime was the subject for them to consider. Could it be wrong to wish for an acquittal for the sinner,—an acquittal before this world's bar, seeing that a true verdict had undoubtedly been given before another bar? Mrs. Orme trusted that no jury would convict her friend. Let Lady Mason go through that ordeal; and then, when the law had declared her innocent, let restitution be made.

'It will be very terrible to all if she be condemned,' said Sir Peregrine.

'Very terrible! But Mr. Furnival——'

'Edith, if it comes to that, she will be condemned. Mr. Furnival is a lawyer and will not say so; but from his countenance, when he speaks of her, I know that he expects it!'

'Oh, father, do not say so.'

'But if it is so——. My love, what is the purport of these courts of law if it be not to discover the truth, and make it plain to the light of day?' Poor Sir Peregrine! His innocence in this respect was perhaps beautiful, but it was very simple. Mr. Aram, could he have been induced to speak out his mind plainly, would have expressed, probably, a different opinion.

'But she escaped before,' said Mrs. Orme, who was clearly at present on the same side with Mr. Aram.

'Yes; she did;—by perjury, Edith. And now the penalty of that further crime awaits her. There was an old poet who said that the wicked man rarely escapes at last. I believe in my heart that he spoke the truth.'

'Father, that old poet knew nothing of our faith.'

Sir Peregrine could not stop to explain, even if he knew how to do so, that the old poet spoke of punishment in this world, whereas the faith on which his daughter relied is efficacious for pardon beyond the grave. It would be much, ay, in one sense everything, if Lady Mason could be brought to repent of the sin she had committed; but no such repentance would stay the bitterness of Joseph Mason or of Samuel Dockwrath. If the property were at once restored, then repentance might commence. If the property were at once restored, then the trial might be stayed. It might be possible that Mr. Round might so act. He felt all this, but he could not argue on it. 'I think, my dear,' he said, 'that I had better see Mr. Round.'

'But you will not tell him?' said Mrs. Orme, sharply.

'No; I am not authorized to do that.'

'But he will entice it from you! He is a lawyer, and he will wind anything out from a plain, chivalrous man of truth and honour.'

'My dear, Mr. Round I believe is a good man.'

'But if he asks you the question, what will you say?'

'I will tell him to ask me no such question.'

'Oh, father, be careful. For her sake be careful. How is it that you know the truth;—or that I know it? She told it here because in that way only could she save you from that marriage. Father, she has sacrificed herself for—for us.'

Sir Peregrine when this was said to him got up from his chair and walked away to the window. He was not angry with her that she so spoke to him. Nay; he acknowledged inwardly the truth of her words, and loved her for her constancy. But nevertheless they were very bitter. How had it come to pass that he was thus indebted to so deep a criminal? What had he done for her but good?

'Do not go from me,' she said, following him. 'Do not think me unkind.'

'No, no, no,' he answered, striving almost ineffectually to repress a sob. 'You are not unkind.'

For two days after that not a word was spoken between them on the subject, and then he did go to Mr. Round. Not a word on the subject was spoken between Sir Peregrine and Mrs. Orme; but she was twice at Orley Farm during the time, and told Lady Mason of the steps which her father-in-law was taking. 'He won't betray me!' Lady Mason had said. Mrs. Orme had answered this with what best assurance she should give; but in her heart of hearts she feared that Sir Peregrine would betray the secret.

It was not a pleasant journey for Sir Peregrine. Indeed it may be said that no journeys could any longer be pleasant for him. He was old and worn and feeble; very much older and much more worn than he had been at the period spoken of in the commencement of this story, though but a few months had passed over his head since that time. For him now it would have been preferable to remain in the arm-chair by the fireside in his own library, receiving such comfort in his old age as might come to him from the affection of his daughter-in-law and grandson. But he thought that it behoved him to do this work; and therefore, old and feeble as he was, he set himself to his task. He reached the station in London, had himself driven to Bedford Row in a cab, and soon found himself in the presence of Mr. Round.

There was much ceremonial talk between them before Sir Peregrine could bring himself to declare the purport which had brought him there. Mr. Round of course protested that he was very sorry for all this affair. The case was not in his hands personally. He had hoped many years since that the matter was closed. His client, Mr. Mason of Groby Park, had insisted that it should be reopened; and now he, Mr. Round, really hardly knew what to say about it.

'But, Mr. Round, do you think it is quite impossible that the trial should even now be abandoned?' asked Sir Peregrine very carefully.

'Well, I fear it is. Mason thinks that the property is his, and is determined to make another struggle for it. I am imputing nothing wrong to the lady. I really am not in a position to have any opinion of my own——'

'No, no, no; I understand. Of course your firm is bound to do the best it can for its client. But, Mr. Round;—I know I am quite safe with you.'

'Well; safe in one way I hope you are. But, Sir Peregrine, you must of course remember that I am the attorney for the other side, —for the side to which you are opposed.'

Sir Peregrine at Mr. Round's office.

' But still ;—all that you can want is your client's interest.'

' Of course we desire to serve his interest.'

' And with that view, Mr. Round, is it not possible that we might come to some compromise ?'

' What ;—by giving up part of the property?'

' By giving up all the property,' said Sir Peregrine, with considerable emphasis.

' Whew—w—w.'   Mr. Round at the moment made no other answer than this, which terminated in a low whistle.

' Better that, at once, than that she should die broken-hearted,' said Sir Peregrine.

There was then silence between them for a minute or two, after which Mr. Round, turning himself round in his chair so as to face his visitor more fully, spoke as follows.   ' I told you just now, Sir Peregrine, that I was Mr. Mason's attorney, and I must now tell you, that as regards this interview between you and me, I will not hold myself as being in that position.   What you have said shall be as though it had not been said ; and as I am not, myself, taking any part in the proceedings, this may with absolute strictness be the case.   But——'

' If I have said anything that I ought not to have said—' began Sir Peregrine.

' Allow me for one moment,' continued Mr. Round.   ' The fault is mine, if there be a fault, as I should have explained to you that the matter could hardly be discussed with propriety between us.'

' Mr. Round, I offer you my apology from the bottom of my heart.'

' No, Sir Peregrine.   You shall offer me no apology, nor will I accept any.   I know no words strong enough to convey to you my esteem and respect for your character.'

' Sir !'

' But I will ask you to listen to me for a moment.   If any compromise be contemplated, it should be arranged by the advice of Mr. Furnival and of Mr. Chaffanbrass, and the terms should be settled between Mr. Aram and my son.   But I cannot myself say that I see any possibility of such a result.   It is not however for me to advise.   If on that matter you wish for advice, I think that you had better see Mr. Furnival.'

' Ah !' said Sir Peregrine, telling more and more of the story by every utterance he made.

' And now it only remains for me to assure you once more that the words which have been spoken in this room shall be as though they had not been spoken.'   And then Mr. Round made it very clear that there was nothing more to be said between them on the subject of Lady Mason.   Sir Peregrine repeated his apology, collected his hat and gloves, and with slow step made his way down to his cab, while Mr. Round absolutely waited upon him till he saw him seated within the vehicle.

'So Mat is right after all,' said the old attorney to himself as he stood alone with his back to his own fire, thursting his hands into his trousers-pockets. 'So Mat is right after all!' The meaning of this exclamation will be plain to my readers. Mat had declared to his father his conviction that Lady Mason had forged the codicil in question, and the father was now also convinced that she had done so. 'Unfortunate woman!' he said; 'poor, wretched woman!' And then he began to calculate what might yet be her chances of escape. On the whole he thought that she would escape. 'Twenty years of possession,' he said to himself; 'and so excellent a character!' But, nevertheless, he repeated to himself over and over again that she was a wretched, miserable woman.

We may say that all the persons most concerned were convinced, or nearly convinced, of Lady Mason's guilt. Among her own friends Mr. Furnival had no doubt of it, and Mr. Chaffanbrass and Mr. Aram but very little; whereas Sir Peregrine and Mrs. Orme of course had none. On the other side Mr. Mason and Mr. Dockwrath were both fully sure of the truth, and the two Rounds, father and son, were quite of the same mind. And yet, except with Dockwrath and Sir Peregrine, the most honest and the most dishonest of the lot, the opinion was that she would escape. These were five lawyers concerned, not one of whom gave to the course of justice credit that it would ascertain the truth, and not one of whom wished that the truth should be ascertained. Surely had they been honest-minded in their profession they would all have so wished;— have so wished, or else have abstained from all professional inter- course in the matter. I cannot understand how any gentleman can be willing to use his intellect for the propagation of untruth, and to be paid for so using it. As to Mr. Chaffanbrass and Mr. Solomon Aram,—to them the escape of a criminal under their auspices would of course be a matter of triumph. To such work for many years had they applied their sharp intellects and legal knowledge. But of Mr. Furnival;—what shall we say of him?

Sir Peregrine went home very sad at heart, and crept silently back into his own library. In the evening, when he was alone with Mrs. Orme, he spoke one word to her. 'Edith,' he said, 'I have seen Mr. Round. We can do nothing for her there.'

'I feared not,' said she.

'No; we can do nothing for her there.'

After that Sir Peregrine took no step in the matter. What step could he take? But he sat over his fire in his library, day after day, thinking over it all, and waiting till those terrible assizes should have come.

CHAPTER XVII.

FELIX GRAHAM, when he left poor Mary Snow, did not go on immediately to the doctor's shop. He had made up his mind that Mary Snow should never be his wife, and therefore considered it wise to lose no time in making such arrangements as might be necessary both for his release and for hers. But, nevertheless, he had not the heart to go about the work the moment that he left her. He passed by the apothecary's, and looking in saw a young man working sedulously at a pestle. If Albert Fitzallen were fit to be her husband and willing to be so, poor as he was himself, he would still make some pecuniary sacrifice by which he might quiet his own conscience and make Mary's marriage possible. He still had a sum of 1,200l. belonging to him, that being all his remaining capital; and the half of that he would give to Mary as her dower. So in two days he returned, and again looking in at the doctor's shop, again saw the young man at his work.

'Yes, sir, my name is Albert Fitzallen,' said the medical aspirant, coming round the counter. There was no one else in the shop, and Felix hardly knew how to accost him on so momentous a subject, while he was still in charge of all that store of medicine, and liable to be called away at any moment to relieve the ailments of Clapham. Albert Fitzallen was a pale-faced, light-haired youth, with an incipient moustache, with his hair parted in equal divisions over his forehead, with elaborate shirt-cuffs elaborately turned back, and with a white apron tied round him so that he might pursue his vocation without injury to his nether garments. His face, however, was not bad, nor mean, and had there not been about him a little air of pretension, assumed perhaps to carry off the combined apron and beard, Felix would have regarded him altogether with favourable eyes.

'Is it in the medical way?' asked Fitzallen, when Graham suggested that he should step out with him for a few minutes. Graham explained that it was not in the medical way,—that it was in a way altogether of a private nature; and then the young man, pulling off his apron and wiping his hands on a thoroughly medicated towel, invoked the master of the establishment from an inner room, and in a few minutes Mary Snow's two lovers were walking together, side by side, along the causeway.

'I believe you know Miss Snow,' said Felix, rushing at once into the middle of all those delicate circumstances.

Albert Fitzallen drew himself up, and declared that he had that honour.

'I also know her,' said Felix. 'My name is Felix Graham——'

'Oh, sir, very well,' said Albert. The street in which they were standing was desolate, and the young man was able to assume a look of decided hostility without encountering any other eyes than those of his rival. 'If you have anything to say to me, sir, I am quite prepared to listen to you—to listen to you, and to answer you. I have heard your name mentioned by Miss Snow.' And Albert Fitzallen stood his ground as though he were at once going to cover himself with his pistol arm.

'Yes, I know you have. Mary has told me what has passed between you. You may regard me, Mr. Fitzallen, as Mary's best and surest friend.'

'I know you have been a friend to her; I am aware of that. But, Mr. Graham, if you will allow me to say so, friendship is one thing, and the warm love of a devoted bosom is another.'

'Quite so,' said Felix.

'A woman's heart is a treasure not to be bought by any efforts of friendship,' said Fitzallen.

'I fully agree with you there,' said Graham.

'Far be it from me to make any boast,' continued the other, 'or even to hint that I have gained a place in that lady's affections. I know my own position too well, and say proudly that I am existing only on hope.' Here, to show his pride, he hit himself with his closed fist on his shirt-front. 'But, Mr. Graham, I am free to declare, even in your presence, though you may be her best and surest friend,'—and there was not wanting, from the tone of his voice a strong flavour of scorn as he repeated these words—'that I do exist on hope, let your claims be what they will. If you desire to make such hope on my part a cause of quarrel, I have nothing to say against it.' And then he twirled all that he could twirl of that incipient moustache.

'By no means,' said Graham.

'Oh, very well,' said Fitzallen. 'Then we understand that the arena of love is open to us both. I do not fail to appreciate the immense advantages which you enjoy in this struggle.' And then Fitzallen looked up into Graham's ugly face, and thought of his own appearance in the looking-glass.

'What I want to know is this,' said Felix. 'If you marry Mary Snow, what means have you of maintaining her? Would your mother receive her into her house? I presume you are not a

partner in that shop; but would it be possible to get you in as a
partner, supposing Mary were to marry you and had a little money
as her fortune?'

'Eh!' said Albert, dropping his look of pride, allowing his hand
to fall from his lips, and standing still before his companion with
his mouth wide open.

'Of course you mean honestly by dear Mary.'

'Oh, sir, yes, on the honour of a gentleman.   My intentions, sir,
are ——.   Mr. Graham, I love that young lady with a devotion of
heart, that—that—that—.   Then you don't mean to marry her
yourself; eh, Mr. Graham?'

'No, Mr. Fitzallen, I do not.   And now, if you will so far
confide in me, we will talk over your prospects.'

'Oh, very well.   I'm sure you are very kind.   But Miss Snow
did tell me——'

'Yes, I know she did, and she was quite right.   But as you said
just now, a woman's heart cannot be bought by friendship.   I have
not been a bad friend to Mary, but I had no right to expect that I
could win her love in that way.   Whether or no you may be able to
succeed, I will not say, but I have abandoned the pursuit.'   In all
which Graham intended to be exceedingly honest, but was, in truth,
rather hypocritical.

'Then the course is open to me,' said Fitzallen.

'Yes, the course is open,' answered Graham.

'But the race has still to be run.   Don't you think that Miss
Snow is of her nature very—very cold?'

Felix remembered the one kiss beneath the lamp-post,—the one
kiss given, and received.   He remembered also that Mary's acquaintance with the gentleman must necessarily have been short; and he
made no answer to this question.   But he made a comparison.
What would Madeline have said and done had he attempted such
an iniquity?   And he thought of her flashing eyes and terrible
scorn, of the utter indignation of all the Staveley family, and of
the wretched abyss into which the offender would have fallen.

He brought back the subject at once to the young man's means,
to his mother, and to the doctor's shop; and though he learned
nothing that was very promising, neither did he learn anything
that was the reverse.   Albert Fitzallen did not ride a very high
horse when he learned that his supposed rival was so anxious to
assist him.   He was quite willing to be guided by Graham, and, in
that matter of the proposed partnership, was sure that old Balsam,
the owner of the business, would be glad to take a sum of money
down.   'He has a son of his own,' said Albert, 'but he don't take
to it at all.   He's gone into wine and spirits; but he don't sell half
as much as he drinks.'

Felix then proposed that he should call on Mrs. Fitzallen, and to this Albert gave a blushing consent. ‘Mother has heard of it,’ said Albert, ‘but I don't exactly know how.’ Perhaps Mrs. Fitzallen was as attentive as Mrs. Thomas had been to stray documents packed away in odd places. ‘And I suppose I may call on—on—Mary?’ asked the lover, as Graham took his leave. But Felix could give no authority for this, and explained that Mrs. Thomas might be found to be a dragon still guarding the Hesperides. Would it not be better to wait till Mary's father had been informed? and then, if all things went well, he might prosecute the affair in due form and as an acknowledged lover.

All this was very nice, and as it was quite unexpected, Fitzallen could not but regard himself as a fortunate young man. He had never contemplated the possibility of Mary Snow being an heiress. And when his mother had spoken to him of the hopelessness of his passion, had suggested that he might perhaps marry his Mary in five or six years. Now the dearest wish of his heart was brought close within his reach, and he must have been a happy man. But yet, though this certainly was so, nevertheless, there was a feeling of coldness about his love, and almost of disappointment as he again took his place behind the counter. The sorrows of Lydia in the play when she finds that her passion meets with general approbation are very absurd, but, nevertheless, are quite true to nature. Lovers would be great losers if the path of love were always to run smooth. Under such a dispensation, indeed, there would probably be no lovers. The matter would be too tame. Albert did not probably bethink himself of a becoming disguise, as did Lydia,—of an amiable ladder of ropes, of a conscious moon, or a Scotch parson ; but he did feel, in some undefined manner, that the romance of his life had been taken away from him. Five minutes under a lamp-post with Mary Snow was sweeter to him than the promise of a whole bevy of evenings spent in the same society, with all the comforts of his mother's drawing-room around him. Ah, yes, dear readers—my male readers of course I mean—were not those minutes under the lamp-post always very pleasant?

But Graham encountered none of this feeling when he discussed the same subject with Albert's mother. She was sufficiently alive to the material view of the matter, and knew how much of a man's married happiness depends on his supplies of bread and butter. Six hundred pounds ! Mr. Graham was very kind—very kind indeed. She hadn't a word to say against Mary Snow. She had seen her, and thought her very pretty and modest looking. Albert was certainly warmly attached to the young lady. Of that she was quite certain. And she would say this of Albert,—that a better-disposed young man did not exist anywhere. He came home quite regular to his meals, and spent ten hours a day behind the counter in Mr. Balsam's shop—ten hours a day, Sundays included, which

Mrs. Fitzallen regarded as a great drawback to the medical line—as should I also, most undoubtedly. But six hundred pounds would make a great difference. Mrs. Fitzallen little doubted but that sum would tempt Mr. Balsam into a partnership, or perhaps the five hundred, leaving one hundred for furniture. In such a case Albert would spend his Sundays at home, of course. After that, so much having been settled, Felix Graham got into an omnibus and took himself back to his own chambers.

So far was so good. This idea of a model wife had already become a very expensive idea, and in winding it up to its natural conclusion poor Graham was willing to spend almost every shilling that he could call his own. But there was still another difficulty in his way. What would Snow père say? Snow père was, he knew, a man with whom dealings would be more difficult than with Albert Fitzallen. And then, seeing that he had already promised to give his remaining possessions to Albert Fitzallen, with what could he bribe Snow père to abandon that natural ambition to have a barrister for his son-in-law? In these days, too, Snow père had derogated even from the position in which Graham had first known him, and had become but little better than a drunken, begging impostor. What a father-in-law to have had! And then Felix Graham thought of Judge Staveley.

He sent, however, to the engraver, and the man was not long in obeying the summons. In latter days Graham had not seen him frequently having bestowed his alms through Mary, and was shocked at the unmistakable evidence of the gin-shop which the man's appearance and voice betrayed. How dreadful to the sight are those watery eyes; that red, uneven, pimpled nose; those fallen cheeks; and that hanging, slobbered mouth! Look at the uncombed hair, the beard half shorn, the weak, impotent gait of the man, and the tattered raiment, all eloquent of gin! You would fain hold your nose when he comes nigh you, he carries with him so foul an evidence of his only and his hourly indulgence. You would do so, had you not still a respect for his feelings, which he himself has entirely forgotten to maintain. How terrible is that absolute loss of all personal dignity which the drunkard is obliged to undergo! And then his voice! Every tone has been formed by gin, and tells of the havoc which the compound has made within his throat. I do not know whether such a man as this is not the vilest thing which grovels on God's earth. There are women whom we affect to scorn with the full power of our contempt; but I doubt whether any woman sinks to a depth so low as that. She also may be a drunkard, and as such may more nearly move our pity and affect our hearts, but I do not think she ever becomes so nauseous a thing as the man that has abandoned all the hopes of life for gin. You can still touch her;—ay, and if the task be in one's way, can touch her gently, striving to bring her back to decency. But the other! Well, one should be willing to touch him too, to make that attempt of bringing back upon him also. I can only say that the task is both nauseous and unpromising. Look at him as he stands there before the foul, reeking, sloppy bar, with the glass in his hand, which he has just emptied. See the grimace with which he puts it down, as though the dram had been almost too unpalatable. It is the last touch of hypocrisy with which he attempts to cover the offence;—as though he were to say, ' I do it for my stomach's sake ; but you know how I abhor it.' Then he skulks sullenly away, speaking a word to no one,—shuffling with his feet, shaking himself in his foul rags, pressing himself into a heap—as though striving to drive the warmth of the spirit into his extremities ! And there he stands lounging at the corner of the street, till his short patience is exhausted, and he returns with his last penny for the other glass. When that has been swallowed the policeman is his guardian.

Reader, such as you and I have come to that, when abandoned by the respect which a man owes to himself. May God in his mercy watch over us and protect us both !

Such a man was Snow père as he stood before Graham in his chambers in the Temple. He could not ask him to sit down, so he himself stood up as he talked to him. At first the man was civil, twirling his old hat about, and shifting from one foot to the other;— very civil, and also somewhat timid, for he knew that he was half drunk at the moment. But when he began to ascertain what was Graham's object in sending for him, and to understand that the gentleman before him did not propose to himself the honour of being his son-in-law, then his civility left him, and, drunk as he was, he spoke out his mind with sufficient freedom.

' You mean to say, Mr. Graham '—and under the effect of gin he turned the name into Gorm—' that you are going to throw that young girl over ?'

' I mean to say no such thing. I shall do for her all that is in my power. And if that is not as much as she deserves, it will, at any rate, be more than you deserve for her.'

' And you won't marry her ?'

' No; I shall not marry her. Nor does she wish it. I trust that she will be engaged, with my full approbation——'

' And what the deuce, sir, is your full approbation to me ? Whose child is she, I should like to know ? Look here, Mr. Gorm ; perhaps you forget that you wrote me this letter when I allowed you to have the charge of that young girl ?' And he took out from his breast a very greasy pocket-book, and displayed to Felix his own much-worn letter,—holding it, however, at a distance, so that it should not be torn from his hands by any sudden raid. ' Do you think, sir, I would have given up my child if I didn't know she was to be married respectable ? My child is as dear to me as another man's.'

' I hope she is. And you are a very lucky fellow to have her so well provided for. I've told you all I've got to say, and now you may go.'

' Mr. Gorm !'

' I've nothing more to say ; and if I had, I would not say it to you now. Your child shall be taken care of.'

' That's what I call pretty cool on the part of any gen'leman. And you're to break your word,—a regular breach of promise, and nothing aint to come of it ! I'll tell you what, Mr. Gorm, you'll find that something will come of it. What do you think I took this letter for ?'

' You took it, I hope, for Mary's protection.'

' And by —— she shall be protected.'

' She shall, undoubtedly ; but I fear not by you. For the present I will protect her ; and I hope that soon a husband will do so who will love her. Now, Mr. Snow, I've told you all I've got to say, and I must trouble you to leave me.'

Nevertheless there were many more words between them before Graham could find himself alone in his chambers. Though Snow père might be a thought tipsy—a sheet or so in the wind, as folks say, he was not more tipsy than was customary with him, and knew pretty well what he was about. ' And what am I to do with myself, Mr. Gorm ?' he asked in a snivelling voice, when the idea began to strike him that it might perhaps be held by the courts of law that his intended son-in-law was doing well by his daughter.

' Work,' said Graham, turning upon him sharply and almost fiercely.

' That's all very well. It's very well to say " Work !" '

' You'll find it well to do it, too. Work, and don't drink. You hardly think, I suppose, that if I had married your daughter I should have found myself obliged to support you in idleness ?'

' It would have been a great comfort in my old age to have had a daughter's house to go to,' said Snow, naïvely, and now reduced to lachrymose distress.

But when he found that Felix would do nothing for him ; that he would not on the present occasion lend him a sovereign, or even half a crown, he again became indignant and paternal, and in this state of mind was turned out of the room.

' Heaven and earth !' said Felix to himself, clenching his hands and striking the table with both of them at the same moment. That was the man with whom he had proposed to link himself in the closest ties of family connection. Albert Fitzallen did not know Mr. Snow ; but it might be a question whether it would not be Graham's duty to introduce them to each other.

CHAPTER XVIII.

THE house at Noningsby was now very quiet. All the visitors had gone, including even the Arbuthnots. Felix Graham and Sophia Furnival, that terrible pair of guests, had relieved Mrs. Staveley of their presence; but, alas! the mischief they had done remained behind them. The house was very quiet, for Augustus and the judge were up in town during the greater part of the week, and Madeline and her mother were alone. The judge was to come back to Noningsby but once before he commenced the circuit which was to terminate at Alston; and it seemed to be acknowledged now on all sides that nothing more of importance was to be done or said in that locality until after Lady Mason's trial.

It may be imagined that poor Madeline was not very happy. Felix had gone away, having made no sign, and she knew that her mother rejoiced that he had so gone. She never accused her mother of cruelty, even within her own heart. She seemed to realize to herself the assurance that a marriage with the man she loved was a happiness which she had no right to expect. She knew that her father was rich. She was aware that in all probability her own fortune would be considerable. She was quite sure that Felix Graham was clever and fit to make his way through the world. And yet she did not think it hard that she should be separated from him. She acknowledged from the very first that he was not the sort of man whom she ought to have loved, and therefore she was prepared to submit.

It was, no doubt, the fact that Felix Graham had never whispered to her a word of love, and that therefore, on that ground, she had no excuse for hope. But, had that been all, she would not have despaired. Had that been all, she might have doubted, but her doubt would have been strongly mingled with the sweetness of hope. He had never whispered a syllable of love, but she had heard the tone of his voice as she spoke a word to him at his chamber door; she had seen his eyes as they fell on her when he was lifted into the carriage; she had felt the tremor of his touch on that evening when she walked up to him across the drawing-room and shook hands with him. Such a girl as Madeline Staveley does not analyze her feelings on such a matter, and then draw her conclusions. But a conclusion is drawn; the mind does receive an impression; and the conclusion and impression are as true as though they had been reached by the aid of logical reasoning. Had the match been such as her mother would have approved, she would have had a hope as to Felix Graham's love—strong enough for happiness.

As it was, there was no use in hoping; and therefore she resolved —having gone through much logical reasoning on this head—that by her all ideas of love must be abandoned. As regarded herself, she must be content to rest by her mother's side as a flower ungathered. That she could marry no man without the approval of her father and mother was a thing to her quite certain; but it was, at any rate, as certain that she could marry no man without her own approval. Felix Graham was beyond her reach. That verdict she herself pronounced, and to it she submitted. But Peregrine Orme was still more distant from her;—Peregrine Orme, or any other of the curled darlings who might come that way playing the part of a suitor. She knew what she owed to her mother, but she also knew her own privileges.

There was nothing said on the subject between the mother and child during three days. Lady Staveley was more than ordinarily affectionate to her daughter, and in that way made known the thoughts which were oppressing her; but she did so in no other way. All this Madeline understood, and thanked her mother with the sweetest smiles and the most constant companionship. Nor was she, even now, absolutely unhappy, or wretchedly miserable; as under such circumstances would be the case with many girls. She knew all that she was prepared to abandon, but she understood also how much remained to her. Her life was her own, and with her life the energy to use it. Her soul was free. And her heart, though burdened with love, could endure its load without sinking. Let him go forth on his career. She would remain in the shade, and be contented while she watched it.

So strictly wise and philosophically serene had Madeline become within a few days of Graham's departure, that she snubbed poor Mrs. Baker, when that goodnatured and sharp-witted housekeeper said a word or two in praise of her late patient.

' We are very lonely, aint we, miss, without Mr. Graham to look after?' said Mrs. Baker.

' I'm sure we are all very glad that he has so far recovered as to be able to be moved.'

' That's in course,—though I still say that he went before he ought. He was such a nice gentleman. Where there's one better, there's twenty worse; and as full of cleverness as an egg's full of meat.' In answer to which Madeline said nothing.

' At any rate, Miss Madeline, you ought to say a word for him,' continued Mrs. Baker; ' for he used to worship the sound of your voice. I've known him lay there and listen, listen, listen, for your very footfall.'

'How can you talk such stuff, Mrs. Baker? You have never known anything of the kind—and even if he had, how could you know it? You should not talk such nonsense to me, and I beg you won't again.' Then she went away, and began to read a paper about sick people written by Florence Nightingale.

But it was by no means Lady Staveley's desire that her daughter should take to the Florence Nightingale line of life. The charities of Noningsby were done on a large scale, in a quiet, handsome, methodical manner, and were regarded by the mistress of the mansion as a very material part of her life's duty; but she would have been driven distracted had she been told that a daughter of hers was about to devote herself exclusively to charity. Her ideas of general religion were the same. Morning and evening prayers, church twice on Sundays, attendance at the Lord's table at any rate once a month, were to herself—and in her estimation for her own family—essentials of life. And they had on her their practical effects. She was not given to backbiting—though, when stirred by any motive near to her own belongings, she would say an illnatured word or two. She was mild and forbearing to her inferiors. Her hand was open to the poor. She was devoted to her husband and her children. In no respect was she self-seeking or self-indulgent. But, nevertheless, she appreciated thoroughly the comforts of a good income—for herself and for her children. She liked to see nice-dressed and nice-mannered people about her, preferring those whose fathers and mothers were nice before them. She liked to go about in her own carriage, comfortably. She liked the feeling that her husband was a judge, and that he and she were therefore above other lawyers and other lawyers' wives. She would not like to have seen Mrs. Furnival walk out of a room before her, nor perhaps to see Sophia Furnival when married take precedence of her own married daughter. She liked to live in a large place like Noningsby, and preferred country society to that of the neighbouring town.

It will be said that I have drawn an impossible character, and depicted a woman who served both God and Mammon. To this accusation I will not plead, but will ask my accusers whether in their life's travail they have met no such ladies as Lady Staveley?

But such as she was, whether good or bad, she had no desire whatever that her daughter should withdraw herself from the world, and give up to sick women what was meant for mankind. Her idea of a woman's duties comprehended the birth, bringing up, education, and settlement in life of children, also due attendance upon a husband, with a close regard to his special taste in cookery. There was her granddaughter Marian. She was already thinking what sort of a wife she would make, and what commencements of education would best fit her to be a good mother. It is hardly too much to say that Marian's future children were already a subject of care to her. Such being her disposition, it was by no means matter of joy to her when she found that Madeline was laying out for herself little ways of life, tending in some slight degree to the monastic. Nothing was said about it, but she fancied that Madeline had doffed a ribbon or two in her usual evening attire. That she read during certain fixed hours in the morning was very manifest. As to that daily afternoon service at four o'clock—she had very often attended that, and it was hardly worthy of remark that she now went to it every day. But there seemed at this time to be a monotonous regularity about her visits to the poor, which told to Lady Staveley's mind—she hardly knew what tale. She herself visited the poor, seeing some of them almost daily. If it was foul weather they came to her, and if it was fair weather she went to them. But Madeline, without saying a word to any one, had adopted a plan of going out exactly at the same hour with exactly the same object, in all sorts of weather. All this made Lady Staveley uneasy; and then, by way of counterpoise, she talked of balls, and offered Madeline *carte blanche* as to a new dress for that special one which would grace the assizes. 'I don't think I shall go,' said Madeline; and thus Lady Staveley became really unhappy. Would not Felix Graham be better than no son-in-law? When some one had once very strongly praised Florence Nightingale in Lady Staveley's presence, she had stoutly declared her opinion that it was a young woman's duty to get married. For myself, I am inclined to agree with her. Then came the second Friday after Graham's departure, and Lady Staveley observed, as she and her daughter sat at dinner alone, that Madeline would eat nothing but potatoes and seakale. 'My dear, you will be ill if you don't eat some meat.'

'Oh no, I shall not,' said Madeline with her prettiest smile.

'But you always used to like minced veal.'

'So I do, but I won't have any to-day, mamma, thank you.'

Then Lady Staveley resolved that she would tell the judge that Felix Graham, bad as he might be, might come there if he pleased. Even Felix Graham would be better than no son-in-law at all.

On the following day, the Saturday, the judge came down with Augustus, to spend his last Sunday at home before the beginning of his circuit, and some little conversation respecting Felix Graham did take place between him and his wife.

'If they are both really fond of each other, they had better marry,' said the judge, curtly.

'But it is terrible to think of their having no income,' said his wife.

'We must get them an income. You'll find that Graham will fall on his legs at last.'

'He's a very long time before he begins to use them,' said Lady Staveley. 'And then you know The Cleeve is such a nice property, and Mr. Orme is——'

'But, my love, it seems that she does not like Mr. Orme.'

'No, she doesn't,' said the poor mother in a tone of voice that was very lachrymose. 'But if she would only wait she might like him,—might she not now? He is such a very handsome young man.'

'If you ask me, I don't think his beauty will do it.'

'I don't suppose she cares for that sort of thing,' said Lady Staveley, almost crying. 'But I'm sure of this, if she were to go and make a nun of herself, it would break my heart,—it would, indeed. I should never hold up my head again.'

What could Lady Staveley's idea have been of the sorrows of some other mothers, whose daughters throw themselves away after a different fashion?

After lunch on Sunday the judge asked his daughter to walk with him, and on that occasion the second church service was abandoned. She got on her bonnet and gloves, her walking-boots and winter shawl, and putting her arm happily and comfortably within his, started for what she knew would be a long walk.

'We'll get as far as the bottom of Cleeve Hill,' said the judge.

Now the bottom of Cleeve Hill, by the path across the fields and the common, was five miles from Noningsby.

'Oh, as for that, I'll walk to the top if you like,' said Madeline.

'If you do, my dear, you'll have to go up alone,' said the judge. And so they started.

There was a crisp, sharp enjoyment attached to a long walk with her father which Madeline always loved, and on the present occasion she was willing to be very happy; but as she started, with her arm beneath his, she feared she knew not what. She had a secret, and her father might touch upon it; she had a sore, though it was not an unwholesome festering sore, and her father might probe the wound. There was, therefore, the slightest shade of hypocrisy in the alacrity with which she prepared herself, and in the pleasant tone of her voice as she walked down the avenue towards the gate.

But by the time that they had gone a mile, when their feet had left the road and were pressing the grassy field-path, there was no longer any hypocrisy in her happiness. Madeline believed that no human being could talk as did her father, and on this occasion he came out with his freshest thoughts and his brightest wit. Nor did he, by any means, have the talk all to himself. The delight of Judge Staveley's conversation consisted chiefly in that—that though he might bring on to the carpet all the wit and all the information going, he rarely uttered much beyond his own share of words. And now they talked of pictures and politics—of the new gallery that was not to be built at Charing Cross, and the great onslaught which was not to end in the dismissal of Ministers. And then they got to books—to novels, new poetry, magazines, essays, and reviews ; and with the slightest touch of pleasant sarcasm the judge passed sentence on the latest efforts of his literary contemporaries. And thus at last they settled down on a certain paper which had lately appeared in a certain Quarterly—a paper on a grave subject, which had been much discussed—and the judge on a sudden stayed his hand, and spared his raillery. ' You have not heard, I suppose, who wrote that ?' said he. No ; Madeline had not heard. She would much like to know. When young people begin their world of reading there is nothing so pleasant to them as knowing the little secrets of literature ; who wrote this and that, of which folk are then talking ;—who manages this periodical, and puts the salt and pepper into those reviews. The judge always knew these events of the inner literary world, and would communicate them freely to Madeline as they walked. No ; there was no longer the slightest touch of hypocrisy in her pleasant manner and eager voice as she answered, ' No, papa, I have not heard. Was it Mr. So-and-so ?' and she named an ephemeral literary giant of the day. ' No,' said the judge, ' it was not So-and-so ; but yet you might guess, as you know the gentleman.' Then the slight shade of hypocrisy came upon her again in a moment. ' She couldn't guess,' she said ; ' she didn't know.' But as she thus spoke the tone of her voice was altered. ' That article,' said the judge, ' was written by Felix Graham. It is uncommonly clever, and yet there are a great many people who abuse it.'

And now all conversation was stopped. Poor Madeline, who had been so ready with her questions, so eager with her answers, so communicative and so inquiring, was stricken dumb on the instant. She had ceased for some time to lean upon his arm, and therefore he could not feel her hand tremble ; and he was too generous and too kind to look into her face ; but he knew that he had touched the fibres of her heart, and that all her presence of mind had for the moment fled from her. Of course such was the case, and of course he knew it. Had he not brought her out there, that they might be alone together when he subjected her to the violence of this shower-bath ?

' Yes,' he continued, ' that was written by our friend Graham. Do you remember, Madeline, the conversation which you and I had about him in the library some time since ?'

' Yes,' she said, ' she remembered it.'

' And so do I,' said the judge, ' and have thought much about it since. A very clever fellow is Felix Graham. There can be no doubt of that.'

'Is he?' said Madeline.

I am inclined to think that the judge also had lost something of his presence of mind, or, at least, of his usual power of conversation. He had brought his daughter out there with the express purpose of saying to her a special word or two; he had beat very wide about the bush with the view of mentioning a certain name; and now that his daughter was there, and the name had been mentioned, it seemed that he hardly knew how to proceed.

'Yes, he is clever enough,' repeated the judge, 'clever enough; and of high principles and an honest purpose. The fault which people find with him is this,—that he is not practical. He won't take the world as he finds it. If he can mend it, well and good; we all ought to do something to mend it; but while we are mending it we must live in it.'

'Yes, we must live in it,' said Madeline, who hardly knew at the moment whether it would be better to live or die in it. Had her father remarked that they must all take wings and fly to heaven, she would have assented.

Then the judge walked on a few paces in silence, bethinking himself that he might as well speak out at once the words which he had to say. 'Madeline, my darling,' said he, 'have you the courage to tell me openly what you think of Felix Graham?'

'What I think of him, papa?'

'Yes, my child. It may be that you are in some difficulty at this moment, and that I can help you. It may be that your heart is sadder than it would be if you knew all my thoughts and wishes respecting you, and all your mother's. I have never had many secrets from my children, Madeline, and I should be pleased now if you could see into my mind and know all my thoughts and wishes as they regard you.'

'Dear papa!'

'To see you happy—you and Augustus and Isabella—that is now our happiness; not to see you rich or great. High position and a plentiful income are great blessings in this world, so that they be achieved without a stain. But even in this world they are not the greatest blessings. There are things much sweeter than them.' As he said this, Madeline did not attempt to answer him, but she put her arm once more within his, and clung to his side.

'Money and rank are only good, if every step by which they are gained be good also. I should never blush to see my girl the wife of a poor man whom she loved; but I should be stricken to the core of my heart if I knew that she had become the wife of a rich man whom she did not love.'

'Papa!' she said, clinging to him. She had meant to assure him that that sorrow should never be his, but she could not get beyond the one word.

'If you love this man, let him come,' said the judge, carried by his feelings somewhat beyond the point to which he had intended to go. 'I know no harm of him. I know nothing but good of him. If you are sure of your own heart, let it be so. He shall be to me as another son,—to me and to your mother. Tell me, Madeline, shall it be so?'

She was sure enough of her own heart; but how was she to be sure of that other heart? 'It shall be so,' said her father. But a man could not be turned into a lover and a husband because she and her father agreed to desire it;—not even if her mother would join in that wish. She had confessed to her mother that she loved this man, and the confession had been repeated to her father. But she had never expressed even a hope that she was loved in return. 'But he has never spoken to me, papa,' she said, whispering the words ever so softly less the winds should carry them.

'No; I know he has never spoken to you,' said the judge. 'He told me so himself. I like him the better for that.'

So then there had been other communications made besides that which she had made to her mother. Mr. Graham had spoken to her father, and had spoken to him about her. In what way had he done this, and how had he spoken? What had been his object, and when had it been done? Had she been indiscreet, and allowed him to read her secret? And then a horrid thought came across her mind. Was he to come there and offer her his hand because he pitied and was sorry for her? The Friday fastings and the evening church and the sick visits would be better far than that. She could not however muster courage to ask her father any question as to that interview between him and Mr. Graham.

'Well, my love,' he said, 'I know it is impertinent to ask a young lady to speak on such a subject; but fathers are impertinent. Be frank with me. I have told you what I think, and your mamma agrees with me. Young Mr. Orme would have been her favourite——'

'Oh, papa, that is impossible.'

'So I perceive, my dear, and therefore we will say no more about it. I only mention his name because I want you to understand that you may speak to your mamma quite openly on the subject. He is a fine young fellow, is Peregrine Orme.'

'I'm sure he is, papa.'

'But that is no reason you should marry him if you don't like him.'

'I could never like him,—in that way.'

'Very well, my dear. There is an end of that, and I'm sorry for him. I think that if I had been a young man at The Cleeve, I should have done just the same. And now let us decide this important question. When Master Graham's ribs, arms, and collar bones are a little stronger, shall we ask him to come back to Noningsby?'

' If you please, papa.'

' Very well, we'll have him here for the assize week. Poor fellow, he'll have a hard job of work on hand just then, and won't have much time for philandering. With Chaffanbrass to watch him on his own side, and Leatherham on the other, I don't envy him his position. I almost think I should keep my arm in the sling till the assizes were over, by way of exciting a little pity.'

' Is Mr. Graham going to defend Lady Mason?'

' To help to do so, my dear.'

' But, papa, she is innocent; don't you feel sure of that?'

The judge was not quite so sure as he had been once. However, he said nothing of his doubts to Madeline. ' Mr. Graham's task on that account will only be the more trying if it becomes difficult to establish her innocence.'

' Poor lady!' said Madeline. ' You won't be the judge; will you, papa?'

' No, certainly not. I would have preferred to have gone any other circuit than to have presided in a case affecting so near a neighbour, and I may almost say a friend. Baron Maltby will sit in that court.'

' And will Mr. Graham have to do much, papa?'

' It will be an occasion of very great anxiety to him, no doubt.' And then they began to return home,—Madeline forming a little plan in her mind by which Mr. Furnival and Mr. Chaffanbrass were to fail absolutely in making out that lady's innocence, but the fact was to be established to the satisfaction of the whole court, and of all the world, by the judicious energy of Felix Graham.

On their homeward journey the judge again spoke of pictures and books, of failures and successes, and Madeline listened to him gratefully. But she did not again take much part in the conversation. She could not now express a very fluent opinion on any subject, and to tell the truth, could have been well satisfied to have been left entirely to her own thoughts. But just before they came out again upon the road, her father stopped her and asked a direct question. ' Tell me, Madeline, are you happy now?'

' Yes, papa.'

' That is right. And what you are to understand is this; Mr. Graham will now be privileged by your mother and me to address you. He has already asked my permission to do so, and I told him that I must consider the matter before I either gave it or withheld it. I shall now give him that permission.' Whereupon Madeline made her answer by a slight pressure upon his arm.

Tell me, Madelaine, are you happy now?

' But you may be sure of this, my dear; I shall be very discreet, and commit you to nothing. If he should choose to ask you any question, you will be at liberty to give him any answer that you may think fit.' But Madeline at once confessed to herself that no such liberty remained to her. If Mr. Graham should choose to ask her a certain question, it would be in her power to give him only one answer. Had he been kept away, had her father told her that such a marriage might not be, she would not have broken her heart. She had already told herself, that under such circumstances, she could live and still live contented. But now,—now if the siege were made, the town would have to capitulate at the first shot. Was it not an understood thing that the governor had been recommended by the king to give up the keys as soon as they were asked for?

' You will tell your mamma of this my dear,' said the judge, as they were entering their own gate.

' Yes,' said Madeline. But she felt that, in this matter, her father was more surely her friend than her mother. And indeed she could understand her mother's opposition to poor Felix, much better than her father's acquiescence.

' Do, my dear. What is anything to us in this world, if we are not all happy together? She thinks that you have become sad, and she must know that you are so no longer.'

' But I have not been sad, papa,' said Madeline, thinking with some pride of her past heroism.

When they reached the hall-door she had one more question to ask; but she could not look in her father's face as she asked.

' Papa, is that review you were speaking of here at Noningsby?'

' You will find it on my study table; but remember, Madeline, I don't above half go along with him.'

The judge went into his study before dinner, and found that the review had been taken.

CHAPTER XIX.

NO SURRENDER.

Sir Peregrine Orme had gone up to London, had had his interview with Mr. Round, and had failed. He had then returned home, and hardly a word on the subject had been spoken between him and Mrs. Orme. Indeed little or nothing was now said between them as to Lady Mason or the trial. What was the use of speaking on a subject that was in every way the cause of so much misery? He had made up his mind that it was no longer possible for him to

take any active step in the matter. He had become bail for her
appearance in court, and that was the last trifling act of friendship
which he could show her? How was it any longer possible that he
could befriend her? He could not speak up on her behalf with
eager voice, and strong indignation against her enemies, as had
formerly been his practice. He could give her no counsel. His
counsel would have taught her to abandon the property in the first
instance, let the result be what it might. He had made his little
effort in that direction by seeing the attorney, and his little effort
had been useless. It was quite clear to him that there was nothing
further for him to do;—nothing further for him, who but a week or
two since was so actively putting himself forward and letting the
world know that he was Lady Mason's champion.

Would he have to go into court as a witness? His mind was
troubled much in his endeavour to answer that question. He had
been her great friend. For years he had been her nearest neighbour. His daughter-in-law still clung to her. She had lived at his
house. She had been chosen to be his wife. Who could speak to
her character, if he could not do so? And yet, what could he say,
if so called on? Mr. Furnival, Mr. Chaffanbrass—all those who
would have the selection of the witnesses, believing themselves in
their client's innocence, as no doubt they did, would of course
imagine that he believed in it also. Could he tell them that it
would not be in his power to utter a single word in her favour?

In these days Mrs. Orme went daily to the Farm. Indeed, she
never missed a day from that on which Lady Mason left The
Cleeve up to the time of the trial. It seemed to Sir Peregrine that
his daughter's affection for this woman had grown with the knowledge of her guilt; but, as I have said before, no discussion on the
matter now took place between them. Mrs. Orme would generally
take some opportunity of saying that she had been at Orley Farm;
but that was all.

Sir Peregrine during this time never left the house once, except
for morning service on Sundays. He hung his hat up on its accustomed peg when he returned from that ill-omened visit to Mr. Round,
and did not move it for days, ay, for weeks,—except on Sunday mornings. At first his groom would come to him, suggesting to him that
he should ride, and the woodman would speak to him about the
young coppices; but after a few days they gave up their efforts.
His grandson also strove to take him out, speaking to him more
earnestly than the servants would do, but it was of no avail. Peregrine, indeed, gave up the attempt sooner, for to him his grandfather
did in some sort confess his own weakness. 'I have had a blow,'
said he; 'Peregrine, I have had a blow. I am too old to bear up
against it;—too old and too weak.' Peregrine knew that he alluded
in some way to that proposed marriage, but he was quite in the

dark as to the manner in which his grandfather had been affected by it.

'People think nothing of that now, sir,' said he, groping in the dark as he strove to administer consolation.

'People will think of it;—and I think of it. But never mind, my boy. I have lived my life, and am contented with it. I have lived my life, and have great joy that such as you are left behind to take my place. If I had really injured you I should have broken my heart—have broken my heart.'

Peregrine of course assured him that let what would come to him the pride which he had in his grandfather would always support him. 'I don't know anybody else that I could be so proud of,' said Peregrine; 'for nobody else that I see thinks so much about other people. And I always was, even when I didn't seem to think much about it;—always.'

Poor Peregrine! Circumstances had somewhat altered him since that day, now not more than six months ago, in which he had pledged himself to abandon the delights of Cowcross Street. As long as there was a hope for him with Madeline Staveley all this might be very well. He preferred Madeline to Cowcross Street with all its delights. But when there should be no longer any hope—and indeed, as things went now, there was but little ground for hoping—what then? Might it not be that his trial had come on him too early in life, and that he would solace himself in his disappointment, if not with Carroty Bob, with companionships and pursuits which would be as objectionable, and perhaps more expensive?

On three or four occasions his grandfather asked him how things were going at Noningsby, striving to interest himself in something as to which the out-look was not altogether dismal, and by degrees learned,—not exactly all the truth—but as much of the truth as Peregrine knew.

'Do as she tells you,' said the grandfather, referring to Lady Staveley's last words.

'I suppose I must,' said Peregrine, sadly. 'There's nothing else for it. But if there's anything that I hate in this world, it's waiting.'

'You are both very young,' said his grandfather.

'Yes; we are what people call young, I suppose. But I don't understand all that. Why isn't a fellow to be happy when he's young as well as when he's old?'

Sir Peregrine did not answer him, but no doubt thought that he might alter his opinion in a few years. There is great doubt as to what may be the most enviable time of life with a man. I am inclined to think that it is at that period when his children have all been born but have not yet began to go astray or to vex him with disappointment; when his own pecuniary prospects are settled, and he knows pretty well what his tether will allow him; when the appetite is still good and the digestive organs at their full power; when he has ceased to care as to the length of his girdle, and before the doctor warns him against solid breakfasts and port wine after dinner; when his affectations are over and his infirmities have not yet come upon him; while he can still walk his ten miles, and feel some little pride in being able to do so; while he has still nerve to ride his horse to hounds, and can look with some scorn on the ignorance of younger men who have hardly yet learned that noble art. As regards men, this, I think, is the happiest time of life; but who shall answer the question as regards women? In this respect their lot is more liable to disappointment. With the choicest flowers that blow the sweetest aroma of their perfection lasts but for a moment. The hour that sees them at their fullest glory sees also the beginning of their fall.

On one morning before the trial Sir Peregrine rang his bell and requested that Mr. Peregrine might be asked to come to him. Mr. Peregrine was out at the moment, and did not make his appearance much before dark, but the baronet had fully resolved upon having this interview, and ordered that the dinner should be put back for half an hour. 'Tell Mrs. Orme, with my compliments,' he said, 'that if it does not put her to inconvenience we will not dine till seven.' It put Mrs. Orme to no inconvenience; but I am inclined to agree with the cook, who remarked that the compliments ought to have been sent to her.

'Sit down, Peregrine,' he said, when his grandson entered his room with his thick boots and muddy gaiters. 'I have been thinking of something.'

'I and Samson have been cutting down trees all day,' said Peregrine. 'You've no conception how the water lies down in the bottom there; and there's a fall every yard down to the river. It's a sin not to drain it.'

'Any sins of that kind, my boy, shall lie on your own head for the future. I will wash my hands of them.'

'Then I'll go to work at once,' said Peregrine, not quite understanding his grandfather.

'You must go to work on more than that, Peregrine.' And then the old man paused. 'You must not think that I am doing this because I am unhappy for the hour, or that I shall repent it when the moment has gone by.'

'Doing what?' asked Peregrine.

'I have thought much of it, and I know that I am right. I cannot get out as I used to do, and do not care to meet people about business.'

'I never knew you more clear-headed in my life, sir.'

'Well, perhaps not. We'll say nothing about that. What I

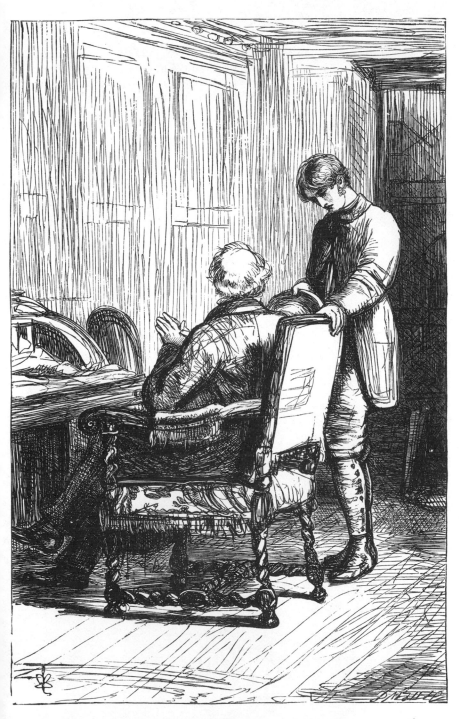

No Surrender.

intend to do is this;—to give up the property into your hands at Lady-day. You shall be master of The Cleeve from that time forth.'

' Sir ?'

' The truth is, you desire employment, and I don't. The property is small, and therefore wants the more looking after. I have never had a regular land steward, but have seen to that myself. If you'll take my advice you'll do the same. There is no better employment for a gentleman. So now, my boy, you may go to work and drain wherever you like. About the Crutchley bottom I have no doubt you're right. I don't know why it has been neglected.' These last words the baronet uttered in a weak, melancholy tone, asking, as it were, forgiveness for his fault; whereas he had spoken out the purport of his great resolution with a clear, strong voice, as though the saying of the words pleased him well.

' I could not hear of such a thing as that,' said his grandson, after a short pause.

' But you have heard it, Perry, and you may be quite sure that I should not have named it had I not fully resolved upon it. I have been thinking of it for days, and have quite made up my mind. You won't turn me out of the house, I know.'

' All the same. I will not hear of it,' said the young man, stoutly.

' Peregrine !'

' I know very well what it all means, sir, and I am not at all astonished. You have wished to do something out of sheer goodness of heart, and you have been balked.'

' We will not talk about that, Peregrine.'

' But I must say a few words about it. All that has made you unhappy, and—and—and——' He wanted to explain that his grandfather was ashamed of his baffled attempt, and for that reason was cowed and down at heart at the present moment; but that in the three or four months when this trial would be over and the wonder passed away, all that would be forgotten, and he would be again as well as ever. But Peregrine, though he understood all this, was hardly able to express himself.

' My boy,' said the old man, ' I know very well what you mean. What you say is partly true, and partly not quite true. Some day, perhaps, when we are sitting here together over the fire, I shall be better able to talk over all this; but not now, Perry. God has been very good to me, and given me so much that I will not repine at this sorrow. I have lived my life, and am content.'

' Oh yes, of course all that's true enough. And if God should choose that you should—die, you know, or I either, some people would be sorry, but we shouldn't complain ourselves. But what I say is this: you should never give up as long as you live. There's a sort of feeling about it which I can't explain. One should always say to oneself, No surrender.' And Peregrine, as he spoke, stood up from his chair, thrust his hands into his trousers-pockets, and shook his head.

Sir Peregrine smiled as he answered him. ' But Perry, my boy, we can't always say that. When the heart and the spirit and the body have all surrendered, why should the voice tell a foolish falsehood ?'

' But it shouldn't be a falsehood,' said Peregrine. ' Nobody should ever knock under of his own accord.'

' You are quite right there, my boy ; you are quite right there. Stick to that yourself. But, remember, that you are not to knock under to any of your enemies. The worst that you will meet with are folly, and vice, and extravagance.'

' That's of course,' said Peregrine, by no means wishing on the present occasion to bring under discussion his future contests with any such enemies as those now named by his grandfather.

' And now, suppose you dress for dinner,' said the baronet. ' I've got ahead of you there you see. What I've told you to-day I have already told your mother.'

' I'm sure she doesn't think you right.'

' If she thinks me wrong, she is too kind and well-behaved to say so,—which is more than I can say for her son. Your mother, Perry, never told me that I was wrong yet, though she has had many occasions ;—too many, too many. But, come, go and dress for dinner.'

' You are wrong in this, sir, if ever you were wrong in your life,' said Peregrine, leaving the room. His grandfather did not answer him again, but followed him out of the door, and walked briskly across the hall into the drawing-room.

' There's Peregrine been lecturing me about draining,' he said to his daughter-in-law, striving to speak in a half-bantering tone of voice, as though things were going well with him.

' Lecturing you !' said Mrs. Orme.

' And he's right, too. There's nothing like it. He'll make a better farmer, I take it, than Lucius Mason. You'll live to see him know the value of an acre of land as well as any man in the county. It's the very thing that he's fit for. He'll do better with the property than ever I did.'

There was something beautiful in the effort which the old man was making when watched by the eyes of one who knew him as well as did his daughter-in-law. She knew him, and understood all the workings of his mind, and the deep sorrow of his heart. In very truth, the star of his life was going out darkly under a cloud ; but he was battling against his sorrow and shame—not that he might be rid of them himself, but that others might not have to share them. That doctrine of ' No surrender ' was strong within his bosom, and he understood the motto in a finer sense than that in which his grandson had used it. He would not tell them that his heart was broken,—not if he could help it. He would not display his wound if it might be in his power to hide it. He would not confess that lands, and houses, and seignorial functions were no longer of value in his eyes. As far as might be possible he would bear his own load till that and the memory of his last folly might be hidden together in the grave.

But he knew that he was no longer fit for a man's work, and that it would be well that he should abandon it. He had made a terrible mistake. In his old age he had gambled for a large stake, and had lost it all. He had ventured to love ;—to increase the small number of those who were nearest and dearest to him, to add one to those whom he regarded as best and purest,—and he had been terribly deceived. He had for many years almost worshipped the one lady who had sat at his table, and now in his old age he had asked her to share her place of honour with another. What that other was need not now be told. And the world knew that this woman was to have been his wife ! He had boasted loudly that he would give her that place and those rights. He had ventured his all upon her innocence and her purity. He had ventured his all,— and he had lost.

I do not say that on this account there was any need that he should be stricken to the ground,—that it behoved him as a man of high feeling to be broken-hearted. He would have been a greater man had he possessed the power to bear up against all this, and to go forth to the world bearing his burden bravely on his shoulders. But Sir Peregrine Orme was not a great man, and possessed few or none of the elements of greatness. He was a man of a singularly pure mind, and endowed with a strong feeling of chivalry. It had been everything to him to be spoken of by the world as a man free from reproach,—who had lived with clean hands and with clean people around him. All manner of delinquencies he could forgive in his dependents which did not tell of absolute baseness ; but it would have half killed him had he ever learned that those he loved had become false or fraudulent. When his grandson had come to trouble about the rats, he had acted, not over-cleverly, a certain amount of paternal anger ; but had Peregrine broken his promise to him, no acting would have been necessary. It may therefore be imagined what were now his feelings as to Lady Mason.

Her he could forgive for deceiving him. He had told his daughter-in-law that he would forgive her; and it was a thing done. But he could not forgive himself in that he had been deceived. He could not forgive himself for having mingled with the sweet current of his Edith's life the foul waters of that criminal

tragedy. He could not now bid her desert Lady Mason; for was
it not true that the woman's wickedness was known to them two,
through her resolve not to injure those who had befriended her?
But all this made the matter worse rather than better to him. It
is all very well to say, ' No surrender;' but when the load placed
upon the back is too heavy to be borne, the back must break or
bend beneath it.

His load was too heavy to be borne, and therefore he said to
himself that he would put it down. He would not again see Lord
Alston and the old friends of former days. He would attend no
more at the magistrates' bench, but would send his grandson out
into his place. For the few days that remained to him in this
world, he might be well contented to abandon the turmoils and
troubles of life. ' It will not be for long,' he said to himself over
and over again. And then he would sit in his arm-chair for hours,
intending to turn his mind to such solemn thoughts as might befit
a dying man. But, as he sat there, he would still think of Lady
Mason. He would remember her as she had leaned against his
breast on that day that he kissed her; and then he would remember her as she was when she spoke those horrid words to him—
' Yes; I did it; at night, when I was alone.' And this was the
woman whom he had loved! This was the woman whom he still
loved,—if all the truth might be confessed.

His grandson, though he read much of his grandfather's mind,
had failed to read it all. He did not know how often Sir Peregrine
repeated to himself those words, ' No Surrender,' or how gallantly
he strove to live up to them. Lands and money and seats of
honour he would surrender, as a man surrenders his tools when
he has done his work; but his tone of feeling and his principle he
would not surrender, though the maintenance of them should crush
him with their weight. The woman had been very vile, desperately false, wicked beyond belief, with premeditated villany, for
years and years;—and this was the woman whom he had wished to
make the bosom companion of his latter days!

' Samson is happy now, I suppose, that he has got the axe in his
hand,' he said to his grandson.

' Pretty well for that, sir, I think.'

' That man will cut down every tree about the place, if you'll
let him.' And in that way he strove to talk about the affairs of the
property.

EVERY day Mrs. Orme went up to Orley Farm and sat for two hours with Lady Mason. We may say that there was now no longer any secret between them, and that she whose life had been so innocent, so pure, and so good, could look into the inmost heart and soul of that other woman whose career had been supported by the proceeds of one terrible life-long iniquity. And now, by degrees, Lady Mason would begin to plead for herself, or, rather, to put in a plea for the deed she had done, acknowledging, however, that she, the doer of it, had fallen almost below forgiveness through the crime. ' Was he not his son as much as that other one; and had I not deserved of him that he should do this thing for me ?' And again ' Never once did I ask of him any favour for myself from the day that I gave myself to him, because he had been good to my father and mother. Up to the very hour of his death I never asked him to spend a shilling on my own account. But I asked him to do this thing for his child; and when at last he refused me, I told him that I myself would cause it to be done.'

' You told him so ?'

' I did; and I think that he believed me. He knew that I was one who would act up to my word. I told him that Orley Farm should belong to our babe.'

' And what did he say ?'

He bade me beware of my soul. My answer was very terrible, and I will not shock you with it. Ah me! it is easy to talk of repentance, but repentance will not come with a word.'

In these days Mrs. Orme became gradually aware that hitherto she had comprehended but little of Lady Mason's character. There was a power of endurance about her, and a courage that was almost awful to the mind of the weaker, softer, and better woman. Lady Mason, during her sojourn at The Cleeve, had seemed almost to sink under her misfortune; nor had there been any hypocrisy, any pretence in her apparent misery. She had been very wretched;— as wretched a human creature, we may say, as any crawling God's earth at that time. But she had borne her load, and, bearing it, had gone about her work, still striving with desperate courage as the ground on which she trod continued to give way beneath her feet, inch by inch. They had known and pitied her misery; they had loved her for misery—as it is in the nature of such people to do;—but they had little known how great had been the cause for it. They had sympathized with the female weakness which had succumbed when there was hardly any necessity for succumbing. Had they then known all, they would have wondered at the strength which made a struggle possible under such circumstances.

Even now she would not yield. I have said that there had been no hypocrisy in her misery during those weeks last past; and I have said so truly. But there had perhaps been some pretences, some acting of a part, some almost necessary pretence as to her weakness. Was she not bound to account to those around her for her great sorrow? And was it not above all things needful that she should enlist their sympathy and obtain their aid? She had been obliged to cry to them for help, though obliged also to confess that there was little reason for such crying. ' I am a woman, and weak,' she had said, 'and therefore cannot walk alone, now that the way is stony.' But what had been the truth with her? How would she have cried, had it been possible for her to utter the sharp cry of her heart? The waters had been closing over her head, and she had clutched at a hand to save her; but the owner of that hand might not know how imminent, how close was the danger.

But in these days, as she sat in her own room with Mrs. Orme, the owner of that hand might know everything. The secret had been told, and there was no longer need for pretence. As she could now expose to view the whole load of her wretchedness, so also could she make known the strength that was still left for endurance. And these two women who had become endeared to each other under such terrible circumstances, came together at these meetings with more of the equality of friendship than had ever existed at The Cleeve. It may seem strange that it should be so—strange that the acknowledged forger of her husband's will should be able to maintain a better claim for equal friendship than the lady who was believed to be innocent and true! But it was so. Now she stood on true ground;—now, as she sat there with Mrs. Orme, she could speak from her heart, pouring forth the real workings of her mind. From Mrs. Orme she had no longer aught to fear; nor from Sir Peregrine. Everything was known to them, and she could now tell of every incident of her crime with an outspoken boldness that in itself was incompatible with the humble bearing of an inferior in the presence of one above her.

And she did still hope. The one point to be gained was this; that her son, her only son, the child on whose behalf this crime had been committed, should never know her shame, or live to be disgraced by her guilt. If she could be punished, she would say, and he left in ignorance of her punishment, she would not care

what indignities they might heap upon her. She had heard of
penal servitude, of years, terribly long, passed in all the misery of
vile companionship ; of solitary confinement, and the dull madness
which it engenders; of all the terrors of a life spent under circumstances bearable only by the uneducated, the rude, and the
vile. But all this was as nothing to her compared with the loss of
honour to her son. ' I should live,' she would say ; ' but he would
die. You cannot ask me to become his murderer !'

It was on this point that they differed always. Mrs. Orme would
have had her confess everything to Lucius, and strove to make her
understand that if he were so told, the blow would fall less heavily
than it would do if the knowledge came to him from her conviction
at the trial. But the mother would not bring herself to believe
that it was absolutely necessary that he should ever know it.
' There was the property ! Yes; but let the trial come, and if she
were acquitted, then let some arrangement be made about that.
The lawyers might find out some cause why it should be surrendered.' But Mrs. Orme feared that if the trial were over, and
the criminal saved from justice, the property would not be surrendered. And then how would that wish of repentance be possible ?
After all was not that the one thing necessary ?

I will not say that Mrs. Orme in these days ever regretted that
her sympathy and friendship had been thus bestowed, but she
frequently acknowledged to herself that the position was too
difficult for her. There was no one whose assistance she could
ask; for she felt that she could not in this matter ask counsel from
Sir Peregrine. She herself was good, and pure, and straight-
minded, and simple in her perception of right and wrong; but
Lady Mason was greater than she in force of character,—a stronger
woman in every way, endowed with more force of will, with more
power of mind, with greater energy, and a swifter flow of words.
Sometimes she almost thought it would be better that she should
stay away from Orley Farm ; but then she had promised to be true
to her wretched friend, and the mother's solicitude for her son still
softened the mother's heart.

In these days, till the evening came, Lucius Mason never made
his way into his mother's sitting-room, which indeed was the
drawing-room of the house,—and he and Mrs. Orme, as a rule,
hardly ever met each other. If he saw her as she entered or left
the place, he would lift his hat to her and pass by without speaking.
He was not admitted to those councils of his mother's, and would
not submit to ask after his mother's welfare or to inquire as to her
affairs from a stranger. On no other subject was it possible that
he should now speak to the daily visitor and the only visitor at
Orley Farm. All this Mrs. Orme understood, and saw that the
young man was alone and comfortless. He passed his hours below,

in his own room, and twice a day his mother found him in the parlour, and then they sat through their silent, miserable meals. She would then leave him, always saying some soft words of motherly love, and putting her hand either upon his shoulder or his arm. On such occasions he was never rough to her, but he would never respond to her caress. She had ill-treated him, preferring in her trouble the assistance of a stranger to his assistance. She would ask him neither for his money nor his counsel, and as she had thus chosen to stand aloof from him, he also would stand aloof from her. Not for always,—as he said to himself over and over again; for his heart misgave him when he saw the lines of care so plainly written on his mother's brow. Not for always should it be so. The day of the trial would soon be present, and the day of the trial would soon be over; then again would they be friends. Poor young man! Unfortunate young man!

Mrs. Orme saw all this, and to her it was very terrible. What would be the world to her, if her boy should frown at her, and look black when she caressed him? And she thought that it was the fault of the mother rather than of the son; as indeed was not all that wretchedness the mother's fault? But then again, there was the one great difficulty. How could any step be taken in the right direction till the whole truth had been confessed to him?

The two women were sitting together in that upstairs room; and the day of the trial was now not a full week distant from them, when Mrs. Orme again tried to persuade the mother to intrust her son with the burden of all her misery. On the preceding day Mr. Solomon Aram had been down at Orley Farm, and had been with Lady Mason for an hour.

'He knows the truth!' Lady Mason had said to her friend. 'I am sure of that.'

'But did he ask you?'

'Oh, no, he did not ask me that. He asked of little things that happened at the time; but from his manner I am sure he knows it all. He says——that I shall escape.'

'Did he say escape?'

'No; not that word, but it was the same thing. He spoke to Lucius, for I saw them on the lawn together.'

'You do not know what he said to him?'

'No; for Lucius would not speak to me, and I could not ask him.' And then they both were silent, for Mrs. Orme was thinking how she could bring about that matter that was so near her heart. Lady Mason was seated in a large old-fashioned arm-chair, in which she now passed nearly all her time. The table was by her side, but she rarely turned herself to it. She sat leaning with her elbow on her arm, supporting her face with her hand; and opposite to her, so close that she might look into her face and watch every movement of her eyes, sat Mrs. Orme,—intent upon that one thing, that the woman before her should be brought to repent the evil she had done.

'And you have not spoken to Lucius?'

'No,' she answered. 'No more than I have told you. What could I say to him about the man?'

'Not about Mr. Aram. It might not be necessary to speak of him. He has his work to do; and I suppose that he must do it in his own way?'

'Yes; he must do it, in his own way. Lucius would not understand.'

'Unless you told him everything, of course he could not understand.'

'That is impossible.'

'No, Lady Mason, it is not impossible. Dear Lady Mason, do not turn from me in that way. It is for your sake,—because I love you, that I press you to do this. If he knew it all——'

'Could you tell your son such a tale?' said Lady Mason, turning upon her sharply, and speaking almost with an air of anger.

Mrs. Orme was for a moment silenced, for she could not at once bring herself to conceive it possible that she could be so circumstanced. But at last she answered. 'Yes,' she said, 'I think I could, if——.' And then she paused.

'If you had done such a deed! Ah, you do not know, for the doing of it would be impossible to you. You can never understand what was my childhood, and how my young years were passed. I never loved anything but him;—that is, till I knew you, and—and——.' But instead of finishing her sentence she pointed down towards The Cleeve. 'How, then, can I tell him? Mrs. Orme, I would let them pull me to pieces, bit by bit, if in that way I could save him.'

'Not in that way,' said Mrs. Orme; 'not in that way.'

But Lady Mason went on pouring forth the pent-up feelings of her bosom, not regarding the faint words of her companion. 'Till he lay in my arms I had loved nothing. From my earliest years I had been taught to love money, wealth, and property; but as to myself the teachings had never come home to me. When they bade me marry the old man because he was rich, I obeyed them,—not caring for his riches, but knowing that it behoved me to relieve them of the burden of my support. He was kinder to me than they had been, and I did for him the best I could. But his money and his wealth were little to me. He told me over and over again that when he died I should have the means to live, and that was enough. I would not pretend to him that I cared for the grandeur of his children who despised me. But then came my baby, and the world was all altered for me. What could I do for the only thing that I had ever called my own? Money and riches they had told me were everything.'

'But they had told you wrong,' said Mrs. Orme, as she wiped the tears from her eyes.

'They had told me falsely. I had heard nothing but falsehoods from my youth upwards,' she answered fiercely. 'For myself I had not cared for these things; but why should not he have money and riches and land? His father had them to give over and above what had already made those sons and daughters so rich and proud. Why should not this other child also be his father's heir? Was he not as well born as they? was he not as fair a child? What did Rebekah do, Mrs. Orme? Did she not do worse; and did it not all go well with her? Why should my boy be an Ishmael? Why should I be treated as the bondwoman, and see my little one perish of thirst in this world's wilderness?'

'No Saviour had lived and died for the world in those days,' said Mrs. Orme.

'And no Saviour had lived and died for me,' said the wretched woman, almost shrieking in her despair. The lines of her face were terrible to be seen as she thus spoke, and an agony of anguish loaded her brow upon which Mrs. Orme was frightened to look. She fell on her knees before the wretched woman, and taking her by both her hands strove all she could to find some comfort for her.

'Ah, do not say so. Do not say that. Whatever may come, that misery—that worst of miseries need not oppress you. If that indeed were true!'

'It was true;—and how should it be otherwise?'

'But now,—now. It need not be true now. Lady Mason, for your soul's sake say that it is so now.'

'Mrs. Orme,' she said, speaking with a singular quiescence of tone after the violence of her last words, 'it seems to me that I care more for his soul than for my own. For myself I can bear even that. But if he were a castaway——!'

I will not attempt to report the words that passed between them for the next half-hour, for they concerned a matter which I may not dare to handle too closely in such pages as these. But Mrs. Orme still knelt there at her feet, pressing Lady Mason's hands, pressing against her knees, as with all the eagerness of true affection she endeavoured to bring her to a frame of mind that would admit of some comfort. But it all ended in this:—Let everything be told to Lucius, so that the first step back to honesty might be taken,— and then let them trust to Him whose mercy can ever temper the wind to the shorn lamb.

But, as Lady Mason had once said to herself, repentance will not come with a word. 'I cannot tell him,' she said at last. 'It is a thing impossible. I should die at his feet before the words were spoken.'

' I will do it for you,' said Mrs. Orme, offering from pure charity to take upon herself a task perhaps as heavy as any that a human creature could perform. ' I will tell him.'

' No, no,' screamed Lady Mason, taking Mrs. Orme by both her arms as she spoke. ' You will not do so : say that you will not. Remember your promise to me. Remember why it is that you know it all yourself.'

' I will not, surely, unless you bid me,' said Mrs. Orme.

' No, no; I do not bid you. Mind, I do not bid you. I will not have it done. Better anything than that, while it may yet be avoided. I have your promise; have I not?'

' Oh, yes; of course I should not do it unless you told me.' And then, after some further short stay, during which but little was said, Mrs. Orme got up to go.

' You will come to me to-morrow,' said Lady Mason.

' Yes, certainly,' said Mrs. Orme.

' Because I feared that I had offended you.'

' Oh, no; I will take no offence from you.'

' You should not, for you know what I have to bear. You know, and no one else knows. Sir Peregrine does not know. He cannot understand. But you know and understand it all. And, Mrs. Orme, what you do now will be counted to you for great treasure,—for very great treasure. You are better than the Samaritan, for he went on his way. But you will stay till the last. Yes; I know you will stay.' And the poor creature kissed her only friend;—kissed her hands and her forehead and her breast. Then Mrs. Orme went without speaking, for her heart was full, and the words would not come to her; but as she went she said to herself that she would stay till the last.

Standing alone on the steps before the front door she found Lucius Mason all alone, and some feeling moved her to speak a word to him as she passed. ' I hope all this does not trouble you much, Mr. Mason,' she said, offering her hand to him. She felt that her words were hypocritical as she was speaking them; but under such circumstances what else could she say to him?

' Well, Mrs. Orme, such an episode in one's family history does give one some trouble. I am unhappy,—very unhappy; but not too much so to thank you for your most unusual kindness to my poor mother.' And then, having been so far encouraged by her speaking to him, he accompanied her round the house on to the lawn, from whence a path led away through a shrubbery on to the road which would take her by the village of Coldharbour to The Cleeve.

' Mr. Mason,' she said, as they walked for a few steps together before the house, ' do not suppose that I presume to interfere between you and your mother.'

' You have a right to interfere now,' he said.

' But I think you might comfort her if you would be more with her. Would it not be better if you could talk freely together about all this?'

' It would be better,' he said; ' but I fear that that is no longer possible. When this trial is over, and the world knows that she is innocent; when people shall see how cruelly she has been used——'

Mrs. Orme might not tell the truth to him, but she could with difficulty bear to hear him dwell thus confidently on hopes which were so false. ' The future is in the hands of God, Mr. Mason; but for the present——'

' The present and the future are both in His hands, Mrs. Orme. I know my mother's innocence, and would have done a son's part towards establishing it;—but she would not allow me. All this will soon be over now, and then, I trust, she and I will once again understand each other. Till then I doubt whether I should be wise to interfere. Good morning, Mrs. Orme; and pray believe that I appreciate at its full worth all that you are doing for her.' Then he again lifted his hat and left her.

Lady Mason from her window saw them as they walked together, and her heart for a moment misgave her. Could it be that her friend was treacherous to her? Was it possible that even now she was telling everything that she had sworn that she would not tell? Why were they two together, seeing that they passed each other day by day without intercourse? And so she watched with anxious eyes till they parted, and then she saw that Lucius stood idly on the terrace swinging his stick as he looked down the hill towards the orchard below him. He would not have stood thus calmly had he already heard his mother's shame. This she knew, and having laid aside her immediate fears she retreated back to her chair. No; she would not tell him: at any rate till the trial should be over.

CHAPTER XXI.

THE day of the trial was now quickly coming on, and the London world, especially the world of lawyers, was beginning to talk much on the subject. Men about the Inns of Court speculated as to the verdict, offering to each other very confident opinions as to the result, and offering, on some occasions, bets as well as opinions. The younger world of barristers was clearly of opinion that Lady Mason was innocent; but a portion, an unhappy portion, was inclined to fear, that, in spite of her innocence, she would be found guilty. The elder world of barristers was not, perhaps, so demonstrative, but in that world the belief in her innocence was not so strong, and the fear of her condemnation much stronger. The attorneys, as a rule, regarded her as guilty. To the policeman's mind every man not a policeman is a guilty being, and the attorneys perhaps share something of this feeling. But the attorneys to a man expected to see her acquitted. Great was their faith in Mr. Furnival; great their faith in Solomon Aram; but greater than in all was their faith in Mr. Chaffanbrass. If Mr. Chaffanbrass could not pull her through, with a prescription of twenty years on her side, things must be very much altered indeed in our English criminal court. To the outer world, that portion of the world which had nothing to do with the administration of the law, the idea of Lady Mason having been guilty seemed preposterous. Of course she was innocent, and of course she would be found to be innocent. And of course, also, that Joseph Mason of Groby Park was, and would be found to be, the meanest, the lowest, the most rapacious of mankind.

And then the story of Sir Peregrine's attachment and proposed marriage, joined as it was to various hints of the manner in which that marriage had been broken off, lent a romance to the whole affair, and added much to Lady Mason's popularity. Everybody had now heard of it, and everybody was also aware, that though the idea of a marriage had been abandoned, there had been no quarrel. The friendship between the families was as close as ever, and Sir Peregrine,—so it was understood—had pledged himself to an acquittal. It was felt to be a public annoyance that an affair of so exciting a nature should be allowed to come off in the little town of

Alston. The court-house, too, was very defective in its arrangements, and ill qualified to give accommodation to the great body of
would-be attendants at the trial. One leading newspaper went so
far as to suggest, that in such a case as this, the antediluvian preju-
dices of the British grandmother—meaning the Constitution —
should be set aside, and the trial should take place in London.
But I am not aware that any step was taken towards the carrying
out of so desirable a project.

Down at Hamworth the feeling in favour of Lady Mason was not
perhaps so strong as it was elsewhere. Dockwrath was a man not
much respected, but nevertheless many believed in him; and
down there, in the streets of Hamworth, he was not slack in
propagating his view of the question. He had no doubt, he said,
how the case would go. He had no doubt, although he was well
aware that Mr. Mason's own lawyers would do all they could to
throw over their own client. But he was too strong, he said, even
for that. The facts as he would bring them forward would confound Round and Crook, and compel any jury to find a verdict of
guilty. I do not say that all Hamworth believed in Dockwrath, but
his energy and confidence did have its effect, and Lady Mason's
case was not upheld so strongly in her own neighbourhood as elsewhere.

The witnesses in these days were of course very important
persons, and could not but feel the weight of that attention which
the world would certainly pay to them. There would be four chief
witnesses for the prosecution; Dockwrath himself, who would be
prepared to speak as to the papers left behind him by old Usbech;
the man in whose possession now remained that deed respecting the
partnership which was in truth executed by old Sir Joseph on that
fourteenth of July; Bridget Bolster; and John Kenneby. Of the
manner in which Mr. Dockwrath used his position we already
know enough. The man who held the deed, one Torrington,
was a relative of Martock, Sir Joseph's partner, and had been
one of his executors. It was not much indeed that he had to say,
but that little sent him up high in the social scale during those
days. He lived at Kennington, and he was asked out to dinner in
that neighbourhood every day for a week running, on the score of
his connection with the great Orley Farm case. Bridget Bolster
was still down at the hotel in the West of England, and being of a
solid, sensible, and somewhat unimaginative turn of mind, probably
went through her duties to the last without much change of manner.
But the effect of the coming scenes upon poor John Kenneby was
terrible. It was to him as though for the time they had made of
him an Atlas, and compelled him to bear on his weak shoulders the
weight of the whole world. Men did talk much about Lady Mason
and the coming trial; but to him it seemed as though men talked of

nothing else. At Hubbles and Grease's it was found useless to put figures into his hands till all this should be over. Indeed it was doubted by many whether he would ever recover his ordinary tone of mind. It seemed to be understood that he would be cross-examined by Chaffanbrass, and there were those who thought that John Kenneby would never again be equal to a day's work after that which he would then be made to endure. That he would have been greatly relieved could the whole thing have been wiped away from him there can be no manner of doubt; but I fancy that he would also have been disappointed. It is much to be great for a day, even though that day's greatness should cause the shipwreck of a whole life.

'I shall endeavour to speak the truth,' said John Kenneby, solemnly.

'The truth, the whole truth, and nothing but the truth,' said Moulder.

'Yes, Moulder, that will be my endeavour; and then I may lay my hand upon my bosom and think that I have done my duty by my country.' And as Kenneby spoke he suited the action to the word.

'Quite right, John,' said Mrs. Smiley. 'Them's the sentiments of a man, and I, as a woman having a right to speak where you are concerned, quite approve of them.'

'They'll get nothing but the truth out of John,' said Mrs. Moulder; 'not if he knows it.' These last words she added, actuated by admiration of what she had heard of Mr. Chaffanbrass, and perhaps with some little doubt as to her brother's firmness.

'That's where it is,' said Moulder. 'Lord bless you, John, they'll turn you round their finger like a bit of red tape. Truth! Gammon! What do they care for truth?'

'But I care, Moulder,' said Kenneby. 'I don't suppose they can make me tell falsehoods if I don't wish it.'

'Not if you're the man I take you to be,' said Mrs. Smiley.

'Gammon!' said Moulder.

'Mr. Moulder, that's an objectionable word,' said Mrs. Smiley. 'If John Kenneby is the man I take him to be,—and who's a right to speak if I haven't, seeing that I am going to commit myself for this world into his hands?'—and Mrs. Smiley, as she spoke, simpered, and looked down with averted head on the fulness of her Irish tabinet—'if he's the man that I take him to be, he won't say on this thrilling occasion no more than the truth, nor yet no less. Now that isn't gammon—if I know what gammon is.'

It will have been already seen that the party in question were assembled at Mr. Moulder's room in Great St. Helen's. There had been a little supper party there to commemorate the final arrangements as to the coming marriage, and the four were now sitting round the fire with their glasses of hot toddy at their elbows.

Moulder was armed with his pipe, and was enjoying himself in that manner which most delighted him. When last we saw him he had somewhat exceeded discretion in his cups, and was not comfortable. But at the present nothing ailed him. The supper had been good, the tobacco was good, and the toddy was good. Therefore when the lovely Thais sitting beside him,—Thais however on this occasion having been provided not for himself but for his brother-in-law,—when Thais objected to the use of his favourite word, he merely chuckled down in the bottom of his fat throat, and allowed her to finish her sentence.

Poor John Kenneby had more—much more, on his hands than this dreadful trial. Since he had declared that the Adriatic was free to wed another, he had found himself devoted and given up to Mrs. Smiley. For some days after that auspicious evening there had been considerable wrangling between Mrs. Moulder and Mrs. Smiley as to the proceeds of the brick-field; and on this question Moulder himself had taken a part. The Moulder interest had of course desired that all right of management in the brick-field should be vested in the husband, seeing that, according to the usages of this country, brick-fields and their belongings appertain rather to men than to women; but Mrs. Smiley had soon made it evident that she by no means intended to be merely a sleeping partner in the firm. At one time Kenneby had entertained a hope of escape; for neither would the Moulder interest give way, nor would the Smiley. But two hundred a year was a great stake, and at last the thing was arranged, very much in accordance with the original Smiley view. And now at this most trying period of his life, poor Kennedy had upon his mind all the cares of a lover as well as the cares of a witness.

' I shall do my best,' said John. ' I shall do my best and then throw myself upon Providence.'

' And take a little drop of something comfortable in your pocket,' said his sister, ' so as to sperrit you up a little when your name's called.'

' Sperrit him up!' said Moulder; ' why I suppose he'll be standing in that box the best part of a day. I knowed a man was a witness; it was a case of horse-stealing; and the man who was the witness was the man who'd took the horse.'

' And he was witness against hisself!' said Mrs. Smiley.

' No; he'd paid for it. That is to say, either he had or he hadn't. That was what they wanted to get out of him, and I'm blessed if he didn't take 'em till the judge wouldn't set there any longer. And then they hadn't got it out of him.'

' But John Kenneby aint one of that sort,' said Mrs. Smiley.

' I suppose that man did not want to unbosom himself,' said Kenneby.

'Well; no. The likes of him seldom do like to unbosom themselves,' said Moulder.

'But that will be my desire. If they will only allow me to speak freely whatever I know about this matter, I will give them no trouble.'

'You mean to act honest, John,' said his sister.

'I always did, Mary Anne.'

'Well now, I'll tell you what it is,' said Moulder. 'As Mrs. Smiley don't like it I won't say anything more about gammon; —not just at present, that is.'

'I've no objection to gammon, Mr. Moulder, when properly used,' said Mrs. Smiley, 'but I look on it as disrespectful; and seeing the position which I hold as regards John Kenneby, anything disrespectful to him is hurtful to my feelings.'

'All right,' said Moulder. 'And now, John, I'll just tell you what it is. You've no more chance of being allowed to speak freely there than—than—than—no more than if you was in church. What are them fellows paid for if you're to say whatever you pleases out in your own way?'

'He only wants to say the truth, M.,' said Mrs. Moulder, who probably knew less than her husband of the general usages of courts of law.

'Truth be ——,' said Moulder.

'Mr. Moulder!' said Mrs. Smiley. 'There's ladies by, if you'll please to remember.'

'To hear such nonsense sets one past oneself,' continued he; 'as if all those lawyers were brought together there—the cleverest and sharpest fellows in the kingdom, mind you—to listen to a man like John here telling his own story in his own way. You'll have to tell your story in their way; that is, in two different ways. There'll be one fellow 'll make you tell it his way first, and another fellow 'll make you tell it again his way afterwards; and its odds but what the first 'll be at you again after that, till you won't know whether you stand on your heels or your head.'

'That can't be right,' said Mrs. Moulder.

'And why can't it be right?' said Moulder. 'They're paid for it; it's their duties; just as it's my duty to sell Hubbles and Grease's sugar. It's not for me to say the sugar's bad, or the samples not equal to the last. My duty is to sell, and I sell;—and it's their duty to get a verdict.'

'But the truth, Moulder ——!' said Kenneby.

'Gammon!' said Moulder. 'Begging your pardon, Mrs. Smiley, for making use of the expression. Look you here, John; if you're paid to bring a man off not guilty, won't you bring him off if you can? I've been at trials times upon times, and listened till I've wished from the bottom of my heart that I'd been brought up a barrister. Not that I think much of myself, and I mean of course with education and all that accordingly. It's beautiful to hear them. You'll see a little fellow in a wig, and he'll get up; and there'll be a man in the box before him,—some swell dressed up to his eyes, who thinks no end of strong beer of himself; and in about ten minutes he'll be as flabby as wet paper, and he'll say—on his oath, mind you,—just anything that that little fellow wants him to say. That's power, mind you, and I call it beautiful.'

'But it aint justice,' said Mrs. Smiley.

'Why not? I say it is justice. You can have it if you choose to pay for it, and so can I. If I buy a greatcoat against the winter, and you go out at night without having one, is it injustice because you're perished by the cold while I'm as warm as a toast? I say it's a grand thing to live in a country where one can buy a greatcoat.'

The argument had got so far, Mr. Moulder certainly having the best of it, when a ring at the outer door was heard.

'Now who on earth is that?' said Moulder.

'Snengkeld, I shouldn't wonder,' said his wife.

'I hope it aint no stranger,' said Mrs. Smiley. 'Situated as John and I are now, strangers is so disagreeable.' And then the door was opened by the maid-servant, and Mr. Kantwise was shown into the room.

'Halloo, Kantwise!' said Mr. Moulder, not rising from his chair, or giving any very decided tokens of welcome. 'I thought you were down somewhere among the iron foundries?'

'So I was, Mr. Moulder, but I came up yesterday. Mrs. Moulder, allow me to have the honour. I hope I see you quite well; but looking at you I need not ask. Mr. Kenneby, sir, your very humble servant. The day's coming on fast; isn't it, Mr. Kenneby? Ma'am, your very obedient. I believe I haven't the pleasure of being acquainted.'

'Mrs. Smiley, Mr. Kantwise. Mr. Kantwise, Mrs. Smiley,' said the lady of the house, introducing her visitors to each other in the appropriate way.

'Quite delighted, I'm sure,' said Kantwise.

'Smiley as is, and Kenneby as will be this day three weeks,' said Moulder; and then they all enjoyed that little joke, Mrs. Smiley by no means appearing bashful in the matter although Mr. Kantwise was a stranger.

'I thought I should find Mr. Kenneby here,' said Kantwise, when the subject of the coming nuptials had been sufficiently discussed, 'and therefore I just stepped in. No intrusion, I hope, Mr. Moulder.'

'All right,' said Moulder; 'make yourself at home. There's the stuff on the table. You know what the tap is.'

'I've just parted from— Mr. Dockwrath,' said Kantwise, speaking in a tone of voice which implied the great importance of the communication, and looking round the table to see the effect of it upon the circle.

'Then you've parted from a very low-lived party, let me tell you that,' said Moulder. He had not forgotten Dockwrath's conduct in the commercial room at Leeds, and was fully resolved that he never would forgive it.

'That's as may be,' said Kantwise. 'I say nothing on that subject at the present moment, either one way or the other. But I think you'll all agree as to this: that at the present moment Mr. Dockwrath fills a conspicuous place in the public eye.'

'By no means so conspicuous as John Kenneby,' said Mrs. Smiley, 'if I may be allowed in my position to hold an opinion.'

'That's as may be, ma'am. I say nothing about that. What I hold by is, that Mr. Dockwrath does hold a conspicuous place in the public eye. I've just parted with him in Gray's Inn Lane, and he says—that it's all up now with Lady Mason.'

'Gammon!' said Moulder. And on this occasion Mrs. Smiley did not rebuke him. 'What does he know about it more than any one else? Will he bet two to one? Because, if so, I'll take it;—only I must see the money down.'

'I don't know what he'll bet, Mr. Moulder; only he says it's all up with her.'

'Will he back his side, even handed?'

'I aint a betting man, Mr. Moulder. I don't think it's right. And on such a matter as this, touching the liberty and almost life of a lady whom I've had the honour of seeing, and acquainted as I am with the lady of the other party, Mrs. Mason that is of Groby Park, I should rather, if it's no offence to you, decline the subject of —betting.'

'Bother!'

'Now M., in your own house, you know!' said his wife.

'So it is bother. But never mind that. Go on, Kantwise. What is this you were saying about Dockwrath?'

'Oh, that's about all. I thought you would like to know what they were doing,—particularly Mr. Kenneby. I do hear that they mean to be uncommonly hard upon him.'

The unfortunate witness shifted uneasily in his seat, but at the moment said nothing himself.

'Well, now, I can't understand it,' said Mrs. Smiley, sitting upright in her chair, and tackling herself to the discussion as though she meant to express her opinion, let who might think differently. 'How is any one to put words into my mouth if I don't choose to speak then? There's John's waistcoat is silk.' Upon which they all looked at Kenneby's waistcoat, and, with the exception of Kantwise, acknowledged the truth of the assertion.

' That's as may be,' said he, looking round at it from the corner of his eyes.

' And do you mean to say that all the barristers in London will make me say that it's made of cloth? It's ridic'lous—nothing short of ridic'lous.'

' You've never tried, my dear,' said Moulder.

' I don't know about being your dear, Mr. Moulder——'

' Nor yet don't I neither, Mrs. Smiley,' said the wife.

' Mr. Kenneby's my dear, and I aint ashamed to own him,—before men and women. But if he allows hisself to be hocussed in that way, I don't know but what I shall be ashamed. I call it hocussing —just hocussing.'

' So it is, ma'am,' said Kantwise, ' only this, you know, if I hocus you, why you hocus me in return ; so it isn't so very unfair, you know.'

' Unfair!' said Moulder. ' It's the fairest thing that is. It's the bulwark of the British Constitution.'

' What! being badgered and browbeat ?' asked Kenneby, who was thinking within himself that if this were so he did not care if he lived somewhere beyond the protection of that blessed Ægis.

' Trial by jury is,' said Moulder. ' And how can you have trial by jury if the witnesses are not to be cross-questioned ?'

To this position no one was at the moment ready to give an answer, and Mr. Moulder enjoyed a triumph over his audience. That he lived in a happy and blessed country Moulder was well aware, and with those blessings he did not wish any one to tamper. ' Mother,' said a fastidious child to his parent, ' the bread is gritty and the butter tastes of turnips.' ' Turnips indeed,—and gritty !' said the mother. ' Is it not a great thing to have bread and butter at all ?' I own that my sympathies are with the child. Bread and butter is a great thing ; but I would have it of the best if that be possible.

After that Mr. Kantwise was allowed to dilate upon the subject which had brought him there. Mr. Dockwrath had been summoned to Bedford Row, and there had held a council of war together with Mr. Joseph Mason and Mr. Matthew Round. According to his own story Mr. Matthew had quite come round and been forced to acknowledge all that Dockwrath had done for the cause. In Bedford Row there was no doubt whatever as to the verdict. ' That woman Bolster is quite clear that she only signed one deed,' said Kantwise.

' I shall say nothing—nothing here,' said Kenneby.

Quite right, John,' said Mrs. Smiley. ' Your feelings on the occasion become you.'

' I'll lay an even bet she's acquitted,' said Moulder. ' And I'll do it in a ten-p'und note.'

CHAPTER XXII.

I HAVE spoken of the state of public opinion as to Lady Mason's coming trial, and have explained that for the most part men's thoughts and sympathies took part with her. But I cannot say that such was the case with the thoughts of those who were most closely concerned with her in the matter,—whatever may have been their sympathies. Of the state of Mr. Furnival's mind on the matter enough has been said. But if he had still entertained any shadow of doubt as to his client's guilt or innocence, none whatever was entertained either by Mr. Aram or by Mr. Chaffanbrass. From the day on which they had first gone into the real circumstances of the case, looking into the evidence which could be adduced against their client, and looking also to their means of rebutting that evidence, they had never felt a shadow of doubt upon the subject. But yet neither of them had ever said that she was guilty. Aram, in discussing with his clerks the work which it was necessary that they should do in the matter, had never expressed such an opinion; nor had Chaffanbrass done so in the consultations which he had held with Aram. As to the verdict they had very often expressed an opinion,—differing considerably. Mr. Aram was strongly of opinion that Lady Mason would be acquitted, resting that opinion, mainly on his great confidence in the powers of Mr. Chaffanbrass. But Mr. Chaffanbrass would shake his head, and sometimes say that things were not now as they used to be.

' That may be so in the City,' said Mr. Aram. ' But you won't find a City jury down at Alston.'

' It's not the juries, Aram. It's the judges. It usedn't to be so, but it is now. When a man has the last word, and will take the trouble to use it, that's everything. If I were asked what point I'd best like to have in my favour, I'd say, a deaf judge. Or if not that, one regularly tired out. I've sometimes thought I'd like to be a judge myself, merely to have the last word.'

' That wouldn't suit you at all, Mr. Chaffanbrass, for you'd be sick of it in a week.'

' At any rate I'm not fit for it,' said the great man meekly. ' I'll tell you what, Aram, I can look back on life and think that I've done a deal of good in my way. I've prevented unnecessary blood-

shed. I've saved the country thousands of pounds in the maintenance of men who've shown themselves well able to maintain
themselves. And I've made the Crown lawyers very careful as to
what sort of evidence they would send up to the Old Bailey. But
my chances of life have been such that they haven't made me fit to
be a judge. I know that.'

'I wish I might see you on the bench to-morrow;—only that we
shouldn't know what to do without you,' said the civil attorney. It
was no more than the fair every-day flattery of the world, for the
practice of Mr. Solomon Aram in his profession was quite as surely
attained as was that of Mr. Chaffanbrass. And it could hardly be
called flattery, for Mr. Solomon Aram much valued the services of
Mr. Chaffanbrass, and greatly appreciated the peculiar turn of that
gentleman's mind.

The above conversation took place in Mr. Solomon Aram's private
room in Bucklersbury. In that much-noted city thoroughfare
Mr. Aram rented the first floor of a house over an eating establishment. He had no great paraphernalia of books and boxes and
clerks' desks, as are apparently necessary to attorneys in general.
Three clerks he did employ, who sat in one room, and he himself
sat in that behind it. So at least they sat when they were to be
found at the parent establishment; but, as regarded the attorney
himself and his senior assistant, the work of their lives was carried
on chiefly in the courts of law. The room in which Mr. Aram was
now sitting was furnished with much more attention to comfort
than is usual in lawyers' chambers. Mr. Chaffanbrass was at
present lying, with his feet up, on a sofa against the wall, in a
position of comfort never attained by him elsewhere till the after-
dinner hours had come to him; and Mr. Aram himself filled an easy
lounging-chair. Some few law papers there were scattered on the
library table, but none of those piles of dusty documents which
give to a stranger, on entering an ordinary attorney's room, so
terrible an idea of the difficulty and dreariness of the profession.
There were no tin boxes with old names labelled on them; there
were no piles of letters, and no pigeon-holes loaded with old memo-
randa. On the whole Mr. Aram's private room was smart and
attractive; though, like himself, it had an air rather of pretence
than of steady and assured well-being.

It is not quite the thing for a barrister to wait upon an attorney,
and therefore it must not be supposed that Mr. Chaffanbrass had
come to Mr. Aram with any view to immediate business; but nevertheless, as the two men understood each other, they could say what
they had to say as to this case of Lady Mason's, although their
present positions were somewhat irregular. They were both to
meet Mr. Furnival and Felix Graham on that afternoon in Mr. Furnival's chambers with reference to the division of those labours

which were to be commenced at Alston on the day but one following, and they both thought that it might be as well that they should say a word to each other on the subject before they went there.

'I suppose you know nothing about the panel down there, eh?' said Chaffanbrass.

'Well, I have made some inquiries; but I don't think there's anything especial to know;—nothing that matters. If I were you, Mr. Chaffanbrass, I wouldn't have any Hamworth people on the jury, for they say that a prophet is never a prophet in his own country.'

'But do you know the Hamworth people?'

'Oh, yes; I can tell you as much as that. But I don't think it will matter much who is or is not on the jury.'

'And why not?'

If those two witnesses break down—that is, Kenneby and Bolster, no jury can convict her. And if they don't——'

'Then no jury can acquit her. But let me tell you, Aram, that it's not every man put into a jury-box who can tell whether a witness has broken down or not.'

'But from what I hear, Mr. Chaffanbrass, I don't think either of these can stand a chance;—that is, if they both come into your hands.'

'But they won't both come into my hands,' said the anxious hero of the Old Bailey.

'Ah! that's where it is. That's where we shall fail. Mr. Furnival is a great man, no doubt.'

'A very great man,—in his way,' said Mr. Chaffanbrass.

'But if he lets one of those two slip through his fingers the thing's over.'

'You know my opinion,' said Chaffanbrass. 'I think it is all over. If you're right in what you say,—that they're both ready to swear in their direct evidence that they only signed one deed on that day, no vacillation afterwards would have any effect on the judge. It's just possible, you know, that their memory might deceive them.'

'Possible! I should think so. I'll tell you what, Mr. Chaffanbrass, if the matter was altogether in your hands I should have no fear,—literally no fear.'

'Ah, you're partial, Aram.'

'It couldn't be so managed, could it, Mr. Chaffanbrass? It would be a great thing; a very great thing.' But Mr. Chaffanbrass said that he thought it could not be managed. The success or safety of a client is a very great thing;—in a professional point of view a very great thing indeed. But there is a matter which in legal eyes is greater even than that. Professional etiquette required that the cross-examination of these two most important witnesses should not be left in the hands of the same barrister.

And then the special attributes of Kenneby and Bridget Bolster were discussed between them, and it was manifest that Aram knew with great accuracy the characters of the persons with whom he had to deal. That Kenneby might be made to say almost anything was taken for granted. With him there would be very great scope for that peculiar skill with which Mr. Chaffanbrass was so wonderfully gifted. In the hands of Mr. Chaffanbrass it was not improbable that Kenneby might be made to swear that he had signed two, three, four—any number of documents on that fourteenth of July, although he had before sworn that he had only signed one. Mr. Chaffanbrass indeed might probably make him say anything that he pleased. Had Kenneby been unsupported the case would have been made safe,—so said Mr. Solomon Aram,—by leaving Kenneby in the hands of Mr. Chaffanbrass. But then Bridget Bolster was supposed to be a witness of altogether a different class of character. To induce her to say exactly the reverse of that which she intended to say might, no doubt, be within the power of man. Mr. Aram thought that it would be within the power of Mr. Chaffanbrass. He thought, however, that it would as certainly be beyond the power of Mr. Furnival; and when the great man lying on the sofa mentioned the name of Mr. Felix Graham, Mr. Aram merely smiled. The question with him was this:— Which would be the safest course?—to make quite sure of Kenneby by leaving him with Chaffanbrass; or to go for the double stake by handing Kenneby over to Mr. Furnival and leaving the task of difficulty to the great master?

' When so much depends upon it, I do detest all this etiquette and precedence,' said Aram with enthusiasm. ' In such a case Mr. Furnival ought not to think of himself.'

' My dear Aram,' said Mr. Chaffanbrass, ' men always think of themselves first. And if we were to go out of the usual course, do you conceive that the gentlemen on the other side would fail to notice it?'

' Which shall it be then?'

' I'm quite indifferent. If the memory of either of these two persons is doubtful,—and after twenty years it may be so,— Mr. Furnival will discover it.'

' Then on the whole I'm disposed to think that I'd let him take the man.'

' Just as you please, Aram. That is, if he's satisfied also.'

' I'm not going to have my client overthrown, you know,' said Aram. ' And then you'll take Dockwrath also, of course. I don't know that it will have much effect upon the case, but I shall like to see Dockwrath in your hands; I shall indeed.'

' I doubt he'll be too many for me.'

' Ha, ha, ha!' Aram might well laugh; for when had any

Mr. Chaffanbrass and Mr. Solomon Aram.

one shown himself able to withstand the powers of Mr. Chaffanbrass?

'They say he is a sharp fellow,' said Mr. Chaffanbrass. 'Well, we
must be off. When those gentlemen at the West End get into Parliament it does not do to keep them waiting. Let one of your
fellows get a cab.' And then the barrister and the attorney started
from Bucklersbury for the general meeting of their forces to be held
in the Old Square, Lincoln's Inn.

We have heard how it came to pass that Felix Graham had been
induced to become one of that legal phalanx which was employed
on behalf of Lady Mason. It was now some days since he had left
Noningsby, and those days with him had been very busy. He had
never yet undertaken the defence of a person in a criminal court,
and had much to learn,—or perhaps he rather fancied that he had.
And then that affair of Mary Snow's new lover was not found to
arrange itself altogether easily. When he came to the details of his
dealings with the different parties, every one wanted from him twice
as much money as he had expected. The chemist was very willing
to have a partner, but then a partnership in his business was, according to his view of the matter, a peculiarly expensive luxury.
Snow père, moreover, came forward with claims which he rested on
such various arguments, that Graham found it almost impossible to
resist them. At first,—that is immediately subsequent to the interview between him and his patron described in a preceding chapter,
Graham had been visited by a very repulsive attorney who had
talked loudly about the cruel wrongs of his ill-used client. This
phasis of the affair would have been by far the preferable one ; but
the attorney and his client probably disagreed. Snow wanted immediate money, and as no immediate money was forthcoming
through the attorney, he threw himself repentant at Graham's
feet, and took himself off with twenty shillings. But his penitence,
and his wants, and his tears, and the thwarted ambition of his
parental mind were endless ; and poor Felix hardly knew where
to turn himself without seeing him. It seemed probable that every
denizen of the courts of law in London would be told before long
the sad tale of Mary Snow's injuries. And then Mrs. Thomas
wanted money,—more money than she had a right to want in
accordance with the terms of their mutual agreement. 'She had
been very much put about,' she said,—' dreadfully put about. She
had had to change her servant three times. There was no knowing
the trouble Mary Snow had given her. She had, in a great measure,
been forced to sacrifice her school.' Poor woman ! she thought she
was telling the truth while making these false plaints. She did not
mean to be dishonest, but it is so easy to be dishonest without meaning it when one is very poor ! Mary Snow herself made no claim on
her lost lover, no claim for money or for aught besides. When he

parted from her on that day without kissing her, Mary Snow knew that all that was over. But not the less did Graham recognize her claim. The very bonnet which she must wear when she stood before the altar with Fitzallen must be paid for out of Graham's pocket. That hobby of moulding a young lady is perhaps of all hobbies the most expensive to which a young gentleman can apply himself.

And in these days he heard no word from Noningsby. Augustus Staveley was up in town, and once or twice they saw each other. But, as may easily be imagined, nothing was said between them about Madeline. As Augustus had once declared, a man does not talk to his friend about his own sister. And then hearing nothing —as indeed how could he have heard anything?—Graham endeavoured to assure himself that that was all over. His hopes had ran high at that moment when his last interview with the judge had taken place; but after all to what did that amount? He had never even asked Madeline to love him. He had been such a fool that he had made no use of those opportunities which chance had thrown in his way. He had been told that he might fairly aspire to the hand of any lady. And yet when he had really loved, and the girl whom he had loved had been close to him, he had not dared to speak to her! How could he now expect that she, in his absence, should care for him?

With all these little troubles around him he went to work on Lady Mason's case, and at first felt thoroughly well inclined to give her all the aid in his power. He saw Mr. Furnival on different occasions, and did much to charm that gentleman by his enthusiasm in this matter. Mr. Furnival himself could no longer be as enthusiastic as he had been. The skill of a lawyer he would still give if necessary, but the ardour of the loving friend was waxing colder from day to day. Would it not be better, if such might be possible, that the whole affair should be given up to the hands of Chaffanbrass who could be energetic without belief, and of Graham who was energetic because he believed? So he would say to himself frequently. But then he would think again of her pale face and acknowledge that this was impossible. He must go on till the end. But, nevertheless, if this young man could believe, would it not be well that he should bear the brunt of the battle? That fighting of a battle without belief is, I think, the sorriest task which ever falls to the lot of any man.

But, as the day grew nigh, a shadow of unbelief, a dim passing shade—a shade which would pass, and then return, and then pass again—flitted also across the mind of Felix Graham. His theory had been, and still was, that those two witnesses, Kenneby and Bolster, were suborned by Dockwrath to swear falsely. He had commenced by looking at the matter with a full confidence in his client's innocence, a confidence which had come from the outer

world, from his social convictions, and the knowledge which he had
of the confidence of others.   Then it had been necessary for him to
reconcile the stories which Kenneby and Bolster were prepared to
tell with this strong confidence, and he could only do so by believing that they were both false and had been thus suborned.
But what if they were not false?   What if he were judging
them wrongfully?   I do not say that he had ceased to believe
in Lady Mason; but a shadow of doubt would occasionally cross
his mind, and give to the whole affair an aspect which to him was
very tragical.

He had reached Mr. Furnival's chambers on this day some few
minutes before his new allies, and as he was seated there discussing
the matter which was now so interesting to them all, he blurted
out a question which nearly confounded the elder barrister

'I suppose there can really be no doubt as to her innocence?'
What was Mr. Furnival to say?   Mr. Chaffanbrass and Mr. Aram
had asked no such question.   Mr. Round had asked no such
question when he had discussed the whole matter confidentially
with him.   It was a sort of question never put to professional men,
and one which Felix Graham should not have asked.   Nevertheless
it must be answered.

'Eh?' he said.

'I suppose we may take it for granted that Lady Mason is really
innocent,—that is, free from all falsehood or fraud in this matter?

'Really innocent!   Oh yes; I presume we take that for granted,
as a matter of course.'

'But you yourself, Mr. Furnival; you have no doubt about it?
You have been concerned in this matter from the beginning, and
therefore I have no hesitation in asking you.'

But that was exactly the reason why he should have hesitated!
At least so Mr. Furnival thought.   'Who; I?   No; I have no
doubt; none in the least,' said he.   And thus the lie which he had
been trying to avoid, was at last told.

The assurance thus given was very complete as far as the words
were concerned; but there was something in the tone of Mr. Furnival's voice, which did not quite satisfy Felix Graham.   It was not
that he thought that Mr. Furnival had spoken falsely, but the
answer had not been made in a manner to set his own mind at rest.
Why had not Mr. Furnival answered him with enthusiasm?   Why
had he not, on behalf of his old friend, shown something like
indignation that any such doubt should have been expressed?   His
words had been words of assurance; but, considering the subject, his
tone had contained no assurance.   And thus the shadow of doubt
flitted backwards and forwards before Graham's mind.

Then the general meeting of the four lawyers was held, and the
various arrangements necessary for the coming contest were settled.

No such impertinent questions were asked then, nor were there any communications between them of a confidential nature. Mr. Chaffan-brass and Solomon Aram might whisper together, as might also Mr. Furnival and Felix Graham; but there could be no whispering when all the four were assembled. The programme of their battle was settled, and then they parted with the understanding that they were to meet again in the court-house at Alston.

CHAPTER XXIII.

THE EVENING BEFORE THE TRIAL.

THE eve of the trial had now come, and still there had been no confidence between the mother and the son. No words of kindness had been spoken with reference to that terrible event which was so near at hand. Lucius had in his manner been courteous to his mother, but he had at the same time been very stern. He had seemed to make no allowance for her sorrows, never saying to her one of those soft words which we all love to hear from those around us when we are suffering. Why should she suffer thus? Had she chosen to lean upon him, he would have borne on her behalf all this trouble and vexation. As to her being guilty—as to her being found guilty by any twelve jurymen in England,—no such idea ever entered his head. I have said that many people had begun to suspect; but no such suspicions had reached his ears. What man, unless it should be some Dockwrath, would whisper to the son the possibility of his mother's guilt? Dockwrath had done more than whisper it; but the words of such a man could have no avail with him against his mother's character.

On that day Mrs. Orme had been with Lady Mason for some hours, and had used all her eloquence to induce the mother even then to divulge her secret to her son. Mrs. Orme had suggested that Sir Peregrine should tell him; she had offered to tell him her-self; she had proposed that Lady Mason should write to Lucius. But all had been of no avail. Lady Mason had argued, and had argued with some truth, that it was too late to tell him now, with the view of obtaining from him support during the trial. If he were now told, he would not recover from the first shock of the blow in time to appear in court without showing on his brow the perturbation of his spirit. His terrible grief would reveal the secret to every one. 'When it is over,'—she had whispered at last, as Mrs. Orme continued to press upon her the absolute necessity that Lucius should give up the property,—'when it is over, you shall do it.'

With this Mrs. Orme was obliged to rest contented. She had not the heart to remind Lady Mason how probable it was that the truth might be told out to all the world during the next two or three days ;—that a verdict of Guilty might make any further telling unnecessary. And indeed it was not needed that she should do so. In this respect Lady Mason was fully aware of the nature of the ground on which she stood.

Mrs. Orme had sat with her the whole afternoon, only leaving herself time to be ready for Sir Peregrine's dinner ; and as she left her she promised to be with her early on the following morning to go with her down to the court. Mr. Aram was also to come to the Farm for her, and a closed carriage had been ordered from the inn for the occasion.

' You won't let him prevent you ?' were the last words she spoke, as Mrs. Orme then left her.

' He will not wish to do so,' said Mrs. Orme. ' He has already given me his permission. He never goes back from his word, you know.'

This had been said in allusion to Sir Peregrine. When Mrs. Orme had first proposed to accompany Lady Mason to the court and to sit by her side during the whole trial, he had been much startled. He had been startled, and for a time had been very unwilling to accede to such a step. The place which she now proposed to fill was one which he had intended to fill himself ;—but he had intended to stand by an innocent, injured lady, not a perpetrator of midnight forgery. He had intended to support a spotless being, who would then be his wife,—not a woman who for years had lived on the proceeds of fraud and felony, committed by herself !

' Edith,' he had said, ' you know that I am unwilling to oppose you ; but I think that in this your feelings are carrying you too far.'

' No, father,' she answered, not giving way at all, or showing herself minded to be turned from her purpose by anything he might say. ' Do not think so ; think of her misery. How could she endure it by herself ?'

' Think of her guilt, Edith !'

' I will leave others to think of that. But, father, her guilt will not stain me. Are we not bound to remember what injury she might have done to us, and how we might still have been ignorant of all this, had not she herself confessed it—for our sakes—for our sakes, father ?'

And then Sir Peregrine gave way. When this argument was used to him, he was forced to yield. It was true that, had not that woman been as generous as she was guilty, he would now have been bound to share her shame. The whole of this affair, taken together, had nearly laid him prostrate ; but that which had gone the farthest

towards effecting this ruin, was the feeling that he owed so much
to Lady Mason. As regarded the outer world, the injury to him
would have been much more terrible had he married her; men
would then have declared that all was over with him; but as
regards the inner man, I doubt whether he would not have borne
that better. It was easier for him to sustain an injury than a
favour,—than a favour from one whom his judgment compelled him
to disown as a friend.

But he had given way, and it was understood at The Cleeve that
Mrs. Orme was to remain by Lady Mason's side during the trial.
To the general household there was nothing in this that was
wonderful. They knew only of the old friendship. To them the
question of her guilt was still an open question. As others had
begun to doubt, so had they; but no one then presumed that Sir
Peregrine or Mrs. Orme had any doubt. That they were assured
of her innocence was the conviction of all Hamworth and its neighbourhood.

'He never goes back from his word, you know,' Mrs. Orme had
said; and then she kissed Lady Mason, and went her way. She
had never left her without a kiss, had never greeted her without a
warm pressure of the hand, since that day on which the secret had
been told in Sir Peregrine's library. It would be impossible to
describe how great had been the worth of this affection to Lady
Mason; but it may almost be said that it had kept her alive. She
herself had said but little about it, uttering but few thanks; but not
the less had she recognized the value of what had been done for her.
She had even become more free herself in her intercourse with Mrs.
Orme,—more open in her mode of speech,—had put herself more on
an equality with her friend, since there had ceased to be anything
hidden between them. Previously Lady Mason had felt, and had
occasionally expressed the feeling, that she was hardly fit to associate on equal terms with Mrs. Orme; but now there was none of
this,—now, as they sat together for hours and hours, they spoke,
and argued, and lived together as though they were equal. But
nevertheless, could she have shown her love by any great deed,
there was nothing which Lady Mason would not have done for
Mrs. Orme.

She was now left alone, and according to her daily custom would
remain there till the servant told her that Mr. Lucius was waiting
for her in the dining-room. In an early part of this story I have
endeavoured to describe how this woman sat alone, with deep
sorrow in her heart and deep thought on her mind, when she first
learned what terrible things were coming on her. The idea, however, which the reader will have conceived of her as she sat there
will have come to him from the skill of the artist, and not from the
words of the writer. If that drawing is now near him, let him go

back to it. Lady Mason was again sitting in the same room—that pleasant room, looking out through the verandah on to the sloping lawn, and in the same chair; one hand again rested open on the arm of the chair, while the other supported her face as she leaned upon her elbow; and the sorrow was still in her heart, and the deep thought in her mind. But the lines of her face were altered, and the spirit expressed by it was changed. There was less of beauty, less of charm, less of softness; but in spite of all that she had gone through there was more of strength,—more of the power to resist all that this world could do to her.

It would be wrong to say that she was in any degree a hypocrite. A man is no more a hypocrite because his manner and gait when he is alone are different from those which he assumes in company, than he is for wearing a dressing-gown in the morning, whereas he puts on a black coat in the evening. Lady Mason in the present crisis of her life endeavoured to be true in all her dealings with Mrs. Orme; but nevertheless Mrs. Orme had not yet read her character. As she now sat thinking of what the morrow would bring upon her, —thinking of all that the malice of that man Dockwrath had brought upon her,—she resolved that she would still struggle on with a bold front. It had been brought home to her that he, her son, the being for whom her soul had been imperilled, and all her hopes for this world destroyed,—that he must be told of his mother's guilt and shame. Let him be told, and then let him leave her while his anguish and the feeling of his shame were hot upon him. Should she be still a free woman when this trial was over she would move herself away at once, and then let him be told. But still it would be well—well for his sake, that his mother should not be found guilty by the law. It was still worth her while to struggle. The world was very hard to her, bruising her to the very soul at every turn, allowing her no hope, offering to her no drop of cool water in her thirst. But still for him there was some future career; and that career perhaps need not be blotted by the public notice of his mother's guilt. She would still fight against her foes, —still show to that court, and to the world that would then gaze at her, a front on which guilt should not seem to have laid its hideous, defacing hand.

There was much that was wonderful about this woman. While she was with those who regarded her with kindness she could be so soft and womanly; and then, when alone, she could be so stern and hard! And it may be said that she felt but little pity for herself. Though she recognized the extent of her misery, she did not complain of it. Even in her inmost thoughts her plaint was this,— that he, her son, should be doomed to suffer so deeply for her sin! Sometimes she would utter to that other mother a word of wailing, in that he would not be soft to her; but even in that she did not mean to complain of him. She knew in her heart of hearts that she had no right to expect such softness. She knew that it was better that it should be as it now was. Had he stayed with her from morn till evening, speaking kind words to her, how could she have failed to tell him? In sickness it may irk us because we are not allowed to take the cool drink that would be grateful; but what man in his senses would willingly swallow that by which his very life would be endangered? It was thus she thought of her son, and what his love might have been to her.

Yes; she would still bear up, as she had borne up at that other trial. She would dress herself with care, and go down into the court with a smooth brow. Men, as they looked at her, should not at once say, 'Behold the face of a guilty woman!' There was still a chance in the battle, though the odds were so tremendously against her. It might be that there was but little to which she could look forward, even though the verdict of the jury should be in her favour; but all that she regarded as removed from her by a great interval. She had promised that Lucius should know all after the trial,—that he should know all, so that the property might be restored to its rightful owner; and she was fully resolved that this promise should be kept. But nevertheless there was a long interval. If she could battle through this first danger,—if by the skill of her lawyers she could avert the public declaration of her guilt, might not the chances of war still take some further turn in her favour? And thus, though her face was pale with suffering and thin with care, though she had realized the fact that nothing short of a miracle could save her,—still she would hope for that miracle.

But the absolute bodily labour which she was forced to endure was so hard upon her! She would dress herself, and smooth her brow for the trial; but that dressing herself, and that maintenance of a smooth brow would impose upon her an amount of toil which would almost overtask her physical strength. O reader, have you ever known what it is to rouse yourself and go out to the world on your daily business, when all the inner man has revolted against work, when a day of rest has seemed to you to be worth a year of life? If she could have rested now, it would have been worth many years of life,—worth all her life. She longed for rest, —to be able to lay aside the terrible fatigue of being ever on the watch. From the burden of that necessity she had never been free since her crime had been first committed. She had never known true rest. She had not once trusted herself to sleep without the feeling that her first waking thought would be one of horror, as the remembrance of her position came upon her. In every word she spoke, in every trifling action of her life, it was necessary that she should ask herself how that word and action might tell upon her chances of escape. She had striven to be true and honest,—true and honest with the exception of that one deed. But that one deed had communicated its poison to her whole life. Truth and honesty — fair, unblemished truth and open-handed, fearless honesty,—had been impossible to her. Before she could be true and honest it would be necessary that she should go back and cleanse herself from the poison of that deed. Such cleansing is to be done. Men have sinned deep as she had sinned, and, lepers though they have been, they have afterwards been clean. But that task of cleansing oneself is not an easy one;—the waters of that Jordan in which it is needful to wash are scalding hot. The cool neighbouring streams of life's pleasant valleys will by no means suffice.

Since she had been home at Orley Farm she had been very scrupulous as to going down into the parlour both at breakfast and at dinner, so that she might take her meals with her son. She had not as yet omitted this on one occasion, although sometimes the task of sitting through the dinner was very severe upon her. On the present occasion, the last day that remained to her before the trial— perhaps the last evening on which she would ever watch the sun set from those windows, she thought that she would spare herself. ' Tell Mr. Lucius,' she said to the servant who came to summon her, ' that I would be obliged to him if he would sit down without me. Tell him that I am not ill, but that I would rather not go down to dinner!' But before the girl was on the stairs she had changed her mind. Why should she now ask for this mercy? What did it matter? So she gathered herself up from the chair, and going forth from the room, stopped the message before it was delivered. She would bear on to the end.

She sat through the dinner, and answered the ordinary questions which Lucius put to her with her ordinary voice, and then, as was her custom, she kissed his brow as she left the room. It must be remembered that they were still mother and son, and that there had been no quarrel between them. And now, as she went up stairs, he followed her into the drawing-room. His custom had been to remain below, and though he had usually seen her again during the evening, there had seldom or never been any social intercourse between them. On the present occasion, however, he followed her, and closing the door for her as he entered the room, he sat himself down on the sofa, close to her chair.

' Mother,' he said, putting out his hand and touching her arm, ' things between us are not as they should be.'

She shuddered, not at the touch, but at the words. Things were not as they should be between them. ' No,' she said. ' But I am sure of this, Lucius, that you never had an unkind thought in your heart towards me.'

'Never, mother. How could I,—to my own mother, who has ever been so good to me? But for the last three months we have been to each other nearly as though we were strangers.'

'But we have loved each other all the same,' said she.

'But love should beget close social intimacy, and above all close confidence in times of sorrow. There has been none such between us.'

What could she say to him? It was on her lips to promise him that such love should again prevail between them as soon as this trial should be over; but the words stuck in her throat. She did not dare to give him so false an assurance. 'Dear Lucius,' she said, 'if it has been my fault, I have suffered for it.'

'I do not say that it is your fault;—nor will I say that it has been my own. If I have seemed harsh to you, I beg your pardon.'

'No, Lucius, no; you have not been harsh. I have understood you through it all.'

'I have been grieved because you did not seem to trust me;—but let that pass now. Mother, I wish that there may be no unpleasant feeling between us when you enter on this ordeal to-morrow.'

'There is none;—there shall be none.'

'No one can feel more keenly,—no one can feel so keenly as I do, the cruelty with which you are treated. The sight of your sorrow has made me wretched.'

'Oh, Lucius!'

'I know how pure and innocent you are——'

'No, Lucius, no.'

'But I say yes; and knowing that, it has cut me to the quick to see them going about a defence of your innocence by quips and quibbles, as though they were struggling for the escape of a criminal.'

'Lucius!' And she put her hands up, praying for mercy, though she could not explain to him how terribly severe were his words.

'Wait a moment, mother. To me such men as Mr. Chaffanbrass and his comrades are odious. I will not, and do not believe that their services are necessary to you——'

'But, Lucius, Mr. Furnival——'

'Yes; Mr. Furnival! It is he that has done it all. In my heart I wish that you had never known Mr. Furnival;—never known him as a lawyer that is,' he added, thinking of his own strong love for the lawyer's daughter.

'Do not upbraid me now, Lucius. Wait till it is all over.'

'Upbraid you! No. I have come to you now that we may be friends. As things have gone so far, this plan of defence must of course be carried on. I will say no more about that. But, mother, I will go into the court with you to-morrow. That support I can

at any rate give you, and they shall see that there is no quarrel between us.'

But Lady Mason did not desire this. She would have wished
that he might have been miles away from the court had that been
possible. ' Mrs. Orme is to be with me,' she said.

Then again there came a black frown upon his brow,—a frown
such as there had often been there of late. ' And will Mrs. Orme's
presence make the attendance of your own son improper ?'

' Oh, no ; of course not. I did not mean that, Lucius.'

' Do you not like to have me near you ?' he asked ; and as he
spoke he rose up, and took her hand as he stood before her.

She gazed for a moment into his face while the tears streamed
down from her eyes, and then rising from her chair, she threw herself on to his bosom and clasped him in her arms. ' My boy ! my
boy !' she said. ' Oh, if you could be near me, and away from this
—away from this !'

She had not intended thus to give way, but the temptation had
been too strong for her. When she had seen Mrs. Orme and Peregrine together,—when she had heard Peregrine's mother, with words
expressed in a joyful tone, affect to complain of the inroads which
her son made upon her, she had envied her that joy. ' Oh, if it
could be so with me also !' she always thought ; and the words too
had more than once been spoken. Now at last, in this last moment,
as it might be, of her life at home, he had come to her with kindly
voice, and she could not repress her yearning.

' Lucius,' she said ; ' dearest Lucius ! my own boy !' And then
the tears from her eyes streamed hot on to his bosom.

' Mother,' he said, ' it shall be so. I will be with you.'

But she was now thinking of more than this—of much more.
Was it possible for her to tell him now? As she held him in her
arms, hiding her face upon his breast, she struggled hard to speak
the word. Then in the midst of that struggle, while there was
still something like a hope within her that it might be done, she
raised her head and looked up into his face. It was not a face
pleasant to look at, as was that of Peregrine Orme. It was hard in
its outlines, and perhaps too manly for his age. But she was his
mother, and she loved it well. She looked up at it, and raising her
hands she stroked his cheeks. She then kissed him again and
again, with warm, clinging kisses. She clung to him, holding him
close to her, while the sobs which she had so long repressed came
forth from her with a violence that terrified him. Then again she
looked up into his face with one long wishful gaze ; and after that
she sank upon the sofa and hid her face within her hands. She
had made the struggle, but it had been of no avail. She could not
tell him that tale with her own voice.

' Mother,' he said, ' what does this mean ? I cannot understand such grief as this.' But for a while she was quite unable to answer. The flood-gates were at length opened, and she could not restrain the torrent of her sobbings.

' You do not understand how weak a woman can be,' she said at last.

But in truth he understood nothing of a woman's strength. He sat down by her, now and then taking her by the hand when she would leave it to him, and in his way endeavoured to comfort her. All comfort, we may say, was out of the question; but by degrees she again became tranquil. ' It shall be to-morrow as you will have it. You will not object to her being with me also ?'

He did object, but he could not say so. He would have much preferred to be the only friend near to her, but he felt that he could not deny her the solace of a woman's aid and a woman's countenance. ' Oh no,' he said, ' if you wish it.' He would have found it impossible to define even to himself the reason for his dislike to any assistance coming from the family of the Ormes; but the feeling was there, strong within his bosom.

' And when this is over, mother, we will go away,' he said. ' If you would wish to live elsewhere, I will sell the property. It will be better perhaps after all that has passed. We will go abroad for a while.'

She could make no answer to this except pressing his hand. Ah, if he had been told—if she had allowed Mrs. Orme to do that kindness for her, how much better for her would it now have been! Sell the property! Ah, me! Were they not words of fearful sound in her ears,—words of terrible import?

' Yes, it shall be so,' she said, putting aside that last proposition of his. ' We will go together to-morrow. Mr. Aram said that he would sit at my side, but he cannot object to your being there between us.' Mr. Aram's name was odious to Lucius Mason. His close presence would be odious to him. But he felt that he could urge nothing against an arrangement that had now become necessary. Mr. Aram, with all his quibbles, had been engaged, and the trial must now be carried through with all the Aram tactics.

After that Lucius left his mother, and took himself out into the dark night, walking up and down on the road between his house and the outer gate, endeavouring to understand why his mother should be so despondent. That she must fear the result of the trial, he thought, was certain, but he could not bring himself to have any such fear. As to any suspicion of her guilt,—no such idea had even for one moment cast a shadow upon his peace of mind.

CHAPTER XXIV.

THE FIRST JOURNEY TO ALSTON.

At that time Sir Richard Leatherham was the Solicitor-general, and he had been retained as leading counsel for the prosecution. It was quite understood by all men who did understand what was going on in the world, that this trial had been in truth instituted by Mr. Mason of Groby with the hope of recovering the property which had been left away from him by his father's will. The whole matter had now been so much discussed, that the true bearings of it were publicly known. If on the former trial Lady Mason had sworn falsely, then there could be no doubt that that will, or the codicil to the will, was an untrue document, and the property would in that case revert to Mr. Mason, after such further legal exercitations on the subject as the lawyers might find necessary and profitable. As far as the public were concerned, and as far as the Masons were concerned, it was known and acknowledged that this was another struggle on the part of the Groby Park family to regain the Orley Farm estate. But then the question had become much more interesting than it had been in the days of the old trial, through the allegation which was now made of Lady Mason's guilt. Had the matter gone against her in the former trial, her child would have lost the property, and that would have been all. But the present issue would be very different. It would be much more tragical, and therefore of much deeper interest.

As Alston was so near to London, Sir Richard, Mr. Furnival, Mr. Chaffanbrass, and others, were able to go up and down by train, —which arrangement was at ordinary assizes a great heartsore to the hotel-keepers and owners of lodging-houses in Alston. But on this occasion the town was quite full in spite of this facility. The attorneys did not feel it safe to run up and down in that way, nor did the witnesses. Mr. Aram remained, as did also Mr. Mat Round. Special accommodation had been provided for John Kenneby and Bridget Bolster, and Mr. Mason of Groby had lodgings of his own.

Mr. Mason of Groby had suggested to the attorneys in Bedford Row that his services as a witness would probably be required, but they had seemed to think otherwise. ' We shall not call you,'

Mr. Round had said, ' and I do not suppose that the other side will do so. They can't if they do not first serve you.' But in spite of this Mr. Mason had determined to be at Alston. If it were true that this woman had robbed him ;—if it could be proved that she had really forged a will, and then by crime of the deepest dye taken from him for years that which was his own, should he not be there to see? Should he not be a witness to her disgrace? Should he not be the first to know and feel his own tardy triumph? Pity! Pity for her! When such a word was named to him, it seemed to him as though the speaker were becoming to a certain extent a partner in her guilt. Pity! Yes; such pity as an Englishman who had caught the Nana Sahib might have felt for his victim. He had complained twenty times since this matter had been mooted of the folly of those who had altered the old laws. That folly had probably robbed him of his property for twenty years, and would now rob him of half his revenge. Not that he ever spoke even to himself of revenge. ' Vengeance is mine, saith the Lord.' He would have been as able as any man to quote the words, and as willing. Justice, outraged justice, was his theme. Whom had he ever robbed? To whom had he not paid all that was owing? ' All that have I done from my youth upwards.' Such were his thoughts of himself; and with such thoughts was it possible that he should willingly be absent from Alston during such a trial?

' I really would stay away if I were you,' Mat Round had said to him.

' I will not stay away,' he had replied, with a look black as a thundercloud. Could there really be anything in those suspicions of Dockwrath, that his own lawyer had wilfully thrown him over once, and was now anxious to throw him over again? ' I will not stay away,' he said; and Dockwrath secured his lodgings for him. About this time he was a good deal with Mr. Dockwrath, and almost regretted that he had not followed that gentleman's advice at the commencement of the trial, and placed the management of the whole concern in his hands.

Thus Alston was quite alive on the morning of the trial, and the doors of the court-house were thronged long before they were opened. They who were personally concerned in the matter, whose presence during the ceremony would be necessary, or who had legal connection with the matter in hand, were of course not driven to this tedious manner of obtaining places. Mr. Dockwrath, for instance, did not stand waiting at the door, nor did his friend Mr. Mason. Mr. Dockwrath was a great man as far as this day was concerned, and could command admittance from the doorkeepers and others about the court. But for the outer world, for men and women who were not lucky enough to be lawyers, witnesses, jurymen, or high sheriff, there was no means of hearing and seeing the events of this stirring day except what might be obtained by exercise of an almost unlimited patience.

There had been much doubt as to what arrangement for her attendance at the court it might be best for Lady Mason to make, and some difficulty too as to who should decide as to these arrangements. Mr. Aram had been down more than once, and had given a hint that it would be well that something should be settled. It had ended in his settling it himself,—he, with the assistance of Mrs. Orme. What would Sir Peregrine have said had he known that on any subject these two had been leagued in council together?

' She can go from hence in a carriage—a carriage from the inn,' Mrs. Orme had said.

' Certainly, certainly; a carriage from the inn; yes. But in the evening, ma'am?'

' When the trial is over?' said Mrs. Orme, inquiring from him his meaning.

' We can hardly expect that it shall be over in one day, ma'am. She will continue to be on bail, and can return home. I will see that she is not annoyed as she leaves the town.'

' Annoyed?' said Mrs. Orme.

' By the people I mean.'

' Will there be anything of that, sir?' she asked, turning pale at the idea. 'I shall be with her, you know.'

' Through the whole affair, ma'am?'

' Yes, through the whole affair.'

' They'll want to have a look at her of course; but,—Mrs. Orme, we'll see that you are not annoyed. Yes; she had better come back home the first day. The expense won't be much; will it?'

' Oh no,' said Mrs. Orme. 'I must return home, you know. How many days will it be, sir?'

' Well, perhaps two,—perhaps three. It may run on all the week. Of course you know, Mrs. Orme——'

' Know what?' she asked.

' When the trial is over, if—if it should go against us,—then you must return alone.'

And so the matter had been settled, and Mr. Aram himself had ordered the carriage from the inn. Sir Peregrine's carriage would have been at their disposal,—or rather Mrs. Orme's own carriage; but she had felt that The Cleeve arms on The Cleeve panels would be out of place in the streets of Hamworth on such an occasion. It would of course be impossible that she should not be recognized in the court, but she would do as little as possible to proclaim her own presence.

When the morning came, the very morning of the terrible day, Mrs. Orme came down early from her room, as it was necessary that she should breakfast two hours before the usual time. She had said nothing of this to Sir Peregrine, hoping that she might have been able to escape in the morning without seeing him. She had told her son to be there; but when she made her appearance in the breakfast parlour, she found that his grandfather was already with him. She sat down and took her cup of tea almost in silence, for they all felt that on such a morning much speech was impossible for them.

' Edith, my dear,' said the baronet, ' you had better eat something. Think of the day that is before you.'

' Yes, father, I have,' said she, and she lifted a morsel of bread to her mouth.

' You must take something with you,' said he, ' or you will be faint in the court. Have you thought how many hours you will be there ?'

' I will see to that,' said Peregrine, speaking with a stern decision in his voice that was by no means natural to him.

' Will you be there, Perry ?' said his mother.

' Of course I shall. I will see that you have what you want. You will find that I will be near you.'

' But how will you get in, my boy ?' asked his grandfather.

' Let me alone for that. I have spoken to the sheriff already. There is no knowing what may turn up; so if anything does turn up you may be sure that I am near you.'

Then another slight attempt at eating was made, the cup of tea was emptied, and the breakfast was finished. ' Is the carriage there, Perry ?' asked Mrs. Orme.

' Yes; it is at the door.'

' Good-bye, father; I am so sorry to have disturbed you.'

' Good-bye, Edith; God bless you, and give you strength to bear it. And, Edith——'

' Sir ?' and she held his hand as he whispered to her.

' Say to her a word of kindness from me ;—a word of kindness. Tell her that I have forgiven her, but tell her also that man's forgiveness will avail her nothing.'

' Yes, father, I will.'

' Teach her where to look for pardon. But tell her all the same that I have forgiven her.'

And then he handed her into the carriage. Peregrine, as he stood aside, had watched them as they whispered, and to his mind also as he followed them to the carriage a suspicion of what the truth might be now made its way. Surely there would be no need of all this solemn mourning if she were innocent. Had she been esteemed as innocent, Sir Peregrine was not the man to believe that any jury of his countrymen could find her guilty. Had this been the reason for that sudden change,—for that breaking off of the intended marriage ? Even Peregrine, as he went down the steps

after his mother, had begun to suspect the truth; and we may say
that he was the last within all that household who did so.   During
the last week every servant at The Cleeve had whispered to her
fellow-servant that Lady Mason had forged the will.

' I shall be near you, mother,' said Peregrine as he put his hand
into the carriage; ' remember that.   The judge and the other fellows
will go out in the middle of the day to get a glass of wine : I'll have
something for both of you near the court.'

Poor Mrs. Orme as she pressed her son's hand felt much relieved
by the assurance.   It was not that she feared anything, but she was
going to a place that was absolutely new to her,—to a place in
which the eyes of many would be fixed on her,—to a place in which
the eyes of all would be fixed on the companion with whom she
would be joined.   Her heart almost sank within her as the carriage
drove away.   She would be alone till she reached Orley Farm, and
there she would take up not only Lady Mason, but Mr. Aram also.
How would it be with them in that small carriage while Mr. Aram
was sitting opposite to them?   Mrs. Orme by no means regretted
this act of kindness which she was doing, but she began to feel that
the task was not a light one.   As to Mr. Aram's presence in the
carriage, she need have been under no uneasiness.   He understood
very well when his presence was desirable, and also when it was
not desirable.

When she arrived at the door of Orley Farm house she found
Mr. Aram waiting there to receive her.   ' I am sorry to say,' said
he, raising his hat, ' that Lady Mason's son is to accompany us.'

' She did not tell me,' said Mrs. Orme, not understanding why
this should make him sorry.

' It was arranged between them last night, and it is very unfortunate.   I cannot explain this to her ; but perhaps——'

' Why is it unfortunate, sir ?'

' Things will be said which—which—which would drive me mad
if they were said about my mother.'   And immediately there was a
touch of sympathy between the high-bred lady and the Old Bailey
Jew lawyer.

' Yes, yes,' said Mrs. Orme.   ' It will be dreadful.'

' And then if they find her guilty !   It may be so, you know.
And how is he to sit there and hear the judge's charge ;—and then
the verdict, and the sentence.   If he is there he cannot escape.
I'll tell you what, Mrs. Orme ; he should not be there at all.'

But what could she do ?   Had it been possible that she should be
an hour alone with Lady Mason, she would have explained all this
to her,—or if not all, would have explained much of it.   But now,
with no minutes to spare, how could she make this understood ?
' But all that will not come to-day, will it, sir ?'

' Not all,—not the charge or the verdict.   But he should not be

there even to-day. He should have gone away; or if he remained
at home, he should not have shown himself out of the house.'

But this was too late now, for as they were still speaking Lady
Mason appeared at the door, leaning on her son's arm. She was
dressed from head to foot in black, and over her face there was a
thick black veil. Mr. Aram spoke no word further as she stepped
up the steps from the hall door to the carriage, but stood back,
holding the carriage-door open in his hand. Lucius merely bowed
to Mrs. Orme as he assisted his mother to take her place; and then
following her, he sat himself down in silence opposite to them.
Mr. Aram, who had carefully arranged his own programme, shut
the door, and mounted on to the box beside the driver.

Mrs. Orme had held out her own hand, and Lady Mason having
taken it, still held it after she was seated. Then they started, and
for the first mile no word was spoken between them. Mrs. Orme
was most anxious to speak, if it might only be for the sake of
breaking the horrid stillness of their greeting; but she could think
of no word which it would be proper on such an occasion to say,
either to Lucius, or even before him. Had she been alone with
Lady Mason there would have been enough of words that she could
have spoken. Sir Peregrine's message was as a burden upon her
tongue till she could deliver it; but she could not deliver it while
Lucius Mason was sitting by her.

Lady Mason herself was the first to speak. 'I did not know
yesterday that Lucius would come,' she said, 'or I should have
told you.'

'I hope it does not inconvenience you,' he said.

'Oh no; by no means.'

'I could not let my mother go out without me on such an occasion as this. But I am grateful to you, Mrs. Orme, for coming
also.'

'I thought it would be better for her to have some lady with
her,' said Mrs. Orme.

'Oh yes, it is better—much better.' And then no further word
was spoken by any of them till the carriage drove up to the court-
house door. It may be hoped that the journey was less painful to
Mr. Aram than to the others, seeing that he solaced himself on the
coach-box with a cigar.

There was still a great crowd round the front of the court-house
when they reached it, although the doors were open, and the court
was already sitting. It had been arranged that this case—the great
case of the assize—should come on first on this day, most of the
criminal business having been completed on that preceding; and
Mr. Aram had promised that his charge should be forthcoming
exactly at ten o'clock. Exactly at ten the carriage was driven up
to the door, and Mr. Aram jumping from his seat directed certain

The Court.

policemen and sheriff's servants to make a way for the ladies up to
the door, and through the hall of the court-house. Had he lived in
Alston all his life, and spent his days in the purlieus of that court,
he could not have been more at home or have been more promptly
obeyed.

'And now I think we may go in,' he said, opening the door and
letting down the steps with his own hands.

At first he took them into a small room within the building, and
then bustled away himself into the court. 'I shall be back in half
a minute,' he said; and in half a dozen half-minutes he was back.
'We are all ready now, and shall have no trouble about our places.
If you have anything to leave,—shawls, or things of that sort,—
they will be quite safe here : Mrs. Hitcham will look after them.'
And then an old woman who had followed Mr. Aram into the room
on the last occasion curtsied to them. But they had nothing to
leave, and their little procession was soon made.

Lucius at first offered his arm to his mother, and she had taken
it till she had gone through the door into the hall. Mr. Aram also
had, with some hesitation, offered his arm to Mrs. Orme; but she,
in spite of that touch of sympathy, had managed, without speaking,
to decline it. In the hall, however, when all the crowd of gazers
had turned their eyes upon them and was only kept off from pressing
on them by the policemen and sheriff's officers, Lady Mason remembered herself, and suddenly dropping her son's arm, she put out her
hand for Mrs. Orme. Mr. Aram was now in front of them, and thus
they two followed him into the body of the court. The veils of
both of them were down ; but Mrs. Orme's veil was not more than
ordinarily thick, and she could see everything that was around her.
So they walked up through the crowded way, and Lucius followed
them by himself.

They were very soon in their seats, the crowd offering them no
impediment. The judge was already on the bench,—not our old
acquaintance Justice Staveley, but his friend and colleague Baron
Maltby. Judge Staveley was sitting in the other court. Mrs. Orme
and Lady Mason soon found themselves seated on a bench, with a
slight standing desk before them, much as though they were seated
in a narrow pew. Up above them, on the same seat, were the three
barristers employed on Lady Mason's behalf; nearest to the judge
was Mr. Furnival ; then came Felix Graham, and below him sat
Mr. Chaffanbrass, somewhat out of the line of precedence, in order
that he might more easily avail himself of the services of Mr. Aram.
Lucius found himself placed next to Mr. Chaffanbrass, and his
mother sat between him and Mrs. Orme. On the bench below them,
immediately facing a large table which was placed in the centre of
the court, sat Mr. Aram and his clerk.

Mrs. Orme as she took her seat was so confused that she could hardly look around her; and it may be imagined that Lady Mason must have suffered at any rate as much in the same way. But they who were looking at her—and it may be said that every one in the court was looking at her—were surprised to see that she raised her veil as soon as she was seated. She raised her veil, and never lowered it again till she left the court, and repassed out into the hall. She had thought much of this day,—even of the little incidents which would occur,—and she was aware that her identification would be necessary. Nobody should tell her to unveil herself, nor would she let it be thought that she was afraid to face her enemies. So there she sat during the whole day, bearing the gaze of the court.

She had dressed herself with great care. It may be said of most women who could be found in such a situation, that they would either give no special heed to their dress on such a morning, or that they would appear in garments of sorrow studiously unbecoming and lachrymose, or that they would attempt to outface the world, and have appeared there in bright trappings, fit for happier days. But Lady Mason had dressed herself after none of these fashions. Never had her clothes been better made, or worn with a better grace; but they were all black, from her bonnet-ribbon down to her boot, and were put on without any attempt at finery or smartness. As regards dress, she had never looked better than she did now; and Mr. Furnival, when his eye caught her as she turned her head round towards the judge, was startled by the grace of her appearance. Her face was very pale, and somewhat hard; but no one on looking at it could say that it was the countenance of a woman overcome either by sorrow or by crime. She was perfect mistress of herself, and as she looked round the court, not with defiant gaze, but with eyes half raised, and a look of modest but yet conscious intelligence, those around her hardly dared to think that she could be guilty.

As she thus looked her gaze fell on one face that she had not seen for years, and their eyes met. It was the face of Joseph Mason of Groby, who sat opposite to her; and as she looked at him her own countenance did not quail for a moment. Her own countenance did not quail; but his eyes fell gradually down, and when he raised them again she had averted her face.

CHAPTER XXV.

'IF you love the man, let him come.' It was thus that the judge had declared to his daughter his opinion of what had better be done in that matter of Felix Graham. Then he had gone on to declare that he had given his permission to Felix Graham to say anything that he had got to say, and finally had undertaken to invite Felix Graham to spend the assize week at Noningsby. Of course in the mind of the judge all this amounted to an actual giving away of his daughter. He regarded the thing now as done, looking upon the young people as betrothed, and his reflections mainly ran on the material part of the business. How should Graham be made to earn an income, and what allowance must be made to him till he did so? There was a certain sum set apart for Madeline's fortune, but that would by no means suffice for the livelihood of a married barrister in London. Graham no doubt earned something as it was, but that was done by his pen rather than by his wig, and the judge was inclined to think that the pen must be abandoned before the wig could be made profitable. Such were the directions which his thoughts took regarding Madeline's lot in life. With him the next week or two, with their events, did not signify much; whereas the coming years did signify a great deal.

At that time, on that Sunday afternoon, there still remained to Madeline the best part of a month to think of it all, before Felix should reappear upon the scene. But then she could not think of it by herself in silence. Her father had desired her to tell her mother what had passed, and she felt that a great difficulty still lay before her. She knew that her mother did not wish her to marry Felix Graham. She knew that her mother did wish her to marry Peregrine Orme. And therefore though no mother and child had ever treated each other with a sweeter confidence, or loved each other with warmer hearts, there was as it were a matter of disunion between them. But nevertheless she must tell her mother, and the dread of this telling weighed heavy upon her as she sat that night in the drawing-room reading the article which Felix had written.

But she need not have been under any alarm. Her father, when he told her to discuss the matter with her mother, had by no means

intended to throw on her shoulders the burden of converting Lady
Staveley to the Graham interest. He took care to do this himself effectually, so that in fact there should be no burden left for Madeline's
shoulders. 'Well, my dear,' he said that same Sunday evening to
his wife, 'I have had it all out with Madeline this afternoon.'

'About Mr. Graham, do you mean?'

'Yes; about Mr. Graham. I have promised that he shall come
here for the assize week.'

'Oh, dear!'

'It's done, my love; and I believe we shall find it all for the
best. The bishops' daughters always marry clergymen, and the
judges' daughters ought to marry lawyers.'

'But you can't give him a practice. The bishops have livings to
give away.'

'Perhaps I may show him how to make a practice for himself,
which would be better. Take my word for it that it will be best
for her happiness. You would not have liked to be disappointed
yourself, when you made up your mind to be married.'

'No, I should not,' said Lady Staveley.

'And she will have a will of her own quite as strong as you had.'
And then there was silence in the room for some time.

'You'll be kind to him when he comes?' said the judge.

'Oh, yes,' said Lady Staveley, in a voice that was by no means
devoid of melancholy.

'Nobody can be so kind as you when you please. And as it is
to be——'

'I always did like him,' said Lady Staveley, 'although he is so
very plain.'

'You'll soon get used to that, my dear.'

'And as for poor young Mr. Orme——'

'As for poor young Mr. Orme, as you call him, he will not die of
a broken heart. Poor young Mr. Orme has all the world before
him and will soon console himself.'

'But he is so attached to her. And then The Cleeve is so near.'

'We must give up all that, my dear.'

'Very well,' said Lady Staveley; and from that moment it may
be said that she had given in her adhesion to the Graham connection. When some time after she gave her orders to Baker as to
preparing a room for Mr. Graham, it was made quite clear to that
excellent woman by her mistress's manner and anxiety as to the
airing of the sheets, that Miss Madeline was to have her own way
in the matter.

But long previous to these preparations Madeline and her mother
had discussed the matter fully. 'Papa says that Mr. Graham is to
come here for the assize week,' said Lady Staveley.

'Yes; so he told me,' Madeline replied, very bashfully.

' I suppose it's all for the best.'

' I hope it is,' said Madeline.   What could she do but hope so?

'Your papa understands everything so very well that I am sure he would not let him come if it were not proper.'

' I suppose not,' said Madeline.

' And now I look upon the matter as all settled.'

' What matter, mamma?'

' That he—that he is to come here as your lover.'

' Oh, no, mamma.   Pray don't imagine that.   It is not so at all. What should I do if you were to say anything to make him think so?'

' But you told me that you loved him.'

' So I do, mamma.'

'And he told your papa that he was desperately in love with you.'

' I don't know, mamma.'

' But he did;—your papa told me so, and that's why he asked him to come down here again.   He never would have done it without.'

Madeline had her own idea about this, believing that her father had thought more of her wants in the matter than he had of those of Felix Graham; but as to this she said nothing.   ' Nevertheless, mamma, you must not say that to any one,' she answered.   ' Mr. Graham has never spoken to me,—not a word.   I should of course have told you had he done so.'

' Yes, I am sure of that.   But, Madeline, I suppose it's all the same.   He asked papa for permission to speak to you, and your papa has given it.'

' I'm sure I don't know, mamma.'

It was a quarter of an hour after that when Lady Staveley again returned to the subject.   ' I am sure Mr. Graham is very clever, and all that.'

' Papa says that he is very clever indeed.'

' I'm quite sure he is, and he makes himself very nice in the house, always talking when there are people to dinner.   Mr. Arbuthnot never will talk when there are people to dinner.   But Mr. Arbuthnot has got a very nice place in Warwickshire, and they say he'll come in for the county some day.'

' Of course, mamma, if there should be anything of that sort, we should not be rich people, like Isabella and Mr. Arbuthnot.'

' Not at first, dear.'

' Neither first nor last.   But I don't care about that.   If you and papa will like him, and—and—if it should come to that!—Oh, mamma, he is so good, and so clever, and he understands things, and talks about things as though he knew how to make himself master of them.   And he is honest and proud.   Oh, mamma, if it should be so, I do hope you will love him.'

And then Lady Staveley promised that she would love him, thinking nevertheless that had things gone differently she would have extended a more motherly warmth of affection to Peregrine Orme.

And about this time Peregrine Orme made another visit to Noningsby. His intention was to see the judge, explaining what steps his grandfather had taken as to The Cleeve property, and then once more to have thrown himself at Madeline's feet. But circumstances as they turned out prevented this. Although he had been at some trouble to ascertain when the judge would be at Noningsby, nevertheless, on his arrival, the judge was out. He would be home, the servant said, to dinner, but not before; and therefore he had again seen Lady Staveley, and after seeing her had not thrown himself at Madeline's feet.

He had made up his mind to give a systematic and detailed account of his pecuniary circumstances, and had selected nearly the very words in which this should be made, not actuated by any idea that such a process would have any weight with Madeline, or by any means assist him with her, but hoping that he might thus procure the judge's permission to press his suit. But all his preparation and all his chosen words were of no use to him. When he saw Lady Staveley's face he at once knew that she had no comfort to offer to him. 'Well,' he said; 'is there any chance for me?' He had intended to speak in a very different tone, but words which have been prepared seldom manage to fit themselves into their appropriate places.

'Oh, Mr. Orme,' she said, taking him by the hand, and holding it. 'I wish it were different; I wish it could be different.'

'There is no hope then?' And as he spoke there was a sound in his voice as though the tidings would utterly unman him.

'I should be wicked to deceive you,' she said. 'There is no hope.' And then as she looked up at the sorrow so plainly written in the lines of his young, handsome face, tears came into her eyes and rolled down her cheeks. How could it be that a daughter of hers should be indifferent to the love of such a suitor as this?

But Peregrine, when he saw her sorrow, repressed his own. 'Very well,' said he; 'I will at any rate know how to take an answer. And for your kindness to me in the matter I am much obliged. I ought to have known myself better than to have supposed she could have cared for me.'

'I am sure she feels that you have done her great honour.'

'Psha! honour! But never mind—Good-bye, Lady Staveley.'

'Will you not see her?'

'No. Why should I see her? Give her my love—my best love——'

'I will—I will.'

' And tell her that I hope she may be happy, and make some fellow happy who is more fortunate than I am. I shall get out of the way somewhere, so that I shall not make a fool of myself when I see it. And then he took his departure, and rode back again to The Cleeve. This happened two days before the commencement of the trial, and the day before that on which Graham was to arrive at Noningsby.

When Graham received the judge's note asking him to put up at Noningsby for the assize week, he was much astonished. It was very short.

' DEAR GRAHAM,

' As you are coming down to Alston, special in Lady Mason's case, you may as well come and stay here. Lady Staveley bids me say that she will be delighted. Your elder brethren will no doubt go back to London each night, so that you will not be expected to remain with them.

' Yours always, &c.'

What could be the intention of the judge in taking so strange a step as this? The judge had undertaken to see him in three months, having given him some faint idea that there then might be a chance of hope. But now, before one month was over, he was actually sending for him to the house, and inviting him to stay there. What would all the bar world say when they found that a young barrister was living at the judge's house during the assizes? Would it not be in every man's mouth that he was a suitor accepted both by the judge's daughter and by the judge? There would be nothing in that to go against the grain with him, if only the fact were so. That the fact should be so he could not venture to hope even on this hint; but he accepted the judge's invitation, sent his grateful thanks to Lady Staveley;—as to Lady Staveley's delight, he was sure that the judge must have romanced a little, for he had clearly recognized Lady Staveley as his enemy;—and then he prepared himself for the chances of war.

On the evening before the trial he arrived at Noningsby just in time for dinner. He had been obliged to remain an hour or two at Alston in conference with Mr. Aram, and was later than he had expected he would be. He had been afraid to come early in the day, lest by doing so he might have seemed to overstep the margin of his invitation. When he did arrive, the two ladies were already dressing, and he found the judge in the hall.

' A pretty fellow you are,' said the judge. ' It's dinner-time already, and of course you take an hour to dress.'

' Mr. Aram—' began Felix.

' Oh, yes, Mr. Aram! I'll give you fifteen minutes, but not a moment more.' And so Felix was hurried on up to his bedroom —the old bedroom in which he had passed so many hours, and been so very uneasy. As he entered the room all that conversation with Augustus Staveley returned upon his memory. He had seen his friend in London, and told him that he was going down to Noningsby. Augustus had looked grave, but had said nothing about Madeline. Augustus was not in his father's confidence in this matter, and had nothing to do but to look grave. On that very morning, moreover, some cause had been given to himself for gravity of demeanour.

At the door of his room he met Mrs. Baker, and, hurried though he was by the judge's strict injunction, he could not but shake hands with his old and very worthy friend.

' Quite strong again,' said he, in answer to her tender inquiries.

' So you are, I do declare. I will say this, Mr. Graham, for wholesomeness of flesh you beat anything I ever come nigh. There's a many would have been weeks and weeks before they could have been moved.'

' It was your good nursing, Mrs. Baker.'

' Well, I think we did take care of you among us. Do you remember the pheasant, Mr. Graham?'

' Remember it! I should think so; and how I improved the occasion.'

' Yes; you did improve fast enough. And the sea-kale, Mr. Graham. Laws! the row I had with John Gardener about that! And, Mr. Graham, do you remember how a certain friend used to come and ask after you at the door? Dear, dear, dear! I nearly caught it about that.'

But Graham in his present frame of mind could not well endure to discuss his remembrances on that subject with Mrs. Baker, so he good-humouredly pushed her out of the room, saying that the judge would be mad if he delayed.

' That's true, too, Mr. Graham. And it won't do for you to take up Mr. Augustus's tricks in the house yet; will it?' And then she left the room. ' What does she mean by " yet " ?' Felix said to himself as he went through the ceremony of dressing with all the haste in his power.

He was in the drawing-room almost within the fifteen minutes, and there he found none but the judge and his wife and daughter. He had at first expected to find Augustus there, but had been told by Mrs. Baker that he was to come down on the following morning. His first greeting from Lady Staveley was something like that he had already received up stairs, only made in less exuberant language. He was congratulated on his speedy recovery and made welcome by a kind smile. Then he shook hands with Madeline, and as he did so he observed that the judge was at the trouble to

turn away, so that he should not watch the greeting. This he did
see, but into Madeline's face he hardly ventured to look. He
touched her hand, however, and said a word; and she also murmured something about his injury. ' And now we'll go to dinner,'
said the judge. ' Give your arm that is not broken to Lady
Staveley.' And so the meeting was over. ' Augustus will be in
Alston to-morrow when the court is opened,' said the judge. ' That
is to say if he finds it possible to get up so soon ; but to-day he had
some engagements in town.' The truth however was that the
judge had chosen to be alone with Felix after dinner.

The dinner was very pleasant, but the judge talked for the whole
party. Madeline hardly spoke at all, nor did Lady Staveley say
much. Felix managed to put in a few words occasionally, as it
always becomes a good listener to do, but the brunt of the battle lay
with the host. One thing Felix observed painfully,—that not a
word was spoken about Lady Mason or Orley Farm. When he had
been last there the judge had spoken of it openly before the whole
party, expressing his opinion that she was a woman much injured ;
but now neither did he say anything nor did Lady Staveley. He
would probably not have observed this had not a feeling crept upon
him during the last fortnight, that that thorough conviction which
men had felt as to her innocence was giving way. While the ladies
were there, however, he did not himself allude to the subject.

When they had left the room and the door had been closed behind
them, the judge began the campaign—began it, and as far as he was
concerned, ended it in a very few minutes. ' Graham,' said he, ' I
am glad to see you.'

' Thank you, judge,' said he.

' Of course you know, and I know, what that amounts to now.
My idea is that you acted as an honest man when you were last
here. You are not a rich man——'

' Anything but that.'

' And therefore I do not think it would have been well had you
endeavoured to gain my daughter's affections without speaking to
me,—or to her mother.' Judge Staveley always spoke of his wife as
though she were an absolute part of himself. ' She and I have discussed the matter now,—and you are at liberty to address yourself
to Madeline if you please.'

' My dear judge——'

' Of course you understand that I am not answering for her ?'

' Oh, of course not.'

' That's your look out. You must fight your own battle there.
What you are allowed to understand is this,—that her father and
mother will give their consent to an engagement, if she finds that
she can bring herself to give hers. If you are minded to ask her,
you may do so.'

' Of course I shall ask her.'

' She will have five thousand pounds on her marriage, settled
upon herself and her children, — and as much more when I die,
settled in the same way. Now fill your glass.' And in his own
easy way he turned the subject round and began to talk about the
late congress at Birmingham.

Felix felt that it was not open to him at the present moment to
say anything further about Madeline; and though he was disappointed at this,—for he would have wished to go on talking about
her all the evening—perhaps it was better for him. The judge
would have said nothing further to encourage him, and he would
have gradually been taught to think that his chance with Madeline
was little, and then less. ' He must have been a fool,' my readers
will say, ' not to have known that Madeline was now his own.'
Probably. But then modest-minded young men are fools.

At last he contrived to bring the conversation round from the
Birmingham congress to the affairs of his new client; and indeed he
contrived to do so in spite of the judge, who was not particularly
anxious to speak on the subject. '·After all that we said and did at
Birmingham, it is odd that I should so soon find myself joined with
Mr. Furnival.'

' Not at all odd. Of course you must take up your profession as
others have taken it up before you. Very many young men dream
of a Themis fit for Utopia. You have slept somewhat longer than
others, and your dreams have been more vivid.'

' And now I wake to find myself leagued with the Empson and
Dudley of our latter-day law courts.'

' Fie, Graham, fie. Do not allow yourself to speak in that tone of
men whom you know to be zealous advocates, and whom you do not
know to be dishonest opponents.'

' It is they and such as they that make so many in these days feel
the need of some Utopia,—as it was in the old days of our history.
But I beg their pardon for nicknaming them, and certainly ought
not to have done so in your presence.'

' Well; if you repent yourself, and will be more charitable for the
future, I will not tell of you.'

' I have never yet even seen Mr. Chaffanbrass in court,' said
Felix, after a pause.

' The more shame for you, never to have gone to the court in
which he practises. A barrister intending to succeed at the common law bar cannot have too wide an experience in such matters.'

' But then I fear that I am a barrister not intending to succeed.'

' I am very sorry to hear it,' said the judge. And then again the
conversation flagged for a minute or two.

' Have you ever seen him at a country assize town before, judge ?'
asked Felix.

' Whom ? Chaffanbrass ? I do not remember that I have.'

' His coming down in this way is quite unusual, I take it.'

' Rather so, I should say. The Old Bailey is his own ground.'

' And why should they think it necessary in such a case as this to have recourse to such a proceeding ?'

' It would be for me to ask you that, seeing that you are one of the counsel.'

' Do you mean to say, judge, that between you and me you are unwilling to give an opinion on such a subject ?'

' Well; you press me hard, and I think I may fairly say that I am unwilling. I would sooner discuss the matter with you after the verdict than before it. Come ; we will go into the drawing-room.'

There was not much in this. Indeed if it were properly looked at there was nothing in it. But nevertheless Graham, as he preceded the judge out of the dining-room, felt that his heart misgave him about Lady Mason. When first the matter had been spoken of at Noningsby, Judge Staveley had been fully convinced of Lady Mason's innocence, and had felt no reserve in expressing his opinion. He had expressed such an opinion very openly. Why should he now affect so much reticence, seeing that the question had been raised in the presence of them two alone? It was he who had persuaded Graham to undertake this work, and now he went back from what he had done, and refused even to speak upon the subject. ' It must be that he thinks she is guilty,' said Graham to himself, as he lay down that night in bed.

But there had been something more for him to do before bedtime came. He followed the judge into the drawing-room, and in five minutes perceived that his host had taken up a book with the honest intention of reading it. Some reference was made to him by his wife, but he showed at once that he did not regard Graham as company, and that he conceived himself to be entitled to enjoy the full luxury of home. ' Upon my word I don't know,' he answered, without taking his eye off the page. And then nobody spoke to him another word.

After another short interval Lady Staveley went to sleep. When Felix Graham had before been at Noningsby, she would have rebelled against nature with all her force rather than have slept while he was left to whisper what he would to her darling. But now he was authorized to whisper, and why should not Lady Staveley sleep if she wished it? She did sleep, and Felix was left alone with his love.

And yet he was not altogether alone. He could not say to her those words which he was now bound to say ; which he longed to say in order that he might know whether the next stage of his life was to be light or dark. There sat the judge, closely intent no doubt upon his book, but wide awake. There also sat Lady

Staveley, fast asleep certainly; but with a wondrous power of hearing even in her sleep. And yet how was he to talk to his love unless he talked of love? He wished that the judge would help them to converse; he wished that some one else was there; he wished at last that he himself was away. Madeline sat perfectly tranquil stitching a collar. Upon her there was incumbent no duty of doing anything beyond that. But he was in a measure bound to talk. Had he dared to do so he also would have taken up a book; but that he knew to be impossible.

'Your brother will be down to-morrow,' he said at last.

'Yes; he is to go direct to Alston. He will be here in the evening,—to dinner.'

'Ah, yes; I suppose we shall all be late to-morrow.'

'Papa always is late when the assizes are going one,' said Madeline.

'Alston is not very far,' said Felix.

'Only two miles,' she answered.

And during the whole of that long evening the conversation between them did not reach a more interesting pitch than that.

'She must think me an utter fool,' said Felix to himself, as he sat staring at the fire. 'How well her brother would have made the most of such an opportunity!' And then he went to bed, by no means in a good humour with himself.

On the next morning he again met her at breakfast, but on that occasion there was no possible opportunity for private conversation. The judge was all alive, and talked enough for the whole party during the twenty minutes that was allowed to them before they started for Alston. 'And now we must be off. We'll say half-past seven for dinner, my dear.' And then they also made their journey to Alston.

CHAPTER XXVI.

SHOWING HOW MISS FURNIVAL TREATED HER LOVERS.

IT is a great thing for young ladies to live in a household in which free correspondence by letter is permitted. 'Two for mamma, four for Amelia, three for Fanny, and one for papa.' When the postman has left his budget they should be dealt out in that way, and no more should be said about it,—except what each may choose to say. Papa's letter is about money of course, and interests nobody. Mamma's contain the character of a cook and an invitation to dinner, and as they interest everybody, are public property. But Fanny's letters and Amelia's should be private; and a well-bred

The Drawing-Room at Noningsby.

mamma of the present day scorns even to look at the handwriting
of the addresses. Now in Harley Street things were so managed
that nobody did see the handwriting of the addresses of Sophia's
letters till they came into her own hand,—that is, neither her
father nor her mother did so. That both Spooner and Mrs. Ball
examined them closely is probable enough.

This was well for her now, for she did not wish it to be known
as yet that she had accepted an offer from Lucius Mason, and she
did wish to have the privilege of receiving his letters. She fancied
that she loved him. She told herself over and over again that she
did so. She compared him within her own mind to Augustus
Staveley, and always gave the preference to Lucius. She liked
Augustus also, and could have accepted him as well, had it been
the way of the world in England for ladies to have two accepted
lovers. Such is not the way of the world in England, and she
therefore had been under the necessity of choosing one. She had
taken the better of the two, she declared to herself very often ; but
nevertheless was it absolutely necessary that the other should be
abandoned altogether? Would it not be well at any rate to wait
till this trial should be over? But then the young men themselves
were in such a hurry!

Lucius, like an honest man, had proposed to go at once to Mr.
Furnival when he was accepted ; but to this Sophia had objected.
' The peculiar position in which my father stands to your mother at
the present moment,' said she, ' would make it very difficult for him
to give you an answer now.' Lucius did not quite understand the
reasoning, but he yielded. It did not occur to him for a moment
that either Mr. or Miss Furnival could doubt the validity of his title
to the Orley Farm property.

But there was no reason why he should not write to her. ' Shall
I address here ?' he had asked. ' Oh yes,' said Sophia; ' my letters
are quite private.' And he had written very frequently, and she had
answered him. His last letter before the trial I propose to publish,
together with Sophia's answer, giving it as my opinion that the
gentleman's production affords by no means a good type of a lover's
letter. But then his circumstances were peculiar. Miss Furnival's
answer was, I think, much better.

' Orley Farm, —— —— ——.

' MY OWN SOPHIA,
          ' MY only comfort—I may really say my only comfort now
—is in writing to you. It is odd that at my age, and having begun
the world early as I did, I should now find myself so much alone.
Were it not for you, I should have no friend. I cannot describe to
you the sadness of this house, nor the wretched state in which my
mother exists. I sometimes think that had she been really guilty

of those monstrous crimes which people lay to her charge, she could hardly have been more miserable. I do not understand it; nor can I understand why your father has surrounded her with lawyers whom he would not himself trust in a case of any moment. To me she never speaks on the subject, which makes the matter worse— worse for both of us. I see her at breakfast and at dinner, and sometimes sit with her for an hour in the evening; but even then we have no conversation. The end of it is I trust soon coming, and then I hope that the sun will again be bright. In these days it seems as though there were a cloud over the whole earth.

' I wish with all my heart that you could have been here with her. I think that your tone and strength of mind would have enabled her to bear up against these troubles with more fortitude. After all, it is but the shadow of a misfortune which has come across her, if she would but allow herself so to think. As it is, Mrs. Orme is with her daily, and nothing I am sure can be more kind. But I can confess to you, though I could do so to no one else, that I do not willingly see an intimacy kept up between my mother and The Cleeve. Why was there that strange proposition as to her marriage ; and why, when it was once made, was it abandoned ? I know that my mother has been not only guiltless, but guileless, in these matters as to which she is accused; but nevertheless her affairs will have been so managed that it will be almost impossible for her to remain in this neighbourhood.

' When all this is over, I think I shall sell this place. What is there to bind me,—to bind me or you to Orley Farm ? Sometimes I have thought that I could be happy here, devoting myself to agriculture,'—' Fiddlesticks !' Sophia exclaimed, as she read this,—' and doing something to lessen the dense ignorance of those around me ; but for such work as that a man should be able to extend himself over a larger surface than that which I can influence. My dream of happiness now carries me away from this to other countries,—to the sunny south. Could you be happy there? A friend of mine whom I well knew in Germany, has a villa on the Lake of Como,'—' Indeed, sir, I'll do no such thing,' said Sophia to herself,—' and there I think we might forget all this annoyance.

' I shall not write again now till the trial is over. I have made up my mind that I will be in court during the whole proceedings. If my mother will admit it, I will remain there close to her, as her son should do in such an emergency. If she will not have this, still I will be there. No one shall say that I am afraid to see my mother in any position to which fortune can bring her, or that I have ever doubted her innocence.

' God bless you, my own one.

' Yours,
' L. M.'

Taking this letter as a whole perhaps we may say that there was
not as much nonsense in it as young gentlemen generally put into
their love-letters to young ladies; but I am inclined to think that
it would have been a better love-letter had there been more nonsense. At any rate there should have been less about himself, and
more about the lady. He should have omitted the agriculture altogether, and been more sure of his loved one's tastes before he suggested the sunny south and the Como villa. It is true that he was
circumstanced as few lovers are, with reference to his mother; but
still I think he might have been less lachrymose. Sophia's answer,
which was sent after the lapse of a day or two, was as follows :—

                                         'Harley Street, —— —— ——.
'MY DEAR LUCIUS,
        'I AM not surprised that you should feel somewhat low-
spirited at the present moment; but you will find, I have no doubt,
that the results of the next week will cure all that. Your mother
will be herself again when this trial is over, and you will then
wonder that it should ever have had so depressing an influence
either upon you or upon her. I cannot but suppose that papa has
done the best as to her advisers. I know how anxious he is about
it, and they say that he is very clever in such matters. Pray give
your mother my love. I cannot but think she is lucky to have
Mrs. Orme with her. What can be more respectable than a connection at such a time with such people ?
        'As to your future residence, do not make up your mind to any-
thing while your spirits are thus depressed. If you like to leave
Orley Farm, why not let it instead of selling it? As for me, if it
should be fated that our lots are to go together, I am inclined to
think that I should still prefer to live in England. In London
papa's position might probably be of some service, and I should like
no life that was not active. But it is too early in the day to talk
thus at present. You must not think me cold hearted if I say that
what has as yet been between us must not be regarded as an
absolute and positive engagement. I, on my part, hope that it may
become so. My heart is not cold, and I am not ashamed to own
that I esteem you favourably; but marriage is a very serious thing,
and there is so much to be considered ! I regard myself as a free
agent, and in a great measure independent of my parents on such a
matter as that; but still I think it well to make no positive promise
without consulting them. When this trial is over I will speak to
my father, and then you will come up to London and see us.
        'Mind you give my love to your mother; and—if it have any
value in your eyes—accept it yourself.
                              'Your affectionate friend,
                                        'SOPHIA FURNIVAL.'

I feel very confident that Mrs. Furnival was right in declining
to inquire very closely into the circumstances of her daughter's
correspondence. A young lady who could write such a letter to
her lover as that requires but little looking after; and in those
points as to which she may require it, will—if she be so minded—
elude it. Such as Miss Furnival was, no care on her mother's part
would, I think, have made her better. Much care might have
made her worse, as, had she been driven to such resources, she
would have received her letters under a false name at the baker's
shop round the corner.

But the last letter was not written throughout without interruption. She was just declaring how on her part she hoped that her
present uncertain tenure of her lover's hand might at some future
time become certain, when Augustus Staveley was announced.
Sophia, who was alone in the drawing-room, rose from her table,
gracefully, slipped her note under the cover of the desk, and courteously greeted her visitor. 'And how are they all at dear Noningsby?' she asked.

'Dear Noningsby is nearly deserted. There is no one there but
my mother and Madeline.'

'And who more would be wanting to make it still dear,—
unless it be the judge? I declare, Mr. Staveley, I was quite in
love with your father when I left. Talk of honey falling from
people's mouths!—he drops nothing less than champagne and pine-
apples.'

'How very difficult of digestion his conversation must be!'

'By no means. If the wine be good and the fruit ripe, nothing
can be more wholesome. And is everybody else gone? Let me
see;—Mr. Graham was still there when I left.'

'He came away shortly afterwards,—as soon, that is, as his arm
would allow him.'

'What a happy accident that was for him, Mr. Staveley!'

'Happy!—breaking three of his ribs, his arm, and his collar-
bone! I thought it very unhappy.'

'Ah, that's because your character is so deficient in true chivalry.
I call it a very happy accident which gives a gentleman an opportunity of spending six weeks under the same roof with the lady of
his love. Mr. Graham is a man of spirit, and I am by no means
sure that he did not break his bones on purpose.'

Augustus for a moment thought of denying the imputation with
regard to his sister, but before he had spoken he had changed his
mind. He was already aware that his friend had been again invited
down to Noningsby, and if his father chose to encourage Graham,
why should he make difficulties? He had conceived some general
idea that Felix Graham was not a guest to be welcomed into a rich
man's family as a son-in-law. He was poor and crotchety, and

"And how are they all at Noningsby?"

as regards professional matters unsteady. But all that was a matter for his father to consider, not for him. So he held his peace as touching Graham, and contrived to change the subject, veering round towards that point of the compass which had brought him into Harley Street.

'Perhaps then, Miss Furnival, it might answer some purpose if I were to get myself run over outside there. I could get one of Pickford's vans, or a dray from Barclay and Perkins', if that might be thought serviceable.'

'It would be of no use in the world, Mr. Staveley. Those very charitable middle-aged ladies opposite, the Miss Mac Codies, would have you into their house in no time, and when you woke from your first swoon, you would find yourself in their best bedroom, with one on each side of you.'

'And you in the mean time—'

'I should send over every morning at ten o'clock to inquire after you—in mamma's name. "Mrs. Furnival's compliments, and hopes Mr. Staveley will recover the use of his legs." And the man would bring back word: "The doctor hopes he may, miss; but his left eye is gone for ever." It is not everybody that can tumble discreetly. Now you, I fancy, would only disfigure yourself.'

'Then I must try what fortune can do for me without the brewer's dray.'

'Fortune has done quite enough for you, Mr. Staveley; I do not advise you to tempt her any further.'

'Miss Furnival, I have come to Harley Street to-day on purpose to tempt her to the utmost. There is my hand——'

'Mr. Staveley, pray keep your hand for a while longer in your own possession.'

'Undoubtedly I shall do so, unless I dispose of it this morning. When we were at Noningsby together, I ventured to tell you what I felt for you——'

'Did you, Mr. Staveley? If your feelings were anything beyond the common, I don't remember the telling.'

'And then,' he continued, without choosing to notice her words, 'you affected to believe that I was not in earnest in what I said to you.'

'And you must excuse me if I affect to believe the same thing of you still.'

Augustus Staveley had come into Harley Street with a positive resolve to throw his heart and hand and fortune at the feet of Miss Furnival. I fear that I shall not raise him in the estimation of my readers by saying so. But then my readers will judge him unfairly. They will forget that they have had a much better opportunity of looking into the character of Miss Furnival than he had had; and they will also forget that they have had no such oppor-

tunity of being influenced by her personal charms. I think I
remarked before that Miss Furnival well understood how best to
fight her own battle. Had she shown herself from the first anxious
to regard as a definite offer the first words tending that way which
Augustus had spoken to her, he would at once have become indifferent about the matter. As a consequence of her judicious conduct
he was not indifferent. We always want that which we can't get
easily. Sophia had made herself difficult to be gotten, and therefore
Augustus fancied that he wanted her. Since he had been in town
he had been frequently in Harley Street, and had been arguing with
himself on the matter. What match could be more discreet or
better? Not only was she very handsome, but she was clever also.
And not only was she handsome and clever, but moreover she was
an heiress. What more could his friends want for him, and what
more could he want for himself? His mother did in truth regard
her as a nasty, sly girl; but then his mother did not know Sophia,
and in such matters mothers are so ignorant!

Miss Furnival, on his thus repeating his offer, again chose to
affect a belief that he was not in earnest. I am inclined to think
that she rather liked this kind of thing. There is an excitement
in the game; and it is one which may be played without great
danger to either party if it be played cautiously and with some
skill. As regards Augustus at the present moment, I have to say
—with some regret—that he abandoned all idea of caution, and that
he showed very little skill.

'Then,' said he, 'I must beg you to lay aside an affectation which
is so very injurious both to my honour and to my hopes of happiness.'

'Your honour, Mr. Staveley, is quite safe, I am certain.'

'I wish that my happiness were equally so,' said he. 'But at
any rate you will let me have an answer. Sophia——'

And now he stood up, looking at her with something really like
love in his eyes, and Miss Furnival began to understand that if she
so chose it the prize was really within her reach. But then was it
a prize? Was not the other thing the better prize? The other
thing was the better prize;—if only that affair about the Orley
Farm were settled. Augustus Staveley was a good-looking handsome fellow, but then there was that in the manner and gait of
Lucius Mason which better suited her taste. There are ladies who
prefer Worcester ware to real china; and, moreover, the order for
the Worcester ware had already been given.

'Sophia, let a man be ever so light-hearted, there will come to
him moments of absolute and almost terrible earnestness.'

'Even to you, Mr. Staveley.'

'I have at any rate done nothing to deserve your scorn.'

'Fie, now; you to talk of my scorn! You come here with soft

words which run easily from your tongue, feeling sure that I shall
be proud in heart when I hear them whispered into my ears; and
now you pretend to be angry because I do not show you that I am
elated.   Do you think it probable that I should treat with scorn
anything of this sort that you might say to me seriously?'

'I think you are doing so.'

'Have you generally found yourself treated with scorn when you
have been out on this pursuit?'

'By heavens! you have no right to speak to me so.   In what
way shall I put my words to make them sound seriously to you?
Do you want me to kneel at your feet, as our grandfathers used to do?'

'Oh, certainly not.   Our grandmothers were very stupid in
desiring that.'

'If I put my hand on my heart will you believe me better?'

'Not in the least.'

'Then through what formula shall I go?'

'Go through no formula, Mr. Staveley.   In such affairs as these
very little, as I take it, depends on the words that are uttered.
When heart has spoken to heart, or even head to head, very little
other speaking is absolutely necessary.'

'And my heart has not spoken to yours?'

'Well;—no;—not with that downright plain open language
which a heart in earnest always knows how to use.   I suppose you
think you like me?'

'Sophia, I love you well enough to make you my wife to-
morrow.'

'Yes; and to be tired of your bargain on the next day.   Has it
ever occurred to you that giving and taking in marriage is a very
serious thing?'

'A very serious thing; but I do not think that on that account it
should be avoided.'

'No; but it seems to me that you are always inclined to play at
marriage.   Do not be angry with me, but for the life of me I can
never think you are in earnest.'

'But I shall be angry—very angry—if I do not get from you some
answer to what I have ventured to say.'

'What, now; to-day;—this morning?   If you insist upon that,
the answer can only be of one sort.   If I am driven to decide this
morning on the question that you have asked me, great as the
honour is—and coming from you, Mr. Staveley, it is very great—I
must decline it.   I am not able, at any rate at the present moment,
to trust my happiness altogether in your hands.'   When we think
of the half-written letter which at this moment Miss Furnival had
within her desk, this was not wonderful.

And then, without having said anything more that was of note,
Augustus Staveley went his way.   As he walked up Harley Street,

he hardly knew whether or no he was to consider himself as bound to Miss Furnival; nor did he feel quite sure whether or no he wished to be so bound. She was handsome, and clever, and an heiress; but yet he was not certain that she possessed all those womanly charms which are desirable in a wife. He could not but reflect that she had never yet said a soft word to him.

CHAPTER XXVII.

MR. MOULDER BACKS HIS OPINION.

As the day of the trial drew nigh, the perturbation of poor John Kenneby's mind became very great. Moulder had not intended to frighten him, but had thought it well to put him up to what he believed to be the truth. No doubt he would be badgered and bullied. 'And,' as Moulder said to his wife afterwards, 'wasn't it better that he should know what was in store for him?' The consequence was, that had it been by any means possible, Kenneby would have run away on the day before the trial.

But it was by no means possible, for Dockwrath had hardly left him alone for an instant. Dockwrath at this time had crept into a sort of employment in the case from which Matthew Round had striven in vain to exclude him. Mr. Round had declared once or twice that if Mr. Mason encouraged Dockwrath to interfere, he, Round, would throw the matter up. But professional men cannot very well throw up their business, and Round went on, although Dockwrath did interfere, and although Mr. Mason did encourage him. On the eve of the trial he went down to Alston with Kenneby and Bolster; and Mr. Moulder, at the express instance of Kenneby, accompanied them.

'What can I do? I can't stop the fellow's gab,' Moulder had said. But Kenneby pleaded hard that some friend might be near him in the day of his trouble, and Moulder at last consented.

'I wish it was me,' Mrs. Smiley had said, when they talked the matter over in Great St. Helens; 'I'd let the barrister know what was what when he came to knock me about.' Kenneby wished it also, with all his heart.

Mr. Mason went down by the same train, but he travelled by the first class. Dockwrath, who was now holding his head up, would have gone with him, had he not thought it better to remain with Kenneby. 'He might jump out of the carriage and destroy himself,' he said to Mr. Mason.

'If he had any of the feelings of an Englishman within his breast,' said Mason, 'he would be anxious to give assistance towards the punishment of such a criminal as that.'

' He has only the feelings of a tomtit,' said Dockwrath.

Lodgings had been taken for the two chief witnesses together, and Moulder and Dockwrath shared the accommodation with them. As they sat down to tea together, these two gentlemen doubtless felt that Bridget Bolster was not exactly fitting company for them. But the necessities of an assize week, and of such a trial as this, level much of these distinctions, and they were both prepared to condescend and become affable.

' Well, Mrs. Bolster, and how do you find yourself?' asked Dockwrath.

Bridget was a solid, square-looking woman, somewhat given to flesh, and now not very quick in her movements. But the nature of her past life had given to her a certain amount of readiness, and an absence of that dread of her fellow-creatures which so terribly afflicted poor Kenneby. And then also she was naturally not a stupid woman, or one inclined to be muddle-headed. Perhaps it would be too much to say that she was generally intelligent, but what she did understand, she understood thoroughly.

' Pretty well, I thank you, Mr. Dockwrath. I sha'n't be sorry to have a bit of something to my tea.'

Bridget Bolster perfectly understood that she was to be well fed when thus brought out for work in her country's service. To have everything that she wanted to eat and drink at places of public entertainment, and then to have the bills paid for her behind her back, was to Bridget Bolster the summit of transitory human bliss.

' And you shall have something to your tea,' said Dockwrath. ' What's it to be?'

' A steak's as good as anything at these places,' suggested Moulder.

' Or some ham and eggs,' suggested Dockwrath.

' Kidneys is nice,' said Bridget.

' What do you say, Kenneby?' asked Dockwrath.

' It is nothing to me,' said Kenneby; ' I have no appetite. I think I'll take a little brandy-and-water.'

Mr. Moulder possessed the most commanding spirit, and the steak was ordered. They then made themselves as comfortable as circumstances would admit, and gradually fell into a general conversation about the trial. It had been understood among them since they first came together, that as a matter of etiquette the witnesses were not to be asked what they had to say. Kenneby was not to divulge his facts in plain language, nor Bridget Bolster those which belonged to her; but it was open to them all to take a general view of the matter, and natural that at the present moment they should hardly be able to speak of anything else. And there was a very divided opinion on the subject in dispute; Dockwrath, of course, expressing a strong conviction in favour of a verdict of guilty, and

Moulder being as certain of an acquittal. At first Moulder had been very unwilling to associate with Dockwrath; for he was a man who maintained his animosities long within his breast; but Dockwrath on this occasion was a great man, and there was some slight reflection of greatness on the associates of Dockwrath; it was only by the assistance of Dockwrath that a place could be obtained within the court, and, upon the whole, it became evident to Moulder that during such a crisis as this the society of Dockwrath must be endured.

'They can't do anything to one if one do one's best?' said Kenneby, who was sitting apart from the table while the others were eating.

'Of course they can't,' said Dockwrath, who wished to inspirit the witnesses on his own side.

'It aint what they do, but what they say,' said Moulder; 'and then everybody is looking at you. I remember a case when I was young on the road; it was at Nottingham. There had been some sugars delivered, and the rats had got at it. I'm blessed if they didn't ask me backwards and forwards so often that I forgot whether they was seconds or thirds, though I'd sold the goods myself. And then the lawyer said he'd have me prosecuted for perjury. Well, I was that frightened, I could not stand in the box. I aint so green now by a good deal.'

'I'm sure you're not, Mr. Moulder,' said Bridget, who well understood the class to which Moulder belonged.

'After that I met that lawyer in the street, and was ashamed to look him in the face. I'm blessed if he didn't come up and shake hands with me, and tell me that he knew all along that his client hadn't a leg to stand on. Now I call that beautiful.'

'Beautiful!' said Kenneby.

'Yes, I do. He fought that battle just as if he was sure of winning, though he knew he was going to lose. Give me the man that can fight a losing battle. Anybody can play whist with four by honours in his own hand.'

'I don't object to four by honours either,' said Dockwrath; 'and that's the game we are going to play to-morrow.'

'And lose the rubber after all,' said Moulder.

'No, I'm blessed if we do, Mr. Moulder. If I know anything of my own profession——'

'Humph!' ejaculated Moulder.

'And I shouldn't be here in such a case as this if I didn't;—but if I do, Lady Mason has no more chance of escape than—than—than that bit of muffin has.' And as he spoke the savoury morsel in question disappeared from the fingers of the commercial traveller.

For a moment or two Moulder could not answer him. The portion of food in question was the last on his plate; it had been cor-

siderable in size, and required attention in mastication.   Then the
remaining gravy had to be picked up on the blade of the knife, and
the particles of pickles collected and disposed of by the same process.   But when all this had been well done, Moulder replied—

'That may be your opinion, Mr. Dockwrath, and I dare say you
may know what you're about.'

'Well; I rather think I do, Mr. Moulder.'

'Mine's different.   Now when one gentleman thinks one thing
and another thinks another, there's nothing for it in my mind but for
each gentleman to back his own.   That's about the ticket in this
country, I believe.'

'That's just as a gentleman may feel disposed,' said Dockwrath.

'No it aint.   What's the use of a man having an opinion if he
won't back it?   He's bound to back it, or else he should give way,
and confess he aint so sure about it as he said he was.   There's no
coming to an end if you don't do that.   Now there's a ten-pound
note,' and Moulder produced that amount of the root of all evil;
'I'll put that in John Kenneby's hands, and do you cover it.'   And
then he looked as though there were no possible escape from the
proposition which he had made.

'I decline to have anything to do with it,' said Kenneby.

'Gammon,' said Moulder; 'two ten-pound notes won't burn a
hole in your pocket.'

'Suppose I should be asked a question about it to-morrow; where
should I be then?'

'Don't trouble yourself, Mr. Kenneby,' said Dockwrath; 'I'm not
going to bet.'

'You aint, aint you?' said Moulder.

'Certainly not, Mr. Moulder.   If you understood professional
matters a little better, you'd know that a professional gentleman
couldn't make a bet as to a case partly in his own hands without
very great impropriety.'   And Dockwrath gathered himself up,
endeavouring to impress a sense of his importance on the two witnesses, even should he fail of doing so upon Mr. Moulder.

Moulder repocketed his ten-pound note, and laughed with a long,
low chuckle.   According to his idea of things, he had altogether got
the better of the attorney upon that subject.   As he himself put it so
plainly, what criterion is there by which a man can test the validity
of his own opinion if he be not willing to support it by a bet?   A
man is bound to do so, or else to give way and apologize.   For
many years he had insisted upon this in commercial rooms as a fun-
damental law in the character and conduct of gentlemen, and never
yet had anything been said to him to show that in such a theory he
was mistaken.

During all this Bridget Bolster sat there much delighted.   It was
not necessary to her pleasure that she should say much herself.

There she was seated in the society of gentlemen and of men of the world, with a cup of tea beside her, and the expectation of a little drop of something warm afterwards. What more could the world offer to her, or what more had the world to offer to anybody? As far as her feelings went she did not care if Lady Mason were tried every month in the year! Not that her feelings towards Lady Mason were cruel. It was nothing to her whether Lady Mason should be convicted or acquitted. But it was much to her to sit quietly on her chair and have nothing to do, to eat and drink of the best, and be made much of; and it was very much to her to hear the conversation of her betters.

On the following morning Dockwrath breakfasted by appointment with Mr. Mason,—promising, however, that he would return to his friends whom he left behind him, and introduce them into the court in proper time. As I have before hinted, Mr. Mason's confidence in Dockwrath had gone on increasing day by day since they had first met each other at Groby Park, till he now wished that he had altogether taken the advice of the Hamworth attorney and put this matter entirely into his hands. By degrees Joseph Mason had learned to understand and thoroughly to appreciate the strong points in his own case; and now he was so fully convinced of the truth of those surmises which Dockwrath had been the first to make, that no amount of contrary evidence could have shaken him. And why had not Round and Crook found this out when the matter was before investigated? Why had they prevented him from appealing to the Lord Chancellor when, through their own carelessness, the matter had gone against him in the inferior court? And why did they now, even in these latter days, when they were driven to reopen the case by the clearness of the evidence submitted to them,—why did they even now wound his ears, irritate his temper, and oppose the warmest feelings of his heart by expressing pity for this wicked criminal, whom it was their bounden duty to prosecute to the very utmost? Was it not by their fault that Orley Farm had been lost to him for the last twenty years? And yet young Round had told him, with the utmost composure, that it would be useless for him to look for any of those moneys which should have accrued to him during all those years! After what had passed, young Round should have been anxious to grind Lucius Mason into powder, and make money of his very bones! Must he not think, when he considered all these things, that Round and Crook had been wilfully dishonest to him, and that their interest had been on the side of Lady Mason? He did so think at last, under the beneficent tutelage of his new adviser, and had it been possible would have taken the case out of the hands of Round and Crook even during the week before the trial.

'We mustn't do it now,' Dockwrath had said, in his triumph. 'If we did, the whole thing would be delayed. But they shall be so watched that they shall not be able to throw the thing over. I've got them in a vice, Mr. Mason; and I'll hold them so tight that they must convict her whether they will or no.'

And the nature and extent of Mr. Dockwrath's reward had been already settled. When Lucius Mason should be expelled from Orley Farm with ignominy, he, Dockwrath, should become the tenant. The very rent was settled with the understanding that it should be remitted for the first year. It would be pleasant to him to have back his two fields in this way;—his two fields, and something else beyond! It may be remembered that Lucius Mason had once gone to his office insulting him. It would now be his turn to visit Lucius Mason at his domicile. He was disposed to think that such visit would be made by him with more effect than had attended that other.

' Well, sir, we're all right,' he said, as he shook hands with Mr. Mason of Groby; ' there's no screw loose that I can find.'

' And will that man be able to speak ?' Mr. Mason was alluding to John Kenneby.

' I think he will, as corroborating the woman Bolster. That's all we shall want. We shall put up the woman first; that is, after I have done. I don't think they'll make much of her, Mr. Mason.'

' They can't make her say that she signed two deeds if she is willing to tell the truth. There's no danger, you think, that she's been tampered with,—that she has taken money.'

' No, no; there's been nothing of that.'

' They'd do anything, you know,' said Mr. Mason. ' Think of such a man as Solomon Aram! He's been used to it all his life, you know.'

' They could not do it, Mr. Mason; I've been too sharp on them. And I tell you what,—they know it now. There isn't one of them that doesn't know we shall get a verdict.' And then for a few minutes there was silence between the two friends.

' I'll tell you what, Dockwrath,' said Mr. Mason, after a while; ' I've so set my heart upon this—upon getting justice at last—that I do think it would kill me if I were to be beaten. I do, indeed. I've known this, you know, all my life; and think what I've felt! For twenty-two years, Dockwrath! By ——! in all that I have read I don't think I ever heard of such a hardship! That she should have robbed me for two-and-twenty years!—And now they say that she will be imprisoned for twelve months!'

' She'll get more than that, Mr. Mason.'

' I know what would have been done to her thirty years ago, when the country was in earnest about such matters. What did they do to Fauntleroy ?'

' Things are changed since then, aint they ?' said Dockwrath, with a laugh. And then he went to look up his flock, and take them into court. 'I'll meet you in the hall, Mr. Mason, in twenty minutes from this time.'

And so the play was beginning on each side.

CHAPTER XXVIII.

THE FIRST DAY OF THE TRIAL.

AND now the judge was there on the bench, the barristers and the attorneys were collected, the prisoner was seated in their presence, and the trial was begun. As is usual in cases of much public moment, when a person of mark is put upon his purgation, or the offence is one which has attracted notice, a considerable amount of time was spent in preliminaries. But we, who are not bound by the necessities under which the court laboured, will pass over these somewhat rapidly. The prisoner was arraigned on the charge of perjury, and pleaded 'not guilty' in a voice which, though low, was audible to all the court. At that moment the hum of voices had stayed itself, and the two small words, spoken in a clear, silver tone, reached the ears of all that then were there assembled. Some had surmised it to be possible that she would at the last moment plead guilty, but such persons had not known Lady Mason. And then by slow degrees a jury was sworn, a considerable number of jurors having been set aside at the instance of Lady Mason's counsel. Mr. Aram had learned to what part of the county each man belonged, and upon his instructions those who came from the neighbourhood of Hamworth were passed over.

The comparative lightness of the offence divested the commencement of the trial of much of that importance and apparent dignity which attach themselves to most celebrated criminal cases. The prisoner was not bidden to look upon the juror, nor the juror to look upon the prisoner, as though a battle for life and death were to be fought between them. A true bill for perjury had come down to the court from the grand jury, but the court officials could not bring themselves on such an occasion to open the case with all that solemnity and deference to the prisoner which they would have exhibited had she been charged with murdering her old husband. Nor was it even the same as though she had been accused of forgery. Though forgery be not now a capital crime, it was so within our memories, and there is still a certain grandeur in the name. But perjury sounds small and petty, and it was not therefore till the trial had advanced a stage or two that it assumed that importance which it afterwards never lost. That this should

be so cut Mr. Mason of Groby to the very soul. Even Mr. Dockwrath had been unable to make him understand that his chance of
regaining the property was under the present circumstances much
greater than it would have been had Lady Mason been arraigned
for forgery. He would not believe that the act of forgery might
possibly not have been proved. Could she have been first whipped
through the street for the misdemeanour, and then hung for the
felony, his spirit would not have been more than sufficiently
appeased.

The case was opened by one Mr. Steelyard, the junior counsel for
the prosecution; but his work on this occasion was hardly more
than formal. He merely stated the nature of the accusation
against Lady Mason, and the issue which the jury were called
upon to try. Then got up Sir Richard Leatherham, the solicitor-
general, and at great length and with wonderful perspicuity
explained all the circumstances of the case, beginning with the
undoubted will left by Sir Joseph Mason, the will independently
of the codicil, and coming down gradually to the discovery of that
document in Mr. Dockwrath's office, which led to the surmise that
the signature of those two witnesses had been obtained, not to a
codicil to a will, but to a deed of another character. In doing this
Sir Richard did not seem to lean very heavily upon Lady Mason,
nor did he say much as to the wrongs suffered by Mr. Mason of
Groby. When he alluded to Mr. Dockwrath and his part in these
transactions, he paid no compliment to the Hamworth attorney;
but in referring to his learned friend on the other side he protested
his conviction that the defence of Lady Mason would be conducted
not only with zeal, but in that spirit of justice and truth for which
the gentlemen opposite to him were so conspicuous in their profession. All this was wormwood to Joseph Mason; but nevertheless, though Sir Richard was so moderate as to his own side, and so
courteous to that opposed to him, he made it very clear before he
sat down that if those witnesses were prepared to swear that which
he was instructed they would swear, either they must be utterly
unworthy of credit—a fact which his learned friends opposite were
as able to elicit as any gentlemen who had ever graced the English
bar—or else the prisoner now on her trial must have been guilty of
the crime of perjury now imputed to her.

Of all those in court now attending to the proceedings, none
listened with greater care to the statement made by Sir Richard
than Joseph Mason, Lady Mason herself, and Felix Graham. To
Joseph Mason it appeared that his counsel was betraying him . Sir
Richard and Round were in a boat together and were determined to
throw him over yet once again. Had it been possible he would
have stopped the proceedings, and in this spirit he spoke to Dockwrath. To Joseph Mason it would have seemed right that Sir

Richard sho uld begin by holding up Lady Mason to the scorn and
indignation of the twelve honest jurymen before him.   Mr. Dockwrath, whose intelligence was keener in such matters, endeavoured
to make his patron understand that he was wrong; but in this he
did not succeed.   'If he lets her escape me,' said Mason, 'I think
it will be the death of me.'

To Lady Mason it appeared as though the man who was now
showing to all the crowd there assembled the chief scenes of her
past life, had been present and seen everything that she had ever done.
He told the jury of all who had been present in the room when
that true deed had been signed; he described how old Usbech had
sat there incapable of action; how that affair of the partnership had
been brought to a close; how those two witnesses had thereupon
appended their name to a deed; how those witnesses had been
deceived, or partially deceived, as to their own signatures when
called upon to give their testimony at a former trial; and he told
them also that a comparison of the signatures on the codicil with
those signatures which were undoubtedly true would lead an expert
and professional judge of writing to tell them that the one set of
signatures or the other must be forgeries.   Then he went on to
describe how the pretended codicil must in truth have been
executed—speaking of the solitary room in which the bad work had
been done, of the midnight care and terrible solicitude for secrecy.
And then, with apparent mercy, he attempted to mitigate the
iniquity of the deed by telling the jury that it had not been done
by that lady with any view to self-aggrandisement, but had been
brought about by a lamentable, infatuated, mad idea that she might
in this way do that justice to her child which that child's father
had refused to do at her instance.   He also, when he told of this,
spoke of Rebekah and her son; and Mrs. Orme when she heard him
did not dare to raise her eyes from the table.   Lucius Mason, when
he had listened to this, lifted his clenched hand on high, and
brought it down with loud violence on the raised desk in front of
him.   'I know the merits of that young man,' said Sir Richard,
looking at him; 'I am told that he is a gentleman, good, indus-
trious, and high spirited.   I wish he were not here; I wish with
all my heart he were not here.'   And then a tear, an absolute and
true drop of briny moisture, stood in the eye of that old experienced
lawyer.   Lucius, when he heard this, for a moment covered his
face.   It was but for a moment, and then he looked up again,
turning his eyes slowly round the entire court, and as he did so
grasping his mother by the arm.   'He'll look in a different sort of
fashion by to-morrow evening, I guess,' said Dockwrath into his
neighbour's ear.   During all this time no change came over Lady
Mason's face.   When she felt her son's hand upon her arm her
muscles had moved involuntarily; but she recovered herself at the

moment, and then went on enduring it all with absolute composure. Nevertheless it seemed to her as though that man who stood before her, telling his tale so calmly, had read the secrets of her very soul. What chance could there be for her when everything was thus known?

To every word that was spoken Felix Graham gave all his mind. While Mr. Chaffanbrass sat fidgeting, or reading, or dreaming, caring nothing for all that his learned brother might say, Graham listened to every fact that was stated, and to every surmise that was propounded. To him the absolute truth in this affair was matter of great moment, but yet he felt that he dreaded to know the truth. Would it not be better for him that he should not know it? But yet he listened, and his active mind, intent on the various points as they were evolved, would not restrain itself from forming opinions. With all his ears he listened, and as he did so Mr. Chaffanbrass, amidst his dreaming, reading, and fidgeting, kept an attentive eye upon him. To him it was a matter of course that Lady Mason should be guilty. Had she not been guilty, he, Mr. Chaffanbrass, would not have been required. Mr. Chaffanbrass well understood that the defence of injured innocence was no part of his mission.

Then at last Sir Richard Leatheram brought to a close his long tale, and the examination of the witnesses was commenced. By this time it was past two o'clock, and the judge went out of court for a few minutes to refresh himself with a glass of wine and a sandwich. And now young Peregrine Orme, in spite of all obstacles, made his way up to his mother and led her also out of court. He took his mother's arm, and Lady Mason followed with her son, and so they made their way into the small outer room which they had first entered. Not a word was said between them on the subject which was filling the minds of all of them. Lucius stood silent and absorbed while Peregrine offered refreshment to both the ladies. Lady Mason, doing as she was bid, essayed to eat and to drink. What was it to her whether she ate and drank or was a-hungered? To maintain by her demeanour the idea in men's minds that she might still possibly be innocent—that was her work. And therefore, in order that those two young men might still think so, she ate and drank as she was bidden.

On their return to court Mr. Steelyard got up to examine Dockwrath, who was put into the box as the first witness. The attorney produced certain documents supposed to be of relevancy, which he had found among his father-in-law's papers, and then described how he had found that special document which gave him to understand that Bolster and Kenneby had been used as witnesses to a certain signature on that 14th of July. He had known all the circumstances of the old trial, and hence his suspicions had been aroused. Acting

upon this he had gone immediately down to Mr. Mason in Yorkshire,
and the present trial was the result of his care and intelligence.
This was in effect the purport of his direct evidence, and then he
was handed over to the tender mercies of the other side.

On the other side Mr. Chaffanbrass rose to begin the battle.
Mr. Furnival had already been engaged in sundry of those preliminary skirmishes which had been found necessary before the
fight had been commenced in earnest, and therefore the turn had
now come for Mr. Chaffanbrass. All this, however, had been
arranged beforehand, and it had been agreed that if possible Dockwrath should be made to fall into the clutches of the Old Bailey
barrister. It was pretty to see the meek way in which Mr.
Chaffanbrass rose to his work; how gently he smiled, how he
fidgeted about a few of the papers as though he were not at first
quite master of his situation, and how he arranged his old wig in a
modest, becoming manner, bringing it well forward over his forehead. His voice also was low and soft;—so low that it was hardly
heard through the whole court, and persons who had come far to
listen to him began to feel themselves disappointed. And it was
pretty also to see how Dockwrath armed himself for the encounter,—
how he sharpened his teeth, as it were, and felt the points of his
own claws. The little devices of Mr. Chaffanbrass did not deceive
him. He knew what he had to expect; but his pluck was good,
as is the pluck of a terrier when a mastiff prepares to attack him.
Let Mr. Chaffanbrass do his worst; that would all be over in an
hour or so. But when Mr. Chaffanbrass had done his worst, Orley
Farm would still remain.

'I believe you were a tenant of Lady Mason's at one time,
Mr. Dockwrath?' asked the barrister.

'I was; and she turned me out. If you will allow me I will
tell you how all that happened, and how I was angered by the
usage I received.' Mr. Dockwrath was determined to make a clean
breast of it, and rather go before his tormentor in telling all that
there was to be told, than lag behind as an unwilling witness.

'Do,' said Mr. Chaffanbrass. 'That will be very kind of you.
When I have learned all that, and one other little circumstance of
the same nature, I do not think I shall want to trouble you any
more.' And then Mr. Dockwrath did tell it all;—how he had lost
the two fields, how he had thus become very angry, how this anger
had induced him at once to do that which he had long thought of
doing,—search, namely, among the papers of old Mr. Usbech, with
the view of ascertaining what might be the real truth as regarded
that doubtful codicil.

'And you found what you searched for, Mr. Dockwrath?'

'I did,' said Dockwrath.

'Without very much delay, apparently?'

' I was two or three days over the work.'

' But you found exactly what you wanted?'

' I found what I expected to find.'

' And that, although all those papers had been subjected to the scrutiny of Messrs. Round and Crook at the time of that other trial twenty years ago?'

' I was sharper than them, Mr. Chaffanbrass,—a deal sharper.'

' So I perceive,' said Chaffanbrass, and now he had pushed back his wig a little, and his eyes had begun to glare with an ugly red light. ' Yes,' he said, ' it will be long, I think, before my old friends Round and Crook are as sharp as you are, Mr. Dockwrath.'

' Upon my word I agree with you, Mr. Chaffanbrass.'

' Yes; Round and Crook are babies to you, Mr. Dockwrath;' and now Mr. Chaffanbrass began to pick at his chin with his finger, as he was accustomed to do when he warmed to his subject. ' Babies to you! You have had a good deal to do with them, I should say, in getting up this case.'

' I have had something to do with them.'

' And very much they must have enjoyed your society, Mr. Dockwrath! And what wrinkles they must have learned from you! What a pleasant oasis it must have been in the generally somewhat dull course of their monotonous though profitable business! I quite envy Round and Crook having you alongside of them in their inner council-chamber.'

' I know nothing about that, sir.'

' No; I dare say you don't;—but they'll remember it. Well, when you'd turned over your father-in-law's papers for three days you found what you looked for?'

' Yes, I did.'

' You had been tolerably sure that you would find it before you began, eh?'

' Well, I had expected that something would turn up.'

' I have no doubt you did,—and something has turned up. That gentleman sitting next to you there,—who is he?'

' Joseph Mason, Esquire, of Groby Park,' said Dockwrath.

' So I thought. It is he that is to have Orley Farm, if Lady Mason and her son should lose it?'

' In that case he would be the heir.'

' Exactly. He would be the heir. How pleasant it must be to you to find yourself on such affectionate terms with—the heir! And when he comes into his inheritance, who is to be tenant? Can you tell us that?'

Dockwrath here paused for a moment. Not that he hesitated as to telling the whole truth. He had fully made up his mind to do so, and to brazen the matter out, declaring that of course he was to be considered worthy of his reward. But there was that in the manner and eye of Chaffanbrass which stopped him for a moment, and his enemy immediately took advantage of this hesitation. 'Come, sir,' said he, ' out with it. If I don't get it from you, I shall from somebody else. You've been very plain-spoken hitherto. Don't let the jury think that your heart is failing you at last.'

' There is no reason why my heart should fail me,' said Dockwrath, in an angry tone.

' Is there not ? I must differ from you there, Mr. Dockwrath. The heart of any man placed in such a position as that you now hold must, I think, fail him. But never mind that. Who is to be the tenant of Orley Farm when my client has been deprived of it ''

' I am.'

' Just so. You were turned out from those two fields when young Mason came home from Germany ?'

' I was.'

' You immediately went to work and discovered this document ?'

' I did.'

' You put up Joseph Mason to this trial ?'

' I told him my opinion.'

' Exactly. And if the result be successful, you are to be put in possession of the land.'

' I shall become Mr. Mason's tenant at Orley Farm.'

' Yes, you will become Mr. Mason's tenant at Orley Farm. Upon my word, Mr. Dockwrath, you have made my work to-day uncommonly easy for me,—uncommonly easy. I don't know that I have anything else to ask you.' And then Mr. Chaffanbrass, as he sat down, looked up to the jury with an expression of countenance which was in itself worth any fee that could be paid to him for that day's work. His face spoke as plain as a face could speak, and what his face said was this: ' After that, gentlemen of the jury, very little more can be necessary. You now see the motives of our opponents, and the way in which those motives have been allowed to act. We, who are altogether upon the square in what we are doing, desire nothing more than that.' All which Mr. Chaffanbrass said by his look, his shrug, and his gesture, much more eloquently than he could have done by the use of any words.

Mr. Dockwrath, as he left the box and went back to his seat—in doing which he had to cross the table in the middle of the court—endeavoured to look and move as though all were right with him. He knew that the eyes of the court were on him, and especially the eyes of the judge and jury. He knew also how men's minds are unconsciously swayed by small appearances. He endeavoured therefore to seem indifferent; but in doing so he swaggered, and was conscious that he swaggered; and he felt as he gained his seat that Mr. Chaffanbrass had been too much for him.

Then one Mr. Torrington from London was examined by Sir

Richard Leatherham, and he proved, apparently beyond all doubt, that a certain deed which he produced was genuine. That deed bore the same date as the codicil which was now questioned, had been executed at Orley Farm by old Sir Joseph, and bore the signatures of John Kenneby and Bridget Bolster as witnesses. Sir Richard, holding the deed in his hands, explained to the jury that he did not at the present stage of the proceedings ask them to take it as proved that those names were the true signatures of the two persons indicated. ('I should think not,' said Mr. Furnival, in a loud voice.) But he asked them to satisfy themselves that the document as now existing purported to bear those two signatures. It would be for them to judge, when the evidence brought before them should be complete, whether or no that deed were a true document. And then the deed was handed up into the jury-box, and the twelve jurymen all examined it. The statement made by this Mr. Torrington was very simple. It had become his business to know the circumstances of the late partnership between Mason and Martock, and these circumstances he explained. Then Sir Richard handed him over to be cross-examined.

It was now Graham's turn to begin his work; but as he rose to do so his mind misgave him. Not a syllable that this Torrington had said appeared to him to be unworthy of belief. The man had not uttered a word, of the truth of which Graham did not feel himself positively assured; and, more than that,—the man had clearly told all that was within him to tell, all that it was well that the jury should hear in order that they might thereby be assisted in coming to a true decision. It had been hinted in his hearing, both by Chaffanbrass and Aram, that this man was probably in league with Dockwrath, and Aram had declared with a sneer that he was a puzzle-pated old fellow. He might be puzzle-pated, and had already shown that he was bashful and unhappy in his present position; but he had shown also, as Graham thought, that he was anxious to tell the truth.

And, moreover, Graham had listened with all his mind to the cross-examination of Dockwrath, and he was filled with disgust— with disgust, not so much at the part played by the attorney as at that played by the barrister. As Graham regarded the matter, what had the iniquities and greed of Dockwrath to do with it? Had reason been shown why the statement made by Dockwrath was in itself unworthy of belief,—that that statement was in its own essence weak,—then the character of the man making it might fairly affect its credibility. But presuming that statement to be strong,—presuming that it was corroborated by other evidence, how could it be affected by any amount of villainy on the part of Dockwrath? All that Chaffanbrass had done or attempted was to prove that Dockwrath had had his own end to serve. Who had ever doubted it?

But not a word had been said, not a spark of evidence elicited, to show that the man had used a falsehood to further those views of his. Of all this the mind of Felix Graham had been full; and now, as he rose to take his own share of the work, his wit was at work rather in opposition to Lady Mason than on her behalf.

This Torrington was a little old man, and Graham had watched how his hands had trembled when Sir Richard first addressed him. But Sir Richard had been very kind,—as was natural to his own witness, and the old man had gradually regained his courage. But now as he turned his face round to the side where he knew that he might expect to find an enemy, that tremor again came upon him, and the stick which he held in his hand was heard as it tapped gently against the side of the witness-box. Graham, as he rose to his work, saw that Mr. Chaffanbrass had fixed his eye upon him, and his courage rose the higher within him as he felt the gaze of the man whom he so much disliked. Was it within the compass of his heart to bully an old man because such a one as Chaffanbrass desired it of him? By heaven, no!

He first asked Mr. Torrington his age, and having been told that he was over seventy, Graham went on to assure him that nothing which could be avoided should be said to disturb his comfort. And now, Mr. Torrington,' he asked, ' will you tell me whether you are a friend of Mr. Dockwrath's, or have had any acquaintance with him previous to the affairs of this trial?' This question he repeated in various forms, but always in a mild voice, and without the appearance of any disbelief in the answers which were given to him. All these questions Torrington answered by a plain negative. He had never seen Dockwrath till the attorney had come to him on the matter of that partnership deed. He had never eaten or drunk with him, nor had there ever been between them any conversation of a confidential nature. ' That will do, Mr. Torrington,' said Graham; and as he sat down, he again turned round and looked Mr. Chaffanbrass full in the face.

After that nothing further of interest was done that day. A few unimportant witnesses were examined on legal points, and then the court was adjourned.

CHAPTER XXIX.

FELIX GRAHAM as he left the Alston court-house on the close of the first day of the trial was not in a happy state of mind. He did not actually accuse himself of having omitted any duty which he owed to his client; but he did accuse himself of having undertaken a duty for which he felt himself to be manifestly unfit. Would it not have been better, as he said to himself, for that poor lady to have had any other possible advocate than himself? Then as he passed out in the company of Mr. Furnival and Mr. Chaffanbrass, the latter looked at him with a scorn which he did not know how to return. In his heart he could do so; and should words be spoken between them on the subject, he would be well able and willing enough to defend himself. But had he attempted to bandy looks with Mr. Chaffanbrass, it would have seemed even to himself that he was proclaiming his resolution to put himself in opposition to his colleagues.

He felt as though he were engaged to fight a battle in which truth and justice, nay heaven itself must be against him. How can a man put his heart to the proof of an assertion in the truth of which he himself has no belief? That though guilty this lady should be treated with the utmost mercy compatible with the law;—for so much, had her guilt stood forward as acknowledged, he could have pleaded with all the eloquence that was in him. He could still pity her, sympathize with her, fight for her on such ground as that; but was it possible that he, believing her to be false, should stand up before the crowd assembled in that court, and use such intellect as God had given him in making others think that the false and the guilty one was true and innocent, and that those accusers were false and guilty whom he knew to be true and innocent?

It had been arranged that Baron Maltby should stay that night at Noningsby. The brother-judges therefore occupied the Noningsby carriage together, and Graham was driven back in a dog-cart by Augustus Staveley.

'Well, old boy,' said Augustus, 'you did not soil your conscience much by bullying that fellow.'

'No, I did not.' said Graham; and then he was silent.

'Chaffanbrass made an uncommonly ugly show of the Hamworth

attorney,' said Augustus, after a pause; but to this Graham at first made no answer.

' If l were on the jury,' continued the other, ' I would not believe a single word that came from that fellow's mouth, unless it were fully supported by other testimony. Nor will the jury believe him.'

' I tell you what, Staveley,' said Graham, ' you will oblige me greatly in this matter if you will not speak to me of the trial till it is over.'

' I beg your pardon.'

' No; don't do that. Nothing can be more natural than that you and I should discuss it together in all its bearings. But there are reasons, which I will explain to you afterwards, why I would rather not do so.'

' All right,' said Augustus. ' I'll not say another word.'

' And for my part, I will get through the work as well as I may.' And then they both sat silent in the gig till they came to the corner of Noningsby wall.

' And is that other subject tabooed also ?' said Augustus.

' What other subject ?'

' That as to which we said something when you were last here,—touching my sister Madeline.'

Graham felt that his face was on fire, but he did not know how to answer. ' In that it is for you to decide whether or no there should be silence between us,' he said at last.

' I certainly do not wish that there should be any secret between us,' said Augustus.

' Then there shall be none. It is my intention to make an offer to her before I leave Noningsby. I can assure you for your satisfaction, that my hopes do not run very high.'

' For my satisfaction, Felix! I don't know why you should suppose me to be anxious that you should fail.' And as he so spoke he stopped his horse at the hall-door, and there was no time for further speech.

' Papa has been home a quarter of an hour,' said Madeline, meeting them in the hall.

' Yes, he had the pull of us by having his carriage ready,' said her brother. ' We had to wait for the ostler.'

' He says that if you are not ready in ten minutes he will go to dinner without you. Mamma and I are dressed.' And as she spoke she turned round with a smile to Felix, making him feel that both she and her father were treating him as though he were one of the family.

' Ten minutes will be quite enough for me,' said he.

' If the governor only would sit down,' said Augustus, ' it would be all right. But that's just what he won't do. Mad, do send somebody to help me to unpack.' And then they all bustled away, so that the pair of judges might not be kept waiting for their food.

Felix Graham hurried up stairs, three steps at a time, as though all his future success at Noningsby depended on his being down in the drawing-room within the period of minutes stipulated by the judge. As he dressed himself with the utmost rapidity, thinking perhaps not so much as he should have done of his appearance in the eyes of his lady-love, he endeavoured to come to some resolve as to the task which was before him. How was he to find an opportunity of speaking his mind to Madeline, if, during the short period of his sojourn at Noningsby, he left the house every morning directly after breakfast, and returned to it in the evening only just in time for dinner?

When he entered the drawing-room both the judges were there, as was also Lady Staveley and Madeline. Augustus alone was wanting. 'Ring the bell, Graham,' the judge said, as Felix took his place on the corner of the rug. 'Augustus will be down about supper-time.' And then the bell was rung and the dinner ordered.

'Papa ought to remember,' said Madeline, 'that he got his carriage first at Alston.'

'I heard the wheels of the gig,' said the judge. 'They were just two minutes after us.'

'I don't think Augustus takes longer than other young men,' said Lady Staveley.

'Look at Graham there. He can't be supposed to have the use of all his limbs, for he broke half a dozen of them a month ago; and yet he's ready. Brother Maltby, give your arm to Lady Staveley. Graham, if you'll take Madeline, I'll follow alone.' He did not call her Miss Staveley, as Felix specially remarked, and so remarking, pressed the little hand somewhat closer to his side. It was the first sign of love he had ever given her, and he feared that some mark of anger might follow it. There was no return to his pressure;—not the slightest answer was made with those sweet finger points; but there was no anger. 'Is your arm quite strong again?' she asked him as they sat down, as soon as the judge's short grace had been uttered.

'Fifteen minutes to the second,' said Augustus, bustling into the room, 'and I think that an unfair advantage has been taken of me. But what can a juvenile barrister expect in the presence of two judges?' And then the dinner went on, and a very pleasant little dinner-party it was.

Not a word was said, either then or during the evening, or on the following morning, on that subject which was engrossing so much of the mind of all of them. Not a word was spoken as to that trial which was now pending, nor was the name of Lady Mason mentioned. It was understood even by Madeline that no allusion could with propriety be made to it in the presence of the judge before whom the cause was now pending, and the ground was considered too sacred for feet to tread upon it. Were it not that this feeling is so general an English judge and English counsellors would almost be forced to subject themselves in such cases to the close custody which jurymen are called upon to endure. But, as a rule, good taste and good feeling are as potent as locks and walls.

'Do you know, Mr. Graham,' said Madeline, in that sort of whisper which a dinner-table allows, 'that Mrs. Baker says you have cut her since you got well.'

'I! I cut one of my very best friends! How can she say anything so untrue? If I knew where she lived I'd go and pay her a visit after dinner.'

'I don't think you need do that,—though she has a very snug little room of her own. You were in it on Christmas-day when we had the snapdragon,—when you and Marion carried away the dishes.'

'I remember. And she is base enough to say that I have cut her? I did see her for a moment yesterday, and then I spoke to her.'

'Ah, but you should have had a long chat with her. She expects you to go back over all the old ground, how you were brought in helpless, how the doctor came to you, and how you took all the messes she prepared for you like a good boy. I'm afraid, Mr. Graham, you don't understand old women.'

'Nor young ones either,' it was on his tongue to say, but he did not say it.

'When I was a young man,' said the baron, carrying on some conversation which had been general at the table, 'I never had an opportunity of breaking my ribs out hunting.'

'Perhaps if you had,' said Augustus, 'you might have used it with more effect than my friend here, and have deprived the age of one of its brightest lights, and the bench of one of its most splendid ornaments.'

'Hear, hear, hear!' said his father.

'Augustus is coming out in a new character,' said his mother.

'I am heartily obliged to him,' said the baron. 'But, as I was saying before, these sort of things never came in my way. If I remember right, my father would have thought I was mad had I talked of going out hunting. Did you hunt, Staveley?'

When the ladies were gone the four lawyers talked about law, though they kept quite clear of that special trial which was going on at Alston. Judge Staveley, as we know, had been at the Birmingham congress; but not so his brother the baron. Baron Maltby, indeed, thought but little of the Birmingham doings, and was inclined to be a little hard upon his brother in that he had taken a part in it.

'I think that the matter is one open to discussion,' said the host.

'Well, I hope so,' said Graham. 'At any rate I have heard no arguments which ought to make us feel that our mouths are closed.'

'Arguments on such a matter are worth nothing at all,' said the baron. 'A man with what is called a logical turn of mind may prove anything or disprove anything; but he never convinces anybody. On any matter that is near to a man's heart, he is convinced by the tenour of his own thoughts as he goes on living, not by the arguments of a logician, or even by the eloquence of an orator. Talkers are apt to think that if their listener cannot answer them they are bound to give way; but non-talkers generally take a very different view of the subject.'

'But does that go to show that a question should not be ventilated?' asked Felix.

'I don't mean to be uncivil,' said the baron, 'but of all words in the language there is none which I dislike so much as that word ventilation. A man given to ventilating subjects is worse than a man who has a mission.'

'Bores of that sort, however,' said Graham, 'will show themselves from time to time and are not easily put down. Some one will have a mission to reform our courts of law, and will do it too.'

'I only hope it may not be in my time,' said the baron.

'I can't go quite so far as that,' said the other judge. 'But no doubt we all have the same feeling more or less. I know pretty well what my friend Graham is driving at.'

'And in your heart you agree with me,' said Graham.

'If you would carry men's heads with you they would do you more good than their hearts,' said the judge. And then as the wine bottles were stationary, the subject was cut short and they went into the drawing-room.

Graham had no opportunity that evening of telling his tale to Madeline Staveley. The party was too large for such tale-telling or else not large enough. And then the evening in the drawing-room was over before it had seemed to begin; and while he was yet hoping that there might be some turn in his favour, Lady Staveley wished him good-night, and Madeline of course did the same. As he again pressed her hand he could not but think how little he had said to her since he had been in the house, and yet it seemed to him as though that little had made him more intimate with her than he had ever found himself before. He had made an attempt to separate himself from the company by proposing to go and call on Mrs. Baker in her own quarters; but Madeline had declared it to be too late for such an expedition, explaining that when Mrs. Baker had no patient on hand she was accustomed to go early to her bed. In the present

instance, however, she had been wrong, for when Felix reached the
door of his own room, Mrs. Baker was coming out of it.

'I was just looking if everything was right,' said she.   'It seems
natural to me to come and look after you, you know.'

'And it is quite as natural to me to be looked after.'

'Is it though? But the worst of you gentlemen when you get
well is that one has done with you.   You go away, and then there's
no more about it.   I always begrudge to see you get well for that
reason.'

'When you have a man in your power you like to keep him there.'

'That's always the way with the women you know.   I hope we
shall see one of them tying you by the leg altogether before long.'

'I don't know anything about that,' said Felix, sheepishly.

'Don't you? Well, if you don't I suppose nobody don't.   But
nevertheless I did hear a little bird say——eh! Mr. Graham.'

'Those little birds are the biggest liars in the world.'

'Are they now? Well perhaps they are.   And how do you think
our Miss Madeline is looking? She wasn't just well for one short
time after you went away.'

'Has she been ill?'

'Well, not ill; not so that she came into my hands.   She's looking
herself again now, isn't she?'

'She is looking, as she always does, uncommonly well.'

'Do you remember how she used to come and say a word to you
standing at the door? Dear heart! I'll be bound now I care
more for her than you do.'

'Do you?' said Graham.

'Of course I do.   And then how angry her ladyship was with me,
—as though it were my fault.   I didn't do it.   Did I, Mr. Graham?
But, Lord love you, what's the use of being angry? My lady ought
to have remembered her own young days, for it was just the same
thing with her.   She had her own way, and so will Miss Madeline.'
And then with some further inquiries as to his fire, his towels, and
his sheets, Mrs. Baker took herself off.

Felix Graham had felt a repugnance to taking the gossiping old
woman openly into his confidence, and yet he had almost asked her
whether he might in truth count upon Madeline's love.   Such at
any rate had been the tenour of his gossiping; but nevertheless he
was by no means certified.   He had the judge's assurance in allowing him to be there; he had the assurance given to him by Augustus
in the few words spoken to him at the door that evening; and he
ought to have known that he had received sufficient assurance from
Madeline herself.   But in truth he knew nothing of the kind.
There are men who are much too forward in believing that they are
regarded with favour; but there are others of whom it may be said
that they are as much too backward.   The world hears most of the

former, and talks of them the most, but I doubt whether the latter are not the more numerous.

The next morning of course there was a hurry and fuss at breakfast in order that they might get off in time for the courts. The judges were to take their seats at ten, and therefore it was necessary that they should sit down to breakfast some time before nine. The achievement does not seem to be one of great difficulty, but nevertheless it left no time for lovemaking.

But for one instant Felix was able to catch Madeline alone in the breakfast-parlour. 'Miss Staveley,' said he, 'will it be possible that I should speak to you alone this evening;—for five minutes?'

'Speak to me alone?' she said, repeating his words; and as she did so she was conscious that her whole face had become suffused with colour.

'Is it too much to ask?'

'Oh, no!'

'Then if I leave the dining-room soon after you have done so——'

'Mamma will be there, you know,' she said. Then others came into the room and he was able to make no further stipulation for the evening.

Madeline, when she was left alone that morning, was by no means satisfied with her own behaviour, and accused herself of having been unnecessarily cold to him. She knew the permission which had been accorded to him, and she knew also—knew well—what answer would be given to his request. In her mind the matter was now fixed. She had confessed to herself that she loved him, and she could not now doubt of his love to her. Why then should she have answered him with coldness and doubt? She hated the missishness of young ladies, and had resolved that when he asked her a plain question she would give him a plain answer. It was true that the question had not been asked as yet; but why should she have left him in doubt as to her kindly feeling?

'It shall be but for this one day,' she said to herself as she sat alone in her room.

CHAPTER XXX.

HOW AM I TO BEAR IT?

WHEN the first day's work was over in the court, Lady Mason and Mrs. Orme kept their seats till the greater part of the crowd had dispersed, and the two young men, Lucius Mason and Peregrine,

remained with them.　Mr. Aram also remained, giving them sundry
little instructions in a low voice as to the manner in which they
should go home and return the next morning,—telling them the
hour at which they must start, and promising that he would meet
them at the door of the court.　To all this Mrs. Orme endeavoured
to give her best attention, as though it were of the last importance;
but Lady Mason was apparently much the more collected of the
two, and seemed to take all Mr. Aram's courtesies as though they
were a matter of course.　There she sat, still with her veil up, and
though all those who had been assembled there during the day
turned their eyes upon her as they passed out, she bore it all without quailing.　It was not that she returned their gaze, or affected
an effrontery in her conduct; but she was able to endure it without
showing that she suffered as she did so.

'The carriage is there now,' said Mr. Aram, who had left the
court for a minute; 'and I think you may get into it quietly.'
This accordingly they did, making their way through an avenue of
idlers who still remained that they might look upon the lady who
was accused of having forged her husband's will.

'I will stay with her to-night,' whispered Mrs. Orme to her son
as they passed through the court.

'Do you mean that you will not come to the Cleeve at all?'

'Not to-night; not till the trial be over.　Do you remain with
your grandfather.'

'I shall be here to-morrow of course to see how you go on.'

'But do not leave your grandfather this evening.　Give him my
love, and say that I think it best that I should remain at Orley
Farm till the trial be over.　And, Peregrine, if I were you I would
not talk to him much about the trial.'

'But why not?'

'I will tell you when it is over.　But it would only harass him
at the present moment.'　And then Peregrine handed his mother
into the carriage and took his own way back to the Cleeve.

As he returned he was bewildered in his mind by what he had
heard, and he also began to feel something like a doubt as to Lady
Mason's innocence.　Hitherto his belief in it had been as fixed and
assured as that of her own son.　Indeed it had never occurred to
him as possible that she could have done the thing with which she
was charged.　He had hated Joseph Mason for suspecting her, and
had hated Dockwrath for his presumed falsehood in pretending to
suspect her.　But what was he to think of this question now,
after hearing the clear and dispassionate statement of all the
circumstances by the solicitor-general?　Hitherto he had understood
none of the particulars of the case; but now the nature of the accusation had been made plain, and it was evident to him that at any
rate that far-sighted lawyer believed in the truth of his own state-

ment. Could it be possible that Lady Mason had forged the will,—
that this deed had been done by his mother's friend, by the woman
who had so nearly become Lady Orme of the Cleeve ? The idea
was terrible to him as he rode home, but yet he could not rid himself
of it. And if this were so, was it also possible that his grandfather
suspected it ? Had that marriage been stopped by any such
suspicion as this ? Was it this that had broken the old man down
and robbed him of all his spirit ? That his mother could not have
any such suspicion seemed to him to be made clear by the fact that
she still treated Lady Mason as her friend. And then why had he
been specially enjoined not to speak to his grandfather as to the
details of the trial ?

But it was impossible for him to meet Sir Peregrine without
speaking of the trial. When he entered the house, which he did by
some back entrance from the stables, he found his grandfather
standing at his own room door. He had heard the sounds of the
horse, and was unable to restrain his anxiety to learn.

' Well,' said Sir Peregrine, ' what has happened ?'

' It is not over as yet. It will last, they say, for three days.'

' But come in, Peregrine ;' and he shut the door, anxious rather
that the servants should not witness his own anxiety than that they
should not hear tidings which must now be common to all the
world. ' They have begun it ?'

' Oh, yes! they have begun it.'

' Well, how far has it gone ?'

' Sir Richard Leatherham told us the accusation they make
against her, and then they examined Dockwrath and one or two
others. They have not got further than that.'

' And the—Lady Mason—how does she bear it ?'

' Very well I should say. She does not seem to be nearly as
nervous now, as she was while staying with us.'

' Ah! indeed. She is a wonderful woman,—a very wonderful
woman. So she bears up ? And your mother, Peregrine ?'

' I don't think she likes it.'

' Likes it ! Who could like such a task as that ?'

' But she will go through with it.'

' I am sure she will. She will go through with anything that she
undertakes. And—and—the judge said nothing—I suppose ?'

' Very little, sir.'

And Sir Peregrine again sat down in his arm-chair as though the
work of conversation were too much for him. But neither did he
dare to speak openly on the subject; and yet there was so much
that he was anxious to know. Do you think she will escape ?
That was the question which he longed to ask but did not dare to
utter.

And then, after a while, they dined together. And Peregrine

determined to talk of other things; but it was in vain. While the servants were in the room nothing was said. The meat was carved and the plates were handed round, and young Orme ate his dinner; but there was a constraint upon them both which they were quite unable to dispel, and at last they gave it up and sat in silence till they were alone.

When the door was closed, and they were opposite to each other over the fire, in the way which was their custom when they two only were there, Sir Peregrine could restrain his desire no longer. It must be that his grandson, who had heard all that had passed in court that day, should have formed some opinion of what was going on,—should have some idea as to the chance of that battle which was being fought. He, Sir Peregrine, could not have gone into the court himself. It would have been impossible for him to show himself there. But there had been his heart all the day. How had it gone with that woman whom a few weeks ago he had loved so well that he had regarded her as his wife?

' Was your mother very tired?' he said, again endeavouring to draw near the subject.

' She did look fagged while sitting in court.'

' It was a dreadful task for her,—very dreadful.'

' Nothing could have turned her from it,' said Peregrine.

' No,—you are right there. Nothing would have turned her from it. She thought it to be her duty to that poor lady. But she— Lady Mason—she bore it better, you say?'

' I think she bears it very well,—considering what her position is.'

' Yes, yes. It is very dreadful. The solicitor-general when he opened,—was he very severe upon her?'

' I do not think he wished to be severe.'

' But he made it very strong against her.'

' The story, as he told it, was very strong against her;—that is, you know, it would be if we were to believe all that he stated.'

' Yes, yes, of course. He only stated what he has been told by others. You could not see how the jury took it?'

' I did not look at them. I was thinking more of her and of Lucius.'

' Lucius was there?'

' Yes; he sat next to her. And Sir Richard said, while he was telling the story, that he wished her son were not there to hear it. Upon my word, sir, I almost wished so too.'

' Poor fellow,—poor fellow! It would have been better for him to stay away.'

' And yet had it been my mother——'

' Your mother, Perry! It could not have been your mother. She could not have been so placed.'

' If it be Lady Mason's misfortune, and not her fault——'

'Ah, well; we will not talk about that. And there will be two days more you say?'

'So said Aram, the attorney.'

'God help her;—may God help her! It would be very dreadful for a man, but for a woman the burden is insupportable.'

Then they both sat silent for a while, during which Peregrine was engrossed in thinking how he could turn his grandfather from the conversation.

'And you heard no one express any opinion?' asked Sir Peregrine, after a pause.

'You mean about Lady Mason?' And Peregrine began to perceive that his mother was right, and that it would have been well if possible to avoid any words about the trial.

'Do they think that she will,—will be acquitted? Of course the people there were talking about it?'

'Yes, sir, they were talking about it. But I really don't know as to any opinion. You see, the chief witnesses have not been examined.'

'And you, Perry, what do you think?'

'I, sir! Well, I was altogether on her side till I heard Sir Richard Leatherham.'

'And then——?'

'Then I did not know what to think. I suppose it's all right; but one never can understand what those lawyers are at. When Mr. Chaffanbrass got up to examine Dockwrath, he seemed to be just as confident on his side as the other fellow had been on the other side. I don't think I'll have any more wine, sir, thank you.'

But Sir Peregrine did not move. He sat in his old accustomed way, nursing one leg over the knee of the other, and thinking of the manner in which she had fallen at his feet, and confessed it all. Had he married her, and gone with her proudly into the court,—as he would have done,—and had he then heard a verdict of guilty given by the jury;—nay, had he heard such proof of her guilt as would have convinced himself, it would have killed him. He felt, as he sat there, safe over his own fireside, that his safety was due to her generosity. Had that other calamity fallen upon him, he could not have survived it. His head would have fallen low before the eyes of those who had known him since they had known anything, and would never have been raised again. In his own spirit, in his inner life, the blow had come to him; but it was due to her effort on his behalf that he had not been stricken in public. When he had discussed the matter with Mrs. Orme, he had seemed in a measure to forget this. It had not at any rate been the thought which rested with the greatest weight upon his mind. Then he had considered how she, whose life had been stainless as driven snow, should bear herself in the presence of such deep guilt. But now,—now as he sat alone, he thought only of Lady Mason. Let her be ever so guilty,—and her guilt had been very terrible,—she had behaved very nobly to him. From him at least she had a right to sympathy. And what chance was there that she should escape? Of absolute escape there was no chance whatever. Even should the jury acquit her, she must declare her guilt to the world,—must declare it to her son, by taking steps for the restoration of the property. As to that Sir Peregrine felt no doubt whatever. That Joseph Mason of Groby would recover his right to Orley Farm was to him a certainty. But how terrible would be the path over which she must walk before this deed of retribution could be done! 'Ah, me! ah, me!' he said, as he thought of all this,—speaking to himself, as though he were unconscious of his grandson's presence. 'Poor woman! poor woman!' Then Peregrine felt sure that she had been guilty, and was sure also that his grandfather was aware of it.

'Will you come into the other room, sir?' he said.

'Yes, yes; if you like it.' And then the one leg fell from the other, and he rose to do his grandson's bidding. To him now and henceforward one room was much the same as another.

In the mean time the party bound for Orley Farm had reached that place, and to them also came the necessity of wearing through that tedious evening. On the mind of Lucius Mason not even yet had a shadow of suspicion fallen. To him, in spite of it all, his mother was still pure. But yet he was stern to her, and his manner was very harsh. It may be that had such suspicion crossed his mind he would have been less stern, and his manner more tender. As it was he could understand nothing that was going on, and almost felt that he was kept in the dark at his mother's instance. Why was it that a man respected by all the world, such as Sir Richard Leatherham, should rise in court and tell such a tale as that against his mother; and that the power of answering that tale on his mother's behalf should be left to such another man as Mr. Chaffanbrass? Sir Richard had told his story plainly, but with terrible force; whereas Chaffanbrass had contented himself with browbeating another lawyer with the lowest quirks of his cunning. Why had not some one been in court able to use the language of passionate truth and ready to thrust the lie down the throats of those who told it?

Tea and supper had been prepared for them, and they sat down together; but the nature of the meal may be imagined. Lady Mason had striven with terrible effort to support herself during the day, and even yet she did not give way. It was quite as necessary that she should restrain herself before her son as before all those others who had gazed at her in court. And she did sustain herself. She took a knife and fork in her hand and ate a few morsels. She drank her cup of tea, and remembering that there in that house she was still hostess, she made some slight effort to welcome her guest. ' Surely after such a day of trouble you will eat something,' she said to her friend. To Mrs. Orme it was marvellous that the woman should even be alive,—let alone that she should speak and perform the ordinary functions of her daily life. ' And now,' she said—Lady Mason said—as soon as that ceremony was over, 'now as we are so tired I think we will go up stairs. Will you light our candles for us, Lucius?' And so the candles were lit, and the two ladies went up stairs.

A second bed had been prepared in Lady Mason's room, and into this chamber they both went at once. Mrs. Orme, as soon as she had entered, turned round and held out both her hands in order that she might comfort Lady Mason by taking hers; but Lady Mason, when she had closed the door, stood for a moment with her face towards the wall, not knowing how to bear herself. It was but for a moment, and then slowly moving round, with her two hands clasped together, she sank on her knees at Mrs. Orme's feet, and hid her face in the skirt of Mrs. Orme's dress.

' My friend—my friend!' said Lady Mason.

' Yes, I am your friend—indeed I am. But, dear Lady Mason—' And she endeavoured to think of words by which she might implore her to rise and compose herself.

' How is it you can bear with such a one as I am? How is it that you do not hate me for my guilt?'

' He does not hate us when we are guilty.'

' I do not know. Sometimes I think that all will hate me,—here and hereafter—except you. Lucius will hate me, and how shall I bear that? Oh, Mrs. Orme, I wish he knew it!'

' I wish he did. He shall know it now,—to-night, if you will allow me to tell him.'

' No. It would kill me to bear his looks. I wish he knew it, and was away, so that he might never look at me again.'

' He too would forgive you if he knew it all.'

' Forgive! How can he forgive?' And as she spoke she rose again to her feet, and her old manner came upon her. ' Do you think what it is that I have done for him? I,—his mother,—for my only child? And after that, is it possible that he should forgive me?'

' You meant him no harm.'

' But I have ruined him before all the world. He is as proud as your boy; and could he bear to think that his whole life would be disgraced by his mother's crime?'

' Had I been so unfortunate he would have forgiven me.'

' We are speaking of what is impossible. It could not have been so. Your youth was different from mine.'

'God has been very good to me, and not placed temptation in my way;—temptation, I mean, to great faults. But little faults require repentance as much as great ones.'

'But then repentance is easy; at any rate it is possible.'

'Oh, Lady Mason, is it not possible for you?'

'But I will not talk of that now. I will not hear you compare yourself with such a one as I am. Do you know I was thinking to-day that my mind would fail me, and that I should be mad before this is over? How can I bear it? how can I bear it?' And rising from her seat, she walked rapidly through the room, holding back her hair from her brows with both her hands.

And how was she to bear it? The load on her back was too much for any shoulders. The burden with which she had laden herself was too heavy to be borne. Her power of endurance was very great. Her strength in supporting the extreme bitterness of intense sorrow was wonderful. But now she was taxed beyond her power. 'How am I to bear it?' she said again, as still holding her hair between her fingers, she drew her hands back over her head.

'You do not know. You have not tried it. It is impossible,' she said in her wildness, as Mrs. Orme endeavoured to teach her the only source from whence consolation might be had. 'I do not believe in the thief on the cross, unless it was that he had prepared himself for that day by years of contrition. I know I shock you,' she added, after a while. 'I know that what I say will be dreadful to you. But innocence will always be shocked by guilt. Go, go and leave me. It has gone so far now that all is of no use.' Then she threw herself on the bed, and burst into a convulsive passion of tears.

Once again Mrs. Orme endeavoured to obtain permission from her to undertake that embassy to her son. Had Lady Mason acceded, or been near acceding, Mrs. Orme's courage would probably have been greatly checked. As it was she pressed it as though the task were one to be performed without difficulty. Mrs. Orme was very anxious that Lucius should not sit in the court throughout the trial. She felt that if he did so the shock,—the shock which was inevitable, —must fall upon him there; and than that she could conceive nothing more terrible. And then also she believed that if the secret were once made known to Lucius, and if he were for a time removed from his mother's side, the poor woman might be brought to a calmer perception of her true position. The strain would be lessened, and she would no longer feel the necessity of exerting so terrible a control over her feelings.

'You have acknowledged that he must know it sooner or later,' pleaded Mrs. Orme.

'But this is not the time,—not now, during the trial. Had he known it before——'

' It would keep him away from the court.'

' Yes, and I should never see him again ! What will he do when he hears it? Perhaps it would be better that he should go without seeing me.'

' He would not do that.'

' It would be better. If they take me to the prison, I will never see him again. His eyes would kill me. Do you ever watch him and see the pride that there is in his eye? He has never yet known what disgrace means; and now I, his mother, have brought him to this !'

It was all in vain as far as that night was concerned. Lady Mason would give no such permission. But Mrs. Orme did exact from her a kind of promise that Lucius should be told on the next evening, if it then appeared, from what Mr. Aram should say, that the result of the trial was likely to be against them.

Lucius Mason spent his evening alone; and though he had as yet heard none of the truth, his mind was not at ease, nor was he happy at heart. Though he had no idea of his mother's guilt, he did conceive that after this trial it would be impossible that they should remain at Orley Farm. His mother's intended marriage with Sir Peregrine, and then the manner in which that engagement had been broken off; the course of the trial, and its celebrity; the enmity of Dockwrath; and lastly, his own inability to place himself on terms of friendship with those people who were still his mother's nearest friends, made him feel that in any event it would be well for them to change their residence. What could life do for him there at Orley Farm, after all that had passed? He had gone to Liverpool and bought guano, and now the sacks were lying in his barn unopened. Be had begun to drain, and the ugly unfinished lines of earth were lying across his fields. He had no further interest in it, and felt that he could no longer go to work on that ground as though he were in truth its master.

But then, as he thought of his future hopes, his place of residence and coming life, there was one other beyond himself and his mother to whom his mind reverted. What would Sophia wish that he should do?—his own Sophia,—she who had promised him that her heart should be with his through all the troubles of this trial? Before he went to bed that night he wrote to Sophia, and told her what were his troubles and what his hopes. ' This will be over in two days more,' he said, ' and then I will come to you. You will see me, I trust, the day after this letter reaches you; but nevertheless I cannot debar myself from the satisfaction of writing. I am not happy, for I am dissatisfied with what they are doing for my mother; and it is only when I think of you, and the assurance of your love, that I can feel anything like content. It is not a pleasant thing to sit by and hear one's mother charged with the foulest

frauds that practised villains can conceive! Yet I have had to
bear it, and have heard no denial of the charge in true honest language. To-day, when the solicitor-general was heaping falsehoods
on her name, I could hardly refrain myself from rushing at his
throat. Let me have a line of comfort from you, and then I will be
with you on Friday.'

That line of comfort never came, nor did Lucius on the Friday
make his intended visit. Miss Furnival had determined, some day
or two before this, that she would not write to Lucius again till
this trial was over; and even then it might be a question whether
a correspondence with the heir of Noningsby would not be more to
her taste.

CHAPTER XXXI.

SHOWING HOW JOHN KENNEBY AND BRIDGET BOLSTER BORE THEMSELVES
IN COURT.

On the next morning they were all in their places at ten o'clock,
and the crowd had been gathered outside the doors of the court
from a much earlier hour. As the trial progressed the interest in
it increased, and as people began to believe that Lady Mason had
in truth forged a will, so did they the more regard her in the light
of a heroine. Had she murdered her husband after forging his
will, men would have paid half a crown apiece to have touched her
garments, or a guinea for the privilege of shaking hands with her.
Lady Mason had again taken her seat with her veil raised, with
Mrs. Orme on one side of her and her son on the other. The
counsel were again ranged on the seats behind, Mr. Furnival
sitting the nearest to the judge, and Mr. Aram again occupied the
intermediate bench, so placing himself that he could communicate
either with his client or with the barristers. These were now their
established places, and great as was the crowd, they found no difficulty in reaching them. An easy way is always made for the chief
performers in a play.

This was to be the great day as regarded the evidence. ' It is a
case that depends altogether on evidence,' one young lawyer said
to another. ' If the counsel know how to handle the witnesses, I
should say she is safe.' The importance of this handling was felt
by every one, and therefore it was understood that the real game
would be played out on this middle day. It had been all very well
for Chaffanbrass to bully Dockwrath and make the wretched attorney
miserable for an hour or so, but that would have but little bearing
on the verdict. There were two persons there who were prepared

How can I bear it

to swear that on a certain day they had only signed one deed. So much the solicitor-general had told them, and nobody doubted that it would be so. The question now was this, would Mr. Furnival and Mr. Chaffanbrass succeed in making them contradict themselves when they had so sworn? Could they be made to say that they had signed two deeds, or that they might have done so?

It was again the duty of Mr. Furnival to come first upon the stage,—that is to say, he was to do so as soon as Sir Richard had performed his very second-rate part of eliciting the evidence in chief. Poor John Kenneby was to be the first victim, and he was placed in the box before them all very soon after the judge had taken his seat. Why had he not emigrated to Australia, and escaped all this,—escaped all this, and Mrs. Smiley also? That was John Kenneby's reflection as he slowly mounted the two steps up into the place of his torture. Near to the same spot, and near also to Dockwrath who had taken these two witnesses under his special charge, sat Bridget Bolster. She had made herself very comfortable that morning with buttered toast and sausages; and when at Dockwrath's instance Kenneby had submitted to a slight infusion of Dutch courage,—a bottle of brandy would not have sufficed for the purpose,—Bridget also had not refused the generous glass. 'Not that I wants it,' said she, meaning thereby to express an opinion that she could hold her own, even against the great Chaffanbrass, without any such extraneous aid. She now sat quite quiet, with her hands crossed on her knees before her, and her eyes immovably fixed on the table which stood in the centre of the court. In that position she remained till her turn came; and one may say that there was no need for fear on account of Bridget Bolster.

And then Sir Richard began. What would be the nature of Kenneby's direct evidence the reader pretty well knows. Sir Richard took a long time in extracting it, for he was aware that it would be necessary to give his witness some confidence before he came to his main questions. Even to do this was difficult, for Kennedy would speak in a voice so low that nobody could hear him; and on the second occasion of the judge enjoining him to speak out, he nearly fainted. It is odd that it never occurs to judges that a witness who is naturally timid will be made more so by being scolded. When I hear a judge thus use his authority, I always wish that I had the power of forcing him to some very uncongenial employment,—jumping in a sack, let us say; and then when he jumped poorly, as he certainly would, I would crack my whip and bid him go higher and higher. The more I so bade him, the more he would limp; and the world looking on, would pity him and execrate me. It is much the same thing when a witness is sternly told to speak louder.

But John Kenneby at last told his plain story. He remembered

the day on which he had met old Usbech and Bridget Bolster and
Lady Mason in Sir Joseph's chamber. He had then witnessed a
signature by Sir Joseph, and had only witnessed one on that day;—
of that he was perfectly certain. He did not think that old Usbech
had signed the deed in question, but on that matter he declined to
swear positively. He remembered the former trial. He had not
then been able to swear positively whether Usbech had or had not
signed the deed. As far as he could remember, that was the point
to which his cross-examination on that occasion had chiefly been
directed. So much John Kenneby did at last say in language that
was sufficiently plain.

And then Mr. Furnival arose. The reader is acquainted with the
state of his mind on the subject of this trial. The enthusiasm on
behalf of Lady Mason, which had been aroused by his belief in her
innocence, by his old friendship, by his ancient adherence to her
cause, and by his admiration for her beauty, had now greatly faded.
It had faded much when he found himself obliged to call in such
fellow-labourers as Chaffanbrass and Aram, and had all but perished
when he learned from contact with them to regard her guilt as
certain. But, nevertheless, now that he was there, the old fire
returned to him. He had wished twenty times that he had been
able to shake the matter from him and leave his old client in the
hands of her new advisers. It would be better for her, he had said
to himself. But on this day—on these three days—seeing that he
had not shaken the matter off, he rose to his work as though he
still loved her, as though all his mind was still intent on pre-
serving that ill-gotten inheritance for her son. It may almost be
doubted whether at moments during these three days he did not
again persuade himself that she was an injured woman. Aram, as
may be remembered, had felt misgivings as to Mr. Furnival's
powers for such cross-examination; but Chaffanbrass had never
doubted it. He knew that Mr. Furnival could do as much as himself in that way; the difference being this,—that Mr. Furnival could
do something else besides.

'And now, Mr. Kenneby, I'll ask you a few questions,' he said :
and Kenneby turned round to him. The barrister spoke in a mild
low voice, but his eye transfixed the poor fellow at once; and though
Kenneby was told a dozen times to look at the jury and speak to the
jury, he never was able to take his gaze away from Mr. Furnival's face.

'You remember the old trial,' he said ; and as he spoke he held
in his hand what was known to be an account of that transaction.
Then there arose a debate between him and Sir Richard, in which
Chaffanbrass, and Graham, and Mr. Steelyard all took part, as to
whether Kenneby might be examined as to his former examination ;
and on this point Graham pleaded very volubly, bringing up pre-
cedents without number,—striving to do his duty to his client on a

point with which his own conscience did not interfere. And at last it was ruled by the judge that this examination might go on;— whereupon both Sir Richard and Mr. Steelyard sat down as though they were perfectly satisfied. Kenneby, on being again asked, said that he did remember the old trial.

'It is necessary, you know, that the jury should hear you, and if you look at them and speak to them, they would stand a better chance.' Kenneby for a moment allowed his eye to travel up to the jury box, but it instantly fell again, and fixed itself on the lawyer's face. 'You do remember that trial?'

'Yes, sir, I remember it,' whispered Kenneby.

'Do you remember my asking you then whether you had been in the habit of witnessing Sir Joseph Mason's signature?'

'Did you ask me that, sir?'

'That is the question which I put to you. Do you remember my doing so?'

'I dare say you did, sir.'

'I did, and I will now read your answer. We shall give to the jury a copy of the proceedings of that trial, my lord, when we have proved it,—as of course we intend to do.'

And then there was another little battle between the barristers. But as Lady Mason was now being tried for perjury, alleged to have been committed at that other trial, it was of course indispensable that all the proceedings of that trial should be made known to the jury.

'You said on that occasion,' continued Furnival, 'that you were sure you had witnessed three signatures of Sir Joseph's that summer,—that you had probably witnessed three in July, that you were quite sure you had witnessed three in one week in July, that you were nearly sure you had witnessed three in one day, that you could not tell what day that might have been, and that you had been used as a witness so often that you really did not remember anything about it. Can you say whether that was the purport of the evidence you gave then?'

'If it's down there ——' said John Kenneby, and then he stopped himself.

'It is down here; I have read it.'

'I suppose it's all right,' said Kenneby.

'I must trouble you to speak out,' said the judge; 'I cannot hear you, and it is impossible that the jury should do so.' The judge's words were not uncivil, but his voice was harsh, and the only perceptible consequence of the remonstrance was to be seen in the thick drops of perspiration standing on John Kenneby's brow.

'That is the evidence which you gave on the former trial? May the jury presume that you then spoke the truth to the best of your knowledge?'

' I tried to speak the truth, sir.'

' You tried to speak the truth? But do you mean to say that you failed ?'

' No, I don't think I failed.'

' When, therefore, you told the jury that you were nearly sure that you had witnessed three signatures of Sir Joseph's in one day, that was truth ?'

' I don't think I ever did.'

' Ever did what ?'

' Witness three papers in one day.'

' You don't think you ever did ?'

' I might have done, to be sure.'

' But then, at that trial, about twelve months after the man's death, you were nearly sure you had done so.'

' Was I ?'

' So you told the jury.'

' Then I did, sir.'

' Then you did what ?'

' Did witness all those papers.'

' You think then now that it is probable you witnessed three signatures on the same day ?'

' No, I don't think that.'

' Then what do you think ?'

' It is so long ago, sir, that I really don't know.'

' Exactly. It is so long ago that you cannot depend on your memory.'

' I suppose I can't, sir.'

' But you just now told the gentleman who examined you on the other side, that you were quite sure you did not witness two deeds on the day he named,—the 14th of July. Now, seeing that you doubt your own memory, going back over so long a time, do you wish to correct that statement ?'

' I suppose I do.'

' What correction do you wish to make ?'

' I don't think I did.'

' Don't think you did what ?'

' I don't think I signed two——'

' I really cannot hear the witness,' said the judge.

' You must speak out louder,' said Mr. Furnival, himself speaking very loudly.

' I mean to do it as well as I can,' said Kenneby.

' I believe you do,' said Furnival ; ' but in so meaning you must be very careful to state nothing as a certainty, of the certainty of which you are not sure. Are you certain that on that day you did not witness two deeds ?'

' I think so.'

' And yet you were not certain twenty years ago, when the fact was so much nearer to you ?'

' I don't remember.'

' You don't remember whether you were certain twelve months after the occurrence, but you think you are certain now.'

' I mean, I don't think I signed two.'

' It is, then, only a matter of thinking ?'

' No ;—only a matter of thinking.'

' And you might have signed the two ?'

' I certainly might have done so.'

' What you mean to tell the jury is this : that you have no remembrance of signing twice on that special day, although you know that you have acted as witness on behalf of Sir Joseph Mason more than twice on the same day ?'

' Yes.'

' That is the intended purport of your evidence ?'

' Yes, sir.'

And then Mr. Furnival travelled off to that other point of Mr. Usbech's presence and alleged handwriting. On that matter Kenneby had not made any positive assertion, though he had expressed a very strong opinion. Mr. Furnival was not satisfied with this, but wished to show that Kenneby had not on that matter even a strong opinion. He again reverted to the evidence on the former trial, and read various questions with their answers ; and the answers as given at that time certainly did not, when so taken, express a clear opinion on the part of the person who gave them : although an impartial person on reading the whole evidence would have found that a very clear opinion was expressed. When first asked, Kenneby had said that he was nearly sure that Mr. Usbech had not signed the document. But his very anxiety to be true had brought him into trouble. Mr. Furnival on that occasion had taken advantage of the word ' nearly,' and had at last succeeded in making him say that he was not sure at all. Evidence by means of torture,—thumbscrew and such-like,—we have for many years past abandoned as barbarous, and have acknowledged that it is of its very nature useless in the search after truth. How long will it be before we shall recognize that the other kind of torture is equally opposed both to truth and civilization ?'

' But Mr. Usbech was certainly in the room on that day ?' continued Mr. Furnival.

' Yes, he was there.'

' And knew what you were all doing, I suppose ?'

' Yes, I suppose he knew.'

' I presume it was he who explained to you the nature of the deed you were to witness ?'

' I dare say he did.'

'As he was the lawyer, that would be natural.'

'I suppose it would.'

'And you don't remember the nature of that special deed, as explained to you on the day when Bridget Bolster was in the room ?'

'No, I don't.'

'It might have been a will?'

'Yes, it might. I did sign one or two wills for Sir Joseph, I think.'

'And as to this individual document, Mr. Usbech might have signed it in your presence, for anything you know to the contrary?'

'He might have done so.'

'Now, on your oath, Kenneby, is your memory strong enough to enable you to give the jury any information on this subject upon which they may firmly rely in convicting that unfortunate lady of the terrible crime laid to her charge.' Then for a moment Kenneby glanced round and fixed his eyes upon Lady Mason's face. 'Think a moment before you answer; and deal with her as you would wish another should deal with you if you were so situated. Can you say that you remember that Usbech did not sign it ?'

'Well, sir, I don't think he did.'

'But he might have done so ?'

'Oh, yes ; he might.'

'You do not remember that he did do so ?'

'Certainly not.'

'And that is about the extent of what you mean to say ?'

'Yes, sir.'

'Let me understand,' said the judge—and then the perspiration became more visible on poor Kenneby's face ;—'do you mean to say that you have no memory on the matter whatever? — that you simply do not remember whether Usbech did or did not sign it ?'

'I don't think he signed it.'

'But why do you think he did not, seeing that his name is there ?'

'I didn't see him.'

'Do you mean,' continued the judge, 'that you didn't see him, or that you don't remember that you saw him ?'

'I don't remember that I saw him.'

'But you may have done so ? He may have signed, and you may have seen him do so, only you don't remember it ?'

'Yes, my lord.'

And then Kenneby was allowed to go down. As he did so, Joseph Mason, who sat near to him, turned upon him a look black as thunder. Mr. Mason gave him no credit for his timidity, but believed that he had been bought over by the other side. Dockwrath, however, knew better. 'They did not quite beat him about his own signature,' said he ; 'but I knew all along that we must depend chiefly upon Bolster.'

Bridget Boister in Court.

Then Bridget Bolster was put into the box, and she was examined by Mr. Steelyard. She had heard Kenneby instructed to look up, and she therefore fixed her eyes upon the canopy over the judge's seat. There she fixed them, and there she kept them till her examination was over, merely turning them for a moment on to Mr. Chaffanbrass, when that gentleman became particularly severe in his treatment of her. What she said in answer to Mr. Steelyard, was very simple. She had never witnessed but one signature in her life, and that she had done in Sir Joseph's room. The nature of the document had been explained to her. 'But,' as she said, 'she was young and giddy then, and what went in at one year went out at another.' She didn't remember Mr. Usbech signing, but he might have done so. She thought he did not. As to the two signatures purporting to be hers, she could not say which was hers and which was not. But this she would swear positively, that they were not both hers. To this she adhered firmly, and Mr. Steelyard handed her over to Mr. Chaffanbrass.

Then Mr. Chaffanbrass rose from his seat, and every one knew that his work was cut out for him. Mr. Furnival had triumphed. It may be said that he had demolished his witness; but his triumph had been very easy. It was now necessary to demolish Bridget Bolster, and the opinion was general that if anybody could do it Mr. Chaffanbrass was the man. But there was a doggedness about Bridget Bolster which induced many to doubt whether even Chaffanbrass would be successful. Mr. Aram trusted greatly; but the bar would have preferred to stake their money on Bridget.

Chaffanbrass as he rose pushed back his small ugly wig from his forehead, thrusting it rather on one side as he did so, and then, with his chin thrown forward, and a wicked, ill-meaning smile upon his mouth, he looked at Bridget for some moments before he spoke to her. She glanced at him, and instantly fixed her eyes back upon the canopy. She then folded her hands one on the other upon the rail before her, compressed her lips, and waited patiently.

'I think you say you're—a chambermaid?' That was the first question which Chaffanbrass asked, and Bridget Bolster gave a little start as she heard his sharp, angry, disagreeable voice.

'Yes, I am, sir, at Palmer's Imperial Hotel, Plymouth, Devonshire; and have been for nineteen years, upper and under.'

'Upper and under! What do upper and under mean?'

'When I was under, I had another above me; and now, as I'm upper, why there's others under me.' So she explained her position at the hotel, but she never took her eyes from the canopy.

'You hadn't begun being—chambermaid, when you signed these documents?'

'I didn't sign only one of 'em.'

'Well, one of them. You hadn't begun being chambermaid then?'

'No, I hadn't; I was housemaid at Orley Farm.'

'Were you upper or under there?'

'Well, I believe I was both; that is, the cook was upper in the house.'

'Oh, the cook was upper. Why wasn't she called to sign her name?'

'That I can't say. She was a very decent woman,—that I can say, —and her name was Martha Mullens.'

So far Mr. Chaffanbrass had not done much; but that was only the preliminary skirmish, as fencers play with their foils before they begin.

'And now, Bridget Bolster, if I understand you,' he said, 'you have sworn that on the 14th of July you only signed one of these documents.'

'I only signed once, sir. I didn't say nothing about the 14th of July, because I don't remember.'

'But when you signed the one deed, you did not sign any other?'

'Neither then nor never.'

'Do you know the offence for which that lady is being tried— Lady Mason?'

'Well, I aint sure; it's for doing something about the will.'

'No, woman, it is not.' And then, as Mr. Chaffanbrass raised his voice, and spoke with savage earnestness, Bridget again started, and gave a little leap up from the floor. But she soon settled herself back in her old position. 'No one has dared to accuse her of that,' continued Mr. Chaffanbrass, looking over at the lawyers on the other side. 'The charge they have brought forward against her is that of perjury—of having given false evidence twenty years ago in a court of law. Now look here, Bridget Bolster; look at me, I say.' She did look at him for a moment, and then turned her eyes back to the canopy. 'As sure as you're a living woman, you shall be placed there and tried for the same offence,—for perjury,—if you tell me a falsehood respecting this matter.'

'I won't say nothing but what's right,' said Bridget.

'You had better not. Now look at these two signatures;' and he handed to her two deeds, or rather made one of the servants of the court hold them for him; 'which of those signatures is the one which you did not sign?'

'I can't say, sir.'

'Did you write that further one,—that with your hand on it?'

'I can't say, sir.'

'Look at it, woman, before you answer me.'

Bridget looked at it, and then repeated the same words—

'I can't say, sir.'

'And now look at the other.' And she again looked down for a moment. 'Did you write that?'

' I can't say, sir.'

' Will you swear that you wrote either?'

' I did write one once.'

' Don't prevaricate with me, woman. Were either of those signatures there written by you?'

' I suppose that one was.'

' Will you swear that you wrote either the one or the other?'

' I'll swear I did write one, once.'

' Will you swear you wrote one of those you have before you? You can read, can't you?'

' Oh yes, I can read.'

' Then look at them.' Again she turned her eyes on them for half a moment. ' Will you swear that you wrote either of those?'

' Not if there's another anywhere else,' said Bridget, at last.

' Another anywhere else,' said Chaffanbrass, repeating her words; ' what do you mean by another?'

' If you've got another that anybody else has done, I won't say which of the three is mine. But I did one, and I didn't do no more.'

Mr. Chaffanbrass continued at it for a long time, but with very indifferent success. That affair of the signatures, which was indeed the only point on which evidence was worth anything, he then abandoned, and tried to make her contradict herself about old Usbech. But on this subject she could say nothing. That Usbeck was present she remembered well, but as to his signing the deed, or not signing it, she would not pretend to say anything.

' I know he was cram full of gout,' she said; ' but I don't remember nothing more.'

But it may be explained that Mr. Chaffanbrass had altogether altered his intention and the very plan of his campaign with reference to this witness, as soon as he saw what was her nature and disposition. He discovered very early in the affair that he could not force her to contradict herself and reduce her own evidence to nothing, as Furnival had done with the man. Nothing would flurry this woman, or force her to utter words of which she herself did not know the meaning. The more he might persevere in such an attempt, the more dogged and steady she would become. He therefore soon gave that up. He had already given it up when he threatened to accuse her of perjury, and resolved that as he could not shake her he would shake the confidence which the jury might place in her. He could not make a fool of her, and therefore he would make her out to be a rogue. Her evidence would stand alone, or nearly alone; and in this way he might turn her firmness to his own purpose, and explain that her dogged resolution to stick to one plain statement arose from her having been specially instructed so to do, with the object of ruining his client. For more

than half an hour he persisted in asking her questions with this
object; hinting that she was on friendly terms with Dockwrath;
asking her what pay she had received for her evidence; making her
acknowledge that she was being kept at free quarters, and on the
fat of the land. He even produced from her a list of the good
things she had eaten that morning at breakfast, and at last succeeded in obtaining information as to that small but indiscreet glass
of spirits. It was then, and then only, that poor Bridget became
discomposed. Beefsteaks, sausages, and pigs' fry, though they were
taken three times a day, were not disgraceful in her line of life;
but that little thimbleful of brandy, taken after much pressing and
in the openness of good fellowship, went sorely against the grain
with her. 'When one has to be badgered like this, one wants a
drop of something more than ordinary,' she said at last. And they
were the only words which she did say which proved any triumph
on the part of Mr. Chaffanbrass. But nevertheless Mr. Chaffanbrass
was not dissatisfied. Triumph, immediate triumph over a poor
maid-servant could hardly have been the object of a man who had
been triumphant in such matters for the last thirty years. Would
it not be practicable to make the jury doubt whether that woman
could be believed? That was the triumph he desired. As for himself, Mr. Chaffanbrass knew well enough that she had spoken
nothing but the truth. But had he so managed that the truth might
be made to look like falsehood,—or at any rate to have a doubtful
air? If he had done that, he had succeeded in the occupation of his
life, and was indifferent to his own triumph.

<hr/>

CHAPTER XXXII.

MR. FURNIVAL'S SPEECH.

ALL this as may be supposed disturbed Felix Graham not a little.
He perceived that each of those two witnesses had made a great
effort to speak the truth;—an honest, painful effort to speak the
truth, and in no way to go beyond it. His gall had risen within
him while he had listened to Mr. Furnival, and witnessed his success
in destroying the presence of mind of that weak wretch who was
endeavouring to do his best in the cause of justice. And again,
when Mr. Chaffanbrass had seized hold of that poor dram, and
used all his wit in deducing from it a self-condemnation from the
woman before him;—when the practised barrister had striven to
show that she was an habitual drunkard, dishonest, unchaste, evil in
all her habits, Graham had felt almost tempted to get up and take
her part. No doubt he had evinced this, for Chaffanbrass had
understood what was going on in his colleague's mind, and had

looked round at him from time to time with an air of scorn that had been almost unendurable.

And then it had become the duty of the prosecutors to prove the circumstances of the former trial. This was of course essentially necessary, seeing that the offence for which Lady Mason was now on her defence was perjury alleged to have been committed at that trial. And when this had been done at considerable length by Sir Richard Leatherham,—not without many interruptions from Mr. Furnival and much assistance from Mr. Steelyard,—it fell upon Felix Graham to show by cross-examination of Crook the attorney, what had been the nature and effect of Lady Mason's testimony. As he arose to do this, Mr. Chaffanbrass whispered into his ear, 'If you feel yourself unequal to it I'll take it up. I won't have her thrown over for any etiquette,—nor yet for any squeamishness.' To this Graham vouchsafed no answer. He would not even reply by a look, but he got up and did his work. At this point his conscience did not interfere with him, for the questions which he asked referred to facts which had really occurred. Lady Mason's testimony at that trial had been believed by everybody. The gentleman who had cross-examined her on the part of Joseph Mason, and who was now dead, had failed to shake her evidence. The judge who tried the case had declared to the jury that it was impossible to disbelieve her evidence. That judge was still living, a poor old bedridden man, and in the course of this latter trial his statement was given in evidence. There could be no doubt that at the time Lady Mason's testimony was taken as worthy of all credit. She had sworn that she had seen the three witnesses sign the codicil, and no one had then thrown discredit on her. The upshot of all was this, that the prosecuting side proved satisfactorily that such and such things had been sworn by Lady Mason; and Felix Graham on the side of the defence proved that, when she had so sworn, her word had been considered worthy of credence by the judge and by the jury, and had hardly been doubted even by the counsel opposed to her. All this really had been so, and Felix Graham used his utmost ingenuity in making clear to the court how high and unassailed had been the position which his client then held.

All this occupied the court till nearly four o'clock, and then as the case was over on the part of the prosecution, the question arose whether or no Mr. Furnival should address the jury on that evening, or wait till the following day. 'If your lordship will sit till seven o'clock,' said Mr. Furnival, 'I think I can undertake to finish what remarks I shall have to make by that time.' 'I should not mind sitting till nine for the pleasure of hearing Mr. Furnival,' said the judge, who was very anxious to escape from Alston on the day but one following. And thus it was decided that Mr. Furnival should commence his speech.

I have said that in spite of some previous hesitation his old fire had returned to him when he began his work in court on behalf of his client. If this had been so when that work consisted in the cross-examination of a witness, it was much more so with him now when he had to exhibit his own powers of forensic eloquence. When a man knows that he can speak with ease and energy, and that he will be listened to with attentive ears, it is all but impossible that he should fail to be enthusiastic, even though his cause be a bad one. It was so with him now. All his old fire came back upon him, and before he had done he had almost brought himself again to believe Lady Mason to be that victim of persecution as which he did not hesitate to represent her to the jury.

'Gentlemen of the jury,' he said, 'I never rose to plead a client's cause with more confidence than I now feel in pleading that of my friend Lady Mason. Twenty years ago I was engaged in defending her rights in this matter, and I then succeeded. I little thought at that time that I should be called on after so long an interval to renew my work. I little thought that the pertinacity of her opponent would hold out for such a period. I compliment him on the firmness of his character, on that equable temperament which has enabled him to sit through all this trial, and to look without dismay on the unfortunate lady whom he has considered it to be his duty to accuse of perjury. I did not think that I should live to fight this battle again. But so it is; and as I had but little doubt of victory then,—so have I none now. Gentlemen of the jury, I must occupy some of your time and of the time of the court in going through the evidence which has been adduced by my learned friend against my client; but I almost feel that I shall be detaining you unnecessarily, so sure I am that the circumstances, as they have been already explained to you, could not justify you in giving a verdict against her.'

As Mr. Furnival's speech occupied fully three hours, I will not trouble my readers with the whole of it. He began by describing the former trial, and giving his own recollections as to Lady Mason's conduct on that occasion. In doing this, he fully acknowledged on her behalf that she did give as evidence that special statement which her opponents now endeavoured to prove to have been false. 'If it were the case,' he said, 'that that codicil —or that pretended codicil, was not executed by old Sir Joseph Mason, and was not witnessed by Usbech, Kenneby, and Bridget Bolster,—then, in that case, Lady Mason has been guilty of perjury.' Mr. Furnival, as he made this acknowledgment, studiously avoided the face of Lady Mason. But as he made this assertion, almost everybody in the court except her own counsel did look at her. Joseph Mason opposite and Dockwrath fixed their gaze closely upon her. Sir Richard Leatherham and Mr. Steelyard turned their eyes towards her, probably without meaning to do so. The judge looked over his spectacles at her. Even Mr. Aram glanced round at her surreptitiously; and Lucius turned his face upon his mother's, almost with an air of triumph. But she bore it all without flinching;—bore it all without flinching, though the state of her mind at that moment must have been pitiable. And Mrs. Orme, who held her hand all the while, knew that it was so. The hand which rested in hers was twitched as it were convulsively, but the culprit gave no outward sign of her guilt.

Mr. Furnival then read much of the evidence given at the former trial, and especially showed how the witnesses had then failed to prove that Usbech had not been required to write his name. It was quite true, he said, that they had been equally unable to prove that he had done so; but that amounted to nothing; the 'onus probandi' lay with the accusing side. There was the signature, and it was for them to prove that it was not that which it pretended to be. Lady Mason had proved that it was so; and because that had then been held to be sufficient, they now, after twenty years, took this means of invalidating her testimony. From that he went to the evidence given at the present trial, beginning with the malice and interested motives of Dockwrath. Against three of them only was it needful that he should allege anything, seeing that the statements made by the others were in no way injurious to Lady Mason,—if the statements made by those three were not credible. Torrington, for instance, had proved that other deed; but what of that, if on the fatal 14th of July Sir Joseph Mason had executed two deeds? As to Dockwrath,—that his conduct had been interested and malicious there could be no doubt; and he submitted to the jury that he had shown himself to be a man unworthy of credit. As to Kenneby, —that poor weak creature, as Mr. Furnival in his mercy called him, —he, Mr. Furnival, could not charge his conscience with saying that he believed him to have been guilty of any falsehood. On the contrary, he conceived that Kenneby had endeavoured to tell the truth. But he was one of those men whose minds were so inconsequential that they literally did not know truth from falsehood. He had not intended to lie when he told the jury that he was not quite sure he had never witnessed two signatures by Sir Joseph Mason on the same day, nor did he lie when he told them again that he had witnessed three. He had meant to declare the truth; but he was, unfortunately, a man whose evidence could not be of much service in any case of importance, and could be of no service whatever in a criminal charge tried, as was done in this instance, more than twenty years after the alleged commission of the offence. With regard to Bridget Bolster, he had no hesitation whatever in telling the jury that she was a woman unworthy of belief,—unworthy of that credit which the jury must place in her before they could convict any one on her unaided testimony. It must have been clear to them all that she had come into court drilled and instructed to make one point-blank statement, and to stick to that. She had refused to give any evidence as to her own signature. She would not even look at her own name as written by herself; but had contented herself with repeating over and over again those few words which she had been instructed so to say;—the statement namely, that she had never put her hand to more than one deed.

Then he addressed himself, as he concluded his speech, to that part of the subject which was more closely personal to Lady Mason herself. 'And now, gentlemen of the jury,' he said, 'before I can dismiss you from your weary day's work, I must ask you to regard the position of the lady who has been thus accused, and the amount of probability of her guilt which you may assume from the nature of her life. I shall call no witnesses as to her character, for I will not submit her friends to the annoyance of those questions which the gentlemen opposite might feel it their duty to put to them. Circumstances have occurred—so much I will tell you, and so much no doubt you all personally know, though it is not in evidence before you;—circumstances have occurred which would make it cruel on my part to place her old friend Sir Peregrine Orme in that box. The story, could I tell it to you, is one full of romance, but full also of truth and affection. But though Sir Peregrine Orme is not here, there sits his daughter by Lady Mason's side,—there she has sat through this tedious trial, giving comfort to the woman that she loves,—and there she will sit till your verdict shall have made her further presence here unnecessary. His lordship and my learned friend there will tell you that you cannot take that as evidence of character. They will be justified in so telling you; but I, on the other hand, defy you not to take it as such evidence. Let us make what laws we will, they cannot take precedence of human nature. There too sits my client's son. You will remember that at the beginning of this trial the solicitor-general expressed a wish that he were not here. I do not know whether you then responded to that wish, but I believe I may take it for granted that you do not do so now. Had any woman dear to either of you been so placed through the malice of an enemy, would you have hesitated to sit by her in her hour of trial? Had you doubted of her innocence you might have hesitated; for who could endure to hear announced in a crowded court like this the guilt of a mother or a wife? But he has no doubt. Nor, I believe, has any living being in this court,—unless it be her kinsman opposite, whose life for the last twenty years has been made wretched by a wicked longing after the patrimony of his brother.

'Gentlemen of the jury, there sits my client with as loving a friend on one side as ever woman had, and with her only child on the other. During the incidents of this trial the nature of the life she has led during the last twenty years,—since the period of that terrible crime with which she is charged,—has been proved before you. I may fearlessly ask you whether so fair a life is compatible with the idea of guilt so foul? I have known her intimately during all those years,—not as a lawyer, but as a friend,—and I confess that the audacity of this man Dockwrath, in assailing such a character with such an accusation, strikes me almost with admiration. What! Forgery!—for that, gentlemen of the jury, is the crime with which she is substantially charged. Look at her, as she sits there! That she, at the age of twenty, or not much more,—she who had so well performed the duties of her young life, that she should have forged a will,—have traced one signature after another in such a manner as to have deceived all those lawyers who were on her track immediately after her husband's death! For, mark you, if this be true, with her own hand she must have done it! There was no accomplice there. Look at her! Was she a forger? Was she a woman to deceive the sharp bloodhounds of the law? Could she, with that young baby on her bosom, have wrested from such as him'—and as he spoke he pointed with his finger, but with a look of unutterable scorn, to Joseph Mason, who was sitting opposite to him—'that fragment of his old father's property which he coveted so sorely? Where had she learned such skilled artifice? .Gentlemen, such ingenuity in crime as that has never yet been proved in a court of law, even against those who have spent a life of wretchedness in acquiring such skill; and now you are asked to believe that such a deed was done by a young wife, of whom all that you know is that her conduct in every other respect had been beyond all praise! Gentlemen, I might have defied you to believe this accusation had it even been supported by testimony of a high character. Even in such case you would have felt that there was more behind than had been brought to your knowledge. But now, having seen, as you have, of what nature are the witnesses on whose testimony she has been impeached, it is impossible that you should believe this story. Had Lady Mason been a woman steeped in guilt from her infancy, had she been noted for cunning and fraudulent ingenuity, had she been known as an expert forger, you would not have convicted her on this indictment, having had before you the malice and greed of Dockwrath, the stupidity—I may almost call it idiocy, of Kenneby, and the dogged resolution to conceal the truth evinced by the woman Bolster. With strong evidence you could not have believed such a charge against so excellent a lady. With such evidence as you have had before you, you could not have believed the charge against a previously convicted felon.

'And what has been the object of this terrible persecution,—of the dreadful punishment which has been inflicted on this poor lady?

For remember, though you cannot pronounce her guilty, her sufferings have been terribly severe. Think what it must have been
for a woman with habits such as hers, to have looked forward for
long, long weeks to such a martyrdom as this! Think what she
must have suffered in being dragged here and subjected to the gaze
of all the county as a suspected felon! Think what must have
been her feelings when I told her, not knowing how deep an ingenuity might be practised against her, that I must counsel her to
call to her aid the unequalled talents of my friend Mr. Chaffanbrass'——'Unequalled no longer, but far surpassed,' whispered
Chaffanbrass, in a voice that was audible through all the centre of
the court. 'Her punishment has been terrible,' continued Mr.
Furnival. 'After what she has gone through, it may well be
doubted whether she can continue to reside at that sweet spot
which has aroused such a feeling of avarice in the bosom of her
kinsman. You have heard that Sir Joseph Mason had promised his
eldest son that Orley Farm should form a part of his inheritance.
It may be that the old man did make such a promise. If so, he
thought fit to break it. But is it not wonderful that a man wealthy
as is Mr. Mason—for his fortune is large ; who has never wanted
anything that money can buy ; a man for whom his father did so
much,—that he should be stirred up by disappointed avarice to
carry in his bosom for twenty years so bitter a feeling of rancour
against those who are nearest to him by blood and ties of family !
Gentlemen, it has been a fearful lesson ; but it is one which neither
you nor I will ever forget !

'And now I shall leave my client's case in your hands. As to
the verdict which you will give, I have no apprehension. You
know as well as I do that she has not been guilty of this terrible
crime. That you will so pronounce I do not for a moment doubt.
But I do hope that that verdict will be accompanied by some expression on your part which may show to the world at large how
great has been the wickedness displayed in the accusation.'

And yet as he sat down he knew that she had been guilty! To
his ear her guilt had never been confessed ; but yet he knew that
it was so, and, knowing that, he had been able to speak as though
her innocence were a thing of course. That those witnesses had
spoken truth he also knew, and yet he had been able to hold them
up to the execration of all around them as though they had committed the worst of crimes from the foulest of motives ! And more
than this, stranger than this, worse than this,—when the legal world
knew—as the legal world soon did know—that all this had been so,
the legal world found no fault with Mr. Furnival, conceiving that
he had done his duty by his client in a manner becoming an
English barrister and an English gentleman.

CHAPTER XXXIII.

It was late when that second day's work was over, and when Mrs. Orme and Lady Mason again found themselves in the Hamworth carriage. They had sat in court from ten in the morning till past seven, with a short interval of a few minutes in the middle of the day, and were weary to the very soul when they left it. Lucius again led out his mother, and as he did so he expressed to her in strong language his approval of Mr. Furnival's speech. At last some one had spoken out on his mother's behalf in that tone which should have been used from the first. He had been very angry with Mr. Furnival, thinking that the barrister had lost sight of his mother's honour, and that he was playing with her happiness. But now he was inclined to forgive him. Now at last the truth had been spoken in eloquent words, and the persecutors of his mother had been addressed in language such as it was fitting that they should hear. To him the last two hours had been two hours of triumph, and as he passed through the hall of the court he whispered in his mother's ear that now, at last, as he hoped, her troubles were at an end.

And another whisper had been spoken as they passed through that hall. Mrs. Orme went out leaning on the arm of her son, but on the other side of her was Mr. Aram. He had remained in his seat till they had begun to move, and then he followed them. Mrs. Orme was already half way across the court when he made his way up to her side and very gently touched her arm.

'Sir?' said she, looking round.

'Do not let her be too sure,' he said. 'Do not let her be over confident. All that may go for nothing with a jury.' Then he lifted his hat and left her.

All that go for nothing with a jury! She hardly understood this, but yet she felt that it all should go for nothing if right were done. Her mind was not argumentative, nor yet perhaps was her sense of true justice very acute. When Sir Peregrine had once hinted that it would be well that the criminal should be pronounced guilty, because in truth she had been guilty, Mrs. Orme by no means agreed with him. But now, having heard how those wretched witnesses had been denounced, knowing how true had been the words they had spoken, knowing how false were those assurances of innocence with which Mr. Furnival had been so fluent, she felt something of that spirit which had actuated Sir Peregrine, and had almost thought that justice demanded a verdict against her friend.

'Do not let her be over-confident,' Mr. Aram had said. But in truth Mrs. Orme, as she had listened to Mr. Furnival's speech, had become almost confident that Lady Mason would be acquitted. It had seemed to her impossible that any jury should pronounce her to be guilty after that speech. The state of her mind as she listened to it had been very painful. Lady Mason's hand had rested in her own during a great portion of it; and it would have been natural that she should give some encouragement to her companion by a touch, by a slight pressure, as the warm words of praise fell from the lawyer's mouth. But how could she do so, knowing that the praise was false? It was not possible to her to show her friendship by congratulating her friend on the success of a lie. Lady Mason also had, no doubt, felt this, for after a while her hand had been withdrawn, and they had both listened in silence, giving no signs to each other as to their feelings on the subject.

But as they sat together in the carriage Lucius did give vent to his feelings. 'I cannot understand why all that should not have been said before, and said in a manner to have been as convincing as it was to-day.'

'I suppose there was no opportunity before the trial,' said Mrs. Orme, feeling that she must say something, but feeling also how impossible it was to speak on the subject with any truth in the presence both of Lady Mason and her son.

'But an occasion should have been made,' said Lucius. 'It is monstrous that my mother should have been subjected to this accusation for months and that no one till now should have spoken out to show how impossible it is that she should have been guilty.'

'Ah! Lucius, you do not understand,' said his mother.

'And I hope I never may,' said he. 'Why did not the jury get up in their seats at once and pronounce their verdict when Mr. Furnival's speech was over? Why should they wait there, giving another day of prolonged trouble, knowing as they must do what their verdict will be? To me all this is incomprehensible, seeing that no good can in any way come from it.'

And so he went on, striving to urge his companions to speak upon a subject which to them did not admit of speech in his presence. It was very painful to them, for in addressing Mrs. Orme he almost demanded from her some expression of triumph. 'You at least have believed in her innocence,' he said at last, 'and have not been ashamed to show that you did so.'

'Lucius,' said his mother, 'we are very weary; do not speak to us now. Let us rest till we are at home.' Then they closed their eyes and there was silence till the carriage drove up to the door of Orley Farm House.

The two ladies immediately went up-stairs, but Lucius, with more cheerfulness about him than he had shown for months past, remained below to give orders for their supper. It had been a joy to him to hear Joseph Mason and Dockwrath exposed, and to listen to those words which had so clearly told the truth as to his mother's history. All that torrent of indignant eloquence had been to him an enumeration of the simple facts,—of the facts as he knew them to be,—of the facts as they would now be made plain to all the world. At last the day had come when the cloud would be blown away. He, looking down from the height of his superior intellect on the folly of those below him, had been indignant at the great delay;—but that he would now forgive.

They had not been long in the house, perhaps about fifteen minutes, when Mrs. Orme returned down stairs and gently entered the dining-room. He was still there, standing with his back to the fire and thinking over the work of the day.

'Your mother will not come down this evening, Mr. Mason.'

'Not come down?'

'No; she is very tired,—very tired indeed. I fear you hardly know how much she has gone through.'

'Shall I go to her?' said Lucius.

'No, Mr. Mason, do not do that. I will return to her now. And —but;—in a few minutes, Mr. Mason, I will come back to you again, for I shall have something to say to you.'

'You will have tea here?'

'I don't know. I think not. When I have spoken to you I will go back to your mother. I came down now in order that you might not wait for us.' And then she left the room and again went up-stairs. It annoyed him that his mother should thus keep away from him, but still he did not think that there was any special reason for it. Mrs. Orme's manner had been strange; but then everything around them in these days was strange, and it did not occur to him that Mrs. Orme would have aught to say in her promised interview which would bring to him any new cause for sorrow.

Lady Mason, when Mrs. Orme returned to her, was sitting exactly in the position in which she had been left. Her bonnet was off and was lying by her side, and she was seated in a large arm-chair, again holding both her hands to the sides of her head. No attempt had been made to smooth her hair or to remove the dust and soil which had come from the day's long sitting in the court. She was a woman very careful in her toilet, and scrupulously nice in all that touched her person. But now all that had been neglected, and her whole appearance was haggard and dishevelled.

'You have not told him?' she said.

'No; I have not told him yet; but I have bidden him expect me. He knows that I am coming to him.'

'And how did he look?'

'I did not see his face.' And then there was silence between them for a few minutes, during which Mrs. Orme stood at the back of Lady Mason's chair with her hand on Lady Mason's shoulder. 'Shall I go now, dear?' said Mrs. Orme.

'No; stay a moment; not yet. Oh, Mrs. Orme!'

'You will find that you will be stronger and better able to bear it when it has been done.'

'Stronger! Why should I wish to be stronger? How will he bear it?'

'It will be a blow to him, of course.'

'It will strike him to the ground, Mrs. Orme. I shall have murdered him. I do not think that he will live when he knows that he is so disgraced.'

'He is a man, and will bear it as a man should do. Shall I do anything for you before I go?'

'Stay a moment. Why must it be to-night?'

'He must not be in the court to-morrow. And what difference will one day make? He must know it when the property is given up.'

Then there was a knock at the door, and a girl entered with a decanter, two wine-glasses, and a slice or two of bread and butter. 'You must drink that,' said Mrs. Orme, pouring out a glass of wine.

'And you?'

'Yes, I will take some too. There. I shall be stronger now. Nay, Lady Mason, you shall drink it. And now if you will take my advice you will go to bed.'

'You will come to me again?'

'Yes; directly it is over. Of course I shall come to you. Am I not to stay here all night?'

'But him;—I will not see him. He is not to come.'

'That will be as he pleases.'

'No. You promised that. I cannot see him when he knows what I have done for him.'

'Not to hear him say that he forgives you?'

'He will not forgive me. You do not know him. Could you bear to look at your boy if you had disgraced him for ever?'

'Whatever I might have done he would not desert me. Nor will Lucius desert you. Shall I go now?'

'Ah, me! Would that I were in my grave!'

Then Mrs. Orme bent over her and kissed her, pressed both her hands, then kissed her again, and silently creeping out of the room made her way once more slowly down the stairs.

Mrs. Orme, as will have been seen, was sufficiently anxious to perform the task which she had given herself, but yet her heart

sank within her as she descended to the parlour. It was indeed a
terrible commission, and her readiness to undertake it had come not
from any feeling on her own part that she was fit for the work and
could do it without difficulty, but from the eagerness with which
she had persuaded Lady Mason that the thing must be done by
some one. And now who else could do it? In Sir Peregrine's
present state it would have been a cruelty to ask him; and then
his feelings towards Lucius in the matter were not tender as were
those of Mrs. Orme. She had been obliged to promise that she
herself would do it, or otherwise she could not have urged the
doing. And now the time had come. Immediately on their return
to the house Mrs. Orme had declared that the story should be told
at once; and then Lady Mason, sinking into the chair from which
she had not since risen, had at length agreed that it should be so.
The time had now come, and Mrs. Orme, whose footsteps down the
stairs had not been audible, stood for a moment with the handle of
the door in her hand.

Had it been possible she also would now have put it off till the
morrow,—would have put it off till any other time than that which
was then present. All manner of thoughts crowded on her during
those few seconds. In what way should she do it? What words
should she use? How should she begin? She was to tell this
young man that his mother had committed a crime of the very
blackest dye, and now she felt that she should have prepared herself and resolved in what fashion this should be done. Might it not
be well, she asked herself for one moment, that she should take the
night to think of it and then see him in the morning? The idea,
however, only lasted her for a moment, and then, fearing lest she
might allow herself to be seduced into some weakness, she turned
the handle and entered the room.

He was still standing with his back to the fire, leaning against
the mantelpiece, and thinking over the occurrences of the day that
was past. His strongest feeling now was one of hatred to Joseph
Mason,—of hatred mixed with thorough contempt. What must
men say of him after such a struggle on his part to ruin the fame
of a lady and to steal the patrimony of a brother! 'Is she still determined not to come down?' he said as soon as he saw Mrs. Orme.

'No; she will not come down to-night, Mr. Mason. I have
something that I must tell you.'

'What! is she ill? Has it been too much for her?'

'Mr. Mason,' she said, 'I hardly know how to do what I have
undertaken.' And he could see that she actually trembled as she
spoke to him.

'What is it, Mrs. Orme? Is it anything about the property? I
think you need hardly be afraid of me. I believe I may say I
could bear anything of that kind.'

'Mr. Mason——' And then again she stopped herself. How was she to speak this horrible word?

'Is it anything about the trial?' He was now beginning to be frightened, feeling that something terrible was coming; but still of the absolute truth he had no suspicion.

'Oh! Mr. Mason, if it were possible that I could spare you I would do so. If there were any escape,—any way in which it might be avoided.'

'What is it?' said he. And now his voice was hoarse and low, for a feeling of fear had come upon him. 'I am a man and can bear it, whatever it is.'

'You must be a man then, for it is very terrible. Mr. Mason, that will, you know——'

'You mean the codicil?'

'The will that gave you the property——'

'Yes.'

'It was not done by your father.'

'Who says so?'

'It is too sure. It was not done by him,—nor by them,—those other people who were in the court to-day.'

'But who says so? How is it known? If my father did not sign it, it is a forgery; and who forged it? Those wretches have bought over some one and you have been deceived, Mrs. Orme. It is not of the property I am thinking, but of my mother. If it were as you say, my mother must have known it?'

'Ah! yes.'

'And you mean that she did know it; that she knew it was a forgery?'

'Oh! Mr. Mason.'

'Heaven and earth! Let me go to her. If she were to tell me so herself I would not believe it of her. Ah! she has told you?'

'Yes; she has told me.'

'Then she is mad. This has been too much for her, and her brain has gone with it. Let me go to her, Mrs. Orme.'

'No, no; you must not go her.' And Mrs. Orme put herself directly before the door. 'She is not mad,—not now. Then, at that time, we must think she was so. It is not so now.'

'I cannot understand you.' And he put his left hand up to his forehead as though to steady his thoughts. 'I do not understand you. If the will be a forgery, who did it?'

This question she could not answer at the moment. She was still standing against the door, and her eyes fell to the ground. 'Who did it?' he repeated. 'Whose hand wrote my father's name?'

'You must be merciful, Mr. Mason.'

'Merciful;—to whom?'

'To your mother.'

'Merciful to my mother! Mrs. Orme, speak out to me. If the will was forged, who forged it? You cannot mean to tell me that she did it!'

She did not answer him at the moment in words, but coming close up to him she took both his hands in hers, and then looked steadfastly up into his eyes. His face had now become almost convulsed with emotion, and his brow was very black. 'Do you wish me to believe that my mother forged the will herself?' Then again he paused, but she said nothing. 'Woman, it's a lie,' he exclaimed; and then tearing his hands from her, shaking her off, and striding away with quick footsteps, he threw himself on a sofa that stood in the furthest part of the room.

She paused for a moment and then followed him very gently. She followed him and stood over him in silence for a moment, as he lay with his face from her. 'Mr. Mason,' she said at last, 'you told me that you would bear this like a man.'

But he made her no answer, and she went on. 'Mr. Mason, it is, as I tell you. Years and years ago, when you were a baby, and when she thought that your father was unjust to you—for your sake,—to remedy that injustice, she did this thing.'

'What; forged his name! It must be a lie. Though an angel came to tell me so, it would be a lie! What; my mother!' And now he turned round and faced her, still however lying on the sofa.

'It is true, Mr. Mason. Oh, how I wish that it were not! But you must forgive her. It is years ago, and she has repented of it, Sir Peregrine has forgiven her,—and I have done so.'

And then she told him the whole story. She told him why the marriage had been broken off, and described to him the manner in which the truth had been made known to Sir Peregrine. It need hardly be said, that in doing so, she dealt as softly as was possible with his mother's name; but yet she told him everything. 'She wrote it herself, in the night.'

'What all; all the names herself?'

'Yes, all.'

'Mrs. Orme it cannot be so. I will not believe it. To me it is impossible. That you believe it I do not doubt, but I cannot. Let me go to her. I will go to her myself. But even should she say so herself, I will not believe it.'

But she would not let him go up-stairs even though he attempted to move her from the door, almost with violence. 'No; not till you say that you will forgive her and be gentle with her. And it must not be to-night. We will be up early in the morning, and you can see her before we go ;—if you will be gentle to her.'

He still persisted that he did not believe the story, but it became clear to her, by degrees, that the meaning of it all had at last sunk into his mind, and that he did believe it. Over and over again she told him all that she knew, explaining to him what his mother had suffered, making him perceive why she had removed herself out of his hands, and had leant on others for advice. And she told him also that though they still hoped that the jury might acquit her, the property must be abandoned.

'I will leave the house this night if you wish it,' he said.

'When it is all over, when she has been acquitted and shall have gone away, then let it be done. Mr. Mason, you will go with her; will you not?' and then again there was a pause.

'Mrs. Orme, it is impossible that I should say now what I may do. It seems to me as though I could not live through it. I do not believe it. I cannot believe it.'

As soon as she had exacted a promise from him that he would not go to his mother, at any rate without further notice, she herself went up stairs and found Lady Mason lying on her bed. At first Mrs. Orme thought that she was asleep, but no such comfort had come to the poor woman. 'Does he know it?' she asked.

Mrs. Orme's task for that night was by no means yet done. After remaining for a while with Lady Mason she again returned to Lucius, and was in this way a bearer of messages between them. There was at last no question as to doubting the story. He did believe it. He could not avoid the necessity for such belief. 'Yes,' he said, when Mrs. Orme spoke again of his leaving the place, 'I will go and hide myself; and as for her——'

, 'But you will go with her,—if the jury do not say that she was guilty——'

'Oh, Mrs. Orme!'

'If they do, you will come back for her, when the time of her punishment is over? She is still your mother, Mr. Mason.'

At last the work of the night was done, and the two ladies went to their beds. The understanding was that Lucius should see his mother before they started in the morning, but that he should not again accompany them to the court. Mrs. Orme's great object had been,—her great object as regarded the present moment,—to prevent his presence in court when the verdict should be given. In this she had succeeded. She could now wish for an acquittal with a clear conscience; and could as it were absolve the sinner within her own heart, seeing that there was no longer any doubt as to the giving up of the property. Whatever might be the verdict of the jury Joseph Mason of Groby would, without doubt, obtain the property which belonged to him.

'Good-night, Mr. Mason,' Mrs. Orme said at last, as she gave him her hand.

'Good-night. I believe that in my madness I spoke to you tonight like a brute.'

'No, no. It was nothing. I did not think of it.'

Lucius Mason, as he leaned on the Gate that was no longer his own.

' When you think of how it was with me, you will forgive me.'

She pressed his hand and again told him that she had not thought of it. It was nothing. And indeed it had been as nothing to her. There may be moments in a man's life when any words may be forgiven, even though they be spoken to a woman.

When Mrs. Orme was gone, he stood for a while perfectly motionless in the dining-room, and then coming out into the hall he opened the front door, and taking his hat, went out into the night. It was still winter, but the night, though cold and very dark, was fine, and the air was sharp with the beginning frost. Leaving the door open he walked forth, and passing out on to the road went down from thence to the gate. It had been his constant practice to walk up and down from his own hall door to his own gate on the high road, perhaps comforting himself too warmly with the reflection that the ground on which he walked was all his own. He had no such comfort now, as he made his way down the accustomed path and leaned upon the gate, thinking over what he had heard.

A forger! At some such hour as this, with patient premeditated care, she had gone to work and committed one of the vilest crimes known to man. And this was his mother! And he, he, Lucius Mason, had been living for years on the fruit of this villainy;—had been so living till this terrible day of retribution had come upon him! I fear that at that moment he thought more of his own misery than he did of hers, and hardly considered, as he surely should have done, that mother's love which had led to all this guilt. And for a moment he resolved that he would not go back to the house. His head, he said to himself, should never again rest under a roof which belonged of right to Joseph Mason. He had injured Joseph Mason;—had injured him innocently, indeed, as far as he himself was concerned; but he had injured him greatly, and therefore now hated him all the more. ' He shall have it instantly,' he said, and walked forth into the high road as though he would not allow his feet to rest again on his brother's property.

But he was forced to remember that this could not be so. His mother's trial was not yet over, and even in the midst of his own personal trouble he remembered that the verdict to her was still a matter of terrible import. He would not let it be known that he had abandoned the property, at any rate till that verdict had been given. And then as he moved back to the house he tried to think in what way it would become him to behave to his mother. ' She can never be my mother again,' he said to himself. They were terrible words;—but then was not his position very terrible?

And when at last he had bolted the front door, going through the accustomed task mechanically, and had gone up stairs to his own room, he had failed to make up his mind on this subject. Perhaps it would be better that he should not see her. What could he say

to her? What word of comfort could he speak? It was not only
that she had beggared him! Nay; it was not that at all! But she
had doomed him to a life of disgrace which no effort of his own could
wipe away. And then as he threw himself on his bed he thought
of Sophia Furnival. Would she share his disgrace with him? Was
it possible that there might be solace there?

Quite impossible, we should say, who know her well.

CHAPTER XXXIV.

YOUNG LOCHINVAR.

JUDGE STAVELEY, whose court had not been kept siting to a late
hour by any such eloquence as that of Mr. Furnival, had gone home
before the business of the other court had closed. Augustus, who
was his father's marshal, remained for his friend, and had made his
way in among the crowd, so as to hear the end of the speech.

' Don't wait dinner for us,' he had said to his father. ' If you do
you will be hating us all the time; and we sha'n't be there till
between eight and nine.'

' I should be sorry to hate you,' said the judge, ' and so I won't.'
When therefore Felix Graham escaped from the court at about half-
past seven, the two young men were able to take their own time
and eat their dinner together comfortably, enjoying their bottle of
champagne between them perhaps more thoroughly than they would
have done had the judge and Mrs. Staveley shared it with them.

But Felix had something of which to think besides the champagne—something which was of more consequence to him even
than the trial in which he was engaged. Madeline had promised
that she would meet him that evening;—or rather had not so
promised. When asked to do so she had not refused, but even
while not refusing had reminded him that her mother would be
there. Her manner to him had, he thought, been cold, though she
had not been ungracious. Upon the whole, he could not make up
his mind to expect success. ' Then he must have been a fool!' the
reader learned in such matters will say. The reader learned in
such matters is, I think, right. In that respect he was a fool.

' I suppose we must give the governor the benefit of our company
over his wine,' said Augustus, as soon as their dinner was over.

' l suppose we ought to do so.'

' And why not? Is there any objection?'

' To tell the truth,' said Graham, ' I have an appointment which
I am very anxious to keep.'

' An appointment? Where? Here at Noningsby, do you mean?'

' In this house. But yet I cannot say that it is absoutely an appointment. I am going to ask your sister what my fate is to be.'

' And that is the appointment! Very well, my dear fellow; and may God prosper you. If you can convince the governor that it is all right, I shall make no objection. I wish, for Madeline's sake, that you had not such a terrible bee in your bonnet.'

' And you will go to the judge alone?'

' Oh, yes. I'll tell him——. What shall I tell him?'

' The truth, if you will. Good-bye, old fellow. You will not see me again to-night, nor yet to-morrow in this house, unless I am more fortunate than I have any right to hope to be.'

' Faint heart never won fair lady, you know,' said Augustus.

' My heart is faint enough then; but nevertheless I shall say what I have got to say.' And then he got up from the table.

' If you don't come down to us,' said Augustus, ' I shall come up to you. But may God speed you. And now I'll go to the governor.'

Felix made his way from the small breakfast-parlour in which they had dined across the hall into the drawing-room, and there he found Lady Staveley alone. ' So the trial is not over yet, Mr. Graham?' she said.

' No; there will be another day of it.'

' And what will be the verdict? Is it possible that she really forged the will?'

' Ah! that I cannot say. You know that I am one of her counsel, Lady Staveley?'

' Yes; I should have remembered that, and been more discreet. If you are looking for Madeline, Mr. Graham, I think that she is in the library.'

' Oh! thank you;—in the library.' And then Felix got himself out of the drawing-room into the hall again not in the most graceful manner. He might have gone direct from the drawing-room to the library, but this he did not remember. It was very odd, he thought, that Lady Staveley, of whose dislike to him he had felt sure, should have thus sent him direct to her daughter, and have become a party, as it were, to an appointment between them. But he had not much time to think of this before he found himself in the room. There, sure enough, was Madeline waiting to listen to his story. She was seated when he entered, with her back to him; but as she heard him she rose, and, after pausing for a moment, she stepped forward to meet him.

' You and Augustus were very late to-day,' she said.

' Yes. I was kept there, and he was good enough to wait for me.'

' You said you wanted to——speak to me,' she said, hesitating a little, but yet very little; ' to speak to me alone; and so mamma said I had better come in here. I hope you are not vexed that I should have told her.'

' Certainly not, Miss Staveley.'

' Because I have no secrets from mamma.'

' Nor do I wish that anything should be secret. I hate all secrecies. Miss Staveley, your father knows of my intention.'

On this point Madeline did not feel it to be necessary to say anything. Of course her father knew of the intention. Had she not received her father's sanction for listening to Mr. Graham she would not have been alone with him in the library. It might be that the time would come in which she would explain all this to her lover, but that time had not come yet. So when he spoke of her father she remained silent, and allowing her eyes to fall to the ground she stood before him, waiting to hear his question.

' Miss Staveley,' he said;—and he was conscious himself of being very awkward. Much more so, indeed, than there was any need, for Madeline was not aware that he was awkward. In her eyes he was quite master of the occasion, and seemed to have everything his own way. He had already done all that was difficult in the matter, and had done it without any awkwardness. He had already made himself master of her heart, and it was only necessary now that he should enter in and take possession. The ripe fruit had fallen, as Miss Furnival had once chosen to express it, and there he was to pick it up,—if only he considered it worth his trouble to do so. That manner of the picking would not signify much, as Madeline thought. That he desired to take it into his garner and preserve it for his life's use was everything to her, but the method of his words at the present moment was not much. He was her lord and master. He was the one man who had conquered and taken possession of her spirit; and as to his being awkward, there was not much in that. Nor do I say that he was awkward. He spoke his mind in honest, plain terms, and I do not know he could have done better.

' Miss Staveley,' he said, ' in asking you to see me alone, I have made a great venture. I am indeed risking all that I most value.' And then he paused, as though he expected that she would speak. But she still kept her eyes upon the ground, and still stood silent before him. ' I cannot but think you must guess my purpose,' he said, ' though I acknowledge that I have had nothing that can warrant me in hoping for a favourable answer. There is my hand; if you can take it you need not doubt that you have my heart with it.' And then he held out to her his broad, right hand.

Madeline still stood silent before him and still fixed her eyes upon the ground, but very slowly she raised her little hand and allowed her soft slight fingers to rest upon his open palm. It was as though she thus affixed her legal signature and seal to the deed of gift. She had not said a word to him; not a word of love or a word of assent; but no such word was now necessary.

' Madeline, my own Madeline,' he said; and then taking unfair advantage of the fingers which she had given him he drew her to his breast and folded her in his arms.

It was nearly an hour after this when he returned to the drawing-room. 'Do go in now,' she said. 'You must not wait any longer; indeed you must go.'

'And you——; you will come in presently.'

'It is already nearly eleven. No, I will not show myself again to-night. Mamma will soon come up to me, I know. Good-night, Felix. Do you go now, and I will follow you.' And then after some further little ceremony he left her.

When he entered the drawing-room Lady Staveley was there, and the judge with his teacup beside him, and Augustus standing with his back to the fire. Felix walked up to the circle, and taking a chair sat down, but at the moment said nothing.

'You didn't get any wine after your day's toil, Master Graham,' said the judge.

'Indeed I did, sir. We had some champagne.'

'Champagne, had you? Then I ought to have waited for my guest, for I got none. You had a long day of it in court.'

'Yes, indeed, sir.'

'And I am afraid not very satisfactory.' To this Graham made no immediate answer, but he could not refrain from thinking that the day, taken altogether, had been satisfactory to him.

And then Baker came into the room, and going close up to Lady Staveley, whispered something in her ear. 'Oh, ah, yes,' said Lady Staveley. 'I must wish you good night, Mr. Graham.' And she took his hand, pressing it very warmly. But though she wished him good night then, she saw him again before he went to bed. It was a family in which all home affairs were very dear, and a new son could not be welcomed into it without much expression of affection.

'Well, sir! and how have you sped since dinner?' the judge asked as soon as the door was closed behind his wife.

'I have proposed to your daughter and she has accepted me.' And as he said so he rose from the chair in which had just now seated himself.

'Then, my boy, I hope you will make her a good husband;' and the judge gave him his hand.

'I will try to do so. I cannot but feel, however, how little right I had to ask her, seeing that I am likely to be so poor a man.'

'Well, well, well—we will talk of that another time. At present we will only sing your triumphs—

'So faithful in love, and so dauntless in war,
There never was knight like the young Lochinvar.'

'Felix, my dear fellow, I congratulate you with all my heart,' said Augustus. 'But I did not know you were good as a warrior.'

'Ah, but he is though,' said the judge. 'What do you think of his wounds? And if all that I hear be true, he has other battles on hand. But we must not speak about that till this poor lady's trial is over.'

'I need hardly tell you, sir,' said Graham, with that sheep-like air which a man always carries on such occasions, 'that I regard myself as the most fortunate man in the world.'

'Quite unnecessary,' said the judge. 'On such occasions that is taken as a matter of course.' And then the conversation between them for the next ten minutes was rather dull and flat.

Up-stairs the same thing was going on, in a manner somewhat more animated, between the mother and daughter,—for ladies on such occasions can be more animated than men.

'Oh, mamma, you must love him,' Madeline said.

'Yes, my dear; of course I shall love him now. Your papa says that he is very clever.'

'I know papa likes him. I knew that from the very first. I think that was the reason why——'

'And I suppose clever people are the best,—that is to say, if they are good.'

'And isn't he good?'

'Well—I hope so. Indeed, I'm sure he is. Mr. Orme was a very good young man too;—but it's no good talking about him now.'

'Mamma, that never could have come to pass.'

'Very well, my dear. It's over now, and of course all that I looked for was your happiness.'

'I know that, mamma; and indeed I am very happy. I'm sure I could not ever have liked any once else since I first knew him.'

Lady Staveley still thought it very odd, but she had nothing else to say. As regarded the pecuniary considerations of the affair she left them altogether to her husband, feeling that in this way she could relieve herself from misgivings which might otherwise make her unhappy. 'And after all I don't know that his ugliness signifies,' she said to herself. And so she made up her mind that she would be loving and affectionate to him, and sat up till she heard his footsteps in the passage, in order that she might speak to him, and make him welcome to the privileges of a son-in-law.

'Mr. Graham,' she said, opening her door as he passed by.

'Of course she has told you,' said Felix.

'Oh yes, she has told me. We don't have many secrets in this house. And I'm sure I congratulate you with all my heart; and I think you have got the very best girl in all the world. Of course I'm her mother; but I declare, if I was to talk of her for a week, I could not say anything of her but good.'

'I know how fortunate I am.'

'Yes, you are fortunate. For there is nothing in the world equal to a loving wife who will do her duty. And I'm sure you'll be good to her.'

'I will endeavour to be so.'

'A man must be very bad indeed who would be bad to her,—and I don't think that of you. And it's a great thing, Mr. Graham, that Madeline should have loved a man of whom her papa is so fond. I don't know what you have done to the judge, I'm sure.' This she said, remembering in the innocence of her heart that Mr. Arbuthnot had been a son-in-law rather after her own choice, and that the judge always declared that his eldest daughter's husband had seldom much to say for himself.

'And I hope that Madeline's mother will receive me as kindly as Madeline's father,' said he, taking Lady Staveley's hand and pressing it.

'Indeed I will. I will love you very dearly if you will let me. My girls' husbands are the same to me as sons.' Then she put up her face and he kissed it, and so they wished each other good night.

He found Augustus in his own room, and they two had hardly sat themselves down over the fire, intending to recall the former scenes which had taken place in that very room, when a knock was heard at the door, and Mrs. Baker entered.

'And so it's all settled, Mr. Felix,' said she.

'Yes,' said he; 'all settled.'

'Well now! didn't I know it from the first?'

'Then what a wicked old woman you were not to, tell,' said Augustus.

'That's all very well, Master Augustus. How would you like me to tell of you;—for I could, you know?'

'You wicked old woman, you couldn't do anything of the kind.'

'Oh, couldn't I? But I defy all the world to say a word of Miss Madeline but what's good,—only I did know all along which way the wind was blowing. Lord love you, Mr. Graham, when you came in here all of a smash like, I knew it wasn't for nothing.'

'You think he did it on purpose then,' said Staveley.

'Did it on purpose? What; make up to Miss Madeline? Why, of course he did it on purpose. He's been a-thinking of it ever since Christmas night, when I saw you, Master Augustus, and a certain young lady when you came out into the dark passage together.'

'That's a downright falsehood, Mrs. Baker.'

'Oh—very well. Perhaps I was mistaken. But now, Mr. Graham, if you don't treat our Miss Madeline well——'

'That's just what I've been telling him,' said her brother. 'If he uses her ill, as he did his former wife—breaks her heart as he did with that one——'

'His former wife!' said Mrs. Baker.

'Haven't you heard of that? Why, he's had two already.'

'Two wives already! Oh now, Master Augustus, what an old fool I am ever to believe a word that comes out of your mouth.' Then having uttered her blessing, and having had her hand cordially grasped by this new scion of the Staveley family, the old woman left the young men to themselves, and went to her bed.

'Now that it is done——,' said Felix.

'You wish it were undone.'

'No, by heaven! I think I may venture to say that it will never come to me to wish that. But now that it is done, I am astonished at my own impudence almost as much as at my success. Why should your father have welcomed me to his house as his son-in-law, seeing how poor are my prospects?'

'Just for that reason; and because he is so different from other men. I have no doubt that he is proud of Madeline for having liked a man with an ugly face and no money.'

'If I had been beautiful like you, I shouldn't have had a chance with him.'

'Not if you'd been weighted with money also. Now, as for myself, I confess I'm not nearly so magnanimous as my father; and, for Mad's sake, I do hope you will get rid of your vagaries. An income, I know, is a very commonplace sort of thing; but when a man has a family there are comforts attached to it.'

'I am at any rate willing to work,' said Graham somewhat moodily.

'Yes, if you may work exactly in your own way. But men in the world can't do that. A man, as I take it, must through life allow himself to be governed by the united wisdom of others around him. He cannot take upon himself to judge as to every step by his own lights. If he does, he will be dead before he has made up his mind as to the preliminaries.' And in this way Augustus Staveley from the depth of his life's experience spoke words of worldly wisdom to his future brother-in-law.

On the next morning before he started again for Alston and his now odious work, Graham succeeded in getting Madeline to himself for five minutes. 'I saw both your father and mother last night,' said he, 'and I shall never forget their goodness to me.'

'Yes, they are good.'

'It seems like a dream to me that they should have accepted me as their son-in-law.'

'But it is no dream to me, Felix;—or if so, I do not mean to wake any more. I used to think that I should never care very much for anybody out of my own family;—but now——' And she then pressed her little hand upon his arm.

'And Felix,' she said, as he prepared to leave her, 'you are not to go away from Noningsby when the trial is over. I wanted mamma to tell you, but she said I'd better do it.'

CHAPTER XXXV

THE LAST DAY.

Mrs. Orme was up very early on that last morning of the trial, and had dressed herself before Lady Mason was awake. It was now March, but yet the morning light was hardly sufficient for her as she went through her toilet. They had been told to be in the court very punctually at ten, and in order to do so they must leave Orley Farm at nine. Before that, as had been arranged over night, Lucius was to see his mother.

'You haven't told him! he doesn't know!' were the first words which Lady Mason spoke as she raised her head from the pillow. But then she remembered. 'Ah! yes,' she said, as she again sank back and hid her face, 'he knows it all now.'

'Yes, dear; he knows it all; and is it not better so? He will come and see you, and when that is over you will be more comfortable than you have been for years past.'

Lucius also had been up early, and when he learned that Mrs. Orme was dressed, he sent up to her begging that he might see her. Mrs. Orme at once went to him, and found him seated at the breakfast-table with his head resting on his arm. His face was pale and haggard, and his hair was uncombed. He had not been undressed that night, and his clothes hung on him as they always do hang on a man who has passed a sleepless night in them. To Mrs. Orme's inquiry after himself he answered not a word, nor did he at first ask after his mother. 'That was all true that you told me last night?'

'Yes, Mr. Mason; it was true.'

'And she and I must be outcasts for ever. I will endeavour to bear it, Mrs. Orme. As I did not put an end to my life last night I suppose that I shall live and bear it. Does she expect to see me?'

'I told her that you would come to her this morning.'

'And what shall I say? I would not condemn my own mother; but how can I not condemn her?'

'Tell her at once that you will forgive her.'

'But it will be a lie. I have not forgiven her. I loved my mother and esteemed her as a pure and excellent woman. I was proud of my mother. How can I forgive her for having destroyed such feelings as those?'

'There should be nothing that a son would not forgive his mother.'

'Ah! that is so easily spoken. Men talk of forgiveness when their anger rankles deepest in their hearts. In the course of years I shall forgive her. I hope I shall. But to say that I can forgive her now would be a farce. She has broken my heart, Mrs. Orme.'

'And has not she suffered herself? Is not her heart broken?'

'I have been thinking of that all night. I cannot understand how she should have lived for the last six months. Well; is it time that I should go to her?'

Mrs. Orme again went up stairs, and after another interval of half an hour returned to fetch him. She almost regretted that she had undertaken to bring them together on that morning, thinking that it might have been better to postpone the interview till the trial should be over. She had expected that Lucius would have been softer in his manner. But it was too late for any such thought.

'You will find her dressed now, Mr. Mason,' said she; 'but I conjure you, as you hope for mercy yourself, to be merciful to her. She is your mother, and though she has injured you by her folly, her heart has been true to you through it all. Go now, and remember that harshness to any woman is unmanly.'

'I can only act as I think best,' he replied in that low stern voice which was habitual to him; and then with slow steps he went up to his mother's room.

When he entered it she was standing with her eyes fixed upon the door and her hands clasped together. So she stood till he had closed the door behind him, and had taken a few steps on towards the centre of the room. Then she rushed forward, and throwing herself on the ground before him clasped him round the knees with her arms. 'My boy, my boy!' she said. And then she lay there bathing his feet with her tears.

'Oh! mother, what is this that she has told me?'

But Lady Mason at the moment spoke no further words. It seemed as though her heart would have burst with sobs, and when for a moment she lifted up her face to his, the tears were streaming down her cheeks. Had it not been for that relief she could not have borne the sufferings which were heaped upon her.

'Mother, get up,' he said. 'Let me raise you. It is dreadful that you should lie there. Mother, let me lift you.' But she still clung to his knees, grovelling on the ground before him. 'Lucius, Lucius,' she said, and she then sank away from him as though the strength of her muscles would no longer allow her to cling to him. She sank away from him and lay along the ground hiding her face upon the floor.

'Mother,' he said, taking her gently by the arm as he knelt at her side, 'if you will rise I will speak to you.'

'Your words will kill me,' she said. 'I do not dare to look at you. Oh! Lucius, will you ever forgive me?'

And yet she had done it all for him. She had done a rascally deed, an hideous cut-throat deed, but it had been done altogether for him. No thought of her own aggrandisement had touched her mind when she resolved upon that forgery. As Rebekah had deceived her lord and robbed Esau, the first-born, of his birthright, so had she robbed him who was as Esau to her. How often had she thought of that, while her conscience was pleading hard against her! Had it been imputed as a crime to Rebekah that she had loved her own son well, and loving him had put a crown upon his head by means of her matchless guile? Did she love Lucius, her babe, less than Rebekah had loved Jacob? And had she not striven with the old man, struggling that she might do this just thing without injustice, till in his anger he had thrust her from him. 'I will not break my promise for the brat,' the old man had said;—and then she did the deed. But all that was as nothing now. She felt no comfort now from that Bible story which had given her such encouragement before the thing was finished. Now the result of evil-doing had come full home to her, and she was seeking pardon with a broken heart, while burning tears furrowed her cheeks,—not from him whom she had thought to injure, but from the child of her own bosom, for whose prosperity she had been so anxious.

Then she slowly arose and allowed him to place her upon the sofa. 'Mother,' he said, 'it is all over here.'

'Ah! yes.'

'Whither we had better go, I cannot yet say,—or when. We must wait till this day is ended.'

'Lucius, I care nothing for myself,—nothing. It is nothing to me whether or no they say that I am guilty. It is of you only that I am thinking.'

'Our lot, mother, must still be together. If they find you guilty you will be imprisoned, and then I will go, and come back when they release you. For you and me the future world will be very different from the past.'

'It need not be so,—for you, Lucius. I do not wish to keep you near me now.'

'But I shall be near you. Where you hide your shame there will I hide mine. In this world there is nothing left for us. But there is another world before you,—if you can repent of your sin.' This too he said very sternly, standing somewhat away from her, and frowning the while with those gloomy eyebrows. Sad as was her condition he might have given her solace, could he have taken her by the hand and kissed her. Peregrine Orme would have done so, or Augustus Staveley, could it have been possible that they should have found themselves in that position. Though Lucius

Mason could not do so, he was not less just than they, and, it may be, not less loving in his heart. He could devote himself for his mother's sake as absolutely as could they. But to some is given and to some is denied that cruse of heavenly balm with which all wounds can be assuaged and sore hearts ever relieved of some portion of their sorrow. Of all the virtues with which man can endow himself surely none other is so odious as that justice which can teach itself·to look down upon mercy almost as a vice!

'I will not ask you to forgive me,' she said, plaintively.

'Mother,' he answered, 'were I to say that I forgave you my words would be a mockery. I have no right either to condemn or to forgive. I accept my position as it has been made for me, and will endeavour to do my duty.'

It would have been almost better for her that he should have upbraided her for her wickedness. She would then have fallen again prostrate before him, if not in body at least in spirit, ànd her weakness would have stood for her in the place of strength. But now it was necessary that she should hear his words and bear his looks,—bear them like a heavy burden on her back without absolutely sinking. It had been that necessity of bearing and never absolutely sinking which, during years past, had so tried and tested the strength of her heart and soul. Seeing that she had not sunk, we may say that her strength had been very wonderful.

And then she stood up and came close to him. 'But you will give me your hand, Lucius?'

'Yes, mother; there is my hand. I shall stand by you through it all.' But he did not offer to kiss her; and there was still some pride in her heart which would not allow her to ask him for an embrace.

'And now,' he said, 'it is time that you should prepare to go. Mrs. Orme thinks it better that I should not accompany you.'

'No, Lucius, no; you must not hear them proclaim my guilt in court.'

'That would make but little difference. But nevertheless I will not go. Had I known this before I should not have gone there. It was to testify my belief in your innocence; nay, my conviction——

'Oh, Lucius, spare me!'

'Well, I will speak of it no more. I shall be here to-night when you come back.'

'But if they say that I am guilty they will take me away.'

'If so I will come to you,—in the morning if they will let me. But, mother, in any case I must leave this house to-morrow.' Then again he gave her his hand, but he left her without touching her with his lips.

When the two ladies appeared in court together without Lucius Mason there was much question among the crowd as to the cause of his absence. Both Dockwrath and Joseph Mason looked at it in the right light, and accepted it as a ground for renewed hope. 'He dare not face the verdict,' said Dockwrath. And yet when they had left the court on the preceding evening, after listening to Mr. Furnival's speech, their hopes had not been very high. Dockwrath had not admitted with words that he feared defeat, but when Mason had gnashed his teeth as he walked up and down his room at Alston, and striking the table with his clenched fist had declared his fears, 'By heavens they will escape me again!' Dockwrath had not been able to give him substantial comfort. 'The jury are not such fools as to take all that for gospel,' he had said. But he had not said it with that tone of assured conviction which he had always used till Mr. Furnival's speech had been made. There could have been no greater attestation to the power displayed by Mr. Furnival than Mr. Mason's countenance as he left the court on that evening. ' I suppose it will cost me hundreds of pounds,' he said to Dockwrath that evening. 'Orley Farm will pay for it all,' Dockwrath had answered; but his answer had shown no confidence. And, if we think well of it, Joseph Mason was deserving of pity. He wanted only what was his own; and that Orley Farm ought to be his own he had no smallest doubt. Mr. Furnival had not in the least shaken him; but he had made him feel that others would be shaken. ' If it could only be left to the judge,' thought Mr. Mason to himself. And then he began to consider whether this British palladium of an unanimous jury had not in it more of evil than of good.

Young Peregrine Orme again met his mother at the door of the court, and at her instance gave his arm to Lady Mason. Mr. Aram was also there; but Mr. Aram had great tact, and did not offer his arm to Mrs. Orme, contenting himself with making a way for her and walking beside her. 'I am glad that her son has not come to-day,' he said, not bringing his head suspiciously close to hers, but still speaking so that none but she might hear him. 'He has done all the good that he could do, and as there is only the judge's charge to hear, the jury will not notice his absence. Of course we hope for the best, Mrs. Orme, but it is doubtful.'

As Felix Graham took his place next to Chaffanbrass, the old lawyer scowled at him, turning his red old savage eyes first on him and then from him, growling the while, so that the whole court might notice it. The legal portion of the court did notice it and were much amused. 'Good morning, Mr. Chaffanbrass,' said Graham quite aloud as he took his seat; and then Chaffanbrass growled again. Considering the lights with which he had been lightened, there was a species of honesty about Mr. Chaffanbrass which certainly deserved praise. He was always true to the man whose money he had taken, and gave to his customer, with all the power at his command, that assistance which he had professed to sell. But we may give the same praise to the hired bravo who goes through with truth and courage the task which he has undertaken. I knew an assassin in Ireland who professed that during twelve years of practice in Tipperary he had never failed when he had once engaged himself. For truth and honesty to their customers—which are great virtues—I would bracket that man and Mr. Chaffanbrass together.

And then the judge commenced his charge, and as he went on with it he repeated all the evidence that was in any way of moment, pulling the details to pieces, and dividing that which bore upon the subject from that which did not. This he did with infinite talent and with a perspicuity beyond all praise. But to my thinking it was remarkable that he seemed to regard the witnesses as a dissecting surgeon may be supposed to regard the subjects on which he operates for the advancement of science. With exquisite care he displayed what each had said and how the special saying of one bore on that special saying of another. But he never spoke of them as though they had been live men and women who were themselves as much entitled to justice at his hands as either the prosecutor in this matter or she who was being prosecuted; who, indeed, if anything, were better entitled unless he could show that they were false and suborned; for unless they were suborned or false they were there doing a painful duty to the public, for which they were to receive no pay and from which they were to obtain no benefit. Of whom else in that court could so much be said? The judge there had his ermine and his canopy, his large salary and his seat of honour. And the lawyers had their wigs, and their own loud voices, and their places of precedence. The attorneys had their seats and their big tables, and the somewhat familiar respect of the tipstaves. The jury, though not much to be envied, were addressed with respect and flattery, had their honourable seats, and were invariably at least called gentlemen. But why should there be no seat of honour for the witnesses? To stand in a box, to be bawled after by the police, to be scowled at and scolded by the judge, to be browbeaten and accused falsely by the barristers, and then to be condemned as perjurers by the jury,—that is the fate of the one person who during the whole trial is perhaps entitled to the greatest respect, and is certainly entitled to the most public gratitude. Let the witness have a big arm-chair, and a canopy over him, and a man behind him with a red cloak to do him honour and keep the flies off; let him be gently invited to come forward from some inner room where he can sit before a fire. Then he will be able to speak out, making himself heard without scolding, and will perhaps be able to make a fair fight with the cocks who can crow so loudly on their own dunghills.

The judge in this case did his work with admirable skill, blowing aside the froth of Mr. Furnival's eloquence, and upsetting the sophistry and false deductions of Mr. Chaffanbrass. The case for the jury, as he said, hung altogether upon the evidence of Kenneby and the woman Bolster. As far as he could see, the evidence of Dockwrath had little to do with it; and alleged malice and greed on the part of Dockwrath could have nothing to do with it. The jury might take it as proved that Lady Mason at the former trial had sworn that she had been present when her husband signed the codicil and had seen the different signatures affixed to it. They might also take it as proved, that that other deed—the deed purporting to close a partnership between Sir Joseph Mason and Mr. Martock,—had been executed on the 14th of July, and that it had been signed by Sir Joseph, and also by those two surviving witnesses, Kenneby and Bolster. The question, therefore, for the consideration of the jury had narrowed itself to this: had two deeds been executed by Sir Joseph Mason, both bearing the same date? If this had not been done, and if that deed with reference to the partnership were a true deed, 'then must the other be false and fraudulent; and if false and fraudulent, then must Lady Mason have sworn falsely, and been guilty of that perjury with which she was now charged. There might, perhaps, be one loophole to this argument by which an escape was possible. Though both deeds bore the date of 14th July, there might have been error in this. It was possible, though no doubt singular, that that date should have been inserted in the partnership deed, and the deed itself be executed afterwards. But then the woman Bolster told them that she had been called to act as witness but once in her life, and if they believed her in that statement, the possibility of error as to the date would be of little or no avail on behalf of Lady Mason. For himself, he could not say that adequate ground had been shown for charging Bolster with swearing falsely. No doubt she had been obstinate in her method of giving her testimony, but that might have arisen from an honest resolution on her part not to allow herself to be shaken. The value of her testimony must, however, be judged by the jury themselves. As regarded Kenneby, he must say that the man had been very stupid. No one who had heard him would accuse him for a moment of having intended to swear falsely, but the jury might perhaps think that the testimony of such a man could not be taken as having much value with reference to circumstances which happened more than twenty years since.

The charge took over two hours, but the substance of it has been stated. Then the jury retired to consider their verdict, and the judge, and the barristers, and some other jury proceeded to the business of some other and less important trial. Lady Mason and Mrs. Orme sat for a while in their seats—perhaps for a space of twenty minutes—and then, as the jury did not at once return into

court, they retired to the sitting-room in which they had first been
placed. Here Mr. Aram accompanied them, and here they were of
course met by Peregrine Orme.

'His lordship's charge was very good—very good, indeed,' said
Mr. Aram.

'Was it?' asked Peregrine.

'And very much in our favour,' continued the attorney.

'You think then,' said Mrs. Orme, looking up into his face, 'you
think that——' But she did not know how to go on with her
question.

'Yes, I do. I think we shall have a verdict; I do, indeed. I
would not say so before Lady Mason if my opinion was not very
strong. The jury may disagree. That is not improbable. But I
cannot anticipate that the verdict will be against us.'

There was some comfort in this; but how wretched was the
nature of the comfort! Did not the attorney, in every word which
he spoke, declare his own conviction of his client's guilt. Even
Peregrine Orme could not say out boldly that he felt sure of an
acquittal because no other verdict could be justly given. And then
why was not Mr. Furnival there, taking his friend by the hand and
congratulating her that her troubles were so nearly over? Mr.
Furnival at this time did not come near her; and had he done so,
what could he have said to her?'

He and Sir Richard Leatherham left the court together, and the
latter went at once back to London without waiting to hear the
verdict. Mr. Chaffanbrass also, and Felix Graham retired from the
scene of their labours, and as they did so, a few words were spoken
between them.

'Mr. Graham,' said the ancient hero of the Old Bailey, 'you are
too great for this kind of work I take it. If I were you, I would
keep out of it for the future.'

'I am very much of the same way of thinking, Mr. Chaffanbrass,'
said the other.

'If a man undertakes a duty, he should do it. That's my
opinion, though I confess it's a little old fashioned; especially if he
takes money for it, Mr. Graham.' And then the old man glowered
at him with his fierce eyes, and nodded his head and went on.
What could Graham say to him? His answer would have been
ready enough had there been time or place in which to give it.
But he had no answer ready which was fit for the crowded hall of
the court-house, and so Mr. Chaffanbrass went on his way. He will
now pass out of our sight, and we will say of him, that he did his
duty well according to his lights.

There, in that little room, sat Lady Mason and Mrs. Orme till
late in the evening, and there, with them, remained Peregrine.
Some sort of refreshment was procured for them, but of the three

days they passed in the court, that, perhaps, was the most oppressive. There was no employment for them, and then the suspense was terrible! That suspense became worse and worse as the hours went on, for it was clear that at any rate some of the jury were anxious to give a verdict against her. 'They say that there's eight and four,' said Mr. Aram, at one of the many visits which he made to them; 'but there's no saying how true that may be.'

'Eight and four!' said Peregrine.

'Eight to acquit, and four for guilty,' said Aram. 'If so, we're safe, at any rate, till the next assizes.'

But it was not fated that Lady Mason should be sent away from the court in doubt. At eight o'clock Mr. Aram came to them, hot with haste, and told them that the jury had sent for the judge. The judge had gone home to his dinner, but would return to court at once when he heard that the jury had agreed.

'And must we go into court again?' said Mrs. Orme.

'Lady Mason must do so.'

'Then of course I shall go with her. Are you ready now, dear?'

Lady Mason was unable to speak, but she signified that she was ready, and then they went into court. The jury were already in the box, and as the two ladies took their seats, the judge entered. But few of the gas-lights were lit, so that they in the court could hardly see each other, and the remaining ceremony did not take five minutes.

'Not guilty, my lord,' said the foreman. Then the verdict was recorded, and the judge went back to his dinner. Joseph Mason and Dockwrath were present and heard the verdict. I will leave the reader to imagine with what an appetite they returned to their chamber.

CHAPTER XXXVI.

I LOVE HER STILL.

IT was all over now, and as Lucius had said to his mother, there was nothing left for them but to go and hide themselves. The verdict had reached him before his mother's return, and on the moment of his hearing it he sat down and commenced the following letter to Mr. Furnival:—

'Orley Farm, March —, 18—.

' DEAR SIR,

' I beg to thank you, in my mother's name, for your great exertions in the late trial. I must acknowledge that I have been wrong in thinking that you gave her bad advice, and am now convinced that you acted with the best judgment on her behalf. May I beg that you will add to your great kindness by inducing the gentlemen who undertook the management of the case as my mother's attorneys to let me know as soon as possible in what sum I am indebted to them?

'I believe I need trouble you with no preamble as to my reasons when I tell you that I have resolved to abandon immediately any title that I may have to the possession of Orley Farm, and to make over the property at once, in any way that may be most efficacious, to my half-brother, Mr. Joseph Mason, of Groby Park. I so strongly feel the necessity of doing this at once, without even a day's delay, that I shall take my mother to lodgings in London to-morrow, and shall then decide on what steps it may be best that we shall take. My mother will be in possession of about 200*l.* a year, subject to such deduction as the cost of the trial may make from it.

'I hope that you will not think that I intrude upon you too far when I ask you to communicate with my brother's lawyers on the subject of this surrender. I do not know how else to do it; and of course you will understand that I wish to screen my mother's name as much as may be in my power with due regard to honesty. I hope I need not insist on the fact,—for it is a fact,—that nothing will change my purpose as to this. If I cannot have it done through you, I must myself go to Mr. Round. I am, moreover, aware that in accordance with strict justice my brother should have upon me a claim for the proceeds of the estate since the date of our father's death. If he wishes it I will give him such claim, making myself his debtor by any form that may be legal. He must, however, in such case be made to understand that his claim will be against a beggar; but, nevertheless, it may suit his views to have such a claim upon me. I cannot think that, under the circumstances, I should be justified in calling on my mother to surrender her small income; but should you be of a different opinion, it shall be done.

'I write thus to you at once as I think that not a day should be lost. I will trouble you with another line from London, to let you know what is our immediate address.

'Pray believe me to be
'Yours, faithfully and obliged,
'Lucius Mason.
'T. Furnival, Esq.,
'Old Square, Lincoln's Inn Fields.'

As soon as he had completed this letter, which was sufficiently good for its purpose, and clearly explained what was the writer's will on the subject of it, he wrote another, which I do not think was equally efficacious. The second was addressed to Miss Furnival, and being a love letter, was not so much within the scope of the writer's peculiar powers.

' DEAREST SOPHIA,

' I hardly know how to address you ; or what I should tell you or what conceal. Were we together, and was that promise renewed which you once gave me, I should tell you all;—but this I cannot do by letter. My mother's trial is over, and she is acquitted ; but that which I have learned during the trial has made me feel that I am bound to relinquish to my brother-in-law all my title to Orley Farm, and I have already taken the first steps towards doing so. Yes, Sophia, I am now a beggar on the face of the world. I have nothing belonging to me, save those powers of mind and body which God has given me; and I am, moreover, a man oppressed with a terribly heavy load of grief. For some short time I must hide myself with my mother; and then, when I shall have been able to brace my mind to work, I shall go forth and labour in whatever field may be open to me.

' But before I go, Sophia, I wish to say a word of farewell to you, that I may understand on what terms we part. Of course I make no claim. I am aware that that which I now tell you must be held as giving you a valid excuse for breaking any contract that there may have been between us. But, nevertheless, I have hope. That I love you very dearly I need hardly now say; and I still venture to think that the time may come when I shall again prove myself to be worthy of your hand. If you have ever loved me you cannot cease to do so merely because I am unfortunate ; and if you love me still, perhaps you will consent to wait. If you will do so,— if you will say that I am rich in that respect,—I shall go to my banishment not altogether a downcast man.

' May I say that I am still your own
' LUCIUS MASON ?'

No; he decidedly might not say so. But as the letter was not yet finished when his mother and Mrs. Orme returned, I will not anticipate matters by giving Miss Furnival's reply.

Mrs. Orme came back that night to Orley Farm, but without the intention of remaining there. Her task was over, and it would be well that she should return to the Cleeve. Her task was over; and as the hour must come in which she should leave the mother in the hands of her son, the present hour would be as good as any.

They again went together to the room which they had shared for the last night or two, and there they parted. They had not been there long when the sound of wheels was heard on the gravel, and Mrs. Orme got up from her seat. ' There is Peregrine with the carriage,' said she.

' And you are going?' said Lady Mason.

' If I could do you good, I would stay,' said Mrs. Orme.

' No, no ; of course you must go. Oh, my darling, oh, my friend,' and she threw herself into the other's arms.

' Of course I will write to you,' said Mrs. Orme. ' I will do so regularly.'

' May God bless you for ever. But it is needless to ask for blessings on such as you. You are blessed.'

' And you too ;—if you will turn to Him you will be blessed.'

' Ah me. Well, I can try now. I feel that I can at any rate try.'

' And none who try ever fail. And now, dear, good-bye.'

' Good-bye, my angel. But, Mrs. Orme, I have one word I must first say ; a message that I must send to him. Tell him this, that never in my life have I loved any man as well as I have loved him and as I do love him. That on my knees I beg his pardon for the wrong I have done him.'

' But he knows how great has been your goodness to him.'

' When the time came I was not quite a devil to drag him down with me to utter destruction !'

' He will always remember what was your conduct then.'

' But tell him, that though I loved him, and though I loved you with all my heart,—with all my heart, I knew through it all, as I know now, that I was not a fitting friend for him or you. No ; do not interrupt me, I always knew it ; and though it was so sweet to me to see your faces, I would have kept away ; but that he would not have it. I came to him to assist me because he was great and strong, and he took me to his bosom with his kindness, till I destroyed his strength ; though his greatness nothing can destroy.'

' No, no ; he does not think that you have injured him.'

' But tell him what I say ; and tell him that a poor bruised, broken creature, who knows at least her own vileness, will pray for him night and morning. And now good-bye. Of my heart towards you I cannot speak.'

' Good-bye then, and, Lady Mason, never despair. There is always room for hope ; and where there is hope there need not be unhappiness.'

Then they parted, and Mrs. Orme went down to her son.

' Mother, the carriage is here,' he said.

' Yes, I heard it. Where is Lucius ? Good-bye, Mr. Mason.'

' God bless you, Mrs. Orme. Believe me I know how good you have been to us.'

As she gave him her hand, she spoke a few words to him. ' My last request to you, Mr. Mason, is to beg that you will be tender to your mother.'

' I will do my best, Mrs. Orme.'

' All her sufferings and your own, have come from her great love for you.'

'That I know and feel, but had her ambition for me been less it would have been better for both of us.' And there he stood bare-headed at the door while Peregrine Orme handed his mother into the carriage. Thus Mrs. Orme took her last leave of Orley Farm, and was parted from the woman she had loved with so much truth and befriended with so much loyalty.

Very few words were spoken in the carriage between Peregrine and his mother while they were being taken back through Hamworth to the Cleeve. To Peregrine the whole matter was unintelligible. He knew that the verdict had been in favour of Lady Mason, and yet there had been no signs of joy at Orley Farm, or even of contentment. He had heard also from Lucius, while they had been together for a few minutes, that Orley Farm was to be given up.

'You'll let it I suppose,' Peregrine had asked.

'It will not be mine to let. It will belong to my brother,' Lucius had answered. Then Peregrine had asked no further question; nor had Lucius offered any further information.

But his mother, as he knew, was worn out with the work she had done, and at the present moment he felt that the subject was one which would hardly bear questions. So he sat by her side in silence; and before the carriage had reached the Cleeve his mind had turned away from the cares and sorrows of Lady Mason, and was once more at Noningsby. After all, as he said to himself, who could be worse off than he was. He had nothing to hope.

They found Sir Peregrine standing in the hall to receive them, and Mrs. Orme, though she had been absent only three days, could not but perceive the havoc which this trial had made upon him. It was not that the sufferings of those three days had broken him down, but that now, after that short absence, she was able to perceive how great had been upon him the effect of his previous sufferings. He had never held up his head since the day on which Lady Mason had made to him her first confession. Up to that time he had stood erect, and though as he walked his steps had shown that he was no longer young, he had walked with a certain air of strength and manly bearing. Till Lady Mason had come to the Cleeve no one would have said that Sir Peregrine looked as though his energy and life had passed away. But now, as he put his arm round his daughter's waist, and stooped down to kiss her cheek, he was a worn-out, tottering old man.

During these three days he had lived almost altogether alone, and had been ashamed to show to those around him the intense interest which he felt in the result of the trial. His grandson had on each day breakfasted alone, and had left the house before his grandfather was out of his room; and on each evening he had returned late,— as he now returned with his mother,—and had dined alone. Then he had sat with his grandfather for an hour or two, and had been

constrained to talk over the events of the day without being allowed
to ask Sir Peregrine's opinion as to Lady Mason's innocence or to
express his own. These three days had been dreadful to Sir Peregrine. He had not left the house, but had crept about from room to
room, ever and again taking up some book or paper and putting it
down unread, as his mind reverted to the one subject which now
for him bore any interest. On the second of these three days a
note had been brought to him from his old friend Lord Alston.
' Dear Orme,' the note had run, ' I am not quite happy as I think of
the manner in which we parted the other day. If I offended in any
degree, I send this as a peacemaker, and beg to shake your hand
heartily. Let me have a line from you to say that it is all right
between us. Neither you nor I can afford to lose an old friend at
our time of life. Yours always, Alston.' But Sir Peregrine had
not answered it. Lord Alston's servant had been dismissed with a
promise that an answer should be sent, but at the end of the three
days it had not yet been written. His mind indeed was still sore
towards Lord Alston. The counsel which his old friend had given
him was good and true, but it had been neglected, and its very
truth and excellence now made the remembrance of it unpalatable.
He had, nevertheless, intended to write; but the idea of such exertion from hour to hour had become more distressing to him.

He had of course heard of Lady Mason's acquittal; and indeed
tidings of the decision to which the jury had come went through
the country very quickly. There is a telegraphic wire for such
tidings which has been very long in use, and which, though always
used, is as yet but very little understood. How is it that information will spread itself quicker than men can travel, and make its
way like water into all parts of the world? It was known all
through the country that night that Lady Mason was acquitted; and
before the next night it was as well known that she had acknowledged her guilt by giving up the property.

Little could be said as to the trial while Peregrine remained in
the room with his mother and his grandfather; but this he had the
tact to perceive, and soon left them together. ' I shall see you,
mother, up stairs before you go to bed,' he said as he sauntered out.
' But you must not keep her up,' said his grandfather. ' Remember all that she has gone through.' With this injunction he
went off, and as he sat alone in his mother's room he tried to come
to some resolution as to Noningsby. He knew he had no ground
for hope;—no chance, as he would have called it. And if so,
would it not be better that he should take himself off? Nevertheless he would go to Noningsby once more. He would not be such
a coward but that he would wish her good-bye before he went, and
hear the end of it all from her own lips.

When he had left the room Lady Mason's last message was given to Sir Peregrine. 'Poor soul, poor soul!' he said, as Mrs. Orme began her story. 'Her son knows it all then now.'

'I told him last night,—with her consent; so that he should not go into the court to-day. It would have been very bad, you know, if they had—found her guilty.'

'Yes, yes; very bad—very bad indeed. Poor creature! And so you told him. How did he bear it?'

'On the whole, well. At first he would not believe me.'

'As for me, I could not have done it. I could not have told him.'

'Yes, sir, you would;—you would, if it had been required of you.'

'I think it would have killed me. But a woman can do things for which a man's courage would never be sufficient. And he bore it manfully.'

'He was very stern.'

'Yes;—and he will be stern. Poor soul!—I pity her from my very heart. But he will not desert her; he will do his duty by her.'

'I am sure he will. In that respect he is a good young man.'

'Yes, my dear. He is one of those who seem by nature created to bear adversity. No trouble or sorrow would I think crush him. But had prosperity come to him, it would have made him odious to all around him. You were not present when they met?'

'No—I thought it better to leave them.'

'Yes, yes. And he will give up the place at once.'

'To-morrow he will do so. In that at any rate he has true spirit. To-morrow early they will go to London, and she I suppose will never see Orley Farm again.' And then Mrs. Orme gave Sir Peregrine that last message.—'I tell you everything as she told me.' Mrs. Orme said, seeing how deeply he was affected. 'Perhaps I am wrong.'

'No, no, no,' he said.

'Coming at such a moment, her words seemed to be almost sacred.'

'They are sacred. They shall be sacred. Poor soul, poor soul!'

'She did a great crime.'

'Yes, yes.'

'But if a crime can be forgiven,—can be excused on account of its motives——'

'It cannot, my dear. Nothing can be forgiven on that ground.'

'No; we know that; we all feel sure of that. But yet how can one help loving her? For myself, I shall love her always.'

'And I also love her.' And then the old man made his confession. 'I loved her well;—better than I had ever thought to love any one again, but you and Perry. I loved her very dearly, and felt that I should have been proud to have called her my wife. How beautiful she was in her sorrow, when we thought that her life had been pure and good!'

' And it had been good,—for many years past.'

' No; for the stolen property was still there. But yet how graceful she was, and how well her sorrows sat upon her ! What might she not have done had the world used her more kindly, and not sent in her way that sore temptation ! She was a woman for a man to have loved to madness.'

' And yet how little can she have known of love !'

' I loved her.' And as the old man said so he rose to his feet with some show of his old energy. ' I loved her,—with all my heart ! It is foolish for an old man so to say; but I did love her; nay, I love her still. But that I knew that it would be wrong,—for your sake, and for Perry's——' And then he stopped himself, as though he would fain hear what she might say to him.

' Yes; it is all over now,' she said in the softest, sweetest, lowest voice. She knew that she was breaking down a last hope, but she knew also that that hope was vain. And then there was silence in the room for some ten minutes' space.

' It is all over,' he then said, repeating her last words.

' But you have us still,—Perry and me. Can any one love you better than we do?' And she got up and went over to him and stood by him, and leaned upon him.

' Edith, my love, since you came to my house there has been an angel in it watching over me. I shall know that always; and when I turn my face to the wall, as I soon shall, that shall be my last earthly thought.' And so in tears they parted for that night. But the sorrow that was bringing him to his grave came from the love of which he had spoken. It is seldom that a young man may die from a broken heart; but if an old man have a heart still left to him, it is more fragile.

CHAPTER XXXVII.

JOHN KENNEBY'S DOOM.

On the evening but one after the trial was over Mr. Moulder entertained a few friends to supper at his apartments in Great St. Helen's, and it was generally understood that in doing so he intended to celebrate the triumph of Lady Mason. Through the whole affair he had been a strong partisan on her side, had expressed a very loud opinion in favour of Mr. Furnival, and had hoped that that scoundrel Dockwrath would get all that he deserved from the hands of Mr. Chaffanbrass. When the hour of Mr. Dockwrath's punishment had come he had been hardly contented, but the inadequacy of Kenneby's testimony had restored him to good humour, and the verdict had made him triumphant.

'Didn't I know it, old fellow?' he had said, slapping his friend Snengkeld on the back. When such a low scoundrel as Dockwrath is pitted against a handsome woman like Lady Mason he'll not find a jury in England to give a verdict in his favour.' Then he asked Snengkeld to come to his little supper; and Kantwise also he invited, though Kantwise had shown Dockwrath tendencies throughout the whole affair;—but Moulder was fond of Kantwise as a butt for his own sarcasm. Mrs. Smiley, too, was asked, as was natural, seeing that she was the betrothed bride of one of the heroes of the day; and Moulder, in the kindness of his heart, swore that he never was proud, and told Bridget Bolster that she would be welcome to take a share of what was going.

'Laws, M.,' said Mrs. Moulder, when she was told of this. 'A chambermaid from an inn! What will Mrs. Smiley say?'

'I aint going to trouble myself with what Mother Smiley may say or think about my friends. If she don't like it, she may do the other thing. What was she herself when you first knew her?'

'Yes, Moulder; but then money do make a difference, you know.'

Bridget Bolster, however, was invited, and she came in spite of the grandeur of Mrs. Smiley. Kenneby also of course was there, but he was not in a happy frame of mind. Since that wretched hour in which he had heard himself described by the judge as too stupid to be held of any account by the jury he had become a melancholy, misanthropic man. The treatment which he received from Mr. Furnival had been very grievous to him, but he had borne with that, hoping that some word of eulogy from the judge would set him right in the public mind. But no such word had come, and poor John Kenneby felt that the cruel hard world was too much for him. He had been with his sister that morning, and words had dropped from him which made her fear that he would wish to postpone his marriage for another space of ten years or so. ' Brickfields!' he had said. ' What can such a one as I have to do with landed property? I am better as I am.'

Mrs. Smiley, however, did not at all seem to think so, and welcomed John Kenneby back from Alston very warmly in spite of the disgrace to which he had been subjected. It was nothing to her that the judge had called her future lord a fool; nor indeed was it anything to any one but himself. According to Moulder's views it was a matter of course that a witness should be abused. For what other purpose was he had into the court? But deep in the mind of poor Kenneby himself the injurious words lay festering. He had struggled hard to tell the truth, and in doing so had simply proved himself to be an ass. ' I aint fit to live with anybody else but myself,' he said to himself, as he walked down Bishopsgate Street.

At this time Mrs. Smiley was not yet there. Bridget had arrived, and had been seated in a chair at one corner of the fire. Mrs. Moulder occupied one end of a sofa opposite, leaving the place of honour at the other end for Mrs. Smiley. Moulder sat immediately in front of the fire in his own easy chair, and Snengkeld and Kantwise were on each side of him. They were of course discussing the trial when Mrs. Smiley was announced; and it was well that she made a diversion by her arrival, for words were beginning to run high.

' A jury of her countrymen has found her innocent,' Moulder had said with much heat; ' and any one who says she's guilty after that is a libeller and a coward, to my way of thinking. If a jury of her countrymen don't make a woman innocent, what does?'

' Of course she's innocent,' said Snengkeld; ' from the very moment the words was spoken by the foreman. If any newspaper was to say she wasn't she'd have her action.'

' That's all very well,' said Kantwise, looking up to the ceiling with his eyes nearly shut. ' But you'll see. What'll you bet me, Mr. Moulder, that Joseph Mason don't get the property?'

' Gammon!' answered Moulder.

' Well, it may be gammon; but you'll see.'

' Gentlemen, gentlemen!' said Mrs. Smiley, sailing into the room; ' upon my word one hears all you say ever so far down the street.'

' And I didn't care if they heard it right away to the Mansion House,' said Moulder. ' We aint talking treason, nor yet highway robbery.'

Then Mrs. Smiley was welcomed;—her bonnet was taken from her and her umbrella, and she was encouraged to spread herself out over the sofa. ' Oh, Mrs. Bolster ; the witness !' she said, when Mrs. Moulder went through some little ceremony of introduction. And from the tone of her voice it appeared that she was not quite satisfied that Mrs. Bolster should be there as a companion for herself. ·

' Yes, ma'am. I was the witness as had never signed but once,' said Bridget, getting up and curtsying. Then she sat down again, folding her hands one over the other on her lap.

' Oh, indeed !' said Mrs. Smiley. ' But where's the other witness, Mrs. Moulder? He's the one who is a deal more interesting to me. Ha, ha, ha! But as you all know it here, what's the good of not telling the truth? Ha, ha, ha !'

' John's here,' said Mrs. Moulder. ' Come, John, why don't you show yourself ?'

' He's just alive, and that's about all you can say for him,' said Moulder.

' Why, what's there been to kill him ?' said Mrs. Smiley. ' Well, John, I must say you're rather backward in coming forward, considering what there's been between us. You might have come and taken my shawl, I'm.thinking.'

' Yes, I might,' said Kenneby gloomily. ' I hope I see you pretty well, Mrs. Smiley.'

' Pretty bobbish, thank you. Only I think it might have been Maria between friends like us.'

' He's sadly put about by this trial,' whispered Mrs. Moulder. ' You know he is so tender-hearted that he can't bear to be put upon like another.'

' But you didn't want her to be found guilty; did you, John ?'

' That I'm sure he didn't,' said Moulder. ' Why it was the way he gave his evidence that brought her off.'

' It wasn't my wish to bring her off,' said Kenneby; ' nor was it my wish to make her guilty. All I wanted was to tell the truth and do my duty. But it was no use. I believe it never is any use.'

' I think you did very well,' said Moulder.

' I'm sure Lady Mason ought to be very much obliged to you,' said Kantwise.

' Nobody needn't care for what's said to them in a court,' said Snengkeld. ' I remember when once they wanted to make out that I'd taken a parcel of teas——'

' Stolen, you mean, sir,' suggested Mrs. Smiley.

' Yes; stolen. But it was only done by the opposite side in court, and I didn't think a halfporth of it. They knew where the teas was well enough.'

' Speaking for myself,' said Kenneby, ' I must say I don't like it.'

' But the paper as we signed,' said Bridget, ' wasn't the old gentleman's will,—no more than this is;' and she lifted up her apron. ' I'm rightly sure of that.'

Then again the battle raged hot and furious, and Moulder became angry with his guest, Bridget Bolster. Kantwise finding himself supported in his views by the principal witness at the trial took heart against the tyranny of Moulder and expressed his opinion, while Mrs. Smiley, with a woman's customary dislike to another woman, sneered ill-naturedly at the idea of Lady Mason's innocence. Poor Kenneby had been forced to take the middle seat on the sofa between his bride and sister; but it did not appear that the honour of his position had any effect in lessening his gloom or mitigating the severity of the judgment which had been passed on him.

'Wasn't the old gentleman's will!' said Moulder, turning on poor Bridget in his anger with a growl. 'But I say it was the old gentleman's will. You never dared say as much as that in court.'

'I wasn't asked,' said Bridget.

'You weren't asked! Yes, you was asked often enough.'

'I'll tell you what it is,' said Kantwise, 'Mrs. Bolster's right in what she says as sure as your name's Moulder.'

'Then as sure as my name's Moulder she's wrong. I suppose we're to think that a chap like you knows more about it than the jury! We all know who your friend is in the matter. I haven't forgot our dinner at Leeds, nor sha'n't in a hurry.'

'Now, John,' said Mrs. Smiley, 'nobody can know the truth of this so well as you do. You've been as close as wax, as was all right till the lady was out of her troubles. That's done and over, and let us hear among friends how the matter really was.' And then there was silence among them in order that his words might come forth freely.

'Come, my dear,' said Mrs. Smiley with a tone of encouraging love. 'There can't be any harm now; can there?'

'Out with it, John,' said Moulder. 'You're honest, anyways.'

'There aint no gammon about you,' said Snengkeld.

'Mr. Kenneby can speak if he likes, no doubt,' said Kantwise; 'though maybe it mayn't be very pleasant to him to do so after all that's come and gone.'

'There's nothing that's come and gone that need make our John hold his tongue,' said Mrs. Moulder. 'He mayn't be just as bright as some of those lawyers, but he's a deal more true-hearted.'

'But he can't say as how it was the old gentleman's will as we signed. I'm well assured of that,' said Bridget.

But Kenneby, though thus called upon by the united strength of the company to solve all their doubts, still remained silent. 'Come, lovey,' said Mrs. Smiley, putting forth her hand and giving his arm a tender squeeze.

'If you've anything to say to clear that woman's character,' said Moulder, 'you owe it to society to say it; becauses she is a woman, and because her enemies is villains.' And then again there was silence while they waited for him.

' I think it will go with him to his grave,' said Mrs. Smiley, very solemnly.

' I shouldn't wonder,' said Snengkeld.

' Then he must give up all idea of taking a wife,' said Moulder.

' He won't do that I'm sure,' said Mrs. Smiley.

' That he won't. Will you, John ?' said his sister.

' There's no knowing what may happen to me in th's world,' said Kenneby, ' but sometimes I almost think I aint fit to live in it, along with anybody else.'

' You'll make him fit, won't you, my dear ?' said Mrs. Moulder.

' I don't exactly know what to say about it,' said Mrs. Smiley. ' If Mr. Kenneby aint willing, I'm not the 'woman to bind him to his word, because I've had his promise over and over again, and could prove it by a number of witnesses before any jury in the land. I'm a independent woman as needn't be beholden to any man, and I should never think of damages. Smiley left me comfortable before all the world, and I don't know but what I'm a fool to think of changing. Anyways if Mr. Kenneby——'

' Come, John. Why don't you speak to her ?' said Mrs. Moulder.

' And what am I to say ?' said Kenneby, thrusting himself forth from between the ample folds of the two ladies' dresses. ' I'm a blighted man ; one on whom the finger of scorn has been pointed. His lordship said that I was——stupid ; and perhaps I am.'

' She don't think nothing of that, John.'

' Certainly not,' said Mrs. Smiley.

' As long as a man can pay twenty shillings in the pound and a trifle over, what does it matter if all the judges in the land was to call him stupid ?' said Snengkeld.

' Stupid is as stupid does,' said Kantwise.

' Stupid be d——,' said Moulder.

' Mr. Moulder, there's ladies present,' said Mrs. Smiley.

' Come, John, rouse yourself a bit,' said his sister. ' Nobody here thinks the worse of you for what the judge said.'

' Certainly not,' said Mrs. Smiley. ' And as it becomes me to speak, I'll say my mind. I'm accustomed to speak freely before friends, and as we are all friends here, why should I be ashamed ?'

' For the matter of that nobody says you are,' said Moulder.

' And I don't mean, Mr. Moulder. Why should I ? I can pay my way, and do what I like with my own, and has people to mind me when I speak, and needn't mind nobody else myself ;—and that's more than everybody can say. Here's John Kenneby and I, is engaged as man and wife. He won't say as it's not so, I'll be bound.'

' No,' said Kenneby, ' I'm engaged I know.'

' When I accepted John Kenneby's hand and heart,—and well I remember the beauteous language in which he expressed his feelings, and always shall,—I told him, that I respected him as a

man that would do his duty by a woman, though perhaps he mightn't
be so cute in the way of having much to say for himself as some
others. "What's the good," said I, " of a man's talking, if so be he's
ashamed to meet the baker at the end of the week?" So I listened
to the vows he made me, and have considered that he and I was as
good as one. Now that he's been put upon by them lawyers, I'm
not the woman to turn my back upon him.'

' That you're not,' said Moulder.

' No I aint, Mr. Moulder, and so, John, there's my hand again,
and you're free to take it if you like.' And so saying she put forth
her hand almost into his lap.

' Take it, John!' said Mrs. Moulder. But poor Kenneby himself
did not seem to be very quick in availing himself of the happiness
offered to him. He did raise his right arm slightly; but then
he hesitated, and allowed it to fall again between him and his
sister.

' Come, John, you know you mean it,' said Mrs. Moulder. And
then with both her hands she lifted his, and placed it bodily within
the grasp of Mrs. Smiley's, which was still held forth to receive it.

' I know I'm engaged,' said Kenneby.

' There's no mistake about it,' said Moulder.

' There needn't be none,' said Mrs. Smiley, softly blushing; ' and I
will say this of myself—as I have been tempted to give a promise,
I'm not the woman to go back from my word. There's my hand,
John; and I don't care though all the world hears me say so.'
And then they sat hand in hand for some seconds, during which
poor Kenneby was unable to escape from the grasp of his bride
elect. One may say that all chance of final escape for him was
now gone by.

' But he can't say as how it was the old gentlemen's will as we
signed,' said Bridget, breaking the silence which ensued.

' And now, ladies and gentlemen,' said Kantwise, ' as Mrs. Bolster
has come back to that matter, I'll tell you something that will
surprise you. My friend Mr. Moulder here, who is as hospitable a
gentleman as I know anywhere wouldn't just let me speak before.'

' That's gammon, Kantwise. I never hindered you from speaking.'

' How I do hate that word. If you knew my aversion, Mr.
Moulder—'

' I can't pick my words for you, old fellow.'

' But what were you going to tell us, Mr. Kantwise?' said Mrs.
Smiley.

' Something that will make all your hairs stand on end, I think.'
And then he paused and looked round upon them all. It was at
this moment that Kenneby succeeded in getting his hand once more
to himself. ' Something that will surprise you all, or I'm very
much mistaken. Lady Mason has confessed her guilt.'

He had surprised them all. 'You don't say so,' exclaimed Mrs. Moulder.

'Confessed her guilt,' said Mrs. Smiley. 'But what guilt, Mr. Kantwise?'

'She forged the will,' said Kantwise.

'I knew that all along,' said Bridget Bolster.

'I'm d—— if I believe it,' said Moulder.

'You can do as you like about that,' said Kantwise; 'but she has. And I'll tell you what's more : she and young Mason have already left Orley Farm and given it all up into Joseph Mason's hands.'

'But didn't she get a verdict?' asked Snengkeld.

'Yes, she got a verdict. There's no doubt on earth about that.'

'Then it's my opinion she can't make herself guilty if she wished it; and as for the property, she can't give it up. The jury has found a verdict, and nobody can go beyond that. If anybody tries she'll have her action against 'em.' That was the law as laid down by Snengkeld.

'I don't believe a word of it,' said Moulder. 'Dockwrath has told him. I'll bet a hat that Kantwise got it from Dockwrath.'

It turned out that Kantwise had received his information from Dockwrath; but nevertheless, there was that in his manner, and in the nature of the story as it was told to them, that did produce belief. Moulder for a long time held out, but it became clear at last that even he was shaken : and now, even Kenneby acknowledged his conviction that the signature to the will was not his own.

'I know'd very well that I never did it twice,' said Bridget Bolster triumphantly, as she sat down to the supper table.

I am inclined to think, that upon the whole the company in Great St. Helen's became more happy as the conviction grew upon them that a great and mysterious crime had been committed, which had baffled two courts of law, and had at last thrust itself forth into the open daylight through the workings of the criminal's conscience. When Kantwise had completed his story, the time had come in which it behoved Mrs. Moulder to descend to the lower regions, and give some aid in preparation of the supper. During her absence the matter was discussed in every way, and on her return, when she was laden with good things, she found that all the party was contented except Moulder and her brother.

'It's a very terrible thing,' said Mrs. Smiley, later in the evening, as she sat with her steaming glass of rum and water before her. 'Very terrible indeed; aint it, John? I do wish now I'd gone down and see'd her, I do indeed. Don't you, Mrs. Moulder?'

'If all this is true I should like just to have had a peep at her.'

'At any rate we shall have pictures of her in all the papers,' said Mrs. Smiley.

CHAPTER XXXVIII.

THE LAST OF THE LAWYERS.

'I should have done my duty by you, Mr. Mason, which those men have not, and you would at this moment have been the owner of Orley Farm.'

It will easily be known that these words were spoken by Mr. Dockwrath, and that they were addressed to Joseph Mason. The two men were seated together in Mr. Mason's lodgings at Alston, late on the morning after the verdict had been given, and Mr. Dockwrath was speaking out his mind with sufficient freedom. On the previous evening he had been content to put up with the misery of the unsuccessful man, and had not added any reproaches of his own. He also had been cowed by the verdict, and the two had been wretched and crestfallen together. But the attorney since that had slept upon the matter, and had bethought himself that he at any rate would make out his little bill. He could show that Mr. Mason had ruined their joint affairs by his adherence to those London attorneys. Had Mr. Mason listened to the advice of his new adviser all would have been well. So at least Dockwrath was prepared to declare, finding that by so doing he would best pave the way for his own important claim.

But Mr. Mason was not a man to be bullied with tame endurance. 'The firm bears the highest name in the profession, sir,' he said; 'and I had just grounds for trusting them.'

'And what has come of your just grounds, Mr. Mason? Where are you? That's the question. I say that Round and Crook have thrown you over. They have been hand and glove with old Furnival through the whole transaction; and I'll tell you what's more, Mr. Mason. I told you how it would be from the beginning.'

'I'll move for a new trial.'

'A new trial; and this a criminal prosecution! She's free of you now for ever, and Orley Farm will belong to that son of hers till he chooses to sell it. It's a pity; that's all. I did my duty by you in a professional way, Mr. Mason; and you won't put the loss on my shoulders.'

'I've been robbed;—damnably robbed, that's all that I know.'

'There's no mistake on earth about that, Mr. Mason; you have been robbed; and the worst of it is, the costs will be so heavy! You'll be going down to Yorkshire soon I suppose, sir.'

'I don't know where I shall go?' said the squire of Groby, not content to be cross-questioned by the attorney from Hamworth.

' Because it's as well, I suppose, that we should settle something about the costs before you leave. I don't want to press for my money exactly now, but I shall be glad to know when I'm to get it.'

' If you have any claim on me, Mr. Dockwrath, you can send it to Mr. Round.'

' If I have any claim! What do you mean by that, sir? And I shall send nothing in to Mr. Round. I have had quite enough of Mr. Round already. I told you from the beginning, Mr. Mason, that I would have nothing to do with this affair as connected with Mr. Round. I have devoted myself entirely to this matter since you were pleased to engage my services at Groby Park. It is not by my fault that you have failed. I think, Mr. Mason, you will do me the justice to acknowledge that.' And then Dockwrath was silent for a moment, as though waiting for an answer.

' I have nothing to say upon the subject, Mr. Dockwrath,' said Mason.

' But, by heaven, something must be said. That won't do at all, Mr. Mason. I presume you do not think that I have been working like a slave for the last four months for nothing.'

Mr. Mason was in truth an honest man, and did not wish that any one should work on his account for nothing;—much less did he wish that such a one as Dockwrath should do so. But then, on the other side, in his present frame of mind he was by no means willing to yield anything to any one. ' I neither deny nor allow your claim, Mr. Dockwrath,' said he. ' But I shall pay nothing except through my regular lawyers. You can send your account to me if you please, but I shall send it on to Mr. Round without looking at it.'

' Oh, that's to be the way, is it? That's your gratitude. Very well, Mr. Mason; I shall now know what to do. And I think you'll find——'

Here Mr. Dockwrath was interrupted by the lodging-house servant, who brought in a note for Mr. Mason. It was from Mr. Furnival, and the girl who delivered it said that the gentleman's messenger was waiting for an answer.

' Sir,' said the note,

'A communication has been made to me this morning on the part of your brother, Mr. Lucius Mason, which may make it desirable that I should have an interview with you. If not inconvenient to you, I would ask you to meet me to-morrow morning at eleven o'clock at the chambers of your own lawyer, Mr. Round, in Bedford Row. I have already seen Mr. Round, and find that he can meet us.

'I am, sir,

'J. Mason, Esq., J.P.   'Your very obedient servant,
(of Groby Park).'   ' THOMAS FURNIVAL.

Mr. Furnival when he wrote this note had already been over to
Orley Farm, and had seen Lucius Mason.   He had been at the farm
almost before daylight, and had come away with the assured conviction that the property must be abandoned by his client.

'We need not talk about it, Mr. Furnival,' Lucius had said.   'It
must be so.'

'You have discussed the matter with your mother?'

'No discussion is necessary, but she is quite aware of my intention.   She is prepared to leave the place—for ever.'

'But the income——'

'Belongs to my brother Joseph.   Mr. Furnival, I think you may
understand that the matter is one in which it is necessary that I
should act, but as to which I trust I may not have to say many
words.   If you cannot arrange this for me, I must go to Mr. Round.'

Of course Mr. Furnival did understand it all.   His client had
been acquitted, and he had triumphed; but he had known for many
a long day that the estate did belong of right to Mr. Mason of
Groby; and though he had not suspected that Lucius would have
been so told, he could not be surprised at the result of such telling.
It was clear to him that Lady Mason had confessed, and that restitution would therefore be made.

'I will do your bidding,' said he.

'And, Mr. Furnival,—if it be possible, spare my mother.'   Then
the meeting was over, and Mr. Furnival returning to Hamworth
wrote his note to Mr. Joseph Mason.

Mr. Dockwrath had been interrupted by the messenger in the
middle of his threat, but he caught the name of Furnival as the
note was delivered.   Then he watched Mr. Mason as he read it and
read it again.

'If you please, sir, I was to wait for an answer,' said the girl.

Mr. Mason did not know what answer it would behove him to
give.   He felt that he was among Philistines while dealing with all
these lawyers, and yet he was at a loss in what way to reply to one
without leaning upon another.   'Look at that,' he said, sulkily
handing the note to Dockwrath.

'You must see Mr. Furnival, by all means,' said Dockwrath.
'But——'

'But what?'

'In your place I should not see him in the presence of Mr.
Round,—unless I was attended by an adviser on whom I could
rely.'   Mr. Mason, having given a few moments' consideration to
the matter, sat himself down and wrote a line to Mr. Furnival,
saying that he would be in Bedford Row at the appointed time.

'I think you are quite right,' said Dockwrath.

'But I shall go alone,' said Mr. Mason.

'Oh, very well; you will of course judge for yourself.   I cannot say what may be the nature of the communication to be made; but if it be anything touching the property, you will no doubt jeopardize your own interests by your imprudence.'

'Good morning, Mr. Dockwrath,' said Mr. Mason.

'Oh, very well. Good morning, sir. You shall hear from me very shortly, Mr. Mason; and I must say that, considering everything, I do not know that I ever came across a gentleman who behaved himself worse in a peculiar position than you have done in yours.' And so they parted.

Punctually at eleven o'clock on the following day Mr. Mason was in Bedford Row. 'Mr. Furnival is with Mr. Round,' said the clerk, 'and will see you in two minutes.' Then he was shown into the dingy office waiting-room, where he sat with his hat in his hand, for rather more than two minutes.

At that moment Mr. Round was describing to Mr. Furnival the manner in which he had been visited some weeks since by Sir Peregrine Orme. 'Of course, Mr. Furnival, I knew which way the wind blew when I heard that.'

'She must have told him everything.'

'No doubt, no doubt. At any rate he knew it all.'

'And what did you say to him?'

'I promised to hold my tongue;—and I kept my promise. Mat knows nothing about it to this day.'

The whole history thus became gradually clear to Mr. Furnival's mind, and he could understand in what manner that marriage had been avoided. Mr. Round also understood it, and the two lawyers confessed together, that though the woman had deserved the punishment which had come upon her, her character was one which might have graced a better destiny. 'And now, I suppose, my fortunate client may come in,' said Mr. Round. Whereupon the fortunate client was released from his captivity, and brought into the sitting-room of the senior partner.

'Mr. Mason, Mr. Furnival,' said the attorney, as soon as he had shaken hands with his client. 'You know each other very well by name, gentlemen.'

Mr. Mason was very stiff in his bearing and demeanour, but remarked that he had heard of Mr. Furnival before.

'All the world has heard of him,' said Mr. Round. 'He hasn't hid his light under a bushel.' Whereupon Mr. Mason bowed, not quite understanding what was said to him.

'Mr. Mason,' began the barrister, 'I have a communication to make to you, very singular in its nature, and of great importance. It is one which I believe you will regard as being of considerable importance to yourself, and which is of still higher moment to my—my friend, Lady Mason.'

'Lady Mason, sir—' began the other; but Mr. Furnival stopped him.

'Allow me to interrupt you, Mr. Mason. I think it will be better that you should hear me before you commit yourself to any expression as to your relative.'

'She is no relative of mine.'

'But her son is. However,—if you will allow me, I will go on. Having this communication to make, I thought it expedient for your own sake that it should be done in the presence of your own legal adviser and friend.'

'Umph!' grunted the disappointed litigant.

'I have already explained to Mr. Round that which I am about to explain to you, and he was good enough to express himself as satisfied with the step which I am taking.'

'Quite so, Mr. Mason. Mr. Furnival is behaving, and I believe has behaved throughout, in a manner becoming the very high position which he holds in his profession.'

'I suppose he has done his best on his side,' said Mason.

'Undoubtedly I have,—as I should have done on yours, had it so chanced that I had been honoured by holding a brief from your attorneys. But the communication which I am going to make now I make not as a lawyer but as a friend. Mr. Mason, my client Lady Mason, and her son Lucius Mason, are prepared to make over to you the full possession of the estate which they have held under the name of Orley Farm.'

The tidings, as so given, were far from conveying to the sense of the hearer the full information which they bore. He heard the words, and at the moment conceived that Orley Farm was intended to come into his hands by some process to which it was thought desirable that he should be brought to agree. He was to be induced to buy it, or to be bought over from further opposition by some concession of an indefinitely future title. But that the estate was to become his at once, without purchase, and by the mere free will of his hated relatives, was an idea that he did not realize.

'Mr. Furnival,' he said, 'what future steps I shall take I do not yet know. That I have been robbed of my property I am as firmly convinced now as ever. But I tell you fairly, and I tell Mr. Round so too, that I will have no dealings with that woman.'

'Your father's widow, sir,' said Mr. Furnival, 'is an unhappy lady, who is now doing her best to atone for the only fault of which I believe her to have been guilty. If you were not unreasonable as well as angry, you would understand that the proposition which I am now making to you is one which should force you to forgive any injury which she may hitherto have done to you. Your half-brother Lucius Mason has instructed me to make over to you the possession of Orley Farm.' These last words Mr. Furnival uttered very slowly, fixing his keen grey eyes full upon the face of Joseph Mason as he did so, and then turning round to the attorney he said, 'I presume your client will understand me now.'

'The estate is yours, Mr. Mason,' said Round. 'You have nothing to do but to take possession of it.'

'What do you mean?' said Mason, turning round upon Furnival.

'Exactly what I say. Your half brother Lucius surrenders to you the estate.'

'Without payment?'

'Yes; without payment. On his doing so you will of course absolve him from all liability on account of the proceeds of the property while in his hands.'

'That will be a matter of course,' said Mr. Round.

'Then she has robbed me,' said Mason, jumping up to his feet. 'By ——, the will was forged after all.'

'Mr. Mason,' said Mr. Round, 'if you have a spark of generosity in you, you will accept the offer made to you without asking any question. By no such questioning can you do yourself any good,— nor can you do that poor lady any harm.'

'I knew it was so,' he said loudly, and as he spoke he twice walked the length of the room. 'I knew it was so;—twenty years ago I said the same. She forged the will. I ask you, as my lawyer, Mr. Round,—did she not forge the will herself?'

'I shall answer no such question, Mr. Mason.'

'Then by heavens I'll expose you. If I spend the whole value of the estate in doing it I'll expose you, and have her punished yet. The slippery villain! For twenty years she has robbed me.'

'Mr. Mason, you are forgetting yourself in your passion,' said Mr. Furnival. 'What you have to look for now is the recovery of the property.' But here Mr. Furnival showed that he had not made himself master of Joseph Mason's character.

'No,' shouted the angry man;—'no, by heaven. What I have first to look to is her punishment, and that of those who have assisted her. I knew she had done it,—and Dockwrath knew it. Had I trusted him, she would now have been in gaol.'

Mr. Furnival and Mr. Round were both desirous of having the matter quietly arranged, and with this view were willing to put up with much. The man had been ill used. When he declared for the fortieth time that he had been robbed for twenty years, they could not deny it. When with horrid oaths he swore that that will had been a forgery, they could not contradict him. When he reviled the laws of his country, which had done so much to facilitate the escape of a criminal, they had no arguments to prove that he was wrong. They bore with him in his rage, hoping that a sense of his own self-interest might induce him to listen to reason. But it was

all in vain. The property was sweet, but that sweetness was taste-
less when compared to the sweetness of revenge.

'Nothing shall make me tamper with justice;—nothing,' said he.

'But even if it were as you say, you cannot do anything to her,'
said Round.

'I'll try,' said Mason. 'You have been my attorney, and what
you know in the matter you are bound to tell. And I'll make
you tell, sir.'

'Upon my word,' said Round, 'this is beyond bearing. Mr.
Mason, I must trouble you to walk out of my office.' And then he
rang the bell. 'Tell Mr. Mat I want to see him.' But before that
younger partner had joined his father Joseph Mason had gone.
'Mat,' said the old man, 'I don't interfere with you in many things,
but on this I must insist. As long as my name is in the firm Mr.
Joseph Mason of Groby shall not be among our customers.'

'The man's a fool,' said Mr. Furnival. 'The end of all that will
be that two years will go by before he gets his property; and, in
the meantime, the house and all about it will go to ruin.'

In these days there was a delightful family concord between
Mr. Furnival and his wife, and perhaps we may be allowed to hope
that the peace was permanent. Martha Biggs had not been in
Harley Street since we last saw her there, and was now walking
round Red Lion Square by the hour with some kindred spirit, complaining bitterly of the return which had been made for her friendship. 'What I endured, and what I was prepared to endure for
that woman, no breathing creature can ever know,' said Martha
Biggs, to that other Martha; 'and now——'

'I suppose the fact is he don't like to see you there,' said the
other.

'And is that a reason?' said our Martha. 'Had I been in her
place I would not have put my foot in his house again till I was
assured that my friend should be as welcome there as myself. But
then, perhaps, my ideas of friendship may be called romantic.'

But though there were heart-burnings and war in Red Lion
Square, there was sweet peace in Harley Street. Mrs. Furnival had
learned that beyond all doubt Lady Mason was an unfortunate
woman on whose behalf her husband was using his best energies as
a lawyer; and though rumours had begun to reach her that were
very injurious to the lady's character, she did not on that account
feel animosity against her. Had Lady Mason been guilty of all the
sins in the calendar except one, Mrs. Furnival could find it within
her heart to forgive her.

But Sophia was now more interested about Lady Mason than was
her mother, and during those days of the trial was much more eager
to learn the news as it became known. She had said nothing to her
mother about Lucius, nor had she said anything as to Augustus

Staveley. Miss Furnival was a lady who on such subjects did not want the assistance of a mother's counsel. Then, early on the morning that followed the trial, they heard the verdict and knew that Lady Mason was free.

'I am so glad,' said Mrs. Furnival; 'and I am sure it was your papa's doing.'

'But we will hope that she was really innocent,' said Sophia.

'Oh, yes; of course; and so I suppose she was. I am sure I hope so. But, nevertheless, we all know that it was going very much against her.'

'I believe papa never thought she was guilty for a moment.'

'I don't know, my dear; your papa never talks of the clients for whom he is engaged. But what a thing it is for Lucius! He would have lost every acre of the property.'

'Yes; it's a great thing for him, certainly.' And then she began to consider whether the standing held by Lucius Mason in the world was not even yet somewhat precarious.

It was on the same day—in the evening—that she received her lover's letter. She was alone when she read it, and she made herself quite master of its contents before she sat herself to think in what way it would be expedient that she should act. 'I am bound to relinquish to my brother-in-law my title to Orley Farm.' Why should he be so bound, unless—? And then she also came to that conclusion which Mr. Round had reached, and which Joseph Mason had reached, when they heard that the property was to be given up. 'Yes, Sophia, I am a beggar,' the letter went on to say. She was very sorry, deeply sorry;—so, at least, she said to herself. As she sat there alone, she took out her handkerchief and pressed it to her eyes. Then, having restored it to her pocket, after moderate use, she refolded her letter, and put that into the same receptacle.

'Papa,' said she, that evening, 'what will Mr. Lucius Mason do now? will he remain at Orley Farm?'

'No, my dear. He will leave Orley Farm, and, I think, will go abroad with his mother.'

'And who will have Orley Farm?'

'His brother Joseph, I believe.'

'And what will Lucius have?'

'I cannot say. I do not know that he will have anything. His mother has an income of her own, and he, I suppose, will go into some profession.'

'Oh, indeed. Is not that very sad for him, poor fellow?' In answer to which her father made no remark.

That night, in her own room, she answered her lover's letter, and her answer was as follows:—

Harley Street, March, 18—.

' MY DEAR MR. MASON,

'I need hardly tell you that I was grieved to the heart by the tidings conveyed in your letter. I will not ask you for that secret which you withhold from me, feeling that I have no title to inquire into it; nor will I attempt to guess at the cause which induces you to give up to your brother the property which you were always taught to regard as your own. That you are actuated by noble motives I am sure; and you may be sure of this, that I shall respect you quite as highly in your adversity as I have ever done in your prosperity. That you will make your way in the world, I shall never doubt; and it may be that the labour which you will now encounter will raise you to higher standing than any you could have achieved, had the property remained in your possession.

'I think you are right in saying, with reference to our mutual regard for each other, that neither should be held as having any claim upon the other. Under present circumstances, any such claim would be very silly. Nothing would hamper you in your future career so much as a long marriage engagement; and for myself, I am aware that the sorrow and solicitude thence arising would be more than I could support. Apart from this, also, I feel certain that I should never obtain my father's sanction for such an engagement, nor could I make it, unless he sanctioned it. I feel so satisfied that you will see the truth of this, that I need not trouble you, and harass my own heart by pursuing the subject any further.

' My feelings of friendship for you—of affectionate friendship— will be as true as ever. I shall look to your future career with great hope, and shall hear of your success with the utmost satisfaction. And I trust that the time may come, at no very distant date, when we may all welcome your return to London, and show you that our regard for you has never been diminished.

'May God bless and preserve you in the trials which are before you, and carry you through them with honour and safety. Wherever you may be I shall watch for tidings of you with anxiety, and always hear them with gratification. I need hardly bid you remember that you have no more affectionate friend

' Than yours always most sincerely,

' SOPHIA FURNIVAL.

' P.S.—I believe that a meeting between us at the present moment would only cause pain to both of us. It might drive you to speak of things which should be wrapped in silence. At any rate, I am sure that you will not press it on me.'

Lucius, when he received this letter, was living with his mother in lodgings near Finsbury Circus, and the letter had been redirected from Hamworth to a post-office in that neighbourhood. It was his

Farewell !

intention to take his mother with him to a small town on one of the rivers that feed the Rhine, and there remain hidden till he could find some means by which he might earn his bread. He was sitting with her in the evening, with two dull tallow candles on the table between them, when his messenger brought the letter to him. He read it in silence very deliberately, then crushed it in his hand, and threw it from him with violence into the fire.

' I hope there is nothing further to distress you, Lucius,' said his mother, looking up into his face as though she were imploring his confidence.

' No, nothing ; nothing that matters. It is an affair quite private to myself.'

Sir Peregrine had spoken with great truth when he declared that Lucius Mason was able to bear adversity. This last blow had now come upon him, but he made no wailings as to his misery, nor did he say a word further on the subject. His mother watched the paper as the flame caught it and reduced it to an ash ; but she asked no further question. She knew that her position with him did not permit of her asking, or even hoping, for his confidence.

' I had no right to expect it would be otherwise,' he said to himself. But even to himself he spoke no word of reproach against Miss Furnival. He had realized the circumstances by which he was surrounded, and had made up his mind to bear their result.

As for Miss Furnival, we may as well declare here that she did not become Mrs. Staveley. Our old friend Augustus conceived that he had received a sufficient answer on the occasion of his last visit to Harley Street, and did not repeat it immediately. Such little scenes as that which took place there had not been uncommon in his life ; and when in after months he looked back upon the affair, he counted it up as one of those miraculous escapes which had marked his career.

CHAPTER XXXIX.

FAREWELL.

' THAT letter you got this morning, my dear, was it not from Lady Mason ?'

' It was from Lady Mason, father ; they go on Thursday.'

' On Thursday ; so soon as that.' And then Sir Peregrine, who had asked the question, remained silent for a while. The letter, according to the family custom, had been handed to Mrs. Orme over the breakfast-table ; but he had made no remark respecting it till they were alone together and free from the servants. It had been a farewell letter, full of love and gratitude, and full also of repentance.

Lady Mason had now been for three weeks in London, and once during that time Mrs. Orme had gone up to visit her. She had then remained with her friend for hours, greatly to Lady Mason's comfort, and now this letter had come, bringing a last adieu.

'You may read it, sir, if you like,' said Mrs. Orme, handing him the letter. It was evident, by his face, that he was gratified by the privilege; and he read it, not once only, but over and over again. As he did so, he placed himself in the shade, and sat with his back to Mrs. Orme; but nevertheless she could see that from time to time he rubbed his eyes with the back of his hand, and gradually raised his handkerchief to his face.

'Thank you, dearest,' he said, as he gave the letter back to her.

'I think that we may forgive her now, even all that she has done,' said Mrs. Orme.

'Yes—yes—yes,' he answered. 'For myself, I forgave her from the first.'

'I know you did. But as regards the property,—it has been given up now.' And then again they were silent.

'Edith,' he said, after a while, 'I have forgiven her altogether. To me she is the same as though she had never done that deed. Are we not all sinners?'

'Surely, father.'

'And can I say because she did one startling thing that the total of her sin is greater than mine? Was I ever tempted as she was tempted? Was my youth made dangerous for me as was hers? And then she did nothing for herself; she did it all for another. We may think of that now.'

'I have thought of it always.'

'It did not make the sin the less; but among her fellow-mortals ——' And then he stopped himself, wanting words to express his meaning. The sin, till it was repented, was damning; but now that it was repented, he could almost love the sinner for the sin.

'Edith,' he said, again. And he looked at her so wishfully! She knew well what was the working of his heart, and she knew also that she did not dare to encourage him.

'I trust,' said Mrs. Orme, 'that she will bear her present lot for a few years; and then, perhaps——'

'Ah! then I shall be in my grave. A few months will do that.'

'Oh, sir!'

'Why should I not save her from such a life as that?'

'From that which she had most to fear she has been saved.'

'Had she not so chosen it herself, she could now have demanded from me a home. Why should I not give it to her now?'

'A home here, sir?'

'Yes; why not? But I know what you would say. It would be wrong,—to you and Parry.'

'It would be wrong to yourself, sir. Think of it, father. It is the fact that she did that thing. We may forgive her, but others will not do so on that account. It would not be right that you should bring her here.'

Sir Peregrine knew that it would not be right. Though he was old, and weak in body, and infirm in purpose, his judgment had not altogether left him. He was well aware that he would offend all social laws if he were to do that which he contemplated, and ask the world around him to respect as Lady Orme—as his wife, the woman who had so deeply disgraced herself. But yet he could hardly bring himself to confess that it was impossible. He was as a child who knows that a coveted treasure is beyond his reach, but still covets it, still longs for it, hoping against hope that it may yet be his own. It seemed to him that he might yet regain his old vitality if he could wind his arm once more about her waist, and press her to his side, and call her his own. It would be so sweet to forgive her; to make her sure that she was absolutely forgiven; to teach her that there was one at least who would not bring up against her her past sin, even in his memory. As for his grandson, the property should be abandoned to him altogether. 'Twas thus he argued with himself; but yet, as he argued, he knew that it could not be so.

'I was harsh to her when she told me,' he said, after another pause—'cruelly harsh.'

'She does not think so.'

'No. If I had spurned her from me with my foot, she would not have thought so. She had condemned herself, and therefore I should have spared her.'

'But you did spare her. I am sure she feels that from the first to the last your conduct to her has been more than kind.'

'And I owed her more than kindness, for I loved her;—yes, I loved her, and I do love her. Though I am a feeble old man, tottering to my grave, yet I love her—love her as that boy loves the fair girl for whom he longs. He will overcome it, and forget it, and some other one as fair will take her place. But for me it is all over.'

What could she say to him? In truth, it was all over,—such love at least as that of which his old heart was dreaming in its dotage. There is no Medea's caldron from which our limbs can come out young and fresh; and it were well that the heart should grow old as does the body.

'It is not all over while we are with you,' she said, caressing him. But she knew that what she said was a subterfuge.

'Yes, yes; I have you, dearest,' he answered. But he also knew that that pretence at comfort was false and hollow.

'And she starts on Thursday,' he said; 'on next Thursday.'

'Yes, on Thursday. It will be much better for her to be away from London. While she is there she never ventures even into the street.'

'Edith, I shall see her before she goes.'

'Will that be wise, sir?'

'Perhaps not. It may be foolish,—very foolish; but still I shall see her. I think you forget, Edith, that I have never yet bidden her farewell. I have not spoken to her since that day when she behaved so generously.'

'I do not think that she expects it, father.'

'No; she expects nothing for herself. Had it been in her nature to expect such a visit, I should not have been anxious to make it. I will go to-morrow. She is always at home you say?'

'Yes, she is always at home.'

'And, Lucius——'

'You will not find him there in the daytime.'

'I shall go to-morrow, dear. You need not tell Peregrine.'

Mrs. Orme still thought that he was wrong, but she had nothing further to say. She could not hinder his going, and therefore, with his permission she wrote a line to Lady Mason, telling her of his purpose. And then, with all the care in her power, and with infinite softness of manner, she warned him against the danger which she so much feared. What might be the result, if, overcome by tenderness, he should again ask Lady Mason to become his wife? Mrs. Orme firmly believed that Lady Mason would again refuse; but, nevertheless, there would be danger.

'No,' said he, 'I will not do that. When I have said so you may accept my word.' Then she hastened to apologize to him, but he assured her with a kiss that he was in nowise angry with her.

He held by his purpose, and on the following day he went up to London. There was nothing said on the matter at breakfast, nor did she make any further endeavour to dissuade him. He was infirm, but still she knew that the actual fatigue would not be of a nature to injure him. Indeed her fear respecting him was rather in regard to his staying at home than to his going abroad. It would have been well for him could he have been induced to think himself fit for more active movement.

Lady Mason was alone when he reached the dingy little room near Finsbury Circus, and received him standing. She was the first to speak, and this she did before she had even touched his hand. She stood to meet him, with her eyes turned to the ground, and her hands tightly folded together before her: 'Sir Peregrine,' she said, 'I did not expect from you this mark of your—kindness.'

'Of my esteem and affection, Lady Mason,' he said. 'We have known each other too well to allow of our parting without a word. I am an old man, and it will probably be for ever.'

Then she gave him her hand, and gradually lifted her eyes to his face. 'Yes,' she said; 'it will be for ever. There will be no coming back for me.'

'Nay, nay; we will not say that. That's as may be hereafter. But it will not be at once. It had better not be quite at once. Edith tells me that you go on Thursday.'

'Yes, sir; we go on Thursday.'

She had still allowed her hand to remain in his, but now she withdrew it, and asked him to sit down. 'Lucius is not here,' she said. 'He never remains at home after breakfast. He has much to settle as to our journey; and then he has lawyers to see.'

Sir Peregrine had not at all wished to see Lucius Mason, but he did not say so. 'You will give him my regards,' he said, 'and tell him that I trust that he may prosper.'

'Thank you. I will do so. It is very kind of you to think of him.'

'I have always thought highly of him as an excellent young man.'

'And he is excellent. Where is there any one who could suffer without a word as he suffers? No complaint ever comes from him; and yet—I have ruined him.'

'No, no. He has his youth, his intellect, and his education. If such a one as he cannot earn his bread in the world—ay, and more than his bread—who can do so? Nothing ruins a young man but ignorance, idleness, and depravity.'

'Nothing;—unless those of whom he should be proud disgrace him before the eyes of the world. Sir Peregrine, I sometimes wonder at my own calmness. I wonder that I can live. But, believe me, that never for a moment do I forget what I have done. I would have poured out for him my blood like water, if it would have served him; but instead of that I have given him cause to curse me till the day of his death. Though I still live, and eat, and sleep, I think of that always. The remembrance is never away from me. They bid those who repent put on sackcloth, and cover themselves with ashes. That is my sackcloth, and it is very sore. Those thoughts are ashes to me, and they are very bitter between my teeth.'

He did not know with what words to comfort her. It all was as she said, and he could not bid her even try to free herself from that sackcloth and from those ashes. It must be so. Were it not so with her, she would not have been in any degree worthy of that love which he felt for her. 'God tempers the wind to the shorn lamb,' he said.

'Yes,' she said, 'for the shorn lamb—' And then she was silent again. But could that bitter, biting wind be tempered for the she-wolf who, in the dead of night, had broken into the fold, and with prowling steps and cunning clutch had stolen the fodder from the sheep? That was the question as it presented itself to her; but she sat silent, and refrained from putting it into words. She sat silent, but he read her heart. 'For the shorn lamb—' she had said, and he had known her thoughts, as they followed, quick, one upon another, through her mind. 'Mary,' he said, seating himself now close beside her on the sofa, 'if his heart be as true to you as mine, he will never remember these things against you.'

'It is my memory, not his, that is my punishment,' she said.

Why could he not take her home with him, and comfort her, and heal that festering wound, and stop that ever-running gush of her heart's blood? But he could not. He had pledged his word and pawned his honour. All the comfort that could be his to bestow must be given in those few minutes that remained to him in that room. And it must be given, too, without falsehood. He could not bring himself to tell her that the sackcloth need not be sore to her poor lacerated body, nor the ashes bitter between her teeth. He could not tell her that the cup of which it was hers to drink might yet be pleasant to the taste, and cool to the lips! What could he tell her? Of the only source of true comfort others, he knew, had spoken,—others who had not spoken in vain. He could not now take up that matter, and press it on her with available strength. For him there was but one thing to say. He had forgiven her; he still loved her; he would have cherished her in his bosom had it been possible. He was a weak, old, foolish man; and there was nothing of which he could speak but of his own heart.

'Mary,' he said, again taking her hand, 'I wish—I wish that I could comfort you.'

'And yet on you also have I brought trouble, and misery—and—all but disgrace!'

'No, my love, no; neither misery nor disgrace,—except this misery, that I shall be no longer near to you. Yes, I will tell you all now. Were I alone in the world, I would still beg you to go back with me.'

'It cannot be; it could not possibly be so.'

'No; for I am not alone. She who loves you so well, has told me so. It must not be. But that is the source of my misery. I have learned to love you too well, and do not know how to part with you. If this had not been so, I would have done all that an old man might to comfort you.'

'But it has been so,' she said. 'I cannot wash out the past. Knowing what I did of myself, Sir Peregrine, I should never have put my foot over your threshold.'

'I wish I might hear its step again upon my floors. I wish I might hear that light step once again.'

'Never, Sir Peregrine. No one again ever shall rejoice to hear

Farewell!

either my step or my voice, or to see my form, or to grasp my hand. The world is over for me, and may God soon grant me relief from my sorrow. But to you—in return for your goodness——'

' For my love.'

' In return for your love, what am I to say? I could have loved you with all my heart had it been so permitted. Nay, I did do so. Had that dream been carried out, I should not have sworn falsely when I gave you my hand. I bade her tell you so from me, when I parted with her.'

' She did tell me.'

' I have known but little love. He—Sir Joseph—was my master rather than my husband. He was a good master, and I served him truly—except in that one thing. But I never loved him. But I am wrong to talk of this, and I will not talk of it longer. May God bless you, Sir Peregrine! It will be well for both of us now that you should leave me.'

' May God bless you, Mary, and preserve you, and give back to you the comforts of a quiet spirit, and a heart at rest! Till you hear that I am under the ground you will know that there is one living who loves you well.' Then he took her in his arms, twice kissed her on the forehead, and left the room without further speech on either side.

Lady Mason, as soon as she was alone, sat herself down, and her thoughts ran back over the whole course of her life. Early in her days, when the world was yet beginning to her, she had done one evil deed, and from that time up to those days of her trial she had been the victim of one incessant struggle to appear before the world as though that deed had not been done,—to appear innocent of it before the world, but, beyond all things, innocent of it before her son. For twenty years she had striven with a labour that had been all but unendurable; and now she had failed, and every one knew her for what she was. Such had been her life; and then she thought of the life which might have been hers. In her earlier days she had known what it was to be poor, and had seen and heard those battles after money which harden our hearts, and quench the poetry of our natures. But it had not been altogether so with her. Had things gone differently with her it might afterwards have been said that she had gone through the fire unscathed. But the beast had set his foot upon her, and when the temptation came it was too much for her. Not for herself would she have sinned, or have robbed that old man, who had been to her a kind master. But when a child was born to her, her eyes were blind, and she could not see that wealth ill gotten for her child would be as sure a curse as wealth ill gotten for herself. She remembered Rebekah, and with the cunning of a second Rebekah she filched a world's blessing for her baby. Now she thought of all this as pictures of that life which might have been hers passed before her mind's eye.

And they were pleasant pictures, had they not burnt into her very soul as she looked at them. How sweet had been that drawing-room at the Cleeve, as she sat there in luxurious quiet with her new friend! How sweet had been that friendship with a woman pure in all her thoughts, graceful to the eye, and delicate in all her ways! She knew now, as she thought of this, that to her had been given the power to appreciate such delights as these. How full of charm to her would have been that life, in which there had been so much of true, innocent affection;—had the load ever been absent from her shoulders! And then she thought of Sir Peregrine, with his pleasant, ancient manner and truth of heart, and told herself that she could have been happy with the love of even so old a man as that,—had that burden been away from her! But the burden had never been away—never could be away. Then she thought once more of her stern but just son, and as she bowed her head and kissed the rod, she prayed that her release might come to her soon.

And now we will say farewell to her, and as we do so the chief interest of our tale will end. I may, perhaps, be thought to owe an apology to my readers in that I have asked their sympathy for a woman who had so sinned as to have placed her beyond the general sympathy of the world at large. If so, I tender my apology, and perhaps feel that I should confess a fault. But as I have told her story that sympathy has grown upon myself till I have learned to forgive her, and to feel that I too could have regarded her as a friend. Of her future life I will not venture to say anything. But no lesson is truer than that which teaches us to believe that God does temper the wind to the shorn lamb. To how many has it not seemed, at some one period of their lives, that all was over for them, and that to them in their afflictions there was nothing left but to die! And yet they have lived to laugh again, to feel that the air was warm and the earth fair, and that God in giving them ever-springing hope had given everything. How many a sun may seem to set on an endless night, and yet rising again on some morrow—

> 'He tricks his beams, and with new spangled ore
> Flames in the forehead of the morning sky!'

For Lady Mason let us hope that the day will come in which she also may once again trick her beams in some modest, unassuming way, and that for her the morning may even yet be sweet with a glad warmth. For us, here in these pages, it must be sufficient to say this last kindly farewell.

As to Lucius Mason and the arrangement of his affairs with his step-brother a very few concluding words will suffice. When Joseph Mason left the office of Messrs. Round and Crook he would gladly have sacrificed all hope of any eventual pecuniary benefit from the possession of Orley Farm could he by doing so have secured the condign punishment of her who had so long kept him out of his inheritance. But he soon found that he had no means of doing this. In the first place he did not know where to turn for advice. He had quarrelled absolutely with Dockwrath, and though he now greatly distrusted the Rounds, he by no means put implicit trust in him of Hamworth. Of the Rounds he suspected that they were engaged to serve his enemy, of Dockwrath he felt sure that he was anxious only to serve himself. Under these circumstances he was driven into the arms of a third attorney, and learned from him, after a delay that cut him to the soul, that he could take no further criminal proceeding against Lady Mason. It would be impossible to have her even indicted for the forgery,—seeing that two juries, at the interval of twenty years, had virtually acquitted her,—unless new evidence which should be absolute and positive in its kind should be forthcoming. But there was no new evidence of any kind. The offer made to surrender the property was no evidence for a jury whatever it might be in the mind of the world at large.

'And what am I to do?' asked Mason.

'Take the goods the gods provide you,' said the attorney. 'Accept the offer which your half-brother has very generously made you.'

'Generously!' shouted Mason of Groby.

'Well, on his part it is generous. It is quite within his power to keep it; and were he to do so no one would say he was wrong. Why should he judge his mother?'

Then Mr. Joseph Mason went to another attorney; but it was of no avail. The time was passing away, and he learned that Lady Mason and Lucius had actually started for Germany. In his agony for revenge he had endeavoured to obtain some legal order that should prevent her departure;—'ne exeat regno,' as he repeated over and over again to his advisers learned in the law. But it was of no avail. Lady Mason had been tried and acquitted, and no judge would interfere.

'We should soon have her back again, you know, if we had evidence of forgery,' said the last attorney.

'Then, by —— ! we will have her back again,' said Mason.

But the threat was vain; nor could he get any one even to promise him that she could be prosecuted and convicted. And by degrees the desire for vengeance slackened as the desire for gain resumed its sway. Many men have threatened to spend a property upon a lawsuit who have afterwards felt grateful that their threats were made abortive. And so it was with Mr. Mason. After remaining in town over a month he took the advice of the first of those new lawyers and allowed that gentleman to put himself in communication with Mr. Furnival. The result was that by the end of six months he again came out of Yorkshire to take upon himself the duties and privileges of the owner of Orley Farm.

And then came his great fight with Dockwrath, which in the end ruined the Hamworth attorney, and cost Mr. Mason more money than he ever liked to confess. Dockwrath claimed to be put in possession of Orley Farm at an exceedingly moderate rent, as to the terms of which he was prepared to prove that Mr. Mason had already entered into a contract with him. Mr. Mason utterly ignored such contract, and contended that the words contained in a certain note produced by Dockwrath amounted only to a proposition to let him the land in the event of certain circumstances and results—which circumstances and results never took place.

This lawsuit Mr. Joseph Mason did win, and Mr. Samuel Dockwrath was, as I have said, ruined. What the attorney did to make it necessary that he should leave Hamworth I do not know; but Miriam, his wife, is now the mistress of that lodging-house to which her own mahogany furniture was so ruthlessly removed.

CHAPTER XL.

SHOWING HOW AFFAIRS SETTLED THEMSELVES AT NONINGSBY.

WE must now go back to Noningsby for one concluding chapter, and then our work will be completed.

'You are not to go away from Noningsby when the trial is over, you know. Mamma said that I had better tell you so.' It was thus that Madeline had spoken to Felix Graham as he was going out to the judge's carriage on the last morning of the celebrated great Orley Farm case, and as she did so she twisted one of her little fingers into one of his buttonholes. This she did with a prettiness of familiarity, and the assumption of a right to give him orders and hold him to obedience, which was almost intoxicating in its sweetness. And why should she not be familiar with him? Why should she not hold him to obedience by his buttonhole? Was he not her own? Had she not chosen him and taken him up to the exclusion of all other such choosings and takings?

'I shall not go till you send me,' he said, putting up his hand as though to protect his coat, and just touching her fingers as he did so.

'Mamma says it will be stupid for you in the mornings, but it will not be worse for you than for Augustus. He stays till after Easter.'

'And I shall stay till after Whitsuntide unless I am turned out.'

'Oh! but you will be turned out. I am not going to make myself answerable for any improper amount of idleness. Papa says you have got all the law courts to reform.'

'There must be a double Hercules for such a set of stables as that,' said Felix; and then with the slight ceremony to which I have before adverted he took his leave for the day.

'I suppose there will be no use in delaying it,' said Lady Staveley on the same morning as she and her daughter sat together in the drawing-room. They had already been talking over the new engagement by the hour, together; but that is a subject on which mothers with marriageable daughters never grow tired, as all mothers and marriageable daughters know full well.

'Oh! mamma, I think it must be delayed.'

'But why, my love? Mr. Graham has not said so?'

'You must call him Felix, mamma. I'm sure it's a nice name.'

'Very well, my dear, I will.'

'No; he has said nothing yet. But of course he means to wait till,—till it will be prudent.'

'Men never care for prudence of that kind when they are really in love;—and I'm sure he is.'

'Is he, mamma?'

'He will marry on anything or nothing. And if you speak to him he tells you of how the young ravens were fed. But he always forgets that he's not a young raven himself.'

'Now you're only joking, mamma.'

'Indeed I'm quite in earnest. But I think your papa means to make up an income for you,—only you must not expect to be rich.'

'I do not want to be rich. I never did.'

'I suppose you will live in London, and then you can come down here when the courts are up. I do hope he won't ever want to take a situation in the colonies.'

'Who, Felix? Why should he go to the colonies?'

'They always do,—the clever young barristers who marry before they have made their way. That would be very dreadful. I really think it would kill me.'

'Oh! mamma, he sha'n't go to any colony.'

'To be sure there are the county courts now, and they are better I suppose you wouldn't like to live at Leeds or Merthyr-Tydvil?'

'Of course I shall live wherever he goes; but I don't know why you should send him to Merthyr-Tydvil.'

'Those are the sort of places they do go to. There is young Mrs. Bright Newdegate,—she had to go to South Shields, and her babies are all dreadfully delicate. She lost two, you know. I do think the Lord Chancellor ought to think about that. Reigate, or Maidstone, or anywhere about Great Marlow would not be so bad.'

And in this way they discussed the coming event and the happy future, while Felix himself was listening to the judge's charge and thinking of his client's guilt.

Then there were two or three days passed at Noningsby of almost unalloyed sweetness. It seemed that they had all agreed that Prudence should go by the board, and that Love with sweet promises, and hopes bright as young trees in spring, should have it all her own way. Judge Staveley was a man who on such an occasion—knowing with whom he had to deal—could allow ordinary prudence to go by the board. There are men, and excellent men too, from whose minds the cares of life never banish themselves, who never seem to remember that provision is made for the young ravens. They toil and spin always, thinking sternly of the worst and rarely hoping for the best. They are ever making provision for rainy days, as though there were to be no more sunshine. So anxious are they for their children that they take no pleasure in them, and their fear is constant that the earth will cease to produce her fruits. Of such was not the judge. 'Dulce est desipere in locis,' he would say, 'and let the opportunities be frequent and the occasions many.' Such a love-making opportunity as this surely should be one.

So Graham wandered about through the dry March winds with his future bride by his side, and never knew that the blasts came from the pernicious east. And she would lean on his arm as though he had been the friend of her earliest years, listening to and trusting him in all things. That little finger, as they stood together, would get up to his buttonhole, and her bright frank eyes would settle themselves on his, and then her hand would press closely upon his arm, and he knew that she was neither ashamed nor afraid of her love. Her love to her was the same as her religion. When it was once acknowledged by her to be a thing good and trustworthy, all the world might know it. Was it not a glory to her that he had chosen her, and why should she conceal her glory? Had it been that some richer, greater man had won her love,—some one whose titles were known and high place in the world approved, —it may well be that then she would have been less free with him.

'Papa would like it best if you would give up your writing, and think of nothing but the law,' she said to him. In answer to which he told her, with many compliments to the special fox in question, that story of the fox who had lost his tail and thought it well that other foxes should dress themselves as he was dressed.

'At any rate papa looks very well without his tail,' said Madeline with somewhat of a daughter's pride. 'But you shall wear yours all the same, if you like it,' she added with much of a young maiden's love.

As they were thus walking near the house on the afternoon of

the third or fourth day after the trial, one of the maids came to
them and told Madeline that a gentleman was in the house who
wished to see her.

' A gentleman !' said Madeline.

' Mr. Orme, miss. My lady told me to ask you up if you were
anywhere near.'

' I suppose I must go,' said Madeline, from whom all her pretty
freedom of manner and light happiness of face departed on the
moment. She had told Felix everything as to poor Peregrine in
return for that story of his respecting Mary Snow. To her it
seemed as though that had made things equal between them,—for
she was too generous to observe that though she had given nothing
to her other lover, Felix had been engaged for many months to
marry his other love. But girls, I think, have no objection to
this. They do not desire first fruits, or even early fruits, as men
do. Indeed, I am not sure whether experience on the part of a
gentleman in his use of his heart is not supposed by most young
ladies to enhance the value of the article. Madeline was not in the
least jealous of Mary Snow ; but with great goodnature promised
to look after her, and patronize her when she should have become
Mrs. Albert Fitzallen. ' But I don't think I should like that Mrs.
Thomas,' she said.

' You would have mended the stockings for her all the same.'

' O yes, I would have done that ;—and so did Miss Snow.
But I would have kept my box locked. She should never have
seen my letters.'

It was now absolutely necessary that she should return to the
house, and say to Peregrine Orme what words of comfort might be
possible for her. If she could have spoken simply with her heart,
she would have said much that was friendly, even though it might
not be comfortable. But it was necessary that she should express
herself in words, and she felt that the task was very difficult. ' Will
you come in ?' she said to Felix.

' No, I think not. But he's a splendid fellow, and to me was
a stanch friend. If I can catch him as he comes out I will speak
to him.' And then Madeline, with hesitating steps, with her
hat still on her head, and her gloves on her hands, walked
through the hall into the drawing-room. There she found her
mother seated on the sofa, and Peregrine Orme standing before her.
Madeline walked up to him with extended hand and a kindly
welcome, though she felt that the colour was high in her cheeks.
Of course it would be impossible to come out from such an interview as this without having confessed her position, or hearing it
confessed by her mother in her presence. That, however, had
been already done, and Peregrine knew that the prize was gone.

' How do you do, Miss Staveley ?' said he. ' As I am going to leave the Cleeve for a long time, I have come over to say good-bye to Lady Staveley—and to you.'

'Are you going away, Mr. Orme?'

'Yes, I shall go abroad,—to Central Africa, I think. It seems a wild sort of place with plenty of animals to kill.'

'But isn't it very dangerous?'

'No, I don't think so. The people always come back alive. I've a sort of idea that nothing will kill me. At any rate I couldn't stay here.'

'Madeline, dear, I've told Mr. Orme that you have accepted Mr. Graham. With a friend such as he is I know that you will not be anxious to keep this a secret.'

'No, mamma.'

'I was sure of that; and now that your papa has consented to it, and that it is quite fixed, I am sure that it is better that he should know it. We shall always look upon him as a very dear friend—if he will allow us.'

Then it was necessary that Peregrine should speak, which he did as follows, holding Madeline's hand for the first three or four seconds of the time:—'Miss Staveley, I will say this of myself, that if ever a fellow loved a girl truly, I loved you;—and I do so now as well or better than ever. It is no good my pretending to be contented, and all that sort of thing. I am not contented, but very unhappy. I have never wished for but one thing in my life; and for that I would have given all that I have in the world. I know that I cannot have it, and that I am not fit to have it.'

'Oh, Mr. Orme, it is not that.'

'But it is that. I knew you before Graham did, and loved you quite as soon. I believe—though of course I don't mean to ask any questions—but I believe I told you so before he ever did.'

'Marriages, they say, are planned in heaven,' said Lady Staveley.

'Perhaps they are. I only wish this one had not been planned there. I cannot help it,—I cannot express my satisfaction, though I will heartily wish for your happiness. I knew from the first how it would be, and was always sure that I was a fool to love you. I should have gone away when I first thought of it, for I used to feel that you never cared to speak to me.'

'Oh, indeed I did,' said poor Madeline.

'No, you did not. And why should you when I had nothing to say for myself? I ought to have fallen in love with some foolish chit with as little wit about her as I have myself.'

'I hope you will fall in love with some very nice girl,' said Lady Staveley; 'and that we shall know her and love her very much.'

'Oh, I dare say I shall marry some day. I feel now as though I should like to break my neck, but I don't suppose I shall. Good-bye, Lady Staveley.'

' Good-bye, Mr. Orme; and may God send that you may be happy.'

' Good-bye, Madeline. I shall never call you so again,—except to myself. I do wish you may be happy,—I do indeed. As for him,— he has been before me, and taken away all that I wanted to win.'

By this time the tears were in his eyes, and his voice was not free from their effect. Of this he was aware, and therefore, pressing her hand, he turned upon his heel and abruptly left the room. He had been unable to say that he wished also that Felix might be happy; but this omission was forgiven him by both the ladies. Poor Madeline, as he went, muttered a kind farewell, but her tears had mastered her also, so that she could hardly speak.

He went directly to the stables, there got upon his horse, and then walked slowly down the avenue towards the gate. He had got the better of that tear-compelling softness as soon as he found himself beyond the presence of the girl he loved, and was now stern in his mood, striving to harden his heart. He had confessed himself a fool in comparison with Felix Graham; but yet,—he asked himself,—in spite of that, was it not possible that he would have made her a better husband than the other? It was not to his title or his estate that he trusted as he so thought, but to a feeling that he was more akin to her in circumstances, in ways of life, and in tenderness of heart. As all this was passing through his mind, Felix Graham presented himself to him in the road.

' Orme,' said he, ' I heard that you were in the house, and have come to shake hands with you. I suppose you have heard what has taken place. Will you not shake hands with me ?'

' No,' said Peregrine, ' I will not.'

' I am sorry for that, for we were good friends, and I owe you much for your kindness. It was a fair stand-up fight, and you should not be angry.'

' I am angry, and I don't want your friendship. Go and tell her that I say so, if you like.'

' No, I will not do that.'

' I wish with all my heart that we had both killed ourselves at that bank.'

' For shame, Orme, for shame !'

' Very well, sir; let it be for shame.' And then he passed on, meaning to go through the gate, and leaving Graham on the grass by the road-side. But before he had gone a hundred yards down the road his better feelings came back upon him, and he returned.

' I am unhappy,' he said, ' and sore at heart. You must not mind what words I spoke just now.'

' No, no; I am sure you did not mean them,' said Felix, putting his hand on the horse's mane.

' I did mean them then, but I do not mean them now. I won't say anything about wishes. Of course you will be happy with her.

Anybody would be happy with her.   I suppose you won't die, and give a fellow another chance.'

' Not if I can help it,' said Graham.

' Well, if you are to live, I don't wish you any evil.   I do wish you hadn't come to Noningsby, that's all.   Good-bye to you.'   And he held out his hand, which Graham took.

' We shall be good friends yet, for all that is come and gone,' said Graham ; and then there were no more words between them.

Peregrine did as he said, and went abroad, extending his travels to many wild countries, in which, as he used to say, any one else would have been in danger.   No danger ever came to him,—so at least he frequently wrote word to his mother.   Gorillas he slew by scores, lions by hundreds, and elephants sufficient for an ivory palace.   The skins, and bones, and other trophies, he sent home in various ships ; and when he appeared in London as a lion, no man doubted his word.   But then he did not write a book, nor even give lectures ; nor did he presume to know much about the huge brutes he had slain, except that they were pervious to powder and ball.

Sir Peregrine had endeavoured to keep him at home by giving up the property into his hands ; but neither for grandfather, nor for mother, nor for lands and money would he remain in the neigh-bourhood of Noningsby.   ' No, mother,' he said ; ' it will be better for me to be away.'   And away he went.

The old baronet lived to see him return, though with plaintive wail he often declared to his daughter-in-law that this was impossible. He lived, but he never returned to that living life which had been his before he had taken up the battle for Lady Mason.   He would sometimes allow Mrs. Orme to drive him about the grounds, but otherwise he remained in the house, sitting solitary over his fire,— with a book, indeed, open before him, but rarely reading.   He was waiting patiently, as he said, till death should come to him.

Mrs. Orme kept her promise, and wrote constantly to Lady Mason,—hearing from her as constantly.   When Lucius had been six months in Germany, he decided on going to Australia, leaving his mother for the present in the little German town in which they were staying.   For her, on the whole, the change was for the better.   As to his success in a thriving colony, there can be but little doubt.

Felix Graham was soon married to Madeline ; and as yet I have not heard of any banishment either to Patagonia or to Merthyr-Tydvil.

And now I may say, Farewell.

A CATALOGUE OF
SELECTED DOVER BOOKS
IN ALL FIELDS OF INTEREST

A CATALOGUE OF SELECTED DOVER
BOOKS IN ALL FIELDS OF INTEREST

CONDITIONED REFLEXES, Ivan P. Pavlov. Full translation of most complete statement of Pavlov's work; cerebral damage, conditioned reflex, experiments with dogs, sleep, similar topics of great importance. 430pp. 5⅜ x 8½. 60614-7 Pa. $4.50

NOTES ON NURSING: WHAT IT IS, AND WHAT IT IS NOT, Florence Nightingale. Outspoken writings by founder of modern nursing. When first published (1860) it played an important role in much needed revolution in nursing. Still stimulating. 140pp. 5⅜ x 8½. 22340-X Pa. $2.50

HARTER'S PICTURE ARCHIVE FOR COLLAGE AND ILLUSTRATION, Jim Harter. Over 300 authentic, rare 19th-century engravings selected by noted collagist for artists, designers, decoupeurs, etc. Machines, people, animals, etc., printed one side of page. 25 scene plates for backgrounds. 6 collages by Harter, Satty, Singer, Evans. Introduction. 192pp. 8⅞ x 11¾. 23659-5 Pa. $5.00

MANUAL OF TRADITIONAL WOOD CARVING, edited by Paul N. Hasluck. Possibly the best book in English on the craft of wood carving. Practical instructions, along with 1,146 working drawings and photographic illustrations. Formerly titled *Cassell's Wood Carving*. 576pp. 6½ x 9¼. 23489-4 Pa. $7.95

THE PRINCIPLES AND PRACTICE OF HAND OR SIMPLE TURNING, John Jacob Holtzapffel. Full coverage of basic lathe techniques—history and development, special apparatus, softwood turning, hardwood turning, metal turning. Many projects—billiard ball, works formed within a sphere, egg cups, ash trays, vases, jardiniers, others—included. 1881 edition. 800 illustrations. 592pp. 6⅛ x 9¼. 23365-0 Clothbd. $15.00

THE JOY OF HANDWEAVING, Osma Tod. Only book you need for hand weaving. Fundamentals, threads, weaves, plus numerous projects for small board-loom, two-harness, tapestry, laid-in, four-harness weaving and more. Over 160 illustrations. 2nd revised edition. 352pp. 6½ x 9¼. 23458-4 Pa. $5.00

THE BOOK OF WOOD CARVING, Charles Marshall Sayers. Still finest book for beginning student in wood sculpture. Noted teacher, craftsman discusses fundamentals, technique; gives 34 designs, over 34 projects for panels, bookends, mirrors, etc. "Absolutely first-rate"—E. J. Tangerman. 33 photos. 118pp. 7¾ x 10⅝. 23654-4 Pa. $3.00

DRAWINGS OF WILLIAM BLAKE, William Blake. 92 plates from Book of Job, *Divine Comedy, Paradise Lost,* visionary heads, mythological figures, Laocoon, etc. Selection, introduction, commentary by Sir Geoffrey Keynes. 178pp. 8⅛ x 11.   22303-5 Pa. $4.00

ENGRAVINGS OF HOGARTH, William Hogarth. 101 of Hogarth's greatest works: *Rake's Progress, Harlot's Progress, Illustrations for Hudibras, Before and After, Beer Street and Gin Lane,* many more. Full commentary. 256pp. 11 x 13¾.   22479-1 Pa. $7.95

DAUMIER: 120 GREAT LITHOGRAPHS, Honore Daumier. Wide-ranging collection of lithographs by the greatest caricaturist of the 19th century. Concentrates on eternally popular series on lawyers, on married life, on liberated women, etc. Selection, introduction, and notes on plates by Charles F. Ramus. Total of 158pp. 9⅜ x 12¼.   23512-2 Pa. $5.50

DRAWINGS OF MUCHA, Alphonse Maria Mucha. Work reveals drafts-man of highest caliber: studies for famous posters and paintings, render-ings for book illustrations and ads, etc. 70 works, 9 in color; including 6 items not drawings. Introduction. List of illustrations. 72pp. 9⅜ x 12¼. (Available in U.S. only)   23672-2 Pa. $4.00

GIOVANNI BATTISTA PIRANESI: DRAWINGS IN THE PIERPONT MORGAN LIBRARY, Giovanni Battista Piranesi. For first time ever all of Morgan Library's collection, world's largest. 167 illustrations of rare Piranesi drawings—archeological, architectural, decorative and visionary. Essay, detailed list of drawings, chronology, captions. Edited by Felice Stampfle. 144pp. 9⅜ x 12¼.   23714-1 Pa. $7.50

NEW YORK ETCHINGS (1905-1949), John Sloan. All of important American artist's N.Y. life etchings. 67 works include some of his best art; also lively historical record—Greenwich Village, tenement scenes. Edited by Sloan's widow. Introduction and captions. 79pp. 8⅜ x 11¼.
                                                  23651-X Pa. $4.00

CHINESE PAINTING AND CALLIGRAPHY: A PICTORIAL SURVEY, Wan-go Weng. 69 fine examples from John M. Crawford's matchless private collection: landscapes, birds, flowers, human figures, etc., plus calligraphy. Every basic form included: hanging scrolls, handscrolls, album leaves, fans, etc. 109 illustrations. Introduction. Captions. 192pp. 8⅞ x 11¾.
                                                  23707-9 Pa. $7.95

DRAWINGS OF REMBRANDT, edited by Seymour Slive. Updated Lipp-mann, Hofstede de Groot edition, with definitive scholarly apparatus. All portraits, biblical sketches, landscapes, nudes, Oriental figures, classical studies, together with selection of work by followers. 550 illustrations. Total of 630pp. 9⅛ x 12¼.   21485-0, 21486-9 Pa., Two-vol. set $15.00

THE DISASTERS OF WAR, Francisco Goya. 83 etchings record horrors of Napoleonic wars in Spain and war in general. Reprint of 1st edition, plus 3 additional plates. Introduction by Philip Hofer. 97pp. 9⅜ x 8¼.
                                                  21872-4 Pa. $3.75

THE EARLY WORK OF AUBREY BEARDSLEY, Aubrey Beardsley. 157 plates, 2 in color: *Manon Lescaut, Madame Bovary, Morte Darthur, Salome,* other. Introduction by H. Marillier. 182pp. 8⅛ x 11. 21816-3 Pa. $4.50

THE LATER WORK OF AUBREY BEARDSLEY, Aubrey Beardsley. Exotic masterpieces of full maturity: *Venus and Tannhauser, Lysistrata, Rape of the Lock, Volpone,* Savoy material, etc. 174 plates, 2 in color. 186pp. 8⅛ x 11. 21817-1 Pa. $4.50

THOMAS NAST'S CHRISTMAS DRAWINGS, Thomas Nast. Almost all Christmas drawings by creator of image of Santa Claus as we know it, and one of America's foremost illustrators and political cartoonists. 66 illustrations. 3 illustrations in color on covers. 96pp. 8⅜ x 11¼. 23660-9 Pa. $3.50

THE DORÉ ILLUSTRATIONS FOR DANTE'S DIVINE COMEDY, Gustave Doré. All 135 plates from Inferno, Purgatory, Paradise; fantastic tortures, infernal landscapes, celestial wonders. Each plate with appropriate (translated) verses. 141pp. 9 x 12. 23231-X Pa. $4.50

DORÉ'S ILLUSTRATIONS FOR RABELAIS, Gustave Doré. 252 striking illustrations of *Gargantua and Pantagruel* books by foremost 19th-century illustrator. Including 60 plates, 192 delightful smaller illustrations. 153pp. 9 x 12. 23656-0 Pa. $5.00

LONDON: A PILGRIMAGE, Gustave Doré, Blanchard Jerrold. Squalor, riches, misery, beauty of mid-Victorian metropolis; 55 wonderful plates, 125 other illustrations, full social, cultural text by Jerrold. 191pp. of text. 9⅜ x 12¼. 22306-X Pa. $6.00

THE RIME OF THE ANCIENT MARINER, Gustave Doré, S. T. Coleridge. Dore's finest work, 34 plates capture moods, subtleties of poem. Full text. Introduction by Millicent Rose. 77pp. 9¼ x 12. 22305-1 Pa. $3.50

THE DORE BIBLE ILLUSTRATIONS, Gustave Doré. All wonderful, detailed plates: Adam and Eve, Flood, Babylon, Life of Jesus, etc. Brief King James text with each plate. Introduction by Millicent Rose. 241 plates. 241pp. 9 x 12. 23004-X Pa. $6.00

THE COMPLETE ENGRAVINGS, ETCHINGS AND DRYPOINTS OF ALBRECHT DURER. "Knight, Death and Devil"; "Melencolia," and more—all Dürer's known works in all three media, including 6 works formerly attributed to him. 120 plates. 235pp. 8⅜ x 11¼. 22851-7 Pa. $6.50

MAXIMILIAN'S TRIUMPHAL ARCH, Albrecht Dürer and others. Incredible monument of woodcut art: 8 foot high elaborate arch—heraldic figures, humans, battle scenes, fantastic elements—that you can assemble yourself. Printed on one side, layout for assembly. 143pp. 11 x 16. 21451-6 Pa. $5.00

CATALOGUE OF DOVER BOOKS

THE COMPLETE WOODCUTS OF ALBRECHT DURER, edited by
Dr. W. Kurth. 346 in all: "Old Testament," "St. Jerome," "Passion,"
"Life of Virgin," Apocalypse," many others. Introduction by Campbell
Dodgson. 285pp. 8½ x 12¼.   21097-9 Pa. $6.95

DRAWINGS OF ALBRECHT DURER, edited by Heinrich Wölfflin. 81
plates show development from youth to full style. Many favorites; many
new. Introduction by Alfred Werner. 96pp. 8⅛ x 11.   22352-3 Pa. $5.00

THE HUMAN FIGURE, Albrecht Dürer. Experiments in various techniques—stereometric, progressive proportional, and others. Also life studies
that rank among finest ever done. Complete reprinting of *Dresden Sketch-
book.* 170 plates. 355pp. 8⅜ x 11¼.   21042-1 Pa. $7.95

OF THE JUST SHAPING OF LETTERS, Albrecht Dürer. Renaissance
artist explains design of Roman majuscules by geometry, also Gothic lower
and capitals. Grolier Club edition. 43pp. 7⅞ x 10¾   21306-4 Pa. $3.00

TEN BOOKS ON ARCHITECTURE, Vitruvius. The most important book
ever written on architecture. Early Roman aesthetics, technology, classical
orders, site selection, all other aspects. Stands behind everything since.
Morgan translation. 331pp. 5⅜ x 8½.   20645-9 Pa. $4.00

THE FOUR BOOKS OF ARCHITECTURE, Andrea Palladio. 16th-century
classic responsible for Palladian movement and style. Covers classical architectural remains, Renaissance revivals, classical orders, etc. 1738 Ware
English edition. Introduction by A. Placzek. 216 plates. 110pp. of text.
9½ x 12¾.   21308-0 Pa. $8.95

HORIZONS, Norman Bel Geddes. Great industrialist stage designer, "father
of streamlining," on application of aesthetics to transportation, amusement,
architecture, etc. 1932 prophetic account; function, theory, specific projects.
222 illustrations. 312pp. 7⅞ x 10¾.   23514-9 Pa. $6.95

FRANK LLOYD WRIGHT'S FALLINGWATER, Donald Hoffmann. Full,
illustrated story of conception and building of Wright's masterwork at
Bear Run, Pa. 100 photographs of site, construction, and details of completed structure. 112pp. 9¼ x 10.   23671-4 Pa. $5.00

THE ELEMENTS OF DRAWING, John Ruskin. Timeless classic by great
Vitlorian; starts with basic ideas, works through more difficult. Many
practical exercises. 48 illustrations. Introduction by Lawrence Campbell.
228pp. 5⅜ x 8½.   22730-8 Pa. $2.75

GIST OF ART, John Sloan. Greatest modern American teacher, Art Stu-
dents League, offers innumerable hints, instructions, guided comments to
help you in painting. Not a formal course. 46 illustrations. Introduction
by Helen Sloan. 200pp. 5⅜ x 8½.   23435-5 Pa. $3.50

THE ANATOMY OF THE HORSE, George Stubbs. Often considered the great masterpiece of animal anatomy. Full reproduction of 1766 edition, plus prospectus; original text and modernized text. 36 plates. Introduction by Eleanor Garvey. 121pp. 11 x 14¾. 23402-9 Pa. $6.00

BRIDGMAN'S LIFE DRAWING, George B. Bridgman. More than 500 illustrative drawings and text teach you to abstract the body into its major masses, use light and shade, proportion; as well as specific areas of anatomy, of which Bridgman is master. 192pp. 6½ x 9¼. (Available in U.S. only) 22710-3 Pa. $3.00

ART NOUVEAU DESIGNS IN COLOR, Alphonse Mucha, Maurice Verneuil, Georges Auriol. Full-color reproduction of *Combinaisons ornementales* (c. 1900) by Art Nouveau masters. Floral, animal, geometric, interlacings, swashes—borders, frames, spots—all incredibly beautiful. 60 plates, hundreds of designs. 9⅜ x 8-1/16. 22885-1 Pa. $4.00

FULL-COLOR FLORAL DESIGNS IN THE ART NOUVEAU STYLE, E. A. Seguy. 166 motifs, on 40 plates, from *Les fleurs et leurs applications decoratives* (1902): borders, circular designs, repeats, allovers, "spots." All in authentic Art Nouveau colors. 48pp. 9⅜ x 12¼. 23439-8 Pa. $5.00

A DIDEROT PICTORIAL ENCYCLOPEDIA OF TRADES AND IN- DUSTRY, edited by Charles C. Gillispie. 485 most interesting plates from the great French Encyclopedia of the 18th century show hundreds of working figures, artifacts, process, land and cityscapes; glassmaking, paper- making, metal extraction, construction, weaving, making furniture, clothing, wigs, dozens of other activities. Plates fully explained. 920pp. 9 x 12. 22284-5, 22285-3 Clothbd., Two-vol. set $40.00

HANDBOOK OF EARLY ADVERTISING ART, Clarence P. Hornung. Largest collection of copyright-free early and antique advertising art ever compiled. Over 6,000 illustrations, from Franklin's time to the 1890's for special effects, novelty. Valuable source, almost inexhaustible.
Pictorial Volume. Agriculture, the zodiac, animals, autos, birds, Christmas, fire engines, flowers, trees, musical instruments, ships, games and sports, much more. Arranged by subject matter and use. 237 plates. 288pp. 9 x 12. 20122-8 Clothbd. $13.50

Typographical Volume. Roman and Gothic faces ranging from 10 point to 300 point, "Barnum," German and Old English faces, script, logotypes, scrolls and flourishes, 1115 ornamental initials, 67 complete alphabets, more. 310 plates. 320pp. 9 x 12. 20123-6 Clothbd. $15.00

CALLIGRAPHY (CALLIGRAPHIA LATINA), J. G. Schwandner. High point of 18th-century ornamental calligraphy. Very ornate initials, scrolls, borders, cherubs, birds, lettered examples. 172pp. 9 x 13. 20475-8 Pa. $6.00

ART FORMS IN NATURE, Ernst Haeckel. Multitude of strangely beautiful natural forms: Radiolaria, Foraminifera, jellyfishes, fungi, turtles, bats, etc. All 100 plates of the 19th-century evolutionist's *Kunstformen der Natur* (1904). 100pp. 9⅜ x 12¼. 22987-4 Pa. $4.50

CHILDREN: A PICTORIAL ARCHIVE FROM NINETEENTH-CENTURY SOURCES, edited by Carol Belanger Grafton. 242 rare, copyright-free wood engravings for artists and designers. Widest such selection available. All illustrations in line. 119pp. 8⅜ x 11¼.
23694-3 Pa. $3.50

WOMEN: A PICTORIAL ARCHIVE FROM NINETEENTH-CENTURY SOURCES, edited by Jim Harter. 391 copyright-free wood engravings for artists and designers selected from rare periodicals. Most extensive such collection available. All illustrations in line. 128pp. 9 x 12.
23703-6 Pa. $4.50

ARABIC ART IN COLOR, Prisse d'Avennes. From the greatest ornamentalists of all time—50 plates in color, rarely seen outside the Near East, rich in suggestion and stimulus. Includes 4 plates on covers. 46pp. 9⅜ x 12¼. 23658-7 Pa. $6.00

AUTHENTIC ALGERIAN CARPET DESIGNS AND MOTIFS, edited by June Beveridge. Algerian carpets are world famous. Dozens of geometrical motifs are charted on grids, color-coded, for weavers, needleworkers, craftsmen, designers. 53 illustrations plus 4 in color. 48pp. 8¼ x 11. (Available in U.S. only) 23650-1 Pa. $1.75

DICTIONARY OF AMERICAN PORTRAITS, edited by Hayward and Blanche Cirker. 4000 important Americans, earliest times to 1905, mostly in clear line. Politicians, writers, soldiers, scientists, inventors, industrialists, Indians, Blacks, women, outlaws, etc. Identificatory information. 756pp. 9¼ x 12¾. 21823-6 Clothbd. $40.00

HOW THE OTHER HALF LIVES, Jacob A. Riis. Journalistic record of filth, degradation, upward drive in New York immigrant slums, shops, around 1900. New edition includes 100 original Riis photos, monuments of early photography. 233pp. 10 x 7⅞. 22012-5 Pa. $6.00

NEW YORK IN THE THIRTIES, Berenice Abbott. Noted photographer's fascinating study of city shows new buildings that have become famous and old sights that have disappeared forever. Insightful commentary. 97 photographs. 97pp. 11⅜ x 10. 22967-X Pa. $5.00

MEN AT WORK, Lewis W. Hine. Famous photographic studies of construction workers, railroad men, factory workers and coal miners. New supplement of 18 photos on Empire State building construction. New introduction by Jonathan L. Doherty. Total of 69 photos. 63pp. 8 x 10¾.
23475-4 Pa. $3.00

THE DEPRESSION YEARS AS PHOTOGRAPHED BY ARTHUR ROTH-STEIN, Arthur Rothstein. First collection devoted entirely to the work of outstanding 1930s photographer: famous dust storm photo, ragged children, unemployed, etc. 120 photographs. Captions. 119pp. 9¼ x 10¾.
23590-4 Pa. $5.00

CAMERA WORK: A PICTORIAL GUIDE, Alfred Stieglitz. All 559 illustrations and plates from the most important periodical in the history of art photography, Camera Work (1903-17). Presented four to a page, reduced in size but still clear, in strict chronological order, with complete captions. Three indexes. Glossary. Bibliography. 176pp. 8⅜ x 11¼.
23591-2 Pa. $6.95

ALVIN LANGDON COBURN, PHOTOGRAPHER, Alvin L. Coburn. Revealing autobiography by one of greatest photographers of 20th century gives insider's version of Photo-Secession, plus comments on his own work. 77 photographs by Coburn. Edited by Helmut and Alison Gernsheim. 160pp. 8⅛ x 11.
23685-4 Pa. $6.00

NEW YORK IN THE FORTIES, Andreas Feininger. 162 brilliant photographs by the well-known photographer, formerly with Life magazine, show commuters, shoppers, Times Square at night, Harlem nightclub, Lower East Side, etc. Introduction and full captions by John von Hartz. 181pp. 9¼ x 10¾.
23585-8 Pa. $6.00

GREAT NEWS PHOTOS AND THE STORIES BEHIND THEM, John Faber. Dramatic volume of 140 great news photos, 1855 through 1976, and revealing stories behind them, with both historical and technical information. Hindenburg disaster, shooting of Oswald, nomination of Jimmy Carter, etc. 160pp. 8¼ x 11.
23667-6 Pa. $5.00

THE ART OF THE CINEMATOGRAPHER, Leonard Maltin. Survey of American cinematography history and anecdotal interviews with 5 masters—Arthur Miller, Hal Mohr, Hal Rosson, Lucien Ballard, and Conrad Hall. Very large selection of behind-the-scenes production photos. 105 photographs. Filmographies. Index. Originally Behind the Camera. 144pp. 8¼ x 11.
23686-2 Pa. $5.00

DESIGNS FOR THE THREE-CORNERED HAT (LE TRICORNE), Pablo Picasso. 32 fabulously rare drawings—including 31 color illustrations of costumes and accessories—for 1919 production of famous ballet. Edited by Parmenia Migel, who has written new introduction. 48pp. 9⅜ x 12¼. (Available in U.S. only)
23709-5 Pa. $5.00

NOTES OF A FILM DIRECTOR, Sergei Eisenstein. Greatest Russian filmmaker explains montage, making of Alexander Nevsky, aesthetics; comments on self, associates, great rivals (Chaplin), similar material. 78 illustrations. 240pp. 5⅜ x 8½.
22392-2 Pa. $4.50

HOLLYWOOD GLAMOUR PORTRAITS, edited by John Kobal. 145 photos capture the stars from 1926-49, the high point in portrait photography. Gable, Harlow, Bogart, Bacall, Hedy Lamarr, Marlene Dietrich, Robert Montgomery, Marlon Brando, Veronica Lake; 94 stars in all. Full background on photographers, technical aspects, much more. Total of 160pp. 8⅜ x 11¼. 23352-9 Pa. $5.00

THE NEW YORK STAGE: FAMOUS PRODUCTIONS IN PHOTO-GRAPHS, edited by Stanley Appelbaum. 148 photographs from Museum of City of New York show 142 plays, 1883-1939. *Peter Pan, The Front Page, Dead End, Our Town,* O'Neill, hundreds of actors and actresses, etc. Full indexes. 154pp. 9½ x 10. 23241-7 Pa. **$6.00**

MASTERS OF THE DRAMA, John Gassner. Most comprehensive history of the drama, every tradition from Greeks to modern Europe and America, including Orient. Covers 800 dramatists, 2000 plays; biography, plot summaries, criticism, theatre history, etc. 77 illustrations. 890pp. 5⅜ x 8½. 20100-7 Clothbd. $10.00

THE GREAT OPERA STARS IN HISTORIC PHOTOGRAPHS, edited by James Camner. 343 portraits from the 1850s to the 1940s: Tamburini, Mario, Caliapin, Jeritza, Melchior, Melba, Patti, Pinza, Schipa, Caruso, Farrar, Steber, Gobbi, and many more—270 performers in all. Index. 199pp. 8⅜ x 11¼. 23575-0 Pa. $6.50

J. S. BACH, Albert Schweitzer. Great full-length study of Bach, life, background to music, music, by foremost modern scholar. Ernest Newman translation. 650 musical examples. Total of 928pp. 5⅜ x 8½. (Available in U.S. only) 21631-4, 21632-2 Pa., Two-vol. set **$10.00**

COMPLETE PIANO SONATAS, Ludwig van Beethoven. All sonatas in the fine Schenker edition, with fingering, analytical material. One of best modern editions. Total of 615pp. 9 x 12. (Available in U.S. only) 23134-8, 23135-6 Pa., Two-vol. set $15.00

KEYBOARD MUSIC, J. S. Bach. Bach-Gesellschaft edition. For harpsichord, piano, other keyboard instruments. English Suites, French Suites, Six Partitas, Goldberg Variations, Two-Part Inventions, Three-Part Sinfonias. 312pp. 8⅛ x 11. (Available in U.S. only) 22360-4 Pa. **$6.00**

FOUR SYMPHONIES IN FULL SCORE, Franz Schubert. Schubert's four most popular symphonies: No. 4 in C Minor ("Tragic"); No. 5 in B-flat Major; No. 8 in B Minor ("Unfinished"); No. 9 in C Major ("Great"). Breitkopf & Hartel edition. Study score. 261pp. 9⅜ x 12¼. 23681-1 Pa. $6.50

THE AUTHENTIC GILBERT & SULLIVAN SONGBOOK, W. S. Gilbert, A. S. Sullivan. Largest selection available; 92 songs, uncut, original keys, in piano rendering approved by Sullivan. Favorites and lesser-known fine numbers. Edited with plot synopses by James Spero. 3 illustrations. 399pp. 9 x 12. 23482-7 Pa. $7.95

PRINCIPLES OF ORCHESTRATION, Nikolay Rimsky-Korsakov. Great classical orchestrator provides fundamentals of tonal resonance, progression of parts, voice and orchestra, tutti effects, much else in major document. 330pp. of musical excerpts. 489pp. 6½ x 9¼. 21266-1 Pa. $6.00

TRISTAN UND ISOLDE, Richard Wagner. Full orchestral score with complete instrumentation. Do not confuse with piano reduction. Commentary by Felix Mottl, great Wagnerian conductor and scholar. Study score. 655pp. 8⅛ x 11. 22915-7 Pa. $12.50

REQUIEM IN FULL SCORE, Giuseppe Verdi. Immensely popular with choral groups and music lovers. Republication of edition published by C. F. Peters, Leipzig, n. d. German frontmaker in English translation. Glossary. Text in Latin. Study score. 204pp. 9⅜ x 12¼. 23682-X Pa. $6.00

COMPLETE CHAMBER MUSIC FOR STRINGS, Felix Mendelssohn. All of Mendelssohn's chamber music: Octet, 2 Quintets, 6 Quartets, and Four Pieces for String Quartet. (Nothing with piano is included). Complete works edition (1874-7). Study score. 283 pp. 9⅜ x 12¼. 23679-X Pa. $6.95

POPULAR SONGS OF NINETEENTH-CENTURY AMERICA, edited by Richard Jackson. 64 most important songs: "Old Oaken Bucket," "Arkansas Traveler," "Yellow Rose of Texas," etc. Authentic original sheet music, full introduction and commentaries. 290pp. 9 x 12. 23270-0 Pa. $6.00

COLLECTED PIANO WORKS, Scott Joplin. Edited by Vera Brodsky Lawrence. Practically all of Joplin's piano works—rags, two-steps, marches, waltzes, etc., 51 works in all. Extensive introduction by Rudi Blesh. Total of 345pp. 9 x 12. 23106-2 Pa. $14.95

BASIC PRINCIPLES OF CLASSICAL BALLET, Agrippina Vaganova. Great Russian theoretician, teacher explains methods for teaching classical ballet; incorporates best from French, Italian, Russian schools. 118 illustrations. 175pp. 5⅜ x 8½. 22036-2 Pa. $2.50

CHINESE CHARACTERS, L. Wieger. Rich analysis of 2300 characters according to traditional systems into primitives. Historical-semantic analysis to phonetics (Classical Mandarin) and radicals. 820pp. 6⅛ x 9¼. 21321-8 Pa. $10.00

EGYPTIAN LANGUAGE: EASY LESSONS IN EGYPTIAN HIEROGLYPHICS, E. A. Wallis Budge. Foremost Egyptologist offers Egyptian grammar, explanation of hieroglyphics, many reading texts, dictionary of symbols. 246pp. 5 x 7½. (Available in U.S. only) 21394-3 Clothbd. $7.50

AN ETYMOLOGICAL DICTIONARY OF MODERN ENGLISH, Ernest Weekley. Richest, fullest work, by foremost British lexicographer. Detailed word histories. Inexhaustible. Do not confuse this with Concise Etymological Dictionary, which is abridged. Total of 856pp. 6½ x 9¼. 21873-2, 21874-0 Pa., Two-vol. set $12.00

A MAYA GRAMMAR, Alfred M. Tozzer. Practical, useful English-language grammar by the Harvard anthropologist who was one of the three greatest American scholars in the area of Maya culture. Phonetics, grammatical processes, syntax, more. 301pp. 5⅜ x 8½.   23465-7 Pa. $4.00

THE JOURNAL OF HENRY D. THOREAU, edited by Bradford Torrey, F. H. Allen. Complete reprinting of 14 volumes, 1837-61, over two million words; the sourcebooks for *Walden*, etc. Definitive. All original sketches, plus 75 photographs. Introduction by Walter Harding. Total of 1804pp. 8½ x 12¼.   20312-3, 20313-1 Clothbd., Two-vol. set $50.00

CLASSIC GHOST STORIES, Charles Dickens and others. 18 wonderful stories you've wanted to reread: "The Monkey's Paw," "The House and the Brain," "The Upper Berth," "The Signalman," "Dracula's Guest," "The Tapestried Chamber," etc. Dickens, Scott, Mary Shelley, Stoker, etc. 330pp. 5⅜ x 8½.   20735-8 Pa. $3.50

SEVEN SCIENCE FICTION NOVELS, H. G. Wells. Full novels. *First Men in the Moon, Island of Dr. Moreau, War of the Worlds, Food of the Gods, Invisible Man, Time Machine, In the Days of the Comet*. A basic science-fiction library. 1015pp. 5⅜ x 8½. (Available in U.S. only)
     20264-X Clothbd. $8.95

ARMADALE, Wilkie Collins. Third great mystery novel by the author of *The Woman in White* and *The Moonstone*. Ingeniously plotted narrative shows an exceptional command of character, incident and mood. Original magazine version with 40 illustrations. 597pp. 5⅜ x 8½.
     23429-0 Pa. $5.00

MASTERS OF MYSTERY, H. Douglas Thomson. The first book in English (1931) devoted to history and aesthetics of detective story. Poe, Doyle, LeFanu, Dickens, many others, up to 1930. New introduction and notes by E. F. Bleiler. 288pp. 5⅜ x 8½. (Available in U.S. only)
     23606-4 Pa. $4.00

FLATLAND, E. A. Abbott. Science-fiction classic explores life of 2-D being in 3-D world. Read also as introduction to thought about hyperspace. Introduction by Banesh Hoffmann. 16 illustrations. 103pp. 5⅜ x 8½.
     20001-9 Pa. $1.75

THREE SUPERNATURAL NOVELS OF THE VICTORIAN PERIOD, edited, with an introduction, by E. F. Bleiler. Reprinted complete and unabridged, three great classics of the supernatural: *The Haunted Hotel* by Wilkie Collins, *The Haunted House at Latchford* by Mrs. J. H. Riddell, and *The Lost Stradivarius* by J. Meade Falkner. 325pp. 5⅜ x 8½.
     22571-2 Pa. $4.00

AYESHA: THE RETURN OF "SHE," H. Rider Haggard. Virtuoso sequel featuring the great mythic creation, Ayesha, in an adventure that is fully as good as the first book, *She*. Original magazine version, with 47 original illustrations by Maurice Greiffenhagen. 189pp. 6½ x 9¼.
     23649-8 Pa. $3.50

UNCLE SILAS, J. Sheridan LeFanu. Victorian Gothic mystery novel, considered by many best of period, even better than Collins or Dickens. Wonderful psychological terror. Introduction by Frederick Shroyer. 436pp. 5⅜ x 8½.   21715-9 Pa. $6.00

JURGEN, James Branch Cabell. The great erotic fantasy of the 1920's that delighted thousands, shocked thousands more. Full final text, Lane edition with 13 plates by Frank Pape. 346pp. 5⅜ x 8½.
23507-6 Pa. $4.50

THE CLAVERINGS, Anthony Trollope. Major novel, chronicling aspects of British Victorian society, personalities. Reprint of Cornhill serialization, 16 plates by M. Edwards; first reprint of full text. Introduction by Norman Donaldson. 412pp. 5⅜ x 8½.   23464-9 Pa. $5.00

KEPT IN THE DARK, Anthony Trollope. Unusual short novel about Victorian morality and abnormal psychology by the great English author. Probably the first American publication. Frontispiece by Sir John Millais. 92pp. 6½ x 9¼.   23609-9 Pa. $2.50

RALPH THE HEIR, Anthony Trollope. Forgotten tale of illegitimacy, inheritance. Master novel of Trollope's later years. Victorian country estates, clubs, Parliament, fox hunting, world of fully realized characters. Reprint of 1871 edition. 12 illustrations by F. A. Faser. 434pp. of text. 5⅜ x 8½.   23642-0 Pa. $5.00

YEKL and THE IMPORTED BRIDEGROOM AND OTHER STORIES OF THE NEW YORK GHETTO, Abraham Cahan. Film *Hester Street* based on *Yekl* (1896). Novel, other stories among first about Jewish immigrants of N.Y.'s East Side. Highly praised by W. D. Howells—Cahan "a new star of realism." New introduction by Bernard G. Richards. 240pp. 5⅜ x 8½.   22427-9 Pa. $3.50

THE HIGH PLACE, James Branch Cabell. Great fantasy writer's enchanting comedy of disenchantment set in 18th-century France. Considered by some critics to be even better than his famous *Jurgen*. 10 illustrations and numerous vignettes by noted fantasy artist Frank C. Pape. 320pp. 5⅜ x 8½.   23670-6 Pa. $4.00

ALICE'S ADVENTURES UNDER GROUND, Lewis Carroll. Facsimile of ms. Carroll gave Alice Liddell in 1864. Different in many ways from final Alice. Handlettered, illustrated by Carroll. Introduction by Martin Gardner. 128pp. 5⅜ x 8½.   21482-6 Pa. $2.00

FAVORITE ANDREW LANG FAIRY TALE BOOKS IN MANY COLORS, Andrew Lang. The four Lang favorites in a boxed set—the complete *Red*, *Green*, *Yellow* and *Blue* Fairy Books. 164 stories; 439 illustrations by Lancelot Speed, Henry Ford and G. P. Jacomb Hood. Total of about 1500pp. 5⅜ x 8½.   23407-X Boxed set, Pa. $14.95

CATALOGUE OF DOVER BOOKS

HOUSEHOLD STORIES BY THE BROTHERS GRIMM. All the great Grimm stories: "Rumpelstiltskin," "Snow White," "Hansel and Gretel," etc., with 114 illustrations by Walter Crane. 269pp. 5⅜ x 8½.
21080-4 Pa. $3.00

SLEEPING BEAUTY, illustrated by Arthur Rackham. Perhaps the fullest, most delightful version ever, told by C. S. Evans. Rackham's best work. 49 illustrations. 110pp. 7⅞ x 10¾.
22756-1 Pa. $2.50

AMERICAN FAIRY TALES, L. Frank Baum. Young cowboy lassoes Father Time; dummy in Mr. Floman's department store window comes to life; and 10 other fairy tales. 41 illustrations by N. P. Hall, Harry Kennedy, Ike Morgan, and Ralph Gardner. 209pp. 5⅜ x 8½.
23643-9 Pa. $3.00

THE WONDERFUL WIZARD OF OZ, L. Frank Baum. Facsimile in full color of America's finest children's classic. Introduction by Martin Gardner. 143 illustrations by W. W. Denslow. 267pp. 5⅜ x 8½.
20691-2 Pa. $3.50

THE TALE OF PETER RABBIT, Beatrix Potter. The inimitable Peter's terrifying adventure in Mr. McGregor's garden, with all 27 wonderful, full-color Potter illustrations. 55pp. 4¼ x 5½. (Available in U.S. only)
22827-4 Pa. $1.25

THE STORY OF KING ARTHUR AND HIS KNIGHTS, Howard Pyle. Finest children's version of life of King Arthur. 48 illustrations by Pyle. 131pp. 6⅛ x 9¼.
21445-1 Pa. $4.95

CARUSO'S CARICATURES, Enrico Caruso. Great tenor's remarkable caricatures of self, fellow musicians, composers, others. Toscanini, Puccini, Farrar, etc. Impish, cutting, insightful. 473 illustrations. Preface by M. Sisca. 217pp. 8⅜ x 11¼.
23528-9 Pa. $6.95

PERSONAL NARRATIVE OF A PILGRIMAGE TO ALMADINAH AND MECCAH, Richard Burton. Great travel classic by remarkably colorful personality. Burton, disguised as a Moroccan, visited sacred shrines of Islam, narrowly escaping death. Wonderful observations of Islamic life, customs, personalities. 47 illustrations. Total of 959pp. 5⅜ x 8½.
21217-3, 21218-1 Pa., Two-vol. set $12.00

INCIDENTS OF TRAVEL IN YUCATAN, John L. Stephens. Classic (1843) exploration of jungles of Yucatan, looking for evidences of Maya civilization. Travel adventures, Mexican and Indian culture, etc. Total of 669pp. 5⅜ x 8½.
20926-1, 20927-X Pa., Two-vol. set $7.90

AMERICAN LITERARY AUTOGRAPHS FROM WASHINGTON IRVING TO HENRY JAMES, Herbert Cahoon, et al. Letters, poems, manuscripts of Hawthorne, Thoreau, Twain, Alcott, Whitman, 67 other prominent American authors. Reproductions, full transcripts and commentary. Plus checklist of all American Literary Autographs in The Pierpont Morgan Library. Printed on exceptionally high-quality paper. 136 illustrations. 212pp. 9⅛ x 12¼.
23548-3 Pa. $7.95

YUCATAN BEFORE AND AFTER THE CONQUEST, Diego de Landa. First English translation of basic book in Maya studies, the only significant account of Yucatan written in the early post-Conquest era. Translated by distinguished Maya scholar William Gates. Appendices, introduction, 4 maps and over 120 illustrations added by translator. 162pp. 5⅜ x 8½.
23622-6 Pa. $3.00

THE MALAY ARCHIPELAGO, Alfred R. Wallace. Spirited travel account by one of founders of modern biology. Touches on zoology, botany, ethnography, geography, and geology. 62 illustrations, maps. 515pp. 5⅜ x 8½.
20187-2 Pa. $6.95

THE DISCOVERY OF THE TOMB OF TUTANKHAMEN, Howard Carter, A. C. Mace. Accompany Carter in the thrill of discovery, as ruined passage suddenly reveals unique, untouched, fabulously rich tomb. Fascinating account, with 106 illustrations. New introduction by J. M. White. Total of 382pp. 5⅜ x 8½. (Available in U.S. only) 23500-9 Pa. $4.00

THE WORLD'S GREATEST SPEECHES, edited by Lewis Copeland and Lawrence W. Lamm. Vast collection of 278 speeches from Greeks up to present. Powerful and effective models; unique look at history. Revised to 1970. Indices. 842pp. 5⅜ x 8½. 20468-5 Pa. $8.95

THE 100 GREATEST ADVERTISEMENTS, Julian Watkins. The priceless ingredient; His master's voice; 99 44/100% pure; over 100 others. How they were written, their impact, etc. Remarkable record. 130 illustrations. 233pp. 7⅞ x 10 3/5. 20540-1 Pa. $5.00

CRUICKSHANK PRINTS FOR HAND COLORING, George Cruickshank. 18 illustrations, one side of a page, on fine-quality paper suitable for watercolors. Caricatures of people in society (c. 1820) full of trenchant wit. Very large format. 32pp. 11 x 16. 23684-6 Pa. $5.00

THIRTY-TWO COLOR POSTCARDS OF TWENTIETH-CENTURY AMERICAN ART, Whitney Museum of American Art. Reproduced in full color in postcard form are 31 art works and one shot of the museum. Calder, Hopper, Rauschenberg, others. Detachable. 16pp. 8¼ x 11.
23629-3 Pa. $2.50

MUSIC OF THE SPHERES: THE MATERIAL UNIVERSE FROM ATOM TO QUASAR SIMPLY EXPLAINED, Guy Murchie. Planets, stars, geology, atoms, radiation, relativity, quantum theory, light, antimatter, similar topics. 319 figures. 664pp. 5⅜ x 8½.
21809-0, 21810-4 Pa., Two-vol. set $10.00

EINSTEIN'S THEORY OF RELATIVITY, Max Born. Finest semi-technical account; covers Einstein, Lorentz, Minkowski, and others, with much detail, much explanation of ideas and math not readily available elsewhere on this level. For student, non-specialist. 376pp. 5⅜ x 8½.
60769-0 Pa. $4.50

AMERICAN ANTIQUE FURNITURE, Edgar G. Miller, Jr. The basic coverage of all American furniture before 1840: chapters per item chronologically cover all types of furniture, with more than 2100 photos. Total of 1106pp. 7⅞ x 10¾.   21599-7, 21600-4 Pa., Two-vol. set $17.90

ILLUSTRATED GUIDE TO SHAKER FURNITURE, Robert Meader. Director, Shaker Museum, Old Chatham, presents up-to-date coverage of all furniture and appurtenances, with much on local styles not available elsewhere. 235 photos. 146pp. 9 x 12.   22819-3 Pa. $5.00

ORIENTAL RUGS, ANTIQUE AND MODERN, Walter A. Hawley. Persia, Turkey, Caucasus, Central Asia, China, other traditions. Best general survey of all aspects: styles and periods, manufacture, uses, symbols and their interpretation, and identification. 96 illustrations, 11 in color. 320pp. 6⅛ x 9¼.   22366-3 Pa. $6.95

CHINESE POTTERY AND PORCELAIN, R. L. Hobson. Detailed descriptions and analyses by former Keeper of the Department of Oriental Antiquities and Ethnography at the British Museum. Covers hundreds of pieces from primitive times to 1915. Still the standard text for most periods. 136 plates, 40 in full color. Total of 750pp. 5⅜ x 8½.
23253-0 Pa. $10.00

THE WARES OF THE MING DYNASTY, R. L. Hobson. Foremost scholar examines and illustrates many varieties of Ming (1368-1644). Famous blue and white, polychrome, lesser-known styles and shapes. 117 illustrations, 9 full color, of outstanding pieces. Total of 263pp. 6⅛ x 9¼. (Available in U.S. only)   23652-8 Pa. $6.00

Prices subject to change without notice.

Available at your book dealer or write for free catalogue to Dept. GI, Dover Publications, Inc., 180 Varick St., N.Y., N.Y. 10014. Dover publishes more than 175 books each year on science, elementary and advanced mathematics, biology, music, art, literary history, social sciences and other areas.